How Children Lea

Written for pre-service and in-service educators of children in preschool through grade five, this book connects research in cognitive development and math education to offer an accessibly written and practical introduction to the science of elementary math learning.

Structured according to children's mathematical development, *How Children Learn Math* systematically reviews and synthesizes the latest developmental research on mathematical cognition into accessible sections that explain both the scientific evidence available and its practical classroom application. Written by an author team with decades of collective experience in cognitive learning research, clinical learning evaluations, and classroom experience working with both teachers and children, this amply illustrated text offers a powerful resource for understanding children's mathematical development, from quantitative intuition to word problems, and helps readers understand and identify math learning difficulties that may emerge in later grades.

Aimed at pre-service and in-service teachers and educators with little background in cognitive development, the book distills important findings in cognitive development into clear, accessible language and practical suggestions. The book therefore serves as an ideal text for pre-service early childhood, elementary, and special education teachers, as well as early career researchers, or as a professional development resource for in-service teachers, supervisors and administrators, school psychologists, homeschool parents, and other educators.

Nancy Krasa is a clinical psychologist and Adjunct Assistant Professor of Psychology at The Ohio State University, USA. She is the author, with Sara Shunkwiler, of *Number Sense and Number Nonsense: Understanding the Challenges of Learning Math*.

Karen Tzanetopoulos is a speech and language therapist, math learning specialist, lecturer, and owner of Learning to Full Potential, LLC.

Colleen Maas is Assistant Professor of Early Childhood Education and Human Development at the University of Cincinnati, USA, and an affiliate member of the Development and Research in Early Math Education network.

How Children Learn Math

The Science of Math Learning in Research and Practice

Nancy Krasa, Karen Tzanetopoulos, and Colleen Maas

Routledge
Taylor & Francis Group

NEW YORK AND LONDON

Cover image: © Getty Images

First published 2023
by Routledge
605 Third Avenue, New York, NY 10158

and by Routledge
4 Park Square, Milton Park, Abingdon, Oxon, OX14 4RN

Routledge is an imprint of the Taylor & Francis Group, an informa business

ISBN: 978-0-367-74409-0 (hbk)
ISBN: 978-0-367-74408-3 (pbk)
ISBN: 978-1-003-15765-6 (ebk)

DOI: 10.4324/9781003157656

Typeset in Times New Roman
by Apex CoVantage, LLC

Access the Support Material: www.routledge.com/9780367744083

All unattributed figures were created by Colleen Maas.

FSC
www.fsc.org

MIX
Paper | Supporting
responsible forestry
FSC™ C013985

Printed in the United Kingdom
by Henry Ling Limited

Contents

About the Authors

Nancy Krasa, PhD, is a clinical psychologist specializing in the assessment of learning difficulties. She is also an adjunct assistant professor of psychology at The Ohio State University, where she conducts research on learning. She received her AB in mathematics from Smith College and her PhD in clinical psychology from New York University. She is the author, with Sara Shunkwiler, of *Number Sense and Number Nonsense: Understanding the Challenges of Learning Math*.

Karen Tzanetopoulos, MS, is a speech and language therapist who specializes in treating children with dyslexia and in helping children learn math. Her interest in math began while working in the public schools, as she observed that many of her students with language disorders also struggled to learn math and noticed a connection between the two. The Polsky Center for Entrepreneurship and Innovation at the University of Chicago awarded her and two teammates an Innovation Corps grant funded by the National Science Foundation in 2016 to study the problems of teaching math across the United States and to discover ways to teach math more effectively. Her focus on brain-based therapy began while working at the Rehabilitation Institute of Chicago and the Chicago Institute for Neurosurgery and Neuroresearch. Currently, she owns a private practice in the Chicago area and presents her findings at a variety of conferences and to school districts.

Colleen (née Uscianowski) Maas, PhD, is an assistant professor in the Early Childhood and Human Development program at the University of Cincinnati. She began her career as an elementary special education teacher in the New York City public schools. She earned her master's degree in learning disabilities in the School of Education at Hunter College and her doctorate in cognitive science in education in the Department of Human Development at Teachers College Columbia University. She is an affiliate member of the Development and Research in Early Math Education (DREME) network, where she works on the Family Math project and contributes to the development and research of early math resources for professionals serving families. She served as a consultant on the U.S. Department of Education Math and Science Partnership Title IIB grant, which focused on improving teachers' knowledge of math in high-needs schools. In addition, she conducts mixed-methods research involving children's mathematical thinking, teacher preparation, and the home math environment.

Preface

As of this writing, all indicators show that American children are not doing well in math. In the United States, only 41 percent of fourth-graders, 34 percent of eighth-graders, and 24 percent of high school seniors scored at or above the proficiency level in math, according to the 2019 National Assessment of Educational Progress (NAEP), with scores holding steady for at least a decade.[1] Internationally, American children have not fared any better. On the 2018 Programme for International Student Assessment (PISA) international math assessment, American 15-year-olds scored below the international average, with children from 36 other countries scoring higher and trend lines stable since 2003.[2] On average, U.S. students trailed those in other English-speaking countries and Europe, all of whom scored, on average, significantly below students in China and other East Asian countries—deeply troubling findings in a global, technology-driven economy. Moreover, these results predate the extensive disruption in education due to COVID-19, and early indications are that math learning has fallen even further behind. This is discouraging news for teachers, who spend long days in the classroom, and a serious problem for our children.

We wrote this book with the philosophy that, in life as in math, the best way to solve a problem is to first understand it, and that is the first purpose of this book. In the two decades leading up to this writing, the scientific research on how children learn math has exploded, with thousands of new studies focused on how children come to understand numbers, how they approach problems, how memory and attention affect their ability to learn, how language and spatial skills influence their mathematical understanding, and how their brains grow and change as they take on the mathematical challenges of the classroom and daily life. Yet little of this work has been accessible to the teachers on the front lines.

For the most part, we limited our review of the research to cross-sectional and longitudinal empirical studies of large numbers of children, as well as to intensive observations of a relatively small number of children over many, many trials (microgenetic studies), because the more information we have, the more reliably the findings can be generalized to other children.

We chose to focus on the early years, from toddlerhood through fifth grade, for two reasons. First, a great deal of the math cognition research during the past two decades concerns children's math learning during those formative years. Second, many children run into math difficulty later in school because they never really mastered the fundamental early concepts. If we are going to get it right, we must start from the beginning.

We also chose to focus on the cognitive aspects of math learning, not because we think the social and emotional aspects are unimportant or separable from the cognitive, but because they could easily fill a book of their own, and we simply do not have room to cover all facets of math learning in one volume. The research on mathematical cognition is vast. What we share with you here is a small but pedagogically relevant part of that work. Some of it is cited directly and appears in the chapter reference lists; other studies, just as important and relevant, can be found in the supplemental lists on the book's website. We offer there, in addition, a discussion of the issues around the diagnosis of mathematics learning disorder (dyscalculia), as well as a number line template to be used for learning multiplication and division.

We also wrote this book in the conviction that all children of average-range intelligence can learn math despite whatever challenges they may bring to the classroom, including poverty, reading and language disability, weak spatial skills, and attentional issues. Thus, the second purpose of the book is to offer teachers a way to apply the insights gleaned from research to sharpen the mathematical understanding of students at all ability levels. Eleven of the chapters contain home and classroom activities that were developed based on the research findings and, where possible, on classroom intervention research. The overarching goal of the activities is to explicitly teach children foundational mathematical concepts that are often not explicitly taught in school, as well as to help children develop problem-solving strategies. Most of the activities take a "back to basics" approach and are meant to enhance the standard curriculum, not replace it. The activities are not based on grade levels, but rather on what students may or may not have already mastered, so that teachers have ways to fill in the gaps for their struggling students and expand on skills for those who excel.

One goal in designing and presenting these activities is to make them accessible to all children. Math learning opportunities are all around us. The activities suggested in this book are simple and straightforward and require few special props or expensive materials; as such, they should be affordable for any school or parent. In activities for which specific materials, such as number blocks, are essential, we have suggested various alternatives to guarantee access for all.

We profoundly hope that readers will get as much out of reading this book as we did from writing it, to the benefit of all children. The stakes are high.

NOTES

1 National Assessment of Educational Progress (NAEP). Retrieved Feb. 1, 2021 from https://nationsreportcard.gov/mathematics/nation/scores/

2 Programme for International Student Assessment (PISA). Retrieved Feb. 1, 2021 from www.oecd.org/pisa/publications/PISA2018-CN-USA.pdf

Acknowledgments

Nancy Krasa would like to convey a wholehearted thank-you to:

A long list of incredible scholars, too numerous to list individually here, but whose names appear throughout the long reference lists at the end of each chapter, who patiently and graciously responded to questions about their work. We have tried to honor their contributions by getting it right. (Where we didn't, the fault is entirely our own, with apologies.) Special thanks to Daniel Ansari, John Opfer, and Bob Siegler, mensches all.

Educators Linda Swarlis, Jennifer Martin-Gledhill, and erstwhile co-author Sara Shunkwiler for their support and help with this project; the late Catherine and Margaret Stern for their inspiration; and the students who kindly stepped up to "teach teachers something" by donating their stories and their work.

Dear friends, including mathematician Bob Mendelson, for his enthusiasm; colleagues Fred Stern and Lois Feldman, for their abiding encouragement; and writers Vivian Witkind Davis, Bob Simon, and Carla Stockton, who were always willing to commiserate, laugh, and advise on punctuation.

Colleen Maas, who, in addition to her expertise in mathematics education, volunteered her astounding graphic design skills to this project, producing most of the figures in this book!

Terri Welch, my long-suffering assistant, for her patience and around-the-clock availability.

My children and their spouses, Hannah, Lila, Jeff, Bill, and Jillian, all in STEM or tech-dependent fields, for understanding what this project means.

My husband, Bob, without whose patience, devotion, and willingness to take clean-up duty for the duration, this book would never, ever have happened.

Karen Tzanetopoulos would like to extend her heartfelt gratitude to:

The Polsky Center for Entrepreneurship and Innovation at the University of Chicago for awarding their Innovation-Corps (I-Corps) grant to me and my teammates in 2016 to investigate the challenges of teaching math across the

United States. Gorana Kolar, senior associate director at the Polsky Center, was especially helpful and kind. My role in this book would not be possible without all that I learned through this grant and the many teachers, administrators, parents, and researchers whom I interviewed.

The National Science Foundation (NSF) for funding the I-Corps grant and providing invaluable feedback during the entire experience.

My I-Corps teammates, Lane Nelson and Jeanne Century, for their outstanding work and perseverance on the grant. Words cannot express my gratitude.

My many amazing students over the years. It has been a great joy to watch you learn and grow and conquer the many challenges you have faced. I have learned from each one of you.

MaryBeth Jones, an exceptional speech and language therapist, for referring some very special children and their families to me.

Dala Aavik Lucas, an exceptional occupational therapist, for collaborating on the topic of visual-spatial skills, dyslexia, and motor integration and for helping improve the lives of so many children.

John Sandberg and Liz Roche, for keeping me going through a variety of challenges.

Haywood Nelson, my father, for always believing in me and my work and for caring about my students almost as much as I do.

George Tzanetopoulos, for his frequent technical assistance, encouragement, and many delicious meals.

Colleen Maas would like to share her deep appreciation for:

My mentors and collaborators in the Development and Research in Early Math Education network, particularly Herb Ginsburg, Michèle Mazzocco, and Eric Dearing. You've shown me what it looks like to work tirelessly to ensure that every child has equal access to high-quality—and fun!—early math learning.

My research collaborators and friends Mia Almeda, Colleen Oppenzato, and Xia (Lisa) Li, who share a curiosity for the fascinating depths of a child's mathematical thinking.

My wonderful colleagues in the Early Childhood Education program in the School of Education at the University of Cincinnati, especially Beth Kouche, whose passion for math teaching is inspiring.

The endless encouragement of Marshall, whose mathematical mind never ceases to surprise me. Your love, patience, and laughter have fueled me. The enthusiasm and support of my family: Mom, Dad, Darren, Rose, Nana, Sing, Hong-Chin, and Phoenix.

Finally, to my students over the years, from elementary school through graduate school, who have generously allowed me to observe their thinking and learn from their insights. They remind me that everyone can think like a mathematician.

And thank you from all three of us to:

Our remarkable editors, Simon Jacobs and AnnaMary Goodall at Routledge, who answered endless lists of silly questions with patience, encouragement, and baffling good cheer. It has been a joy to work with you! Helen Strain, Marie Louise Roberts, our copy editor, and the rest of the production team: thank you for your patience and diligence on this complex project.

Chapter 1

Setting the Stage
Attention, Mental Control, Memory, and Understanding

THIS book tells the story of how children learn math. And like any story, it has a setting. In the case of this story, the setting is the child's mind, and that is where this story will begin: What are the mental resources that a child brings to the study of mathematics?

Children are born into a complex world that will demand much of them, and thus in the first dozen years or so—the years considered in this volume—they must learn a great deal. Fortunately, most children's brains are hardwired to make that possible. Moreover, as the brain grows it is also shaped by experience, which in turn determines how the child learns going forward. One of the most important things that young children learn as they grow is language—how to speak and understand it. Another is learning how their physical world is arranged—where things are, how things move in it, and how to navigate it. Both of these skill sets are exceptionally important for learning math and will be discussed at length throughout the book.

This chapter will focus on additional aspects of thinking and learning that are crucial not only for learning math but for learning anything at all. They are so pervasively important that it is easy to take them for granted; indeed, their importance is often appreciated only in their absence. These skills include attention and the executive functions that control it, memory, and understanding. They are introduced here so that readers can keep them in mind as they read the chapters that follow.

ATTENTION AND MENTAL CONTROL

Basic attention is simple and innate, and even the youngest babies have some ability to attend. From the time their eyes can focus, one can usually catch a baby's attention, albeit sometimes for only a brief moment. As children develop, their attention range expands, but not by much. By the time they get to kindergarten, young children can

DOI: 10.4324/9781003157656-1

typically focus their attention on two or three things at once, such as their shoes and jacket when they are getting ready for school. Surprisingly, adults can attend to only about three or four things at once, a level most, but not all, children achieve around age ten.[1] As we will discuss in subsequent chapters, this ability to focus attention is crucial for learning math.[2] Indeed, the ability to pay attention in class in *kindergarten* is a significant predictor of math performance as late as *fifth grade*.[3]

While the capacity for paying attention is innate, however, the ability to pay attention over time (what we call *sustained attention*) is not. Indeed, as most teachers will attest, one of the most time-consuming and exhausting parts of the job is simply keeping children on task. (They are paying attention but not necessarily to the lesson.) Rather, the ability to sustain attention to something varies enormously not only across development but also across individuals and circumstances. To illustrate, let's try this thought experiment: Suppose that you are at a baseball game. And let's say, for argument's sake, that you are alone in the stands and that all you know about the game is that the object is to hit the ball with the bat, run around the bases to home plate, and avoid being tagged out. A batter is up. You have a normal adult attention range, and thus you should be able to attend to the location of the runner, the ball, the outfielder in the ball's path, and the player covering first and to follow the play without any problem.

But now let's see what happens. Suppose two friends join you. One played baseball in college and explains the rules of play. He also has been tracking the players all season, fills you in on the runner's and fielders' stats, and engages you in speculation about the batter's chances of hitting a home run. Your other friend, a fan of the opposing team, challenges you to a bet on the game's outcome. It is the seventh game of the World Series. The bottom of the ninth. The score is tied. What has happened to your ability to attend to the play?

Let's run this experiment again. Suppose the stands are full. You are hungry, and the hotdog hawker is approaching. You cannot find your wallet. You see friends three rows ahead; they wave. You notice that the batter's number is *13* and start to worry. The pitcher throws, you hear the crack of the bat on the ball, and a fight breaks out in the stands directly in front of you. Now what has happened to your ability to attend to the play?

As these thought experiments should make clear, experience and background knowledge, as well as personal importance, or *salience*, can intensify the focus of attention and help sustain it (although probably not expand it), while distractions can divert it. Being able to ignore distractions and not respond to them (what we call *inhibitory control* or *inhibition*) is crucially important for both focusing and sustaining attention.[4]

As these experiments also illustrate, some distractions are external, such as the fight breaking out in the stands. And as all teachers know, potential distractions both in the classroom and out the window are practically limitless. Other distractions are internal, such as hunger, random thoughts, or worries. In fact, mind-wandering is remarkably common in the classroom (and is normal for adults, as well).[5] In one study, nine- to 11-year-olds listened to a teacher read aloud while the researcher periodically interrupted to ask the children what they were thinking about at that moment. The children reported task-unrelated thoughts on 20 to 25 percent of the thought probes. Moreover, the weaker a child's ability to inhibit distraction, as measured by a separate task, the more frequently she reported mind wandering.[6]

Both internal and external distractions can interfere with learning. As early as preschool, inhibition has been linked to math learning, in particular—remarkably, a preschooler's capacity for inhibitory control predicts her math learning as late as fourth grade.[7] In studies of elementary students, children's computational strategy development and accuracy, math-fact errors, and procedural bugs were linked to the teacher's ratings of inattention evident in the children's general behavior.[8]

One kind of distraction particular to the math classroom is the irrelevant and misleading information often found in the math problems themselves. Here is a non-math example: *Emily's father has three daughters. The first two are named Monday and Tuesday. What is the third daughter's name?* And here is what you may well have thought: "Wednesday! . . . Oh, wait . . . No! . . . Emily!" The answer "Wednesday" comes from passive verbal association to the days of the week, not from active, rational thought. Cognitive inhibition buys the time necessary for rational thought. Not surprisingly, it also predicts success in mathematics.[9] As we discuss in Chapter 12, this issue most commonly presents itself in the context of story problems, where such decoys are often included. Irrelevant information can also interfere in math tasks as wide-ranging as comparing set sizes, calculating, reading graphs, and comparing proportions.[10] Preconceived notions and habits may also serve as distractions.[11] For example, try this: *If there are 3 apples and you take away 2, how many do you have?*[12] Only blind habit would produce the answer "one." (Would it help if the question were worded, "If there are 3 apples on the grocer's shelf and you take away 2, ..."?) For another example, habits and assumptions established during years of basic arithmetic practice risk facilitating the almost universal experience of later mistakenly treating fractions as whole numbers, as discussed in Chapter 11.[13] Research has demonstrated that children with weak inhibitory control are more likely to be lured into math errors than children with stronger inhibition. Indeed, upon reviewing the research, one scholar suggested that what sets experts apart is that they simply get to be very good at ignoring their initial impulses.[14]

Furthermore, while it is important that lessons and materials hold students' attention, there is a fine line between attention-grabbing and attention-stealing. This can be a general problem with classroom décor and especially troublesome in the design of some manipulatives and educational software, in which the effort to grab children's attention with (irrelevant) perceptual attractions may simultaneously distract it from the mathematical point to be made.[15]

One note of clarification: The term *inhibitory control* is sometimes used to refer to behavioral self-control, as well as cognitive self-control. Here we are referring to cognitive inhibition. In preschoolers and kindergartners, the two forms of self-control are closely related—those who have trouble sitting still and controlling their impulses tend to have trouble with staying on task, and vice versa. By first grade, the two forms of inhibition begin to operate more independently of one another.[16]

Finally, to stretch the baseball analogy precariously close to its limits, imagine this. You are at a baseball game. A batter is up and the bases are loaded. But this time, the batter is a southpaw, and to make things easier for him, the rules have changed: Instead of running counterclockwise, the runner is to proceed clockwise around the bases. What happens to your ability to follow the play? Or how about this: As the bat hits the ball, your cell phone rings. Someone is calling to tell you that your house is on fire. Are you able to let go of the play altogether and scramble out of the stadium?

As these improbable examples illustrate, another influence on one's ability to sustain attention is the ability to quickly switch gears from one set of rules to another, from one task to another, or from one goal to another. Such a turn-around also means that information that used to be relevant may no longer be so, while once-irrelevant information may now suddenly become important. The mental agility required (what is variously called *cognitive flexibility*, *shifting*, or *switching*) first appears in children around age four or five. Its increase during the early school years may reflect the growing role of "inner speech" in guiding the switch—that is, talking one's way through it. The youngest children may have difficulty switching because they are stuck on the first task, whereas among primary-grade children, one begins to see active preparation for the new task. Improved cognitive flexibility in the school years may also reflect the fact that learning and experience can make it easier to be flexible: Experienced first responders may be better prepared to make a smooth transition from ball-game attendance to tackling a house fire than would an untrained homeowner. The relative difficulty of the two tasks is also likely to influence the ease of transition—it is understandably more difficult to switch from an easy task to a hard one than vice versa.[17] Cognitive flexibility can also make it easier to persevere on a difficult problem, particularly one whose solution may depend on viewing the problem from a different angle.[18] Improvements seen during the elementary-school years also reflect greater efficiency in all aspects of problem-solving. Because cognitive flexibility is built on so many factors, its developmental trajectory is long; research finds that even 13-year-olds are not yet as mentally flexible as adults.[19]

It should not be surprising that mental flexibility is directly linked to math achievement.[20] It helps to be mentally flexible, for example, when faced with a series of arithmetic problems requiring different operations or multiple steps. Or in understanding how a story problem that includes the word *more* might not necessarily require addition to arrive at the solution, a topic of Chapter 12. As will be discussed in relation to arithmetic in Chapter 10, but which applies to all problem-solving, children with a variety of strategies do better than those with only one.[21] To approach a problem from different perspectives requires mental flexibility.

Inhibitory control and mental flexibility are two of what are called the mind's *executive functions*. Unlike the capacity for attention that we are born with, which is passive, the executive functions are active but develop relatively slowly.[22] Importantly, they make possible many other crucial aspects of learning: planning strategies, imagining potential consequences, analyzing results, and staying alert to errors and correcting them, as well as the "working" aspect of memory, a topic of the next section. In essence, the executive functions are the brain's orchestra conductor—they initiate, direct, coordinate, and control behavior, including attention. As such, they are critical for problem-solving, as we have seen.[23] Indeed, growth in problem-solving ability is closely tied to the development of the executive functions.[24]

Executive functions are also fragile. Deficits in executive functions have been associated with stress, as well as with the exigencies of poverty, including frequent school changes, diminished resources for cognitive stimulation, and sleep problems, with the expected effects on math learning.[25] In some young children, they can also be symptoms of autism or of conditions brought on by very premature birth or very low birth weight, compromising school readiness and math learning.[26]

The most common condition with prominent attention-control symptoms is attention-deficit-hyperactivity disorder (ADHD), a neurodevelopmental disorder involving multiple brain networks, including diminished activity in the front portion of the brain affecting the executive functions.[27] While some children with ADHD also exhibit hyperactivity and impulsiveness, research has found that difficulty regulating attention is the symptom that significantly affects math learning in children with ADHD.[28] Interestingly, a mind-wandering study of children with ADHD found that during an activity requiring attention, their minds were focused some of the time and wandered at other times, just like children without ADHD, as noted previously. However, unlike their typical peers, sometimes their minds just went blank and had no thoughts at all.[29] Children with ADHD can also occasionally hyperfocus—that is, attend so intensely that they are able to screen out everything else. As would be expected, the rate of significant math learning difficulties among children with ADHD is relatively high: nearly one in five, versus one in 15 to 20 children without ADHD. While not all children who have trouble paying attention have ADHD (its prevalence in the general population is about seven percent), its chronicity may help explain the long-lasting effects of early inattention on math performance in the large-scale studies noted earlier.[30] See Textbox 1.1 for the story of one student whose ADHD was not diagnosed until late in college.

TEXTBOX 1.1

Victor was a college senior when he was referred for assessment. A bright math major at a competitive university, he had an avid interest in economics and aspired to work in that field after college. Yet his grades in math and in math-heavy economics courses were highly uneven—he sometimes managed more difficult tasks but not easier ones, despite very hard work. In fact, for as long as he could remember, math class and math exams had made him extremely anxious. (Classes and exams in other subjects did not make him anxious.) He attributed his anxiety to his difficulty sustaining attention and mentally holding onto verbal and written information in class, where he always felt a few steps behind the other students. He also complained of difficulty with the extended thought processes required for mathematical proofs and frequently worked on them with classmates, who helped him stay focused. For the same reason, only "chewing gum like crazy" helped him get through exams, and even then he was often unable to do so in the allotted time. An exhaustive evaluation strongly suggested a diagnosis of ADHD dating from childhood, with no other underlying cause of math difficulty. Following the evaluation, he consulted with a physician, who began treating the ADHD with medication. During Victor's final semester, he took two of his most challenging math courses and performed better on them than he had on any previous ones. He graduated and currently works successfully (and calmly) as a data analyst.

Researchers caution that even such children with relatively mild inattention may have unusual difficulty with math.[31] Just as important, teachers and parents should know that many children with serious attention difficulties do not exhibit disruptive classroom behavior. Their mental disengagement may be more difficult to discover, but it can be just as deleterious to their math learning as that of their more disruptive classmates. For the most part, while trials of classroom interventions aimed at improving general executive functioning have been disappointing,[32] those that are adaptive or integrate physical activity into the classroom have had some success in increasing children's time on task and improving academic performance.[33] Teachers concerned about a student's persistent inattention should discuss the situation with the child's parents, for whom consultation with a clinical psychologist or neuropsychologist and the child's pediatrician would be appropriate next steps.[34]

Thus attention, along with the ability to focus, sustain, and control it, is essential for math learning.

MEMORY

Another mental function essential for learning is memory. Indeed, some would say that memory *is* learning, for what we do not remember, we have not learned. But memory is not just a single ability, and it is as important for the very process of learning as it is for holding onto what we already know.[35]

Long-Term Memory

One kind of memory is long-term memory, the vast store of information we accumulate over time. It includes the people and events in our lives, as well as the information (who was president during the War of 1812, the correct spelling of *accept* and *except*, the result of adding $7 + 6$) that we took pains to memorize in school. Because we were consciously aware of learning this information and can describe it, it is termed *explicit memory*. Also stored away in long-term memory, however, are other sorts of information—ideas, images, even habits and skills—that we pick up without conscious effort and are less easily put into words, referred to as *implicit memory*.[36] While this sort of ability may not be relevant to math learning, there is an interesting kind of implicit memory that is quite relevant, called *statistical learning*. Through simple exposure, the human brain is capable of picking up and remembering regularities in the environment—that is, patterns in the sights and sounds of daily life. Infants begin to learn speech from the statistical regularities in the speech sounds they hear, for example, before they know what it means or can use it themselves.[37] Kindergartners learn spelling conventions from words they see, even before they can read or are taught how to spell.[38] Similarly, as we discuss in Chapter 10, children pick up regularities in the way that numbers are associated with each other in arithmetic fact patterns. The more frequently they see *2 + 3* associated with *5*, the easier the sum is to remember. Thus, if the child himself solves it sometimes as *5* but other times as *4* or *6*, it will be more difficult to remember than if he always solves it as *5*. We discuss ways to provide error-free practice to ensure well-established memory.

Long-term memory, once established, lasts a long time. However, it does require effort and executive control, both in the study and practice needed to set down the memories and in their retrieval. Without mental focus, older, better established memories can dominate newer ones. As we discuss in Chapter 10, children often confuse newly learned multiplication facts with the already-mastered addition facts involving the same numbers (e.g., *5 × 6 = 11*). The reverse (*5 + 6 = 30*) can also occur if a child has more recently been practicing multiplication. These mistakes are referred to as *table errors*. Similarly, younger children occasionally lapse from an addition fact into the overlearned counting sequence (e.g., *3 + 6 = 7*). Interestingly, one small study demonstrated that children with untreated ADHD often have difficulty with the effortful demands of explicit memory but not with implicit memory.[39]

Of course, the primary goal of math education is for children to understand mathematics. How that happens will be the topic of the next section of this chapter. However, it is important for math development that some information, such as basic arithmetic facts, be committed to long-term memory for rapid, automatic retrieval during complex problem-solving. A child may be able to solve *3 + 6 = __* accurately and understand what it means but may still not have rapid, automatic access to its result. Without such automatic recall, the attention needed to solve *43 + 66 = __* will be siphoned off by these more basic calculations, increasing the likelihood of error and frustration.

Establishing information in long-term memory for ready access requires effortful strategizing. Research has revealed some useful classroom strategies that work as well for arithmetic facts as spelling lists. Their particulars may become more varied, ambitious, and sophisticated as children develop, of course, but these are some of the basics.[40]

One approach is to tie the bits of to-be-memorized information together in meaningful clusters (e.g., addition-subtraction "fact families") or to other already-mastered information. As noted earlier, if children practice these simple arithmetic combinations with few errors, implicit statistical learning should help them retain the associations and facilitate retrieval. Teacher-directed cueing ("If seven and three is the same amount as ten, then . . .") can help.

Another perhaps surprising approach is effortful retrieval in the form of periodic, no-stakes quizzing, which has proven remarkably effective in establishing information in long-term memory—indeed, more effective than just studying. Teacher questioning can also spur effortful retrieval. Crucially, immediate corrective feedback and self-correction are imperative to prevent erroneous information from being stored in long-term memory instead. Children also benefit from charting their own progress on the quizzes. Quizzing is more likely to be effective for long-term retention if accomplished in brief episodes spaced out over time (*distributed practice*) than if done all at one time (*massed practice*), with longer intervals more effective than short ones.[41] Most importantly, however, quizzing is ill-advised until accuracy has been fully achieved under untimed conditions, lest quizzing becomes an occasion for practicing errors.

Finally, understanding *how* one remembers can facilitate memory. Cognitive research reveals that a teacher's questions and reflections can help a child develop the memory and self-monitoring skills necessary to master all kinds of information. For example, teachers can simply ask, "How did you remember that?" when a child retrieves correct information. Or, "What are some strategies you could use to help you figure that out?" Or, "How did you solve that problem?" Or, "How did we do that yesterday?" Or, "What is the first thing you need to do?" These sorts of questions are exercises in what is called *meta-cognition*, which simply means teaching a child to think about thinking.[42] Providing the child with a reminder, however, should be undertaken cautiously: It will take some time for the child to absorb the reminder, and moving on to something else too quickly afterward will defeat its purpose.[43]

The ability to set down long-term memories is hardwired in our brains. It is evident as early as infancy, and the brain's capacity for storing memories is practically unlimited.

Short-Term and Working Memory

There is another kind of memory, however—*short-term memory*—that is stored elsewhere in the brain and serves a very different purpose.[44] Short-term memory pertains to the very small amount of information that we can hold in mind at one time. In that sense, it is not much different from attention and is similarly limited and affected by distraction.[45] If long-term memory is remembering what the three branches of government are, then short-term memory is remembering someone's phone number just long enough to enter it into Contacts, with no final exam or even a quiz at the end of the week. Short-term memories in auditory form are stored separately in the brain from those in visual imagery or spatial configurations. Given the close dependence of short-term memory on attention, it is not surprising that many children with ADHD have trouble with it as well.[46]

Short-term memory is also an intrinsic part of what is called *working memory*—that is, the ability to hold onto information while using it; and here again, the brain handles auditory and visual-spatial information separately. Working memory is required in arithmetic tasks such as mentally adding *15 + 7*—remembering the two numbers while adding them and remembering the result—particularly if the strategy involves trading.[47] More complex problems, such as adding *9 + 7 + 8 + 6* in one's head, additionally require one to keep track of the running totals: *9 + 7 = 16; 16 + 8 = 24; 24 + 6 = 30,* or any arrangement of subtotals: *9 + 6 = 15; 7 + 8 = 15; 15 + 15 = 30*. Further, to make room in one's head for the subtotals, one needs to let go of the addends. Tracking the resulting new information and letting go of no-longer-needed bits of old information constitute an executive function called *updating*. Moreover, as you no doubt discovered if you tried this problem yourself, working memory requires a great deal of attention. Indeed, it can feel as though remembering the numbers and adding them at the same time compete for whatever attention you can give, and doing both simultaneously can feel like mental juggling.[48] Directing attention with this kind of mental agility requires executive control, as does filtering out of this very limited mental space all irrelevant information, as discussed in relation to attention. This directing-and-filtering part of working memory is called the *central executive*, which one scholarly wag likened to a bouncer at a very exclusive club.[49] The more information involved and the more complex its manipulation—mentally adding *367 + 458*, say—the more mental control that is required and thus the higher the chance of failure.

A vast amount of research attests to the close tie between working memory and math ability.[50] Arithmetic tasks that depend most on working memory include, among others, writing multi-digit numbers, solving story problems, using a decomposition strategy efficiently, and executing both exact and estimated calculations, particularly those that involve trading, as one might imagine. Fractional comparisons and computations can be especially challenging before about age 11 or so, because they generally consist of at least four different numerical elements (e.g., $\frac{2}{3} = \frac{6}{9}$)—a lot to keep in mind.[51] As with the executive functions discussed in the previous section, the central executive of working memory (particularly verbal working memory) is fragile and vulnerable to stress and anxiety.[52] For some children with serious math difficulties, trouble with short-term and working memory, including updating, can be specific to numerical information. The reason for this is not well understood but may pertain to difficulty with the verbal counting sequence or the concept of number, topics taken up in later chapters.[53]

For most children, both short- and long-term memory improve throughout childhood. Research reveals that short-term memory capacity increases two- to three-fold between the ages of four and 14. Working memory also develops rapidly during childhood. However, because working memory requires more executive control, which is governed by more slowly developing brain regions, its development lags behind that of short-term memory.[54]

If a child's attention is limited to only two or three things at a time, what accounts for the ability of short-term and even working memory to expand beyond that limit? According to one study, about 15 percent of the difference is accounted for by brain maturation. Indeed, some scholars think that there may be some true differences in capacity, both among peers and over time.[55] The rest, however, is accounted for by strengthened executive controls and efficiency, as well as by human ingenuity in the form of strategies.

What can one do to hold onto such ephemeral information?[56] Of course, one strategy, which applies as well to grocery lists, driving directions, and addition subtotals, is to simply outfox working memory altogether and write it down. In math class, committing mental calculations to paper, jotting down subtotals, or, as we discuss in Chapter 12, sketching a diagram of relevant story-problem information, will relieve working memory that is either overloaded or poorly defended against irrelevant distractions. In a similar vein, letting go of information no longer needed also frees up memory space—once the bread is in the shopping cart, one no longer needs to keep it on the mental grocery list.

The most common way to keep verbal information alive in short-term memory is to rehearse it, either aloud or in one's head. Some children tend to scramble numbers in their heads between seeing or hearing them and writing them down or punching them into a calculator. Verbal rehearsal may help maintain accuracy during the transition. Research has shown that children under age seven or so do not spontaneously rehearse to remember.[57] However, like other strategies discussed here, it can easily be taught, with good results.

One of the skills that develops throughout childhood is *processing speed*, the rate at which a person can do a mental task. Research has shown that adults can remember as many things as they can recite in two seconds and that older children can recite (rehearse) faster and thus remember more than younger children. In fact, there is a direct association between processing speed and working memory from preschool through young adulthood. With increased speed of rehearsal, however, comes a greater chance that number words that sound similar—"five" and "nine," or "thirty" and "thirteen," for example—will get confused.[58] The other note of caution is that children with developmental language deficits may find verbal rehearsal difficult: Even if they can remember a list, they may have trouble keeping the order of items straight.[59]

It is also the case that mentally grouping items to be remembered allows one to remember more—for example, remembering a shopping list by thinking of the sections of the grocery store in which the items can be found. Thus, the natural grouping of digits into multi-digit numbers means that remembering three two-digit numbers (*37–58–92*) should be easier than remembering six digits (*3-7-5-8-9-2*). Both the verbal and visual place-value distinctions, as well as the natural pauses or spaces between such numbers, should make their grouping evident. Children begin to use grouping cues to help them remember around age eight,[60] which is when they typically are mastering multi-digit addition and subtraction.

As noted earlier, the human mind is capable of remembering visual and spatial, as well as auditory, information for short-term use. Examples include a planned route while driving, or the appearance of *3 + 5 = 8* on the screen, or the location of *7* on a mental number line. Spatial skills, in particular, including spatial working memory, are perhaps surprisingly crucial for math learning, as discussed in Chapters 4 and 5. Indeed, visual-spatial working memory and arithmetic share brain circuits in both children and adults.[61] The growth rate of spatial working memory through the elementary-school years has been shown to predict fifth-grade math achievement.[62] Weak spatial working memory has been repeatedly linked to weak math skills, while especially strong spatial working memory has been linked to high math achievement and more sophisticated arithmetic strategies.[63] Children with non-verbal learning difficulties, developmental coordination disorder, or Turner syndrome often have particularly weak spatial working memory.[64] Like short-term verbal memories, visual-spatial memories must also be refreshed to stay alive in the mind, as can be done by repeatedly visualizing them in one's mind. Mentally including a verbal description of the elements along with one's mental visual image of them significantly boosts their memorability—for example, thinking "three plus five equals eight" while visualizing $3 + 5 = 8$. Note, however, that children with hearing or language deficits may require extra support.[65]

Short-term and working memory can also be stops along the way to long-term memory. For example, young children at first remember the counting-word sequence, "one-two-three-four-five" (as if it were a single word) just long enough to repeat it and then through practice get it into long-term storage. Because working memory requires so much attention, regular practice keeping information in working memory can help secure it in long-term memory as well. But beware: Overloading working memory with more than two or three bits of such information will create a bottleneck en route to long-term memory and thus will be self-defeating.[66]

Finally, one's well-learned knowledge can be enormously useful on tasks requiring short-term recall. Knowing by heart the addition-subtraction fact combinations, for example, can take a load off working memory while one is doing complex, multi-digit sums—much the same way that knowing a favorite cake recipe by heart can make baking it much more efficient. For this reason, children who can nimbly jump back and forth from working to long-term memory are quicker to adopt more sophisticated calculation strategies, such as decomposition. In this sense, long-term memory is working memory's best friend.[67] It is also the most cogent argument for the importance of committing basic arithmetic facts to memory. Moreover, the sheer burden on working memory in learning without the support of established knowledge has led some scholars to argue against the wisdom of minimal-guidance ("constructivist") pedagogy in favor of highly structured approaches for children new to a concept and for those slower to catch on.[68]

Children's discovery of strategies to improve recall increases significantly through the course of childhood and varies considerably from child to child, as do children's efficiency, flexibility, and adaptiveness in using them.[69] As we discuss in relation to arithmetic strategies in Chapter 10, the larger the number of strategies available to a child, the better position she is in to tackle a problem, including the challenge of remembering. And provided that a child does not have seriously impaired attention, strategies to improve memory can be taught.[70] (We distinguish here between teaching memory strategies and "training working memory," which has largely been unsuccessful.[71]) Moreover, with continuing brain maturation (and sufficient attention), children's judgments about the wisdom of their strategy choices—for remembering and for arithmetic problem-solving—improve, along with their confidence in those judgments. Their keener awareness of their own mistakes makes it possible to learn from them.[72]

UNDERSTANDING

Attention and memory are two essential ingredients of learning. A third essential ingredient is understanding—making an idea one's own, being able to apply and explain it, and, of course, remembering it.

The discussion here will focus on two key components of mathematical understanding. The first is relationships. Elementary mathematics is about quantitative and spatial relationships. As discussed in the early chapters, one of the first things the youngest children understand about quantity is that one quantity can be more or less than another. By sometime in preschool, children learn to match groups of objects and discover that two amounts can also be the same. These three relational ideas about quantity—more than, less than, and the same amount as—are foundational for mathematics from preschool through high school. For this reason, children require a thorough understanding of what numbers mean and how they relate to each other, the critical underpinning of arithmetic.[73] Indeed, there is some evidence that children's ability to think relationally about many things, not just numbers, predicts their success in high school math and science and is central to work in all areas of math, science, engineering, and technology (the STEM fields).[74] The ability to think relationally grows with education and brain maturation.[75]

The second critical component is problem-solving. To solve a quantitative problem, one must understand what it is asking. One must also understand the various strategies that are available to solve it—not just how to use them but also *why* one strategy might be better than another for any particular problem. Thus, the three questions that a child should be able to answer in solving any problem are: 1) What is the problem asking? 2) What are some ways I can solve it? and 3) Which strategy is best for this problem?

Cognitive science has much to offer mathematical pedagogy.[76] Here, we discuss three general routes to relational reasoning and problem-solving: language and gesture, comparison, and patterns.

Language and Gesture

One way to help children think relationally is to use relational language. With the youngest children, specifying objects' relationship as spatial (*on top*, *in*, *under*, rather than *there*) or functional (*rabbits eat carrots*, rather than *rabbits and carrots go together*) is an effective way to demonstrate a relationship in a way that children can then generalize it to other objects.[77] In that sense, specifying a relationship makes it more usefully abstract. In the elementary math classroom, the most pervasively available yet undervalued tool for conveying numerical relationships is the humble = sign.[78] Unfortunately, most children translate it as *equals, is, adds up to*, or *makes*. However, translated as *is the same amount as* conveys the relational meaning of = much more transparently: *3 + 5 is the same amount as 8*. In fact, mathematical notational language provides symbols for all three of the most basic quantitative relationships: <, >, and =. Inequality is usually introduced relatively late in the curriculum. This is surprising, because even the youngest children are familiar with those quantitative relationships, a good argument for introducing them earlier. Indeed, one study found that third- and fourth-graders who were taught to use them made greater gains in math than did those who were not,[79] leading one to wonder whether they could be introduced even earlier, right along with the concept of equivalence. Research on this question is warranted. One note of caution is in order, however. For neurodevelopmental reasons discussed in Chapter 8, children may confuse the mirrored symbols > and < prior to third grade, but the concepts of more than and less than should not be a problem.

Gesture is another highly effective route to understanding. For younger children, teachers' gestures can suggest both spatial and quantitative relationships. Among older students, teachers can gesture to direct students' attention to the critical aspects of written problems, as well as synchronize gesture with verbal instruction to influence what students learn from it.[80] In the next few chapters, we will also see how gestures can help explain all manner of spatial quantitative features, such as relative size, distance, shape, and so on. Just as important, children can use it themselves to help them explain their thinking when they do not yet have the proper words to do so, to retrieve words they may have forgotten, and to understand. Moreover, there are many ways that fingers can tag items and communicate numerosities, as we will discuss in Chapter 7. Studies of the youngest children show that pointing leads to more accurate object-counting than just trying to coordinate visual attention and the number sequence. Pointing also reinforces the idea of a one-to-one relationship between number words and items.[81] The more difficult the counting task, the more likely a preschooler will gesture, suggesting that she is using it to help her think.[82] Research with older children who are learning to solve missing-addend problems (involving quantitative relationships across the = sign) reveals that simply encouraging them to gesture while doing a problem gets them to arrive at new strategies and prepares them for learning. Moreover, those children who were told to gesture while explaining their strategy performed significantly better on a test four weeks later than those who were told to describe their strategy in words only.[83] The researchers speculated that the gestures represent an underlying, implicit understanding and that the synergy between this implicit understanding and explicit, verbal understanding can facilitate learning.[84] Importantly, a mismatch between a child's speech and gestures while solving a problem often indicates that the child is dealing with conflicting ideas. This is a transitional state that makes it highly likely that she will learn[85]; as such, it is a useful signal to teachers.

Comparison

Coming to understand something by comparing it to something more familiar is one of the most effective ways that children learn. And comparing two relationships—that is, reasoning by *analogy*—is one of the best ways to learn about relative quantity.[86] As will be discussed in full in this book, children can compare quantities in many ways. For example, they can compare them non-symbolically with sets of objects or fingers, verbally by noting where the number words fall relative to each other in the counting sequence, and spatially by their relative locations on the number line. Indeed, the number line provides one of the most powerful analogies for understanding number in that it portrays the relationship between quantities in terms of the more familiar and accessible idea of distance and direction between two points on a line. Scaling—a form of analogy that explains the relationships between large, unfamiliar quantities in terms of those between smaller, familiar ones, like map reading—can foster understanding of the structure of the written number system and number lines in different ranges,[87] as we discuss in Chapter 9 and in relation to fractions in Chapter 11. The best manipulatives, such as rods or number blocks, if properly designed to focus the child's attention on length/quantity, can also provide a familiar length analogy to number and numerical relations.[88]

Comparison is also a powerful route to understanding both the nature of quantitative problems and their various solution strategies.[89] (We make no distinction here between concepts and procedures, since understanding one facilitates understanding the other.[90]) Studying correctly worked solutions is an excellent way to introduce a new type of problem or strategy that minimizes the working memory load and allows the child to focus on the nature of the problem.[91] However, once the problem and one solution strategy become a bit more familiar, a route to deeper understanding is to compare one worked example to others that use different strategies and to figure out how they are different and under what circumstances one strategy would be more useful than another.[92] Or to compare (contrast) correctly and incorrectly worked examples and explain why an incorrect strategy does not work.[93] Or to compare (contrast) solutions of easily confused types of problems, such as *1 + 0* and *1 × 0*.

In East Asian classrooms, teachers often devote the entire class time to an open, full-class discussion of a single problem, looking at it from different angles, with the emphasis on reasoning rather than answers.[94] In this setting, children produce their own alternative correct—and incorrect—strategies to compare and contrast. Another key feature of the East Asian approach to teaching by analogy is the abundant use of gestures and other familiar visual and spatial cues—for example, a balance scale while balancing equations—to provide an ongoing reminder of the familiar analog and reduce the load on children's long-term and working memory.[95] Indeed, some children make the connection simply by practicing on familiar problems immediately before attempting a new, analogous problem in the same format. Seeing those familiar cues in place while doing so is sufficient to help them make the connection.[96]

Finally, the extent to which practice incorporates comparison and contrast can strongly affect how much a child learns from it. Blocked practice, the most common textbook assignment in which the child solves only similar problems, can foster procedural familiarity but not necessarily understanding. (Successfully completing a blocked practice can also leave a child with an overestimation of how well he fully understands it.) Once blocked practice has established a basic familiarity, interleaving (intermixing) recently learned problems with well-learned problems, where a child has to decide the best strategy for each problem in turn, can significantly strengthen her understanding. Interleaved practice takes more time than blocked exercises and typically requires considerably more thought. However, when the problems vary in their fundamental structure, the essential similarities and differences between problem types will foster deeper understanding of them and greater flexibility in solving them.[97]

A few words of caution are in order. The best approach to introducing a new idea will depend entirely on the age of the children, how quickly they tend to catch on to new ideas, an estimate of their executive-function development, and how dissimilar the new idea is to what they are already familiar with. The younger the class, the more likely they will struggle with new ideas and the more distracted they are likely to be by irrelevant information. Moreover, the more dissimilar the new idea is to the ones they are familiar with, the more structured the introduction of a new idea will need to be (worked problems, blocked practice, teacher guidance). The youngest children need to learn from problems highly similar to what they already know, although this will set them up for more distant comparisons in the future. Finally, if the relationship involves a change or transformation, the youngest children will likely not understand it unless the *cause* of the change is made clear.[98] For example, the idea that adding *1* to *2* produces the same kind of change as adding *1* to *3* may need to be illustrated with countable objects. The brain is capable of supporting thinking by analogy by age six. However, with close linguistic, gestural, and other instructional support, even younger children can benefit from such comparisons.[99]

Among older children, the degree of "newness" may help determine how much structure they need at the start. If the problem is similar to types they are already familiar with, they may benefit from a chance to explore it before formal instruction. The newer the problem type, the more structure required. An adult analogy here may help: Your dishwasher breaks down. If you have never repaired an appliance before, you will need step-by-step written instructions with diagrams, and it might take you all day to figure it out. A professional appliance repair person will either know what to do or, if the machine is a new brand, may need a quick look at the manual. Being confronted with a problem that is brand new without support can lead, at best, to befuddlement and, at worst, to serious misconceptions and injured self-confidence. The critical element is that the teacher keep his ears and eyes open for misunderstandings and intervene right away. A similar benefit accrues from the immediate feedback provided by *adaptive* computer instruction.[100]

Patterns

Mathematics is full of patterns. Indeed, one scholar termed it "the science of patterns."[101] There are predictable patterns everywhere in math, even at the most elementary level: Adding *one* to a number produces the same amount as the next number in the counting sequence. Adding or subtracting *zero* leaves you with the same amount you started with. Adding *a* to *b* comes to the same amount as adding *b* to *a*. The even and odd numbers alternate predictably. Decimal notation is based on a highly predictable system (the number words somewhat less so). And so on. Thus, having an eye for predictable patterns, being in the habit of looking for them, or even appreciating a pattern when it is brought to one's attention can greatly broaden one's numerical vista and provide a shortcut to any number of problem solutions.

As of this writing, there are more than a dozen studies of young children's ability to identify, extend, and abstract predictable sequential patterns.[102] The children in these studies are typically in the age range of four to six years old, and the sequences, usually consisting of pictures, colors, or geometric shapes, are repeating (e.g., ABAB, ABBABB, ABCABC) or growing/shrinking (e.g., ABAABAAAB, ABBBABBAB). The children are asked to copy them with the same or different figures, identify the pattern units (e.g., ABB), and, where possible, extend them—in other words, to reason about the relationships among their parts. In general, preschoolers could copy and extend the patterns and abstract them to different figures, abilities that improved with age. Only a few, however, could explicitly identify the pattern units (i.e., the pattern, such as red blue blue, that repeats, grows, or shrinks), a skill that does not typically emerge until the end of kindergarten.[103] Moreover, these skills were found to depend significantly on working memory.[104]

Most importantly for our purposes, however, young children's patterning skills, along with their tendency to create patterns in their play, were significantly associated with their general numerical ability.[105] Studies that followed children's progress found that the association held over time—preschool patterning skill was an important predictor of math achievement as late as middle school.[106]

The repeating and growing patterns discussed here are typically based on logical analogy—that is, a fundamental similarity between two relationships. As children approach middle school, however, additional relational patterns and tasks become relevant—for example, picking out of a set an item that does *not* belong, or finding an opposite relationship, or identifying which items do and do not belong to a particular category. By middle school, this more expanded relational reasoning becomes relevant to math ability.[107]

Furthermore, several studies have found that patterning skills can be taught. For example, using the same sort of concrete patterning tasks, teachers can point out the regularities in the sequences ("See, there's one of these and two of these, one of these and two of these"); to do so, it was found that labeling the pattern using abstract, generalizable language ("See, it goes A, B, B") was more effective than labeling the particular figures in the task ("It goes one red, two blue").[108] Moreover, among first graders with weak patterning skills, six months' intervention in patterning significantly improved children's math performance, probably because it helped children focus on underlying relationships.[109] This success is particularly good news, because the students in these studies were largely from low-income households and were missing key early math skills.

As with comparisons, a word of caution is in order here as well, which is that children tend to overgeneralize new information and may assume that patterns applicable to one mathematical situation automatically apply to all mathematical situations. Many mathematical patterns do *not* universally generalize. For example, numbers can be added or multiplied, but not subtracted, in any order. Adding *zero* to a number does not work the same way as multiplying a number by *zero*. Number-word patterns above "twenty" do not apply to those between "ten" and "nineteen." Rational numbers often do not behave the way whole numbers do.

Conversely, some patterns apply more widely than children are frequently led to believe. For example, just because numerical operations are located to the left of the = sign in many equations does not mean they cannot also be located on the right. *More* is often used in word problems requiring addition for solution but can be used in word problems requiring other operations as well. Teachers need to anticipate such overgeneralizations and concreteness and make them explicit as such in the classroom. Moreover, children with an eye for patterns may also implicitly pick up on math-irrelevant regularities in textbooks. For example, in a study of textbook presentations of rational numbers, researchers found that textbooks feature equal denominators significantly more frequently in addition than multiplication problems, leading children to associate equal denominators with the fraction addition procedure.[110] Such insidious, uneven distribution of examples and practice opportunities abound in math textbooks and can have a profound effect on how children come to understand the material, particularly when teachers absorb those regularities into their lesson plans and homework assignments.[111]

CONCLUSION

The mental setting in which a child begins her mathematical education is a-buzz with work in progress. The abilities to focus attention; to fend off distractions long enough to track, manipulate, and remember information; and to make sense of how things work are all undergoing rapid development, particularly in the early years. And all of these abilities will help determine how any given child learns mathematics (and learning mathematics, in turn, will help strengthen those abilities). The mathematical skill and knowledge acquired during the early years of schooling depend heavily on attention and memory and call upon a multitude of strategies and ways of understanding problems. The remaining chapters in this book focus on the mathematics, but the reader is strongly urged to keep in mind the mental setting in which it is learned.

Moreover, these skills do not develop in a vacuum. Far from it. Teachers and parents play a critical role in facilitating them. For this reason, all but the last of the forthcoming chapters offer research-supported interventions that focus on understanding and take into account children's ability to attend and remember.

With that said, the story now begins.

NOTES

1 Halford et al., 2007.
2 Commodari & DiBlasi, 2014; Dulaney et al., 2015.
3 Claessens et al., 2009.
4 Reck & Hund, 2011.
5 Smallwood et al., 2008.
6 Keulers & Jonkman, 2019.
7 Birgisdottir et al., 2020.

8 Geary et al., 2012; Raghubar et al., 2009; but see, Moffett & Morrison, 2020.

9 Young & Shtulman, 2020.

10 Gilmore et al., 2015; Kaminski & Sloutsky, 2013.

11 Robinson & Dubé, 2013.

12 Young & Shtulman, 2020.

13 Alibali & Sidney, 2015.

14 Mareschal, 2016.

15 Chan & Mazzocco, 2017; Donovan & Alibali, 2021; Fisher et al., 2014; Mazzocco et al., 2020; Willingham, 2017.

16 Oeri et al., 2018.

17 Cragg & Chevalier, 2012.

18 Oeri et al., 2020.

19 Davidson et al., 2006.

20 Yeniad et al., 2013.

21 Siegler, 1996.

22 Albert & Steinberg, 2011.

23 Andersson, 2007; Ellefson et al., 2020.

24 Swanson, 2020.

25 Lawson et al., 2018.

26 Aarnoudse-Moens et al., 2009; Pellicano et al., 2017.

27 Bastos Vieira deMelo et al., 2018; Wiersema et al., 2005.

28 Merrell et al., 2017.

29 Van den Driessche et al., 2017.

30 Thomas et al., 2015.

31 Merrell et al., 2017.

32 Diamond & Ling, 2016.

33 Kibbe et al., 2011; Peng & Miller, 2016.

34 Zentall et al., 2013.

35 Schneider, 2014.

36 Lloyd & Newcombe, 2009.

37 Aslin, 2017.

38 Krasa & Bell, 2021.

39 Aloisi et al., 2004.

40 Bjorkland et al., 2009; Booth et al., 2017.

41 Fazio & Marsh, 2019; Gerbier & Toppino, 2015.

42 Bellon et al., 2019; Ornstein & Coffman, 2020.

43 Katzoff et al., 2020.

44 Cowan, 2014.

45 Beattie et al., 2018.

46 Andersen et al., 2013.

47 Gathercole et al., 2004.

48 Barrouillet & Camos, 2012.

49 Awh & Vogel, 2008.

50 Ahmed et al., 2019; Geary et al., 2012; Peng et al., 2016.

51 Halford et al., 2007.

52 Cargnelutti et al., 2017.

53 Pelegrina et al., 2015.

54 Cowan, 2014.

55 Barriga-Paulino et al., 2017; Luck & Vogel, 2013.

56 Cowan, 2014.

57 Camos & Barrouillet, 2011.

58 Hulme & Tordoff, 1989.

59 Gillam et al., 1995.

60 Towse et al., 1999.

61 Matejko & Ansari, 2021.

62 Li & Geary, 2013.

63 Hammerstein et al., 2021; Mammarella et al., 2018; Menon, 2016.

64 Brankaer et al., 2017; Mammarella et al., 2010; Wang et al., 2017.

65 Botting et al., 2017; Kibbe & Feigenson, 2014.

66 Forsberg et al., 2021.

67 Miller-Cotto & Byrnes, 2020; Rhodes & Cowan, 2018.

68 Kirschner et al., 2006; Sweller, 2016.

69 Schneider & Ornstein, 2015.

70 Schneider, 2014; Swanson, 2015.

71 Melby-Lervåg et al., 2016; Roberts et al., 2016; Soveri et al., 2017.

72 Tamnes et al., 2013.

73 Smith, 2002.

74 Blums et al., 2017.

75 Singley & Bunge, 2014.

76 Booth et al., 2017.

77 Gentner et al., 2011.

78 Chesney et al., 2018.

79 Hattikudur & Alibali, 2010.

80 Wakefield et al., 2018.

81 Alibali & DiRusso, 1999.

82 Gordon et al., 2019.

83 Cook et al., 2008.

84 Broaders et al., 2007.

85 Church, 1999.

86 Gentner & Hoyos, 2017.

87 Thompson & Opfer, 2010.

88 Willingham, 2017.

89 Gray & Holyoak, 2021; Rittle-Johnson et al., 2020.

90 Rittle-Johnson & Schneider, 2014.

91 Kirschner et al., 2006.

92 Brown & Alibali, 2018.

93 Durkin & Rittle-Johnson, 2012.

94 Stevenson & Stigler, 1992.

95 Richland et al., 2007.

96 Sidney & Thompson, 2019; Yu et al., in press.

97 Rohrer, 2012; Rohrer et al., 2020.

98 Goddu et al., 2020.

99   Vendetti et al., 2015; Yuan et al., 2017.
100 Fyfe & Rittle-Johnson, 2016; Kalyuga et al., 2001.
101 Steen, 1988.
102 Burgoyne et al., 2017.
103 Clarke et al., 2006.
104 Miller et al., 2016.
105 Rittle-Johnson et al., 2017; Wijns et al., 2020.
106 Claessens & Engel, 2013; Rittle-Johnson et al., 2017.
107 Zhao et al., 2021.
108 Flynn et al., 2020.
109 Kidd et al., 2014.
110 Braithwaite et al., 2017.
111 Siegler et al., 2020.

REFERENCES

The following references were cited in this chapter. For additional selected references relevant to this chapter, please see Chapter 1 Supplemental References in eResources.

Aarnoudse-Moens, C.S.H., Weisglas-Kuperus, N., vanGoudoever, J.B., & Oosterlaan, J. (2009). Meta-analysis of neurobehavioral outcomes in very preterm and/or very low birth weight children. *Pediatrics, 124,* 717–728.

Ahmed, S.F., Tang, S., Waters, N.E., & Davis-Kean, P. (2019). Executive function and academic achievement: Longitudinal relations from early childhood to adolescence. *Journal of Educational Psychology, 111,* 446–458.

Albert, D., & Steinberg, L. (2011). Age differences in strategic planning as indexed by the Tower of London. *Child Development, 82,* 1501–1517.

Alibali, M.W., & DiRusso, A.A. (1999). The function of gesture in learning to count: More than keeping track. *Cognitive Development, 14,* 37–56.

Alibali, M.W., & Sidney, P.G. (2015). Variability in the natural number bias: Who, when, how, and why. *Learning and Instruction, 37,* 56–61.

Aloisi, B.A., McKone, E., & Heubeck, B.G. (2004). Implicit and explicit memory performance in children with attention deficit/hyperactivity disorder. *British Journal of Developmental Psychology, 22,* 275–292.

Andersen, P.N., Egeland, J., & Øie, M. (2013). Learning and memory impairments in children and adolescents with attention-deficit/hyperactivity disorder. *Journal of Learning Disabilities, 46,* 453–460.

Andersson, U. (2007). The contribution of working memory to children's mathematical word problem solving. *Applied Cognitive Psychology, 21,* 1201–1216.

Aslin, R.N. (2017). Statistical learning: A powerful mechanism that operates by mere exposure. *Wiley Interdisciplinary Reviews: Cognitive Science, 8,* e1373.

Awh, E., & Vogel, E.K. (2008). The bouncer in the brain. *Nature Neuroscience, 11,* 5–6.

Barriga-Paulino, C.I., Rodríguez-Martínez, E.I., Arjona, A., Morales, M., & Gómez, C.M. (2017). Developmental trajectories of event related potentials related to working memory. *Neuropsychologia, 95,* 215–226.

Barrouillet, P., & Camos, V. (2012). As time goes by: Temporal constraints in working memory. *Current Directions in Psychological Science, 21,* 413–419.

Bastos Vieira deMelo, B., Trigueiro, M.J., & Rodrigues, P.P. (2018). Systematic overview of neuroanatomical differences in ADHD: Definitive evidence. *Developmental Neuropsychology, 43,* 52–68.

Beattie, H.L., Schutte, A.R., & Cortesa, C.S. (2018). The relationship between spatial working memory precision and attention and inhibitory control in young children. *Cognitive Development, 47*, 32–45.

Bellon, E., Fias, W., & DeSmedt, B. (2019). More than number sense: The additional role of executive functions and metacognition in arithmetic. *Journal of Experimental Child Psychology, 182*, 38–60.

Birgisdottir, F., Gestsdottir, S., & Geldhof, G.J. (2020). Early predictors of first and fourth grade reading and math: The role of self-regulation and early literacy skills. *Early Childhood Research Quarterly, 53*, 507–519.

Bjorkland, D.F., Dukes, C., & Brown, R.D. (2009). The development of memory strategies. In M.L. Courage & N. Cowan (Eds.), *The development of memory in infancy and childhood* (pp. 145–175). Psychology Press.

Blums, A., Belsky, J., Grimm, K., & Chen, Z. (2017). Building links between early socioeconomic status, cognitive ability, and math and science achievement. *Journal of Cognition and Development, 18*, 16–40.

Booth, J.L., McGinn, K.M., Barbieri, C., Begolli, K.N., Chang, B., Miller-Cotto, D., Young, L.K., & Davenport, J.L. (2017). Evidence for cognitive science principles that impact learning in mathematics. In D.C. Geary, D.B. Berch, R. Ochsendorf, & K.M. Koepke (Eds.), *Acquisition of complex arithmetic skills and higher-order mathematics concepts* (pp. 297–325). Academic Press.

Botting, N., Jones, A., Marshall, C., Denmark, T., Atkinson, J., & Morgan, G. (2017). Nonverbal executive function is mediated by language: A study of deaf and hearing children. *Child Development, 88*, 1689–1700.

Braithwaite, D.W., Pyke, A.A., & Siegler, R.S. (2017). A computational model of fraction arithmetic. *Psychological Review, 124*, 603–625.

Brankaer, C., Ghesquière, P., DeWel, A., Swillen, A., & DeSmedt, B. (2017). Numerical magnitude processing impairments in genetic syndromes: A cross-syndrome comparison of Turner and 22q11.2 deletion syndromes. *Developmental Science, 20*, e12458.

Broaders, S.C., Cook, S.W., Mitchell, Z., & Goldin-Meadow, S. (2007). Making children gesture brings out implicit knowledge and leads to learning. *Journal of Experimental Psychology: General, 136*, 539–550.

Brown, S.A., & Alibali, M.W. (2018). Promoting strategy change: Mere exposure to alternative strategies helps, but feedback can hurt. *Journal of Cognition and Development, 19*, 301–324.

Burgoyne, K., Witteveen, K., Tolan, A., Malone, S., & Hulme, C. (2017). Pattern understanding: Relationships with arithmetic and reading development. *Child Development Perspectives, 11*, 239–244.

Camos, V., & Barrouillet, P. (2011). Developmental change in working memory strategies: From passive maintenance to active refreshing. *Developmental Psychology, 47*, 898–904.

Cargnelutti, E., Tomasetto, C., & Passolunghi, M.C. (2017). The interplay between affective and cognitive factors in shaping early proficiency in mathematics. *Trends in Neuroscience and Education, 8–9*, 28–36.

Chan, J.Y.-C., & Mazzocco, M.M.M. (2017). Competing features influence children's attention to number. *Journal of Experimental Child Psychology, 156*, 62–81.

Chesney, D.L., McNeil, N.M., Petersen, L.A., & Dunwiddie, A.E. (2018). Arithmetic practice that includes relational words promotes understanding of symbolic equations. *Learning and Individual Differences, 64*, 104–112.

Church, R.B. (1999). Using gesture and speech to capture transition in learning. *Cognitive Development, 14*, 313–342.

Claessens, A., Duncan, G.J., & Engel, M. (2009). Kindergarten skills and fifth grade achievement: Evidence from the ECLS-K. *Economics of Education Review, 28*, 415–427.

Claessens, A., & Engel, M. (2013). How important is where you start? Early mathematics knowledge and later school success. *Teachers College Record, 115*, 060306.

Clarke, B., Clarke, D., & Cheeseman, J. (2006). The mathematical knowledge and understanding young children bring to school. *Mathematics Education Research Journal, 18*, 78–102.

Commodari, E., & DiBlasi, M. (2014). The role of the different components of attention on calculation skill. *Learning and Individual Differences, 32*, 225–232.

Cook, S.W., Mitchell, Z., & Goldin-Meadow, S. (2008). Gesturing makes learning last. *Cognition, 106*, 1047–1058.

Cowan, N. (2014) Short-term and working memory in childhood. In P.J. Bauer & R. Fivush (Eds.), *The Wiley handbook on the development of children's memory* (Vol. I, pp. 202–229). Wiley-Blackwell.

Cragg, L., & Chevalier, N. (2012). The processes underlying flexibility in childhood. *The Quarterly Journal of Experimental Psychology, 65*, 209–232.

Davidson, M.C., Amso, D., Anderson, L.C., & Diamond, A. (2006). Development of cognitive control and executive functions from 4 to 13 years: Evidence from manipulations of memory, inhibition, and task switching. *Neuropsychologia, 44*, 2037–2078.

Diamond, A., & Ling, D.S. (2016). Conclusions about interventions, programs, and approaches for improving executive functions that appear justified and those that, despite much hype, do not. *Developmental Cognitive Neuroscience, 18*, 34–48.

Donovan, A.M., Alibali, M.W. (2021). Toys or math tools: Do children's views of manipulatives affect their learning? *Journal of Cognition and Development, 22*, 281–304.

Dulaney, A., Vasilyeva, M., & O'Dwyer, L. (2015). Individual differences in cognitive resources and elementary school mathematics achievement: Examining the roles of storage and attention. *Learning and Individual Differences, 37*, 55–63.

Durkin, K., & Rittle-Johnson, B. (2012). The effectiveness of using incorrect examples to support learning about decimal magnitude. *Learning and Instruction, 22*, 206–214.

Ellefson, M.R., Zachariou, A., Ng, F.F.-Y., Wang, Q., & Hughes, C. (2020). Do executive functions mediate the link between socioeconomic status and numeracy skills? A cross-site comparison of Hong Kong and the United Kingdom. *Journal of Experimental Child Psychology, 194*, 104734.

Fazio, L.K., & Marsh, E.J. (2019). Retrieval-based learning in children. *Psychological Science, 28*, 111–116.

Fisher, A.V., Godwin, K.E., & Seltman, H. (2014). Visual environment, attention allocation, and learning in young children: When too much of a good thing may be bad. *Psychological Science, 25*, 1362–1370.

Flynn, M.E., Guba, T.P., & Fyfe, E.R. (2020). ABBABB or 1212: Abstract language facilitates children's early patterning skills. *Journal of Experimental Child Psychology, 193*, 104791.

Forsberg, A., Guitard, D., & Cowan, N. (2021). Working memory limits severely constrain long-term retention. *Psychonomic Bulletin & Review, 28*, 537–547.

Fyfe, E.R., & Rittle-Johnson, B. (2016). The benefits of computer-generated feedback for mathematics problem solving. *Journal of Experimental Child Psychology, 147*, 140–151.

Gathercole, S.E., Pickering, S.J., Ambridge, B., & Wearing, H. (2004). The structure of working memory from 4 to 15 years of age. *Developmental Psychology, 40*, 177–190.

Geary, D.C., Hoard, M.K., & Nugent, L. (2012). Independent contributions of the central executive, intelligence, and in-class attentive behavior to developmental change in the strategies used to solve addition problems. *Journal of Experimental Child Psychology, 113*, 49–65.

Gentner, D., Anggoro, F.K., & Klibanoff, R.S. (2011). Structure mapping and relational language support children's learning of relational categories. *Child Development, 82*, 1173–1188.

Gentner, D., & Hoyos, C. (2017). Analogy and abstraction. *Topics in Cognitive Science, 9*, 672–693.

Gerbier, E., & Toppino, T.C. (2015). The effect of distributed practice: Neuroscience, cognition, and education. *Trends in Neuroscience and Education, 4,* 49–59.

Gillam, R.B., Cowan, N., & Day, L.S. (1995). Sequential memory in children with and without language impairment. *Journal of Speech & Hearing Research, 38,* 393–402.

Gilmore, C., Keeble, S., Richardson, S., & Cragg, L. (2015). The role of cognitive inhibition in different components of arithmetic. *ZDM: Mathematics Education, 47,* 771–782.

Goddu, M.K., Lombrozo, T., & Gopnick, A. (2020). Transformations and transfer: Preschool children understand abstract relations and reason analogically in a causal task. *Child Development, 91,* 1898–1915.

Gordon, R., Chernyak, N., & Cordes, S. (2019). Get to the point: Preschoolers' spontaneous gesture use during a cardinality task. *Cognitive Development, 52,* 100818.

Gray, M.E., & Holyoak, K.J. (2021). Teaching by analogy: From theory to practice. *Mind, Brain, and Education, 15,* 250–263.

Halford, G.S., Cowan, N., & Andrews, G. (2007). Separating cognitive capacity from knowledge: A new hypothesis. *Trends in Cognitive Sciences, 11,* 236–242.

Hammerstein, S., Poloczek, S., Lösche, P., & Büttner, G., (2021). Individual differences in children's strategy selection in a computational estimation task with two versus three available strategies. *Journal of Experimental Child Psychology, 208,* 105132.

Hattikudur, S., & Alibali, M.W. (2010). Learning about the equal sign: Does comparing with inequality symbols help? *Journal of Experimental Child Psychology, 107,* 15–30.

Hulme, C., & Tordoff, V. (1989). Working memory development: The effects of speech rate, word length, and acoustic similarity on serial recall. *Journal of Experimental Child Psychology, 47,* 72–87.

Kalyuga, S., Chandler, P., Tuovinen, J., & Sweller, J. (2001). When problem solving is superior to studying worked examples. *Journal of Educational Psychology, 93,* 579–588.

Kaminski, J.A., & Sloutsky, V.M. (2013). Extraneous perceptual information interferes with children's acquisition of mathematical knowledge. *Journal of Educational Psychology, 105,* 351–363.

Katzoff, A., Zigdon, N.M., & Ashkenazi, S. (2020). Difficulties in retrieval multiplication facts: The case of interference to reconsolidation. *Trends in Neuroscience and Education, 20,* 100137.

Keulers, E.H.H., & Jonkman, L.M. (2019). Mind wandering in children: Examining task-unrelated thoughts in computerized tasks and a classroom lesson, and the association with different executive functions. *Journal of Experimental Child Psychology, 179,* 276–290.

Kibbe, D.L., Hackett, J., Hurley, M., McFarland, A., Schubert, K.G., Schultz, A., & Harris, S. (2011). Ten years of Take 10!®: Integrating physical activity with academic concepts in elementary school classrooms. *Preventive Medicine, 52,* 543–550.

Kibbe, M.M., & Feigenson, L. (2014). Developmental origins of recoding and decoding in memory. *Cognitive Psychology, 75,* 55–79.

Kidd, J.K., Pasnak, R., Gadzichowski, K.M., Gallington, D.A., McKnight, P., Boyer, C.E., & Carlson, A. (2014). Instructing first-grade children on patterning improves reading and mathematics. *Early Education and Development, 25,* 134–151.

Kirschner, P.A., Sweller, J., & Clark, R.E. (2006). Why minimal guidance during instruction does not work: An analysis of the failure of constructivist, discovery, problem-based, experiential, and inquiry-based teaching. *Educational Psychologist, 41,* 75–86.

Krasa, N., & Bell, Z. (2021). Silent word-reading fluency is strongly associated with orthotactic sensitivity among elementary school children. *Journal of Experimental Child Psychology, 205,* 105061.

Lawson, G.M., Hook, C.J., & Farah, M.J. (2018). A meta-analysis of the relationship between socioeconomic status and executive function performance among children. *Developmental Science, 21,* e12529.

Li, Y., & Geary, D.C. (2013). Developmental gains in visuospatial memory predict gains in mathematics achievement. *PLoS ONE, 8*(7), e70160.

Lloyd, M.E., & Newcombe, N.S. (2009). Implicit memory in childhood: Reassessing developmental invariance. In M.L. Courage & N. Cowan (Eds.), *The development of memory in infancy and childhood* (pp. 93–113). Psychology Press.

Luck, S.J., & Vogel, E.K. (2013). Visual working memory capacity: From psychophysics and neurobiology to individual differences. *Trends in Cognitive Science, 17,* 391–400.

Mammarella, I.C., Caviola, S., Giofrè, D., & Szűcs, D. (2018). The underlying structure of visuospatial working memory in children with mathematical learning disability. *British Journal of Developmental Psychology, 36,* 220–235.

Mammarella, I.C., Lucangeli, D., & Cornoldi, C. (2010). Spatial working memory and arithmetic deficits in children with nonverbal learning difficulties. *Journal of Learning Disabilities, 43,* 455–468.

Mareschal, D. (2016). The neuroscience of conceptual learning in science and mathematics. *Current Opinion in Behavioral Sciences, 10,* 114–118.

Matejko, A.A., & Ansari, D. (2021). Shared neural circuits for visuospatial working memory and arithmetic in children and adults. *Journal of Cognitive Neuroscience, 33,* 1003–1019.

Mazzocco, M.M.M., Chan, J.Y.-C., Bye, J.K., Padrutt, E.R., Praus-Singh, T., Lukowski, S., Brown, E., & Olson, R.E. (2020). Attention to numerosity varies across individuals and task contexts. *Mathematical Thinking and Learning, 22,* 258–280.

Melby-Lervåg, M., Redick, T.S., & Hulme, C. (2016). Working memory training does not improve performance on measures of intelligence or other measures of "far transfer": Evidence from a meta-analytic review. *Perspectives on Psychological Science, 11,* 512–534.

Menon, V. (2016). Working memory in children's math learning and its disruption in dyscalculia. *Current Opinion in Behavioral Sciences, 10,* 125–132.

Merrell, C., Sayal, K., Tymms, P., & Kasim, A. (2017). A longitudinal study of the association between inattention, hyperactivity and impulsivity and children's academic attainment at age 11. *Learning and Individual Differences, 53,* 156–161.

Miller, M.R., Rittle-Johnson, B., Loehr, A.M., & Fyfe, E.R. (2016). The influence of relational knowledge and executive function on preschoolers' repeating pattern knowledge. *Journal of Cognition and Development, 17,* 85–104.

Miller-Cotto, D., & Byrnes, J.P. (2020). What's the best way to characterize the relationship between working memory and achievement?: An initial examination of competing theories. *Journal of Educational Psychology, 112,* 1074–1084.

Moffett, L., & Morrison, F.J. (2020). Off-task behavior in kindergarten: Relations to executive function and academic achievement. *Journal of Educational Psychology, 112,* 938–955.

Oeri, N., Kälin, S., & Buttelmann, D. (2020). The role of executive functions in kindergarteners' persistent and non-persistent behaviour. *British Journal of Developmental Psychology, 38,* 337–343.

Oeri, N., Voelke, A.E., & Roebers, C.M. (2018). Inhibition and behavioral self-regulation: An inextricably linked couple in preschool years. *Cognitive Development, 47,* 1–7.

Ornstein, P.A., & Coffman, J.L. (2020). Toward an understanding of the development of skilled remembering: The role of teachers' instructional language. *Current Directions in Psychological Science, 29,* 445–452.

Pelegrina, S., Capodieci, A., Carretti, B., & Cornoldi, C. (2015). Magnitude representation and working memory updating in children with arithmetic and reading comprehension disabilities. *Journal of Learning Disabilities, 48,* 658–668.

Pellicano, E., Kenny, L., Brede, J., Klaric, E., Lichwa, H., & McMillin, R. (2017). Executive function predicts school readiness in autistic and typical preschool children. *Cognitive Development, 43,* 1–13.

Peng, P., & Miller, A.C. (2016). Does attention training work? A selective meta-analysis to explore the effects of attention training and moderators. *Learning and Individual Differences, 45,* 77–87.

Peng, P., Namkung, J., Barnes, M., & Sun, C. (2016). A meta-analysis of mathematics and working memory: Moderating effects of working memory domain, type of mathematics skill, and sample characteristics. *Journal of Educational Psychology, 108,* 455–473.

Raghubar, K., Cirino, P., Barnes, M., Ewing-Cobbs, L., Fletcher, J., & Fuchs, L. (2009). Errors in multi-digit arithmetic and behavioral inattention in children with math difficulties. *Journal of Learning Disabilities, 42,* 356–371.

Reck, S.G., & Hund, A.M. (2011). Sustained attention and age predict inhibitory control during early childhood. *Journal of Experimental Child Psychology, 108,* 504–512.

Rhodes, S., & Cowan, N. (2018). Attention in working memory: Attention is needed but it yearns to be free. *Annals of the New York Academy of Sciences, 1424,* 52–63.

Richland, L.E., Zur, O., & Holyoak, K.J. (2007). Cognitive supports for analogies in the mathematics classroom. *Science, 316,* 1128–1129.

Rittle-Johnson, B., Fyfe, E.R., Hofer, K.G., & Farran, D.C. (2017). Early math trajectories: Low-income children's mathematics knowledge from ages 4 to 11. *Child Development, 88,* 1727–1742.

Rittle-Johnson, B., & Schneider, M. (2014). Developing conceptual and procedural knowledge of mathematics. In R. Cohen Kadosh & A. Dowker (Eds.), *Oxford handbook of numerical cognition* (pp. 1118–1134). Oxford University Press.

Rittle-Johnson, B., Star, J.R., & Durkin, K. (2020). How can cognitive-science research help improve education? The case of comparing multiple strategies to improve mathematics learning and teaching. *Current Directions in Psychological Science, 29,* 599–609.

Roberts, G., Quach, J., Spencer-Smith, M., Anderson, P.J., Gathercole, S., Gold, L., Sia, K.-L., Mensah, F., Rickards, F., Ainley, J., & Wake, M. (2016). Academic outcomes 2 years after working memory training for children with low working memory: A randomized clinical trial. *JAMA Pediatrics, 170,* e154568.

Robinson, K.M., & Dubé, A.K. (2013). Children's additive concepts: Promoting understanding and the role of inhibition. *Learning and Individual Differences, 23,* 101–107.

Rohrer, D. (2012). Interleaving helps students distinguish among similar concepts. *Educational Psychology Review, 24,* 355–367.

Rohrer, D., Dedrick, R.F., & Hartwig, M.K. (2020). The scarcity of interleaved practice in mathematics textbooks. *Educational Psychology Review, 32,* 873–883.

Schneider, W. (2014). Individual differences in memory development and educational implications: Cross-sectional and longitudinal evidence. In P.J. Bauer & R. Fivush (Eds.), *The Wiley handbook on the development of children's memory* (Vol. II, pp. 947–971). John Wiley & Sons, Ltd.

Schneider, W., & Ornstein, P.A. (2015). The development of children's memory. *Child Development Perspectives, 9,* 190–195.

Sidney, P.G., & Thompson, C.A. (2019). Implicit analogies in learning: Supporting transfer by warming up. *Current Directions in Psychological Science, 28,* 619–625.

Siegler, R.S. (1996). *Emerging minds: The process of change in children's thinking.* Oxford University Press.

Siegler, R.S., Im, S.-H., Schiller, L., Tian, J., & Braithwaite, D. (2020). The sleep of reason produces monsters: How and when biased input shapes mathematics learning. *Annual Review of Developmental Psychology, 2,* 413–435.

Singley, A.T.M., & Bunge, S.A. (2014). Neurodevelopment of relational reasoning: Implications for mathematical pedagogy. *Trends in Neuroscience and Education, 3,* 33–37.

Smallwood, J., Beach, E., Schooler, J.W., & Handy, T.C. (2008). Going AWOL in the brain: Mind wandering reduces cortical analysis of external events. *Journal of Cognitive Neuroscience, 20,* 458–469.

Smith, F. (2002). *The glass wall: Why mathematics can seem difficult.* Teachers College Press.

Soveri, A., Antfolk, J., Karlsson, L., Salo, B., & Laine, M. (2017). Working memory training revisited: A multi-level meta-analysis of n-back training studies. *Psychonomic Bulletin & Review, 24,* 1077–1096.

Steen, L.A. (1988). The science of patterns. *Science, 240,* 611–616.

Stevenson, H.W., & Stigler, J.W. (1992). *The learning gap: Why our schools are failing and what we can learn from Japanese and Chinese education.* Summit.

Swanson, H.L. (2015). Cognitive strategy interventions improve word problem solving and working memory in children with math disabilities. *Frontiers in Psychology, 6,* 1099.

Swanson, H.L. (2020). The relationship between executive processing and computational growth among monolingual and English learners with and without math difficulties: Does it help to be bilingual? *Cognitive Development, 56,* 100961.

Sweller, J. (2016). Cognitive load theory, evolutionary educational psychology, and instructional design. In D.C. Geary & D.B. Berch (Eds.), *Evolutionary perspectives on education and child development* (pp. 291–306). Springer.

Tamnes, C.K., Walhovd, K.B., Torstveit, M., Sells, V.T., & Fjell, A.M. (2013). Performance monitoring in children and adolescents: A review of developmental changes in the error-related negativity and brain maturation. *Developmental Cognitive Neuroscience, 6,* 1–13.

Thomas, R., Sanders, S., Doust, J., Beller, E., & Glasziou, P. (2015). Prevalence of Attention-Deficit/Hyperactivity Disorder: A systematic review and meta-analysis. *Pediatrics, 135,* e994-e1001.

Thompson, C.A., & Opfer, J.E. (2010). How 15 hundred is like 15 cherries: Effect of progressive alignment on representational changes in numerical cognition. *Child Development, 81,* 1768–1786.

Towse, J.N., Hitch, G.J., & Skeates, S. (1999). Developmental sensitivity to temporal grouping effects in short-term memory. *International Journal of Behavioral Development, 23,* 391–411.

Van den Driessche, C., Bastian, M., Peyre, H., Stordeur, C., Acquaviva, É., Bahadori, S., Delorme, R., & Sackur, J. (2017). Attentional lapses in Attention-Deficit/Hyperactivity Disorder: Blank rather than wandering thoughts. *Psychological Science, 28,* 1375–1386.

Vendetti, M.S., Matlen, B.J., Richland, L.E., & Bunge, S.A. (2015). Analogical reasoning in the classroom: Insights from cognitive science. *Mind, Brain, and Education, 9,* 100–106.

Wakefield, E., Novack, M.A., Congdon, E.L., Franconeri, S., & Goldin-Meadow, S. (2018). Gesture helps learners learn, but not merely by guiding their visual attention. *Developmental Science, 21,* e12664.

Wang, C.-H., Tseng, Y.-T., Liu, D., & Tsai, C.-L. (2017). Neural oscillation reveals deficits in visuospatial working memory in children with developmental coordination disorder. *Child Development, 88,* 1716–1726.

Wiersema, J.R., van der Meere, J.J., & Roeyers, H. (2005). ERP correlates of impaired error monitoring in children with ADHD. *Journal of Neural Transmission, 112,* 1417–1430.

Wijns, N., DeSmedt, B., Verschaffel, L., Torbeyns, J. (2020). Are preschoolers who spontaneously create patterns better in mathematics? *British Journal of Educational Psychology, 90,* 753–769.

Willingham, D.T. (2017, Fall). Do manipulatives help students learn? *American Educator.* Retrieved from www.aft.org/ae/fall2017/willingham

Yeniad, N., Malda, M., Mesman, J., vanIJzendoorn, M.H., & Pieper, S. (2013). Shifting ability predicts math and reading performance in children: A meta-analytical study. *Learning and Individual Differences, 23,* 1–9.

Young, A.G., & Shtulman, A. (2020). Children's cognitive reflection predicts conceptual understanding in science and mathematics. *Psychological Science, 31,* 1396–1408.

Yu, S., Kim, D., Fitzsimmons, C.J., Mielicki, M.K., Thompson, C.A., & Opfer, J.E. (in press). From integers to fractions: Developing a coherent understanding of proportional magnitude. *Developmental Psychology, 59.*

Yuan, L., Uttal, D., & Gentner, D. (2017). Analogical processes in children's understanding of spatial representations. *Developmental Psychology, 53,* 1098–1114.

Zentall, S.S., Tom-Wright, K., & Lee, J. (2013). Psychostimulant and sensory stimulation interventions that target the reading and math deficits of students with ADHD. *Journal of Attention Disorders, 17,* 308–329.

Zhao, H., Alexander, P.A., & Sun, Y. (2021). Relational reasoning's contributions to mathematical thinking and performance in Chinese elementary and middle-school students. *Journal of Educational Psychology, 113,* 279–303.

Part I

Mathematical Headwaters

"God created the natural numbers; everything else is the work of man."

Leopold Kronecker, 19th-century German
mathematician[1]

DOI: 10.4324/9781003157656-2

Scientists have long sought the intuitive headwaters of mathematical thought. More than any other, that question—what is *number sense?*—has sparked the curiosity and imagination of contemporary researchers in mathematical cognition. Indeed, *number sense* has been defined in, well, numerous ways. For our purposes throughout the book, we take it in its broadest sense to signify "an understanding of what numbers mean and of numerical relationships."[2] In this section, we will review some recent scientific findings regarding our earliest numerical abilities and most basic intuitions about number and suggest some ways to nurture them in young children.

As of this writing, developmental psychologists generally agree that children enter school with two great reservoirs of natural ability that contribute to intuition or early knowledge about quantity.[3] The first is a general feel for the quantity of what is perceived through the senses. Pre-numerate children, who have not yet learned to count or measure, have no way to answer the questions *how many?* or *how much?* But what they can do is differentiate between two amounts (i.e., notice that they are different) and, if they seem different, identify which amount is more. That is, the pre-numerate sense of quantity is *relative*—one amount can only be judged in relation to another. It is also *approximate*: If amounts are very similar, pre-numerate children may not notice their difference. And it applies not only to *how much*—physical size, duration, loudness, weight, brightness, and so forth—but also to *how many*—the quantity of individual things in a group, or *numerosity*. Researchers refer to this ability as a general *sense of magnitude* and to the mental mechanism that differentiates quantities as the *Approximate Number System* (*ANS*). In any given situation, young children differentiate quantities not by measuring or counting, of course, but by a process akin to what is colloquially referred to as "eyeballing" or "sizing up." Since a verb will be more useful for our purposes here than the official noun phrases, we will call it *sizing up*. For babies and very young children, sizing up is not a thought process, but an implicit perceptual skill that gradually, with experience and language development, becomes a way of consciously differentiating and comparing quantities in the world around them.

The second kind of quantitative intuition emerges from children's ability to attend to and keep track of two or three objects or events simultaneously. These perceptual skills are referred to, respectively, as *parallel individuation* and *tracking*. In contrast to sizing up, these skills involve absolute—but, of course, extremely limited—numerosities. Again, with experience and the development of language, as well as attention, memory, and other skills, parallel individuation and tracking serve as the perceptual foundation of object-counting.

Even before they learn to count, children attentive to their social and physical surroundings acquire perceptual, cognitive, and linguistic resources they can bring with them to school to understand quantity. *Contra* Kronecker, who had the ordinal feature of whole numbers in mind, this natural treasury will contribute to children's understanding of not just numerical order but of counting, natural-number arithmetic, the positive rational numbers, *zero*, and perhaps even the negative numbers. Part I will review each of these natural resources and the language development that supports them, along with activities to nurture them in the early years.

NOTES

1 Cited in Boniface, 2005, pp. 145–146.
2 Malofeeva et al., 2004, p. 648.
3 Mix et al., 2016.

REFERENCES

The following references were cited in this introduction. For additional selected references relevant to this introduction, please see Part I Supplemental References in eResources.

Boniface, J. (2005). Leopold Kronecker's conception of the foundations of mathematics. *Philosophia Scientiæ, CS 5*. Retrieved from http://philosophiascientiae.revues.org/384

Malofeeva, E., Day, J., Saco, X., Young, L., & Ciancio, D. (2004). Construction and evaluation of a number sense test with Head Start children. *Journal of Educational Psychology, 96*, 648–659.

Mix, K.S., Levine, S.C., & Newcombe, N.S. (2016). Development of quantitative thinking across correlated dimensions. In A. Henik (Ed.), *Continuous issues in numerical cognition: How many or how much?* (pp. 3–35). Academic Press.

Chapter 2

Sizing Up

SCIENCE has demonstrated that humans are not alone in the ability to quantify. Animals, who do not have words or symbols with which to count or measure, rely on their ability to size up quantity every day for survival. Across the phylogenetic spectrum from insects to chimpanzees, survival of both the individual and the species depends on this quantitative skill to communicate, navigate, socialize, forage, hunt, evaluate threat, optimize breeding, track offspring, save time, conserve energy, and even make collective decisions.[1] Indeed, some of this animal "math" is quite complex. Take, for example, the case of the coot, a territorial marsh bird. The female, who can control how many eggs she lays, will produce only the number of offspring that her territory can feed.[2] Needless to say, this complex breeding behavior requires a reliable ability to evaluate the size of her territory and the number of eggs in the nest and to base her behavior on that information.

These primitive sizing-up skills apply not only to numerosities* of objects (e.g., eggs) but also to those of actions, events, and even sounds. For example, a lion can compare the size of a rival pride hiding in the bush to that of her own pride by the numerosity of different roars she hears,[3] an important signal to fight or flee. Moreover, sizing up applies not only to quantities of individual (*discrete*) things that humans might count, such as eggs or roars, but also to amounts of (*continuous*) stuff that humans might measure, such as the area of a territory. That is, in their own way, animals can ask and answer the questions *how many?* and *how much?*

What about humans? Are we born with the same quantitative intuitions? Can babies size up quantities? The answer will begin with a discussion of the *how many?* question in relation to discrete objects.

HOW MANY? SIZING UP DISCRETE QUANTITIES

Studying infants' quantitative intuitions is naturally impeded by the fact that infants cannot tell us what they are thinking. They do, however, tend to spend more time looking at something new or unexpected than at something highly familiar. Thus, by

---

* Numerosity refers to a quantity of discrete items.

DOI: 10.4324/9781003157656-3

familiarizing an infant with one thing and then presenting something else, researchers can determine whether the infant views the second thing as something new and different or as pretty much the same as the first by whether he looks longer at it or not. In this way, researchers have discovered that infants as young as six months can detect a difference between two arrays with different numerosities of identical dots, for example.[4] We cannot know whether one set of dots looks like "more" than another to a young infant, but we do know that the infant can recognize the two collections as different—a necessary first step in comparing quantities. Moreover, like animals, infants can discriminate the numerosities of sequential sounds they hear, such as chirps, whistles, or drumbeats.[5] Indeed, congenitally blind adults can do so as well,[6] indicating that sizing up is not tied to vision. By toddlerhood, children can usually determine which is "more" and adapt their behavior accordingly. For example, a two-year-old knows that it takes more strength to lift a plate piled high with cookies than a plate with only two cookies.[7]

Adults often size up situations in the same relative and approximate way. For example, suppose one wants to figure out the larger of two amounts, such as the numerosity of students in Ms. Smith's class versus the numerosity in Mr. Jones's class, but one does not have time to count or to pair the students up. How accurate is one likely to be, just using visual inspection? The likelihood of one's judgment's being correct typically depends, at least in part, on the *ratio* of the two collections (known as *Weber's law*).[8] The more similar in size the two classes—that is, the closer the ratio is to one—the harder the amounts are to differentiate from each other. Thus, if Mr. Jones has seven students and Ms. Smith has ten—a ratio of 7:10—one will probably notice the difference and correctly conclude that the classes are different sizes and that Ms. Smith has the bigger class. But if Mr. Jones has 33 students and Ms. Smith has 36 (again a difference of three but a *ratio*—33:36—much closer to one), one might not see a difference. The ability to detect such differences generally improves with age, such that a three-year-old can typically detect differences at a ratio of 3:4, a six-year-old can do so at a ratio of 5:6, while a typical adult can see differences at a ratio of 10:11.[9]

However, the ability to differentiate numerosities also varies widely from person to person. Thus, from a practical point of view, without counting or one-to-one matching, distinctions such as "different" and "more" can be somewhat blurry concepts. In fact, scientists refer to the ability to differentiate numerosities as *numerosity acuity*, like eyesight or hearing. Researchers debate whether individual differences in numerosity acuity are primarily due to fundamental differences in attention and perception[10] or in the ability to grasp the numerical meaning of what is seen or heard.[11] Nevertheless, most people are equipped to size up relative numerosities in daily life.

HOW MANY? VERSUS HOW MUCH?

The same principles of approximate comparison apply when animals and humans size up differences in quantities of continuous stuff, or *dimensions*, that cannot be counted— more like territory than eggs—where quantification answers the question *how much?* rather than *how many?*. These principles also apply to continuous *features* of countable objects—the circumference of a cookie, the length of a pencil, the weight of a book, the loudness or duration of a tone—that, unlike the objects themselves, are quantifiable only in terms of *how much*. Later in school, with the acquisition of counting and the concept of standard units, children will learn to measure them, as will be discussed in Chapter 9. In the laboratory, however, even infants demonstrate an ability to differentiate two amounts of sand, durations of sound, extents of area, and speeds of rolling balls. When more than two amounts are presented—such as three piles of sand, say—there is even some evidence that infants are sensitive to their order from small to large.[12]

All of which brings up an interesting question: When a toddler chooses a plate with three cookies over a plate with only two, is it because there are more cookies or because there is more cookie stuff? (See Figure 2.1a.) In other words, since discrete things have continuous properties—in the cookie case, physical size—perhaps what seems like counting to the adult observer is just a sizing up of those continuous features. Would the toddler choose the same plate if the two cookies were each a lot bigger than each of the three cookies—that is, if their numerosity and size were incongruous? (See Figure 2.1b.) Which of these competing features, size or numerosity, helps determine which is *more* in the eyes of young children?

The relative salience (i.e., perceived importance) of size, say, versus numerosity in children's comparisons, along with the question of whether young children can even distinguish between those two dimensions, has been the subject of considerable scholarly head-scratching and debate. There is evidence, for example, that with numerical experience and education, older children become more aware of numerosity. However, some scholars are now coming around to the idea that this may not be an either/or issue, but rather that young children arrive at their judgments by weighing all available cues—numerosity *and* extent, *how many* and *how much*—together, relying on a general sense of magnitude. That is, sometimes physical size might influence one's numerosity judgment—we know, for example, that seven-year-olds can be so dazzled by the size of the bigger cookies that they fail to realize that there are only two of them.[13] But it can also work the other way around: Numerosity can influence one's ability to correctly

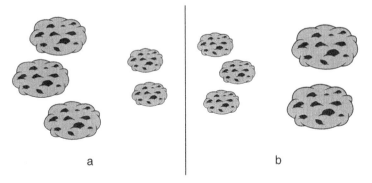

a   b

FIGURE 2.1 a) Numerosity of cookies and amount of cookie stuff congruous. b) Numerosity of cookies and amount of cookie stuff incongruous.

size up other features such as area. For the most part, it depends on the problem at hand. Since these judgments are usually eyeballed anyway, the cues that get a close enough answer the most quickly are the cues that get used. Even preschoolers seem to rely on whichever cues make the job easier,[14] although when asked to shift nimbly from one set of cues to another, many have trouble.[15] This notion of using all available information appears to hold true for animals as well,[16] as it does for human adults when counting is not an option: Imagine trying to sing the correct number of "*la*'s" in the *Deck the Halls* refrain without the cues of rhythm or pitch.[17]

In fact, in the wild, discrete and continuous features tend to be highly correlated. Eight eggs take up more space and are heavier than four eggs. A roaring pride of lions is louder than one lion. A class of 30 children typically takes up more space, is louder, and takes longer to come back through the door after recess than does a class of 15 children. Using all available cues provides more reliable information more efficiently and thus, from an evolutionary perspective, at least, is more likely to lead to survival. Hence, some scientists reason, we are probably wired to do so.[18]

As children develop, however, they acquire the perceptual, cognitive, and attentional skills that make it possible to focus on the magnitude of one dimension apart from that of other dimensions—to think about the numerosity of cookies apart from their size, and vice versa, or the distance from home to school apart from the time it takes to get there. Importantly, children learn—at home and in the classroom—the language in which they can think about, count, measure, and describe quantities of duration, spatial extent, and numerosity, allowing these dimensions to eventually diverge from each other in their minds.[19]

Children also get better at answering *how many?* and *how much?* at different rates. One study of children and adults found that sizing up area and length typically develops by adolescence, duration by early adulthood, and numerosity by sometime in between.[20] Moreover, perceptual and cognitive impairments can take a differential toll on those skills.[21]

SIZING UP AND MATH DEVELOPMENT

One might reasonably be thinking that the foregoing is all very interesting, but what does sizing up have to do with conventional mathematics? In the math classroom, children are expected to arrive at exact answers—what do rough and relative quantitative judgments have to do with that? Do early sizing-up skills lead to school math achievement? Researchers have wondered the same thing, and their findings have been inconclusive.[22] Scholars disagree about the effectiveness of intensive training in comparing numerosities for improving symbolic arithmetic.[23] In fact, a cogent argument has even been made against the possibility that a system of exact numerical quantity could be based on relative and approximate magnitudes.[24] Indeed, there is growing evidence that experience with school math improves numerosity acuity (not the other way around), just as it helps to disentangle discrete from continuous quantity, as discussed earlier.[25]

Interestingly, however, there is some evidence that students with significant math learning disabilities may have trouble detecting numerosity differences.[26] In particular, their problem in detecting the more numerous of two sets occurs on sets where perceptual features, such as object size, are incongruent with numerosity (e.g., a few big dots or many small dots, like the cookie problem), a confusion resembling that of typically developing younger children who have not yet disentangled those dimensions. Being able to focus on the set's numerosity under such distracting circumstances requires being able to mentally screen out those other features, a form of mental control discussed in Chapter 1.[27] While it is hard to know whether this difficulty contributes *to* or stems *from* these students' persistent difficulties with school math—or indeed, whether both problems are caused by some other factor—it is evident that children (and adults) with persistent math difficulties may have particular trouble disentangling numerosity from other perceptual information.[28] By contrast, adults with strong arithmetic skills have trouble *ignoring* numerosity when comparing incongruent size, for example—that is, they would be dazzled by three cookies and not as aware of their smaller size.[29]

Scientists have also speculated whether children who have difficulty with the dimension of numerosity also have difficulty with the dimension of time. Several studies of children with or at risk for significant math learning trouble found that they had trouble reproducing and comparing short durations and that their everyday time-related habits were poor.[30]

For most children, however, quantitative intuitions and general sizing-up experience seem to provide a powerful base from which even the youngest students can make sense of, and derive meaning from, school math. Most kindergartners already understand something about quantitative change and can roughly answer the questions *How much now?* and *How many now?* They have an approximate idea of how much you wind up with when you combine two amounts or take one amount away from another, and they know that when you put in an amount and take the same amount out again, nothing changes.[31] Indeed, research has shown that four- and five-year-old preschoolers can benefit from experience with such exercises.[32] In social contexts, they understand about fair sharing, an intuitive foundation of division.[33] And although as yet unschooled in the averaging algorithm, they can judge which of two trees has on average the fatter fruit.[34]

Thus, down the road, while good sizing-up skills may not necessarily lead directly to a correct solution on a school arithmetic problem, those skills may well help the young mathematician decide whether his or her answer makes sense. For example, take a common addition problem, executed with an algorithmic carrying error (*19 + 7 = 16*). If you add a counting number to *19* and come up with an answer that is *less* than *19, does that make sense?* It will not to a child who understands how numerosities relate to each other. This is the most fundamental meaning of *number sense* and serves to undergird all of elementary mathematics.[35]

Moreover, outside the classroom children and adults alike use their sizing-up skills in eyeballed comparisons all the time: What is the most popular restaurant on the block? Which is the quickest check-out line at the grocery store? Where am I most likely to get a parking spot? Which is the quietest reading room in the library? These comparisons encompass countable (people, cars) and uncountable (density, loudness) features. None of them, however, requires formal counting or measuring, which would create an unnecessary and time-consuming obstacle anyway. That is not to say that knowing *how* to count does not help: Among one Amazonian tribe, whose only enumeration words are "one," "two," and "many," those without access to schooling were not quite as sharp at making these eyeballed comparisons as were those exposed to numerical language and arithmetic.[36] Moreover, kindergartners do get better at such comparison as they learn conventional math.[37] But these rough comparisons do not require actual counting, and intensive conventional math training of children who are already numerate does not seem to improve them.[38]

Another kind of daily-life task that is related to sizing up is *cognitive estimation* (or what is colloquially called "guess-timation"): On a typical day, how many dogs are in the dog park? How many apples typically come in a bag? How many children can a school bus carry? How many sticks of spaghetti are in a package? How heavy is traffic at this time of day? These are estimates based not just on a perceptual comparison but on memory of past experiences. In a study of adults, the accuracy of such numerosity "guess-timates" was predicted by performance on a dot-array test of numerosity acuity.[39] Interestingly, in that study, similar estimates of continuous amounts—weight, speed, height, and so forth—were not related to numerosity acuity, suggesting that numerosity and continuous magnitudes had diverged, as predicted, in the mental life of these adults.

Finally, comparing continuous amounts—length, weight, duration, temperature, and so on—forms the basis of *measurement*. Primitive man first measured by comparing the length of small objects directly to the length of his own body parts—a foot, for example—and other handy common objects. Over time and use, these comparators became more precise, portable, and standardized—the distance from England's King Henry I's nose to the thumb of his outstretched hand was decreed to be a yard, for example.[40] However, measuring with today's ruler, thermometer, or scale still requires the comparison of continuous amounts. Standardized measurement units will be discussed in Chapter 9.

RANK ORDERING

One early skill resulting from the ability to make rough comparisons of amounts, with a potentially powerful impact on conventional math learning, is ordering, or ranking by amount. Both continuous and discrete amounts can be thought of as going from less (or fewer) to more, or the other way around, in orderly fashion. Even infants can detect when a familiar ascending or descending sequence has been reversed. Laboratory studies have demonstrated that by the end of their first year, infants are sensitive to order based on numerosity, size, and area. And as with two-item comparisons, the more cues, the better.[41] The preschool years see significant growth in Goldilocks-type sorting of things into small, medium, and large such that by sometime in the fifth year, children can order and match all manner of dimensions and experiences—physical size, temperature, loudness, pitch, hardness, and the like.

FIGURE 2.2   Number line: Compatibility of number sequence and line length.

Two of the earliest and easiest dimensions for preschoolers to sort and match are numerosities and lengths (provided the amounts are easily differentiated without counting or measuring), suggesting that those two dimensions may have a special relationship.[42] Indeed, looking ahead, rank ordering of numerosity and of length may be particularly important to conventional math because of the similarity in the growth pattern of *length* and the *whole-number sequence*: Each grows at a steady rate (linearly), as shown in Figure 2.2. As children acquire the written and spoken words and symbols for the counting numbers, the straight line serves as a concrete, continuous *analog*, or model, of the orderly, abstract whole-number sequence and a potent tool for teaching numerical relations. While comparing and ordering numerosities and lengths are cognitive skills that predate formal education developmentally, the association between symbolic numbers and length—what has been called the mental number line—typically emerges out of the formal process of learning the exact, symbolic, ordered whole-number system explicitly and systematically taught, a topic to be discussed in Part III. Moreover, the ability to efficiently judge the order of symbolic numerical sequences (e.g., is *2-7-5* in the correct order?) is one of the strongest predictors of arithmetic achievement.[43] The ordered nature of *non*-symbolic numerosity and of all manner of continuous features such as length—a key building block of the mental number line—is within young children's grasp and should be nurtured. Moreover, a child's feel for line length as a continuous dimension can provide intuitive access to a number's infinite divisibility in the realm of rational numbers.[44]

Time and the temporal order of events are another dimension that young children can begin to think of in terms of order. Do you eat breakfast before you wake up in the morning? Which comes first in a day, breakfast or lunch? Which day is between yesterday and tomorrow? In a one-year longitudinal study, researchers found that a child's ability to judge the correct order of daily events at age five predicted their counting ability at age six.[45]

PROPORTION

One more particularly important early sizing-up skill with potential for providing intuitive support for difficult mathematics is the ability to compare *proportions* of both discrete and continuous amounts—the uneaten proportion of a box of chocolates or of a pint of ice cream, say. Animals can be trained to do so, and even six-month-old infants can detect a difference in proportions (provided one is at least twice the other, just as in comparing absolute amounts).[46] The fact that very young children have an intuitive eye for such proportions has prompted one scientist to suggest that "fractions may in some sense be natural numbers, too."[47]

A technical note is in order here. To an adult mathematician, fractions, proportions, decimals, ratios, and probabilities are all decidedly different from each other. However, at their most fundamental level, they all describe the relation of two amounts, and that is the level at which the youngest children intuitively grasp them.[48] For example, given a two-colored spinner (see Figure 2.3), three-year-olds have no trouble guessing the likely result of a spin, and five-year-olds can compare the chances across two such spinners.[49]

By kindergarten, children have become increasingly competent at comparing proportions of things and probabilities of events, and even at recognizing the results of adding and subtracting them; in personally salient situations, they know when the odds are in their favor.[50] Among children in the primary grades, before any formal fraction instruction, the concept of "half" serves as a useful anchor for proportional comparisons (i.e., young children find it easier to compare two proportions if one is less than half and the other is more than half). Even children from primitive cultures with no more than a few number words know what it means to cut an amount down the middle.[51]

As we have seen, early quantitative understanding is not only approximate, it is also relative. For that reason, many young children find it easier to think in terms of proportions than of absolute amounts (see Figure 2.4). For example, when asked to

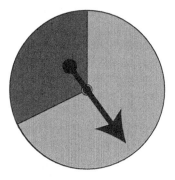

FIGURE 2.3   Spinner with unequal probabilities.

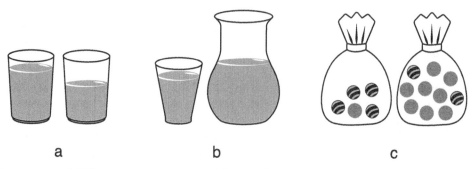

a   b   c

FIGURE 2.4   a) Different proportions, equal frame of reference. b) Different proportions, different frames of reference. c) Different proportions of discrete amounts, different frames of reference.

compare the quantity of juice in two containers, they are more likely to compare how full the two containers are than to compare the absolute amounts of juice in them. The distinction between absolute and proportional approaches is confounded, of course, when the containers are the same size (where the smaller proportion is necessarily also the smaller amount, Figure 2.4a), but can be seen with unequal containers, where the smaller proportion in the larger container could still be the larger amount (Figure 2.4b). As children develop, they become increasingly able to compare amounts apart from their frames of reference, such as containers.[52]

Importantly, however, children who are old enough to know how to count usually find it easier to compare continuous rather than discrete proportions—for example, the proportions of juice in two glasses versus the proportions of red marbles in two bags (Figure 2.4c). Discrete proportions are difficult because when confronted with discrete objects, children find it hard to resist the temptation to count and compare only the items of interest, ignoring the proportional, relation-of-relations crux of the task.[53]

Understanding the nature of proportion in these intuitive ways is as important for math learning as is detecting numerosity differences. It forms the foundation of rational numbers (fractions and decimals), probability, function, and rates of change, which in turn undergird algebra and calculus, all gnarly math topics for many students.[54] Proportion and its difficulties will be picked up again in Chapter 11.

NEGATIVE QUANTITIES

So far, we have seen evidence of intuitive precursors for the natural numbers and for positive rational numbers. But what about negative quantity? While negative-number arithmetic is beyond the scope of this book, speculating about its intuitive precursors in early childhood is not. Is there some sort of perceptual support familiar to pre-numerate children that they can later lean on to understand negative numbers? To qualify, such an example would need to be readily accessible to young children and to feature both natural bidirectionality and a stationary, nonarbitrary *zero* point.

Mathematicians struggled with the idea of negative quantity for centuries. Twelfth-century Hindu mathematicians suggested place (east-west, north-south), time (prior and subsequent), and ownership (mine, his) as natural illustrations of things that could be quantified in positive and negative terms.[55] Leaving aside the question of whether these examples make sense, one would have to acknowledge that they are not the sorts of mental images that could be readily called upon by young children. Indeed, Western mathematicians found the whole concept of negative numbers so counterintuitive—in their words, "ridiculous," "absurd," "impossible," "jargon at which common sense recoils"—that they wrestled with it well into the 19th century.[56] Modern middle-schoolers seem to feel the same way.[57] Moreover, there has been very little psychological research on the subject, and most of the educational literature concerns methods for teaching the notation and operations to children who are already numerate, rather than supporting pre-numeracy intuitions.

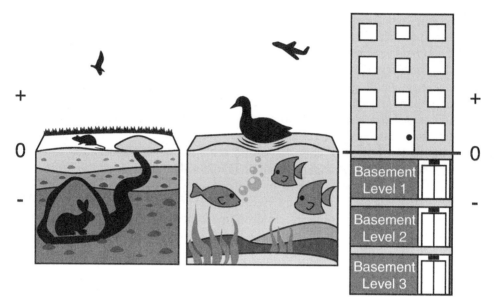

FIGURE 2.5   Illustrations of positive and negative, with *zero* at ground and water surface level, positive above and negative below.

Closer to a young child's experience, however, one might consider two general sets of candidate illustrations of negativity that satisfy the natural bidirectionality and stationary and nonarbitrary *zero*-point requirements. The first is spatial: above and below ground, or above and under water, both continuous examples with the *zero*-point at ground or sea level. The stairs or elevator in a high-rise building with several basement levels might provide a discrete, countable version of those examples, using the ground floor as *zero* (see Figure 2.5). The Celsius thermometer, whose *zero* is familiarly set at water's freezing point, might also work, even without the degree markings, which would be meaningless to pre-numerate children. (One potential problem with the example of a thermometer, however, is the temptation to think in terms of the height of the mercury column rather than the distance of its top from *zero*.) On the horizontal axis, the game of tug-of-war might be another familiar example.

The second set of candidates consists of what has felicitously been called "things and un-things,"[58] of which a time-honored, grown-up example is credit and debt. Indeed, the mathematician Leonhard Euler deemed this commercial application so valuable that for him it justified a place in mathematics for negative numbers.[59] But for young children, who do not know the meaning of "owe," researchers have instead used happy and sad thoughts or good and bad behavior.[60] Critically, however, both these examples rest on the assumption, which must be made explicit, that one cancels out the other. In the classroom, their use also depends on counting, as do the elevator and stairs examples. For the time being, however, young children's attention may profitably be drawn to holes in the ground or being under water, common metaphors for debt.

CONCLUSION

Most children begin formal schooling not as blank slates, but with abundant perceptual and intuitive resources to support emerging formal arithmetic skills. These include not only an eye for more and less and a sense of rank order, but also (*contra* Kronecker) a feel for relative proportions, and even, perhaps, an intuition about negative quantity. These pre-numerate young children expect that when you add to something, you wind up with more of it; that when you take something away, you wind up with less of it; and that when you break things in half, there will be more bits than before. Here, then, are the seeds of whole-number and rational-number arithmetic and measurement. As we shall see in the next chapter, young children also come to school with the precursors of counting.

ACTIVITIES

How Many? Sizing Up Discrete Quantities

ACTIVITY 2.1: Compare Sets of Discrete Objects: More and Fewer

Objective: To compare the numerosities of two sets of items without counting. Each set must contain more than four items.

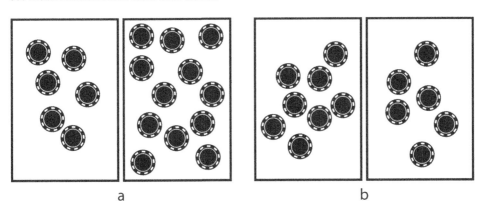

a   b

■ **First:** Create two sets of objects with different amounts and ask children which set has more and which set has fewer. Use readily available objects such as plastic chips, large beads or buttons, or small blocks. Begin with sets that have a large difference in quantity such as six and 12 (see Figure a). Progress to sets with a ratio of 3:4, such as six and eight objects (see Figure b).

■ **Next:** Progress to sets shown using abstract images, such as sets of dots on cards, instead of physical manipulatives. Dot cards can be found online or made with index cards. Show the children two cards at a time and ask them to identify which card has more dots and which card has fewer dots. Make sure the dots are all the same size.

■ **Next:** Once the children can easily identify which set has more or fewer items, add a memory component to the task. Show the children a set of objects such as buttons, then hide them in an opaque container. Show the children a second set of the same kind of buttons and ask them to point to the more numerous set—the buttons in the container or the visible buttons.

How Many? **Versus** *How Much?*

ACTIVITY 2.2: Compare Continuous Dimensions: More and Less

Objective: To compare continuous dimensions of size. Children will eventually learn to *measure* these dimensions, which is a topic taken up in Chapter 9. However, children can compare these dimensions long before they can measure them.

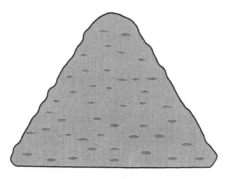 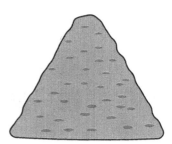

■ **First:** Compare two different sized piles of sand or dirt. Ask children to point to the pile that has more sand and to the pile that has less sand. Have the children make their own two piles and talk about them. Other materials that you could use include Play-Doh, clay, slime, or Silly Putty.

■ **Next:** Compare two of the same objects of different sizes, such as blocks, nesting cups, leaves, or rocks. Ask the children which object is taller, longer, shorter, wider, thinner, thicker, etc.

■ **Next:** Using two of the same type of object that differ significantly in size, present one and then hide it with a cloth or place it out of view. Then present the second object and ask whether it is taller, longer, shorter, wider, thinner, thicker, etc., than the hidden one. Bring out the hidden object and compare.

■ **Next:** Pour water into two clear containers of the same size and mark the water level in each with a line on the outside of the container. Say that you are going to pour some water from one container into the other container (point to indicate the direction) and ask the children to predict whether the new water levels will be the same, higher, or lower than the initial levels in each container. Then pour some water from one container to the other and observe the changes.

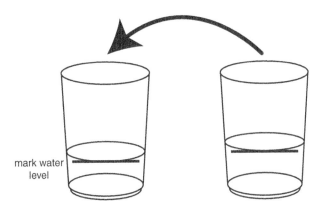

mark water level

ACTIVITY 2.3: Compare Continuous Dimensions: Length, Distance, Weight, and Time

Objective: To compare distances, lengths, heights, weights, and durations.

■ Compare two different lengths of tape on the floor. Ask, "Which one goes farther? Which one is longer? Which one is shorter?" Have children draw lines of different lengths with chalk on a sidewalk or playground and have them tell which one is shorter, longer, or goes farther.

■ Find sticks of different lengths. Line up the sticks and talk about which is longer and which is shorter. Stand the sticks up in the ground, sand table, or bucket of sand and talk about which is taller and which is shorter.

■ Look outside for flowers, trees, or buildings of different heights. Talk about which is taller and which is shorter.

■ Have the children hold a finger alongside a pencil and say which is longer, the pencil or their finger. In the same way, have them compare their body parts to other objects in the room: their hand and a pencil or a book, their foot and a book, their arm and the width of a desk, their leg and the height of a desk.

■ Have the children walk or run between two points set at longer and shorter distances. Discuss which is farther or closer.

■ Using two identical containers, have the children add different amounts of liquid or sand. Have them show their containers and talk about which has more and less and which is heavier or lighter. Have the children lift the containers at the same time to compare the weight, then lift them one at a time to compare.

■ Introduce the concept of time by exposing the children to two sounds of shorter and longer duration. Make the durations sufficiently different to be noticeable to the children. Ask which sound was longer, as well as which one took more time or less time.

■ Have the children sing and hold a note /ahhh/ for shorter and longer amounts of time. The teacher and children can take turns being the director and gesture when to start and stop singing. Ask how it feels to hold a note for a long time versus a short amount of time.

■ Use different sand timers that run for different lengths of time. Have the children watch the timers to see which one will run out first. The children can also do different physical movements for the duration of the different timers to add depth of comparison. Ask which timer took longer. Notice and talk about a new meaning for the word *longer*. Talk about which timer took more time to run out and which timer was faster or slower.

ACTIVITY 2.4: Compare Sets of Discrete Objects in Which Numerosity and Object Size Are Incongruent: More and Fewer

Objective: To compare *without counting* the numerosities of two sets in which the smaller set has larger items and the larger set has smaller items. Once children feel comfortable comparing the numerosities of sets of identical objects and comparing the relative sizes of individual objects, they are ready to tackle this more difficult task. The challenge here is focusing on numerosity while ignoring the size of the objects.

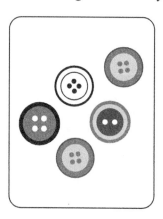 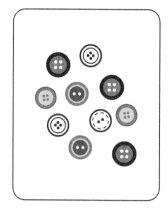

■ **First:** Have the children compare the numerosities of two sets of objects that are identical except for size, such as different-sized buttons or rocks. In one set, place a few of the larger objects; in the other set, place a larger collection of the small objects. For example, one set might have five large rocks, while the other has ten small rocks. Ask the children which set has more rocks. Start with a very large difference in numerosity to draw attention to it.

- **Next:** Progress to more abstract sets, such as dots on two cards, with fewer large dots on one card and more small dots on the other. As earlier, these sets vary on two dimensions: numerosity and size. Ask which card has more dots or fewer dots.

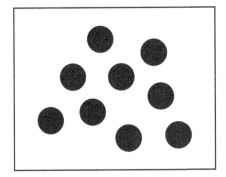 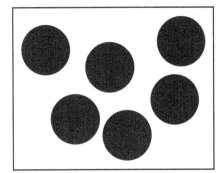

- **Next:** Compare two sets of objects that differ on three dimensions: numerosity, size, and type of object—for example, five apples versus nine blueberries. Ask which set has more items or fewer items. The children can create their own sets made up of different objects in bigger and smaller sizes. They can exchange sets with a partner and discuss which of their partner's sets has more items or fewer items.
- **Next:** Progress to more abstract sets that differ in numerosity, size, and type of object using pictures instead of physical objects. Compare cards with different pictured items, such as many small rabbits and a few large elephants.

Sizing Up and Math Development

ACTIVITY 2.5: Non-Symbolic Arithmetic

Objective: To learn the effect of adding to or taking away from sets of four or more items. This activity begins where Activity 2.1 left off and introduces a non-symbolic arithmetic element. Without counting, children determine the result of adding or subtracting manipulatives, such as plastic chips, by sizing up sets with a ratio of 2:1.

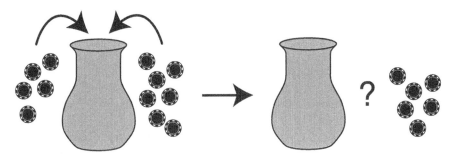

■ **First:** Present a set of five chips and put them in an opaque container. Then present a set of seven chips and put them in the same container with the first set. Next show a set of six chips and have the children decide which has more chips, the container or the visible set. (Alternatively, the third set could have 24 or more chips instead of six.)

■ **Next:** Present a set of 20 chips and then put them in an opaque container. Then say, "Watch as I take out these chips." Remove six chips and place them on the table. Now show the children a new set of 28 chips and have the children decide which has more chips, the container or the visible set. (Alternatively, the third set could have seven chips instead of 28.)

■ **Next:** Present a set of six plastic chips and then put them in an opaque container. Then hide ten more chips in your hand and add them to the container without the children watching. Dump all the chips from the container onto the table and say, "Now we have this many chips altogether." Show the children a set of five chips and have them decide which set has more chips: the amount you secretly added or the new set. (Alternatively, the third set could have 20 chips instead of five.)

■ **Next:** Present a set of 15 chips and then put them in an opaque container. Remove ten chips without the children watching and place the chips out of view. Dump the remaining chips in the container onto the table and say, "Now we have this many chips left." Show the children a set of five chips and have them decide which set has more chips, the amount you secretly took out of the container or the new set. (Alternatively, the third set could have 20 chips instead of five.)

Rank Ordering

ACTIVITY 2.6: Rank Ordering by Size of Individual Objects

Objective: To learn to rank order by size. As children become familiar with the ideas of more or less, adults can begin to introduce ordering multiple objects by size. Have children place objects in a row from smallest to largest going from left to right, which helps build the foundation of numeracy and the number line, discussed in Chapter 9. Use comparative language to discuss the size relationships. Suggested materials include blocks, rocks, leaves, straws, nesting dolls or cups, graduated rings on a post, measuring cups, stuffed animals, dolls, etc. Montessori sensorial materials include a variety of graduated series, the most common being the cylinders and the pink tower.

■ **First:** Have the children place items in order of size, such as a small, medium, and large ball. Compare their sizes, using such terms as *smaller, smallest, bigger, biggest, taller, tallest.*

■ **Next:** Progress to placing up to five items in order of size.

■ **Next:** Begin using *different* items of different sizes to line up in order of size. Introduce a variety of size words such as *wide, wider, widest; thin, thinner, thinnest; short, shorter, shortest.*

■ **Next:** Have the children choose any item in the room and have them take turns placing their items on a table in order of size. After the children order the items according to one dimension, have them reorder the items based on a different dimension: "Look at how we lined up the objects from thinnest to widest. Let's start again, and this time we'll line up the objects from shortest to tallest."

Proportion

ACTIVITY 2.7: Compare Proportions of Continuous Substances

Objective: To compare proportions of continuous amounts. These activities compare proportions in relation to their frames of reference, which are the containers in these cases. Use containers of different sizes so that children do not confuse the absolute amount of substance with proportion. The guiding questions should all refer to how full or empty the containers are, rather than how much substance is in them. Suggested materials, here referred to as "substances," include water, dirt, sand, sugar, flour, salt, and rice. Containers could include cups, pitchers, sandwich bags, or other transparent containers.

■ **First:** Fill two different-sized containers with different amounts of a substance and have children point to the container that is most full and the one that is least full. Ask the children to describe what they see. Use gestures to indicate more and less full. Use terms such as *full, half-full, empty, a little, a lot, almost empty, almost full.*

■ **Next:** Have the children put different amounts of a substance, from a little bit to full, in three or more containers. Arrange the containers from left to right in order of amount from least to most full. Talk about which container is *most full* and which is *least full, empty, somewhat empty, almost empty, half-full, almost full, mostly full, full.* Also include an empty container at times to include a discussion of *empty, none, zero.*

ACTIVITY 2.8: Compare Proportions of Discrete Objects

Objective: To compare proportions of discrete amounts. In this activity, children judge proportions of discrete objects within single containers by eyeballing the different amounts. At least one numerosity should be large to discourage counting, and the numerosity difference should be large. Materials you could use include two different colors of marbles, buttons, or pom poms.

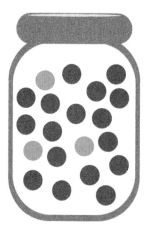

■ **First:** Fill two identical, transparent jars with opposite proportions—for example, 17 red marbles to three green marbles, and three red marbles to 17 green marbles, as in the Figure above. Tell the children that they will close their eyes and pick one marble from one jar without looking. Explain that if they pick a red marble, there will be a prize but if they pick a green marble, there will not. Then ask, "Which jar would you like to pick the marble from?" and "Why that jar?" As the children achieve success with this task, proceed gradually to more similar proportions.

■ **Next:** Use jars of different sizes with different total numbers of marbles but still with opposite proportions.

Negative Quantities

ACTIVITY 2.9: Negative Quantity: Digging Holes

Objective: To develop a notion of negative quantity. In the following example, level ground or water surface serves the function of a familiar, natural, stable *zero*-point—a necessary component of early negative number concepts—in a way that children can relate to in their daily lives (see Figure 2.5).

- Dig holes of varying depths. Place the same stick in turn into the different holes and talk about which hole goes below the surface more, or is the deepest, and which is shallowest. Other options include using a sandbox or a planter, pot, or box with potting soil or sand. Supplement with stories of burrowing animals that nest underground.
- Have the children play with a variety of objects that float or sink using a large, clear bowl, water table, or baby pool filled with water. Talk about the toys that sink being below the water surface. The children can push the toys that float below the surface of the water.

NOTES

1   Nieder, 2017.
2   Andersson, 2003.
3   McComb et al., 1994.
4   Xu & Spelke, 2000.
5   Lipton & Spelke, 2003.
6   Kanjlia et al., 2021.
7   Krause et al., 2019.
8   Testolin & McClelland, 2021.
9   Halberda & Feigenson, 2008.
10 Cheng et al., 2020.
11 Halberda, 2019.
12 Cassia et al., 2012; Hespos et al., 2012; Möhring et al., 2012.
13 Szűcs et al., 2013.
14 Leibovich et al., 2017; Newcombe et al., 2015.
15 Fuhs et al., 2021.
16 Franks et al., 2006.
17 Thanks to Davis & Pérusse, 1988, p. 564, for this example.
18 Bueti & Walsh, 2009.

19 Piazza et al., 2018.

20 Odic, 2018.

21 Crollen et al., 2017.

22 Schneider et al., 2017.

23 Bugden et al., 2016; Szűcs & Myers, 2017.

24 Carey & Barner, 2019.

25 Lau et al., 2021.

26 DeSmedt et al., 2013.

27 Viarouge et al., 2019; Wilkey et al., 2020.

28 Bugden & Ansari, 2016.

29 Nys & Content, 2012.

30 Cester et al., 2017; Tobia et al., 2018.

31 Canobi & Bethune, 2008.

32 Park et al., 2016.

33 Hamamouche et al., 2020.

34 Sweeny et al., 2015.

35 Dowker, 1992.

36 Piazza et al., 2013.

37 Lyons et al., 2018.

38 Sullivan et al., 2016.

39 Ashkenazi & Tsyganov, 2017.

40 Cooperrider & Gentner, 2019.

41 Suanda et al., 2008.

42 Starr & Brannon, 2015.

43 Lyons & Ansari, 2015.

44 Smith et al., 2005.

45 O'Connor et al., 2018.

46 Eckert et al., 2018; McCrink & Wynn, 2007.

47 Matthews & Chesney, 2015.

48 Matthews & Ellis, 2018.

49 Hurst & Cordes, 2018.

50 Doan et al., 2020.

51 McCrink et al., 2012; Spinillo & Bryant, 1999.

52 Vasilyeva et al., 2007.

53 Begolli et al., 2020.

54 Matthews & Ellis, 2018; Möhring et al., 2016.

55 Colebrooke, 1817, p. 132, footnote 3.

56 Martinez, 2006, pp. 18–44.

57 Mukhopadhyay, 1997.

58 Sawyer, 1964/2003, pp. 309ff.

59 Martinez, 2006, p. 31.

60 Whitacre et al., 2012.

REFERENCES

The following references were cited in this chapter. For additional selected references relevant to this chapter, please see Chapter 2 Supplemental References in eResources.

Andersson, M. (2003, Apr. 3). Behavioural ecology: Coots count. *Nature, 422,* 483, 485.

Ashkenazi, S., & Tsyganov, Y. (2017). The Cognitive Estimation Task is nonunitary: Evidence for multiple magnitude representation mechanisms among normative and ADHD college students. *Journal of Numerical Cognition, 2,* 220–246.

Begolli, K.N., Booth, J.L., Holmes, C.A., & Newcombe, N.S. (2020). How many apples make a quarter? The challenge of discrete proportional formats. *Journal of Experimental Child Psychology, 192,* 104774.

Bueti, D., & Walsh, V. (2009). The parietal cortex and the representation of time, space, number and other magnitudes. *Philosophical Transactions of the Royal Society B, 364,* 1831–1840.

Bugden, S., & Ansari, D. (2016). Probing the nature of deficits in the "approximate number system" in children with persistent Developmental Dyscalculia. *Developmental Science, 19,* 817–833.

Bugden, S., DeWind, N.K., & Brannon, E.M. (2016). Using cognitive training studies to unravel the mechanisms by which the approximate number system supports symbolic math ability. *Current Opinion in Behavioral Sciences, 10,* 73–80.

Canobi, K.H., & Bethune, N.E. (2008). Number words in young children's conceptual and procedural knowledge of addition, subtraction and inversion. *Cognition, 108,* 675–686.

Carey, S., & Barner, D. (2019). Ontogenetic origins of human integer representations. *Trends in Cognitive Sciences, 23,* 823–835.

Cassia, V.M., Picozzi, M., Girelli, L., & DeHevia, M.D. (2012). Increasing magnitude *counts* more: Asymmetrical processing of ordinality in 4-month-old infants. *Cognition, 124,* 183–193.

Cester, I., Mioni, G., & Cornoldi, C. (2017). Time processing in children with mathematical difficulties. *Learning and Individual Differences, 58,* 22–30.

Cheng, D., Xiao, Q., Cui, J., Chen, C., Zeng, J., Chen, Q., & Zhou, X. (2020). Short-term numerosity training promotes symbolic arithmetic in children with developmental dyscalculia: The mediating role of visual form perception. *Developmental Science, 23,* e12910.

Colebrooke, H.T. (1817). *Algebra, with arithmetic and mensuration, from the Sanscrit of Brahmagupta and Bháscara* [Electronic version]. John Murray, Albemarle. Retrieved 02/01/2018, from http://books.google.com/books/about/ Algebra.html?id=A3cAAAAAMAAJ

Cooperrider, K., & Gentner, D. (2019). The career of measurement. *Cognition, 191,* 103942.

Crollen, V., Collignon, O., & Noël, M.-P. (2017). Visual-spatial processes as a domain-general factor impacting numerical development in atypical populations. *Journal of Numerical Cognition, 3,* 344–364.

Davis, H., & Pérusse, R. (1988). Numerical competence in animals: Definitional issues, current evidence, and a new research agenda. *Behavioral and Brain Sciences, 11,* 561–615.

DeSmedt, B., Noël, M.-P., Gilmore, C., & Ansari, D. (2013). How do symbolic and non-symbolic numerical magnitude processing skills relate to individual differences in children's mathematical skills? A review of evidence from brain and behavior. *Trends in Neuroscience and Education, 2,* 48–55.

Doan, T., Friedman, O., & Denison, S. (2020). Young children use probability to infer happiness and the quality of outcomes. *Psychological Science, 31,* 149–159.

Dowker, A.D. (1992). Computational estimation strategies of professional mathematicians. *Journal for Research in Mathematics Education, 23,* 45–55.

Eckert, J., Call, J., Hermes, J., Herrmann, E., & Rakoczy, H. (2018). Intuitive statistical inferences in chimpanzees and humans follow Weber's law. *Cognition, 180,* 99–107.

Franks, N.R., Dornhaus, A.R., Metherell, B.G., Nelson, T.R., Lanfear, S.A.J., & Symes, W.S. (2006). Not everything that counts can be counted: Ants use multiple metrics for a single nest trait. *Proceedings of the Royal Society B, 273,* 165–169.

Fuhs, M.W., Tavassolie, N., Wang, Y., Bartek, V., Sheeks, N.A., & Gunderson, E.A. (2021). Children's flexible attention to numerical and spatial magnitudes in early childhood. *Journal of Cognition and Development, 22,* 22–47.

Halberda, J. (2019). Perceptual input is not conceptual content. *Trends in Cognitive Sciences, 23,* 636–638.

Halberda, J., & Feigenson, L. (2008). Developmental change in the acuity of the "number sense": The approximate number system in 3-, 4-, 5-, and 6-year-olds and adults. *Developmental Psychology, 44,* 1457–1465.

Hamamouche, K., Chernyak, N., & Cordes, S. (2020). Sharing scenarios facilitate division performance in preschoolers. *Cognitive Development, 56,* 100954.

Hespos, S.J., Dora, B., Rips, L.J., & Christie, S. (2012). Infants make quantity discriminations for substances. *Child Development, 83,* 554–567.

Hurst, M.A., & Cordes, S. (2018). Attending to relations: Proportional reasoning in 3- to 6-year-old children. *Developmental Psychology, 54,* 428–439.

Kanjlia, S., Feigenson, L., & Bedny, M. (2021). Neural basis of approximate number in congenital blindness. *Cortex, 142,* 342–356.

Krause, F., Meyer, M., Bekkering, H., Hunnius, S., & Lindemann, O. (2019). Interaction between perceptual and motor magnitudes in early childhood. *Cognitive Development, 49,* 11–19.

Lau, N.T.T., Merkley, R., Tremblay, P., Zhang, S., DeJesus, S., & Ansari, D. (2021). Kindergarteners' symbolic number abilities predict nonsymbolic number abilities and math achievement in Grade 1. *Developmental Psychology, 57,* 471–488.

Leibovich, T., Katzin, N., Harel, M., & Henik, A. (2017). From "sense of number" to "sense of magnitude": The role of continuous magnitudes in numerical cognition. *Behavioral and Brain Sciences, 40,* e164.

Lipton, J.S., & Spelke, E.S. (2003). Origins of number sense: Large number discrimination in human infants. *Psychological Science, 14,* 396–401.

Lyons, I.M., & Ansari, D. (2015). Numerical order processing in children: From reversing the distance-effect to predicting arithmetic. *Mind, Brain, and Education, 9,* 207–221.

Lyons, I.M., Bugden, S., Zheng, S., DeJesus, S., & Ansari, D. (2018). Symbolic number skills predict growth in nonsymbolic number skills in kindergarteners. *Developmental Psychology, 54,* 440–457.

Martinez, A.A. (2006). *Negative math: How mathematical rules can be positively bent.* Princeton University Press.

Matthews, P.G., & Chesney, D.L. (2015). Fractions as percepts? Exploring cross-format distance effects for fractional magnitudes. *Cognitive Psychology, 78,* 28–56.

Matthews, P.G., & Ellis, A.B. (2018). Natural alternatives to natural number: The case of ratio. *Journal of Numerical Cognition, 4,* 19–58.

McComb, K., Packer, C., & Pusey, A. (1994). Roaring and numerical assessment in contests between groups of female lions, *Panthera leo. Animal Behaviour, 47,* 379–387.

McCrink, K., Spelke, E.S., Dehaene, S., & Pica, P. (2012). Non-symbolic halving in an Amazonian indigene group. *Developmental Science, 16,* 451–462.

McCrink, K., & Wynn, K. (2007). Ratio abstraction by 6-month-old infants. *Psychological Science, 18,* 740–745.

Möhring, W., Libertus, M.E., & Bertin, E. (2012). Speed discrimination in 6- and 10-month-old infants follows Weber's Law. *Journal of Experimental Child Psychology, 111,* 405–418.

Möhring, W., Newcombe, N.S., Levine, S.C., & Frick, A. (2016). Spatial proportional reasoning is associated with formal knowledge about fractions. *Journal of Cognition and Development, 17,* 67–84.

Mukhopadhyay, S. (1997). Story telling as sense-making: Children's ideas about negative numbers. *Hiroshima Journal of Mathematics Education, 5,* 35–50.

Newcombe, N.S., Levine, S.C., & Mix, K.S. (2015). Thinking about quantity: The intertwined development of spatial and numerical cognition. *Wiley Interdisciplinary Reviews (WIREs): Cognitive Science, 6,* 491–505.

Nieder, A. (2017). Evolution of cognitive and neural solutions enabling numerosity judgements: Lessons from primates and corvids. *Philosophical Transactions of the Royal Society B, 373,* 20160514.

Nys, J., & Content, A. (2012). Judgement of discrete and continuous quantity in adults: Number counts! *The Quarterly Journal of Experimental Psychology, 65,* 675–690.

O'Connor, P.A., Morsanyi, K., & McCormack, T. (2018). Young children's non-numerical ordering ability at the start of formal education longitudinally predicts their symbolic number skills and academic achievement in maths. *Developmental Science, 21,* e12645.

Odic, D. (2018). Children's intuitive sense of number develops independently of their perception of area, density, length, and time. *Developmental Science, 21,* e12533.

Park, J., Bermudez, V., Roberts, R.C., & Brannon, E.M. (2016). Non-symbolic approximate arithmetic training improves math performance in preschoolers. *Journal of Experimental Child Psychology, 152,* 278–293.

Piazza, M., DeFeo, V., Panzeri, S., & Dehaene, S. (2018). Learning to focus on number. *Cognition, 181,* 35–45.

Piazza, M., Pica, P., Izard, V., Spelke, E.S., & Dehaene, S. (2013). Education enhances the acuity of the nonverbal approximate number system. *Psychological Science, 24,* 1037–1043.

Sawyer, W.W. (1964/2003). *Vision in elementary mathematics* (pp. 291–311). Dover Publications.

Schneider, M., Beeres, K., Coban, L., Merz, S., Schmidt, S.S., Stricker, J., & DeSmedt, B. (2017). Associations of non-symbolic and symbolic numerical magnitude processing with mathematical competence: A meta-analysis. *Developmental Science, 20,* e12372.

Smith, C.L., Solomon, G.E.A., & Carey, S. (2005). Never getting to zero: Elementary school students' understanding of the infinite divisibility of number and matter. *Cognitive Psychology, 51,* 101–140.

Spinillo, A.G., & Bryant, P.E. (1999). Proportional reasoning in young children: Part-part comparisons about continuous and discontinuous quantity. *Mathematical Cognition, 5,* 181–197.

Starr, A., & Brannon, E.M. (2015). Developmental continuity in the link between sensitivity to numerosity and physical size. *Journal of Numerical Cognition, 1,* 7–20.

Suanda, S.H., Tompson, W., & Brannon, E.M. (2008). Changes in the ability to detect ordinal numerical relationships between 9 and 11 months of age. *Infancy, 13,* 308–337.

Sullivan, J., Frank, M.C., & Barner, D. (2016). Intensive math training does not affect approximate number acuity: Evidence from a three-year longitudinal curriculum intervention. *Journal of Numerical Cognition, 2,* 57–76.

Sweeny, T.D., Wurnitsch, N., Gopnik, A., & Whitney, D. (2015). Ensemble perception of size in 4–5-year-old children. *Developmental Science, 18,* 556–568.

Szűcs, D., & Myers, T. (2017). A critical analysis of design, facts, bias and interference in the approximate number system training literature: A systematic review. *Trends in Neuroscience and Education, 6,* 187–203.

Szűcs, D., Nobes, A., Devine, A., Gabriel, F.C., & Gebuis, T. (2013). Visual stimulus parameters seriously compromise the measurement of approximate number system acuity and comparative effects between adults and children. *Frontiers in Psychology, 4,* 444. Doi:10.3389/fpsyg.2013.00444.

Testolin, A., & McClelland, J.L. (2021). Do estimates of numerosity really adhere to Weber's law? A reexamination of two case studies. *Psychonomic Bulletin & Review, 28,* 158–168.

Tobia, V., Rinaldi, L., & Marzocchi, G.M. (2018). Time processing impairments in preschoolers at risk of developing difficulties in mathematics. *Developmental Science, 21,* e12526.

Vasilyeva, M., Duffy, S., & Huttenlocher, J. (2007). Developmental changes in the use of absolute and relative information: The case of spatial extent. *Journal of Cognition and Development, 8,* 455–471.

Viarouge, A., Houdé, O., & Borst, G. (2019). Evidence for the role of inhibition in numerical comparison: A negative priming study in 7- to 8-year-olds and adults. *Journal of Experimental Child Psychology, 186,* 131–141.

Whitacre, I., Bishop, J.P., Lamb, L.L.C., Philipp, R.A., Schappelle, B.P., & Lewis, M.L. (2012). Happy and sad thoughts: An exploration of children's integer reasoning. *Journal of Mathematical Behavior, 31,* 356–365.

Wilkey, E.D., Pollack, C., & Price, G.R. (2020). Dyscalculia and typical math achievement are associated with individual differences in number-specific executive function. *Child Development, 91,* 596–619.

Xu, F., & Spelke, E.S. (2000). Large number discrimination in 6-month-old infants. *Cognition, 74,* B1–B11.

Chapter 3

The Prelude to Counting

"ONE great blooming, buzzing confusion." That's how William James, the 19th-century psychologist, described the world as experienced by the newborn baby.[1] But as focus, muscle control, and working memory develop,[2] infants begin to make out people and things around them as separate and distinct from the rest of their surroundings. Specifically, the first things that come into focus are things with fixed boundaries, spatial coherence and location, and the ability to move on their own trajectories—in other words, discrete objects such as cookies but not continuous substances such as ice cream, as discussed in Chapter 2. Before the end of the first few months of life, infants can perceptually isolate and attend to up to as many as three such objects at once, nearly the same level of attention as adults, a skill referred to as *parallel individuation*. Moreover, infants can visually track these objects through different trajectories over time, much as a baseball fan might track multiple baserunners, an ability referred to as the *object tracking system*. That is not to say that these skills are products of conscious thought or effort; rather, they emerge from a baby's natural attention and perceptual abilities in the course of adapting to the new environment.[3]

SMALL NUMEROSITIES: ONE, TWO, AND THREE

As we saw in Chapter 2, researchers can spot when infants notice a difference in the numerosities of two collections of things by how long they look at them. In the same way, scientists have figured out that babies can detect a quantitative difference between sets of one, two, or three things.[4] Using the same strategy, researchers familiarized a group of four- to six-month-olds with an image of two dots. When they then showed the infants an image with three dots, the babies took notice of the change—three dots looked different than two dots to them. Similarly, babies familiarized with an image of three dots then took notice of a new two-dot image.[5] Six-month-old babies can also differentiate two versus three sounds, as well as two versus three events.[6] Again, these are perceptual, not mathematical, feats; even salamanders can see a difference between two fruit flies and three.[7]

DOI: 10.4324/9781003157656-4

The attentive reader may remember that six-month-old infants typically cannot detect a difference in numerosities any smaller than a ratio of 1:2, as noted in the previous chapter on sizing up. Yet here is evidence that they can see a difference between two dots and three—a ratio of 2:3! Moreover, other experiments have produced equally intriguing results. In one study, for example, six-month-olds could differentiate four items versus eight (a 1:2 ratio), but *not* two items versus four (also a 1:2 ratio).[8] In other studies (see Figure 3.1), ten- and 12-month-old infants observed researchers place different numerosities of equal-sized crackers one by one into two opaque containers and were then allowed to crawl to whichever container they chose to retrieve the crackers. The crackers looked delicious, and the infants reliably chose the container with the larger numerosity of them when the choice was one versus two crackers or two versus three crackers. However, they failed to do so when the choices were three versus four, two versus four, one versus four, or three versus six, suggesting that they could not tell the difference between these amounts.[9]

Results such as these prompted the researchers to conclude that the mental system that detects differences between small numerosities (one, two, and three) is different and separate from the system that detects differences between large numerosities (more than three) and that same/different judgments across the boundary between the two ranges (e.g., two versus four) are exceptionally difficult for infants.[10] Later on, toddlers and young preschoolers seem to find comparisons of small-range numerosities easier than the sized-up comparisons of numerosities in the larger range.[11] Learning how to compare sets of items up to three will be discussed later in this chapter.

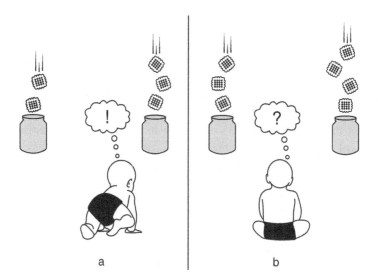

a   b

FIGURE 3.1   a) Older infants can distinguish three crackers from two crackers, (b) but not from four crackers.

Source: Adapted from Feigenson et al., 2002.

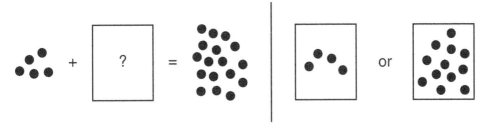

FIGURE 3.2 Without counting, estimate which of the two sets of dots on the right would more likely solve the equation on the left. Adapted from Kibbe & Feigenson, 2017.

While detecting a difference between small numerosities is within an infant's skill set, non-symbolic small-numerosity arithmetic is slow to develop. In one study, researchers found that even though four- to six-year-olds could correctly pick out the answer to the problem • + •• = ? (given the choices ••• and ••), they could not identify what they would have to add to • to get ••• (given the same choices). By contrast, most of them knew that they would have to add a large pile of buttons to a small pile of buttons to wind up with a much larger pile of buttons (see Figure 3.2). In this sense, these youngsters' large-numerosity approximate arithmetic was significantly better than their small-numerosity exact arithmetic.[12]

Among older children and adults who already know how to count, human perception serves to facilitate more efficient counting of exact quantities up to three or four.[13] This skill—recognizing at a glance that there are only three apples in a basket, for example—is called *subitizing* (pronounced /soo´-bitizing/), from the Latin *subitus*, meaning "sudden." Interestingly, it applies not only to visible items but to those enumerated by touch and hearing as well, although the subitizing limit may be somewhat different for each of the senses. The subitizing limit also depends on whether the items are all perceived at the same time (e.g., a visual array of dots) or one at a time (e.g., a series of tones), which would require keeping the perceptions in working memory. For any given sensory mode and presentation, the numerosity limit is typically one more for adults than for children; in the case of visual arrays, the limit is about three for children and four for adults.[14]

Subitizing is further facilitated by other perceptual skills, such as the tendency to mentally "chunk" into clusters items that are near each other and to recognize familiar patterns, such as the iconic arrangements on the faces of dice or playing cards (see Figure 3.3). Both of these skills—"chunking" and recognizing patterns—contribute to higher subitizing ranges.[15] One example of a system built on subitizing is the Morse code, a means of telegraphic communication in which letters are represented by combinations of short *dits* (.) and longer *dahs* (-). Designed for supreme efficiency, the code contains only one letter with more than three *dits* or *dahs* in a row.[16]

Subitizing will be discussed again in relation to counting in Chapter 6. We mention it here to draw attention to its perceptual underpinnings.

FIGURE 3.3 Canonical numerosity patterns can be enumerated quickly and precisely by children and adults familiar with them.

ZERO

As we have just seen, there is a perceptual basis for learning the smallest numerosities—*one*, *two*, and *three*. But this raises an interesting question: *Is there a perceptual basis for zero?* This may seem like a silly question—how can there be a perceptual basis for seeing nothing? However, infants' ability to track objects through time and space allows them to predict where an object might be. Thus, if an object is not at its predicted location, they take notice. To understand how that could happen, we return to the baseball stadium. The bases are loaded. The pitch is good, the batter hits a long one, and you watch as the players take off. But then your attention gets diverted by a kerfuffle at third, or the fan in front of you stands up, obscuring your view, while the runner is tagged out at first and trots off the field. By the time your attention returns, first base is empty, and your response is, "Wait! What just happened?" That is, the runner is not where you expected, and you notice.

Human infants are not alone in realizing when something has gone missing. Many animals, including monkeys, some birds, and even honeybees, demonstrate an appreciation for the "empty set."[17] Researchers have shown that both great apes and 12-month-old human infants often request something that is absent by pointing to the empty place where it once was, and four-year-old children will search intensively for an object that has gone missing.[18] Moreover, even though they have not yet been taught about *zero*, most preschoolers know that *zero* is less than any other amount, and many can accurately rank order *zero* below *one* as a numerosity.[19] When asked to label three containers in which they had put five cookies, a half a cookie, and no cookies, respectively, four-year-olds perceptively placed a blank sign on the "no cookies" jar, the meaning of which they still understood two weeks later.[20] Thus, by age four or so, children comprehend the quantitative meaning of an empty set as the absence of something that could reasonably be expected to be there.

That is also an accurate understanding of the nontrivial way in which *zero* is used by adults. For example, one might meaningfully report that the polar bear census on a particular arctic iceberg is zero, but it would be trivial (albeit true) to say the same for the polar bear census on the island of Oahu or the Congo River. It is also how *zero* is understood in place-value notation: The *0* in the numeral *305* signifies the absence of tens: Since 90 percent of the whole numbers between *100* and *999* have a component expressible in tens, one could reasonably expect a counting digit to be there. By contrast, *0* would not be used to express *496* as *0496*, because zero percent of the numbers less than *1,000* are expressed in thousands—that is, it would be *un*reasonable to expect a counting digit to be there, and so the use of *0* in the thousands place would be trivial.

Thus, even *zero* has its foundation in the earliest human perceptions.

QUANTITATIVE LANGUAGE

A critical element in counting development is the emergence of quantitative language, beginning with basic quantifiers (*some, many*), size descriptors (*big, little*), and plurals (*doggies, they*), as well as spatial words (discussed in Chapter 4), commensurate with children's developing sense of relative magnitude. Indeed, in the preschool years, quantitative-language knowledge is associated with all basic numeracy skills, and a quantitative-language *deficit* is one of the strongest predictors of math difficulty.[21]

Language development starts in utero, as the brain begins to detect patterns in the incoming speech sounds. Two-way verbal communication emerges with speech typically sometime during the child's second year. Having words for things, features of things, actions, and events draws attention to those experiences. It also turns implicitly sensed things into explicit information, allowing a child to think about them. For example, having a word for the color red draws attention not only to the redness of fire engines and stop signs but to the color differences of grass and bluebirds. As an added plus, language gives scientists another window into what a child is thinking.

One can see these linguistic developments in children's earliest efforts to understand quantity. One of the first things toddlers begin to grasp, sometime around their second birthday, is the linguistic plural: When told, "Look, there are some toys!" they expect to see more than one. Of the quantitative clues in that sentence (*are, some, toys*), the *is-are* verb distinction is typically understood first, developmentally speaking.[22] However, by age three or so, most children have picked up the basic vocabulary and word-form rules of quantity and know, for example, that plural nouns (*kitties*) and demonstratives (*these, those*) refer to more than one individual thing.[23] English is not the only language that contains built-in numerosity clues. In fact, several hundred of the world's languages do, and many students for whom English is their second language should already understand these distinctions well in their native language.[24]

Everyday language is replete with simple words that convey quantitative information about individual items and continuous stuff that toddlers and preschoolers pick up in their routine activities and interactions as a natural part of general language development.[25] For example, common adjectives that describe physical size and/or time (*big, little, long, short, fast*), as well as their comparative and superlative forms (*bigger, fastest*), are all familiar words in American households. These words form a critical component of the activities in Chapter 2. Other words and phrases, called articles—*a(n), the*—and quantifiers—*some, any, many, most, all, more, less, enough, another, both, half, a lot of, a little bit, a few*—convey quantitative information and are typically also part of common language around the home. For example, while *more!* is often one of the first words exclaimed by still-hungry toddlers, soon after their third birthday children also begin to use *more* to compare different quantities, appropriately referring to both discrete (cookies) and continuous (ice cream) amounts.[26] *Some* and *most* seem to be particularly tricky for preschoolers but emerge gradually in the fourth year, independently of children's knowledge of large number words. In one study, for example, some children understood *most* but not *four*, while others understood *nine* but not *most*.[27] Learning the words *less* and *fewer* is intimately tied to learning the difference between continuous stuff (*less* ice cream) and discrete objects (*fewer* cookies), along with the ways they are quantified. Talking about sharing continuous amounts (milk, ice cream) is one effective way to foster the use of quantifiers, just as talking about sharing things (cookies, crayons) can prompt the use of number words.[28] Children also figure out that such quantifiers come first in a series of descriptors (*more red hats, some pretty flowers*). Around age four or five, about the time they are learning to count, preschoolers begin to understand collective nouns (*class, army, flock*). In fact, counting and learning collective nouns may be related because number words in their total-amount (cardinal) sense describe groups (e.g., a flock of five birds), and learning to think in terms of total amounts may draw attention to collections.[29]

Children catch on to the place of number words in language and the rules for using them considerably before they begin to understand their meaning. In an intensive study of the verbal interactions of three children, aged one and two years, and their mothers, researchers found that the children understood very early on the distinction between continuous and discrete properties and used number words only regarding the latter (*three cookies*, but never *three ice creams*). They also understood that number words, like other quantifiers, come before adjectives in describing objects (*three chocolate cookies*) and that phrases such as ___ *of the cookies* can only be used with a number word or quantifier.[30] This general understanding of types of words and their place in spoken grammar, then, sets the stage for learning their specific meanings.

Typically, children learn the three smallest number words (*one, two, three*) first, but how that happens exactly has eluded orderly sequencing. For example, some researchers report a strict sequence—*one*, then *two*, then *three*. Others, however, suggest that *one* and *two* emerge more or less at the same time, around age two, or that *one* becomes exact by contrast to *two*. Research efforts have also produced conflicting results about the relative preciseness or fuzziness of children's interpretations of singular nouns (*banana*), quantifiers (*some bananas*), and number words (*two bananas*).[31]

Toddlerhood is also the developmental period when children begin to understand the linguistic plural, as we have seen. But how or even whether enumeration and grammar are related is unclear. Some children use "two" to signify plurality generally or, more specifically, "a pair of," or even general similarity. Two-year-olds are also more likely to use the plural form of nouns quantified by "four" ("four froggies") than by "two" ("two froggy") and for identical, not just similar, objects.[32] Some scholars argue that two-year-olds use "two" for counting but not yet in its cardinal (*how many*) sense, so their understanding is not related to the linguistic plural.[33] (Of course, this is the time when toddlers also learn that "Two!" is the correct answer to the question, "How old are you?" even though they do not yet know the meaning of "two"—or "old," for that matter.) Others, however, argue that the importance of the singular-plural linguistic distinction for numerical understanding is highlighted by the evidence that Chinese and Japanese children, whose languages do not distinguish between singular and plural, on average learn the meaning of the number word for *one* and can distinguish between one and more than one object later developmentally than do English-speaking children.[34] And others have found that English-speaking preschoolers' understanding of the singular form of nouns is somewhat fuzzier than their notions of the plural forms.[35]

As fine-grained diary studies show (see Textbox 3.1), it can take time and a great deal of linguistic experimentation for children to grasp the exact numerical meanings of the first few number words, which may explain why the research attempts to pin down their development have been so conflicting.

TEXTBOX 3.1

In addition to data from formal studies, we have one researcher's (Kelly Mix) observations of her own child, Spencer.[36] Spencer was cared for solely by his parents for his first 18 months and then additionally by a part-time nanny at home for the rest of the study's duration. The researcher/mother kept a detailed diary of Spencer's efforts to count or label sets numerically in her presence between the ages of 12 and 38 months. As the only adult who knew the questions that she hoped the diary would answer, she did not initiate numerical conversations around her son in order to avoid contaminating the findings. None of the adults made any special effort to teach him, and on repeated standard measures of numerical development during this period, Spencer's performance was in the normal range for his age. One of the study's most striking findings was that number language appeared in spontaneous chatter long before it could be measured by performance on formal testing by strangers in a laboratory. For that reason, it is a particularly valuable window on how children actually figure it all out.

Spencer's first number utterance was at 18 months, when he began learning the names of the digits in his board books, starting with *zero* and which, by 22 months, included *one* through *eight* and *ten*. He learned them as names of the digit shapes, just as he learned the names of other objects, without any symbolic significance or numerical meaning. Shortly thereafter, he began to use number words in reference to other objects. Like many toddlers, he began with "two" in direct imitation of his nanny, who said, "Two shoes. One. Two.," tagging each shoe by touching or pointing to it. After a week, he generalized the phrase and gestures to other objects (dogs, spoons, straws), and soon after that added *one*: "One noodle"; "One eye. Two eyes"; "One foot. Two foots." He also modified the original phrase ("Shoe. Shoe. Two shoes.") and used it to refer to various objects as well as to continuous features ("Yellow. Yellow. Two yellows." [things]), discrete formations of continuous stuff ("Blood. Blood. Two bloods." [spots]), and even remembered events ("Ow. Ow. Two ows." [falls]). Occasionally, he said "two" to refer to three objects ("Apple. Apple. Apple. Two apples.") but more frequently applied the word to exactly two objects. This closely timed emergence of *one* and *two* in his vocabulary coincided with the more general linguistic development of the singular-plural distinction, and as with most new developments, this distinction was initially overgeneralized, both grammatically and conceptually. The other notable aspect of Spencer's use of *two* is that it could as easily signify similarity as numerosity, as in "Here's one shoe, and here's another just the same"—an accomplishment of abstraction rather than, or perhaps in addition to, that of number.

During the course of his third year, Spencer experimented with simpler phrasing, saying "one _____" and "two _____" and still occasionally using *two* to refer to larger groups. By age two and a half, he was fairly accurate in his spontaneous number word use but rarely correct in response to the question *How many?*—even on sets of one and two—and he responded "two" on most groups bigger than two. Indeed, if he understood *two* to mean *the same*, his answers made sense. Moreover, and to this point, over the next few months he demonstrated that he could correctly produce a set of two or three items matching a given such set—but only if the items were *identical* to those in the model set. Around 28 months, he also began experimenting with *three* and *four*, although for many months he used *two* and *three* interchangeably, as if they were fungible synonyms for *same*. Around that time, he also occasionally used number words in reference to *anticipated* events, the work of his newly emerging imagination.

Shortly before Spencer's third birthday, a full year after he began experimenting with *two*, he used both *two* and *three* correctly, the first evidence of the *numerical* understanding of those words. About that time, too, he used *four* correctly for the first time and then shortly thereafter used it reliably as well. And for the first time on formal testing, he could correctly answer the question *How many?* referring to groups of one, two, or three. Moreover, for the first time he could now match two groups of two, three, and even four items each that were *not identical*, suggesting both that his abstracting ability had expanded, such that objects could be "the same" in some way without being identical, and that numerosity was now a feature that could identify a group. Thus, for Spencer, his third birthday marked the beginning of a true *concept* of number.

Interestingly, young children growing up bilingual learn the meanings of "one," "two," and "three" independently in each language, suggesting perhaps the same muddled and concrete understanding of them that Spencer showed in his second year (see Textbox 3.1). However, they learn the number words above "three" and the logic and process of counting simultaneously in both languages, suggesting that in that range, number concept drives the learning.[37]

DEVELOPING PRECISION AND ABSTRACTION

As Spencer clearly demonstrates (Textbox 3.1), during their second and third years, children begin to connect the number words "one," "two," "three," and "four" to objects—at first in vague reference to their identity but increasingly in relation to their numerosity. Moreover, young children initially use these number words to indicate numerosity imprecisely, at times to indicate the correct amount but at other times to indicate some other small amount.[38] Over time, children become more precise in their use.

Before young children learn how to use those number words reliably to count, however, researchers have three windows into their (non-verbal) quantitative thinking.[39] One such window is children's behavior when asked to copy what they see, such as an array of objects. Can they line up the same numerosity of buttons as in a model array of buttons? Alternatively, researchers show a set of objects and then hide them one at a time, asking the child to produce or point to a matching set from memory.[40] What researchers found is that sometime around age two and a half years, children can copy a small array of objects—buttons, for example—but can only do so *approximately*, even for arrays of two or three. By age three, however, many children can match small sets *exactly*, but only if the objects are all identical to each other (i.e., buttons of the same size, shape, and color). That is, the matching is global and literal, not specifically quantitative. Over time and with the natural increases in attention and working memory, the numerosity of the successfully copied arrays increases. By age four, most children can copy sets of three objects, and many can do so with sets of four, whether or not they know the appropriate number word.[41] And as with number-word use, their copying ability becomes more precise with age. Moreover, with the development of abstraction and imagination, the range of types of quantifiable items expands. Thus, by age four, most preschoolers can match a set of tokens to a sequence of sounds, such as claps, or visual events, such as flashes of light. And by age four and a half or so, they can match a set of tokens to a set of random objects. Does this mean that they can count? Not necessarily, since it appears that they accomplish these feats by one-to-one matching. The same thing can be seen in their one-for-you, one-for-me fair-sharing strategy. Importantly, the fact that they can eventually execute these matches regardless of the nature of the items—matching a set of beans to a set of poker chips, for example—suggests that they are beginning to disentangle numerosity from other features of the set and the identity of the objects.

A second window into children's quantitative thinking is their behavior when asked to compare two numerosities, as discussed in Chapter 2. Thus, if two-and-a-half-year-olds are taught that "two is the winner over one," they can use that information to recognize the same relation between other sets of two and one items. However, it typically takes until kindergarten for children to use the same information to figure out that "four is the winner over three." The same pattern holds for other quantifiable features, such as size. For example, four-year-olds can relate three circles of increasing size to three squares of increasing size. By age six, children can relate three circles of increasing size to three circles of increasing color saturation—that is, across different dimensions. Thus, just as set-matching is an important beginning for understanding quantity, comparison is an important beginning for understanding ordered quantitative relationships.

Finally, a third window into young children's quantitative thinking is their behavior when asked to match the result of adding items or taking items away. In these experiments, researchers show children a set of three marbles, for example. They then hide the three marbles in a box. While the child is watching, the researcher then adds, say, one marble to the box. When asked to construct or point to a set that is the same amount as the result, the solutions of two-year-olds were only approximate—they might point to a card with five dots on it—while solutions of three- and four-year-olds became increasingly more accurate. The older children were also increasingly more successful on such problems with larger sets of objects.

Most of the foregoing discussion has concerned the development of discrete quantification that leads up to counting, begging the question: *How and when do children learn to quantify continuous dimensions—size, weight, distance, time, and so forth?* Children begin to learn that there is a difference between countable things and both uncountable stuff and uncountable dimensions of objects around the middle of their third year, when they figure out what sorts of things can be matched exactly or can be easily and fairly shared and what cannot, as discussed earlier. As children become more and more aware of what they can know about, and do with, discrete objects, the distinction between things and stuff (and dimensions) becomes clearer. Down the developmental and educational road, the challenge will be to learn how to apply counting to the quantification of uncountable stuff.[42] Measurement will be taken up in Chapter 9.

Observations of individual children over time show that quantitative learning proceeds over an uneven course, as we see with Spencer, wherein competence in a skill is demonstrated in one context but not another until, after much time and experimentation, the skill can be consolidated and generalized.[43] Children's early math language plays a major role in that development. Research that includes home visits reveals that parental and caretaker math language and number talk have a significant impact on a child's progress toward counting.[44] Unfortunately, that means that children whose parents have had minimal education often begin school at a math-language disadvantage. Reading books about numbers together, particularly the numbers *one* to *three*, promotes early number knowledge.[45] However, as much as 40 percent of a parent's number-word use is in incidental conversation.[46] In particular, verbal prompts ("Two then three then . . ." or "Are these the same amount?") rather than statements ("We each get two") seem to be especially effective in eliciting number talk from a child and in extending parent-child conversations about number.[47] In these simple ways, young children acquire the basic perceptual, cognitive, and linguistic skills upon which counting and conventional arithmetic can build.

NOTICING NUMEROSITY

Finally, one line of research has begun to explore the idea that at least some of children's success in math may be associated with their tendency to simply and spontaneously *notice numerosity* (and among older elementary students, to *notice quantitative relations*). Studies have looked at this question in children from as young as three through the elementary-school years.[48] Methods for learning the extent to which children spontaneously pay attention to numerosity (from among all the available attractions) are quite simple. While the child watches, the adult wordlessly performs a simple task and then, giving the child identical materials, asks the child to "Do the same as I just did." (Older children are given a picture and asked to "describe it in as many ways as possible.") Tasks might include arranging blocks in an array, feeding "carrots" to a toy rabbit, putting different colored envelopes into a mailbox, drawing spikes on a picture of a dinosaur, or finding objects hidden in containers laid out in a semicircle. For very young children, the numerosities involved do not need to be higher than three. The open nature of the adult's question allows children to respond in any way they are inclined to, and what they do and say next are recorded. While preschoolers do not tend to verbalize their quantitative thoughts, the extent to which they match the numerosity of items, or point or gesture as if matching item to item, is noted.

One study that followed children from preschool through fifth grade found that their spontaneous attention to numerosity in preschool predicted their fifth-grade arithmetic fluency and number-line estimation skills.[49] However, it is difficult to assess causality: Do children learn number skills because they pay attention to number? Or do they find numbers interesting because they know something about them? Or does some third common factor affect both? There is some evidence that the relationship is reciprocal, but the question remains open.[50] Another caveat is that the nature of the task can strongly influence a child's attention to numerosity: If a child finds the alternatives more salient, that is where her attention will go. Thus, studies asking young children to describe busy pictures have been much less successful in eliciting comments regarding numerosity.[51]

Some readers may be familiar with Piaget's number conservation task. In this simple activity, the child is asked to judge whether the numerosity of a set of objects arrayed in a row is the same as or different from that of the same set of objects that have been spread out to make a longer row (see Figure 3.4). Piaget held that

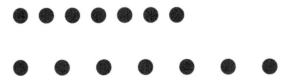

FIGURE 3.4 Piaget's number conservation array.

a conceptual shift produces the realization that, even though the row is longer, the numerosity of objects is the same. More recently, researchers gave a group of six-year-olds the same task, but in a separate exercise assessed their spontaneous attention to numerosity, spacing, or object size. The researchers found that the children who in general attended more to spacing than to numerosity were less likely to accept the idea that the numerosity remained the same than were those who in general paid more attention to numerosity, particularly as the spacing increased. That is, the more salient numerosity is—on that task and for that child—the easier it is to disentangle it from the other features. The research team concluded that the behavior that Piaget observed did not represent a sudden conceptual shift, but rather evolved as a progressive extrication of numerosity from other dimensions as numerosity became more salient.[52]

The important question for the classroom is: *Is it possible to get children into the habit of noticing numerosity?* As of this writing, we do not yet have the answer to that question for the long term. However, we have some preliminary evidence that children's awareness of numerosity can be induced in the short term. Researchers looked at the effect of five minutes of parent-guided play in a children's museum "grocery store." Specifically, parents and their preschoolers were asked to plan a meal and shop for food within a 20-dollar budget. The children's spontaneous attention to numerosity was tested before and after this exercise. Compared to children who were given a non-numerical task (find ingredients from all the food groups), the children who spent the five allotted minutes on a task involving numerical content (shopping under budget constraints) showed sharper attention to numerosity afterward.[53] The results of this and other work[54] reinforce the idea that parental number talk and prompts in the course of their daily routine—shopping, cooking, managing time—can have a significant influence on a child's relationship with number and the place of quantity in a child's mental life. More research on this important matter is warranted.

CONCLUSION

Babies are born with perceptual equipment that allows them to isolate individual objects, sounds, and events around them. Their visual sense eventually allows them to track up to three individual objects through space and time, to be aware when an object goes missing, and to remember where missing objects used to be. Their emerging linguistic skills give them the tools with which to think explicitly and communicate about quantity. These are the perceptual and linguistic underpinnings of preschoolers' earliest experience of exact numerosities *zero* to *three* and of counting. We will pick up counting again in Chapter 6.

ACTIVITIES

Small Numerosities

ACTIVITY 3.1: Matching and Naming Small Sets of Identical Objects

Objective: To discover that numerosity is a category that characterizes a set of discrete objects and that each numerosity has a unique name. In other words, any set with exactly three things belongs to the category *three*, no matter what those things are. These activities will open the door to one-to-one counting (one number word per object) and to the cardinality principle (the last number named in counting the objects tells how many objects there are).

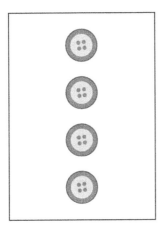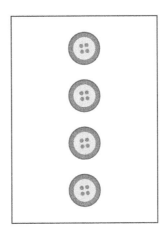

- **First:** Gather a group of eight identical items and place them between the adult and child. Here we use buttons, but tokens or counters will work as well. Tell the child, "Now watch what I do, then you do the same." Take one item from the pile and place it in front of you. Then touch it and say, "One, one button. I have one button. Now you do the same with your button." If the child does not automatically say "one" or touch the button, provide hand-over-hand assistance while saying "one."[55]
- **Next:** Line up two (then subsequently three and then four) identical buttons. Then simultaneously count and touch each button in turn, ending with "Two, I

have two buttons." Emphasizing the final word in the counting sequence ("one, *two*") and then attaching it to the name of the object ("*two* buttons") facilitates the child's understanding of counting and cardinality.[56] Instruct the child to match fresh buttons one-to-one with your set and to touch and count them, in turn, the same way (see Figure above). It is important that the child touch each button while counting, as this will help ensure accuracy.[57] If the child places an inaccurate number of buttons (say, one or three buttons instead of two in the present exercise), provide feedback by saying, "That is not two buttons. Can you show me two buttons?" This "not two" language has been shown to help children extend their number knowledge to unfamiliar numerosities.[58]

■ **Next:** After multiple successes with matching these small sets of items, remove them, point to the space where the items had been and say, "Look! Zero! Here are zero buttons! That means there are no buttons here. How many buttons do you have? You have zero buttons too!" Use gestures to indicate there is nothing, or zero items, in front of them.

ACTIVITY 3.2: Matching Numerosities of Unlike Items

Objective: To distinguish numerosity from item type and to extend counting to any set of discrete items.

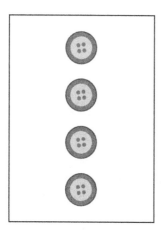

■ **First:** Repeat the exercises in Activity 3.1, but this time the child has different items than those of the adult (see Figure). Refer to the items generically: "One . . . two . . . three. I have three *things*. Now you show me three things!" This approach facilitates the idea that counting applies to any discrete thing.

■ **Next:** Do the same thing, but this time use a variety of different objects in both sets. Have the child match the quantity using any combination of objects chosen from a shared pile.

- **Next:** Line up one to four items on the table (beginning with one or two), touch and count each item, and then count and clap that many times. Ask the child to also count and clap the same number of times.
- **Next:** Count while clapping one to four times (beginning with one or two times), then line up that many items on the table in front of the child. After a few rounds, count and clap again and tell the child it is their turn to line up the items on the table. If they do not understand, use hand-over-hand assistance. Then switch and have the child count and clap one to four times, after which you line up the corresponding number of items.

ACTIVITY 3.3: Matching and Naming Quantities of Zero to Four Using Dot Cards

Objective: To extend number knowledge from concrete objects to more abstract dots on a card that are not arranged in a single line. In this activity, children match cards featuring zero to four dots with other cards and small objects, such as tokens or buttons. It is important to provide images of dots in various configurations.

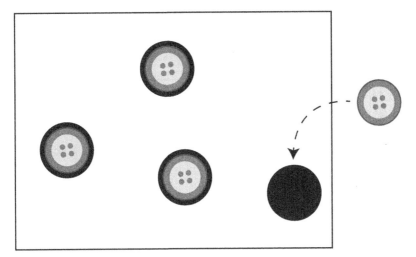

- **First:** Match tokens to dots on cards. Lay out a card with one, two, three, or four dots. Demonstrate placing one token on each dot while counting aloud. Give the children their own card and have them do the same.
- **Next:** The *zero* card can be confusing, so it was not previously included. Show a card without dots and say, "Look! There are no dots on this card! There are zero dots!" Touch the card and say, "Zero. Zero dots. We'll put zero tokens on this card—that means no tokens."
- **Next:** Create a second set of dot cards for numbers *zero* through *four*, which should be identical in configuration to the first set of dot cards. Have the children find matching cards with the same number of dots.

- **Next:** Create a third set of dot cards for numbers *zero* through *four*. The dots should be shown in different arrangements than the previous sets of dot cards. Have the children match cards with the same numerosity.
- **Next:** Have the children copy the dot cards by placing the same number of tokens on a blank card.
- **Next:** Have the children make their own dot cards using markers, crayons, or stickers.

ACTIVITY 3.4: Memory for Small Numerosities

Objective: To develop mental images of small numerosities.

- **First:** Hold up a dot card for a few seconds and then place it face down on the table. The children then replicate the number of dots on a blank card with dots or tokens. Take turns holding up a card (and then placing it face down) and replicating the numerosity on the card.
- **Next:** Place three or more pairs of matching dot cards face down on the table, randomly arrayed. Play a memory matching game in which players take turns flipping over two cards at a time. If the numerosities on the two cards match, the player keeps the cards. The player with the most cards at the end wins. Increase the number of card pairs and players in the game as tolerated.

ACTIVITY 3.5: Matching and Naming Quantities of Zero to Four Using Labeled Containers

Objective: To match item numerosity to dot numerosity. Children fill containers with items that correspond to the number of dots on each container. Use quantitative language to describe the quantity in the containers: "Which container has the *most*? Which has the *least*? Which has *zero*? Which containers have *more* than this one? Which containers have *fewer* than this one?"

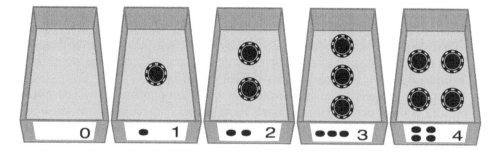

- **First:** Set out ten identical items. Have five containers labeled with cards marked with zero to four dots. Draw the children's attention to each of the labels and have them place the corresponding number of items into the containers in sequential order until each container is filled with the correct numerosity (see Figure above). Once the containers are filled, check the number of items in each of them by counting aloud the items along with the child. Encourage the children to fix any errors using terminology like *two* and *not-two*, as suggested in Activity 3.1. By starting with the exact number of objects to fit in the containers—in this case, ten—the activity can be self-correcting: "Uh-oh! We ran out of buttons before we finished! We must have put too many in one of the containers." Or "We have some left! We must not have put enough in one of the containers. Let's look and fix it."

■ **Next:** Provide a variety of different objects for the children to place in the containers. This level is more abstract and reinforces the concept of number as a category. Learning numerical symbols will be discussed in Chapter 8; here, however, include the Arabic numerals *0* to *4* on the container labels along with the corresponding numerosity of dots to provide the children with some exposure to the numerals before formal instruction.

ACTIVITY 3.6: Non-Symbolic +1 and −1

Objective: To introduce arithmetic transformation. Children watch as you add or subtract one from a small set that is hidden beneath a cloth or in an opaque container. Then the children create their own set to show the total after one item has been added or subtracted.

■ **First:** Show the children a small collection of zero to three items. Count the items aloud with the children, then place the items in an opaque container or cover them with a cloth. While the children watch, add one more item to the container or under the cloth. Ask them to make their own set of objects that has the same amount as the hidden set of objects, without looking at the original set. For example, if you start with two marbles and add one more to an opaque container, the children need to create their own set of three marbles.

■ **Next:** Repeat the previous procedure with two to four items but take away one object from the container or under the cloth.

Zero

ACTIVITY 3.7: The Empty Set: Zero. All Gone!

Objective: To reinforce the empty set. Young children begin to experience the empty set—the absence of something expected—at an early age, which helps with their understanding of the abstract concept of *zero*. Develop the concept of *zero* using everyday experiences of nothing left, all gone, no more, and empty.

■ **First:** Show and talk about *no more*, *none left*, and *all gone* at snack and mealtime when plates and cups become empty. Ask them how much is left when nothing is left. Model the language of "zero" by saying, "There are zero blueberries left. They are all gone. None left." Note that "zero" is followed by a plural noun in the English language (e.g., "zero things"), which may confuse the children and cause them to misunderstand "zero" as depicting an amount greater than "one."

■ **Next:** Demonstrate the empty set with an empty box, bucket, pan, etc. Have the children fill containers and then dump them out. "The box is empty, there are zero things inside now."

■ **Next:** Go on a hunt for empty containers or spaces of any kind: sinks, bathtubs, drawers, shelves, pockets, etc. Tell the children, "Let's look for things that are empty, that have zero things." Ask questions for both filled and empty containers: "Is it empty? No, it is not empty. It is not zero." Or, "Yes, it's empty, it has zero things in it."

Noticing Numerosity

ACTIVITY 3.8: Noticing Numerosity

Objective: To draw children's attention to numerosity. Some children more naturally notice numerosity, while others do not. Yet doing so predicts later arithmetic fluency and number line estimation.[59] For children who do not spontaneously pay attention to numerosity, the following tasks will encourage them to do so. Although these exercises explicitly prompt children to attend to numerosity, with practice, the children should begin to spontaneously focus on numerosity without prompting. Begin these tasks using numerosities of one to four and then increase to larger numerosities with time and practice.

■ Pretend to feed a stuffed animal with a few pieces of pretend food and then direct the children to replicate your actions. Immediately point out whether they fed the animal the same amount and encourage them if they did. Keep practicing until they are more consistent. The children can also feed the animal first and then monitor whether the adult feeds the animal the same amount.

■ Draw a simple picture, such as of a sun, flower, or dinosaur while the children are watching. Tell them to pay attention to how many rays from the sun, petals or leaves on the flower, or spikes on the dinosaur you draw, but do not count them aloud. Turn the drawing over and then have the children draw the picture. Compare drawings, notice and discuss the numerosity, and if it is different, have the child try again.

■ Draw or look at a more complex picture with small numerosities of people, animals, or things. Direct the children to pay attention to the various numerosities. Turn the image over, and have them talk about how many are in each category in the image, such as the number of animals, clouds, cars, etc. As the children improve, provide less direction for them to notice the numerosity and determine if they do so spontaneously.

- Make a design with blocks, stones, shapes, pentominoes, or other objects. Encourage the children to pay attention to the number of objects used in the design as well as the design itself. The number of objects may increase as the age of the children increases. Cover the design and have the children replicate it. Compare designs and discuss whether they used the same number of objects as in the original design, as well as how well they replicated the design.
- Using pretend food for "shopping," instruct the children that they are allowed to "buy" a specific number of food items. When they "check out," have them determine whether they have the correct number of food items and provide encouragement if they do. If not, have them adjust their "purchases" to the correct number.
- Set up a tea party with pretend plates, cups, and food. Set a varying number of items on the plate, and have the children replicate the plate for one of the other members of the tea party (such as a stuffed animal). Direct the children that the food items chosen can be different but that the number of items must be the same to be fair.
- Research suggests that math picture books may be useful for guiding children's attention to numerosity.[60] Read counting books aloud with the children, modeling how you notice the numbers in the text and illustrations, and count objects in the illustrations aloud. Encourage the children to make their own numerical observations about the story. Over time, start to notice and discuss numerosity in picture books without explicit reference to number (non-counting books).

NOTES

1 James, 1890, p. 488.
2 Ross-Sheehy et al., 2003.
3 Carey & Xu, 2001; Mix et al., 2016.
4 Smyth & Ansari, 2020.
5 Starkey & Cooper, 1980.
6 Starkey et al., 1983; Wynn, 1996.
7 Uller et al., 2003.
8 Xu, 2003.
9 Feigenson et al., 2002; vanMarle, 2013.
10 Cordes & Brannon, 2009.
11 Cheung & LeCorre, 2018.
12 Kibbe & Feigenson, 2017.
13 Gelman & Gallistel, 1978/1986.

14 Anobile et al., 2019; Katzin et al., 2019.
15 Bloechle et al., 2018; Jansen et al., 2014.
16 International Telecommunications Union, 2009.
17 Nieder, 2018.
18 Bohn et al., 2015; Watson et al., 2001.
19 Merritt & Brannon, 2013.
20 Bialystok & Codd, 2000.
21 Hornburg et al., 2018; Purpura et al., 2017.
22 Kouider et al., 2006.
23 Davies et al., 2019.
24 Franzon et al., 2019; Katsos et al., 2016.
25 Spelke, 2017.
26 Odic et al., 2013.
27 Halberda et al., 2008.
28 Chernyak, 2020.
29 Mix et al., 2002.
30 Bloom & Wynn, 1997.
31 Barner et al., 2009, 2012; Sarnecka & Lee, 2009; Shusterman et al., 2010.
32 Zapf & Smith, 2008.
33 Barner et al., 2012; Shusterman et al., 2010.
34 LeCorre et al., 2016; Sensaki et al., 2019.
35 Davies et al., 2019.
36 Mix, 2009.
37 Wagner et al., 2015.
38 Wagner et al., 2019.
39 For a review covering the material in the ensuing three paragraphs, see Mix et al., 2002, pp. 23–36.
40 Sella et al., 2016.
41 Rodríguez et al., 2018.
42 Mix et al., 2016.
43 Mix, 2002.
44 Levine et al., 2010; Purpura & Reid, 2016.
45 Gibson et al., 2020.
46 Durkin et al., 1986.
47 Eason et al., 2021.
48 McMullen et al., 2019.
49 Nanu et al., 2018.
50 Hannula & Lehtinen, 2005; Savelkouls et al., 2020.
51 Chan & Mazzocco, 2017; Mazzocco et al., 2020.
52 Viarouge et al., 2019.
53 Braham et al., 2018.
54 Zhang et al., 2020.
55 Casey et al., 2018; Lombardi et al., 2017.
56 Paliwal & Baroody, 2018.
57 Alibali & DiRusso, 1999.
58 Posid & Cordes, 2018.
59 Nanu et al., 2018.
60 Rathé et al., 2018.

REFERENCES

The following references were cited in this chapter. For additional selected references relevant to this chapter, please see Chapter 3 Supplemental References in eResources.

Alibali, M.W., & DiRusso, A.A. (1999). The function of gesture in learning to count: More than keeping track. *Cognitive Development, 14,* 37–56.

Anobile, G., Arrighi, R., & Burr, D.C. (2019). Simultaneous and sequential subitizing are separate systems, and neither predicts math abilities. *Journal of Experimental Child Psychology, 178,* 86–103.

Barner, D., Chow, K., & Yang, S.-J. (2009). Finding one's meaning: A test of the relation between quantifiers and integers in language development. *Cognitive Psychology, 58,* 195–219.

Barner, D., Lui, T., & Zapf, J. (2012). Is *two* a plural marker in early child language? *Developmental Psychology, 48,* 10–17.

Bialystok, E., & Codd, J. (2000). Representing quantity beyond whole numbers: Some, none, and part. *Canadian Journal of Experimental Psychology, 54,* 117–128.

Bloechle, J., Huber, S., Klein, E., Bahnmueller, J., Moeller, K., Rennig, J. (2018). Neuro-cognitive mechanisms of global Gestalt perception in visual quantification. *NeuroImage, 181,* 359–369.

Bloom, P., & Wynn, K. (1997). Linguistic cues in the acquisition of number words. *Journal of Child Language, 24,* 511–533.

Bohn, M., Call, J., & Tomasello, M. (2015). Communication about absent entities in great apes and human infants. *Cognition, 145,* 63–72.

Braham, E.J., Libertus, M.E., & McCrink, K. (2018). Children's spontaneous focus on number before and after guided parent-child interactions in a children's museum. *Developmental Psychology, 54,* 1492–1498.

Carey, S., & Xu, F. (2001). Infants' knowledge of objects: Beyond object files and object tracking. *Cognition, 80,* 179–213.

Casey, B.M., Lombardi, C.M., Thomson, D., Nguyen, H.N., Paz, M., Theriault, C.A., & Dearing, E. (2018). Maternal support of children's early numerical concept learning predicts preschool and first-grade math achievement. *Child Development, 89,* 156–173.

Chan, J.Y.-C., & Mazzocco, M.M.M. (2017). Competing features influence children's attention to number. *Journal of Experimental Child Psychology, 156,* 62–81.

Chernyak, N. (2020). Number-based sharing: Conversation about quantity in the context of resource distribution. *Early Childhood Research Quarterly, 50,* 90–96.

Cheung, P., & LeCorre, M. (2018). Parallel individuation supports numerical comparisons in preschoolers. *Journal of Numerical Cognition, 4,* 380–409.

Cordes, S., & Brannon, E.M. (2009). Crossing the divide: Infants discriminate small from large numerosities. *Developmental Psychology, 45,* 1583–1594.

Davies, B., Rattanasone, N.X., Schembri, T., & Demuth, K. (2019). Preschoolers' developing comprehension of the plural: The effects of number and allomorphic variation. *Journal of Experimental Child Psychology, 185,* 95–108.

Durkin, K., Shire, B., Riem, R., Crowther, R.D., & Rutter, D.R. (1986). The social and linguistic context of early number word use. *British Journal of Developmental Psychology, 4,* 269–288.

Eason, S.H., Nelson, A.E., Dearing, E., & Levine, S.C. (2021). Facilitating young children's numeracy talk in play: The role of parent prompts. *Journal of Experimental Child Psychology, 207,* 105124.

Feigenson, L., Carey, S., & Hauser, M. (2002). The representations underlying infants' choice of more: Object files versus analog magnitudes. *Psychological Science, 13,* 150–156.

Franzon, F., Zanini, C., & Rugani, R. (2019). Do non-verbal number systems shape grammar? Numerical cognition and number morphology compared. *Mind & Language, 34,* 37–58.

Gelman, R., & Gallistel, C.R. (1978/1986). *The child's understanding of number* (Rev.). Harvard University Press.

Gibson, D.J., Gunderson, E.A., & Levine, S.C. (2020). Causal effects of parent number talk on preschoolers' number knowledge. *Child Development, 91*, e1162–e1177.

Halberda, J., Taing, L., & Lidz, J. (2008). The development of "most" comprehension and its potential dependence on counting ability in preschoolers. *Language Learning and Development, 42*, 99–121.

Hannula, M.M., & Lehtinen, E. (2005). Spontaneous focusing on numerosity and mathematical skills of young children. *Learning and Instruction, 15*, 237–256.

Hornburg, C.B., Schmitt, S.A., & Purpura, D.J. (2018). Relations between preschoolers' mathematical language understanding and specific numeracy skills. *Journal of Experimental Child Psychology, 176*, 84–100.

International Telecommunications Union (2009, Oct.). *International Morse code recommendation ITU-R M.1677–1.*

James, W. (1890/1950). *The principles of psychology* (Vol. 1). Dover Publications (Original work published by Henry Holt and Company).

Jansen, B.R.J., Hofman, A.D., Straatemeier, M., vanBers, B.M.C.W., Raijmakers, M.E.J., & van der Maas, H.L.J. (2014). The role of pattern recognition in children's exact enumeration of small numbers. *British Journal of Developmental Psychology, 32*, 178–194.

Katsos, N., Cummins, C., Ezeizabarrena, M.-J., Gavarró, A., Kraljević, J.K., Hrzica, G., . . . Noveck, I. (2016). Cross-linguistic patterns in the acquisition of quantifiers. *Proceedings of the National Academy of Sciences, 113*, 9244–9249.

Katzin, N., Cohen, Z.Z., & Henik, A. (2019). If it looks, sounds, or feels like subitizing, is it subitizing? A modulated definition of subitizing. *Psychonomic Bulletin & Review, 26*, 790–797.

Kibbe, M.M., & Feigenson, L. (2017). A dissociation between small and large numbers in young children's ability to "solve for x" in non-symbolic math problems. *Cognition, 160*, 82–90.

Kouider, S., Halberda, J., Wood, J.N., & Carey, S. (2006). Acquisition of English number marking: The singular-plural distinction. *Language Learning and Development, 2*, 1–25.

LeCorre, M., Li, P., Huang, B.H., Jia, G., & Carey, S. (2016). Numerical morphology supports early number word learning: Evidence from a comparison of young Mandarin and English learners. *Cognitive Psychology, 88*, 162–186.

Levine, S.C., Suriyakham, L.W., Rowe, M.L., Huttenlocher, J., & Gunderson, E.A. (2010). What counts in the development of young children's number knowledge? *Developmental Psychology, 46*, 1309–1319.

Lombardi, C.M., Casey, B.M., Thomson, D., Nguyen, H.N., & Dearing, E. (2017). Maternal support of young children's planning and spatial concept learning as predictors of later math (and reading) achievement. *Early Childhood Research Quarterly, 41*, 114–125.

Mazzocco, M.M.M., Chan, J.Y.-C., Bye, J.K., Padrutt, E.R., Praus-Singh, T., Lukowski, S., Brown, E., & Olson, R.E. (2020). Attention to numerosity varies across individuals and task contexts. *Mathematical Thinking and Learning, 22*, 258–280.

McMullen, J., Chan, J.Y.-C., Mazzocco, M.M.M., & Hannula-Sormunen, M.M. (2019). Spontaneous mathematical focusing tendencies in mathematical development and education. In A. Norton & M.W. Alibali (Eds.), *Constructing number: Merging perspectives from psychology and mathematics education* (pp. 69–86). Springer Nature.

Merritt, D.J., & Brannon, E.M. (2013). Nothing to it: Precursors to a zero concept in preschoolers. *Behavioural Processes, 93*, 91–97.

Mix, K.S. (2002). The construction of number concepts. *Cognitive Development, 17*, 1345–1363.

Mix, K.S. (2009). How Spencer made number: First uses of the number words. *Journal of Experimental Child Psychology, 102*, 427–444.

Mix, K.S., Huttenlocher, J., & Levine, S. (2002). *Quantitative development in infancy and early childhood.* Oxford University Press.

Mix, K.S., Levine, S.C., & Newcombe, N.S. (2016). Development of quantitative thinking across correlated dimensions. In A. Henik (Ed.), *Continuous issues in numerical cognition* (pp. 1–33). Academic Press.

Nanu, C.E., McMullen, J., Munck, P., Pipari Study Group, Hannula-Sormunen, M.M. (2018). Spontaneous focusing on numerosity in preschool as a predictor of mathematical skills and knowledge in the fifth grade. *Journal of Experimental Child Psychology, 169,* 42–58.

Nieder, A. (2018, June 8). Honey bees zero in on the empty set. *Science, 360*(6393), 1069–1070.

Odic, D., Pietroski, P., Hunter, T., Lidz, J., & Halberda, J. (2013). Young children's understanding of "more" and discrimination of number and surface area. *Journal of Experimental Psychology: Learning, Memory, and Cognition, 39,* 451–461.

Paliwal, V., & Baroody, A.J. (2018). How best to teach the cardinality principle? *Early Childhood Research Quarterly, 44,* 152–160.

Posid, T., & Cordes, S. (2018). How high can you count? Probing the limits of children's counting. *Developmental Psychology, 54,* 875–889.

Purpura, D.J., Day, E., Napoli, A.R., & Hart, S.A. (2017). Identifying domain-general and domain-specific predictors of low mathematics performance: A classification and regression tree analysis. *Journal of Numerical Cognition, 3,* 365–399.

Purpura, D.J., & Reid, E.E. (2016). Mathematics and language: Individual and group differences in mathematical language skills in young children. *Early Childhood Research Quarterly, 36,* 259–268.

Rathé, S., Torbeyns, J., DeSmedt, B., Hannula-Sormunen, M.M., & Verschaffel, L. (2018). Kindergartners' spontaneous focus on number during picture book reading. In I. Elia, J. Mulligan, A. Anderson, A. Baccaglini-Frank, & C. Benz (Eds.), *Contemporary research and perspectives on early childhood mathematics education* (pp. 87–99). Springer International Publishing.

Rodríguez, J., Martí, E., & Salsa, A. (2018). Symbolic representations and cardinal knowledge in 3- and 4-year-old children. *Cognitive Development, 48,* 235–243.

Ross-Sheehy, S., Oakes, L.M., & Luck, S.J. (2003). The development of visual short-term memory capacity in infants. *Child Development, 74,* 1807–1822.

Sarnecka, B.W., & Lee, M.D. (2009). Levels of number knowledge during early childhood. *Journal of Experimental Child Psychology, 103,* 325–337.

Savelkouls, S., Hurst, M.A., & Cordes, S. (2020). Preschoolers' number knowledge relates to spontaneous focusing on number for small, but not large, sets. *Developmental Psychology, 56,* 1879–1893.

Sella, F., Berteletti, I., Lucangeli, D., & Zorzi, M. (2016). Spontaneous non-verbal counting in toddlers. *Developmental Science, 19,* 329–337.

Sensaki, S., Lanter, J., & Shimizu, Y. (2019). The development of attention to singular vs. plural sets in preschool children: Insights from a cross-linguistic comparison between English and Japanese. *Cognitive Development, 52,* 100810.

Shusterman, A., Gibson, D., & Finder, B. (2010). *Acquiring first number words: The developmental trajectory of children's meaning for "two".* Proceedings of the 34th Annual Boston University Conference on Language Development. Cascadilla Press.

Smyth, R.E., & Ansari, D. (2020). Do infants have a sense of numerosity? A *p*-curve analysis of infant numerosity discrimination studies. *Developmental Science, 23,* e12897.

Spelke, E.S. (2017). Core knowledge, language, and number. *Language Learning and Development, 13,* 147–170.

Starkey, P., & Cooper, R.G. Jr. (1980). Perception of numbers by human infants. *Science, 210,* 1033–1035.

Starkey, P., Spelke, E.S., & Gelman, R. (1983, Oct. 14). Detection of intermodal correspondences by human infants. *Science, 222,* 179–181.

Uller, C., Jaeger, R., Guidry, G., & Martin, C. (2003). Salamanders (*Plethodon cinereus*) go for more: Rudiments of number in an amphibian. *Animal Cognition, 6,* 105–112.

VanMarle, K. (2013). Infants use different mechanisms to make small and large number ordinal judgments. *Journal of Experimental Child Psychology, 114,* 102–110.

Viarouge, A., Houdé, O., & Borst, G. (2019). The progressive 6-year-old conserver: Numerical saliency and sensitivity as core mechanisms of numerical abstraction in a Piaget-like estimation task. *Cognition, 190,* 137–142.

Wagner, K., Chu, J., & Barner, D. (2019). Do children's number words begin noisy? *Developmental Science, 22,* e12752.

Wagner, K., Kimura, K., Cheung, P., & Barner, D. (2015). Why is number word learning hard? Evidence from bilingual learners. *Cognitive Psychology, 83,* 1–21.

Watson, J.S., Gergely, G., Csanyi, V., Topal, J., Gacsi, M., Sarkozi, Z. (2001). Distinguishing logic from association in the solution of an invisible displacement task by children (*Homo sapiens*) and dogs (*Canis familiaris*): Using negation of disjunction. *Journal of Comparative Psychology, 115,* 219–226.

Wynn, K. (1996). Infants' individuation and enumeration of actions. *Psychological Science, 7,* 164–169.

Xu, F. (2003). Numerosity discrimination in infants: Evidence for two systems of representations. *Cognition, 89,* B15–B25.

Zapf, J.A., & Smith, L.B. (2008). Meaning matters in children's plural productions. *Cognition, 108,* 466–476.

Zhang, X., Hu, B.Y., Zou, X., & Ren, L. (2020). Parent-child number application activities predict children's math trajectories from preschool to primary school. *Journal of Educational Psychology, 112,* 1521–1531.

Part II | Spatial Skills

The psychical entities which seem to serve as elements in thought are certain signs and more or less clear images which can be "voluntarily" reproduced and combined.

Albert Einstein[1]

DOI: 10.4324/9781003157656-5

Alert readers who have made it past the title of this section are probably scratching their heads, wondering what spatial skills are doing in a book about children and math. Of course, it makes sense that spatial abilities might have something to do with geometry; after all, geometry is about shapes, and shapes are spatial. And one would certainly expect that spatial skills are important for architects, carpenters, surgeons, sculptors, engineers, and many others. But math students?

Yes, says the research, math students! The connection between spatial skills and math runs deep. In a longitudinal study of 400,000 intellectually talented high school students, those with the strongest spatial skills in high school were the ones who later wound up with careers in math, engineering, and physical science.[2] In this section, you will find a description of a wide variety of spatial skills and their important links to mathematical thinking.

This section will also discuss the discouraging findings that children growing up in low-income homes with diminished exposure to spatial language often have more difficulty than children from higher-income homes on tasks requiring spatial skill and that some spatial tasks are, on average, more difficult for females than they are for males.[3] The potential long-range consequences for poor children and girls include difficulty with math throughout their schooling; the lack of range and flexibility of problem-solving strategies necessary for advanced math and lucrative careers in science, technology, engineering and mathematics, known as the STEM fields; or even difficulty with the math tasks of daily adult life. Fortunately, it is possible to improve spatial skills.[4] Thus, this section suggests abundant classroom spatial activities, including the use of spatial language, to help mitigate those obstacles.

This topic is introduced here because, like the quantitative intuitions reviewed in Chapters 2 and 3, spatial skills emerge early in development and can be nurtured along to great benefit before formal math education begins.[5] Readers will return to numbers in Chapter 6.

One additional—but important—point. If you are a teacher or aspiring teacher, you may be thinking, "Uh oh. I'm not very good at solving spatial problems myself. How am I going to guide my students through them?" You are not alone. The same study of intellectually talented high-school students noted earlier found that those with the weakest spatial ability had gone into the field of education.[6] That is not to say that all teachers are uncomfortable around spatial tasks, but many are, which may have significant consequences and needs to be considered in any plans to improve students' spatial abilities.[7] In fact, teachers' spatial anxiety has a measurable effect on their students' spatial skills as early as first and second grade.[8] Thus, it is highly recommended that spatial skill training be made available for teachers, as well as their students. Indeed, conducting such training might be an ideal job for those teachers who do gravitate to spatial activities naturally and would enjoy sharing their enthusiasm.

NOTES

1 Cited in Hadamard, 1945.

2 Wai et al., 2009.

3 Johnson et al., 2022; Peters et al., 2006; Voyer et al., 1995.
4 Uttal et al., 2013.
5 Verdine et al., 2014.
6 Wai et al., 2009.
7 Atit & Rocha, 2021.
8 Gunderson et al., 2013.

REFERENCES

The following references were cited in this introduction. For additional selected references relevant to this introduction, please see Part II Supplemental References in eResources.

Atit, K., & Rocha, K. (2021). Examining the relations between spatial skills, spatial anxiety, and K-12 teacher practice. *Mind, Brain, and Education*, 15, 139–148.

Gunderson, E.A., Ramirez, G., Beilock, S.L., & Levine, S.C. (2013). Teachers' spatial anxiety relates to 1st and 2nd-graders' spatial learning. *Mind, Brain, and Education*, 7, 196–199.

Hadamard, J. (1945). *An essay on the psychology of invention in the mathematical field* (pp. 142–143). Princeton University Press.

Johnson, T., Burgoyne, A.P., Mix, K.S., Young, C.J., & Levine, S.C. (2022). Spatial and mathematics skills: Similarities and differences related to age, SES, and gender. *Cognition*, 218, 104918.

Peters, M., Lehmann, W., Takahira, S., Takeuchi, Y., & Jordan, K. (2006). Mental rotation test performance in four cross-cultural samples (N = 3367): Overall sex differences and the role of academic program in performance. *Cortex*, 42, 1005–1014.

Uttal, D.H., Meadow, N.G., Tipton, E., Hand, L.L., Alden, A.R., Warren, C., & Newcombe, N.S. (2013). The malleability of spatial skills: A meta-analysis of training studies. *Psychological Bulletin*, 139, 352–402.

Verdine, B.N., Golinkoff, R.M., Hirsh-Pasek, K., & Newcombe, N.S. (2014). Finding the missing piece: Blocks, puzzles, and shapes fuel school readiness. *Trends in Neuroscience and Education*, 3, 7–13.

Voyer, D., Voyer, S., & Bryden, M.P. (1995). Magnitude of sex differences in spatial ability: A meta-analysis and consideration of critical variables. *Psychological Bulletin*, 117, 250–270.

Wai, J., Lubinski, D., & Benbow, C.P. (2009). Spatial ability for STEM domains: Aligning over 50 years of cumulative psychological knowledge solidifies its importance. *Journal of Educational Psychology*, 101, 817–835.

Chapter 4

Visual-Spatial Skills

FROM the time a baby leaves the simplicity of the womb, she must begin to answer some basic questions for herself: "Where am I?" and "What are all these things I see?" When a baby learns to reach for a toy, she must answer, "How far away is it?" "In what direction?" "Is it moving?" "How fast?" "How do I catch it?" "How big is it?" "Can I wrap my hand around it?" "If so, how do I do that?" When she begins to crawl and walk, she must answer even more questions: "Which way am I going?" "Where is my toy?" "How do I get to it?" "What is in my way, and what do I do about it?" "What is nearby that I can hold on to?" "Which of these things can move on their own?" "How do other things move?" "What do I have to do to make something move?"[1] And many others. With lots of experimentation and support from adults and older children, most babies eventually arrive at the answers to these questions.

The abilities children develop along the way are referred to as *visual-spatial skills* or *spatial skills*. This chapter will describe some of them. The sheer variety of spatial questions to be answered and problems to be solved is reflected in the large number of such abilities emerging from them. Over the years, researchers have tried to categorize these skills, with the idea that one sort of spatial task might be different from other sorts of spatial tasks in some way that makes it easier or more difficult for some people. Several schemes for categorizing spatial skills have been proposed and tested in children and adults, with mixed results.[2] They are grouped here according to shapes, people in motion, and objects in motion only because that seemed one sensible way to break up the topic. But there are many other ways to do so.

Importantly, most of these skills, in one way or another, play a role in mathematics understanding. Their relevance to math learning is the topic of Chapter 5. Here we will describe them.

SHAPES

Since we all studied geometry in school, it is likely that the first visual-spatial skill that comes to mind has to do with shapes—the shapes of flat (*two-dimensional*) things, like puzzle pieces, crackers, and print on paper; and the shapes of un-flat (*three-dimensional*)

DOI: 10.4324/9781003157656-6

things, like balls, building blocks, and party hats. As with children's understanding of quantity discussed in Part I, research over the past few decades has revealed that even the youngest children have a wealth of intuition about shape.

Children's sense of shape has been studied in different ways to suit the ages of the children being studied. To study infants, who are too young to communicate their perceptions in any other way, researchers have used eye-tracking methods to see what holds their attention. As with numerosities, for example, if one shows an infant a series of squares until she gets bored with them and then shows her a circle, she will perk up and gaze longer at this unexpected new shape—but only if she perceives it as different from a square. By this method, researchers have discovered that, remarkably, even newborns can distinguish between open (+) and closed (□ Δ O) shapes. By four months they can distinguish triangles, squares, and circles as different from each other.[3]

Children aged three years and older can let researchers in on their geometric thinking more directly. One interesting method that researchers have devised is to present children with a set of drawings, all but one of which illustrate a particular geometric property or rule and the remaining one of which violates it. The task, then, is to pick the drawing that is "different" or "weird" in the set. (See Figure 4.1 for a few examples. Go ahead and try them yourself.) Preschoolers proved remarkably sensitive to differences in line length and angle, as well as to features of connectedness, curvature, and convexity. By age six, children could distinguish curvy from straight lines and by age nine, lines that are parallel from those that are not. Around that age, too, children began to view right angles as special among angles. Children's performance on this test improved steadily until it reached adult levels around age 12. While adults performed better overall than children, there was a striking consistency across development from preschool to adulthood: What preschoolers could distinguish (e.g., line length and angles) was also easiest for adults, and what was difficult or impossible for preschoolers (e.g., telling the difference between a shape and its mirror image, or *sense*) was also difficult for adults.[4] Perhaps even more intriguing was this finding: Uneducated children and adults from a primitive culture performed as well as American children (aged six to 13 years old) when given the same task. The only group that performed significantly better was educated American adults.[5] These findings suggest that, as with number, most children bring an intuitive sensitivity to shapes to the formal study of geometric principles. Everyday experience and, as we will discuss later, language also play significant roles in geometric development. Moreover, geometric intuition does not come from vision alone: Children and adults who were blind since birth performed as well as sighted children and adults on touch (*haptic*) versions of these items.[6]

Indeed, observations of preschoolers' play suggest that preschoolers *use* geometric properties, even though they may not be aware of them or be able to demonstrate such knowledge on command. Preschoolers seem most aware of the length of lines and objects, but they also use parallel and perpendicular alignments intuitively when playing with blocks. In their artwork, they can create a picture out of a two-dimensional shape and by first grade can combine shapes to make new shapes. Preschoolers also

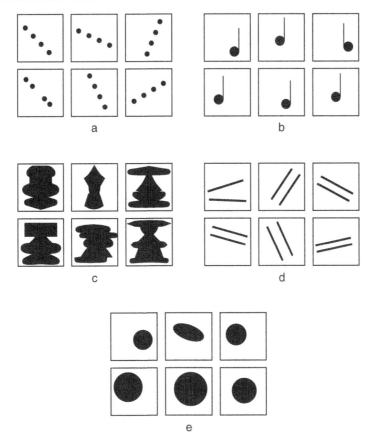

FIGURE 4.1 Odd-one-out geometry test. a) Equidistance. b) Chirality. c) Symmetry. d) Parallelism. e) Circularity.

Source: Adapted from Dehaene et al., 2006.

notice and associate the same shapes in different sizes (their *similarity*), an early insight into scaling and proportionality. Not long after that, they begin to develop strategies to determine if a shape is *symmetrical* and also if two shapes are identical (*congruent*). The easiest strategy is sliding one figure over another (*translation*); flipping the figure over to its mirror image (*reflection*) is a bit more difficult. Turning the figure around a point in the plane (*rotation*) is the most difficult such strategy and will be discussed later.[7]

As we saw in Chapter 3 with early number names, however, explicitly understanding differences among shapes also depends on language. Although spatial skills as a whole are independent of verbal skills as a whole, such that a person can be weak (or skilled) in one and not the other, *spatial language* strongly facilitates spatial thinking. Among primitive cultures, those with words to describe shapes (e.g., "a figure with at least three corners" or "a figure with at least four corners")

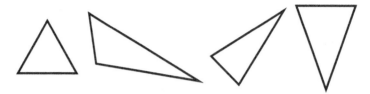

FIGURE 4.2 Canonical (left) and non-canonical triangles.

are able to distinguish those shapes,[8] while those whose language contains no words for geometric forms are not.[9] Closer to home, children who are exposed to shape names begin picking them up in the months following their second birthday, with "circle," "square," "triangle," and "star" being the easiest. "Rectangle" (perhaps more difficult to pronounce) and "pentagon" (which would also require more counting skill than two-year-olds are capable of) take longer to learn. By the middle of their third year, children also begin to apply the appropriate words to variations of those shapes (*non-canonical* forms), such as triangles in which not all the sides are equal in length (Figure 4.2), and to find familiar shapes embedded in pictures and objects around the house.[10]

Interestingly, the one open question about geometric intuition is the idea of an angle. Children and uneducated adults are certainly aware of points or corners (*vertices*), as noted earlier, and perhaps of straight-line distances between the legs, but angles (*subtended arcs*) per se do not seem to catch their attention.[11] Part of that difficulty may come from being unclear as to whether *angle* refers to the extent of the angle spread, the straight-line distance between the legs, or the size of the total figure, including the lengths of the lines that define it. But words can help here, too. One study of four- and five-year-olds found that teaching the children *angle* to mean the size of the spread and a separate invented word (e.g., *toma*) to signify the size of the whole figure helped children understand the correct meaning of *angle*.[12]

However, it typically takes several years before children can use geometric words accurately and reliably.[13] One common way for toddlers to learn their shapes is through age-appropriate books about shapes and by playing with a physical or digital touchscreen form board or shape sorter. Unfortunately, a review of those products reveals that they offer examples of very few shape categories or their atypical variants and are seldom defined in terms of similarities and differences between shapes.[14] The best learning method is still old-school: an adult and child playing together with blocks, puzzles, cookie cutters, and other household objects that represent both canonical and non-canonical versions of each shape, with on-going discussion about their similarities and differences.[15] Indeed, researchers found that parents' use of language conveying the size, shape, and other spatial features of common objects around the house during the early years directly influences children's own use of spatial language, which in turn predicts their spatial problem-solving ability in preschool.[16]

PEOPLE IN MOTION

As noted at the beginning of this chapter, one of babies' first tasks in life is to figure out where they are. Once they are mobile, they need to know not only where they are but also where they are going and how to get there. They learn their way around their room, their family's home, their yard, and their playground. During the earliest months of walking, they learn from experience which objects tend to stay in one place. Using their sense of distance and of relative size—two important geometric properties—as well as other features, they learn where those objects are in relation to themselves and to each other.

Then, shortly before their second birthday, they begin to figure out where they are based on a process called *dead reckoning*. Dead reckoning is a strategy that sailors and other navigators use to figure out where they are at any given moment based on estimates of their distance from a stable object (*landmark*) and the direction (*heading*) and speed at which they are traveling.[17] Over time, toddlers get more skilled at estimating distances, as well as picking useful landmarks and navigable routes. In fact, somewhat older children can even imagine a map based on their movement alone, without the aid of vision: When researchers blindfolded children aged five to nine one at a time and led them from one place straight to another seven meters away, almost all of them could find their way back to their starting point while still blindfolded. If they had been led to the goal *in*directly, about two-thirds of them could take a shortcut back—all from "maps" they contrived in their heads from the physical experience.[18] (However, it may take until age eight or so before they can figure out and express coherently what a listener would need to know in order to get from one place to another efficiently.[19]) By around age nine, children can create a mental map from their experience navigating a series of rooms.[20] The memory skills necessary to learn a route and to keep track of where one is at any given time, as well as the mental flexibility to switch course if necessary, develop gradually over the whole course of childhood, as discussed in Chapter 1.

As with shapes, a key element of navigation development is language—in particular, prepositions, the words that describe where people and things are located in relation to other people and things.[21] Like the earliest navigation skills, prepositions make their first appearance in children's speech during the second year of life but take years to master.[22] The earliest prepositions learned are those that are most visually accessible, beginning with *on*, *in*, and *under* (and the related adjectives *top*, *middle*, and *bottom*), then *beside* and *between*, and later *in front of* and *behind*. (As it turns out, *middle* and *between* are particularly tricky for preschoolers,[23] a fact which could conceivably have repercussions in mastering numerical ordering.) Navigation and preposition knowledge develop hand in hand: Without physical experience, the prepositions would be meaningless; conversely, finding one's way around without prepositions is significantly more difficult than with them, as studies of deaf children reveal.[24] Young children can learn navigation-related words easily. In one laboratory study, four-year-olds were taught a made-up pair of novel words meaning north and south. The children had little trouble learning those words and using them appropriately to indicate directions.[25] In another study, kindergartners were able to use verbal descriptions to place landmarks appropriately in a model of a route through an amusement park.[26] And in yet another experiment in which four-year-olds were shown three objects and a mouse arrayed across the computer screen, the children were instructed to "Sit on your hands and tell me where the mouse is." The study found that the children's *adaptive use* of language in describing the mouse's location in relation to the other objects was closely related to their spatial skills, which were tested separately. Importantly, it was more closely linked to spatial skills than were the number of spatial words produced.[27] Thus, it is not the sheer number of spatial words that children know, but how well they can actually use them to get around and to communicate about their experience, that matters in the development of navigation skills.

There is one exception to the ease with which young children pick up navigation-related language—an exception that should be very familiar to parents and preschool teachers—and that is *left* and *right*. They are usually among the last such words learned, sometimes with much difficulty.[28] In a study in which four-year-olds were taught novel words meaning left and right, researchers found that the children had little difficulty learning the words, provided that the words were first introduced in reference to their own bodies and then extended to their surroundings. However, they had difficulty applying the terms to the left and right sides of a doll—a problem even six-year-olds struggle with—even though they could label the doll's front and back.[29] While there has been some scholarly debate, this difficulty likely has to do with the young brain's natural inability to distinguish objects from their mirror images, to be discussed more fully in Chapter 8.

Images in the familiar form of floor plans and maps are also useful and important navigation tools. A floor plan or map is a two-dimensional illustration of a real spatial arrangement drawn to scale. This means that any distance between two points on a plan or map is a particular proportion of the distance between the same two points in the real world—like the relationship between a person and his shadow on a wall. For example, a floor plan may be drawn so that one inch on the plan equals one foot in the room; a road map might use one inch to represent one mile. Three-dimensional models work the same way. To understand the idea of scaling is one way of understanding proportion. For our purposes here, all such illustrations will be referred to as maps. Unlike verbal directions, the information on a map, including directions and relative distances, is conveyed visually at a glance, rather than in sequence (e.g., "turn left, then right").

Children's map skills begin to develop remarkably early.[30] Two-year-olds, for example, can recognize a room whether they are looking down on it, say from a flight of stairs, or at it from a spot in the room itself. Before they turn three years old, they can recognize a drawing or photograph of a familiar room. By their fifth birthday, most can grasp the scaling idea on maps of simple spaces, understand that objects can be represented by symbols, solve a maze or retrieve objects from memory using a map, and create a map to identify an object's location.[31] Moreover, they can scale up (from map to room) as well as down (from room to map).[32] One large study showed that children typically make significant strides in spatial scaling between the ages of five and eight years, suggesting that those years may be a good time for highlighting those activities in the classroom.[33] From that point on, with practice, they simply get better at reading more complex maps and planning navigation routes using them. Not surprisingly, young children's ability to comprehend the notion of scaling on maps is closely related to their ability to gauge proportional quantities, as discussed in Chapter 2.[34] Moreover, their comprehension of distances and directions on maps, as it develops through their elementary-school years, is closely linked to their geometric intuitions about shapes, as discussed earlier in this chapter.[35]

Perhaps one of the biggest challenges for children in reading maps is the problem of misalignment—that is, reading a map that is not facing the same way as the real space represented on it appears from the child's point of view. For anyone who has ever tried to find a location using a poorly placed "you are here"–type of map in a park or shopping mall, this will be a familiar problem. Often the only way to succeed is to rotate the map physically or mentally or cock one's head to align it with the space. Five-year-olds understand enough about their position in relation to other objects to realize the need to align the map to their own viewpoint. (Younger preschoolers may do better viewing a space from a spot outside it and using a map that is already aligned.) With the increased development of the mental rotation abilities needed to *imagine* the map and scene properly aligned (a topic discussed later), children in the first few grades of elementary school can begin to use maps that are somewhat misaligned.[36] Using a map that is 180 degrees out of alignment without physically rotating it, however, is exceptionally difficult even for older children and adults. Fortunately, unlike paper maps, most global positioning systems (GPSs) have a function that can align the map with the user's heading, relieving the user of the burden of realignment.

Finally, a skill closely related to navigation and map reading is being able to imagine a scene from a different vantage point, or *perspective-taking*. Try this: Stand just inside the door to a classroom and survey the scene. Now imagine what that same room would look like if you peered in at it from the window on the opposite wall. You would see the other side of each chair and desk, and the furniture and walls seen on the left side from the doorway would now appear on your right, and vice versa. Or think about how the rooms of your house look when you enter through the front door versus the back door. Imagining scenes from a different perspective has been examined in young children in several ways. For example, researchers showed children a scene (Figure 4.3) and asked them what they would see if they looked at it from above, like a bird.[37] Other researchers, using immersive virtual reality, showed the child a space with two landmark objects and a third object of interest. The object of interest then disappeared. The child was then "teleported" to a new position and asked to point to where the object had been.[38] Most five-year-olds could manage the first task, and all succeeded at the second.

A more difficult variation of perspective-taking involves imagining what an object would look like on the inside. A common version of this exercise is to mentally slice open an object and imagine what the shape of the cut surfaces would look like. This task is quite difficult for preschoolers but becomes significantly easier between ages four and eight. Moreover, imagining the appearance of an object's cross-section is related to both mental rotation skill (discussed later) and math.[39] In later grades, teachers typically ask

There is a tree with a flower and a picnic basket underneath it. An owl is inside the tree. What do you see if you look from above like a bird?

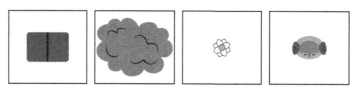

FIGURE 4.3   Perspective-taking.

Source: Adapted from Van den Heuvel-Panhuizen et al., 2015.

students to imagine slices of geometric solids—spheres, prisms, cones (see Figure 4.4), and the like—but in the meantime, experiments with fruits, vegetables, or other familiar solid objects can help them get ready.

Learning shapes and routes and maps of routes involves remembering in the mind's eye what is seen by the eye. Conjuring up images of what something unseen *would* look like or *might* look like, however, involves more than just memory; it requires *imagination*. This kind of imagination is more tied to reality than, say, imagining fairies and unicorns. In fact, the imagined outcomes required in math and science are tightly constrained by logic and principles. Nevertheless, they do require being able to conjure up an image that does not (yet) exist. Perspective-taking and slicing involve imagining what something would look like when seen from a different location or point of view. Likewise, planning a route involves imagining oneself traveling along it, as well as

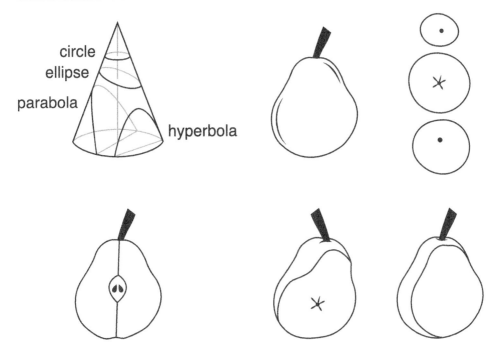

FIGURE 4.4   Sections of a cone and a pear.

imagining the consequences—will it get me where I want to go? The ability to mentally project and transform images in space and time develops gradually with imagination in general. For example, preschoolers begin to experiment mentally with different routes before they take a step, such that by the end of kindergarten, a child can plan the best way to get where he is going through complicated spaces with several possible routes (think of a path across a typical kindergarten classroom). The skills described in the next section on objects in motion also depend heavily on visual-spatial imagination.

OBJECTS IN MOTION

A skill closely related to navigation and map reading, as well as to perspective-taking, is mental rotation.[40] While perspective-taking involves the viewer imagining the way a scene would look if she changed locations, mental rotation is the ability to imagine what an object would look like if she rotated the object. Technically, of course, the effect is the same; the difference generally has to do with the size and manipulability of the thing being observed.

Mental rotation ability has been detected in infants as young as six months. Importantly, this skill is linked to babies' motor development, with significant improvements noted as they learn to sit by themselves, reach for and manipulate objects, and crawl.[41] Observations of children during the two years between their first and third birthdays

FIGURE 4.5 Two-dimensional rotation. Is the bear on the right the same as the bear on the left, or its mirror image?

Source: Adapted from Perrucci et al., 2008.

reveal that their exploration and manipulation of nesting toys and blocks that can be fitted together become increasingly complex.[42] Close observation of their efforts to insert shape toys into similarly shaped openings shows that as these toddlers develop, they get better at both predicting which object will fit and orienting the object into the correct position *before* attempting to insert it, requiring less trial and error.[43]

The mental rotation skills of young children are usually assessed using two-dimensional figures. In experiments, children are sometimes shown an upright target object along with one or more rotated objects and are asked to determine whether the rotated objects are the same as or different from the target (Figure 4.5), where the rotated objects are either identical to or a mirror image of the upright target.[44] However, prior to learning how to read, children think of identical and mirror-image objects as "the same" because orientation does not yet have significance for them, as it will when they have mastered the difference between *b* and *d*, for example.[45] A more effective method is to ask the child to mentally rotate an asymmetric puzzle piece to fit into a matching or mirror-oriented slot or hole.[46] In this way, the child must decide only if it fits, not if it is the "same," a more abstract and ambiguous question. Another two-dimensional problem often requiring mental rotation involves mentally fitting geometric pieces together to match a target figure (Figure 4.6), much like doing a jigsaw puzzle in one's head.[47] This sort of task is typically free of left-right orientation complications and works well as a measure of young children's mental rotation skill (as long as it does not contain features that invite verbal analysis, an issue discussed in the next paragraph).

By age seven or eight, children begin to make rotation-based judgments on tangible, three-dimensional figures, and eventually on two-dimensional drawings of three-dimensional figures. Children who have an easy time with three-dimensional rotation tasks usually have an easy time with two-dimensional tasks.[48] The classic psychological task employed to evaluate mental rotation in older children and adults involves two-dimensional perspective drawings of cubes attached to each other to form larger, three-dimensional configurations (Figure 4.7). The individual is shown a row of four such configurations and asked to pick the two that are identical to a target configuration

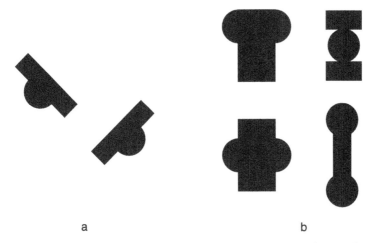

a   b

FIGURE 4.6 a) When these two pieces are put together, b) which of these figures will it look like?

Source: Adapted from Levine et al., 1999.

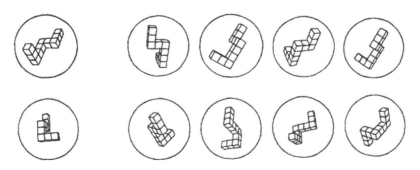

FIGURE 4.7 Mental Rotation Test.

Source: Derived from Vandenberg & Kuse, 1978. © Sage Publications

but in a different orientation. If you try it, you will see that this task is very difficult to coach oneself through verbally—more difficult, in fact, than for most other mental rotation tasks. Thus, it is one of the purest measures of mental rotation ability, as well as of visual-spatial skills in general. By contrast, when using the same forms but with a few cubes shaded a different color, a verbal, analytical strategy can give a significant assist: "Let's see. Flip the blue cube over and move it to the left." Moreover, during this task variation, brain scans show a shift of activity toward regions governing language and feature (e.g., color) identification, rather than mental rotation.[49] Thus, the classic, feature-free mental rotation test is especially valuable for gaining insight into an individual's mental rotation abilities. As will be discussed in Chapter 5, the test has been particularly useful in examining the relationship between visual-spatial abilities and math learning.

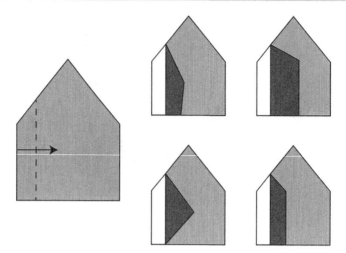

FIGURE 4.8   Which one of the figures on the right is the same as the figure on the left after the paper is folded?

Source: Derived from Harris et al., 2013. © John Wiley, Blackwell Publishing

Another popular mental rotation test is mental paper-folding, in which one is given a flat paper configuration and instructed to imagine it folded up into a box or some other three-dimensional object, similar to origami. In another version, the individual is presented with a folded-up piece of paper with a hole punched through the layers; the task is to figure out where all the holes will be when the paper is unfolded. In the version shown in Figure 4.8, the child is asked to imagine the consequences of a single fold. Children can vary considerably in their skill, but most can begin to imagine folding paper by about age six.[50] Because mental paper-folding tasks often involve multiple folds, which are typically accomplished sequentially, it invites an analytic strategy and thus is not quite as powerful as the classic Mental Rotation Test with cube configurations.

A close cousin of mental rotation is the ability to mentally simulate and manipulate the forces that make objects move and to anticipate their effects, or *mechanical reasoning*.[51] (Figure 4.9. Give it a try.) Like other spatial abilities, ideas about how objects move emerge early in life. Even infants, the most naïve physicists, can distinguish animate objects that can move on their own (their sister, their cat) from inanimate objects that cannot (their crib, their teddy), with a separate, ambiguous category reserved for shadows and powered machines.[52] As noted in Chapter 2, they can also distinguish solid objects with a fixed shape (blocks) from stuff that changes shape (milk, sand). Importantly, infants have different expectations for how these things respond to force. For example, when a container is tipped, they know that blocks will tumble out, but milk will pour. When a solid object is hit or pulled, they know that it will move but otherwise will not, and that when a moving object bumps into a bigger object it will stop. If an object is released in mid-air, they know that it will fall. Sometimes an object will fall off a table on its own, but they know that it will

FIGURE 4.9 Mechanical reasoning problems. a) When the rope is pulled, will the bottom pulley turn clockwise or counterclockwise? b) When the left gear turns clockwise, in what direction will the far-right gear turn?

Source: Derived from Hegarty, 2004.

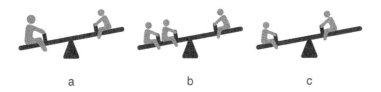

FIGURE 4.10 Development of balance concepts. The side that goes down a) has the larger weight, b) has more weights, and/or c) has the weight farther from the fulcrum. Adapted from balance beam experiments.

Source: Adapted from Case & Griffin, 1990; Siegler, 1976.

not if more than half of it is on the table.[53] As their experience with objects in motion accumulates and their sensory and motor faculties mature, children become increasingly accurate in their predictions. Children's laboratories—their playrooms, hobby tables, playgrounds, gyms, and sports fields—are particularly rich in opportunities to make observations and develop, reject, and revise ideas about motion. Moreover, as children's memories and imaginations increase, so does their ability to simulate and manipulate those motions in their heads, a kind of step-by-step mental rehearsal of the events as they might unfold.

The path to clarity is long and not always straight, however. Take the effect of gravity on the motion of simple levers, for example, a lesson once learned on the playground's teeter-totter (Figure 4.10). Extrapolating from balance beam studies, we know that at age four, a child understands that when he sits on one end and his father sits on the other, Dad (who is heavier) will go down. By age six, children figure out that if two classmates sit on the other side instead of Dad, those friends also make that side go down—that is, children can now make an association between numerosity and weight. Around age eight, they begin to consider relative distances from the fulcrum, although the ability to weigh all three factors—weight, numerosity, and distance—together often does not occur until adolescence.[54]

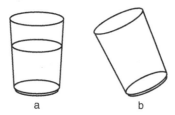

a   b

FIGURE 4.11   Water level task. Here is a glass of water. Draw a line on the empty glass where the water level would be if the glass of water were tilted like this.

Source: Adapted from Papadopoulos & Koustriava, 2011.

Similarly, one's sense of gravity's effect on water can be assessed by the water level task, in which children are shown a picture of a glass of water (Figure 4.11a) and asked to draw on a second glass where they think the water line would be if the glass were tipped as shown (Figure 4.11b). On this task, even some five-year-olds can draw the line correctly, provided they are given a chance to experiment first with a real glass of water.[55]

As we have already seen, sometimes ideas take root implicitly long before they become explicit. For example, when grade-school-aged children were shown two balls of the same size but different weight and were asked to predict their relative speed in rolling down an incline, they tended to pick either the lighter or heavier one as being faster. However, when they were shown doctored videos depicting one ball or the other rolling faster or the balls rolling at the same speed and were asked which video looked correct, more often than not the children recognized the correct depiction (rolling at the same speed).[56] Still, whatever errors they did make reflected their earlier predictions, suggesting that a child's ideas arise from the interplay between their implicit knowledge based on their experience and their explicit understanding (or misunderstanding) at any given point in time. In fact, studies have shown that misconceptions can *increase* as children's experience broadens. Notably, even adults who have been schooled in the relevant mechanical principles frequently perform better by using mental imagery than by applying those (often misremembered) rules, suggesting that the two kinds of information are recruited independently.[57]

Finally, there is the ability to imagine objects' simple relocation in space (without involving force). One such task is to mentally relocate a circular array of objects while retaining their original sequence (Figure 4.12). In this exercise, most children above age eight can remember the original order, but being able to re-create that order with a new starting position is a skill that continues to develop into adulthood.[58] Mentally relocating objects *in relation to each other* in space is another, arguably more difficult, variation of this task best exemplified by jigsaw puzzles, as well as by the games of checkers, chess, and Scrabble. Researchers have found that these games' experts differ

FIGURE 4.12   a) Four figures in a circle. b) The same four figures in the same order but different starting positions.

Source: Adapted from Michaelides & Avraamides, 2017.

from novices by the knowledge, born of long experience and study, that they bring to the game, such as board plays or letter positions in words. Importantly, while novices engage brain structures in only one or the other hemisphere, experts engage the same structures in both hemispheres during play, allowing for highly efficient performance.[59] Being able to imagine the relocation of one object and the consequent realignment of other objects in relation to it can be challenging. But imagining the consequences of multiple simultaneous object relocations—or of multiple such moves over time—takes extraordinary skill. Practice builds not only the knowledge base but also the brain circuits that permit such efficient, expert performance. Other spatial strategy games, including some team sports, do the same. Age-appropriate versions of all such games are available to children.

In addition to imagination, many other more general cognitive skills are involved in strategy games. The best visual-spatial thinkers use mental imagery and imagination, analogies to more familiar situations, (correct) knowledge of rules, and analytic strategies in flexible and adaptive combination.[60] Here, the discussion has focused principally on spatial imagery and imagination, but the same strategies are used in much of mathematics.

LANGUAGE, MOVEMENT, AND GESTURE IN SPATIAL REASONING

As noted in Chapter 1, relational reasoning is key to mathematics, and one route to thinking about relationships, including spatial relationships, is through language.[61] Children's knowledge of spatial language is a vital aspect of learning and communicating about spatial relations. As we have seen, spatial language is rich in relational nouns (*part, whole, portion*) and comparative descriptors (*taller, wider, longer, straighter, curvier*). As noted previously in relation to navigation, it is also abundant in prepositions (*in, on, under, above, through, over, upon, after, before, behind, in front of, left, right, outside, near, far, into, beyond, beside, by, at, inside, toward, beneath, up, down, between*). Except for *left* and *right*, these words are typically learned with use during the preschool years. *Left* and *right* are learned somewhat later, during the elementary years, because the brain must be trained to pay attention to left-right orientation. In a study of children aged four and a half to six and a half, only about 25 percent of them could use *left* and *right* correctly in speech, whereas the majority of children could use the other common prepositions.[62] As we will discuss in Chapter 5, visual-spatial skills are vital to math, and thus children must master spatial language in the early years.

Spatial reasoning in all its forms is also closely linked to bodily movement. We have already seen how infants' mental rotation skills develop right along with their motor skills. In fact, the association between bodily motion and visual-spatial skills holds for preschoolers,[63] older children, and adults as well and are closely related in the brain.[64] In a remarkable study of seven- to 12-year-olds, researchers compared children's mental rotation abilities (tested on drawings of cube configurations) with their speed in a physical steeple chase. The steeple chase involved a forward roll, jumping, crawling, turning, and changing directions. The researchers found that, even taking into consideration the children's sex and straight-track running speed, their steeple-chase completion time was linked to their mental rotation ability: the better their race time, the more efficient their mental rotation performance.[65] In an equally remarkable study, researchers found that training eight- to 12-year-old children who have spina bifida how to juggle significantly improved their performance efficiency on a mental rotation task.[66]

The role of bodily movement in spatial reasoning can often be observed in the gestures people make while they solve spatial problems. (If you have been experimenting with the problems in the figures presented in this chapter, you might even have caught yourself gesturing.) In fact, children's gesturing while solving spatial problems is linked to performance on all sorts of spatial tasks. For example, researchers asked four- to six-year-olds to mentally solve spatial transformation problems or analogies without moving the pieces around. The researchers then asked the children how they had solved the problems and observed their behavior as they explained their strategy. What the study teams found was that the extent to which children produced relevant words *and gestures* during their explanations was linked to their performance on the task, prompting the researchers to consider that gesture training, in addition to spatial language instruction, might improve children's mental rotation skills.[67] Other researchers obtained similar results from preschool and primary-grade children engaged in the odd-one-out geometry task used in studies mentioned earlier (see Figure 4.1). Observations of the children during testing revealed that certain geometric concepts were evident in the children's gestures before they made their choice or articulated their reason. Children sometimes chose the correct item for other geometric properties, even if they could not explain their solution in words or gestures. The researchers concluded that behavior, such as children's gestures and choices, may reflect *implicit* knowledge upon which later explicit geometric reasoning can build.[68] Similar results have been obtained in navigation studies: Preschoolers remembered a route better if they had gestured while learning it, and eight-year-olds could explain the locations of hidden objects better once they were taught to "use your hands."[69] Not only might it be helpful to children if they were encouraged to think with their hands, but vigilant teachers would learn more about their students by watching them think.

CONCLUSION

Children engage in spatial thinking and behavior from when they get out of bed in the morning until they get back into bed at night. It is part of everyday life, and opportunities to learn from those experiences are everywhere—at home, in school, on the sports field and playground, in games and crafts and hobbies. If teachers are puzzled about how they can teach spatial skills in their classroom, perhaps all that is needed is a broader definition of "the classroom." The next section of this chapter offers some specific suggestions.

ACTIVITIES

A Note About Gesture and Language

Physical gestures and spatial language, used separately and together, have been shown to improve children's spatial skills and math performance.[70] Therefore, when engaging children in these activities, it is important to use both gestures and spatial language. In addition to modeling gestures, encourage children to use gestures themselves during each task. If children make mistakes during these activities, use those mistakes as opportunities for learning by discussing and fixing their errors.

Shapes

ACTIVITY 4.1: Shape Search

Objective: To recognize different shapes in everyday environments. Children find, name, take pictures or draw, and label the shapes they find.

- **First:** Search for two-dimensional shapes of increasing complexity, such as circles, squares, rectangles, triangles, ovals, hexagons, and trapezoids. Discuss the properties of the shapes, including the number of sides and vertices (corners), and compare their composition. For example, "The window is a rectangle because it has two shorter sides of the same length, two longer sides of the same length, and four right angles. The window in the door is a big square. It has four sides of the same length." Count how many different shapes the children can find in their environment or how many of the shapes may be within the same object, such as how many shapes there are in a door.
- **Next:** Search for three-dimensional shapes such as spheres, cubes, rectangular prisms, and triangular prisms. Discuss how objects in the children's environments can be made of multiple shapes that are put together. For example, "The trunk of the tree looks like a cylinder, and the top of the tree looks round like a sphere."

ACTIVITY 4.2: Geoboards

Objective: To strengthen understanding of shape composition, spatial relations, and transformations using geoboards. During the activity, talk about shape names, angles (acute, right, obtuse), orientation, proximity (*next to, above, below, to the right, between*), and transformation (*translate, rotate, flip*) and its results (*mirror image*, two squares make a rectangle). Geoboards and designs can be found for free online or used as a physical manipulative.

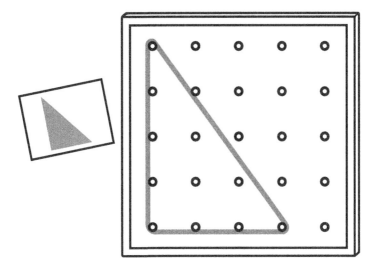

- **First:** Using geoboards, children copy shapes created on other geoboards by the instructor or copy designs from cards or online sources. Begin with a simple, common shape. The children first make an exact replica of the shape, then make it bigger or smaller. After making a shape, turn the geoboard and discuss how the shape looks at various rotations. Repeat with other simple shapes.
- **Next:** Have the children copy two or more shapes on the geoboard. Make sure that they copy the space between shapes and their orientation correctly. You can also put two of the same shape on the grid but with different orientations and/ or sizes for the children to copy.
- **Next:** Provide more complex and irregular shapes. First, the children make an exact replica of one, then mentally rotate, reflect, or change the size of the shape and talk about the transformation. After creating a mental image of the transformation, the children physically reproduce the transformed shape without moving the original geoboard or card. For example, show the children a concave polygon and have them mentally and then physically reproduce it as a mirror image. In addition to copying shapes, the children can create, describe, or transform their own shapes.

ACTIVITY 4.3: Copy and Draw Geometric Shapes and Designs

Objective: To learn about structure, shape, angle, and geometric relationships by drawing two- and three-dimensional shapes and designs on paper. Children compare their drawings to the original and look for differences in angle, proportion, relationship, and points of intersection. If the children cannot see the differences, help them compare their drawing to the original by pointing out the differences using specific spatial language. Have the children redraw the figure and repeat the process of looking for similarities and differences until their drawing is fairly accurate. Emphasize that we learn from our mistakes and then make progress. Through discussion and revision of mistakes, children can learn that there are many ways to visualize, remember, and reconstruct two- and three-dimensional shapes. A wide variety of type and complexity of geometric shapes are available for free from an online search.

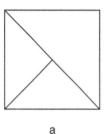
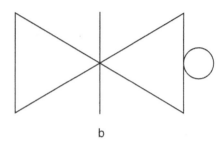

a   b

- **First:** Study-Copy: Show children a simple two-dimensional geometric design and have them study and discuss it (see Figure a as an example), then copy or trace it. If tracing first, then replicate next without tracing.
- **Next:** Replicate from memory: Cover the design and have children draw it from memory. When they are done, compare their drawing with the original design and discuss similarities and fix any differences.
- **Next:** Have children draw a rotated or reflected version of the previous designs. Over time, present the children with increasingly more complex geometric designs (see Figure b as an example).
- **Next:** Hear-Replicate: Describe a two-dimensional geometric design in a step-by-step manner without showing it to the children. The children draw it by following the verbal instructions. They can also describe the design for an adult or another child to draw, using spatial language that describes the properties (*straight, curvy, diagonal*), position (*middle, below*), and parts (*corner, side*) of the design. Compare the finished drawing with the original and comment on any differences to highlight the spatial elements in the design's composition.
- **Next:** Study-Copy in three dimensions: Show children a three-dimensional geometric design such as a cube or prism. The children study the design and then draw it. When they are done, compare their drawing with the original design and discuss. Allow the children to modify their drawings as many times as needed. Many fun three-dimensional drawings can be found online.

ACTIVITY 4.4: Building With Blocks: Guided and Free Play

Objective: To build tall, complex, well-balanced structures. Research shows that children respond to adults who model language that encourages building tall, complex structures and suggests that girls may be particularly motivated by stories with characters that encourage them to do so.[71] The Activities section of Chapter 5 mentions additional ways to build complex block structures.

- **Activity:** Build structures with blocks with as much height, complexity, and balance as possible. Children can create their own structures as well as copy structures from models or images. Adults and children can build their own structures together or side-by-side so that the children can observe and use some of the adult's techniques. Encourage children to tell a story about their structure, including characters that will use it or live in it. Use spatial language and gestures throughout the activity.
- **Talk about:** How tall can we make it? How can we make it stronger? Is it better to use bigger pieces on the top or the bottom? Is there a different way? Will these pieces fit together? Will this piece balance on top? What would happen if . . .?
- **Create motivation through stories:** Make up stories with characters to help motivate children to build tall and complex structures. Use stuffed animals, cutouts, or pictures of characters. *Monkey lost his best friend so let's build a big tower so he can look all around and find his friend. Unicorn wants to know what the clouds feel like, so let's help Unicorn get up to the clouds. Anna needs to get to the top of the castle to find Elsa.*

People in Motion

ACTIVITY 4.5: Scavenger Hunt Using Spatial Language

Objective: To find a hidden object by following location and direction language and gestures. Hide objects around the classroom or outside on the playground for children to find.

- **First:** Provide directions using spatial words related to position (e.g., *in, on, over, under*), direction (e.g., *up, down*), and proximity (e.g., *beside, between, next to*).

Give the children multiple steps to follow: "Go *between* those big bushes, *over* the tree stump, and look *under* the pile of leaves." Use gestures to accompany the language.

■ **Next:** Incorporate spatial language and gesture related to frames of reference (e.g., *behind, in front of, to this side of, above, below*). Introduce *left* and *right*, which are difficult spatial words for children to master. You can support the children by placing a sticker with the letter *L* on their left hand and a sticker with the letter *R* on their right hand. In addition, you can provide further context clues: "Turn *left*, toward the door."

■ **Next:** Incorporate language related to distance. For example, "Walk *five steps forward*. Turn to the *left*. Look *behind* the table." "Walk *halfway* to the slide. Look *between* the two plants."

■ **Next:** After they practice following the adult's directions, the children can take turns giving directions for a partner to navigate the space and to find a hidden object using language indicating position, direction, and distance. Encourage the child providing the instructions to remain stationary and use spatial language and gestures to describe the location of the hidden object.

ACTIVITY 4.6: Mapping With Scaling

Objective: To learn to navigate the classroom or playground using a scaled map of the location. To learn how to create a map of their own. Place signs with the labels *North, South, East*, and *West* on the classroom or playground floor in their respective locations to help children orient themselves using these cardinal points.

■ **First:** The teacher creates a scaled map of the classroom or playground, with notable landmarks (furniture, doors, windows, play centers, etc.) marked on the map along with the cardinal points *North, South, East*, and *West*. Mark a specific location on the map and ask the children to find that location in their physical surroundings. Discuss the distance between objects on the map and their counterparts in children's physical surroundings: "I notice that the block center is near the North windows in our classroom. Does the block center look close to the windows or far away from the windows on the map?"

■ **Next:** After the children have had experience using a scaled map of the classroom or playground, turn the map into a "treasure map." Hide a stuffed animal or other object and mark its location on the map. The children need to read the map and navigate the space to find the treasure.

■ **Next:** Help children create a map of the classroom. Create an outline of the classroom on a large sheet of paper. Draw or cut shapes out of construction paper representing key items in the classroom, such as doors, windows, rugs, desks, and other furniture. Have the children first label *North, South, East*, and *West* on the map, then describe the location of each item in the classroom and decide where to place the item on the map. Estimate and check the distances between objects on the map: "Look at the map and guess how many steps it takes to walk from the door to the bookshelf. Now let's walk and see if your guess is correct."

■ **Next:** Have the children draw their own maps of the classroom, playground, home, or neighborhood. Draw a path to navigate between different locations, such as a path to get from their classroom to the cafeteria. Stage a scavenger hunt using maps.

ACTIVITY 4.7: Taking Pictures of Objects From Different Perspectives

Objective: To view and imagine objects from different perspectives.

■ Have children photograph or draw pictures of the same object from different perspectives (above, beside, beneath) and from different distances. Talk about the objects and how they look the same and different from the various perspectives. Have the children rank-order the images of the objects taken from different distances and discuss how the perspective changes. Have other children guess what the object is when photographed from unusual perspectives or from close up.

Objects in Motion

ACTIVITY 4.8: Jigsaw Puzzle Imagery Task

Objective: To mentally move, rotate, and rearrange segments of an image to create a whole.[72]

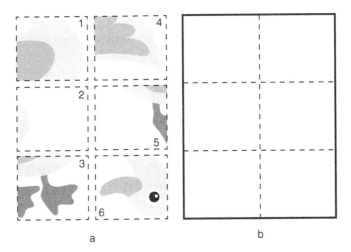

a   b

- **First:** Photocopy drawings of animals or other images. Cut the drawings into four or six equal-sized rectangles, rearrange the pieces and number the pieces (see Figure a). Present the pieces along with a grid in which to mentally arrange them to make the picture (see Figure b). Ask the children to write the number of the puzzle piece that belongs in each location on the grid, such that they create the complete image by visualizing the puzzle only, without moving the puzzle pieces.
- **Next:** Once the children can visualize the pieces on the grid correctly, continue with more puzzles with at least some of the pieces rotated 180 degrees.
- **Next:** Using similar images, cut the picture into four to six segments with non-rectangular shapes.

ACTIVITY 4.9: Create Unique Two-Dimensional and Three-Dimensional Figures

Objective: To create as many unique two-dimensional and three-dimensional figures as they can using square tiles or linking cubes. Have them rotate each novel formation in various ways to look at them from different perspectives.

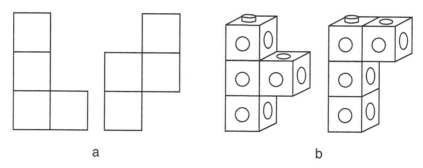

a   b

- **First:** Children make as many unique two-dimensional figures as possible starting with four and later using five or six square tiles (see Figure a). The challenge is to make unique structures that are not rotated versions of one another. When they are done, have them physically reorient the figures, if necessary, to make sure each individual figure is unique and not a rotated version of another structure.
- **Next:** Have children make as many unique three-dimensional figures as possible using four and then eventually five and six linking cubes (see Figure b). Afterward, children can choose a few figures to draw in three dimensions.

ACTIVITY 4.10: Replicate a Three-Dimensional Figure From Verbal Instructions

Objective: To describe the design of a cube figure so that it can be accurately replicated from verbal instructions only.

■ Pair children up and set up a barrier between them such that they cannot see each other's cube formations. Have one child create a novel formation with linking cubes and then give step-by-step instructions, in words and gestures, on how to build it. The second child creates the figure from the instructions only, without seeing it. They remove the barrier to see if they successfully created the figure, and if not, they describe the original figure with words and gestures and fix the copy. Then the children switch roles.

ACTIVITY 4.11: Geometric Rotations and Reflections With Two-Dimensional Materials

Objective: To mentally rotate or reflect a two-dimensional geometric figure. Children use classroom manipulatives to create a rotated or reflected version of a model figure by imagining the transformation. In addition to square tiles and pattern blocks, there are a variety of magnetic boards that come with shapes that can be combined to create different designs and have been used in research.[73] Incorporate spatial language to describe the location, movement, and transformation of the manipulatives. If children are familiar with analog clocks, you can introduce the terms *clockwise* and *counterclockwise* to describe rotational direction.

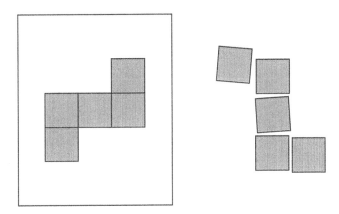

■ **First:** Present children with a two-dimensional figure made of square tiles, pattern blocks, or other shapes. Ask the children to imagine the figure "turned like this" (demonstrate a planar turn, such as a 90-degree, 180-degree, or 45-degree rotation) and to then use manipulatives to create the rotated figure or draw what the rotated figure would look like. Begin with simple figures and progress to more complex figures.
■ **Next:** Present the children with a two-dimensional figure and invite them to look at its reflection in a mirror. Then have them draw or arrange the manipulatives to look like the reflection. When they have mastered that, ask them to *imagine* what a figure would look like in a mirror and to re-create it the same way. Vary

between having children flip the figure over a horizontal and a vertical line. Begin with simple figures and progress to using more complex figures.

ACTIVITY 4.12: Three-Dimensional Mental Rotation Block Task

Objective: To improve mental rotation. Research demonstrated improved math skills using this spatial training activity.[74]

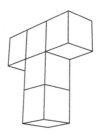

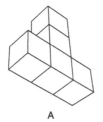

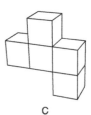

A   B   C

▪ Create different three-dimensional designs with snap cubes. For each design, create three additional designs from which children will choose the one that matches the target: a replica presented in a different orientation and two unrelated designs. The child must identify which of the three figures exactly matches the target figure once rotated. For easy accessibility, use photographs or digital creations of the arrayed configurations.

ACTIVITY 4.13: Object Circular Rotation

Objective: To mentally rotate a circular array of objects while retaining their original sequence.[75]

▪ **First:** Place four pictures of different animals or physical objects in a circle, name them in order, and have children take a mental picture of them (see Figure 4.12). Cover the items and have the children replicate the order with their copies of the animals or objects. Uncover the items in the circle for the children to see, check their order, and fix any errors.

- **Next:** Have children pick up all of their objects except for the one at the top of the circle, and then have them move that piece 90 degrees to the right (show them the new position of that piece). Have them place the rest of their objects in the same sequence as previously but now rotated 90 degrees around the circle. Place the items in the new correct orientation and have the children check their items for accuracy.
- **Next:** Show the original order of the objects, then have the children mentally rotate the objects by 90 degrees to the left. Then children physically rotate their objects by 90 degrees to the left. Show them the new correct order and have the children check to see if their placements are correct.

ACTIVITY 4.14: Visualizing the Results of Paper-Folding and- Unfolding

Objective: To visualize how a piece of paper that has been folded and punctured or cut will look when it is then unfolded.[76]

- **First:** Demonstrate folding a piece of paper at first one time, and later two or more times, then punch a hole in the folded paper. On a separate piece of unfolded paper, have the children mark where the holes will be once the paper is unfolded. Unfold the paper and check for accuracy.
- **Next:** Have the children fold a piece of paper in half, then cut shapes along the fold. Have them draw what the shape will look like when the paper is unfolded, then open the cut paper and compare.
- **Next:** Fold the paper in half, then in half again, and repeat the previous steps.

NOTES

1 Marshall & Fink, 2001.
2 Kozhevnikov & Hegarty, 2001; Mix et al., 2018; Vander Heyden et al., 2016.
3 Quinn et al., 2001.
4 Izard & Spelke, 2009.
5 Dehaene et al., 2006.
6 Marlair et al., 2021.
7 Clements, 2004.
8 Izard & Spelke, 2009.
9 Rosch, 1973.
10 Verdine et al., 2016.
11 Clements, 2004; P. Pica, personal communication, March 25, 2020.

12 Gibson et al., 2015.

13 Clements, 2004.

14 Resnick et al., 2016.

15 Verdine et al., 2019.

16 Pruden et al., 2011.

17 Newcombe & Huttenlocher, 2000, pp. 73–108.

18 Bostelmann et al., 2020.

19 Newcombe & Huttenlocher, 2000, pp. 73–108.

20 Burles et al., 2020.

21 Loewenstein & Gentner, 2005; Miller et al., 2016; Newcombe & Huttenlocher, 2000, pp. 197–206.

22 Balcomb et al., 2011.

23 Simms & Gentner, 2019.

24 Gentner et al., 2013; Hyde et al., 2011.

25 Shusterman & Li, 2016.

26 Meneghetti et al., 2020.

27 Miller et al., 2017.

28 Newcombe & Huttenlocher, 2000, p. 198.

29 Newcombe & Huttenlocher, 2000, p. 202; Shusterman & Li, 2016.

30 Newcombe & Huttenlocher, 2000, pp. 145–178.

31 Frick & Newcombe, 2012; Salsa et al., 2019.

32 Plumert et al., 2019.

33 Gilligan et al., 2018.

34 Möhring et al., 2015.

35 Dillon & Spelke, 2018.

36 Newcombe & Huttenlocher, 2000, pp. 164–166.

37 Van den Heuvel-Panhuizen et al., 2015.

38 Negen et al., 2018.

39 Ratliff et al., 2010; Van den Heuvel-Panhuizen et al., 2015.

40 Meneghetti et al., 2016.

41 Frick & Möhring, 2013; Möhring & Frick, 2013.

42 Oudgenoeg-Paz et al., 2016.

43 Jung et al., 2018; Örnkloo & vonHofsten, 2007.

44 Quaiser-Pohl, 2003.

45 Cronin, 1967.

46 Frick et al., 2013a, 2013b.

47 Levine et al., 1999; Wang et al., 2021.

48 Hawes et al., 2015.

49 Ark, 2005.

50 Harris et al., 2013.

51 Hegarty, 2004.

52 Gelman et al., 1995.

53 Baillargeon & DeJong, 2017; Hespos et al., 2016; Luo et al., 2009.

54 Siegler, 1976.

55 Frick et al., 2009.

56 Hast & Howe, 2017.

57 Howe, 2017.

58 Michaelides & Avraamides, 2017.
59 Bilalić, 2018.
60 Hegarty, 2004.
61 Turan et al., 2021.
62 Georges et al., 2021.
63 Jansen & Heil, 2010.
64 Schlegel et al., 2016.
65 Hoyek et al., 2014.
66 Lehmann & Jansen, 2012.
67 Ehrlich et al., 2006; Miller et al., 2020.
68 Calero et al., 2019.
69 Austin & Sweller, 2014; Sauter et al., 2012.
70 Casasola et al., 2020; Congdon et al., 2017; Levine et al., 2018.
71 Casey et al., 2008.
72 Richardson & Vecchi, 2002.
73 Casasola et al., 2020.
74 Bruce & Hawes, 2015.
75 Michaelides & Avraamides, 2017.
76 Harris et al., 2013.

REFERENCES

The following references were cited in this chapter. For additional selected references relevant to this chapter, please see Chapter 4 Supplemental References in eResources.

Ark, W.S. (2005). Comparing mental rotation and feature matching strategies in adults and children with behavioral and neuroimaging techniques. *Dissertation Abstracts International, 66*(09), 5112B (UMI No. 3190005).

Austin, E.E., & Sweller, N. (2014). Presentation and production: The role of gesture in spatial communication. *Journal of Experimental Child Psychology, 122,* 92–103.

Baillargeon, R., & DeJong, G.F. (2017). Explanation-based learning in infancy. *Psychonomic Bulletin & Review, 24,* 1511–1526.

Balcomb, F., Newcombe, N.S., & Ferrara, K. (2011). Finding where and saying where: Developmental relationships between place learning and language in the second year. *Journal of Cognition & Development, 12,* 315–331.

Bilalić, M. (2018). The double take of expertise: Neural expansion is associated with outstanding performance. *Current Directions in Psychological Science, 27,* 462–469.

Bostelmann, M., Lavenex, P., & Lavenex, P.B. (2020). Children five-to-nine years old use path integration to build a cognitive map without vision. *Cognitive Psychology, 121,* 101307.

Bruce, C.D., & Hawes, Z. (2015). The role of 2D and 3D mental rotation in mathematics for young children: What is it? Why does it matter? And what can we do about it? *ZDM Mathematics Education, 47,* 331–343.

Burles, F., Liu, I., Hart, C., Murias, K., Graham, S.A., & Iaria, G. (2020). The emergence of cognitive maps for spatial navigation in 7- to 10-year-old children. *Child Development, 91,* e733–e744.

Calero, C.I., Shalom, D.E., Spelke, E.S., & Sigman, M. (2019). Language, gesture, and judgment: Children's paths to abstract geometry. *Journal of Experimental Child Psychology, 177,* 70–85.

Casasola, M., Wei, W.S., Suh, D.D., Donskoy, P., & Ransom, A. (2020). Children's exposure to spatial language promotes their spatial thinking. *Journal of Experimental Psychology: General, 149*, 1116–1136.

Case, R., & Griffin, S. (1990). Child cognitive development: The role of central conceptual structures in the development of scientific and social thought. In C.-A. Hauert (Ed.), *Developmental psychology: Cognitive, perceptual-motor and psychological perspectives* (pp. 193–230). Elsevier.

Casey, M., Andrews, N., Schindler, H., Kersh, J.E., Samper, A., & Copley, J. (2008). The development of spatial skills through interventions involving block building activities. *Cognition and Instruction, 26*, 269–309.

Clements, D.H. (2004). Geometric and spatial thinking in early childhood education. In D.H. Clements, J. Sarama (Eds.,), & A.-M. DiBiase (Assoc. Ed.), *Engaging young children in mathematics: Standards for early childhood mathematics education* (pp. 267–297). Erlbaum.

Congdon, E.L., Novack, M.A., Brooks, N., Hemani-Lopez, N., O'Keefe, L., & Goldin-Meadow, S. (2017). Better together: Simultaneous presentation of speech and gesture in math instruction supports generalization and retention. *Learning and Instruction, 50*, 65–74.

Cronin, V. (1967). Mirror-image reversal discrimination in kindergarten and first-grade children. *Journal of Experimental Child Psychology, 5*, 577–585.

Dehaene, S., Izard, V., Pica, P., & Spelke, E. (2006). Core knowledge of geometry in an Amazonian indigene group. *Science, 311*, 381–384.

Dillon, M.R., & Spelke, E.S. (2018). From map reading to geometric intuitions. *Developmental Psychology, 54*, 1304–1316.

Ehrlich, S.B., Levine, S.C., & Goldin-Meadow, S. (2006). The importance of gesture in children's spatial reasoning. *Developmental Psychology, 42*, 1259–1268.

Frick, A., Daum, M.M., Wilson, M., & Wilkening, F. (2009). Effects of action on children's and adults' mental imagery. *Journal of Experimental Child Psychology, 104*, 34–51.

Frick, A., Ferrara, K., & Newcombe, N.S. (2013a). Using a touch screen paradigm to assess the development of mental rotation between 3 ½ and 5 ½ years of age. *Cognitive Processing, 14*, 117–127.

Frick, A., Hansen, M.A., & Newcombe, N.S. (2013b). Development of mental rotation in 3- to 5-year-old children. *Cognitive Development, 28*, 386–399.

Frick, A., & Möhring, W. (2013). Mental object rotation and motor development in 8- and 10-month-old infants. *Journal of Experimental Child Psychology, 115*, 708–720.

Frick, A., & Newcombe, N.S. (2012). Getting the big picture: Development of spatial scaling abilities. *Cognitive Development, 27*, 270–282.

Gelman, R., Durgin, F., & Kaufman, L. (1995). Distinguishing between animates and inanimates: Not by motion alone. In D. Sperber, D. Premack, & A.J. Premack (Eds.), *Causal cognition: A multidisciplinary debate* (pp. 150–184). Clarendon Press.

Gentner, D., Özyürek, A., Gürcanli, Ö., & Goldin-Meadow, S. (2013). Spatial language facilitates spatial cognition: Evidence from children who lack language input. *Cognition, 127*, 318–330.

Georges, C., Cornu, V., & Schiltz, C. (2021). The importance of visuospatial abilities for verbal number skills in preschool: Adding spatial language to the equation. *Journal of Experimental Child Psychology, 201*, 104971.

Gibson, D.J., Congdon, E.L., & Levine, S.C. (2015). The effects of word-learning biases on children's concept of angle. *Child Development, 86*, 319–326.

Gilligan, K.A., Hodgkiss, A., Thomas, M.S.C., & Farran, E.K. (2018). The use of discrimination scaling tasks: A novel perspective on the development of spatial scaling in children. *Cognitive Development, 47*, 133–145.

Harris, J., Newcombe, N.S., & Hirsh-Pasek, K. (2013). A new twist on studying the development of dynamic spatial transformations: Mental paper folding in young children. *Mind, Brain, and Education, 7*, 49–55.

Hast, M., & Howe, C. (2017). Changing predictions, stable recognition: Children's representations of downward incline motion. *British Journal of Developmental Psychology, 35,* 516–530.

Hawes, Z., LeFevre, J.-A., Xu, C., & Bruce, C.D. (2015). Mental rotation with tangible three-dimensional objects: A new measure sensitive to developmental differences in 4- to 8-year-old children. *Mind, Brain, and Education, 9,* 10–18.

Hegarty, M. (2004). Mechanical reasoning by mental simulation. *Trends in Cognitive Sciences, 8,* 280–285.

Hespos, S.J., Ferry, A.L., Anderson, E.M., Hollenbeck, E.N., & Rips, L.J. (2016). Five-month-old infants have general knowledge of how nonsolid substances behave and interact. *Psychological Science, 27,* 244–256.

Howe, C. (2017). Developing understanding of object fall: Going beyond inhibitory processes. *British Journal of Developmental Psychology, 35,* 463–468.

Hoyek, N., Champely, S., Collet, C., Fargier, P., & Guillot, A. (2014). Is mental rotation ability a predictor of success for motor performance? *Journal of Cognition and Development, 15,* 495–505.

Hyde, D.C., Winkler-Rhoades, N., Lee, S.-A., Izard, V., Shapiro, K.A., & Spelke, E.S. (2011). Spatial and numerical abilities without a complete natural language. *Neuropsychologia, 49,* 924–936.

Izard, V., & Spelke, E.S. (2009). Development of sensitivity to geometry in visual forms. *Human Evolution, 23,* 213–248.

Jansen, P., & Heil, M. (2010). The relation between motor development and mental rotation ability in 5- to 6-year-old children. *European Journal of Developmental Science, 4,* 67–75.

Jung, W.P., Kahrs, B.A., & Lockman, J.J. (2018). Fitting handled objects into apertures by 17- to 36-month-old children: The dynamics of spatial coordination. *Developmental Psychology, 54,* 228–239.

Kozhevnikov, M., & Hegarty, M. (2001). A dissociation between object-manipulation spatial ability and spatial orientation ability. *Memory & Cognition, 29,* 745–756.

Lehmann, J., & Jansen, P. (2012). The influence of juggling on mental rotation performance in children with spina bifida. *Brain and Cognition, 80,* 223–229.

Levine, S.C., Goldin-Meadow, S., Carlson, M.T., & Hemani-Lopez, N. (2018). Mental transformation skill in young children: The role of concrete and abstract motor training. *Cognitive Science, 42,* 1207–1228.

Levine, S.C., Huttenlocher, J., Taylor, A., & Langrock, A. (1999). Early sex differences in spatial skill. *Developmental Psychology, 35,* 940–949.

Loewenstein, J., & Gentner, D. (2005). Relational language and the development of relational mapping. *Cognitive Psychology, 50,* 315–353.

Luo, Y., Kaufman, L., & Baillargeon, R. (2009). Young infants' reasoning about physical events involving inert and self-propelled objects. *Cognitive Psychology, 58,* 441–486.

Marlair, C., Pierret, E., & Crollen, V. (2021). Geometry intuitions without vision? A study in blind children and adults. *Cognition, 216,* 104861.

Marshall, J.C., & Fink, G.R. (2001). Spatial cognition: Where we were and where we are. *NeuroImage, 14*(1), S2–S7.

Meneghetti, C., Carretti, B., Lanfranchi, S., & Toffalini, E. (2020). Spatial description learning in preschoolers: The role of perspective and individual factors. *Cognitive Development, 53,* 100841.

Meneghetti, C., Zancada-Menéndez, C., Sampedro-Piquero, P., Lopez, L., Martinelli, M., Ronconi, L., & Rossi, B. (2016). Mental representations derived from navigation: The role of visuo-spatial abilities and working memory. *Learning and Individual Differences, 49,* 314–322.

Michaelides, C.S., & Avraamides, M.N. (2017). Developmental changes in the mental transformation of spatial arrays. *Journal of Experimental Child Psychology, 164,* 152–162.

Miller, H.E., Andrews, C.A., & Simmering, V.R. (2020). Speech and gesture production provide unique insights into young children's spatial reasoning. *Child Development, 91,* 1934–1952.

Miller, H.E., Patterson, R., & Simmering, V.R. (2016). Language supports young children's use of spatial relations to remember locations. *Cognition, 150,* 170–180.

Miller, H.E., Vlach, H.A., & Simmering, V.R. (2017). Producing spatial words is not enough: Understanding the relation between language and spatial cognition. *Child Development, 88,* 1966–1982.

Mix, K.S., Hambrick, D.Z., Satyam, V.R., Burgoyne, A.P., & Levine, S.C. (2018). The latent structure of spatial skill: A test of the 2 x 2 typology. *Cognition, 180,* 268–278.

Möhring, W., & Frick, A. (2013). Touching up mental rotation: Effects of manual experience on 6-month-old infants' mental object rotation. *Child Development, 84,* 1554–1565.

Möhring, W., Newcombe, N.S., & Frick, A. (2015). The relation between spatial thinking and proportional reasoning in preschoolers. *Journal of Experimental Child Psychology, 132,* 213–220.

Negen, J., Roome, H.E., Keenaghan, S., & Nardini, M. (2018). Effects of two-dimensional versus three-dimensional landmark geometry and layout on young children's recall of locations from new viewpoints. *Journal of Experimental Child Psychology, 170,* 1–29.

Newcombe, N., & Huttenlocher, J. (2000). *Making space: The development of spatial representation and reasoning.* The MIT Press.

Örnkloo, H., & vonHofsten, C. (2007). Fitting objects into holes: On the development of spatial cognition skills. *Developmental Psychology, 43,* 404–416.

Oudgenoeg-Paz, O., Boom, J., Volman, M.J.M., & Leseman, P.P.M. (2016). Development of exploration of spatial-relational object properties in the second and third years of life. *Journal of Experimental Child Psychology, 146,* 137–155.

Papadopoulos, K., & Koustriava, E. (2011). Piaget's water-level task: The impact of vision on performance. *Research in Developmental Disabilities, 32,* 2889–2893.

Perrucci, V., Agnoli, F., & Albiero, P. (2008). Children's performance in mental rotation tasks: Orientation-free features flatten the slope. *Developmental Science, 11,* 732–742.

Plumert, J.M., Hund, A.M., & Recker, K.M. (2019). Is scaling up harder than scaling down? How children and adults visually scale distance from memory. *Cognition, 185,* 39–48.

Pruden, S.M., Levine, S.C., & Huttenlocher, J. (2011). Children's spatial thinking: Does talk about the spatial world matter? *Developmental Science, 14,* 1417–1430.

Quaiser-Pohl, C. (2003). The Mental Cutting Test "Schnitte" and the Picture Rotation Test: Two new measures to assess spatial ability. *International Journal of Testing, 3,* 219–231.

Quinn, P.C., Slater, A.M., Brown, E., & Hayes, R.A. (2001). Developmental change in form categorization in early infancy. *British Journal of Developmental Psychology, 19,* 207–218.

Ratliff, K.R., McGinnis, C.R., & Levine, S.C. (2010). *The development and assessment of cross-sectioning ability in young children.* Proceedings of the 32nd annual meeting of the Cognitive Science Society. Portland, OR. Retrieved 10/01/20, from http://csjarchive.cogsci.rpi.edu/Proceedings/2010/papers/0666/paper0666.pdf

Resnick, I., Verdine, B.N., Golinkoff, R., & Hirsh-Pasek, K. (2016). Geometric toys in the attic? A corpus analysis of early exposure to geometric shapes. *Early Childhood Research Quarterly, 36,* 358–365.

Richardson, J.T.E., & Vecchi, T. (2002). A jigsaw-puzzle imagery task for assessing active visuospatial processes in old and young people. *Behavior Research Methods, Instruments, & Computers, 34,* 69–82.

Rosch, E.H. (1973). Natural categories. *Cognitive Psychology, 4,* 328–350.

Salsa, A., Gariboldi, M.B., Vivaldi, R., & Rodríguez, J. (2019). Geometric maps as tools for different purposes in early childhood. *Journal of Experimental Child Psychology, 186,* 33–44.

Sauter, M., Uttal, D.H., Alman, A.S., Goldin-Meadow, S., & Levine, S.C. (2012). Learning what children know about space from looking at their hands: The added value of gesture in spatial communication. *Journal of Experimental Child Psychology, 111,* 587–606.

Schlegel, A., Konuthula, D., Alexander, P., Blackwood, E., & Tse, P.U. (2016). Fundamentally distributed information processing integrates the motor network into the mental workspace during mental rotation. *Journal of Cognitive Neuroscience, 28,* 1139–1151.

Shusterman, A., & Li, P. (2016). Frames of reference in spatial language acquisition. *Cognitive Psychology, 88,* 115–161.

Siegler, R.S. (1976). Three aspects of cognitive development. *Cognitive Psychology, 8,* 481–520.

Simms, N.K., & Gentner, D. (2019). Finding the *middle:* Spatial language and spatial reasoning. *Cognitive Development, 50,* 177–194.

Turan, E., Kobaş, M., & Göksun, T. (2021). Spatial language and mental transformation in preschoolers: Does relational reasoning matter? *Cognitive Development, 57,* 100980.

Vandenberg, S.G., & Kuse, A.R. (1978). Mental rotations, a group test of three-dimensional spatial visualization. *Perceptual and Motor Skills, 47,* 599–604.

Van den Heuvel-Panhuizen, M., Elia, I., & Robitzsch, A. (2015). Kindergartners' performance in two types of imaginary perspective-taking. *ZDM: Mathematics Education, 47,* 345–362.

Vander Heyden, K.M., Huizinga, M., Kan, K.-J., & Jolles, J. (2016). A developmental perspective on spatial reasoning: Dissociating object transformation from viewer transformation ability. *Cognitive Development, 38,* 63–74.

Verdine, B.N., Lucca, K.R., Golinkoff, R.M., Hirsh-Pasek, K., & Newcombe, N.S. (2016). The shape of things: The origin of young children's knowledge of the names and properties of geometric forms. *Journal of Cognition and Development, 17,* 142–161.

Verdine, B.N., Zimmermann, L., Foster, L., Marzouk, M.A., Golinkoff, R.M., Hirsh-Pasek, K., & Newcombe, N. (2019). Effects of geometric toy design on parent-child interactions and spatial language. *Early Childhood Research Quarterly, 46,* 126–141.

Wang, S., Hu, B.Y., & Zhang, X. (2021). Kindergarteners' spatial skills and their reading and math achievement in second grade. *Early Childhood Research Quarterly, 57,* 157–166.

Chapter 5

Spatial Skills, Math, SES, and Sex

WHAT DO SPATIAL SKILLS HAVE TO DO WITH MATH?

W E turn here to the curious fact that spatial skills and math ability are closely related. Abundant research with tens of thousands of infants, preschoolers, school children, adolescents, and college students and covering all the spatial skills reported in Chapter 4 and more attests to the close connection of spatial ability and math performance across a wide range of math skills. Moreover, many of these studies are longitudinal, which means that they look at spatial abilities at one point in time and compare them to math performance anywhere from four months to 20 years later.[1]

For example, a series of longitudinal studies by different research teams paints a picture of the relation between block-building skills and math achievement. One study found that when mothers and their three-year-olds build with blocks together, the amount of spatial language, related gestures, and planning support the mothers provide predicts the children's math skill in first grade.[2] Moreover, a three-year-old's block-building skill is a better predictor of the child's number knowledge at age five than is his number knowledge at age three, suggesting that good spatial skills lead to good math skills and not vice versa.[3] Most remarkably, in a study that followed children from preschool through high school, researchers found that children's *preschool* block-building skills predicted their *high school* math course selections, math grades, and standardized math test scores.[4] Block-building skills of adolescents, in particular the extent to which their structures demonstrate stability and balance, predict students' math scores on standardized exams, including the SAT.[5] The long-range consequences are significant: Among intellectually talented middle- and high-schoolers, spatial ability (more broadly measured) predicts favorite high school courses, leisure interests, undergraduate majors, fields of graduate study, and occupations.[6]

Block-building skills essentially require mental rotation—imagining the effect of placing a block in a certain position in relation to other blocks as one decides where a block should go. As noted in Chapter 4, mental rotation is one of the very few spatial tasks on which a verbal, analytic (step-by-step) approach is typically useless. In a

DOI: 10.4324/9781003157656-7

study of fifth-graders gifted in math or verbal skills, researchers found that while gifted students shared many intellectual traits, the one exception was mental rotation: On the classic Mental Rotation Test, the math-gifted students performed strikingly better (in statistical terms, by nearly two standard deviations) than did students with verbal gifts.[7]

The range of spatial deficits appears to be broad among children with serious math learning difficulties. A study of children aged nine to 12 with and without significant math learning disability revealed that the group with math deficits performed more slowly and less accurately on eight different spatial tasks than did those with typical math development, leading the researchers to recommend including spatial training in math remediation programs.[8]

So it is clear *that* spatial skills are related to math. What is not yet entirely clear is *how* they are related—why do people with good spatial skills have an easier time with math, or those with weak math skills have a harder time with spatial tasks? Research has begun to shed some light on this question as well.[9] One point of connection between the two skill sets pertains to how we think of numbers. In fact, the parts of the human brain most specialized for thinking about numbers overlap significantly with the regions more generally concerned with spatial judgments.[10] As most children learn to count, the ordered and linearly increasing nature of the number sequence prompts a kind of mental sense or image of numbers lined up on what has been called a "mental number line." In an important study, researchers found that the mental rotation skills of five-year-olds predicted the accuracy with which they could place numbers on an unmarked physical number line at age six, which in turn predicted their numerical estimation abilities at age eight.[11] (The number line, Figure 5.1, will be the topic of Chapter 9.)

Among older students, studies of items on the quantitative portions of high-stakes high school and college exams revealed that certain problems are much easier to solve with holistic, visual-spatial strategies than with purely computational ones. Importantly, among students who can use such strategies, these additional resources allow them to use non-algorithmic shortcuts and contrive new strategies for unconventional problems, a clear advantage in the classroom and in life.[12]

Where does that leave children with significant spatial deficits? Some have a difficult time counting, placing numbers accurately on a number line, and even comparing two numbers, such as deciding whether *three* means more or less than *five*.[13] Most schools teach simple addition and subtraction facts verbally or symbolically—"five minus three equals two" or *5 – 3 = 2*, for example—and that is how many children remember them. Indeed, young children with strong verbal skills often do quite well with simple calculations for this reason.[14] However, being able to envision the spatial relation of five and three along a line gives students another way to arrive at the result, to estimate quickly, and to think about numbers and operations in general. Lacking this

FIGURE 5.1

ability, students must rely solely on their verbal skills. A fuller discussion of the number line and its role in arithmetic appears in Chapters 9 through 11.

Students may also reveal their visual-spatial difficulties in the way they arrange their written work on the page. In children with good pencil control, chaotic written organization may reflect difficulty with visual acuity or processing. Alternatively, it may reflect a problem integrating what they see with what their fingers draw or write, a skill known to be linked to math performance.[15] For example, some children may have difficulty aligning digits vertically for computation. Such students should be evaluated by a neuropsychologist and/or developmental ophthalmologist. There is some evidence that occupational therapy can help preschoolers with delays in visual-graphomotor integration catch up with their peers,[16] although as of this writing no research, to our knowledge, answers the question of whether such remediation would also improve arithmetic performance.

Much has been made of what has been called "math anxiety," the often debilitating anxiety that many people feel before taking a math exam or tackling a math assign- ment or even when balancing one's checkbook. And we now know more about the particularly debilitating effects that a teacher's math anxiety can have on students' math performance and achievement.[17] It is beyond the scope of this book to delve into the vast literature on this topic. What is most interesting and relevant to the purpose of this chapter, however, is that researchers are now linking math anxiety to the anxiety gen- erated by having to understand mathematical concepts intuitively and the difficulty in conjuring up the spatial imagery required—or what is being called "spatial anxiety."[18]

The good news is that, despite genetic influences, visual-spatial skills are highly malleable: For most students, spatial skills can be trained. The typical brain is capable of growth, change, and, within limits, rewiring itself well into adulthood.[19] A review of more than two hundred spatial-skill training studies found that training effects are stable over time, that training on one task can often have positive effects on other similar spatial tasks (although getting to that point sometimes requires particularly intensive training), and that spatial skills can be improved across the life span. Moreover, the reviewers found that all the training methods reported in the research led to improve- ment in spatial skills.[20]

The bigger question here, of course, is: *Can spatial-skill training lead to improve- ment in math learning?* On that question, research is less certain but offers grounds for optimism.[21] Although not all classroom efforts have been successful,[22] children from kindergarten through middle school have been shown to benefit from a wide range of classroom spatial activities, with improvement in various aspects of class- room math. For example, earlier we discussed the positive, far-reaching math effects of adult-preschooler block talk. In fact, a study of four- to six-year-olds found that while visual-spatial abilities were related to verbal number skills, what mediated, or *explained*, that relationship was the children's *spatial language*, thereby highlighting the importance of spatial language (as discussed in Chapter 4) for math development.[23] Moreover, a preschool intervention with an emphasis on spatial vocabulary and spatial reasoning was found to significantly increase children's numeracy skills.[24] Another study provided children in grades one and six with six 30-minute training sessions over three to four weeks in one of two different spatial skills (spatial visualization or visual-spatial working memory). The researchers found that the children in both groups improved significantly in a wide range of math skills, and significantly more than did a group without the training.[25] Other studies involving primary-[26] and intermediate-[27] grade-level students have reported similar success. Among middle-schoolers, spatial skills training increased enrollment in math and science classes in high school.[28]

With content-related spatial training, even college students demonstrate improvement in geometry and calculus, as well as in such math-heavy STEM disciplines as physics, organic chemistry, and engineering. In fact, some STEM programs have instituted spatial-skill screening upon matriculation and a booster course in it for those who need it.[29] In as much as course choices in high school often determine access to STEM programs in college, spatial skills—and, just as important, interest and enjoyment in spatial activities—need to be in place before then if the goal is to increase children's STEM opportunities in life. Mathematics education, which is foundational for most STEM disciplines, begins in early childhood. Thus, the ideal place to support a child's ability to think spatially is in the home, at preschool, and throughout elementary and middle school.

Students are keenly aware of their own strengths and weaknesses, which typically become reinforced through the course of their education. When children aged eight to 17 were asked to rate themselves on such questions as "I am good at expressing myself in writing," or "I am good at playing action video games," or "When reading a book, I can usually imagine clear, colorful pictures of the people and places," their self-ratings aligned closely with their actual strengths as measured on cognitive tests (in this case, language, spatial skill, and detailed visual imagery, respectively). They also aligned closely with their favorite classes and their professional ambitions.[30] Thus, the findings of the longitudinal studies cited at the beginning of this chapter are, in some ways, self-fulfilling prophecies. In a discipline such as math, which builds each new skill on old ones, children with weak spatial skills who are never identified and provided with explicit supportive instruction in spatial skills sometimes never really have a chance to fully develop their math skills.

SPATIAL SKILL, SES, AND SEX

In a society that values equal opportunity for all and in which some of the most exciting and lucrative opportunities are in the STEM fields, it is frustrating to have to report that, on average, males and children from higher-income families are better at several important kinds of spatial reasoning than females and children from low-income families.

The body of research on the relation of parental income to spatial skill is still small but growing. One early study surveyed several basic cognitive skills in a group of first-graders from a wide range of parental income levels and found a significant relation between parental income and both visual-spatial skills and visual-spatial working memory, to the advantage of higher-income children.[31] A more ambitious study, which investigated a range of spatial and math skills among a large, diverse group of kindergartners, third-graders, and sixth-graders, found that spatial skills were, indeed, significantly related to parental income, again advantaging higher-income children. Moreover, the income-related gap in spatial skill was similar at each grade level.[32] Since schools generally do not focus on spatial skills, researchers have suggested that the difference is likely related to differences in general opportunities for spatial-type activities at home and in the community. However, research shows that children of low-income families (and of mothers with less education) do not differ from those of higher-income families in the frequency of their spatial play.[33] Rather, the difference appears to be verbal. For example, in one study three-year-olds from low-income/low-education families had more difficulty than children from more prosperous and well-educated families in matching shapes to shape names. Two years later, at age five, those same children had weaker general spatial abilities as well.[34] These findings are consistent with those of other studies linking early spatial language exposure to spatial skill development.[35]

In contrast to this emerging income and parental education evidence, the relation of sex to spatial skills has been the object of wide-ranging scientific investigation and debate for several decades, with abundant evidence supporting the existence of a sex gap in spatial ability favoring males.[36] Studies of the performance of hundreds of thousands of adults around the world on the classic mental rotation test, described in Chapter 4, consistently report this difference, which has been stable over decades.[37] Note that to say that there is a sex gap in spatial skill is not to say that no females are as spatially capable as males—many are, and some are more capable than most males. However, there are fewer females than males in the upper part of the ability range.

Potential explanations for this sex discrepancy include strategy differences and sex stereotyping,[38] activity preferences and experiences,[39] structural brain differences,[40] brain-activation pattern differences during mental rotation or math,[41] genetic patterns of brain lateral dominance,[42] and different hormonal influences on brain development.[43]

Adult navigation studies also demonstrate sex differences.[44] When tested on an assortment of navigation tasks, males on average are more accurate, efficient, and knowledgeable about the geometric properties of a map than are females. Males on average tend to perform best when using distance-and-direction information and like to take shortcuts, while women, who—again, on average—prefer to use a verbal strategy, do best with landmarks and well-learned routes. Moreover, for both sexes, performance is linked to their mental rotation ability, while neither navigation skill nor mental rotation ability is related to landmark recall; thus, remembering landmarks appears to be a less spatial sort of skill.[45] Brain scans during navigation of virtual mazes reveal both shared and sex-specific regions of neuronal activity consistent with those found in male and female rats during a similar task.[46]

Thus, it is clear that men typically do better on certain spatial tasks than do women, perhaps by adopting more effective strategies. But what about children—do they show a similar sex gap in spatial abilities? Here the findings are somewhat mixed, particularly among younger children, although given the wide range of tasks used from study to study, it is difficult to be certain.[47]

Among the youngest infants (three to six months old), boys tend to notice more often than girls do when a mirror image has been substituted for a rotated figure. Noting the link between this test performance and boys' salivary testosterone levels a few months earlier, some researchers speculate that this normal, early testosterone surge may affect the boys' sensitivity to shape orientation, perhaps through reorganization of brain structure or function.[48] (Testosterone surges have notable effects on adults' spatial skills as well.[49])

Among toddlers, both boys and girls begin to anticipate, with equal success, which way a shape block will fit into a hole at around 22 months of age.[50] They also use geometric cues in the environment to figure out where they are, although boys rely on this information more than girls do.[51] In addition, there are differences favoring boys in the quality of parental puzzle play with their two- and three-year-olds. Parents use more size and shape words with their toddler sons than daughters; indeed, by the time those toddlers turn three, boys typically use more of those words in their own speech than do girls.[52] Studies have produced inconsistent findings regarding potential sex differences in early spatial language, however, as well as in the relation of spatial language to early numeracy skills. While spatial language serves a facilitative function for most children, there is some evidence that boys may have an additional, non-verbal path from spatial skills to math that is more direct and which may depend on the particular spatial skill or the child's age.[53]

Observations of preschoolers on a wide range of spatial tasks (including two-dimensional mental transformation, perspective-taking, block play, and paper-folding) have been mixed; where sex differences are observed, however, they favor boys.[54] Two studies of five-year-olds using a test of two-dimensional shape manipulation had some interesting findings. One was that boys tended to gesture more than girls did while explaining how they had solved an item; boys were also more accurate in their solutions than girls were, and their advantage was linked to the amount of gesturing.[55] The other finding of note is that when (and only when) mental rotation was needed to solve the problem, boys and girls demonstrated different patterns of brain activation: boys activated the parietal lobes on the right and left sides of the brain, while girls activated chiefly the left parietal lobe.[56] (This may help explain the fact that spatial ability predicts math performance in older boys and left-handed girls but not in right-handed girls.[57])

While some studies of elementary- and middle-school students reveal a sex gap favoring boys on mental rotation that increases with age from about nine years onward,[58] other studies have found convincing evidence of a sex gap in spatial skill throughout the elementary school years.[59] For example, the large-scale study noted earlier demonstrating a significant income gap found a comparable sex gap, favoring boys, across a range of spatial skills that remained constant from kindergarten to sixth grade.[60] Could these differences be due to social expectation? Researchers tested this idea by announcing to a group of fourth-graders in advance of a mental rotation test that boys (or girls) are generally better at the task. The ruse did not affect performance: Boys outperformed girls regardless of what the researchers tried to lead them to believe.[61]

During adolescence, performance on mental rotation tasks shows a clear male advantage, as it does in adults. One large study of individuals aged nine to 23 years demonstrated male superiority on mental rotation throughout the age range. Test scores increased with age for both sexes, but more so for males.[62] One possible clue to male success on mental rotation is how they go about doing it: comparing the overall configurations of the objects and mentally picturing the whole figure rotating. Females, by contrast, tend to examine the figures in a piecemeal fashion, analyzing the relative positions of their parts, often with the help of verbal self-coaching, a less efficient and more time-consuming and error-prone process.[63] (It may be significant that the brain's left parietal lobe—many girls' sole site of parietal activation during mental rotation, as noted earlier—is near the brain's language circuits.) Boys also tend to build better-balanced block structures than girls do by the time they get to high school.[64] Moreover, a 1992 study revealed a striking male advantage in mechanical reasoning—the male-female ratio among those scoring in the top ten percent on a standardized test was nearly five to one. (By contrast, the strongest female advantage was in spelling, at about two and a half to one.)[65] An updated investigation of those findings would be very interesting and is clearly warranted.

Finally, there is a curious relation between income and sex in terms of spatial skills. An internet survey found that across 53 nations, sex *inequality* in spatial skill was associated, surprisingly, with stronger economic development and general social sex *equality*. That is, in underdeveloped countries, males have as much trouble with mental rotation as females; in more developed economies, the spatial skills of both males and females are stronger, but males' spatial skills are stronger than females'.[66] Similarly, and just as surprising, in the United States sex differences in spatial skill are chiefly apparent among children living above poverty. The reason for this complex relationship is unclear. Researchers speculate that the accessibility of such costly toys as LEGOs, blocks, and video games, often favored by boys, may make the difference.[67] However, even taking into account sex differences in the amount of early spatial play, one large study found that boys' spatial skills remained stronger than girls' on average.[68] Future research is warranted to clarify the complex web of relationships among spatial skill, sex, and wealth.

SPATIAL SKILLS, MATH, SES, AND SEX

We have seen that math and spatial skills are closely linked. We have also just seen that spatial skills are tied to sex, as well as parental income and education. So where does that leave the chances for girls and for children from low-income families to succeed in math? We take up the income issue first.

Several very large-scale studies found a significant income gap in math from the fall of kindergarten through sixth grade.[69] However, unlike the income gap in spatial skills, which remained stable through elementary school, the income gap in math increased from kindergarten to sixth grade.[70] This trajectory has significant repercussions down the road for gate-keeper college and career testing. The College Board, which administers the SAT college admissions exam, reports a breakdown of scores by parental education (arguably the more relevant factor) rather than by income. Strikingly, the SAT Math exam parental-education gap *dwarfs* the sex gap.[71] We will discuss the importance of early math screening and intervention, including spatial skills training, for low-income kindergartners in Chapter 13.

While the sex gap in math achievement is much less pronounced than the income gap, there has been considerably more research attention focused on it. There are many questions. Do girls, on average, have more trouble than boys with math? With certain aspects of math? If so, is their trouble due to differences in spatial ability? In strategy? And how early in development are differences evident? Large-scale statistics suggest that girls do have more trouble than boys with math. One European study found that roughly two out of every three children with an isolated math disability and three out of every four children with a combined math and reading disability are girls.[72] More boys than girls score at the top of the scale on national and international math exams such as the Trends in International Mathematics and Science Study (TIMSS), National Assessment of Educational Progress (NAEP), and Programme for International Student Assessment (PISA), and certain university STEM programs show sharp enrollment discrepancies between the sexes. Faced with these findings, researchers have attempted to understand what they mean.[73] The answers are not yet clear, but here is the evidence to date.

As of this writing, most researchers agree on two important points. One is that there is no sex gap in overall math achievement during the preschool or elementary-school years. Three large-scale studies involving children aged four to 13 found no overall sex differences in performance on basic numeracy skills (counting, naming and ordering digits, symbolic and non-symbolic numerical comparison, and basic arithmetic).[74]

The second point of scholarly agreement is that there are consistent sex differences in arithmetic strategy choices and in the kinds of problems on which girls or boys, on average, tend to perform better. To understand this difference, it is instructive to look at the relative strengths that boys and girls bring to math problem-solving.

We begin with boys' relative strengths. First, primary-grade boys, on average, are more accurate than girls in their number-line placements on both the *0-to-100* number line and especially the *0-to-1,000* number line.[75] This is in keeping with the observation, discussed in the first part of this chapter, of a link between early number-line and spatial skills.[76] That is, boys seem to "see" in their minds the relation of numbers to one another as if spread out along a line (or as researchers put it, they develop a strong *spatial-numerical association*). This ability may have to do with boys' better visual-spatial attention, which was found to account for the sex difference (in favor of boys) in fraction number-line placement and fraction arithmetic among sixth- and seventh-graders.[77] Boys may also have an advantage in visual-spatial working memory. Although some research has pointed to the onset of this male advantage in adolescence,[78] two studies have reported notably strong visual-spatial working memory in preschool and kindergarten boys with strong number skills.[79]

Regarding arithmetic, even in kindergarten, boys who are good with numbers also tend to be good at spatial tasks.[80] Among first-graders, boys on average use a retrieval strategy more often than girls, who may continue to use counting methods for simple addition and subtraction.[81] It is possible that boys remember arithmetic facts better because they have easier access to a mental number line on which they can visualize

TABLE 5.1 Useful Problems for Assessing Strategy Choice

Routine	238 third-graders and 178 fourth-graders marched in the parade. How many children marched in the parade? (Grade 3)
Non-routine	19 plants need to be put into flower pots. They will be potted either 2 or 3 plants to a pot. There are 7 pots. How many plants will have to be potted 3 to a pot, and how many can be planted 2 to a pot? (Grade 1)
Extension	Jamal had 5 dollars. He spent 1 dollar and 72 cents for a toy. How much money did Jamal have left? (Grade 3)

Adapted from Fennema et al., 1998, p. 7.

those quantitative transformations. By third grade, boys can flexibly extend well-known procedures to unpracticed problems. The ability to apply procedures to new problems is related to the use of decomposition, or what some researchers call "invented algorithms," in the earlier primary grades. Decomposition, in the words of a student, goes something like this: "To add twenty-eight plus thirty-seven, you go twenty and thirty is fifty, and eight and seven is fifteen. Ten and fifty makes sixty, so it's sixty-five." The link between the use of decomposition in the early grades and later extended application is true for both boys and girls, but more boys tend to use these more flexible strategies.[82] See Table 5.1 for examples of routine, non-routine, and extension problems.

Boys have also demonstrated strength on measurement problems, particularly in understanding the relations between the object being measured and the unit of measurement, even when there is no illustration accompanying the problem. When showing their work, boys tend to draw pictures.[83] (See Table 5.2 for examples of these spatial-conceptual problems.)

This profile of male strengths—of understanding how numbers relate to each other and how measurement units relate to what is being measured—is consistent with an ability to "see" and manipulate objects in space, all in the mind's eye and in working memory. Unlike the case for girls, the levels of boys' spatial and verbal skills are typically not aligned with each other, suggesting, among other things, that some boys may understand more math than they can communicate in words.[84] Among middle-schoolers, strong spatial skills may be the reason why boys, who tend to be less self-disciplined than girls, wind up doing as well in math class.[85]

By contrast, across studies, girls' strengths center on their better-developed verbal skills. In kindergarten, just as boys' number skills are linked to their spatial ability, so are girls' number skills linked to their verbal ability.[86] In fact, the one exception to the pattern of sex equality in early math achievement is the finding that boys enjoy greater math success in kindergarten than do girls, a difference fully explained by boys' stronger spatial skills.[87] One may speculate that this finding is accounted for by the relatively light burden on verbal memory in early formal math education. By spring of first grade, girls' verbal skills allow them to catch up.[88] A solid foundation in language and reading allows girls to read instructions and story problems.[89] It also gives them a leg up on verbal object-counting in first grade.[90] Note, however, that straightforward object-counting, which depends on a well-learned verbal sequence, is quite different

TABLE 5.2 Formula and Spatial/Conceptual Problems, Grade 4

Formula-based	Ebony drew a rectangle. The length of the rectangle is 6 inches. The perimeter of the rectangle is 18 inches. What is the WIDTH of the rectangle in inches? 12 inches 6 inches 3 inches 2 inches		
	Find the AREA of this shape. 6 inches 4 inches [ ] 4 inches 6 inches 10 square inches 20 square inches 24 square inches 48 square inches		
Spatial/ Conceptual: Measurement	Isabella's little brother is in kindergarten. Isabella made four guesses about how tall her brother is. Which one do you think is her best guess? 10 feet 6 feet 3½ feet 1 foot		
Spatial/ Conceptual: Inverse Rule	Four children measured the length of the same room by counting how many steps it took each of them to cross it. The chart shows their measurements. Who has the longest step? Ana Mateo Imani Liam	Name	Number of Steps
		Ana	10
		Mateo	11
		Imani	9
		Liam	8

Adapted from Vasilyeva et al., 2009, pp. 407–409.

from counting backward, a more complex task requiring a reliable mental picture of the ordered number sequence that one can refer to in generating a response. Indeed, counting backward is associated with spatial skill and is a good predictor of primary-grade math achievement.[91]

Such findings support the speculation that girls are more likely to use a verbal, analytic (step-by-step) approach to solving problems. Indeed, consistent with this verbal strength, counting—counting all, counting on, with fingers, with counters—tends to be their preferred basic arithmetic strategy in first grade.[92] By the end of third grade, they also tend to use standard algorithms routinely, more than the on-the-fly decomposition favored by boys, and do well on routine and even non-routine sorts of problems (see Table 5.1).[93] Moreover, girls have even been shown to use analytic strategies for such spatially relevant skills as measurement. While girls performed as well as boys in one series of experiments involving measurement, their areas of relative strength were different: Girls did better on formula-based measurement and computation but had trouble with the spatial concepts involved, particularly when there were no accompanying pictures (see Table 5.2). Indeed, in showing their work, while boys drew pictures, girls calculated.[94]

Two studies looked closely at girls' math development, following a large group of them from first grade to fifth. In particular, they investigated their verbal, spatial, and arithmetic skills and, in fifth grade, their mathematical reasoning on numerical and algebraic problems (see Table 5.3 for examples). The researchers found that first-grade girls' verbal and spatial skills predicted their use of a decomposition strategy, but that only their spatial skills predicted their use of retrieval. (And poor spatial skills predicted the use of less efficient counting strategies.) This is consistent with the idea, noted earlier in relation to boys' retrieval use, that retrieval may be made easier by

TABLE 5.3 Algebraic and Numerical Problems to Assess Mathematical Reasoning, Grade 5

Algebra		
	Flag-pole height (ft)	Shadow length (in)
	6	16
	8	32
	10	48
	12	64

The table shows the shadow lengths of flag poles of different heights. What is the shadow length of a flag pole that has a height of 9 ft?

36 in   38 in   42 in   40 in

The two number sentences shown here are true.

$$! - * = 7$$

$$* + * = 2$$

Which of the following must also be true?

$! \times * = !$ $* \times 2 = *$ $! + * = !$ $! - ! = *$

Number: Diego brought a bag of cookies to share with Dmitry and DaShawn. Diego ate ½ of the cookies. Dmitry ate ¼ of the cookies. DaShawn ate ⅛ of the cookies. How much of the bag of cookies is left?

½   ⅝   ⅛   ⅞

In the stadium there are 12 times as many fans as players and coaches. There are 124 players and coaches in the stadium. What is the total number of fans, players, and coaches combined in the stadium?

124   2,976   1,488   1,612

Adapted from Casey et al., 2017, pp. 553–554.

ready access to the mental number line. The second important finding was that the girls' first-grade—first-grade!—spatial skills were the strongest predictor of their fifth-grade math reasoning ability. Moreover, in agreement with the study cited previously, their first-grade use of decomposition also predicted fifth-grade math reasoning.[95]

Finally, one research team looked at teachers' effects on their kindergartners' scores on KeyMath, a children's general math diagnostic assessment. A teaching approach that favored explicit instruction, as well as guidance aimed at associating, comparing, and contrasting ideas; at seeing things from a different perspective; and at focusing attention on the relevant evidence was positively linked to girls' math scores. By contrast, boys did best with teachers who encouraged them by simply pointing out what they had done correctly. Moreover, neither teaching style had any effect on the opposite sex. A broad investigation of teachers' math explanations revealed that 72 percent of them were verbal and only 28 percent of them were spatial (drawings, gestures). This suggests that they were typically more suited to girls than to boys.[96] It also suggests that girls received relatively little exposure to spatial instruction.

The question is, how far can a verbal, analytic approach take one through the increasing complexity of school mathematics? On the one hand, a study of eighth-graders found that while boys and girls used different strategies, there was no sex difference in math grades or in the results of a comprehensive state math exam. These outcomes suggest that girls were doing just as well as boys using non-spatial strategies[97] and that teachers would be justified in feeling that they had done their job.

On the other hand, the findings of multiple studies point to a clear achievement advantage emerging from the ability to recruit a spatial strategy. While there is no evidence of a sex gap in *young* children's overall math achievement, as we have seen, further along the developmental path research has demonstrated the cost—to girls and to society—of poorly developed spatial skills and the consequent need to adhere closely to instructed procedures. For example, high-school girls, but not boys, have difficulty noticing and ignoring irrelevant data in algebra word problems.[98] On the quantitative portions of high-stakes, career-determining exams, there is a male advantage on items requiring spatial skills and visual-spatial working memory. As noted in the first section of this chapter, these spatial resources, above and beyond algorithmic knowledge, confer significant benefits in speed, accuracy, and the ability to use non-algorithmic shortcuts and contrive new strategies for unconventional problems, all potential real-world advantages in problem-solving flexibility.[99]

In other words—to borrow a spatial metaphor—these resources allow a student to understand the math in more *depth*.

And indeed, for this reason, math anxiety and spatial anxiety are particularly understandable in girls, many of whom do not have access to that level of understanding. Studies found that even in the primary grades, some children describe feelings of nervousness at the prospect of engaging in spatial activities and math. These feelings were associated with poorer math performance and weak mental rotation skills and were more frequent in girls than in boys. Girls with strong verbal working memory were less vulnerable to such anxiety, suggesting that they successfully relied instead on verbal skills for problem-solving (by recalling facts, rules, etc.).[100] Studies of older college students found that spatial anxiety, above and beyond actual spatial ability, largely explained the high prevalence of math anxiety in females.[101]

How well-founded are girls' concerns in the face of complex math? Apparently quite well-founded, according to studies of the relative effects of spatial skill and math self-confidence on math test scores. On a series of items with the largest male advantage on the eighth-grade TIMSS exam, test-takers' spatial skills accounted for 74 percent of the male advantage, while math self-confidence accounted for only 26 percent.[102] A similar study of the math portion of the SAT had comparable findings.[103] For many anxious young females struggling with math, it is not just their anxiety that is getting in the way.

The classroom implications are significant. As noted in the introduction to Part II of this book, a teacher's math anxiety can be contagious, and the vast majority of early childhood, elementary, and special-education teachers are females.[104] A study of female first- and second-grade teachers demonstrated that the teacher's math anxiety had a deleterious effect on at least some girls' math achievement,[105] and more recent studies of kindergarten through 12th-grade teachers' spatial anxiety have produced similar results. Moreover, as the more recent studies show, such anxiety also affects teachers' willingness to use or encourage spatial approaches in their classrooms.[106] Future research is certainly warranted to disentangle this web and, in particular, to determine whether improving those anxious teachers' spatial skills would redound on their students' math confidence and achievement.

Fortunately, spatial skills training works as well for females as it does for males—and research shows that both sexes have plenty of room to grow.[107] Notably, spatial training for first-year female engineering students produced a robust improvement in grades in a variety of introductory STEM courses and increased their program retention rates.[108] It is still not clear whether such training could close the sex gap. However, as some have pointed out, it is certainly possible to raise girls' spatial abilities to a level of competence that would comfortably put them in the running for STEM careers.[109] Indeed, one review of university majors in male-dominated physics, engineering, and computer science programs found that if graduate programs in these fields admitted students on merit, more than a third of the incoming class would be female.[110]

Boys show an advantage in mental rotation skills as early as preschool,[111] so girls would benefit significantly from an early introduction to spatial activities. Simple steps, such as adults' engaging in spatial language with girls as much as they do with boys, would go a long way.[112] Indeed, in a study of first graders engaged in block building with their fathers, the quality of a father's interactions with his daughter—asking probing questions, suggesting strategies, and providing rich explanations—had a particularly beneficial effect on the growth of her spatial ability.[113] Other activities, such as shape games played around stories, might increase their spatial awareness, skill, and enjoyment.[114] Intriguingly, even music instruction, particularly rhythm, has been shown to provide these same advantages.[115] (Indeed, one study of college music majors failed to find a sex gap in their mental rotation skill.[116]) A study of females in STEM careers found that they had preferred spatial toys as children more than had females in non-STEM careers,[117] and certainly young girls should be introduced to such toys. Incorporating spatial activity throughout the elementary- and middle-school curriculum would make thinking spatially as much a natural part of their mental life as verbal thought.

CONCLUSION

The human brain works in remarkable ways. One key region that allows us to understand quantity and quantitative relationships is embedded in an area that governs our understanding of spatial relationships. This spatial understanding of number permits broad access to a wide range of mathematical concepts and problem-solving strategies. For reasons pertaining to diminished early spatial language exposure, children in low-income families enter school lagging in spatial skill. For some combination of biological and experiential reasons, males, on average, have easier access to those spatial resources than do females—children and adults alike. But the brain is easily influenced by experience, and science has now given us reason for optimism about the power of spatial training to improve those skills. For children, the earlier that begins, the better.

ACTIVITIES

Given the malleable nature of spatial skills and strong evidence that all children can improve these skills, the following are specific ways to help all children, and especially girls, close the gap and succeed in the spatial activities described in Chapter 4. We include a range of strategies, activities, and additional classroom resources in what follows.

Spatial Language

Studies demonstrate that children's spatial ability significantly improves when adults use diverse spatial terms[118] and when children use spatial language themselves[119] while engaging in spatial activities. Children's spatial skills tend to improve the most from hearing adults use specific spatial language, particularly girls and children from low-income families, who tend to have less exposure to spatial language at home when they are young.[120] The following are some types and examples of useful spatial language from which to draw during activities, all of which can be accompanied by gestures. It is helpful to discuss and model the meaning of these terms and how they are similar to and different from related terms.

Two- and three-dimensional shape names: *circle, oval, square, rectangle, triangle (including different types of triangles), pentagon, hexagon, octagon, rhombus, trapezoid, sphere, cylinder, cone, cube, prism, pyramid*

Shape composition and decomposition: Discuss how combining two or more shapes results in a new shape, such as two triangles forming a rectangle

Spatial features and properties: *angles, vertices, sides, faces, edges, apex, symmetrical, parallel, perpendicular, straight, round, curvy, curved, pointy, flat, diagonal, surface*

Size and comparatives: Terms describing length, width, height, depth, and related comparatives, such as *tall/taller/tallest, small/medium/large, wide/narrow/thin, shallow/deep/deeper/deepest*

Distance: *close, far, halfway, part-way, near, farther, faraway*

Location and direction: *middle, center, left, right, above, below, under, beneath, beside, between, adjacent to, behind, opposite, bottom, top, north, south, east, west, in front of, behind, next to, outside, inside*

Orientation and transformation: *horizontal, vertical, perpendicular, right, left, inverted, reverse, upside down, right side up, sideways, upright, upward, downward, flip, turn (around), rotate, facing, fold, clockwise, counterclockwise*

Perspective: *underneath, from the side, from the front, from the top, overhead, aerial*

Order: *first, second, third, next, then, last, finally, before, after*

Gestures

Studies have demonstrated the effectiveness of gestures in improving spatial skills.[121] Children benefit from observing adults use gestures while speaking and performing spatial tasks. Adults should also encourage children to use gestures themselves while talking about spatial activities, especially when they are not yet familiar with spatial language.

Types of gestures include those that show movement, rotation, direction, location, size, transformation, and perspective. For example, children and adults can rotate their index finger in a circular manner to indicate the round shape of a circle or sphere, or trace four straight sides in the air to depict the features of a rectangle. They can hold their arms out wide to illustrate the large width of one object then draw their arms together to illustrate the comparatively smaller width of another object. They can use their hands to make turning and flipping motions to depict rotations and reflections during spatial activities. Deictic, or pointing, gestures can indicate location such as *below, between, above*, and *beside* during activities such as block play.

Stories

Adolescent girls tend to build less complex and shorter structures than boys, requiring less balance, mental rotation, and spatial visualization.[122] Encouraging girls to build tall, complex structures during the preschool and elementary years might help prevent this sex difference in later grades. Using a story or narrative context to provide both motivation and building specifications improves girls' block building ability. Researchers found that when they provided girls with a story context in which a character was given explicit instructions on how to build a complex structure that the character desperately needed, the girls sympathized, followed along, and got involved. In addition, the ratio-nale for the complex building requirements made sense to them, and the children were more open to adult guidance and to asking questions while they were building.[123] The researchers used the storybook *Sneeze Builds a Castle*[124] as the basis for their study, although teachers, parents, and even the children themselves can create other story contexts. The following section provides specific types of complex block building that can be included in a story context.

Block Building Complexity

Adults can instruct children how to build increasingly complex structures to improve their spatial skills and resultant STEM skills through block building. The following are ways to increase that complexity.[125] The goal is to build tall structures with supports.

1. Build structures that require balance.
2. Use counterweights for more complex balance.
3. Balance using center and counterweights.
4. Create a bridge with vertical blocks on the side and horizontal block(s) across the top with an open space between the vertical blocks (see Figure).
5. Build a bridge on a non-flat surface such as the tops of cones.
6. Build enclosures to form a complete perimeter and open space in the middle.
7. Build symmetrical structures.
8. Build asymmetrical structures.
9. Build structures with a roof.

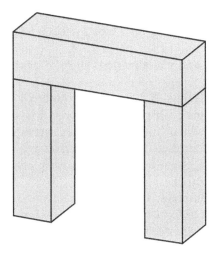

Experience

Girls may or may not choose to spontaneously engage in spatial activities such as building with blocks and are often less likely to do so than boys. Boys and girls improve their math skills through structured or semi-structured building activities.[126] Structured spatial activities for all children, such as block building, should be included in the regular curriculum beginning in preschool and the primary grades, giving girls the experience to improve their spatial skills even if they would not freely choose the activities. Classrooms should have dedicated math centers with spatial materials, such as the games and activities recommended next and in Chapter 4. Teachers can guide students through activities in these spatial centers while modeling the use of gestures and spatial language.

Spatial Programs and Resources

Taking Shape: Activities to Develop Geometric and Spatial Thinking, Grades K-2, **by Joan Moss:** An extensive spatial skills curriculum based on six years of study with the Math for Young Children project that includes online resources with the purchase of the book.

Developing Spatial Thinking, **by Sheryl Sorby:** For middle school and higher and can be accessed online and in a workbook. This research-based intensive program has been shown to improve spatial thinking and mental rotation skills,[127] especially in girls and women, with participants obtaining higher grades in STEM classes.[128]

Spatial Intelligence and Learning Center (SILC): silc.northwestern.edu. This website provides a wide variety of resources to enhance spatial learning.

Examples of Commercially Available Games and Activities

Mental rotation: Q-bitz, Q-bitz Extreme, Blokus, *MindWare* 3D Pattern Play, Pixie Cubes, Mighty Mind, *ThinkFun* Shape by Shape, *ThinkFun* Block by Block, *ThinkFun* MoonSpinner

Spatial relationship and visualization: chess, checkers, Connect 4, Quoridor, Sapphiro, Shifting Stones

Origami: Many books, kits, and free online resources are available from beginning to advanced skill levels.[129] Origami can be a very low-cost activity that has been shown to improve spatial skills,[130] particularly when accompanied by adult support.[131] In fact, NASA scientists have used origami to help solve complex design problems.[132] Use specific spatial language such as *bottom-left corner, center,* and *rotate,* as well as gestures, during origami activities.

Tangrams and pentominoes: Tangram and pentomino pieces can be rotated and arranged in endless ways to form new shapes and designs. Children can copy preset designs included with purchased sets or from many free online resources such as *tangram-channel.com,* and they can also create their own designs. Additionally, children can sketch their completed designs. Teachers and parents can cut out shapes from construction paper, poster board, or cardboard as a low-cost alternative to buying sets.

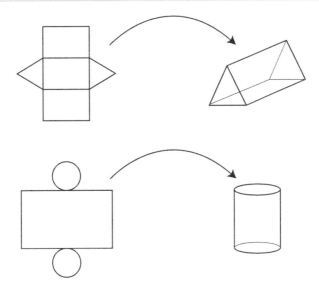

Three-dimensional geometric solids and geometric nets: Children fold plastic and paper nets into their corresponding three-dimensional shapes (see Figure). Plastic nets of geometric shapes are commercially available. *Geometric Nets Mega Project Book Tabbed*[133] has printable paper nets. Other paper net models can be found for free and for purchase online. Nets of cubes and rectangular prisms with designs or letters on them provide an opportunity for children to predict the pattern of the designs or letters once they fold the net. Before folding, children visualize and draw how the net will look with the specific location of the letters or designs when it is folded. The *Developing Spatial Thinking* book by Sheryl Sorby mentioned earlier has an entire section on nets.

Puzzles for all ages: Puzzles give children the experience of physically rotating objects to fit into a given space or to transform shapes. Different types of puzzles include:

- Wooden puzzles with pegs
- Part-whole relation puzzles
- Jigsaw puzzles—wooden or cardboard
- 3D puzzles
- Brain teaser puzzles
- Friedrich Froebel Gifts

One School's Success

Textbox 5.1 gives a brief description of the Columbus School for Girls, which successfully integrates spatial activities throughout their curriculum by implementing many of the strategies and activities described in Chapters 4 and 5 and more.

TEXTBOX 5.1 WHAT'S POSSIBLE: COLUMBUS SCHOOL FOR GIRLS

Columbus School for Girls (CSG), in Columbus, Ohio, was founded in 1898 as a college-preparatory school for girls. It currently educates about 650 girls from pre-kindergarten through 12th grade. Since 2007, the school has woven activities designed to foster spatial skills, particularly mental rotation, into all classes from the earliest grades on. Examples of how they include spatial training include:

- Structured block building, puzzles, and marble runs are part of the curriculum in the early grades, and every child participates. Children then sketch what they build.
- Nature walks include making 2D and 3D bug sculptures, designing and building treehouses, and drawing maps.
- Students draw and follow maps of the classroom, the school, and areas outside of the school.
- Teachers participate in training for spatial vocabulary and gestures.
- The library has spatial learning areas that contain items such as LEGOs, chess sets, and puzzles.
- Teachers provide explicit instruction in reading and creating graphs, charts, and diagrams throughout all classes.
- The *Developing Spatial Thinking* curriculum by Sheryl Sorby is used in the middle school.
- Teachers provide explicit instruction in creating and following maps from the earliest grades, including Google Earth and Google Tour Builder, in a variety of classes including social studies and geography.
- Students create maps for ancient and medieval civilizations.
- Computer science and coding are taught from the earliest grades, using HER Academy, Hour of Code, TinkerCAD, and Makerbot.
- Students participate in robotics teams and LEGO League Competitions.

Since 2014, when class-wide data were first gathered, between 37 percent and 57 percent of CSG graduating seniors each year have expressed the intention of majoring in a STEM field in college. The proportion of the CSG graduates intending to major in engineering, the physical sciences, math, or computer science—the fields with the widest gender gap favoring men—has kept ahead of the national rate for young women.

NOTES

1 Mix et al., 2017; Young et al., 2018.
2 Lombardi et al., 2017.
3 Verdine et al., 2017b.
4 Stannard et al., 2001; Wolfgang et al., 2001.
5 Casey et al., 2012.
6 Wai et al., 2009; Webb et al., 2007 .
7 Lehmann & Jüling, 2002.
8 Yazdani et al., 2021.
9 Hawes & Ansari, 2020; Lourenco et al., 2018; Mix, 2019.
10 Hawes et al., 2019.
11 Gunderson et al., 2012.
12 Gallagher et al., 1992, 2002.
13 Crollen et al., 2017.
14 Wei et al., 2012.
15 Sortor & Kulp, 2003.
16 Dankert et al., 2003.
17 Schaeffer et al., 2021.
18 Lauer et al., 2018; Ramirez et al., 2012.
19 Maguire et al., 2000.
20 Uttal et al., 2013.
21 Lowrie et al., 2020.
22 Cornu et al., 2019; Hawes et al., 2015; Mulligan et al., 2020; Rodán et al., 2019.
23 Georges et al., 2021.
24 Raudenbush et al., 2020.
25 Mix et al., 2021.
26 Cheng & Mix, 2014; Cheung et al., 2020; Gilligan et al., 2020; Hawes et al., 2017; Judd & Klingberg, 2021.
27 Lowrie et al., 2017, 2019
28 Sorby, 2009.
29 Sorby et al., 2018.
30 Blazhenkova et al., 2011.
31 Noble et al., 2007.
32 Johnson et al., 2022.
33 Jirout & Newcombe, 2015.
34 Verdine et al., 2017a.
35 Pruden et al., 2011.
36 Levine et al., 2016.
37 Jansen et al., 2016; Peters et al., 2006; Vandenberg & Kuse, 1978; Voyer et al., 1995.
38 Hegarty, 2018; Heil et al., 2012.
39 Baenninger & Newcombe, 1989.

40 Koscik et al., 2009.

41 Jordan et al., 2002.

42 Casey et al., 1992.

43 Vuoksimaa et al., 2010.

44 Nazareth et al., 2019.

45 Boone et al., 2018; Saucier et al., 2003.

46 Grön et al., 2000.

47 Lauer et al., 2019; Nazareth et al., 2019.

48 Constantinescu et al., 2018.

49 VanGoozen et al., 1995.

50 Örnkloo & vonHofsten, 2007.

51 Lourenco et al., 2011.

52 Pruden & Levine, 2017; Verdine et al., 2019.

53 Bower et al., 2020a; Georges et al., 2021.

54 Levine et al., 1999; Verdine et al., 2017b.

55 Ehrlich et al., 2006.

56 Hahn et al., 2010.

57 Casey et al., 1992.

58 Geiser et al., 2008; Jeng & Liu, 2016.

59 Beilstein & Wilson, 2000.

60 Johnson et al., 2022.

61 Titze et al., 2010.

62 Geiser et al., 2008.

63 Janssen & Geiser, 2010.

64 Casey et al., 2012.

65 Stanley et al., 1992.

66 Lippa et al., 2010.

67 Levine et al., 2005.

68 Jirout & Newcombe, 2015.

69 Denton & West, 2002; Johnson et al., 2022.

70 Johnson et al., 2022.

71 College Board, 2021.

72 Landerl & Moll, 2010.

73 Halpern, 1997.

74 Bakker et al., 2019; Denton & West, 2002; Hutchison et al., 2019.

75 Hutchison et al., 2019; Zhang et al., 2020.

76 Gunderson et al., 2012.

77 Geary et al., 2021b.

78 Voyer et al., 2017.

79 Geary et al., 2009; Robinson et al., 1996.

80 Klein et al., 2010.

81 Carr & Jessup, 1997.

82 Fennema et al., 1998.

83 Vasilyeva et al., 2009.

84 Klein et al., 2010.

85 Duckworth & Seligman, 2006; Geary et al., 2021a.

86 Klein et al., 2010.

87 Johnson et al., 2022.

88 Denton & West, 2002.

89 Denton & West, 2002.

90 Hutchison et al., 2019.

91 Zhang et al., 2014.

92 Carr & Jessup, 1997; Fennema et al., 1998.

93 Fennema et al., 1998.

94 Vasilyeva et al., 2009.

95 Casey et al., 2017; Laski et al., 2013.

96 Klein et al., 2010.

97 Ganley & Vasilyeva, 2011.

98 Low & Over, 1993.

99 Gallagher, 1992; Gallagher et al., 2002.

100 Lauer et al., 2018; Ramirez et al., 2012.

101 Maloney et al., 2012; Sokolowski et al., 2019.

102 Casey et al., 2001.

103 Casey et al., 1997.

104 Bureau of Labor Statistics, 2020.

105 Beilock et al., 2010.

106 Atit & Rocha, 2021; Gunderson et al., 2013.

107 Uttal et al., 2013.

108 Sorby et al., 2018.

109 Newcombe, 2010; Uttal et al., 2013.

110 Cimpian et al., 2020.

111 Jirout & Newcombe, 2015.

112 Pruden & Levine, 2017.

113 Thomson et al., 2020.

114 Casey et al., 2008b.

115 Rauscher, 2003.

116 Pietsch & Jansen, 2012.

117 Moè et al., 2018.

118 Casasola et al., 2020.

119 Miller et al., 2016; Pruden et al., 2011.

120 Verdine et al., 2017a; Verdine et al., 2019.

121 Alibali, 2005; Ehrlich et al., 2006.

122 Casey et al., 2012.

123 Casey et al., 2008b.

124 Casey et al., 2002.

125 Bower et al., 2020b; Casey et al., 2008b; Casey et al., 2012; Gregory et al., 2003.

126 Casey et al., 2008a; Schmitt et al., 2018.

127 Sorby, 2009.

128 Sorby et al., 2018.

129 See www.origami-instructions.com/ for a collection of free origami activities.

130 Boakes, 2009.
131 Casey et al., 2014.
132 See www.nasa.gov/jpl/news/origami-style-solar-power-20140814
133 McAdams, 2016.

REFERENCES

The following references were cited in this chapter. For additional selected references relevant to this chapter, please see Chapter 5 Supplemental References in eResources.

Alibali, M.W. (2005). Gesture in spatial cognition: Expressing, communicating, and thinking about spatial information. *Spatial Cognition and Computation, 5*, 307–331.

Atit, K., & Rocha, K. (2021). Examining the relations between spatial skills, spatial anxiety, and K-12 teacher practice. *Mind, Brain, and Education, 15*, 139–148.

Baenninger, M., & Newcombe, N. (1989). The role of experience in spatial test performance: A meta-analysis. *Sex Roles, 20*, 327–344.

Bakker, M., Torbeyns, J., Wijns, N., Verschaffel, L., & DeSmedt, B. (2019). Gender equality in 4- to 5-year-old preschoolers' early numerical competencies. *Developmental Science, 22*, e12718.

Beilock, S.L., Gunderson, E.A., Ramirez, G., & Levine, S.C. (2010). Female teachers' math anxiety affects girls' math achievement. *Proceedings of the National Academy of Sciences, 107*, 1860–1863.

Beilstein, C.D., & Wilson, J.F. (2000). Landmarks in route learning by girls and boys. *Perceptual & Motor Skills, 91*, 877–882.

Blazhenkova, O., Becker, M., & Kozhevnikov, M. (2011). Object-spatial imagery and verbal cognitive styles in children and adolescents: Developmental trajectories in relation to ability. *Learning and Individual Differences, 21*, 281–287.

Boakes, N.J. (2009). *Origami-mathematics lessons: Researching its impact and influence on mathematical knowledge and spatial ability of students. RMLE Online: Research in Middle Level Education, 32*(7), 1–12.

Boone, A.P., Gong, X., & Hegarty, M. (2018). Sex differences in navigation strategy and efficiency. *Memory & Cognition, 46*, 909–922.

Bower, C.A., Foster, L., Zimmerman, L., Verdine, B.N., Marzouk, M., Islam, S., Golinkoff, R.M., & Hirsh-Pasek, K. (2020a). Three-year-olds' spatial language comprehension and links with mathematics and spatial performance. *Developmental Psychology, 56*, 1894–1905.

Bower, C.A., Odean, R., Verdine, B.N., Medford, J.R., Marzouk, M., Golinkoff, R.M., & Hirsh-Pasek, K. (2020b). Associations of 3-year-olds' block-building complexity with later spatial and mathematical skills. *Journal of Cognition and Development, 21*, 383–405.

Bureau of Labor Statistics (2020). *Household data annual averages. Table II: Employed persons by detailed occupation, sex, race, and Hispanic or Latino ethnicity.* Retrieved from www.bls.gov/cps/cpsaat11.pdf.

Carr, M., & Jessup, D.L. (1997). Gender differences in first grade mathematics strategy use: Social and metacognitive influences. *Journal of Educational Psychology, 89*, 318–328.

Casasola, M., Wei, W.S., Suh, D.D., Donskoy, P., & Ransom, A. (2020). Children's exposure to spatial language promotes their spatial thinking. *Journal of Experimental Psychology: General, 149*, 1116–1136.

Casey, B., Andrews, N., Schindler, H., Kersh, J.E., Samper, A., & Copley, J. (2008a). The development of spatial skills through interventions involving block building activities. *Cognition and Instruction, 26*, 269–309.

Casey, B., Dearing, E., Dulaney, A., Heyman, M., & Springer, R. (2014). Young girls' spatial and arithmetic performance: The mediating role of maternal supportive interactions during joint spatial problem solving. *Early Childhood Research Quarterly, 29*, 636–648.

Casey, B., Erkut, S., Ceder, I., & Young, J.M. (2008b). Use of a storytelling context to improve girls' and boys' geometry skills in kindergarten. *Journal of Applied Developmental Psychology, 29*, 29–48.

Casey, B., Lombardi, C.M., Pollock, A., Fineman, B., & Pezaris, E. (2017). Girls' spatial skills and arithmetic strategies in first grade as predictors of fifth-grade analytical math reasoning. *Journal of Cognition and Development, 18*, 530–555.

Casey, B., Nuttall, R.L., & Pezaris, E. (1997). Mediators of gender differences in mathematics college entrance test scores: A comparison of spatial skills with internalized beliefs and anxieties. *Developmental Psychology, 33*, 669–680.

Casey, B., Nuttall, R.L., & Pezaris, E. (2001). Spatial-mechanical reasoning skills versus mathematics self-confidence as mediators of gender differences on mathematics subtests using cross-national gender-based items. *Journal for Research in Mathematics Education, 32*, 28–57.

Casey, B., Paugh, P., & Ballard, N. (2002). *Sneeze builds a castle*. The Wright Group/McGraw-Hill.

Casey, B., Pezaris, E.E., & Bassi, J. (2012). Adolescent boys' and girls' block constructions differ in structural balance: A block-building characteristic related to math achievement. *Learning and Individual Differences, 22*, 25–36.

Casey, B., Pezaris, E.E., & Nuttall, R.L. (1992). Spatial ability as a predictor of math achievement: The importance of sex and handedness patterns. *Neuropsychologia, 30*, 35–45.

Cheng, Y.-L., & Mix, K.S. (2014). Spatial training improves children's mathematics ability. *Journal of Cognition and Development, 15*, 2–11.

Cheung, C.-N., Sung, J.Y., & Lourenco, S.F. (2020). Does training mental rotation transfer to gains in mathematical competence? Assessment of an at-home visuospatial intervention. *Psychological Research, 84*, 2000–2017.

Cimpian, J.R., Kim, T.H., & McDermott, Z.T. (2020). Understanding persistent gender gaps in STEM: Does achievement matter differently for men and women? *Science, 368*, 1317–1319.

College Board (2021). *SAT suite of assessments annual report*. Retrieved from https://reports.collegeboard.org/pdf/2021-total-group-SAT-suite-assessments-annual-report.pdf.

Constantinescu, M., Moore, D.S., Johnson, S.P., & Hines, M. (2018). Early contributions to infants' mental rotation abilities. *Developmental Science, 21*, e12613.

Cornu, V., Schiltz, C., Pazouki, T., & Martin, R. (2019). Training early visuo-spatial abilities: A controlled classroom-based intervention study. *Applied Developmental Science, 23*, 1–21.

Crollen, V., Collignon, O., & Noël, M.-P. (2017). Visuo-spatial processes as a domain-general factor impacting numerical development in atypical populations. *Journal of Numerical Cognition, 3*, 344–364.

Dankert, H.L., Davies, P.L., & Gavin, W.J. (2003). Occupational therapy effects on visual-motor skills in preschool children. *American Journal of Occupational Therapy, 57*, 542–549.

Denton, K., & West, J. (2002). *Children's reading and mathematics achievement in kindergarten and first grade*. U.S. Department of Education.

Duckworth, A.L., & Seligman, M.E.P. (2006). Self-discipline gives girls the edge: Gender in self-discipline, grades, and achievement test scores. *Journal of Educational Psychology, 98*, 198–208.

Ehrlich, S.B., Levine, S.C., & Goldin-Meadow, S. (2006). The importance of gesture in children's spatial reasoning. *Developmental Psychology, 42*, 1259–1268.

Fennema, E., Carpenter, T.P., Jacobs, V.R., Franke, M.L., & Levi, L.W. (1998). A longitudinal study of gender differences in young children's mathematical thinking. *Educational Researcher, 27*(5), 6–11.

Gallagher, A.M. (1992). *Sex differences in problem-solving used by high-scoring examinees on the SAT-M* (College Board Report No. 92–2, ETS RR No. 92–33). College Board Publications.

Gallagher, A.M., Levin, J., & Cahalan, C. (2002, Sept.). *Cognitive patterns of gender differences on mathematics admissions tests.* ETS Research Report, 02–19. Retrieved 12/19/2021, from www.ets.org/Media/Research/pdf/RR-02-19-Gallagher.pdf.

Ganley, C.M., & Vasilyeva, M. (2011). Sex differences in the relation between math performance, spatial skills, and attitudes. *Journal of Applied Developmental Psychology, 32,* 235–242.

Geary, D.C., Bailey, D.H., Littlefield, A., Wood, P., Hoard, M.K., & Nugent, L.(2009). First-grade predictors of mathematical learning disability: A latent class trajectory analysis. *Cognitive Development, 24,* 411–429.

Geary, D.C., Hoard, M.K., & Nugent, L. (2021a). Boys' visuospatial abilities compensate for their relatively poor in-class attentive behavior in learning mathematics. *Journal of Experimental Child Psychology, 211,* 105222.

Geary, D.C., Scofield, J.E., Hoard, M.K., & Nugent, L. (2021b). Boys' advantage on the fractions number line is mediated by visuospatial attention: Evidence for a parietal-spatial contribution to number line learning. *Developmental Science, 24,* e13063.

Geiser, C., Lehmann, W., & Eid, M. (2008). A note on sex differences in mental rotation in different age groups. *Intelligence, 36,* 556–563.

Georges, C., Cornu, V., & Schiltz, C. (2021). The importance of visuospatial abilities for verbal number skills in preschool: Adding spatial language to the equation. *Journal of Experimental Child Psychology, 201,* 104971.

Gilligan, K.A., Thomas, M.S.C., & Farran, E.K. (2020). First demonstration of effective spatial training for near transfer to spatial performance and far transfer to a range of mathematics skills at 8 years. *Developmental Science, 23,* e12909.

Gregory, K.M., Kim, A.S., & Whiren, A. (2003). The effect of verbal scaffolding on the complexity of preschool children's block constructions. In D.E. Lytle (Ed.), *Play and educational theory and practice* (pp. 117–133). Praeger Publishers/Greenwood Publishing Group.

Grön, G., Wunderlich, A.P., Spitzer, M., Tomczak, R., & Riepe, M.W. (2000). Brain activation during human navigation: Gender-different neural networks as substrate of performance. *Nature Neuroscience, 3,* 404–408.

Gunderson, E.A., Ramirez, G., Beilock, S.L., & Levine, S.C. (2012). The relation between spatial skill and early number knowledge: The role of the linear number line. *Developmental Psychology, 48,* 1229–1241.

Gunderson, E.A., Ramirez, G., Beilock, S.L., & Levine, S.C. (2013). Teachers' spatial anxiety relates to 1st and 2nd-graders' spatial learning. *Mind, Brain, and Education, 7,* 196–199.

Hahn, N., Jansen, P., & Heil, M. (2010). Preschoolers' mental rotation: Sex differences in hemispheric asymmetry. *Journal of Cognitive Neuroscience, 22,* 1244–1250.

Halpern, D.F. (1997). Sex differences in intelligence: Implications for education. *American Psychologist, 52,* 1091–1102.

Hawes, Z., & Ansari, D. (2020). What explains the relationship between spatial and mathematical skills? A review of evidence from brain and behavior. *Psychonomic Bulletin & Review, 27,* 465–482.

Hawes, Z., Moss, J., Caswell, B., & Naqvi, S., & MacKinnon, S. (2017). Enhancing children's spatial and numerical skills through a dynamic spatial approach to early geometry instruction: Effects of a 32-week intervention. *Cognition and Instruction, 35,* 236–264.

Hawes, Z., Moss, J., Caswell, B., & Poliszczuk, D. (2015). Effects of mental rotation training on children's spatial and mathematics performance: A randomized controlled study.

Trends in Neuroscience and Education, 4, 60–68.

Hawes, Z., Sokolowski, H.M., Ononye, C.B., Ansari, D. (2019). Neural underpinnings of numerical and spatial cognition: An fMRI meta-analysis of brain regions associated with symbolic number, arithmetic, and mental rotation. *Neuroscience and Biobehavioral Reviews, 103,* 316–336.

Hegarty, M. (2018). Ability and sex differences in spatial thinking: What does the mental rotation test really measure? *Psychonomic Bulletin & Review, 25,* 1212–1219.

Heil, M., Jansen, P., Quaiser-Pohl, C., & Neuburger, S. (2012). Gender-specific effects of artificially induced gender beliefs in mental rotation. *Learning and Individual Differences, 22,* 350–353.

Hutchison, J.E., Lyons, I.M., & Ansari, D. (2019). More similar than different: Gender differences in children's basic numerical skills are the exception not the rule. *Child Development, 90,* e66–e79.

Jansen, P., Zayed, K., & Osmann, R. (2016). Gender differences in mental rotation in Oman and Germany. *Learning and Individual Differences, 51,* 284–290.

Janssen, A.B., & Geiser, C. (2010). On the relationship between solution strategies in two mental rotation tasks. *Learning and Individual Differences, 20,* 473–478.

Jeng, H.-L., & Liu, G.-F. (2016). Test interactivity is promising in promoting gender equity in females' pursuit of STEM careers. *Learning and Individual Differences, 49,* 201–208.

Jirout, J.J., & Newcombe, N.S. (2015). Building blocks for developing spatial skills: Evidence from a large, representative U.S. sample. *Psychological Science, 26,* 302–310.

Johnson, T., Burgoyne, A.P., Mix, K.S., Young, C.J., & Levine, S.C. (2022). Spatial and mathematics skills: Similarities and differences related to age, SES, and gender. *Cognition, 218,* 104918.

Jordan, K., Wüstenberg, T., Heinze, H.-J., Peters, M., & Jäncke, L. (2002). Women and men exhibit different cortical activation patterns during mental rotation tasks. *Neuropsychologia, 40,* 2397–2408.

Judd, N., & Klingberg, T. (2021). Training spatial cognition enhances mathematical learning in a randomized study of 17,000 children. *Nature Human Behaviour, 5,* 1548–1554.

Klein, P.S., Adi-Japha, E., & Hakak-Benizri, S. (2010). Mathematical thinking of kindergarten boys and girls: Similar achievement, different contributing processes. *Educational Studies in Mathematics, 73,* 233–246.

Koscik, T., O'Leary, D., Moser, D.J., Andreason, N.C., & Nopoulos, P. (2009). Sex differences in parietal lobe morphology: Relationship to mental rotation performance. *Brain and Cognition, 69,* 451–459.

Landerl, K., & Moll, K. (2010). Comorbidity of learning disorders: Prevalence and familial transmission. *The Journal of Child Psychology and Psychiatry, 51,* 287–294.

Laski, E.V., Casey, B.M., Yu, Q., Dulaney, A., Heyman, M., & Dearing, E. (2013). Spatial skills as a predictor of first grade girls' use of higher level arithmetic strategies. *Learning and Individual Differences, 23,* 123–130.

Lauer, J.E., Esposito, A.G., & Bauer, P.J. (2018). Domain-specific anxiety relates to children's math and spatial performance. *Developmental Psychology, 54,* 2126–2138.

Lauer, J.E., Yhang, E., & Lourenco, S.F. (2019). The development of gender differences in spatial reasoning: A meta-analytic review. *Psychological Bulletin, 145,* 537–565.

Lehmann, W., & Jüling, I. (2002). Spatial reasoning and mathematical abilities: Independent constructs or two sides of the same coin? *Psychologie in Erziehung und Unterricht, 49,* 31–43.

Levine, S.C., Foley, A., Lourenco, S., Ehrlich, S., & Ratliff, K. (2016). Sex differences in spatial cognition: Advancing the conversation. *WIREs Cognitive Science, 7,* 127–155.

Levine, S.C., Huttenlocher, J., Taylor, A., & Langrock, A. (1999). Early sex differences in spatial skill. *Developmental Psychology, 35,* 940–949.

Levine, S.C., Vasilyeva, M., Lourenco, S.F., New-combe, N.S., & Huttenlocher, J. (2005). Socioeconomic status modifies the sex difference in spatial skill. *Psychological Science, 16*, 841–845.

Lippa, R.A., Collaer, M.L., & Peters, M. (2010). Sex differences in mental rotation and line angle judgments are positively associated with gender equality and economic development across 53 nations. *Archives of Sexual Behavior, 39*, 990–997.

Lombardi, C.M., Casey, B.M., Thomson, D., Nguyen, H.N., & Dearing, E. (2017). Maternal support of young children's planning and spatial concept learning as predictors of later math (and reading) achievement. *Early Childhood Research Quarterly, 41*, 114–125.

Lourenco, S.F., Addy, D., Huttenlocher, J., & Fabian, L. (2011). Early sex differences in weighting geometric cues. *Developmental Science, 14*, 1365–1378.

Lourenco, S.F., Cheung, C.-N., & Aulet, L.S. (2018). Is visuospatial reasoning related to early mathematical development? A critical review. In A. Henik & W. Fias (Eds.), *Heterogeneity of function in numerical cognition* (pp. 177–210). Academic Press.

Low, R., & Over, R. (1993). Gender differences in solution of algebraic word problems containing irrelevant information. *Journal of Educational Psychology, 85*, 331–339.

Lowrie, T., Logan, T., & Hegarty, M. (2019). The influence of spatial visualization training on students' spatial reasoning and mathematics performance. *Journal of Cognition and Development, 20*, 729–751.

Lowrie, T., Logan, T., & Ramful, A. (2017). Visuospatial training improves elementary students' mathematics performance. *British Journal of Educational Psychology, 87*, 170–186.

Lowrie, T., Resnick, I., Harris, D., & Logan, T. (2020). In search of the mechanisms that enable transfer from spatial reasoning to mathematics understanding. *Mathematics Education Research Journal, 32*, 175–188.

Maguire, E.A., Gadian, D.G., Johnsrude, I.S., Good, C.D., Ashburner, J., Frackowiak, R.S.J., & Frith, C.D. (2000). Navigation-related structural change in the hippocampi of taxi drivers. *Proceedings of the National Academy of Sciences, 97*, 4398–4403.

Maloney, E.A., Waechter, S., Risko, E.F., & Fugelsang, J.A. (2012). Reducing the sex difference in math anxiety; The role of spatial processing ability. *Learning and Individual Differences, 22*, 380–384.

McAdams, D.E. (2016). *Geometric nets mega project book tabbed*. CreateSpace Independent Publishing Platform.

Miller, H.E., Patterson, R., & Simmering, V.R. (2016). Language supports young children's use of spatial relations to remember locations. *Cognition, 150*, 170–180.

Mix, K.S. (2019). Why are spatial skill and mathematics related? *Child Development Perspectives, 13*, 121–126.

Mix, K.S., Levine, S.C., Cheng, Y.-L., Stockton, J.D., & Bower, C. (2021). Effects of spatial training on mathematics in first and sixth grade children. *Journal of Educational Psychology, 113*, 304–314.

Mix, K.S., Levine, S.C., Cheng, Y.-L., Young, C.J., Hambrick, D.Z., & Konstantopoulos, S., (2017). The latent structure of spatial skills and mathematics: A replication of the two-factor model. *Journal of Cognition and Development, 18*, 465–492.

Moè, A., Jansen, P., & Pietsch, S. (2018). Childhood preference for spatial toys: Gender differences and relationships with mental rotation in STEM and non-STEM students. *Learning and Individual Differences, 68*, 108–115.

Mulligan, J., Woolcott, G., Mitchelmore, M., Busatto, S., Lai, J., & Davis, B. (2020). Evaluating the impact of a Spatial Reasoning Mathematics Program (SRMP) intervention in the primary school. *Mathematics Education Research Journal, 32*, 285–305.

Nazareth, A., Huang, X., Voyer, D., & Newcombe, N. (2019). A meta-analysis of sex differences in human navigation skills. *Psychonomic Bulletin & Review, 26,* 1503–1528.

Newcombe, N.S. (2010, June). Picture this: Increasing math and science learning by improving spatial thinking. *American Educator, 34,* 29–35, 43.

Noble, K.G., McCandliss, B.D., & Farah, M.J. (2007). Socioeconomic gradients predict individual differences in neurocognitive abilities. *Developmental Science, 10,* 464–480.

Örnkloo, H., & vonHofsten, C. (2007). Fitting objects into holes: On the development of spatial cognition skills. *Developmental Psychology, 43,* 404–416.

Peters, M., Lehmann, W., Takahira, S., Takeuchi, Y., & Jordan, K. (2006). Mental rotation test performance in four cross-cultural samples (N=3376): Overall sex differences and the role of academic program in performance. *Cortex, 42,* 1005–1014.

Pietsch, S., & Jansen, P. (2012). Different mental rotation performance in students of music, sport and education. *Learning and Individual Differences, 22,* 159–163.

Pruden, S.M., & Levine, S.C. (2017). Parents' spatial language mediates a sex difference in preschoolers' spatial-language use. *Psychological Science, 28,* 1583–1596.

Pruden, S.M., Levine, S.C., & Huttenlocher, J. (2011). Children's spatial thinking: Does talk about the spatial world matter? *Developmental Science, 14,* 1417–1430.

Ramirez, G., Gunderson, E.A., Levine, S.C., & Beilock, S.L. (2012). Spatial anxiety relates to spatial abilities as a function of working memory in children. *The Quarterly Journal of Experimental Psychology, 65,* 474–487.

Raudenbush, S.W., Hernandez, M., Goldin-Meadow, S., Carrazza, C., Foley, A., Leslie, D., Sorkin, J.E., & Levine, S.C. (2020). Longitudinally adaptive assessment and instruction increase numerical skills of preschool children. *Proceedings of the National Academy of Sciences, 117,* 27945–27953.

Rauscher, F.H. (2003). *Effects of piano, rhythm, and singing instruction on the spatial reasoning of at-risk children.* European Society for the Cognitive Sciences of Music, Hannover, Germany.

Robinson, N.M., Abbott, R.D., Berninger, V.W., Busse, J. (1996). The structure of abilities in math-precocious young children: Gender similarities and differences. *Journal of Educational Psychology, 88,* 341–352.

Rodán, A., Gimeno, P., Elosúa, M.R., Montoro, P.R., & Contreras, M.J. (2019). Boys and girls gain in spatial, but not in mathematical ability after mental rotation training in primary education. *Learning and Individual Differences, 70,* 1–11.

Saucier, D., Bowman, M., & Elias, L. (2003). Sex differences in the effect of articulatory or spatial dual task interference during navigation. *Brain and Cognition, 53,* 346–350.

Schaeffer, M.W., Rozek, C.S., Maloney, E.A., Berkowitz, T., Levine, S.C., & Beilock, S.L. (2021). Elementary school teachers' math anxiety and students' math learning: A large-scale replication. *Developmental Science, 24,* e13080.

Schmitt, S.A., Korucu, I., Napoli, A.R., Bryant, L.M., & Purpura, D.J. (2018). Using block play to enhance preschool children's mathematics and executive functioning: A randomized controlled trial. *Early Childhood Research Quarterly, 44,* 181–191.

Sokolowski, H.M., Hawes, Z., & Lyons, I.M. (2019). What explains sex differences in math anxiety? A closer look at the role of spatial processing. *Cognition, 182,* 193–212.

Sorby, S.A. (2009). Developing spatial cognitive skills among middle school students. *Cognitive Processes, 10,* S312-S315.

Sorby, S., Veurink, N., & Streiner, S. (2018). Does spatial skills instruction improve STEM outcomes? The answer is 'yes'. *Learning and Individual Differences, 67,* 209–222.

Sortor, J.M., & Kulp, M.T. (2003). Are the results of the Beery-Buktenica Developmental Test of Visual-Motor Integration and its subtests related to achievement test scores? *Optometry & Visual Science, 80,* 758–763.

Stanley, J.C., Benbow, C.P., Brody, L.E., Dauber, S., & Lupkowski, A. (1992). Gender differences on eighty-six nationally standardized aptitude and achievement tests. In N. Colangelo, S.G. Assouline, & D.L. Ambroson (Eds.), *Talent development, Vol. 1: Proceedings from the 1991 Henry B. and Jocelyn Wallace national research symposium on talent development* (pp. 42–65). Trillium Press.

Stannard, L., Wolfgang, C.H., Jones, I., & Phelps, P. (2001). A longitudinal study of the predicted relations among construction play and mathematical achievement. *Early Childhood Development and Care, 167,* 115–125.

Thomson, D., Casey, B.M., Lombardi, C.M., & Nguyen, H.N. (2020). Quality of fathers' spatial concept support during block building predicts their daughters' early math skills—but not their sons'. *Early Childhood Research Quarterly, 50,* 51–64.

Titze, C., Jansen, P., & Heil, M. (2010). Mental rotation performance in fourth graders: No effects of gender beliefs (yet?). *Learning and Individual Differences, 20,* 459–463.

Uttal, D.H., Meadow, N.G., Tipton, E., Hand, L.L., Alden, A.R., Warren, C., & Newcombe, N.S. (2013). The malleability of spatial skills: A meta-analysis of training studies. *Psychological Bulletin, 139,* 352–402.

Vandenberg, S.G., & Kuse, A.R. (1978). Mental rotations, a group test of three-dimensional spatial visualization. *Perceptual and Motor Skills, 47,* 599–604.

VanGoozen, S.H.M., Cohen-Kettenis, P.T., Gooren, L.J.G., Frijda, N.H., & Van de Poll, N.E. (1995). Gender differences in behaviour: Activating effects of cross-sex hormones. *Psychoneuroendocrinology, 20,* 343–363.

Vasilyeva, M., Casey, B.M., Dearing, E., & Ganley, C.M. (2009). Measurement skills in low-income elementary school students: Exploring the nature of gender differences. *Cognition and Instruction, 27,* 401–428.

Verdine, B.N., Bunger, A., Athanasopoulou, A., Golinkoff, R.M., & Hirsh-Pasek, K. (2017a). Shape up: An eye-tracking study of preschoolers' shape name processing and spatial development. *Developmental Psychology, 53,* 1869–1880.

Verdine, B.N., Golinkoff, R.M., Hirsh-Pasek, K., & Newcombe, N.S. (2017b). Links between spatial and mathematical skills across the preschool years. In *Monographs of the society for research in child development.* John Wiley & Sons, Inc.

Verdine, B.N., Zimmermann, L., Foster, L., Marzouk, M.A., Golinkoff, R.M., Hirsh-Pasek, K., & Newcombe, N. (2019). Effects of geometric toy design on parent-child interactions and spatial language. *Early Childhood Research Quarterly, 46,* 126–141.

Voyer, D., Voyer, S., & Bryden, M.P. (1995). Magnitude of sex differences in spatial abilities: A meta-analysis and consideration of critical variables. *Psychological Bulletin, 117,* 250–270.

Voyer, D., Voyer, S.D., & Saint-Aubin, J. (2017). Sex differences in visual-spatial working memory: A meta-analysis. *Psychonomic Bulletin & Review, 24,* 307–334.

Vuoksimaa, E., Kaprio, J., Kremen, W.S., Hokkanen, L., Viken, R.J., Tuulio-Henriksson, A., & Rose, R.J. (2010). Having a male co-twin masculinizes mental rotation performance in females. *Psychological Science, 21,* 1069–1071.

Wai, J., Lubinski, D., & Benbow, C.P. (2009). Spatial ability for STEM domains: Aligning over 50 years of cumulative psychological knowledge solidifies its importance. *Journal of Educational Psychology, 101,* 817–835.

Webb, R.M., Lubinski, D., & Benbow, C.P. (2007). Spatial ability: A neglected dimension in the talent searches for intellectually precocious youth. *Journal of Educational Psychology, 99,* 397–420.

Wei, W., Lu, H., Zhao, H., Chen, C., Dong, Q., & Zhou, X. (2012). Gender differences in children's arithmetic performance are accounted for by gender differences in language abilities. *Psychological Science, 23,* 320–330.

Wolfgang, C.H., Stannard, L.L., & Jones, I. (2001). Block play performance among preschoolers as a predictor of later school achievement in mathematics. *Journal of Research in Childhood Education, 15*, 173–181.

Yazdani, S., Soluki, S., Arjmandnia, A.A., Fathabadi, J., Hassanzadeh, S., & Nejati, V. (2021). Spatial ability in children with mathematics learning disorder (MLD) and its impact on executive functions. *Developmental Neuropsychology, 46*, 232–248.

Young, C.J., Levine, S.C., & Mix, K.S. (2018). The connection between spatial and mathematical ability across development. *Frontiers in Psychology, 9*, 755.

Zhang, T., Chen, C., Chen, C., & Wei, W. (2020). Gender differences in the development of semantic and spatial processing of numbers. *British Journal of Developmental Psychology, 38*, 391–414.

Zhang, X., Koponen, T., Räsänen, P., Aunola, K., Lerkkanen, M.-K., & Nurmi, J.-E. (2014). Linguistic and spatial skills predict early arithmetic development via counting sequence knowledge. *Child Development, 85*, 1091–1107.

Part III

The Tools of Numeracy

By repeating . . . the idea of an unit, and joining it to another unit, we make thereof one collective idea, marked by the name two. And whosoever can do this, and proceed on still, adding one more to the last collective idea which he had of any number, and give a name to it, may count. . . . For without such names or marks, we can hardly well make use of numbers in reckoning, especially where the combination is made up of any great multitude of units; which put together without a name or mark, to distinguish that precise collection, will hardly be kept from being a heap of confusion.

John Locke, 1689[1]

Perhaps what all of us have, besides the number sense we share with other animals, is just the belief that large, exact numerosities exist, plus better or worse technologies for keeping track of them.

Barbara Sarnecka and Susan Gelman, 2004[2]

DOI: 10.4324/9781003157656-8

When last seen at the end of Chapter 3, our three-year-old hero was on the brink of figuring out how to enumerate more than three objects. He knows some number words, what order to say them in, and how to use the first three to name three objects. He also has some idea of how to match up objects, one for one, to another set of objects. He has probably seen the big kids hold up fingers whenever they say a number word and may even have learned to do so himself. Now what?

This section will take a close look at how children develop the "technologies" to understand and keep track of large, exact quantities. Although most children are born with the mental equipment to do this successfully, the tools themselves are not hard-wired[3]; what they are and how to use them must be taught, and learning this is far from "easy as one, two, three." In fact, mastering them typically takes most of elementary school.

In the grand scheme, these enumerating tools were invented only fairly recently, when humans needed to solve the new problems introduced by farming and trading.[4] As noted briefly in Chapter 2, hunter-gatherer societies, who do not have such problems, typically do not have the tools to solve them, either—only the words *one, two*, and *many*—although the mental capacity to learn them is there.[5]

PRIMITIVE CULTURES DEVELOP SESAME STREET.

Source: xkcd.com. Reprinted with permission.

Our early ancestors often kept track of large quantities—of animals, days of the lunar cycles, or seasons—by making a knot in a rope or a notch in wood or bone for each item, matching knots or notches, one for one, with the items to be enumerated.[6] One-to-one matching is how our modern tools work, too, and each will be reviewed here in turn: number words, fingers, written numerical symbols, and units of length along a line.

NOTES

1 Locke, 1689/1824.
2 Sarnecka & Gelman, 2004.

3 LeCorre et al., 2006.
4 Devlin, 2005, pp. 199–237.
5 Piantadosi et al., 2014.
6 Dehaene, 1997, pp. 92ff.; D'Errico et al., 2017.

REFERENCES

The following references were cited in this introduction. For additional selected references relevant to this introduction, please see Part III Supplemental References in eResources.

Dehaene, S. (1997). *The number sense: How the mind creates mathematics.* Oxford University Press.

D'Errico, F., Doyon, L., Colagé, I., Queffelec, A., LeVraux, E., Giacobini, G., Vandermeersch, B., & Maureille, B. (2017). From number sense to number symbols: An archeological perspective. *Philosophical Transactions of the Royal Society B., 373,* 20160518.

Devlin, K. (2005). *The math instinct: Why you're a mathematical genius (along with lobsters, birds, cats, and dogs).* Thunder's Mouth Press.

LeCorre, M., Van de Walle, G., Brannon, E.M., & Carey, S. (2006). Re-visiting the competence/performance debate in the acquisition of the counting principles. *Cognitive Psychology, 52,* 130–169.

Locke, J. (1689/1824). *The works of John Locke, vol. 1 (An essay concerning human understanding part 1) [1689]* (Chapt. XVI). Retrieved 03/23/2019, from http://oll.libertyfund.org/titles/locke-the-works-vol-1-an-essay-concerning-human-understanding-part-1

Piantadosi, S.T., Jara-Ettinger, J., & Gibson, E. (2014). Children's learning of number words in an indigenous farming-foraging group. *Developmental Science, 17,* 553–563.

Sarnecka, B.W., & Gelman, S.A. (2004). *Six* does not just mean *a lot*: Preschoolers see number words as specific. *Cognition, 92,* 329–352.

Chapter 6

Number Words and Counting

FIVE basic principles define our counting system[1]:

- One-to-one principle: There must be one unique tag (i.e., number word or numeral) per item counted.
- Stable order principle: The tags used must be ordered the same way consistently over time (i.e., we always count in the same sequence, "One, two, three, ...").
- Cardinality principle: The last tag used in the stable order list uniquely represents the cardinal value of the set (i.e., the last number word used answers the question, *How many?*).
- Abstraction principle: It does not matter what you are counting as long as you think of them as entities, real or imagined.
- Order-irrelevance principle: As long as the first two principles are adhered to, it does not matter in what order you count the items (i.e., the tags must be in order, but the items tagged do not).

The remarkable thing about this counting system is that it is completely reliable and unambiguous. It also ensures that record-keeping and communication are clear and simple.

Learning this system, however, is not. Writing this chapter would be easy (and the chapter would be shorter) if children learned these principles in a certain order, in a few lessons, and by a given age. Were that the case, we could present what follows in a simple chart and move on. The truth, however, is that children usually learn these principles somewhat independently of one another, often simultaneously, in what can seem a chaotic fashion, over the course of several years' worth of observations and personal experiments and experience. Although some research has pinpointed ages of expected mastery on some of these tasks, readers should know that in any given preschool or early primary school classroom, counting development can vary widely.[2] Our discussion will start with the second principle, stable order, as it is a feature of the verbal number sequence.

DOI: 10.4324/9781003157656-9

STABLE ORDER NUMBER SEQUENCE

If you learned to sing "Frère Jacques" as a child (but were not lucky enough to have French-speaking parents), you probably understand what it is like for most small children to learn the verbal counting sequence. With enough practice and a good ear for language, you could probably manage to get the words right and remember them in the right order—yet have no idea what they mean. Moreover, while you might be able to sing the words in the right order, if someone stopped the music in the middle, you might have to go back to the beginning and start all over to proceed.[3] And you certainly could not sing them in reverse order.

Like learning songs, learning the counting words is a social activity. Children learn the counting words from parents, older children, teachers, and caregivers. The more that children hear them and see them used, the more likely they are to learn them and use them. One study found that for the first two and a half or three years, a mother typically uses them more than her child does, but from age three on, the child outpaces her in the frequency of saying the number words.[4] Moreover, observations of parent-child interactions during the toddler and preschool years show that parents' use of number words to count (tag) present and visible objects is related to their children's math skills and to their vocabulary in general. Parental counting is particularly effective when it involves numbers just above those with which their children are already familiar.[5]

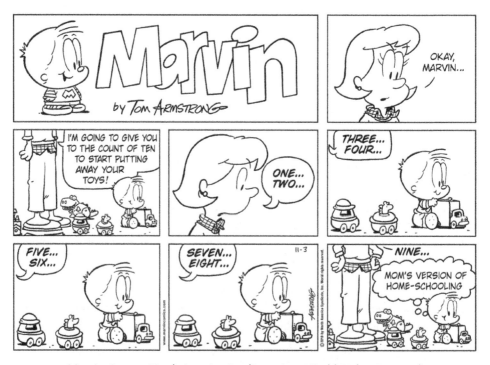

FIGURE 6.1 Marvin © 2019 North America Syndicate, Inc., World Rights Reserved.

The close tie between early numeracy and language leaves some young children at risk for math difficulty. For example, teachers' attention to general receptive and expressive language skills has been found to be particularly critical for preschool counting development among children from low-income homes.[6] Among English-Spanish bilingual preschoolers and kindergartners, expressive language and syntax comprehension are strongly associated with early numeracy skills within each language.[7] At the extreme, children with a developmental language disorder detected in preschool have a one-in-four chance of developing a serious math and/or reading disorder, and often both. Of those who develop a reading disability, about two in three also develop a math disability, and vice versa.[8]

Remarkably, children typically begin to develop an ear for the counting sequence shortly before they turn a year and a half, well before they can say the words themselves. In a series of Australian (English-language) studies, researchers presented toddlers with two videos demonstrating someone counting six objects. A button press triggered the videos, and the children were free to press either button to play the video they preferred. In the first study, one video showed someone speaking the counting words in the usual order ("one, two, three, four, five, six"), while the other video showed them spoken in random order (e.g., "three, one, five, six, four, two"), with a different random order used each time. The 15-month-olds did not seem to have a preference, but the 18-month-olds did: They preferred the video in which the person counted the usual way. In the second study, a group of 18-month-olds watched the same two videos, except the videos were both in Japanese. Here, with this unfamiliar language, the 18-month-olds showed no preference between the videos. In the third study, researchers offered the Japanese videos to a group of 18-month-olds from homes in which two or more languages (but not Japanese) were regularly spoken. Interestingly, these children preferred the Japanese video with the customary counting sequence—even though they had never heard Japanese spoken before. When the same 18-month-olds from multilingual homes were offered videos in which someone recited the English *alphabet* in the usual versus a variable scrambled order, these children had no preference for one or the other versions of the alphabet, suggesting that the toddlers' ears were tuned to the counting sequence in particular.[9]

Other studies have arrived at similar results. When 14- and 18-month-old toddlers watched a researcher hide some objects, the toddlers then found significantly more of them if the researcher had counted them aloud when hiding them, rather than just indicated them by "this, this, and this"—even though the children did not yet know the meaning of the counting words.[10] And when three-year-olds were asked to remember a string of consecutive number words, they remembered them much more easily if the numbers were presented in numerical order, even including those numbers beyond their counting range.[11]

What can we learn from these findings? First, children develop an ear for the standard sequence of counting words to at least "six" in their family's language around age 18 months and expect to hear that stable sequence of sound patterns during counting behavior. Second, hearing more than one language at home seems to make toddlers more sensitive to the regular patterns of sounds in speech and primed to expect to hear such a stable, regular sound pattern during counting behavior in particular. Finally, young toddlers understand that the counting routine is related to numerosity. These findings do not mean that children can speak the word sequence or understand it, but having an ear for it is a good start.

Furthermore, as discussed in Chapter 3, other studies have demonstrated that by the age of three or so, children can distinguish number words from non-number words. They learn this difference while developing an ear for the syntax of everyday language. In particular, they know that number words refer to specific, mutually exclusive numerosities (although they do not yet know which ones), unlike vaguer quantifiers such as "a lot" or "some."[12] And by age five, children can remember "three-hundred forty-five" better than "five three forty hundred," for example, suggesting that they have an ear for conventional multi-digit number names well before the formal study of such numbers.[13]

Distinguishing the regular word pattern of counting, however, requires the ability to discern the individual sounds in spoken language, an ability termed *phonological awareness*. To extend the "Frère Jacques" analogy, most of us have had the experience of singing along to a favorite song and only years later finding out that we have had the lyrics wrong. If a young child is going to master a series of words, he needs to hear them clearly and correctly every time. Moreover, in the math classroom, it will be vital that he can distinguish the sound of "thirty" from "thirteen," say, or "five" from "nine." Psychologists evaluate phonological awareness by asking the child to come up with a word that rhymes with a given word, or to put together two given sounds to make a word, or to decipher a word with a sound missing, or to detect the difference between two similar-sounding words. Using such techniques to assess young children's ear for language, researchers have found that phonological awareness significantly predicts the successful acquisition of the number-word sequence and growth in early calculation skills.[14]

To be able to count efficiently, however, requires not only an ear for language but a mouth for language, as well—a child needs to be able to say the number words fluently. Research with first- and second-graders has shown that verbal counting fluency depends on the general ability to quickly and automatically name familiar objects, a skill that is also necessary for reading.[15]

Unfortunately, some children have significant language impairments, often including deficits in phonological awareness, verbal sequencing and memory, and rapid, automatic word retrieval. Consequently, they find learning the number-word sequence very difficult. When tested at the age of six or seven, a group of such children could count to only "forty-two," while their peers could count to "eighty-five." They were unable to count by *ten*s or recite the number words in reverse order from "twenty." Mentally storing verbal sequences and retrieving them from memory was particularly difficult. Thus, while they understood the counting principles, their actual counting was strained.[16]

Deaf children also have difficulty mastering the counting sequence, which they learn in sign language. This may be, in part, because their memory for sign language is relatively constricted. Research suggests that they do master it, but that it just takes them more time to learn the signed sequence than their hearing peers require to learn the verbal sequence. Once deaf children learn the sequence, however, they count as well as hearing children do with spoken number words.[17]

TABLE 6.1 Pinyin Transliteration of Mandarin Counting Words

Pinyin	yī	èr	sān	sì	wǔ	liù	qī	bā	jiǔ	shí
English	one	two	three	four	five	six	seven	eight	nine	ten
Pinyin	shí-yī	shí-èr	shí-sān	shí-sì	shí-wǔ	shí-liù	shí-qī	shí-bā	shí-jiǔ	èr-shí
English	eleven	twelve	thirteen	fourteen	fifteen	sixteen	seventeen	eighteen	nineteen	twenty
Pinyin	èr-shí-yī	èr-shí-èr	èr-shí-sān	èr-shí-sì	èr-shí-wǔ	èr-shí-liù	èr-shí-qī	èr-shí-bā	èr-shí-jiǔ	sān-shí
English	twenty-one	twenty-two	twenty-three	twenty-four	twenty-five	twenty-six	twenty-seven	twenty-eight	twenty-nine	thirty
Pinyin	dì-yī	dì-èr	dì-sān	dì-sì	dì-wǔ	dì-liù	dì-qī	dì-bā	dì-jiǔ	dì-shí
English	first	second	third	fourth	fifth	sixth	seventh	eighth	ninth	tenth

One of the things that can make learning the counting sequence difficult for many English-speaking children is the word-sound (*phonological*) complexity of the number words. These difficulties become clear when the English number words are compared with those in several East Asian languages.[18] To illustrate, we will take Chinese as an example. As can be seen in Table 6.1, the Chinese words through "ten" are all short and phonologically simple. For children without a language disability, this difference would not be noticeable when learning to count. In fact, a study of Chinese and American preschoolers demonstrated that nearly all of them could count to "ten" in their native language.[19] However, the shorter number words can make a significant difference when a child is trying to remember a string of them, as might be necessary while doing complex calculations.[20] Indeed, Chinese primary students' relatively early abandonment of finger counting has been attributed to their superior digit-word recall.[21]

There are three other ways in which the Chinese number words have a significant advantage over those in English, all having to do with their morphemic structure (i.e., the way the basic number words take on affixes to change their meaning). The first Chinese advantage is that their words for "eleven" to "nineteen" take on the clear base-10 format (see Table 6.1). Thus, while English-speaking children are struggling with such historical relics as "eleven" and "twelve," and remembering that "-teen" means "ten," Chinese children simply use the word for *ten*, "shí," as a prefix. Moreover, while in Chinese the verbal terms are consistent with place-value notation (e.g., "ten-four" = *14*), in English the units *precede* the "-teen," as in "four-teen," the reverse of place-value notation order. The Chinese words also remain perfectly regular in their pronunciation and spelling, unlike, for example, "thirteen" and "fifteen," which undergo phonological as well as spelling changes. Thus, it is not surprising that, in a study of Chinese and American preschoolers, 74 percent of the Chinese children but only 48 percent of the Americans could count to "twenty."[22]

The second Chinese advantage is its simple regularity of terms for numbers above "nineteen" (see Table 6.1). Both English and Chinese express the decades in multiples of ten. However, the Chinese word forms are identical to those used for small numerosities. For example, in Chinese, "ten" is always "shí," while in English, children must

FIGURE 6.2

Source: One Big Happy © By permission of Rick Detorie and Creators Syndicate, Inc.

learn that "ten" converts to "-ty." Additionally, "two" is always "èr," "three" is always "sān," and "five" is always "wǔ"; thus, Chinese children learn "èr-shí," "sān-shí," and "wǔ- shí," instead of the less directly decipherable "twen-ty," "thir-ty," and "fif-ty." (Both Chinese and English append the units to the end of the term: "Twenty-one" in Chinese is "two-ten-one": "èr-shí-yī.") Here again, it should not be surprising that Chinese children on average are counting to "one hundred" for almost a year before English-speaking children reach "forty."[23] Moreover, the Chinese advantage seen in the simple counting words has downstream benefits. For example, to count to "one million," English speakers require 30 different counting words, while Chinese speakers need only 14. The counting advantage extends to arithmetic, as well, since counting is the way that many children start to learn addition and subtraction. Indeed, research has shown that Chinese children's addition strategies are more sophisticated than American children's by the time they start school.[24]

The third Chinese advantage is in their ordinal form, or the form a number word takes to express the order in which something occurs. In English, those forms are "first," "second," "third," and the suffix "-th" added to the rest of the counting words (with a phonemic alteration for "fifth"). This system can be confusing for English-speaking children, who sometimes apply "-th" to the wrong part of larger number words ("twentieth-six"), overgeneralize "-th" to the small units of larger number words ("twenty-oneth"), or use "-teenth" instead of "-th" ("twenty-one-teenth"). By contrast, Chinese ordinals are formed by adding the prefix "dì-" to all number words (see Table 6.1). Thus, it should not be surprising that in a study of young American and Chinese students, fewer than half of the American fourth-graders could recite the ordinal number words up to "thirtieth," while all of the Chinese kindergartners could recite the Chinese terms up to *forty-fifth*, the last term tested.[25]

Regardless of which language a child speaks, knowledge of the rules governing the number-word sequence is significantly associated with a deeper understanding of the number system. For example, discovering the recurring (*recursive*) pattern of starting over from "one" after every decade change ("thirty, thirty-one, thirty-two . . . forty, forty-one, forty-two . . .") is related to children's insight into the *successor function*: that is, an increase of one item in a set means the value of the expanded set is the next number word up in the sequence.[26] While the developmental timing varies with the transparency of the particular language's counting system (speakers of Chinese figure it out early; speakers of Hindi, with its opaque numbering system, discover it later) and other cultural and individual differences, the relationship between insights about the linguistic pattern and the successor function of counting holds.[27] Children can use their insights about counting to form new and more accurate arithmetic strategies as well.[28]

Finally, what does mastery of the counting sequence look like? Research with children aged five to six and a half reveals that when given a number, most of them could name the next number in the sequence. And most of them responded appropriately with the next number word when they watched one item being added to a collection. However, the children also gave the next number word in the sequence when asked for the *previous* number or when shown an item being *removed* from a collection. In the latter situations, very few of them could name the *preceding* number in the sequence. Importantly, being able to name the preceding number was associated with the child's ability to compare two numbers. Thus, concluded the researchers, mastery of the number sequence goes beyond rote memorization of it.[29] In fact, as noted in Chapter 5, counting backward and comparing numbers likely depend on the ability to think of numbers lined up in order. The "mental number line" will be a topic of Chapter 9.

ONE-TO-ONE TAGGING

The counting routine requires matching up, one for one, the items to be counted with words from the counting sequence in their customary order beginning with "one." As previously discussed, children develop an ear for the word sequence by about age one and a half. A similar study found that 18-month-olds (but not 15-month-olds) also have an eye for the item-by-item pointing routine that goes with the verbal sequence. As in the study mentioned earlier, the toddlers had control over the buttons that allowed them to watch whichever of two video clips they preferred. One clip showed a person pointing to each of six pictures of fish in turn while simultaneously saying the words "one" to "six" in the usual order. The other clip showed the same person saying the counting sequence while pointing to only two of the fish in an alternating manner. The 18-month-olds preferred the video of the standard pointing routine, while the 15-month-olds showed no preference between them. Moreover, these children from English-speaking families clearly understood that the pointing was connected to the verbal sequence: When they viewed the same two videos with either beeping sounds or Japanese counting words, they no longer expressed a preference for one video over the other. And when 18-month-olds from Japanese-speaking families viewed the same two videos in English or Japanese, they preferred the correct-routine video in Japanese, but showed no preference when the words were in English.[30] It should be noted that these toddlers' "preferences" were based on perceptual familiarity—other researchers have shown that children do not become *conceptually* (i.e., explicitly) aware of this one-to-one counting requirement until the age of four.[31]

Pointing while counting—as if physically pinning a name tag on each item—helps children to keep track of which items they have already counted and to coordinate the words with the items as they match them up.[32] (Many scholars refer to number words used in counting as "tags" and to counting as "tagging.") Spontaneous hand gestures, including pointing and finger counting, are linked to counting success in the early years.[33] In the brain, finger awareness and counting are closely related neural functions,[34] a topic to be taken up again in Chapter 7.

Some children, however, continue to have trouble coordinating pointing with counting after their classmates have mastered the skill. When a group of first- and second-graders with significant math difficulties were asked to judge a puppet's counting skill, many of them missed the fact that the puppet sometimes pointed to the first item twice, an unexpected error in first-graders.[35] It is easy to imagine how much trouble a child would have in learning basic arithmetic if she still had trouble with the counting routine.

CARDINALITY

So far, we have discussed the stable order of the counting-word sequence and the one-to-one correspondence between the words and the items to be counted. Which gets us to the cardinality principle, the idea that the last number word (tag) used in the stable-order list answers the question, *How many?* Up to this point, children have understood number words as referring to individual items, namely the particular item tagged by the particular word. Understanding that a number word can also refer to a *set* of objects is a major conceptual leap that some scholars describe as "an epiphany."[36]

Trying to figure out how children make that connection and what the consequences are has kept researchers very busy. A child's understanding that the last number word used to count a set is the number word that describes the numerosity of the set is usually tested by asking the child to "give me _____ [objects]." That is, the child must create a set described by that number word. Typically, the researcher places a pile of 30 or so buttons on the table. The researcher then says, "Give me three buttons," for example, and the child picks out three buttons and hands them to the researcher. Observations of children engaged in this task reveal that they may understand this principle as it pertains to "one," "two," and "three," say, but not to "four" or "five." For example, a child might respond correctly if you asked for "three buttons" but then would respond to a request for five buttons as if you had just asked for an unspecified "some buttons."[37] That is, they understand the cardinal value of one number word but not of a somewhat larger number word. Furthermore, children may understand some of the implications of cardinality but not others when applied to larger numbers. For example, in a study of young three-year-olds who could "give" (that is, create sets of) one, two, or three items, researchers found that the children correctly understood that a set labeled "eight" retains this label if the set is unchanged, that it is not also "four," and that "eight" is more than "two." However, they also incorrectly judged that a set of eight objects could just as well be labeled "four" and that "eight" continues to apply even though the set is increased by one, doubled, or halved, but not if it is rearranged—misunderstandings that they do not have in relation to sets of one, two, or three.[38] Moreover, creating a set of a particular cardinality is a surprisingly different task than simply counting the items in a given set, and the disconnect between them can be seen in the different performance levels of three- and four-year-olds when asked to perform these seemingly identical tasks.[39]

In another effort to understand what young children think about numbers, researchers showed the children a puppet ("Farmer Brown") and some plastic bananas, oranges, and strawberries. The researchers then told them, "Give Farmer Brown everything, but don't give him ___ banana(s)," where the blank was filled in by a quantifier ("a" or "some") or a number word inside ("one," "two") or outside ("five") their familiar set-creation range. When asked not to give "a banana" or "some bananas," the children correctly tended to give zero bananas. But when asked not to give a particular number of bananas, they tended to give another number of bananas, suggesting they knew that number words (even those outside their familiar set-creation range) were more specific than quantifiers. In a second experiment, the researchers then showed the children two animals, each with a collection of fish, one within and one outside the child's set-creation range, with a difference of two fish (see Figure 6.3). For illustration purposes, the child here knows how to create sets containing one, two, or three objects. When asked, "Who has four?" the child, who could identify which animal had two, correctly assumed the other one must have four. When asked, "Who does *not* have four?" the child could reason that it must be the animal with two. Finally, the child was asked, "Who has three?" and "Who does *not* have three?" The child correctly identified the animal with four fish and the animal with two fish, respectively, suggesting that the child knew that if you have four fish, you thereby also have three, and if you do not have three fish, you also cannot have four. Remarkably, when the child was pushed to make the same judgments about numbers that were all outside her set-creation range, she was still able to judge correctly, revealing an impressive level of logical and numerical reasoning.[40]

Finally, when other researchers asked preschoolers to give a number of objects just outside their familiar range (say, four in the case of children who were capable of creating sets of up to three), some could correctly and consistently give four; however, they would also sometimes give four in response to a request for another amount, say "five." Interestingly, on other measures of number-word understanding, these children performed better than children who could not give four but not as well as children who

FIGURE 6.3 Who has four? Who does *not* have four? Who has three? Who does *not* have three? *Adapted* from Feiman et al., 2019.

gave four only in response to requests for "four," suggesting that ideas about number expand in very subtle increments.[41]

Because the cardinality principle is the key insight that makes number words such an effective, uniquely human tool for keeping quantities from being just "a heap of confusion," researchers have attempted to see if they could find an effective way to teach it. The target children for these studies were generally those who could create sets of three objects but not of more than three. Several studies focused their efforts on showing children one set of four items at a time, labeling each set as "four," and comparing it to a set with a different number of items. These studies had some success in getting children to differentiate sets of four items from sets with other numerosities, although one of the studies found that even after training, the children still labeled sets of five or six items as "four."[42] Other researchers saw some improvement by labeling the set "four" and then immediately counting the four items—"Four rabbits! One, two, three, four rabbits!"—a strategy that parents actually seldom use.[43] Still, the results of these efforts were limited.

In order to learn more about the timing of cardinality understanding, researchers followed a group of 197 children over two years of preschool, from about age three and a half to five and a half years old. Fifty-six of the children entered preschool able to create sets of five or six objects. and 96 more learned to do so during their fifth year. By the end of the study, sometime early in their sixth year, 18 of the children could not yet create sets of five or six objects. The researchers found that children who mastered this task early tended to have higher general intelligence, know more counting words and numerals, and have a better intuitive grasp of relative non-symbolic quantity (discussed in Chapter 2) than their peers. Those children who lagged behind on the task, by contrast, were weaker in those areas and also had difficulty with letter recognition, as well as with flexible thinking (a topic of Chapter 1).[44]

Early research on the cardinality principle concluded that once children understood the cardinal meaning of "three" or "four," they could generalize this "epiphany" to all larger numbers. And in fact, the study just discussed found that most, but not all, of the children who understood the cardinal meaning of "four" could, in fact, correctly create sets of five and six objects. More recent research, however, has found that fully understanding the cardinality principle and its implications can take years and require a lot of imitation, practice, and reinforcement.[45] For example, one study found that some children can create a small set of objects and do indeed know that the last word says *how many* but have not yet landed on a stable counting sequence. Hence, one child—who on another occasion or in another context could count "one, two, three, four, five"—when asked for five of the objects in front of her, counted out "one, two, five!" and handed over three.[46] Other children do not understand how one would know the next number in the sequence; in one study, even after learning to label a set "four" correctly, the children still could not say whether "five" or "six" comes next. Nor could they correctly order cards with sets of one to seven dots on them.[47] Others could create sets of ten, 12, or even 21 objects, but only a third of those children could name the number that comes next in the counting sequence, while another third started counting again from "one" to figure it out, and the rest had no idea.[48] And many children who can create a set with a small number of objects do not know which of two numbers in their counting-word list stands for a greater number of objects—the later the number word in the sequence, the greater the value, or the *later-greater* principle—unless they actually count out the objects.[49] Nor do many know that the difference between successive numbers in the counting sequence is the same amount as one thing. In fact, it takes years of counting experience for children to arrive at the idea that, regardless of the number you start with, you can always add one to it.[50]

With lots of experience counting objects, however, children do learn how the counting words attach to different numerosities, starting with the smallest amounts and gradually working up. They figure out that each number word belongs with one and only one numerosity and that each number word in turn accounts for one more object than the previous number word. In the process, bigger numbers become progressively less fuzzy in their minds.[51]

In all, then, the "epiphany" that the last number word used to create a set of objects answers the question *How many?* is a very protracted process that does not happen in an instant or automatically generalize to all numbers. Children learn the cardinal meaning of number words one numerosity at time, not just for "one," "two," "three," and "four," but progressively for larger numbers as well, although the process speeds up with time and experience. Moreover, the age when a child finally comes to understand that the cardinality principle—the last number used to create a set tells *how many*—applies to all numerosities is highly variable from child to child and may only come into focus at age six or even later for some children.[52]

This protracted and highly variable developmental trajectory has some practical implications for the preschool playground. Take, for example, all those squabbles about how so-and-so was not sharing something fairly. In a series of studies, the researchers had children share some stickers equally with a puppet; they also asked the children how some candies *should* be shared. Readers who have reached this point in the chapter will not be surprised at their findings: The children all knew that it was morally important to share fairly—and, crucially, they thought that they had! Their errors on the sharing task were largely a reflection of the gaps in their understanding of number and counting. As the researchers reported, there was "little support for the insufficient motivation hypothesis."[53] And indeed, such "resource distribution" activities can be particularly fertile ground for verbal number-word, quantifier,[54] and cardinality practice and instruction.

Before we conclude this section on cardinality, a few words about subitizing are in order. Subitizing, as introduced in Chapter 3, is the highly efficient judgment of the numerosity (cardinal value) of a small set. Preschoolers will count objects one by one at every opportunity. As counting becomes easier with lots and lots of practice and attention, however, most children come to realize that they can enumerate the smallest sets (up to three) more efficiently by drawing on their perceptual skills to subitize. Subitizing is often characterized as instant, at-a-glance recognition of a numerosity. However, close observation reveals a tiny increase in the time it takes to recognize three objects compared to two objects, suggesting that subitizing is simply a highly efficient form of counting. While picking out and tracking small numerosities of objects are perceptual skills, as discussed in Chapter 3, subitizing adds a cognitive component that is facilitated by counting mastery and knowledge of the cardinality principle. The speed and efficiency of subitizing varies depending on the numerosity and the child's level of attention to the task. Above the visual subitizing limit (typically three for children, four for adults), recognition time increases noticeably as the numerosity increases, suggesting that regular counting is necessary above that limit.[55]

Another perceptual skill that can facilitate set-size determination is what has been called *groupitizing*—that is, by visualizing large sets of objects as groups of subitizing-range arrays, such as nine items grouped into three groups of three. As noted in Chapter 3, certain iconic arrays, such as those on dice, playing cards, and finger displays, also facilitate subitizing above the usual range. In fact, a study of ten-year-olds found that the brain registered those amounts automatically as well.[56] Both of these strategies potentially raise the number of subitizable items well over three. Indeed, some scholars have speculated that subitizing is based on general pattern recognition,[57] a speculation that receives some support from the finding that subitizing activates brain regions responsive to visual patterns.[58]

Children become more efficient at subitizing with age, and by age 11 children can typically subitize as efficiently as adults. Indeed, age differences in efficiency are more marked in the counting range (four and more) than in the lower, subitizing range for older children.[59] As to the question of whether subitizing skill is in some way associated with differences in math achievement, the findings are mixed, at least for typical math students.[60] However, there is scientific agreement that some children with severe math difficulties do struggle to subitize efficiently, not only in the range of one to three items but, for some, also in the range of five to nine items arranged in familiar, iconic arrays.[61]

ABSTRACTION

The last two remaining counting principles, the abstraction and order-irrelevance principles, can also take a while to mature. We start with the abstraction principle. To abstract is to find a common thread or overarching category that unites a disparate set of things or ideas. At its most basic, it involves regarding a picture of an object as representing the object, or an object as representing a kind of object. So, for example, a picture of a pig represents a pig, and a pig is an example of things that go "oink" and are called "pigs." More abstractly, a pig is also an example of the larger category of "animals." These are difficult intellectual leaps for small children. Applying a number word to describe a set is an especially difficult example of abstraction. Most children can understand a set of pigs, in which each pig bears the identifying characteristics of a pig. But it is a conceptual leap to understand how the abstract word "six," which does not—cannot—describe an individual pig, could also describe this set. Thus, a study of three-year-olds who were capable of creating small sets of objects found that the children could be taught to tell the numerical difference between a picture of four pigs and pictures of other numerosities of pigs but were unable to apply that knowledge to a new picture of four horses. Their notion of "four" was tied to *that* picture of *those* pigs.[62] Similarly, a group of three- to six-year-olds could identify which of two sets of pigs had six pigs, but unless they verbally counted, they were less accurate in identifying which of two sets had six animals.[63] Yet more abstractly, of course, number words can apply to all manner of things real, remembered, and imagined, including objects, ideas—even counting principles.

ORDER-IRRELEVANCE

The order-irrelevance principle is typically the last counting feature to fall into place. It is unusual for preschoolers, for example, to recognize that it does not matter in what order the items in a set are counted. Some researchers have observed that fixed ideas of order (e.g., left to right) actually help some young children master ordinal tasks, while others have noted that in kindergarten the best math students adhere to their belief in a fixed counting order because structure helps them learn. In fact, some have observed that the rigidity of children's ideas about counting order actually increases in the early grades before it lets up later, as it becomes easier to remember which items have already been counted and children can appreciate the abstract nature of the exercise. Indeed, counting in an orderly fashion often makes it easier—for children and adults—to keep track of what has been counted and what has not.[64] For this reason, we did not include an order-irrelevance activity in this chapter. Some researchers have noted that second-graders with significant math learning difficulties do not recognize the order-irrelevance principle, but other studies have found that typical second-graders have trouble with it, too.[65]

Delving into the question of which unusual counting orders were more or less acceptable for students, researchers asked children in grades two, three, and four to judge the correctness of counting performed by characters in a computer animation game. For half of the children, the character explicitly stated the cardinal value after counting; for the other half, the character did not state the cardinal value. The characters counted with four different pseudo-errors: 1) counting all of the objects but not in adjacent order; 2) tagging each of the objects with a unique number word but saying only some of the words aloud; 3) skipping one item and then returning to it or using the same number word to tag one item three times; and 4) alternating or reversing the usual left-to-right direction. The researchers found that the children were more accepting of the first and fourth methods—that is, of non-adjacent and non–left-right counting—than of the other two options. However, those who were presented with the cardinal value were more tolerant of all of the pseudo-errors and more easily recognized the optional nature of the non-essential counting features.[66] It is typically not until about fifth grade that children can begin to see the more abstract nature of counting.[67]

COUNTING AT THE START OF KINDERGARTEN

If you are a teacher or prospective teacher, you may be wondering where this developmental trajectory leaves children at the end of preschool—what skills do children bring through the door with them on their first day of kindergarten? Some researchers asked that

TABLE 6.2 The Counting Skills of 97 Children at the Beginning of Kindergarten

No. of children	Skill
97	Could begin the counting sequence
9	Could count to 30
84	Could count six items correctly when they were in view
33	Could count six items correctly from memory after they were hidden
13	Could count to six by rote but not apply it
57	Could determine that two sets of objects had the same numerosity, but some children had to count to decide
14	Knew that a set of objects kept the same numerosity even when the pieces were moved around
94	Recognized that a set of five items and a set of seven items were unequal and knew which set was larger
30	Could point to "the third car"
24	Could state the ordinal name for an item in a series
22	Could order four sets of different numerosities correctly

Adapted from Fischer & Beckey, 1990.

question of 97 kindergartners, aged four years 10 months to five years 11 months, at the beginning of the school year. Their findings are reported in Table 6.2. It is important to note that the children in the study were from middle-class homes; children from low-income homes may present a different picture.[68] Table 13.1 in Chapter 13 contains additional data about the general numeracy skills of five-year-olds from a more recent nationally representative demographic sample that includes children in Head Start preschools.

Several studies of children from low-income families have demonstrated the importance of preschool counting for later arithmetic achievement. While some young children may know the verbal counting sequence, delayed understanding of the cardinal values of at least some of the number words as early as the first year of preschool can place children at risk for math difficulties as late as first grade. Even those who catch on to the meaning of number words during the second year of preschool can later show subtle deficits in understanding the quantities represented by numerals and arithmetic manipulations.[69] Conversely, while some young children with weak verbal abilities may understand problems that are presented non-verbally (e.g., with disks)—that is, they understand the values but not the verbal tags—and are able to respond in kind,[70] they find themselves at a distinct disadvantage in a classroom where arithmetic is taught verbally. Success requires knowing both the number words and what they mean.

CONCLUSION

The counting system is a complex machine with many moving parts. Consequently, it can take young children several years of persistent observation, experimentation, and practice to figure out how it works. Once mastered, however, the number words provide a remarkable "technology" for keeping track of large numerosities and communicating about them.

ACTIVITIES

In the following activities, carefully choose the manipulatives and how they are presented. The visual richness and familiarity of the objects influence children's ability to count. Manipulatives that are highly familiar and/or perceptually rich, such as cute animal figures, might distract children from the counting task.[71] Children may be more successful on counting tasks when using simpler manipulatives such as buttons, Popsicle sticks, or plastic chips. In addition, most beginning counters will benefit from using manipulatives that are the same size within a given set and arranged in a line rather than in an array or scattered arrangement.[72] As children become more skilled counters, they should practice counting objects of varying sizes in different arrangements, such as small and large buttons arranged in rows and columns. In the following activities involving objects, make sure to emphasize the cardinal value by repeating the last number counted and the name of the object, such as, "one, two, three—three buttons." Count slowly, pointing to each object one at a time, to emphasize one-to-one correspondence. These activities can be modified based on the age and skill of the children, keeping to smaller numbers with younger children and expanding to greater numbers with older children.

ACTIVITY 6.1: Counting the Base-10 Way

Objective: To learn the counting sequence and meaning of the number names in the English language using the base-10 system.[73] Some English number names are phonologically complex and not directly related to the base-10 system, leading to confusion and slowed rates of learning to count. Children who speak some East Asian languages in which number names are directly related to the base-10 system learn to count accurately and demonstrate mastery of arithmetic sooner. English-speaking children should experience counting the base-10 way as early as possible and continue to have experience doing so over time. All of the activities presented here can be completed counting the base-10 way or alternating with counting in English.

- **First:** Line up ten counters of the same color in a row. Counting from the children's left to their right, slowly touch and count each object to ten. Leave a space before the next set of ten, which will be in a new color. Add a counter in this new color and say, "Ten and one." Add another counter in this new color and say, "Ten and two." Continue in this way to 19 ("ten and nine"). Complete the second group of ten and say, "two tens."
- **Next:** Count on from there, adding counters in a third group of ten with a new color and say, "Two tens and one. Two tens and two." Continue counting to higher numbers as tolerated.

- **Next:** To learn the English number names, start again from the beginning. After the first group of ten, when adding on say, "Ten and one. The name for this number is eleven. It means ten and one." Continue counting the base-10 way first, then saying the English number name and what it means.
- **Next:** This activity can be completed on a number line or number chart with the numerals showing.

The Verbal Number Sequence

ACTIVITY 6.2: Learning the Counting Words With Movement

Objective: To learn the verbal number sequence, the stable order principle, and the cardinality principle. Children experience hearing and saying the count list in the correct order while moving. Prior to these activities, help children process the sounds in the number names by saying them slowly and exaggerating the sounds. Children often first hear the number sequence as all one word, "onetwothreefourfive," so pause between each number such that each name can be easily distinguished as separate while learning the counting words. For higher numbers, exaggerate the final sounds such as in "thirteen" /n/ and "thirty" /ee/ to contrast them. Feel the sounds in the mouth and listen to how the number names "thirteen" and "thirty" are similar and different and demonstrate the difference in their meaning. The same can be done for the other number names that end in "-teen" and their "-ty" corollary. Movement helps to reinforce children's experience and may be helpful to fidgety children with attention deficits.

- **Punch the air:** Call out a number from "four" to "ten," beginning with the smaller numbers. Children punch the air with alternating hands the number of times called. Start punching and counting slowly with a pause between each punch, like a martial artist. Work toward punching more quickly. Once children master punching to "ten," practice counting on: "Let's add two more. Eleven, twelve."
- **Take steps:** Line up children shoulder to shoulder. Going from their left to their right, have children count and take a designated number of steps. The first child takes one step, counting, "one." The second child takes two steps, counting, "one, two" (and is now one step past the first child). Continue until each child steps forward.
- **Pass and shoot:** Line children up shoulder to shoulder and give a ball to the first child on their left. Children pass the ball down the line the number of times the adult calls out, and the child holding the ball at the end runs to shoot the

ball into a basket. Continue until each child gets a turn. Then start at the end of the line and count backward to the number called out, and that child runs to shoot the ball.

- **Line up:** Line children up for a transition such as going outside. Beginning at the front of the line, the children count in turn until reaching the end of the line. On other days, start at the end of the line and count from the total number of children backward.
- **Hopscotch:** Using tape or chalk, play hopscotch to *10*, calling out the numbers as they hop. Then, start at *10* and hop back to *1*.
- **How many?** How many times can you jump? How many times can you pass a ball without dropping it? How many times can you hit a balloon and keep it in the air?

ACTIVITY 6.3: Flexible Verbal Counting

Objective: To learn the verbal number sequence, the stable order principle, and the cardinality principle. Once children learn to recite the counting words in order, they can practice counting flexibly by counting on from mid-sequence, counting backward, and skip counting. We include the use of a number line or number chart in this activity even though we have not formally introduced written numerals to promote a number-rich environment and to provide something for children to count (a visual anchor) while extending their counting to higher numbers. Here are some activities that promote flexible counting:

- **First:** Counting forward and backward by one: Have children sit side by side in a row and count off from their left to their right. The first child says "one" and stands, then the second child says "two" and stands, and so on. When all children are standing, they reverse the sequence by counting backward and sitting down, one by one.
- **Next:** Musical counting: Have children sit in a circle while you play recorded instrumental music. A child starts with "one," then the children proceed to count around the circle. Stop the music intermittently. When the music stops, children reverse the count and start counting backward, going in the opposite direction in the circle. When the music stops again, start counting forward again.
- **Next:** Counting from mid-sequence: Children count aloud together from a starting number. For example, "Let's start counting on from eleven. Eleven, twelve, thirteen. . . ." You may point to the numbers on a number line or number chart as children count to higher and less familiar numbers to provide a visual anchor.
- **Next:** Skip counting: Children count aloud together by *ten*s and then count backward by *ten*s. As children become more fluent counters, they can skip count forward and backward by *five*s and later by *two*s.

One-to-One Tagging (Counting)

ACTIVITY 6.4: Count, Cover, and Make a Set

Objective: To learn the cardinality principle and one-to-one counting. Children improve their ability to count after an adult demonstrates both counting and labeling the amount, reinforcing the cardinality principle.[74] In this activity, children learn by watching an adult count a set, practice counting along with the adult, and immediately make the same set on their own.

■   **First:** Demonstrate how to create a set of items using manipulatives such as plastic chips: "Watch me make a group of five! One, two, three, four, five. Five chips." Ask children to count along with you: "Let's check to make sure there are really five. Count with me and touch each chip. . . . Five chips." Then ask children to create a set that has the same number of objects as your set. "Now you make a group that has the same number of chips as my group." Make sure that children repeat the last count with the label: "five chips."

■   **Next:** After creating and counting a set of items, cover your set with a sheet of paper and invite children to re-create the set themselves from memory. Then uncover yours and check if both groups have the same amount. Give children practice counting increasingly larger sets of objects.

■   **Next:** Have children play with a partner, taking turns creating the set and copying the set.

Cardinality

ACTIVITY 6.5: Count and Produce a Set of Objects

Objective: To learn cardinality and one-to-one counting. Children practice counting and producing a set of objects, with particular emphasis on naming its cardinal value. Use a puppet, stuffed animal, or doll as a prop along with manipulatives, such as Popsicle sticks.

■   **First:** Explain that the puppet wants to share some Popsicle sticks, but it sometimes makes counting mistakes. Children ask for a number of Popsicle sticks between three and five, "May I please have four Popsicle sticks?" Children try to catch the puppet making a mistake by counting to make sure that the puppet gave them the correct amount. Show children a set of one to five Popsicle sticks. For example, "The puppet is supposed to give you four sticks. Can you count to make sure there are really four sticks?" Vary between showing the correct and incorrect quantity. Repeat the process using larger sets of six or more Popsicle sticks.

■ **Next:** Have children give Popsicle sticks to the puppet. Say, "Let's share some sticks! Can you take five sticks out of the bucket and give them to the puppet?" Start with quantities of five or fewer and eventually progress to sets of ten or more.

ACTIVITY 6.6: Egg Carton Math

Objective: To practice counting. An egg carton's distinct compartments and layout of rows and columns make it suitable for activities involving one-to-one correspondence and skip counting by *two*s. Use ten cards, each with a different numeral *0* to *10*.

■ **First:** Cut two compartments off one end of an egg carton so that it resembles a ten-frame with two rows of five compartments. Place the stack of cards face down on the table. Children turn over the top card and count out the number on it. As they count, they place counters into the carton, one per compartment, until they reach the target number. If the child draws the *0* card, they simply say, "Zero. There is nothing in the carton!"

■ **Next:** Practice skip counting by *two*s. Place one counter each in the first two compartments in the egg carton and say "two." Continue to the next two compartments and say "four." Continue until the carton is full.

ACTIVITY 6.7: Counting in the Real World

Objective: To learn to count during common activities. Research suggests that informal math activities embedded in real-world contexts can promote children's understanding of formal math concepts.[75] The following activities provide children with authentic counting experiences that relate math to their everyday lives.

■ **Setting the table:** Have children count out plates, cups, forks, spoons, and napkins to set on the table.

■ **Grocery shopping:** Count out food and grocery items in the store or in the dramatic play center. For example, "Our list says six bananas. Can you count six bananas?"

■ **Storybook reading:** Count how many objects are in the pictures. "Can you find and count the acorns in the picture?"

■ **Cooking:** Estimate and count ingredients as they go into a recipe. For example, first guess how many grapes you'll use in a fruit salad and then count the grapes as you make the salad.

■ **Count while cleaning:** Count items, such as toys, as children put them away. After all the items are put away, have children name how many there are altogether.

■ **Count objects on a walk:** While walking around the neighborhood, find things to count. For example, first count all the red cars, then count all the blue cars.

- **Board games:** Play board games with linear paths, such as Chutes and Ladders or Parcheesi. Using traditional dot dice during the game can improve children's counting skills more than using dice with numerals.[76]

Abstraction

ACTIVITY 6.8: Make a Set of Diverse Objects and Engage Executive Functioning Skills

Objective: To learn the abstraction principle by creating diverse sets. For this activity, use objects that vary across multiple features, such as size, color, and shape. As the activity progresses and children create sets that vary by two or more features, they also exercise their executive functioning skill of inhibition as they focus on relevant information and ignore irrelevant information. Have a variety of objects available from which children can make diverse sets, such as a variety of shapes or blocks of different sizes and colors.

- **First:** Children create a set of objects based on one feature, such as size. "Give me six big objects." The objects do not have to be the same—they just need to be six big objects.
- **Next:** Children create a set of objects based on two features, such as size and shape. "Give me eight small squares."
- **Next:** Children create a set of objects based on three features, such as size, shape, and color. "Give me five small blue triangles."

ACTIVITY 6.9: Counting and Matching Card Games

Objective: To recognize and count objects in diverse configurations. Create dot cards by placing circular stickers on index cards with two configurations of each number. For example, create one card that shows four dots arranged in a row and another card that shows four dots in a scattered arrangement. Each game ends when there are no cards remaining.

- **Match or no match:** Children start with five cards each. They take turns turning over a card from the draw pile and counting the dots. If the card from the draw pile matches one of their cards, they take both cards and put them to the side. A match has the same quantity but a different display. For example, one card in the pair shows seven dots in an orderly array and the other card shows seven scattered dots. If the card from the draw pile does not match one of their cards, children add it to their deck.
- **Go fish:** Children start with five cards each and take turns asking another child for a card that matches one of theirs: "Do you have a six?" If the other player doesn't have the requested card, the child takes a card from the draw pile.
- **Memory:** Lay all the cards face down on the table. Children take turns turning over two cards to find matching cards that show the same quantity but a different arrangement of dots.
- **Not-the-number:** Lay all the cards face-up on the table. Have children identify a card that is not a given number: "Give me a card that is not nine."

NOTES

1   Gelman, 2000.

2   Dowker, 2008; Fischer & Beckey, 1990.

3   Fuson, 1988.

4   Fuson, 1988.

5   Elliott et al., 2017; Gunderson & Levine, 2011.

6   Gjicali et al., 2019.

7   Foster et al., 2019; Méndez et al., 2019.

8   Snowling et al., 2021.

9   Ip et al., 2018.

10 Wang & Feigenson, 2019.

11 VanRinsveld et al., 2020.

12 Hurewitz et al., 2006.

13 Barrouillet et al., 2010.

14 Michalczyk et al., 2013; Soto-Calvo et al., 2015.

15 Koponen et al., 2020.

16 Donlan et al., 2007; Fazio, 1996.

17 Bull, 2008.

18 Guerrero et al., 2020; Miller et al., 2005.

19 Miller et al., 1995.

20 Stigler et al., 1986.

21 Geary et al., 1996.

22 Miller et al., 2005.

23 Miller et al., 2005.

24 Miller et al., 1995.

25 Miller et al., 2000.

26 Schneider et al., 2021.

27 Schneider et al., 2020.

28 Johansson, 2005.

29 Sella & Lucangeli, 2020.

30 Slaughter et al., 2011.

31 Briars & Siegler, 1984.

32 Alibali & DiRusso, 1999.

33 Gordon et al., 2021.

34 Penner-Wilger & Anderson, 2013.

35 Geary et al., 1992.

36 Sarnecka & Gelman, 2004.

37 Gelman et al., 2019.

38 Condry & Spelke, 2008.

39 Mou et al., 2021.

40 Feiman et al., 2019.

41 O'Rear et al., 2020.

42 Carey et al., 2017; Huang et al., 2010.

43 Mix et al., 2012; Posid & Cordes, 2018.

44 Geary et al., 2019.

45 Mix et al., 2005; Sarnecka, 2015.

46 Wynn, 1992.

47 Spaepen et al., 2018.

48 Dowker, 2008.

49 LeCorre, 2014.

50 Cheung et al., 2017; Davidson et al., 2012.

51 Shusterman et al., 2017; Slusser et al., 2013.

52 Rousselle & Vossius, 2021.

53 Chernyak et al., 2019.

54 Chernyak, 2020.

55 Katzin et al., 2019.

56 Marlair et al., 2021.

57 Jansen et al., 2014; Starkey & McCandliss, 2014.

58 Bloechle et al., 2018.

59 Schleifer & Landerl, 2011.

60 Anobile et al., 2019; Starkey & McCandliss, 2021.

61 Ashkenazi et al., 2013; Schleifer & Landerl, 2011.

62 Carey et al., 2017.

63 Posid & Cordes, 2015.

64 Briars & Siegler, 1984; Kamawar et al., 2010.

65 Geary, 2004; Rodríguez et al., 2013.

66 Lago et al., 2016.

67 Kamawar et al., 2010.

68 Klibanoff et al., 2006.

69 Chu et al., 2019.

70 Jordan et al., 1994.

71 McNeil & Jarvin, 2007.

72 See Ward et al., 2017, for a description of the features of objects and images that support counting.
73 Magargee & Beauford, 2016.
74 Mix et al., 2012.
75 Zhang et al., 2020.
76 Gasteiger & Moeller, 2021.

REFERENCES

The following references were cited in this chapter. For additional selected references relevant to this chapter, please see Chapter 6 Supplemental References in eResources.

Alibali, M.W., & DiRusso, A.A. (1999). The function of gesture in learning to count: More than keeping track. *Cognitive Development, 14*, 37–56.

Anobile, G., Arrighi, R., & Burr, D.C. (2019). Simultaneous and sequential subitizing are separate systems, and neither predicts math abilities. *Journal of Experimental Child Psychology, 178*, 86–103.

Ashkenazi, S., Mark-Zigdon, N., & Henik, A. (2013). Do subitizing deficits in developmental dyscalculia involve pattern recognition weakness? *Developmental Science, 16*, 35–46.

Barrouillet, P., Thevenot, C., & Fayol, M. (2010). Evidence for knowledge of the syntax of large numbers in preschoolers. *Journal of Experimental Child Psychology, 105*, 264–271.

Bloechle, J., Huber, S., Klein, E., Bahnmueller, J., Moeller, K., Rennig, J. (2018). Neuro-cognitive mechanisms of global Gestalt perception in visual quantification. *NeuroImage, 181*, 359–369.

Briars, D., & Siegler, R.S. (1984). A featural analysis of preschoolers' counting knowledge. *Developmental Psychology, 20*, 607–618.

Bull, R. (2008). Deafness, numerical cognition, and mathematics. In M. Marschark & P.C. Hauser (Eds.), *Deaf cognition: Foundations and outcomes* (pp. 170–200). Oxford University Press.

Carey, S., Shusterman, A., Haward, P., & Distefano, R. (2017). Do analog number representations underlie the meanings of young children's verbal numerals? *Cognition, 168*, 243–255.

Chernyak, N. (2020). Number-based sharing: Conversation about quantity in the context of resource distribution. *Early Childhood Research Quarterly, 50*, 90–96.

Chernyak, N., Harris, P.L., & Cordes, S. (2019). Explaining early moral hypocrisy: Numerical cognition promotes equal sharing behavior in preschool-aged children. *Developmental Science, 22*, e12695.

Cheung, P., Rubenson, M., & Barner, D. (2017). To infinity and beyond: Children generalize the successor function to all possible numbers years after learning to count. *Cognitive Psychology, 92*, 22–36.

Chu, F.W., vanMarle, K., Hoard, M.K., Nugent, L., Scofield, J.E., & Geary, D.C. (2019). Preschool deficits in cardinal knowledge and executive function contribute to longer-term mathematical learning disability. *Journal of Experimental Child Psychology, 188*, 104668.

Condry, K.F., & Spelke, E.S. (2008). The development of language and abstract concepts: The case of natural number. *Journal of Experimental Psychology: General, 137*, 22–38.

Davidson, K., Eng, K., & Barner, D. (2012). Does learning to count involve a semantic induction? *Cognition, 123*, 162–173.

Donlan, C., Cowan, R., Newton, E.J., & Lloyd, D. (2007). The role of language in mathematical development: Evidence from children with specific language impairments. *Cognition, 103*, 23–33.

Dowker, A. (2008). Individual differences in numerical abilities in preschoolers. *Developmental Science, 11*, 650–654.

Elliott, L., Braham, E.J., & Libertus, M.E. (2017). Understanding sources of individual variability in parents' number talk with young children. *Journal of Experimental Child Psychology, 159*, 1–15.

Fazio, B.B. (1996). Mathematical abilities of children with specific language impairment: A 2-year follow-up study. *Journal of Speech and Hearing Research, 39*, 839–849.

Feiman, R., Hartshorne, J.K., & Barner, D. (2019). Contrast and entailment: Abstract logical relations constrain how 2- and 3-year-old children interpret unknown numbers. *Cognition, 183*, 192–207.

Fischer, F.E., & Beckey, R.D. (1990). Beginning kindergartener's perception of number. *Perceptual and Motor Skills, 70*, 419–425.

Foster, M.E., Anthony, J.L., Zucker, T.A., & Branum-Martin, L. (2019). Prediction of English and Spanish kindergarten mathematics from English and Spanish cognitive and linguistic abilities in Hispanic dual language learners. *Early Childhood Research Quarterly, 46*, 213–227.

Fuson, K.C. (1988). *Children's counting and concepts of number*. Springer-Verlag.

Gasteiger, H., & Moeller, K. (2021). Fostering early numerical competencies by playing conventional board games. *Journal of Experimental Child Psychology, 204*, 105060.

Geary, D.C. (2004). Mathematics and learning disabilities. *Journal of Learning Disabilities, 37*, 4–15.

Geary, D.C., Bow-Thomas, C.C., Liu, F., & Siegler, R.S. (1996). Development of arithmetical competencies in Chinese and American children: Influence of age, language, and schooling. *Child Development, 67*, 2022–2044.

Geary, D.C., Bow-Thomas, C.C., & Yao, Y. (1992). Counting knowledge and skill in cognitive addition: A comparison of normal and mathematically disabled children. *Journal of Experimental Child Psychology, 54*, 372–391.

Geary, D.C., vanMarle, K., Chu, F.W., Hoard, M.K., & Nugent, L. (2019). Predicting age of becoming a cardinal principle knower. *Journal of Educational Psychology, 111*, 256–267.

Gelman, R. (2000). The epigenesis of mathematical thinking. *Journal of Applied Developmental Psychology, 21*, 27–37.

Gelman, S.A., Leslie, S.-J., Gelman, R., & Leslie, A. (2019). Do children recall numbers as generic? A strong test of the generics-as-default hypothesis. *Language Learning and Development, 15*, 217–231.

Gjicali, K., Astuto, J., & Lipnevich, A.A. (2019). Relations among language comprehension, oral counting, and numeral knowledge of ethnic and racial minority young children from low-income communities. *Early Childhood Research Quarterly, 46*, 5–19.

Gordon, R., Scalise, N.R., & Ramani, G.B. (2021). Give yourself a hand: The role of gesture and working memory in preschoolers' numerical knowledge. *Journal of Experimental Child Psychology, 208*, 105145.

Guerrero, D., Hwang, J., Boutin, B., Roeper, T., & Park, J. (2020). Is thirty-two three tens and two ones? The embedded structure of cardinal numbers. *Cognition, 203*, 104331.

Gunderson, E.A., & Levine, S.C. (2011). Some types of parent number talk count more than others: Relations between parents' input and children's cardinal-number knowledge. *Developmental Science, 14*, 1021–1032.

Huang, Y.T., Spelke, E., & Snedeker, J. (2010). When is *four* far more than *three*? Children's generalization of newly acquired number words. *Psychological Science, 21*, 600–606.

Hurewitz, F., Papafragou, A., Gleitman, L., & Gelman, R. (2006). Asymmetries in the acquisition of numbers and quantifiers. *Language Learning and Development, 2*, 77–96.

Ip, M.H.K., Imuta, K., & Slaughter, V. (2018). Which button will I press? Preference for correctly ordered counting sequences in 18-month-olds. *Developmental Psychology, 54*, 1199–1207.

Jansen, B.R.J., Hofman, A.D., Straatemeier, M., vanBers, B.M.C.W., Raijmakers, M.E.J., & van der Maas, H.L.J. (2014). The role of pattern recognition in children's exact enumeration of small numbers. *British Journal of Developmental Psychology, 32*, 178–194.

Johansson, B.S. (2005). Number-word sequence skill and arithmetic performance. *Scandinavian Journal of Psychology, 46,* 157–167.

Jordan, N.C., Huttenlocher, J., & Levine, S.C. (1994). Assessing early arithmetic abilities: Effects of verbal and nonverbal response types on the calculation performance of middle- and low-income children. *Learning and Individual Differences, 6,* 413–432.

Kamawar, D., LeFevre, J.-A., Bisanz, J., Fast, L., Skwarchuk, S.-L., Smith-Chant, B., & Penner-Wilger, M. (2010). Knowledge of counting principles: How relevant is order irrelevance? *Journal of Experimental Child Psychology, 105,* 138–145.

Katzin, N., Cohen, Z.Z., & Henik, A. (2019). If it looks, sounds, or feels like subitizing, is it subitizing? A modulated definition of subitizing. *Psychonomic Bulletin & Review, 26,* 790–797.

Klibanoff, R.S., Levine, S.C., Huttenlocher, J., Vasilyeva, M., & Hedges, L.V. (2006). Preschool children's mathematical knowledge: The effect of teacher "math talk." *Developmental Psychology, 42,* 59–69.

Koponen, T., Eklund, K., Heikkilä, R., Salminen, J., Fuchs, L., Fuchs, D., & Aro, M. (2020). Cognitive correlates of the covariance in reading and arithmetic fluency: Importance of serial retrieval fluency. *Child Development, 91,* 1063–1080.

Lago, M.O., Rodríguez, P., Escudero, A., & Dopico, C. (2016). Detection of counting pseudo-errors: What helps children accept them? *British Journal of Developmental Psychology, 34,* 169–180.

LeCorre, M. (2014). Children acquire the later-greater principle after the cardinal principle. *British Journal of Developmental Psychology, 32,* 163–177.

Magargee, S.D., & Beauford, J.E. (2016). Do explicit number names accelerate pre-kindergarteners' numeracy and place value acquisition? *Educational Studies in Mathematics, 92,* 179–192.

Marlair, C., Lochy, A., Buyle, M., Schiltz, C., & Crollen, V. (2021). Canonical representations of fingers and dots trigger an automatic activation of number semantics: An EEG study on 10-year-old children. *Neuropsychologia, 157,* 107874.

McNeil, N.M., & Jarvin, L. (2007). When theories don't add up: Disentangling the manipulatives debate. *Theory into Practice, 46,* 309–316.

Méndez, L.I., Hammer, C.S., Lopez, L.M., & Blair, C. (2019). Examining language and early numeracy skills in young Latino dual language learners. *Early Childhood Research Quarterly, 46,* 252–261.

Michalczyk, K., Krajewski, K., Preßler, A.-L., & Hasselhorn, M. (2013). The relationships between quantity-number competencies, working memory, and phonological awareness in 5- and 6-year-olds. *British Journal of Developmental Psychology, 31,* 408–424.

Miller, K.F., Kelly, M., & Zhou, X. (2005). Learning mathematics in China and the United States: Cross-cultural insights into the nature and course of preschool mathematical development. In J.I.D. Campbell (Ed.), *Handbook of mathematical cognition* (pp. 163–178). Psychology Press.

Miller, K.F., Major, S.M., Shu, H., & Zhang, H. (2000). Ordinal knowledge: Number names and number concepts in Chinese and English. *Canadian Journal of Experimental Psychology, 54,* 129–139.

Miller, K.F., Smith, C.M., Zhu, J., & Zhang, H. (1995). Preschool origins of cross-national differences in mathematical competence: The role of number-naming systems. *Psychological Science, 6,* 56–60.

Mix, K.S., Sandhofer, C.M., & Baroody, A.J. (2005). Number words and number concepts: The interplay of verbal and nonverbal quantification in early childhood. *Advances in Child Development and Behavior, 33,* 305–346.

Mix, K.S., Sandhofer, C.M., Moore, J.A., & Russell, C. (2012). Acquisition of the cardinal word principle: The role of input. *Early Childhood Research Quarterly, 27,* 274–283.

Mou, Y., Zhang, B., Piazza, M., & Hyde, D.C. (2021). Comparing set-to-number and number-to-set measures of cardinal number knowledge in preschool children using latent variable modeling. *Early Childhood Research Quarterly, 54*, 125–135.

O'Rear, C.D., McNeil, N.M., & Kirkland, P.K. (2020). Partial knowledge in the development of number word understanding. *Developmental Science, 23*, e12944.

Penner-Wilger, M., & Anderson, M.L. (2013). The relation between finger gnosis and mathematical ability: Why redeployment of neural circuits best explains the finding. *Frontiers in Psychology, 4*, 877.

Posid, T., & Cordes, S. (2015). Verbal counting moderates perceptual biases found in children's cardinality judgments. *Journal of Cognition and Development, 16*, 621–637.

Posid, T., & Cordes, S. (2018). How high can you count? Probing the limits of children's counting. *Developmental Psychology, 54*, 875–889.

Rodríguez, P., Lago, M.O., Enesco, I., & Guerrero, S. (2013). Children's understandings of counting: Detection of errors and pseudoerrors by kindergarten and primary school children. *Journal of Experimental Child Psychology, 114*, 35–46.

Rousselle, L., & Vossius, L. (2021). Acquiring the cardinal knowledge of number words: A conceptual replication. *Journal of Numerical Cognition, 7*, 411–434.

Sarnecka, B.W. (2015). Learning to represent exact numbers. *Synthese, 32*, 63–86.

Sarnecka, B.W., & Gelman, S.A. (2004). *Six* does not just mean *a lot*: Preschoolers see number words as specific. *Cognition, 92*, 329–352.

Schleifer, P., & Landerl, K. (2011). Subitizing and counting in typical and atypical development. *Developmental Science, 14*, 280–291.

Schneider, R.M., Sullivan, J., Guo, K., & Barner, D. (2021). What counts? Sources of knowledge in children's acquisition of the successor function. *Child Development, 92*, e476–e492.

Schneider, R.M., Sullivan, J., Marušič, F., Žaucer, R., Biswas, P., Mišmaš, P., Plesničar, V., & Barner, D. (2020). Do children use language structure to discover the recursive rules of counting? *Cognitive Psychology, 117*, 101263.

Sella, F., & Lucangeli, D. (2020). The knowledge of the preceding number reveals a mature understanding of the number sequence. *Cognition, 194*, 104104.

Shusterman, A., Cheung, P., Taggart, J., Bass, I., Berkowitz, T., Leonard, J.A., & Schwartz, A. (2017). Conceptual correlates of counting: Children's spontaneous matching and tracking of large sets reflects their knowledge of the cardinal principle. *Journal of Numerical Cognition, 3*, 1–30

Slaughter, V., Itakura, S., Kutsuki, A., & Siegal, M. (2011). Learning to count begins in infancy: Evidence from 18 month olds' visual preferences. *Proceedings of the Royal Society B, 278*, 2979–2984.

Slusser, E., Ditta, A., & Sarnecka, B. (2013). Connecting numbers to discrete quantification: A step in the child's construction of integer concepts. *Cognition, 129*, 31–41.

Snowling, M.J., Moll, K., & Hulme, C. (2021). Language difficulties are a shared risk factor for both reading disorder and mathematics disorder. *Journal of Experimental Child Psychology, 202*, 105009.

Soto-Calvo, E., Simmons, F.R., Willis, C., & Adams, A.-M. (2015). Identifying the cognitive predictors of early counting and calculation skills: Evidence from a longitudinal study. *Journal of Experimental Child Psychology, 140*, 16–37.

Spaepen, E., Gunderson, E.A., Gibson, D., Goldin-Meadow, S., & Levine, S.C. (2018). Meaning before order: Cardinal principle knowledge predicts improvement in understanding the successor principle and exact ordering. *Cognition, 180*, 59–81.

Starkey, G.S., & McCandliss, B.D. (2014). The emergence of "groupitizing" in children's numerical cognition. *Journal of Experimental Child Psychology, 126*, 120–137.

Starkey, G.S., & McCandliss, B.D. (2021). A probabilistic approach for quantifying children's subitizing span. *Journal of Experimental Child Psychology, 207*, 105118.

Stigler, J.W., Lee, S.Y., & Stevenson, H.W. (1986). Digit memory in Chinese and English: Evidence for a temporally limited store. *Cognition, 23*, 1–20.

VanRinsveld, A., Schiltz, C., Majerus, S., & Fayol, M. (2020). When one-two-three beats two-one-three: Tracking the acquisition of the verbal number sequence. *Psychonomic Bulletin & Review, 27*, 122–129.

Wang, J.J., & Feigenson, L. (2019). Infants recognize counting as numerically relevant. *Developmental Science, 22*, e12805.

Ward, J.M., Mazzocco, M.M., Bock, A.M., & Prokes, N.A. (2017). Are content and structural features of counting books aligned with research on numeracy development? *Early Childhood Research Quarterly, 39*, 47–63.

Wynn, K. (1992). Children's acquisition of the number words and counting system. *Cognitive Psychology, 24*, 220–251.

Zhang, X., Hu, B.Y., Zou, X., & Ren, L. (2020). Parent-child number application activities predict children's math trajectories from preschool to primary school. *Journal of Educational Psychology, 112*, 1521–1531.

Chapter 7

Fingers

IN 2014, a paper appeared in the academic journal *Rock Art Research*, reporting on 27,000-year-old hand stencils found in the caves of France. The resemblance of the hand positions to modern finger-counting practices convinced the author that the similarity "was unlikely due to chance."[1] Scholars agree that counting, at least above three, began with reference to body parts.[2] Even after the invention of written notation, fingers were used for counting, computation, record-keeping, and communication in ancient Greek, Roman, Egyptian, Babylonian, Persian, and Arab marketplaces, arenas, and law courts. Roman youth were schooled in them. In fact, fingers were still the only numeracy tool in much of Europe when Columbus sailed west.[3] Fingers were convenient, portable, independent of language, and hence handy for use by traders.[4] More recently, an ethnographic survey of 33 societies across six continents revealed nearly universal use of fingers (and in some cases toes) for counting. Indeed, in English, the anatomical term *digits* signifies both fingers and toes, as well as numbers below *ten*; and *fist, finger*, and *five* all share a common root.[5] Thus, it is no accident that out of 196 languages, 125 employ a decimal (base-10) numerical system and another 42 a vigesimal (base-20) system,[6] a reflection of the natural structure of human anatomy.

All of which is to say that your students are not the first or only ones to use their fingers for math. Finger counting and calculating are ancient practices and practically universal.

And if you have noticed that your students use several different finger routines in their problem-solving, consider this: Worldwide, finger gestures vary markedly, including palms up or down, starting with the thumb, index finger, or pinky, with fingers folded or extended, on the right or left hand. Some counting routines are analog (one finger per counted object), while others are symbolic (with positions that do not represent such a one-to-one match-up).[7] The Chinese, for example, use only one hand for counting, whereby the numbers *one* through *five* are represented analogically, while *six* through *ten* are symbolic positions.[8] Other symbolic systems include gestures representing multiples of *ten* (see Figure 7.1). Among those using analog systems, most count fingers consecutively, but some count symmetrically across two hands (e.g., beginning with the thumb on each hand), while others count in a continuous pattern like a number line (e.g., ending with the thumb on the first hand and beginning with the thumb on the

DOI: 10.4324/9781003157656-10

second hand).[9] These widely varying routines and customs are determined by several factors: cultural influences, handedness, individual preferences, circumstance (is one hand holding a pencil?), and the task at hand.[10] People also often use different finger patterns for counting, calculating, and displaying a total.[11]

It may also be pertinent to point out that modern, well-educated adults use their fingers all the time for enumeration. Football referees, land surveyors, and stock and commodity traders communicate numbers with them over distances and in noisy environments.[12] The rest of us use them to remember shopping and to-do lists; total up party guests; figure out how many months lie between, say, April and September; and even calculate when one is too distracted or flummoxed to do so in one's head.

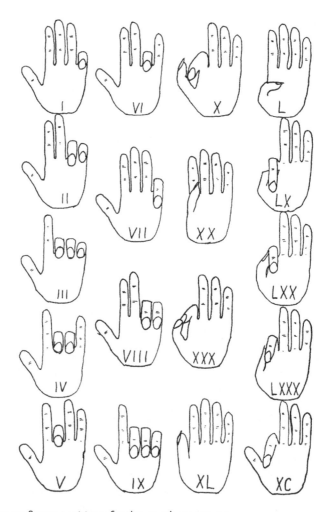

FIGURE 7.1   Roman finger positions for the numbers 1 to 99.

Source: Derived from Turner, 1951. © Classical Association of the Middle West & South

In our modern society, children use these handy numeracy tools in several important ways. First, they use an index finger to physically tag objects as they name each with a number word in counting. This gesture serves several functions. Most concretely, it is a physical enactment of attaching a number name to the object. The routine of touching one object and then moving on to the next one teaches and reinforces the one-to-one counting principle, discussed in Chapter 6. For young children who know the number-word sequence as "onetwothreefourfive," the gesture routine also helps to slow down the verbal string, allowing the individual number words to emerge independently and as phonologically distinct. (Note, however, that synchronizing the finger-pointing gesture with the spoken number word requires coordination that may take time and practice to develop.) Finally, pointing helps a child—or adult—remember which objects have already been counted. This memory aid is especially useful when the counted objects all look the same or are randomly arrayed.

In analog systems, a second numerical finger function involves matching each item to be counted one for one with a different finger in sequence, also for the purpose of counting. (In symbolic systems, each counted item is matched with a unique finger configuration.) Fully analogical systems have the advantage of reinforcing several of the counting principles, discussed in Chapter 6, in the range of *one* to *ten*. The one-to-one principle is embodied in the one-for-one routine itself: one number word or object uniquely paired with one and only one finger. Furthermore, a study of bilingual preschoolers from cultures with somewhat different analogical counting routines demonstrated that children become more sensitive to the one-to-one feature of those gestures if they are exposed to more than one set of finger sequences.[13] With practice, finger counting also comes to embody and reinforce the stable order of the verbal counting sequence and for each number demonstrates a unique successor ($N + 1$) and unique predecessor ($N - 1$). That is, with fingers naturally all lined up, finger counting is a living exhibit of numbers' ordinality. It also demonstrates numbers' cardinality—the number name attached to the last finger counted is the numerosity of the counted fingers. This feature of finger counting will play an important role in finger arithmetic, to be discussed later. Moreover, when fingers are used to stand in for objects, they exemplify the abstraction principle in that one employs the same counting routine for fingers as for the objects they represent, and fingers can represent any object. One of the most useful functions of finger counting is to enumerate items when verbal counting is difficult—for example, when the items to be counted are themselves verbal, such as names of people or things ("April, May, June . . ."). In these instances, the fingers stand in for the number words until the fingers themselves can be counted. While fully analogical finger counting is difficult to use for more than ten items, this very limitation is a clear demonstration of the decimal foundation of the number system. Indeed, it is a more transparent demonstration than the English number names, which begin their second iteration with the inscrutable "eleven" and "twelve." Finally, there is an open question as to whether children should be taught or encouraged to count on their fingers in a particular way or direction. As will be discussed in Chapter 9, in cultures whose writing goes from left to right, people (including young children who do not yet know how to read) tend to think of numbers as growing from left to right and to count objects in that direction.[14] However, one study demonstrated that children with visual-spatial deficits and accompanying math difficulties do not have a firm left-to-right sense of magnitude,[15] raising the question of whether teaching them left-to-right finger counting would help. To our knowledge, as of this writing there have been no experimental interventions addressing the finger-counting-direction question.[16]

A third numerical finger function is to signal the total numerosity of a group of items, so-called *finger montring*. As already noted, for any given number, the gestures a person uses for counting and for montring are not necessarily the same. As with counting, montring reinforces the abstract nature of number, since one holds up three fingers to signal three of anything. Moreover, the gestures embody the cardinal function of numbers, and their use reinforces the cardinality principle of counting: The last verbal tag used in the count answers the question, *How many?* Importantly, however, many preschoolers may not yet connect a number's montring gesture with the actual numerosity of fingers held up in the gesture, since they do not seem to understand the meaning of unconventional montring gestures involving the same number of fingers. That is, they may know that when someone holds up the three central fingers of one hand, it means the same thing as three objects; however, they may not make the same connection if someone holds up one finger on one hand and two on the other.[17] However, even these rote gestures may be easier to learn than the verbal counting sequence. Indeed, studies of preschoolers found that those who did not yet know the cardinality principle were more than twice as accurate in labeling or approximating the numerosities of sets with gestures as with number words. Moreover, children's numerical gesture-word mismatches may signal a readiness to benefit from wide-ranging discussion about counting, cardinal values, and numerical relations. In this sense, the finger gestures may serve as a stepping-stone to the verbal numbers.[18]

A fourth function of these finger tools is to display numerical relations and aid in arithmetic manipulations, particularly addition and subtraction. Counting out the addends on their fingers, for example, reminds children where they are in the count. Interestingly, Chinese children give up using finger counting to solve arithmetic problems well before American children do, perhaps because their short number words are easier to keep in mind without the aid of fingers than are the phonologically more complex English number words, as noted in Chapter 6.[19] Moreover, children can physically experiment on their fingers with strategies for composing and decomposing numbers and can arrive at the result of an operation before those results have been committed to memory. A study of first-graders revealed that children use their fingers most frequently for operations involving values above *four* and for problems, such as math-fact exercises, that do not have associated objects.[20] Thus, finger arithmetic practice may serve to lighten the short-term memory load, aid in memorizing number combinations, and serve as a stepping-stone to abstract operations. Indeed, some scholars have attributed Chinese children's early advantage in arithmetic, evident already in kindergarten, to their early and frequent use of fingers to count and solve problems.[21] The role of fingers in arithmetic will be taken up again in Chapter 10.

What is the connection between fingers and enumeration that makes finger counting so universal? There is substantial evidence that finger awareness and motor control share a cortical neighborhood with a brain region that is particularly active during numerical manipulations.[22] Brain images of both children[23] and adults[24] actively engaged in mental calculation, for example, reveal activation in cortical finger regions specific to the hand on which that person typically starts counting—even when fingers are not being used! Moreover, injury to this region produces a well-known set of symptoms (Gerstmann syndrome) that includes marked deficits in both calculations and finger awareness (that is, the ability to identify without visual feedback which of one's fingers is being touched, a skill known as *finger gnosis*, the second word pronounced with a silent *g*).[25] The functional connection between finger gnosis and numeracy appears to be at least in part visual, however, because most children who are blind from early in life do not spontaneously use their fingers for counting.[26] Astoundingly, however, the finger-math connection apparently does not necessarily require actual fingers. Doctors report a case of an 11-year-old girl born without forearms but whose brain allowed her to *feel* as though she had normal hands (a common phenomenon called *phantom limb*). She learned to place her phantom hands on the table and count and do arithmetic on her vividly imagined outstretched fingers.[27]

These findings raise two intriguing sets of questions. The first is a theoretical and admittedly speculative one: Is it just a coincidence that fingers and number are so intertwined in the brain? Probably not. One compelling theory is that some brain cells (*neurons*) originally developed for finger control and sensation were repurposed, through eons of human finger-counting experience, to respond to numerical demands and now serve both functions.[28] Makes sense.

The second, more important question is a practical one: *How necessary are good finger awareness and control to the math development of the average child?* And related to that: *If it is necessary, is there a way to remediate weak finger skills?* A recent review of the growing body of research concluded that there is indeed a connection between young children's numerical abilities, on the one hand (figuratively speaking), and finger gnosis and finger fine-motor skills, on the other. The reviewers suggest that this connection emerges from the use of finger-based numerical strategies in early childhood serving to connect fingers to numbers in the brain circuits primed for it.[29]

Additionally, there have been a few intriguing reports that bear on the classroom. One is that preschoolers with poor finger fine-motor dexterity that makes it difficult for them to sync up their pointing to objects with the verbal number-word sequence fall behind in understanding what counting is all about,[30] a potentially serious problem for arithmetic. Another study revealed finger-gnosis deficits in a group of eight- to 11-year-old children with severe math learning difficulties. These researchers also point to the importance of fingers for tracking and tagging objects and for reducing the cognitive load on working memory.[31] A third important finding was that, among kindergartners, weak finger gnosis was linked to weak number-line estimations, which in turn explained these children's weak addition skills. Interestingly, finger gnosis was unrelated to a child's overt use of finger counting in solving addition problems,[32] suggesting that the intertwining of fingers and numbers may have more to do with brain activity than with finger activity. Finally, researchers found that simultaneously doing other, unrelated things with one's hands can interfere with mental arithmetic, at least among kindergartners—a heads-up to teachers.[33]

There has been less research on the question of remediation, both in terms of how to do it and who would benefit. Some efforts have been successful,[34] others not as much.[35] All have focused on children in the age range of five to seven. One successful study consisted of a four-week series of interventions with children aged six and seven. The interventions consisted of two components: finger-number activities and number games (dominoes, playing cards, dice, board games). Some children just did the finger activities; these children made gains in finger gnosis. Other children just played the number games; they improved in non-symbolic comparisons (i.e., comparing the numerosities of sets of dots, as described in Chapter 2). But some children did both the finger-number activities *and* the number games; these children saw gains in a whole range of quantitative skills—counting objects; recognizing numerosities on dice and adding them; comparing symbolic magnitudes; ordering numerals to *102*; completing number sequences forward and backward in ones, twos, fives, and tens; splitting numbers into composite parts; and creating a larger number from two or three smaller numbers.[36]

Another intriguing finding was that kindergartners who had some musical training in playing the piano, guitar, or flute demonstrated better finger gnosis than those who had no such training. Moreover, those kindergartners with good finger gnosis added more accurately than those with weaker finger gnosis, as described earlier.[37] It is interesting to note that in a study of ten-year-olds, those who had been learning and practicing a musical instrument since the age of seven had better finger gnosis and performed better on math calculations, problem-solving, and general understanding than those without the instrumental training. This is especially notable because there had been no difference in either finger gnosis or math skills between the groups at age seven.[38] Some researchers have speculated that experience with sequencing (events, numbers, fingers, pitch) and the capacity to understand it is central to early numeracy,[39] and thus may help to explain these results. Sequencing and the number line will be a topic of Chapter 9.

Both of these two successful interventions were undertaken with young children unselected for either finger or math difficulties—that is, an apparently typical range of students. Research on the effect of such interventions on children with weak finger and/ or math skills is certainly warranted.

What does this all mean for early childhood education? The research raises—and suggests the answers to—several important questions. First, is finger counting necessary for later math success? The answer appears to be no. Blind children who do not use their fingers for counting or calculating nevertheless learn the cardinality principle and part/whole relations.[40]

Second, does using one's fingers for counting and calculation provide any benefits for numeracy development in the early years? Most researchers agree that it certainly does.[41] As we hope this chapter has demonstrated, finger gestures illustrate (some would say *embody*) and reinforce most of the counting principles. In their transparency, they help to clarify the verbal counting sequence in terms of both the words' pronunciations and the values they represent. As stand-ins for counted objects, fingers provide a stepping-stone to abstract numbers. And they provide children with a convenient and ever-present literal set of manipulatives that can help them grasp numerical relations and the decimal system. In one longitudinal study, first-graders (many of whom came from low-income families) who had never used their fingers for counting and arithmetic were more likely to use them in first grade than those who had used them in kindergarten.[42] This suggests that early finger use—in preschool and kindergarten—can be particularly effective in opening the door to more efficient arithmetic strategies. Moreover, some scholars speculate that the finger sensorimotor patterns and connections established early in numeracy development play a role in setting up the neural networks serving a lifetime of mathematics.[43] Others point to the significant benefit of what they call *intersensory redundancy*—that is, common information obtained through several senses, such as auditory, visual, and tactile (touch) modes—in teaching the meaning of numbers' values.[44]

Finally, does early finger use inhibit children from learning more efficient calculation strategies? The answer appears to be no. Although finger calculation is a highly reliable system, it does have at least two disadvantages in the long run. First, compared with retrieving results from well-established memory or even employing other strategies in one's head, reckoning on one's fingers is time-consuming. And second, it is limited to small-number operations.

Children's spontaneous use of fingers for counting and calculation is nearly universal. Yet most children, through practice and lots of experience and under the pressure of keeping up, develop multiple more-efficient strategies that gain use with time—if they are, indeed, more efficient. Typically, that shift occurs around the end of first grade or beginning of second grade.[45] However, some children have significant difficulty transitioning to more efficient methods, not because using their fingers is so easy, but because, for one or more reasons, those other methods are particularly difficult and hence even less efficient for them, a topic of Chapters 8, 9, and 10. Finger counting remains their most efficient and reliable method, so they stick with it. For typical students, however, *early* finger use should support, rather than hinder, later development of more efficient strategies for all the reasons cited.

CONCLUSION

Fingers are an ancient and nearly universal tool of numeracy. When used early and often, they support counting and arithmetic acquisition by reinforcing the counting principles, reducing the burden on working memory, introducing the base-10 numbering structure, and providing an opportunity for problem-solving strategy experimentation and math-fact exposure. Without this early experience, children are likely to rely on finger counting long after their classmates have discovered more efficient strategies. Children who persist in using their fingers without developing more efficient strategies should be evaluated.

ACTIVITIES

ACTIVITY 7.1: Finger Counting

Objective: To practice cardinal and ordinal number representations using children's fingers to count. In the following activities, start with numbers *zero* through *five* and eventually progress to numbers *six* through *ten*.

- **Ordinal number knowledge:** The children work in pairs. One child says a number and the other child counts on his or her fingers to that given number. The first child has to monitor and check that the count was done correctly, then the children switch roles.
- **Cardinal number knowledge:** Use a deck of cards with dot representations or numerals. Hold up one card at a time. The children read the number on the card and show that number by extending their fingers simultaneously without counting.
- **Cardinal number knowledge with executive functioning:** Play Simon Says with finger representations. The teacher calls out a number while showing that number of fingers: "Simon says show me five!" or "Show me five!" The children follow the action and hold up that many fingers, but only when Simon says. The children practice their executive functioning skills as they vary their behavior based on whether they hear "Simon says."

ACTIVITY 7.2: Finger Movement

Objective: To improve quantitative skills through finger movement.[46]

- Count verbally forward to and backward from "ten" with finger representations of each number: "One," "two," "three," . . . "ten," "ten," "nine," "eight" . . . "one."
- Count verbally and with fingers by *ten*s, *five*s, and *two*s. For example, hold up all ten fingers and say "ten," close hands and open again and say "twenty," and then continue to one hundred.
- Use fingers to represent a calculation: Show $3 + 2 = 5$ or $8 - 3 = 5$, for example, by showing fingers of the first number and then raising or lowering fingers to add or subtract.
- Count aloud and use finger representations of two-digit numbers such as *24* by showing ten, ten, and then four fingers.

ACTIVITY 7.3: Which Finger Did I Touch?

Objective: To develop finger awareness. Finger awareness (*finger gnosia*) is a significant predictor of calculation skills and number system knowledge.[47] Finger training using the activities in this chapter can improve these numerical skills in children.[48]

- **First:** For a quick screening of finger gnosia, have the children close their eyes and lay their hands flat on the table while the adult touches one of the children's fingers. The children open their eyes and point to the finger perceived to be touched. Next, have the children close their eyes again and the adult touches one finger on each hand consecutively. The children indicate which fingers were touched. Then, the adult touches two fingers simultaneously. If children struggle to identify which finger(s) were touched, do the following activities to increase their finger gnosis.
- **Next:** Repeat the finger touching activities but with the children's eyes open at first to give them visual feedback. Have the children firmly touch their own fingers after the adult has done so. With adult support, the children name the fingers they are touching (index, middle, ring, pinkie, thumb).
- **Next:** Repeat the finger touching activities with the children's eyes closed again and monitor for improvement. If the children continue to struggle, the adult can name the finger as it is touched or return to having the children's eyes open until it becomes easier.

ACTIVITY 7.4: Finger-Counter Correspondence

Objective: To practice one-to-one correspondence and fine motor skills. Children pick up counters one at a time, count them, and place them in a container.

- Place four circular counters on the table alongside a container. The children use their thumb and index finger to pick up the first counter, place it in the container, and count, "one." Then they use their thumb and middle finger to pick up the second counter, place it in the container, and count, "two." Next, they use their thumb and ring finger to pick up the third counter while counting "three," and finally, their thumb and pinky finger to pick up the last counter while counting "four." After all four counters are in the container, empty the container and repeat using the other hand.

ACTIVITY 7.5: Finger to Thumb

Objective: To learn the association of each finger with a particular numeral and number word.

- **First:** Place numeral stickers on children's fingernails, with *1* on the index finger, *2* on the middle finger, *3* on the ring finger, and *4* on the pinkie. Keep the same alignment for both hands. Beginning with the dominant hand, have the children touch each finger with their thumb in order from one to four, saying the number as they touch that finger with their thumb. Repeat with the non-dominant hand. The children should produce a strong pinch with their finger and thumb and hold it for several seconds.

- **Next:** Call out numbers non-sequentially and have the children touch the corresponding finger with their thumb. For example, when you call out "three," the children touch their thumb to their ring finger. Begin with the dominant hand, then the non-dominant hand, and finally both hands simultaneously.

- **Next:** Call out pairs of numbers, such as "one, three," and have the children touch those fingers sequentially with their thumb. Begin with one hand at a time, and then try both hands at the same time.

- **Next:** Remove the numeral stickers from the children's nails and repeat the exercises without the visual cue of the stickers.

ACTIVITY 7.6: Touch-Touch-Go Finger Training[49]

Objective: To improve finger gnosis and fine motor skills. Place colored stickers on the nails of both hands, such as thumb-white, index-green, middle-blue, ring-yellow, pinkie-red. Keep this pattern for all the activities that follow. A printable handout of these activities is available to download for use with children.[50]

- **Labyrinth:** Beginning with two colored markers (white, green, blue, yellow, or red), draw interlinked pathways on a piece of paper. The children trace the pathways with their corresponding-colored finger. Increase the interlinked pathways to include all five colors on each sheet. Following the lines focuses the children's attention on that finger.

- **Pointing game:** Arrange additional colored stickers in a row on a piece of paper, first in corresponding order with each hand. Have the children point to the corresponding stickers, first with their dominant hand and then with their non-dominant hand. To increase the difficulty level, arrange the stickers in a different order and have the children point to the corresponding colored sticker that matches the sticker on their finger.

- **Piano game:** Create a series of colored rectangles (like piano keys) that first correspond to the colors on each finger for both hands. The children touch the rectangles in the corresponding order from left to right and hold their touch for a few seconds. Next, create a sequence of colored rectangles with some of the rectangles of a different color, thus having the children skip that key. Next, rearrange the order of the colors, having the children complete the sequence first with the left hand and then with the right, and finally alternating one key at a time between the two hands.

ACTIVITY 7.7: Number Bracelets

Objective: To develop fine motor skills while using fingers to develop counting skills. Children place a target number of beads on a pipe cleaner and then shape it into a circle, or bracelet. Then they slide and count the beads, which they can later use to compose and decompose numbers.

- **First:** Begin with 11 pipe cleaners and 55 beads. The children twist the first pipe cleaner into a circle without any beads and fold a sticker over the top with the numeral *0*, indicating that this bracelet has no beads. The children place one bead on the next pipe cleaner, then twist the pipe cleaner into a circle, folding a sticker over the top with the numeral *1* on it. Place two beads on the next bracelet. Continue until 11 bracelets are made, with the last bracelet having ten beads and the numeral *10*. The children slide and count the beads on the bracelets. To improve fine motor skills, also practice sliding the beads with each of the different fingers and thumb, beginning with the dominant hand and then the non-dominant hand.
- **Next:** Have the children place 20 beads on one pipe cleaner, ten of one color in a row and then ten of another color in a row. Twist the pipe cleaner into a circle, but without a numeral sticker at the top.
- **Next:** The children slide beads to the top of the circle from each side and both colors, then count the total. Adults can call out or provide index cards with different number combinations such as "three white, four red" (see Figure). The cards can be in sequential order at first and then in random order.
- **Next:** The children slide all ten beads of the color on the left to the top of the circle and say "ten." Then slide one bead from the right to the top and say, "ten and one is eleven," or count in the base-10 way, saying, "ten and one, the name is eleven." Continue through "twenty."

NOTES

1 Overmann, 2014.
2 Dehaene, 1997, pp. 91–95; Devlin, 2005, pp. 199–205.
3 Crosby, 1997, p. 215.
4 Richardson, 1916; Williams & Williams, 1995.
5 The Electronic Textbook of Hand Surgery, e-hand.com/clf/clf522.htm, retrieved 6/4/2021.
6 Comrie, 2011.
7 Bender & Beller, 2012.
8 Domahs et al., 2010.
9 Bender & Beller, 2012.
10 Morrissey et al., 2016; Wasner et al., 2014.
11 Morrissey & Hallett, 2018.
12 Williams & Williams, 1995.
13 Nicoladis et al., 2019.
14 Göbel et al., 2018; Opfer & Furlong, 2011.
15 Bachot et al., 2005.
16 Fischer & Brugger, 2011; Moeller et al., 2011.
17 Nicoladis et al., 2018.
18 Gibson et al., 2019; Gunderson et al., 2015.
19 Geary et al., 1993.
20 Jordan et al., 1994.
21 Siegler & Mu, 2008.
22 Andres et al., 2012.
23 Berteletti & Booth, 2015.
24 Tschentscher et al., 2012.
25 PeBenito et al., 1988.
26 Crollen et al., 2014.
27 Poeck, 1964.
28 Anderson & Penner-Wilger, 2013.
29 Barrocas et al., 2020.
30 Fischer et al., 2018.
31 Costa et al., 2011.
32 Zhang et al., 2020.
33 Crollen & Noël, 2015.
34 Gracia-Bafalluy et al., 2007; Jay & Betenson, 2017.
35 Fischer, 2010; Gracia-Bafalluy & Noël, 2008; Schild et al., 2020.
36 Jay & Betenson, 2017.
37 Zhang et al., 2020.
38 Gracia-Bafalluy et al., 2007.
39 O'Connor et al., 2018; Schild et al., 2020; Xu & LeFevre, 2016.
40 Crollen et al., 2011.
41 Crollen et al., 2011; Moeller et al., 2011; Soylu et al., 2018.
42 Jordan et al., 1994.
43 DeLaCruz et al., 2014.
44 Siegler & Mu, 2008.

45 Jordan et al., 2008.
46 Jay & Betenson, 2017.
47 Barrocas et al., 2020.
48 Jay & Betenson, 2017.
49 Derived from Gracia-Bafalluy & Noël, 2008.
50 Jo Boaler at Stanford University, along with Lang Chen, Cathy Williams, and Montserrat Cordero, adapted
    the research activities, which can be found at www.youcubed.org/wp-content/uploads/2017/03/Finger-
    Activities-vF.pdf with printable directions and handouts for ease of implementation.

REFERENCES

The following references were cited in this chapter. For additional selected references relevant to this chapter, please see Chapter 7 Supplemental References in eResources.

Anderson, M.L., & Penner-Wilger, M. (2013). Neural reuse in the evolution and development of the brain: Evidence for developmental homology? *Developmental Psychobiology, 55*, 42–51.

Andres, M., Michaux, N., & Pesenti, M. (2012). Common substrate for mental arithmetic and finger representation in the parietal cortex. *NeuroImage, 62*, 1520–1528.

Bachot, J., Gevers, W., Fias, W., & Roeyers, H. (2005). Number sense in children with visuospatial disabilities: Orientation of the mental number line. *Psychology Science, 47*, 172–183.

Barrocas, R., Roesch, S., Gawrilow, C., & Moeller, K. (2020). Putting a finger on numerical development: Reviewing the contributions of kindergarten finger gnosis and fine motor skills to numerical abilities. *Frontiers in Psychology, 11*, 1012.

Bender, A., & Beller, S. (2012). Nature and culture of finger counting: Diversity and representational effects of an embodied cognitive tool *Cognition, 124*, 156–182.

Berteletti, I., & Booth, J.R. (2015). Perceiving fingers in single-digit arithmetic problems. *Frontiers in Psychology, 6*, 226.

Comrie, B. (2011). Numeral bases. In M.S. Dryer & M. Haspelmath (Eds.), *The world atlas of language structures online* (Chapter 131). Max Planck Digit Library. Retrieved on 12/26/2021, from http://wals.info/chapter/131

Costa, A.J., Silva, J.B.L., Pinheiro Chagas, P., Krinzinger, H., Lonneman, J., Willmes, K., Wood, G., & Haase, V.G. (2011). A hand full of numbers: A role for offloading in arithmetics learning? *Frontiers in Psychology, 2*, 368.

Crollen, V., & Noël, M.-P. (2015). The role of fingers in the development of counting and arithmetic skills. *Acta Psychologica, 156*, 37–44.

Crollen, V., Noël, M.-P., Seron, X., Mahau, P., Lepore, F., & Collignon, O. (2014). Visual experience influences the interactions between fingers and numbers. *Cognition, 133*, 91–96.

Crollen, V., Seron, X., & Noël, M.-P. (2011). Is finger-counting necessary for the development of arithmetic abilities? *Frontiers in Psychology, 2*, 242.

Crosby, A.W. (1997). *The measure of reality: Quantification and western society, 1250–1600*. Cambridge University Press.

Dehaene, S. (1997). *The number sense: How the mind creates mathematics*. Oxford University Press.

DeLaCruz, V., DiNuovo, A., DiNuovo, S., & Cangelosi, A. (2014). Making fingers and words count in a cognitive robot. *Frontiers in Behavioral Neuroscience, 8*, 13.

Devlin, K. (2005). *The math instinct: Why you're a mathematical genius (along with lobsters, birds, cats, and dogs)*. Thunder's Mouth Press.

Domahs, F., Moeller, K., Huber, S., Willmes, K., & Nuerk, H.-C. (2010). Embodied numerosity:

Implicit hand-based representation influence symbolic number processing across cultures. *Cognition, 116,* 251–266.

Fischer, J.-P. (2010). Numerical performance increased by finger training: A fallacy due to regression toward the mean? *Cortex, 46,* 272–273.

Fischer, M.H., & Brugger, P. (2011). When digits help digits: Spatial-numerical associations point to finger counting as prime example of embodied cognition. *Frontiers in Psychology, 2,* 260.

Fischer, U., Suggate, S.P., Schmirl, J., & Stoeger, H. (2018). Counting on fine motor skills: Links between preschool finger dexterity and numerical skills. *Developmental Science, 21,* e12623.

Geary, D.C., Bow-Thomas, C.C., Liu, F., & Siegler, R.S. (1993). Even before formal instruction, Chinese children outperform American children in mental addition. *Cognitive Development, 8,* 517–529.

Gibson, D.J., Gunderson, E.A., Spaepen, E., Levine, S.C., & Goldin-Meadow, S. (2019). Number gestures predict learning of number words. *Developmental Science, 22,* e12791.

Göbel, S.M., McCrink, K., Fischer, M.H., & Shaki, S. (2018). Observation of directional storybook reading influences young children's counting direction. *Journal of Experimental Child Psychology, 166,* 49–66.

Gracia-Bafalluy, M., Fayol, M., & Noël, M.-P. (2007, June). *Consequences of playing a musical instrument on finger gnosia and number skills in children.* Paper presented at Numbers, Fingers, and the Brain symposium at the Belgian Association for Psychological Sciences annual meeting at the Université Catholique de Louvain.

Gracia-Bafalluy, M., & Noël, M.-P. (2008). Does finger training increase young children's numerical performance? *Cortex, 44,* 368–375.

Gunderson, E.A., Spaepen, E., Gibson, D., Goldin-Meadow, S., & Levine, S.C. (2015). Gesture as a window into children's number knowledge. *Cognition, 144,* 14–28.

Jay, T., & Betenson, J. (2017). Mathematics at your fingertips: Testing a finger training intervention to improve quantitative skills. *Frontiers in Education, 2,* 22.

Jordan, N.C., Kaplan, D., Ramineni, C., & Locuniak, M.N. (2008). Development of number combination skill in the early school years: When do fingers help? *Developmental Science, 11,* 662–668.

Jordan, N.C., Levine, S.C., & Huttenlocher, J. (1994). Development of calculation abilities in middle- and low-income children after formal instruction in school. *Journal of Applied Developmental Psychology, 15,* 223–240.

Moeller, K., Martignon, L., Wessolowski, S., Engel, J., & Nuerk, H.-C. (2011). Effects of finger counting on numerical development: The opposing views of neurocognition and mathematics education. *Frontiers in Psychology, 2,* 328.

Morrissey, K.R., & Hallett, D. (2018). Cardinal and ordinal aspects of finger-counting habits predict different individual differences in embodied numerosity. *Journal of Numerical Cognition, 4,* 613–635.

Morrissey, K.R., Liu, M., Kang, J., Hallett, D., & Wang, Q. (2016). Cross-cultural and intracultural differences in finger-counting habits and number magnitude processing: Embodied numerosity in Canadian and Chinese university students. *Journal of Numerical Cognition, 2,* 1–19.

Nicoladis, E., Marentette, P., & Pika, S. (2019). How many fingers am I holding up? The answer depends on children's language background. *Developmental Science, 22,* e12781.

Nicoladis, E., Marentette, P., Pika, S., & Barbosa, P.G. (2018). Young children show little sensitivity to the iconicity in number gestures. *Language Learning and Development, 14,* 297–319.

O'Connor, P.A., Morsanyi, K., & McCormack, T. (2018). Young children's non-numerical ordering ability at the start of formal education longitudinally predicts their symbolic number skills and academic achievement in maths. *Developmental Science, 21*, e12645.

Opfer, J.E., & Furlong, E.E. (2011). How numbers bias preschoolers' spatial search. *Journal of Cross-Cultural Psychology, 42*, 682–695.

Overmann, K.A. (2014). Finger-counting in the Upper Paleolithic. *Rock Art Research, 31*, 63–80.

PeBenito, R., Fisch, C.B., & Fisch, M.L. (1988). Developmental Gerstmann's Syndrome. *Archives of Neurology, 45*, 977–982.

Poeck, K. (1964). Phantoms following amputation in early childhood and in congenital absence of limbs. *Cortex, 1*, 269–275.

Richardson, L.J., (1916). Digital reckoning among the ancients. *The American Mathematical Monthly, 23*, 7–13.

Schild, U., Bauch, A., & Nuerk, H.-C. (2020). A finger-based numerical training failed to improve arithmetic skills in kindergarten children beyond effects of an active non-numerical control training. *Frontiers in Psychology, 11*, 529.

Siegler, R.S., & Mu, Y. (2008). Chinese children excel on novel mathematics problems even before elementary school. *Psychological Science, 19*, 759–763.

Soylu, F., Lester, F.K. Jr., & Newman, S.D. (2018). You can count on your fingers: The role of fingers in early mathematical development. *Journal of Numerical Cognition, 4*, 107–135.

Tschentscher, N., Hauk, O., Fischer, M.H., & Pulvermüller, F. (2012). You can count on the motor cortex: Finger counting habits modulate motor cortex activation evoked by numbers. *NeuroImage, 59*, 3139–3148.

Turner, J.H. (1951). Roman elementary mathematics: The operations. *Classical Journal, 47*, 63–74, 106–108.

Wasner, M., Moeller, K., Fischer, M.H., & Nuerk, H.-C. (2014). Aspects of situated cognition in embodied numerosity: The case of finger counting. *Cognitive Processing, 15*, 317–328.

Williams, B.P., & Williams, R.S. (1995). Finger numbers in the Greco-Roman world and the early middle ages. *Isis, 86*, 587–608.

Xu, C., & LeFevre, J.-A. (2016). Training young children on sequential relations among numbers and spatial decomposition: Differential transfer to number line and mental transformation tasks. *Developmental Psychology, 52*, 854–866.

Zhang, L., Wang, W., & Zhang, X. (2020). Effect of finger gnosis on young Chinese children's addition skills. *Frontiers in Psychology, 11*, 544543.

Chapter 8

Arabic Digits and Base-10 Notation

A third tool that children acquire to deal with large numerosities consists of the Arabic digits and the base-10 notation system. This notation system is used in most modern societies and as such is the closest thing we have to an international language of mathematical literacy. It permits efficient and reliable record-keeping, problem-solving, and communication. Like number words, digits are symbolic and arbitrary in form. That is, there is nothing about the appearance of *5* that tells you what it means (namely, how many things it stands for) or the order in which it appears in the series. Nor does it reveal the number word that means the same amount. Thus, young children have a complex task: They must learn how to recognize each digit, write it, and distinguish it from other symbols; they must also learn what it is called, what order it appears in, and, finally and most critically, what numerosity it symbolizes. Each of these hurdles will be discussed in turn.

RECOGNIZING AND WRITING DIGITS

Young children can learn to recognize the written digits relatively early. Children typically learn the Arabic digits at the same point in their education as the letters of the alphabet, yet it is surprisingly unusual for children to confuse them. In one study of lower-middle-class children aged three and a half to six and a half, for example, researchers found that all but a few could distinguish between symbol strings that "belong to writing" (letters) versus those that "belong to numbers" versus those that "belong to drawing" (pictures). Most of them also knew that a single symbol or a string of identical symbols was acceptable for numbers but usually not for letters and that linked symbols were permissible for cursive letters but not for numbers.[1] By kindergarten, children typically have no difficulty distinguishing letters from digits.[2]

However, learning to recognize and write individual digits and numerals can take time and effort. One reason is that up until sometime around first or second grade young children are typically confused about the asymmetric symbols' orientation around the

DOI: 10.4324/9781003157656-11

vertical axis, and nearly all children occasionally write digits (and letters) in mirror image. This confusion is not abnormal. The brain is not hardwired to notice left-right asymmetry but is typically "trained" to do so by the normal process of learning to read and write, which is the first time that objects' left-right orientation really matters.[3] In fact, reading and writing are often just as easy in mirror as in conventional notation for young children. This confusion is not an issue of perception or hand function—even four-year-olds can *copy* digits correctly most of the time—but rather of understanding that left-right orientation matters, remembering to begin writing on the left side of the page, and keeping the correct orientation in memory when the digit is not visible, as when writing.[4] In general, mirror confusion should not pose a problem for learning arithmetic at this early stage. Indeed, one study found that when six-year-olds were asked to write the digits, the children who had the hardest time with math were those who declined to write anything at all.[5] It is likely that the children who were brave enough to write something were less confused about digits' names and basic shapes (aside from orientation) and were probably able to read mirror digits just as well as correctly oriented digits, as noted earlier.

Importantly, however, some students continue to reverse digits (and letters) long after their classmates' mirror confusion has resolved. For them, written math assignments are burdened by this additional tax on their cognitive resources, and teachers may be more likely to misinterpret their responses. Children whose reversal errors persist after second grade are most likely to have significant reading difficulties as well, like the third-grader whose digit reversals are shown in Figure 8.1.[6]

The challenge for teachers, then, is not only to build and stabilize a child's mental image of the digits but to do so in their correct orientation. While there have been a few studies on digit-learning, research on letter-learning has consistently found that repeatedly writing the letters by hand is superior to typing, tracing, or simply looking at them for producing lasting improvement in symbol recall and recognition. Various behavioral explanations for the effectiveness of writing by hand have been offered, including having to pay more attention to symbol form and to remember it.[7] However, brain researchers note that in addition to the visual circuit designed to identify objects, there is a second circuit specialized in processing the visual information necessary for action, including gesture and finger motion. And to the point, while object identification does not normally require information about left-right orientation, bodily motion certainly does. Thus, one theory about how children learn to overcome mirror confusion is to involve that second region—by writing.[8] Moreover, brain imaging studies find that writing practice enhances neural activation not only in regions involved in the

FIGURE 8.1   Reprinted with parental permission.

execution, imagery, and observation of actions (motor memory) but also in the visual region sensitive to written characters and in the functional connections to other cortical regions in the reading circuit. Crucially, it has also been shown to produce more reliable visual recognition of the characters' orientation.[9] Also, children are more likely to write digits in their correct orientation if they begin writing on the left side of the paper.[10] Placing a reminder mark by the left margin should help.

MULTI-DIGIT NUMERALS

Learning how to recognize and write multi-digit numerals additionally requires understanding the basic base-10 rules and place-value system upon which they are constructed. In recent years, the base-10 (or *decimal*) numeration system has been taught successfully to first- and second-graders by use of an exponential sequence of concrete base-10 blocks or beads demonstrating the place-values[11] (see Figure 8.2a) and a *1–100* number chart illustrating the iterative nature of the notation (see Figure 8.2b). We will discuss these methods further in relation to the number line in Chapter 9.

Interestingly, however, even prior to formal instruction, some kindergartners seem to understand the meaning of place-value. For example, in one large study, researchers presented unit-blocks and 10-blocks to kindergartners and told them, "These blocks can

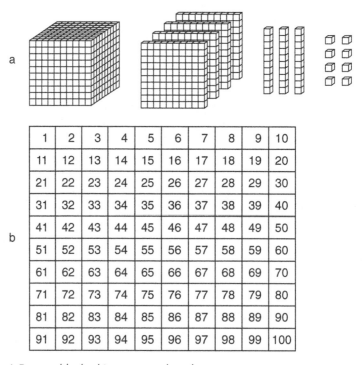

FIGURE 8.2 a) Base-10 blocks. b) *1–100* number chart.

be used to show number." While there was considerable variability in the children's performance, many were able to use the blocks to illustrate two-digit numerals. Moreover, while this international study included children whose language was either opaque (English and Russian) or transparent (Mandarin and Korean) with respect to base-10 numeral naming, as discussed in Chapter 6, language differences did not affect performance, suggesting that these young children may have translated directly from the blocks to the notation.[12] (These children were all from well-educated families; results from children of less well-educated families might be weaker.) However, a study of English-speaking four- to six-year-olds found that children who could name multi-digit numerals stood a better chance of being able to compare their values than those who could not name them, suggesting that the numerals' verbal names provide some access to their values.[13] This topic will be taken up again in the next section.

As would be expected, there is a strong link between correctly writing multi-digit numerals and addition and subtraction ability, particularly in the use of decomposition and retrieval strategies.[14] Some children who have the sort of dyslexia that makes it difficult to keep track of letters' positions within written words can have the same trouble with digit order in written numerals.[15] This is a serious problem not just for calculations but for understanding magnitude and the structure of large-value numerals.

TRANSCODING

Another hurdle for young children is learning the names of the Arabic digits and numerals.[16] For most adults, there is an automatic association between the written digit (*5*), the spoken word ("five"), and the written word (*five*), such that when someone hears or sees one of them, the others automatically come to mind.[17] The translation from one format to another is referred to as *transcoding*. (Most adults also automatically associate these symbolic forms to the numerosity they represent, a form of transcoding taken up later in the section on what the digits mean.) Under normal circumstances, learning the names of the digits comes to children as easily as learning the words for other common objects, which is how young children initially view digits.

Researchers investigating the learning trajectory of using written symbols to express number words presented some cookies and a box to children aged three to seven years. Each child was asked to "put _____ cookies in the box," where the number was "two," "five," or "zero." The examiner then gave the child a blank sticky note and asked him to "put something on this paper to help you remember how many cookies are in the box." When the child had done so, the examiner closed each box and stuck the notes on them. After 20 minutes of a distracting activity, the examiner showed the notes to the child and asked how many cookies were in each box. The child was asked the same question again two weeks later. To answer this question, the child had to read his own markings. The children's markings typically fell into one of four categories: symbolic (*5* or *five*), analog (| | | | |), pictorial (cookies), or blank (typically standing for *zero*). Pictures were most commonly used by the three-year-olds. Analogs were used chiefly by three- and four-year-olds (and some five-year-olds), but were not used by six- and seven-year-olds. Arabic digits were used by some three- and four-year-olds, but more often by five to-seven-year olds. Most children left the sticky note blank (an analog representation) to denote *zero*. Most of the children also expressed whole numbers and *zero* the same way, either both in digits or both in analogs. Their ability to decipher their own marks diminished over time (as one might imagine), but they most easily remembered conventional digit notation. Only the three-year-olds had trouble remembering what their marks for the whole numbers and *zero* meant.[18] Thus, the connection between the number words and the Arabic digits is a work in progress during the early school years, and as we will see in Chapter 11, fraction notation is still several years away.

Where whole-number transcoding becomes tricky is with multi-digit numerals. As noted in Chapter 6, the irregularity of the "-teen" number names in English makes them especially difficult to transcode into numerals. This is equally true for learning the numerals' names, where a large survey found that the ability to name *12* and *15* lagged behind the ability to name the more regular *10* and *14* well into kindergarten.[19] Importantly, most studies have found that the ability to read them and to write them to dictation is directly related to progress in learning arithmetic.[20]

Transcoding large numerals depends on a child's knowledge of their base-10 structure. Studies of young children's transcoding errors find that early efforts most often involve fragmenting (*365* as "thirty six five") or simply leaving one part out. Children who have just learned the word "hundred" often transpose it (*200* as "hundred two"). Later efforts usually involve experimenting with different ways to divide up the digit string (*834* as "eighty thirty four") or mixing up the place-value (*803* as "eight thousand and three").[21] Similar misunderstandings can be seen in their attempts to write the number they hear, in which the correct digits are written in order left to right but are expanded with *zeroes* or other digits to mark place (e.g., "six hundred and forty-two" as *600402* or *610042*). Interestingly, one study found that young girls tend to rely on the spoken structure to guide their written numbers more strongly than boys do, as in this latter example, while boys give more weight to the written form. In all, the researchers concluded that it takes a long time to learn the naming rules, often because they conflict with the most natural strategies.[22]

In a study of elementary-school children, researchers found that those in first grade could, on average, read numerals in the low *hundreds*, those in third grade in the *thousands*, in fifth grade in the *millions*, and in seventh grade in the *billions*. Importantly, however, there were large individual differences in numeral naming and counting skills within each grade. The researchers note that fluency in numeral reading is crucial in arithmetic because the verbal support reduces the demand on visual working memory for the numerals. Indeed, the children's numeral-naming fluency was associated with their arithmetic ability, even as late as seventh grade.[23]

Interestingly, unlike Arabic numerical notation for big numbers, the verbal expressions for quantity retain closer ties to local cultures and language. The term for *94*, for example, is "ninety-four" in English and translates to "four-and-ninety" in German and Dutch and "four-twenty-fourteen" in French—the latter construct a vexing holdover from an archaic base-20 system. These cross-linguistic differences can be reflected in transcoding efficiency differences. Integrating the *ones* and *ten*s elements of multi-digit numerals is particularly tricky for young children in languages such as German and Hebrew, in which the direction of reading words conflicts with that of reading numerals. Among young children, such differences can have pronounced effects on arithmetic performance.[24]

Transcoding is closely related to reading, and abundant research has demonstrated that transcoding between numerals and number words is significantly impaired in many individuals with dyslexia. One study estimated that nearly half of all children with dyslexia in grades three through five had arithmetic deficits related to difficulty with number transcoding, and another study demonstrated that ten- to 14-year-olds with dyslexia took four times as long as their classmates without dyslexia to mentally process five-digit numerals.[25] Or they may say the number correctly but then write it incorrectly. This transcoding problem is thought to be related to the difficulty that individuals with dyslexia have in converting what they see in print into language sounds.[26] By contrast, many children whose difficulties are principally with arithmetic and not with reading have much the same trouble with numerals as they have with number words,[27] although if their reading skills are strong, their transcoding skills may improve over time.[28] Thus, number transcoding difficulties often characterize children with serious reading and/or math learning troubles, albeit somewhat differently.[29] Moreover, children may show problems with naming—not just digits but letters and colors as well—as early as kindergarten.[30] This early manifestation of potential transcoding difficulties and their consequences for arithmetic and reading is fortunate in that it should be possible to screen for them early (a topic of Chapter 13) and intervene in a timely fashion.

Finally, automatically accessing the name of a digit or numeral can be especially problematic for children learning arithmetic in a second language, particularly if they have already learned the number names in their native language. The older an individual is when she learns the second set of number names, the more difficult it may be to achieve automatic access to them in the second language, as demonstrated in a study of bilingual Chinese and Japanese adults who learned English in late childhood and early adolescence.[31] The bilingual transition can be especially challenging if one of the languages inverts number names (e.g., German), has a different grammatical category for small numbers (e.g., Russian), conforms in part to a base other than 10 (e.g., French), or contains number names that are irregular variants of base-10 (e.g., English).[32]

Happily, some American educators have found that adjusting number names so that they conform to the base-10 notation system, as in the East Asian languages (e.g., *21* = "two-tens-and-one"; see Chapter 6), significantly improved arithmetic performance for all children. In one study, explicit base-10 language and instruction brought the math performance of inner-city, English-Spanish bilingual first-graders above their expected grade level.[33]

For three- and four-year-olds, learning to transcode digits and numerals correctly is their most important mathematical task. In a longitudinal study of children this age, researchers found that the ability to identify, read, and write digits and numerals was the strongest predictor—indeed, the only predictor—of arithmetic accuracy and fluency at age six.[34]

NUMERICAL ORDER

Classroom emphasis on arithmetic may focus attention on numerals' cardinal values. However, their ordered arrangement, or *ordinality*, is an important numerical characteristic that plays a significant role in arithmetic thinking.

At first glance, it might seem as though the two questions, "Which (*3* or *6*) is more?" and "Are these digits (*3-8-6*) in the correct order?" are asking the same thing. However, the child's mind handles them a bit differently.[35] In the earliest years of school, children's arithmetic depends chiefly on their understanding of numerical (cardinal) value—the *which is more?* question—and arithmetical procedural knowledge, and their understanding and use of ordinal number words lag somewhat behind that of the cardinal words.[36] But by second grade, their grasp of numerical order begins to take on a more important role, possibly because their arithmetic strategies become more sophisticated and because numerical order facilitates children's long-term and working memory for numerical information.[37] By adulthood, the ability to quickly judge if a set of numbers is correctly ordered is reliably linked to arithmetic fluency.[38]

Importantly, in elementary-age children, difficulty in judging numerical order can be a red flag for a significant math learning disability.[39] But the signs may be evident even earlier. One curious study found that kindergartners' ability to keep track of the order in which daily life events occur (e.g., waking up, getting dressed, going to school, eating lunch, coming home, eating dinner, going to bed) and to remember the chronological order of past events strongly predicted math achievement one year later, in first grade.[40]

WHAT THE DIGITS MEAN

It is one thing to know what a *6* looks like, say its name, and write it or point it out in a picture book. It is quite another to know what it means—that is, how many countable things it stands for, or symbolizes. This is the essence of its usefulness as a "technology" for keeping track of numerosities and manipulating them and is discernable in the ease with which a child can compare the values of two numerals. Indeed, there is now mounting evidence that of all the basic ways of understanding number, thoroughly understanding *how many things* are denoted by a symbolic written numeral is the skill most closely tied to a child's ability to learn formal arithmetic. It is also the biggest math stumbling block for children with mild intellectual disabilities, as well as the core problem for some children with serious math disability.[41]

Digits and letters are often considered as simply different symbol sets, one for math and the other for reading. However, for the most part, they serve quite different functions grammatically: Letters signify speech sounds at the phonemic level, while digits signify meaning, like words, at the lexical level of speech (see Table 8.1). It thus makes sense that, according to one study, knowledge of digit meaning is as important for arithmetic success as phonological awareness is for reading.[42]

TABLE 8.1 Grammatical Levels of Natural Language and Numerical Language

Level	Natural	Numerical
Phonemic	d (/d/)	
Lexical	day	*6*
Morphemic	birthday	*26*
Syntactic	It's my birthday.	*6 + 2 = 8*

Digit comprehension is typically evaluated in one of two ways. The first is to show a child a symbolic digit and a collection of items or dots and ask which represents the greater (or lesser) amount. The child needs to have some understanding of the amount the digit stands for in order to answer correctly. However, that method also necessarily relies on the child's ability to count the items in the compared collection, so it is not a pure measure of symbol comprehension. The second and most frequently employed assessment method is to ask the child which of two symbolic digits means the greater amount. The child must have a pretty good idea of the value of each to answer this question correctly.[43] Of course, for very young children, it is first important to know that the child is familiar with the symbol. Not surprisingly, researchers have found a close association between kindergartners' ability to compare two small sets of dots and their ability to compare two low-value digits, suggesting that knowing how to do one may foster the ability to do the other.[44] For older children who may be unsure but still answer correctly, the comparison test can be given under time constraints. Children for whom the knowledge is automatic will respond more quickly than those whose knowledge is still fragile.[45] Indeed, in one study, children with significant math difficulties in grades two to four were notably slower than their classmates without significant math difficulties.[46]

Learning to compare multi-digit numerals, understandably, takes quite a bit longer. Children's earliest strategy for comparing two two-digit numerals (e.g., *47* versus *52*) is typically to analyze the *ten*s and *one*s digits sequentially (*4*, then *7*) or simply to rely on the *ten*s digit (*4*). With increasing numerical experience, children become able to analyze the two digits more simultaneously and by fifth grade, tend to process the digits in parallel, much as adults do.[47] This progression is quite similar to that in reading, where children start out decoding a word's letters one by one but with practice are eventually able to read the letters in parallel, allowing them to read a word more efficiently. This is not to say that older children never look at numerals one digit at a time; children use whatever strategy seems like it will work best in any given situation. It just means that with enough experience, most children get to the point where they can understand a numeral's value without analyzing each digit separately. However, children with significant math difficulties often have trouble making that transition and continue to rely on a one-digit-at-a-time strategy for dealing with multi-digit numerals. That means that comparing numbers like *47* versus *52*, in which the larger digit in the *ten*s place (*5*) is paired with the smaller digit in the *one*s place (*2*), can pose a particular challenge for them.[48]

A statistical analysis across many different studies found that the ability to compare the values of symbolic numerals is the most powerful predictor of arithmetic competence, at least for arithmetic skills that involve calculating quantities.[49] For this reason, scholars recommend focusing preschoolers' attention on numerical symbols, including identifying them, ordering them, and understanding *how many* each of them stands for.[50] While that may seem early, studies have shown that kindergartners, and even preschoolers, are capable of learning a surprising amount about even multi-digit numerals, both through specific activities such as sorting, matching, copying, and comparing and through simple exposure and having their attention directed to them. For example, one study found that even some three-year-olds knew the spoken names of two- and three-digit numerals and could judge their relative quantities. By age five, many preschoolers know that multi-digit numerals are read from left to right, that the digit on the left means a bigger amount than the digit on the right, that the number of digits in a numeral is related to both its amount and what it is called, and that *zero* is a placeholder. This knowledge may not yet be explicit—most preschoolers would be unable to articulate what they know. However, from their responses to such questions as "Which (*26* or *206*) is twenty-six?" and "Which (*37* or *307*) is more?", it was clear that many understood these base-10 regularities *implicitly*, presumably picked up in their everyday experiences with the symbols. By contrast, when shown arrays of 26 and 206 dots, these children were unable to pick out the array with "twenty-six" dots without counting. Interestingly, these preschoolers also did better with the written numerals than with base-10 blocks, leading the researchers to suggest that base-10 blocks might be more effective for instruction once the child has verbal knowledge of the place-value structure rather than as an introduction to large numbers. By contrast, the five- to seven-year-old kindergartners in another study were nearly all able to name two-digit numerals and construct them with base-10 blocks.[51]

Finally, as discussed in Chapter 3, preschoolers can be introduced to *0*—they can be taught what it looks like, how to write it, and what it is called. Through various activities, young children can also learn that it means the same amount as "none" or "nothing." What may be a bit more difficult, given that they know "one" as the first counting word, is coming to understand that "zero" is a number among other small numbers and that it is the smallest number, even smaller than "one." One way to demonstrate this aspect of "zero" is to count a set of objects backward, removing one item with each count word until none is left.[52]

To say that knowledge of digit meaning is the strongest predictor of arithmetic achievement is not to say that other basic number skills are unimportant for arithmetic. The earlier mastered number skills are all essential foundations for understanding their values. Knowing digits' names, for example, makes it possible to think and talk about them. Indeed, preschoolers seem to learn the quantitative meanings of the numerals through their knowledge of the quantitative meanings of their respective number words. That is, if they know that *3* is called "three" and that "three" means this many (• • •), then they know that *3* also means that many.[53] And knowing the counting-word sequence facilitates learning the order of the numerals. Knowing the cardinality principle of counting is crucial for digit comparison, which improves rapidly once a child begins to understand cardinality.[54] There is also some evidence that young children use their knowledge of digit order to gain information about numerals' relative magnitude: In one study, when the preschoolers, who had begun to grasp cardinality, were shown a row of three consecutive digits, their ability to put them in the correct order was closely related to their ability to indicate the largest one among them.[55] Moreover, as children move through school, their sense of the amounts symbolized by larger and larger numerals deepens as they use base-10 notation and gain experience with arithmetic in the classroom.[56] (This topic will be taken up again in reference to the number line in Chapter 9.)

Understanding (*accessing*) the precise quantities that written symbols stand for, as demonstrated by ease of comparison, is associated with arithmetic performance throughout elementary school. It can also be notably impaired in many children with serious math difficulties from first grade onward. Moreover, for some children, difficulty accessing quantity from written numeric symbols may extend to the quantity represented by number words as well.[57] Indeed, associating the number words with the written numeric symbols may have an important role in accessing the symbols' meaning, as suggested by one study of deaf adults who, despite having no trouble with non-symbolic subtraction, had unusual difficulty subtracting with Arabic numerals.[58] Deficits in accessing numerical meaning are typically noticeable early in a child's schooling; Chapter 13 will review effective means of screening for them.

CONCLUSION

All in all, then, young children have a lot to learn about numerals. They must know what the written digits look like, how to write them, the rules for combining them to symbolize numbers above *9*, and what they are called. And they must learn what order they go in and how many countable things each of them stands for. This is a tall order, and as we have seen, children master these skills over time, in various contexts, and with much experimentation and adult instruction and guidance.

The question arises: *Is there any developmental pattern or trajectory that can be discerned?* Are some skills, on average, easier to master than others? What can early childhood teachers expect? While there has been some disagreement,[59] studies have generally found that children master the verbal number sequence and object counting first (as outlined in Chapter 6), then the names and shapes of the digits. Three- and four-year-olds get to the values and order of the digits, typically the last and most difficult numeracy tasks, via their knowledge of their names. By age five, most children have mastered all of these tasks for the numbers *one* through *six*.[60] Children master numbers, in all their forms, roughly in order beginning with the smallest and gradually working their way through the difficult -*teen*s into higher multi-digit numbers and the base-10 rules for constructing them, as we have seen. This process can take years of instruction and experience. As one research team noted, it is not until late elementary or middle school that "one million" begins to mean something more precise than just "very large amount."[61] We will see that played out quite vividly on the mental number line in Chapter 9.

ACTIVITIES

A Note on Topics

Most of the activities in this section cover several of the topics addressed in the research. Those topics are noted in the objectives for each activity.

ACTIVITY 8.1: Writing Digits With Correct Left-Right Orientation

Objective: To learn how to write digits in the proper orientation. Some children persist with writing digits (and letters) in the mirror image, or reversed left-right orientation, beyond first grade.

- **First:** For any digits that children reverse while writing, have them write the digit as large as possible in the proper orientation on a whiteboard or chalkboard, on a very large piece of paper, or with their finger on a wall, with hand over hand and verbal assistance if needed. Repeat this whole-arm gross-motor action many times, then gradually write the digit smaller and smaller until the digit is mastered in the normal size on paper.
- **Next:** Have the children write the target digit repeatedly on the same line and then check their work for any errors in digit orientation. If they do not recognize their own errors, point to an error and ask if it is the same or different than a digit in the proper orientation. Have them correct their errors.
- **Next:** The children write a variety of digits from teacher dictation, including both the target digit and others that the children do not typically reverse.
- **Next:** Dictate two- and three-digit numbers and have the children check for errors in orientation of the individual digits. Children may be more likely to revert to the mirror image of digits when they must focus on more than one digit at a time.
- **Next:** Have the children complete a variety of equations and then check for digit reversals within their written work.

ACTIVITY 8.2: Numeral Concentration Card Came

Objective: To learn what digits mean. Children match the numerosity shown on a card with a numeral written on another card.

- **First:** Create two decks of cards using index cards or thick card stock of two different colors. Write numerals *0* through *10* on the blank side of one set of the colored cards. Use stickers to show numerosities *zero* through *ten* (e.g., use five star-stickers to show the numerosity *five*) on the blank side of the other colored set. Shuffle the cards and place them face down. The children take turns turning over one numeral card and one card with stickers. If the pair is a match, they keep the cards.

■ **Next:** Expand the deck by adding cards with numerals *11* through *20*. For the cards depicting numerosity, use line and dot representations instead of stickers (see Activity 8.8).

ACTIVITY 8.3: Number Board Game[62]

Objective: To learn numerical order and to read numerals. Playing a linear board game has been shown to improve children's ability to grasp the numerical sequence, and searching for the written numerals improves recognition of them. Create a linear gameboard with squares labeled from *1* to *20*. Two children share the same gameboard, and each child will need a set of 20 numbered square tiles. Create the square tiles out of thick cardstock and make sure that each set is a different color. In the game, the children take turns spinning a spinner and placing one or two numbered tiles on the gameboard.

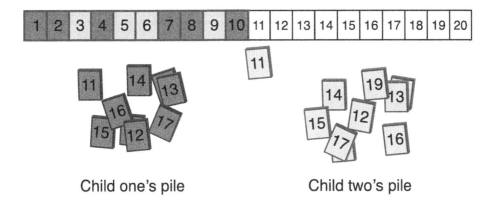

Child one's pile   Child two's pile

■ The children play in pairs. The first child spins a spinner with numbers *1* and *2*. If the spinner lands on *1*, then the tile *1* is placed on the board. If the spinner lands on *2*, then two tiles (*1* and *2*) are placed on the board. As they continue playing, the children must search for the number(s) to pick from their pile of numbered tiles based on the next successive numeral(s) on the gameboard. For example, if there are currently ten tiles on the board and the child rolls a *1*, the child sees that the next number on the gameboard is *11*, looks through their pile to find tile *11*, places tile *11* on the board, and reads the number aloud. The game ends when one child lands on *20*.

ACTIVITY 8.4: Number Naming and Verbal Counting Routines

Objective: To learn multi-digit number names, numerical order, and base-10 rules; to support transcoding. Using a *1–100* number chart that is organized by decades, point to numerals and have children say the number names aloud (see Figure 8.2b).

- First in consecutive order beginning with *1*.
- Then pick any number on the chart and count on and backward from that number.
- Count forward and backward by *10*s.
- Starting at *1*, continue counting on by adding *10* (*1, 11, 21, 31*, etc.).
- Alternate between counting by *10*s and *1*s. Start counting forward by *10*s (*10, 20, 30, 40, 50*) and pause. Then switch to counting from there by *1*s (*51, 52, 53, 54, 55*). Pause again and switch back to counting by *10*s (*65, 75, 85, 95*). Pause again and switch back to counting by *1*s (*96, 97, 98*, etc.).
- Count backward both by *10*s and by *1*s.
- Cover some numbers on the chart and have the children say the missing number.

ACTIVITY 8.5: Stackable Place-Value Number Cards and Counting the Base-10 Way

Objective: To learn base-10 rules and place-value. To learn to read and write multi-digit numerals. Stackable place-value number cards explicitly label the instances of *0* and correspond directly to number names. For example, three cards (*200, 40, 6*) can be stacked sequentially. First show the *200* card and say, "Two hundred." Then stack the *40* card on top so that *240* shows and say, "Two hundred forty." Finally, stack the *6* card on top and say, "Two hundred forty-six." An additional method is to name the numeral using the base-10 way, "Two hundreds, four tens, and six."[63] Commercial place-value cards or flip charts are readily available, or they can be made.

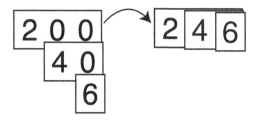

- **First:** Begin with single digits and name the numbers from *0* to *9* as the cards are flipped over.

- **Next:** The most difficult early number names are those from "eleven" to "nineteen," particularly "eleven" and "twelve," which do not follow the same pattern as the subsequent -teen numbers. First, flip the *10* card and say "ten." Next, stack the *1* card such that it covers the *0* of the *10* and shows *11*. Counting the base-10 way, say, "One ten and one, the name is eleven." Then replace the *1* card with the *2* card and say, "One ten and two, the name is twelve." Replace the *2* card with the *3* card and say, "One ten and three, the name is thirteen." For the numbers ending in "-teen," the order of the word parts is reversed, so it can be helpful to be explicit in pointing out that "-teen" really means "ten" and "thir-" represents "three" but that the name is in the flipped order, "thirteen."

- **Next:** Continue with the numbers *20–99*, first counting the base-10 way and then using the English name, such as showing the *20* card and saying, "Two tens, the name is twenty." Then show the *20* card. Place the *1* card on top of the *0* and say, "Two tens and one, the name is twenty-one."

- **Next:** Continue to increase the number of digits in the numerals and proceed in a similar manner, showing the numeral with the *0*s and stacking the additional numerals on top in a consecutive order, such as *5,000* then *400* then *30* then *2*, and say, "Five thousand four hundred and thirty-two."

- **Next:** An alternative to using cards or a flip chart is to use a piece of paper. Write the number *10* at the edge of the left side of the paper (see Figure a). On the back of the far-right side of the paper, write the number *1* such that when the paper is folded over, the *1* covers the *0* of the *10* on the left side, revealing the number *11* (see Figure b). Continue in this manner with multi-digit numerals.

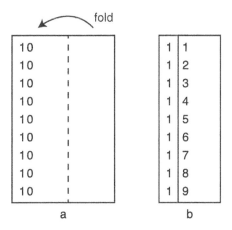

a   b

ACTIVITY 8.6: Reading and Writing Numbers Based on Place-Value

Objective: To learn to read and write multi-digit numerals with different place-values and to improve transcoding.

■ **First:** Draw a line for each digit in a numeral. The teacher fills in the digits one at a time from left to right and the children read the numeral aloud, such as:

$\overline{4}\ \underline{\ }\ \underline{\ }$ and children say "four hundred."
4 3 _ and children say "four hundred thirty."
4 3 2 and children say "four hundred thirty-two."

■ **Next:** Call out a number. The children write lines for the number of digits and then fill in the digits as they say the number. The children can think, "Four hundred thirty-two. That means there are three lines because there are three digits in numbers in the hundreds." Then show the correct number for comparison.

■ **Next:** Extend the numbers into the *1,000*s, with four, then five, then six digits. Children begin to show more confusion with sequencing the number names at this level. At first, it can help the children to practice naming these longer numbers with the word *thousand* written below the space where the *1,000*s digits are written. They learn to say, "Five thousand four hundred thirty-two. Sixty-five thousand four hundred thirty-two. Seven hundred sixty-five thousand four hundred thirty-two." Once the children can name the numbers in the *thousands* range, then they can write the numbers to dictation as described earlier.

$$765,432$$
Thousand

ACTIVITY 8.7: Unitizing With Stick Bundles[64]

Objective: To learn multi-digit numerals, what the digits mean, and that *ten* is a base unit. Children bundle sets of ten Popsicle sticks into "tens." The leftover single Popsicle sticks are called "ones."

■ **First:** Give the children a collection of Popsicle sticks. The children count and bundle groups of ten. Ask, "How many 'tens' do you have? How many 'ones' are left over?" Discuss the total numerical value of the bundles and leftover sticks: "We have six 'tens,' which is sixty, and three 'ones' left over. We have sixty-three sticks."

■ **Next:** After the children have had practice building groups of ten, practice incrementing and decrementing by bundles of ten while counting aloud. Start with a bundle of ten sticks and place more bundles on the table, one at a time, as the children count: "Ten, twenty, thirty, forty, fifty." Take bundles of sticks off the table and count backward: "Fifty, forty, thirty, twenty, ten, zero." Have the children write the numbers as well.

■ **Next:** Include loose sticks, representing the *one*s, in the counting sequence. For example, start with three "ten" bundles and five loose "ones." Add one more "ten" bundle at a time as the children count: "Thirty-five, forty-five, fifty-five, sixty-five, seventy-five, eighty-five." Take bundles away: "Eighty-five, seventy-five, sixty-five, fifty-five, forty-five. . . ." Have the children write the numbers as well.

■ **Next:** Alternate between incrementing or decrementing by "tens" and "ones." For example, start with four bundles and one stick. Add some bundles: "Forty-one, fifty-one, sixty-one." Switch to adding sticks: "Sixty-two, sixty-three, sixty-four, sixty-five, sixty-six." Switch back to adding bundles: "Seventy-six, eighty-six, ninety-six." Take away bundles and sticks in the same way, alternating between the two as the children count backward. Switching between bundles ("tens") and sticks ("ones") will help the children practice shifting flexibly, an important executive function. Have the children write the numbers as well.

ACTIVITY 8.8: Lines and Dots[65]

Objective: To learn what digits mean and to name multi-digit numerals. Children represent sets using line-and-dot drawings as they count sets of objects.

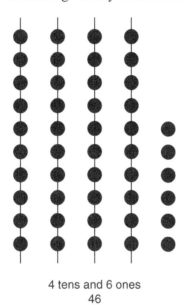

4 tens and 6 ones
46

■ Give each child a collection of more than 11 items to count. As they count, the children represent each object by drawing a dot in a vertical column. When they have a vertical column of ten dots, they draw a line through those ten dots and start a new column of dots to the right. After they are done counting, the children should have a collection of vertical lines with ten dots (representing the *tens*) and single dots (representing the *ones*) drawn on the paper. Read the number aloud by reciting the *tens* and *ones* separately: "One, two, three, four tens and one, two, three, four, five, six ones. That's forty-six." Write the number of lines and dots.

ACTIVITY 8.9: Numeral Pair Comparisons

Objective: To learn what numerals mean.[66] Write out multiple examples of the types of numeral pairs described here, and have children choose which numeral in the pair has the greater magnitude. The numeral pairs provided here are based on common comparison difficulties that children have. Write out the pairs such that sometimes the numeral with greater magnitude is on the left and sometimes on the right of the pair.

- Unit differences such as *12* and *13*, *75* and *74*.
- Single and double digits such as *7* and *17*.
- Double and triple digits such as *23* and *230* and *203*.
- Reverse digits such as *23* and *32*.
- Difference of *10*, such as *12* and *22*, *43* and *53*.

ACTIVITY 8.10: Representing Numbers in Different Ways

Objective: To learn transcoding.[67] You can adapt a place-value chart to show only the place value that the class is currently learning. The place-value chart has five rows: place-value, standard form, base-10 blocks, expanded form, and written form.

245			
Place value	HOW MANY 100s	HOW MANY 10s	HOW MANY 1s
Standard form	2	4	5
Base-10 blocks			
Expanded form	200 +	40 +	5
Written form	two hundred	forty	five

- Have a stack of index cards depicting written numerals *0* through *9*. The children randomly draw three cards, place them on the chart in the standard form row (see Figure), and read the number aloud. They use base-10 blocks or lines and dots (see Activity 8.8) to create the quantity directly below the numeral on the chart. The children write the expanded form and the standard numeral in the row underneath. Practice reading the numeral aloud once more.
- Some children have an especially difficult time reading and writing numerals with *0*s. For example, a child might write *45* as *405*. Have the children practice making numerals such as *45* and *405* on two adjacent place-value charts. Read each number aloud and discuss how the numbers are different.

NOTES

1 Tolchinsky-Landsmann & Karmiloff-Smith, 1992.
2 Mark-Zigdon & Tirosh, 2008.
3 Dehaene et al., 2005.
4 Fischer & Koch, 2016.
5 Johansson, 2005.
6 Krasa & Yu, under review.
7 Cao et al., 2013; Naka, 1998.
8 Dehaene, 2009, pp. 284–299.
9 Vinci-Booher et al., 2016; Zemlock et al., 2018.
10 Krasa et al., in preparation.
11 Mix et al., 2017.
12 Vasilyeva et al., 2015.
13 Cheung & Ansari, 2021.
14 Johansson, 2005.
15 Friedmann et al., 2010.
16 Malone et al., 2019.
17 Cohen et al., 2013.
18 Bialystok & Codd, 2000.
19 Litkowski et al., 2020.
20 Clayton et al., 2020.
21 Power & DalMartello, 1997.
22 Byrge et al., 2014.
23 Skwarchuk & Anglin, 2002.
24 Moeller et al., 2015; Stein et al., 2021; VanRinsveld & Schiltz, 2016.
25 DeClerq-Quaegebeur et al., 2018; Ellis & Miles, 1977.
26 Ziegler et al., 2010.
27 Moura et al., 2013.
28 Erbeli et al., 2021.
29 Raddatz et al., 2017.
30 Mazzocco & Grimm, 2013.
31 Lin et al., 2019.

32 Göbel et al., 2014; Steingold et al., 2003.

33 Fuson et al., 1997.

34 Habermann et al., 2020.

35 Vogel et al., 2015.

36 Colomé & Noël, 2012.

37 Attout & Majerus, 2018; Lyons et al., 2014; Sasanguie & Vos, 2018.

38 Vogel et al., 2017.

39 Morsanyi et al., 2018.

40 O'Connor et al., 2018.

41 DeSmedt & Gilmore, 2011; Schneider et al., 2017; Träff et al., 2020.

42 Vanbinst et al., 2016.

43 Nosworthy et al., 2013.

44 Hutchison et al., 2020.

45 Sasanguie et al., 2012.

46 Landerl, 2013.

47 Mann et al., 2011.

48 Nuerk et al., 2004.

49 Schneider et al., 2017.

50 Merkley & Ansari, 2016.

51 Laski et al., 2016; Yuan et al., 2019.

52 Wellman & Miller, 1986.

53 Hurst et al., 2017.

54 Geary & van Marle, 2018.

55 Sella et al., 2019.

56 Skwarchuk & Anglin, 2002; Vanbinst et al., 2019.

57 Lafay et al., 2017.

58 Masataka, 2006.

59 Benoit et al., 2013.

60 Knudsen et al., 2015; Marinova et al., 2021.

61 Skwarchuk & Anglin, 2002.

62 Derived from Hawes et al., 2020.

63 Adapted from Magargee & Beauford, 2016.

64 Adapted from Ellemor-Collins & Wright, 2011.

65 Adapted from Fuson et al., 1997.

66 Adapted from Cheung & Ansari, 2021.

67 Adapted from Fuson & Briars, 1990; Rojo et al., 2021.

REFERENCES

The following references were cited in this chapter. For additional selected references relevant to this chapter, please see Chapter 8 Supplemental References in eResources.

Attout, L., & Majerus, S. (2018). Serial order working memory and numerical ordinal processing share common processes and predict arithmetic abilities. *British Journal of Developmental Psychology, 36*, 285–298.

Benoit, L., Lehalle, H., Molina, M., Tijus, C., & Jouen, F. (2013). Young children's mapping between arrays, number words, and digits. *Cognition, 129*, 95–101.

Bialystok, E., & Codd, J. (2000). Representing quantity beyond whole numbers: Some, none, and part. *Canadian Journal of Experimental Psychology, 54*, 117–128.

Byrge, L., Smith, L.B., & Mix, K.S. (2014). Beginnings of place value: How preschoolers write three-digit numbers. *Child Development, 85*, 437–443.

Cao, F., Rickles, B., Vu, M., Zhu, Z., Chan, D.H.L., Harris, L.N., Stafura, J., Xu, Y., & Perfetti, C.A. (2013). Early stage visual-orthographic processes predict long-term retention of word form and meaning: A visual encoding training study. *Journal of Neurolinguistics, 26*, 440–461.

Cheung, P., & Ansari, D. (2021). Cracking the code of place value: The relationship between *place* and *value* takes years to master. *Developmental Psychology, 57*, 227–240.

Clayton, F.J., Copper, C., Steiner, A.F., Banfi, C., Finke, S., Landerl, K., & Göbel, S.M. (2020). Two-digit number writing and arithmetic in Year 1 children: Does number word inversion matter? *Cognitive Development, 56*, 100967.

Cohen, D.J., Warren, E., & Blanc-Goldhammer, D. (2013). Cross-format physical similarity effects and their implications for the numerical cognition architecture. *Cognitive Psychology, 66*, 355–379.

Colomé, À., & Noël, M.-P. (2012). One first? Acquisition of the cardinal and ordinal uses of numbers in preschoolers. *Journal of Experimental Child Psychology, 113*, 233–247.

DeClercq-Quaegebeur, M., Casalis, S., Vilette, B., Lemaitre, M.-P., & Vallée, L. (2018). Arithmetic abilities in children with developmental dyslexia: Performance on French ZAREKI-R Test. *Journal of Learning Disabilities, 51*, 236–249.

Dehaene, S. (2009). *Reading in the brain*. Viking Press.

Dehaene, S., Cohen, L., Sigman, M., & Vinckier, F. (2005). The neural code for written words: A proposal. *Trends in Cognitive Sciences, 9*, 335–341.

DeSmedt, B., & Gilmore, C.K. (2011). Defective number module or impaired access? Numerical magnitude processing in first graders with mathematical difficulties. *Journal of Experimental Child Psychology, 108*, 278–292.

Ellemor-Collins, D., & Wright, R. (2011). Developing conceptual place value: Instructional design for intensive intervention. *Australian Journal of Learning Difficulties, 16*, 41–63.

Ellis, N.C., & Miles, T.R. (1977). Dyslexia as a limitation in the ability to process information. *Bulletin of the Orton Society, 27*, 72–81.

Erbeli, F., Shi, Q., Campbell, A.R., Hart, S.A., & Woltering, S. (2021). Developmental dynamics between reading and math in elementary school. *Developmental Science, 24*, e13004.

Fischer, J.-P., & Koch, A.-M. (2016). Mirror writing in typically developing children: A first longitudinal study. *Cognitive Development, 38*, 114–124.

Friedmann, N., Dotan, D., & Rahamim, E. (2010). Is the visual analyzer orthographic-specific? Reading words and numbers in letter position dyslexia. *Cortex, 46*, 982–1004.

Fuson, K.C., & Briars, D.J. (1990). Using a base-ten blocks learning/teaching approach for first- and second-grade place-value and multidigit addition and subtraction. *Journal for Research in Mathematics Education, 21*, 180–206.

Fuson, K.C., Smith, S.T., & LoCicero, A.M. (1997). Supporting Latino first graders' ten-structured thinking in urban classrooms. *Journal for Research in Mathematics Education, 28*, 738–766.

Geary, D.C., & van Marle, K. (2018). Growth of symbolic number knowledge accelerates after children understand cardinality. *Cognition, 177*, 69–78.

Göbel, S.M., Moeller, K., Pixner, S., Kaufmann, L., & Nuerk, H.-C. (2014). Language affects symbolic arithmetic in children: The case of number word inversion. *Journal of Experimental Child Psychology, 119*, 17–25.

Habermann, S., Donlan, C., Göbel, S.M., & Hulme, C. (2020). The critical role of Arabic numeral knowledge as a longitudinal predictor of arithmetic development. *Journal of Experimental Child Psychology, 193*, 104794.

Hawes, Z., Cain, M., Jones, S., Thomson, N., Bailey, C., Seo, J., Caswell, B., & Moss, J. (2020). Effects of a teacher-designed and teacher-led numerical board game intervention: A randomized controlled study with 4- to 6-year-olds. *Mind, Brain and Education, 14,* 71–80.

Hurst, M., Anderson, U., & Cordes, S. (2017). Mapping among number words, numerals, and nonsymbolic quantities in preschoolers. *Journal of Cognition and Development, 18,* 41–62.

Hutchison, J.E., Ansari, D., Zheng, S., DeJesus, S., & Lyons, I.M. (2020). The relation between subitizable symbolic and non-symbolic number processing over the kindergarten school year. *Developmental Science, 23,* e12884.

Johansson, B.S. (2005). Numeral writing skill and elementary arithmetic mental calculations. *Scandinavian Journal of Educational Research, 49,* 3–25.

Knudsen, B., Fischer, M.H., Henning, A., & Aschersleben, G. (2015). The development of Arabic digit knowledge in 4- to 7-year-old children. *Journal of Numerical Cognition, 1,* 21–37.

Krasa, N., Bell, Z., & Qin, J. (in preparation). Mirror invariance in reading and writing in subsequent-alphabet acquisition.

Krasa, N., & Yu, S. (under review). Ƨ ᗺ or not ᗺ Ƨ: The developmental trajectory of mirror discrimination for alphanumeric symbols and its relationship to reading.

Lafay, A., Macoir, J., & St.-Pierre, M.-C. (2017). Impairment of Arabic- and spoken-number processing in children with mathematical learning disability. *Journal of Numerical Cognition, 3,* 620–641.

Landerl, K. (2013). Development of numerical processing in children with typical and dyscalculic arithmetic skills: A longitudinal study. *Frontiers in Psychology, 4,* 459.

Landsmann, L.T., & Karmiloff-Smith, A. (1992). Children's understanding of notations as domains of knowledge versus referential-communicative tools. *Cognitive Development, 7,* 287–300.

Laski, E.V., Schiffman, J., Shen, C., & Vasilyeva, M. (2016). Kindergartners' base-10 knowledge predicts arithmetic accuracy concurrently and longitudinally. *Learning and Individual Differences, 50,* 234–239.

Lin, J.-F.L., Imada, T., & Kuhl, P.K. (2019). Neuroplasticity, bilingualism, and mental mathematics: A behavior-MEG study. *Brain and Cognition, 134,* 122–134.

Litkowski, E.C., Duncan, R.J., Logan, J.A.R., & Purpura, D.J. (2020). When do preschoolers learn specific mathematics skills? Mapping the development of early numeracy knowledge. *Journal of Experimental Child Psychology, 195,* 104846.

Lyons, I.M., Price, G.R., Vaessen, A., Blomert, L., & Ansari, D. (2014). Numerical predictors of arithmetic success in grades 1–6. *Developmental Science, 17,* 714–726.

Magargee, S.D., & Beauford, J.E. (2016). Do explicit number names accelerate pre-kindergarteners' numeracy and place value acquisition? *Educational Studies in Mathematics, 92,* 179–192.

Malone, S.A., Heron-Delaney, M., Burgoyne, K., & Hulme, C. (2019). Learning correspondences between magnitudes, symbols and words: Evidence for a triple code model of arithmetic development. *Cognition, 187,* 1–9.

Mann, A., Moeller, K., Pixner, S., Kaufmann, L., & Nuerk, H.-C. (2011). Attentional strategies in place-value integration: A longitudinal study on two-digit number comparison. *Journal of Psychology, 219,* 42–49.

Marinova, M., Reynvoet, B., & Sasanguie, D. (2021). Mapping between number notations in kindergarten and the role of home numeracy. *Cognitive Development, 57,* 101002.

Mark-Zigdon, N., & Tirosh, D. (2008). Kindergarten and first graders' knowledge of the number symbols: Production and recognition. *Focus on Learning Problems in Mathematics, 30,* 1–11.

Masataka, N. (2006). Differences in arithmetic subtraction of nonsymbolic numerosities by deaf and hearing adults. *Journal of Deaf Studies and Deaf Education*, *11*, 139–143.

Mazzocco, M.M.M., & Grimm, K.J. (2013). Growth in rapid automatized naming from grades K to 8 in children with math or reading disabilities. *Journal of Learning Disabilities*, *46*, 517–533.

Merkley, R., & Ansari, D. (2016). Why numerical symbols count in the development of mathematical skills: Evidence from brain and behavior. *Current Opinion in Behavioral Sciences*, *10*, 14–20.

Mix, K.S., Smith, L.B., Stockton, J.D., Cheng, Y.-L., & Barterian, J.A. (2017). Grounding the symbols for place value: Evidence from training and long-term exposure to base-10 models. *Journal of Cognition and Development*, *18*, 129–151.

Moeller, K., Shaki, S., Göbel, S.M., & Nuerk, H.-C. (2015). Language influences number processing: A quadrilingual study. *Cognition*, *136*, 150–155.

Morsanyi, K., vanBers, B.M.C.W., O'Connor, P.A., & McCormack, T. (2018). Developmental dyscalculia is characterized by order processing deficits: Evidence from numerical and non-numerical ordering tasks. *Developmental Neuropsychology*, *43*, 595–621.

Moura, R., Wood, G., Pinheiro-Chagas, P., Lonnemann, J., Krinzinger, H., Willmes, K., & Haase, V.G. (2013). Transcoding abilities in typical and atypical mathematics achievers: The role of working memory and procedural and lexical competencies. *Journal of Experimental Child Psychology*, *116*, 707–727.

Naka, M. (1998). Repeated writing facilitates children's memory for pseudocharacters and foreign letters. *Memory & Cognition*, *26*, 804–809.

Nosworthy, N., Bugden, S., Archibald, L., Evans, B., & Ansari, D. (2013). A two-minute paper-and-pencil test of symbolic and nonsymbolic numerical magnitude processing explains variability in primary school children's arithmetic competence. *PLoS ONE*, *8*(7), e67918.

Nuerk, H.-C., Kaufmann, L., Zoppoth, S., & Willmes, K. (2004). On the development of the mental number line: More, less, or never holistic with increasing age? *Developmental Psychology*, *40*, 1199–1211.

O'Connor, P. A., Morsanyi, K., & McCormack, T. (2018). Young children's non-numerical ordering ability at the start of formal education longitudinally predicts their symbolic number skills and academic achievement in maths. *Developmental Science*, *21*, e12645.

Power, R., DalMartello, M.F. (1997). From 834 to eight thirty four: The reading of Arabic numerals by seven-year-old children. *Mathematical Cognition*, *3*, 63–85.

Raddatz, J., Kuhn, J.-T., Holling, H., Moll, K., & Dobel, C. (2017). Comorbidity of arithmetic and reading disorder: Basic number processing and calculation in children with learning impairments. *Journal of Learning Disabilities*, *50*, 298–308.

Rojo, M.M., Knight, B., & Bryant, D.P. (2021). Teaching place value to students with learning disabilities in mathematics. *Intervention in School and Clinic*, *57*, 32–40.

Sasanguie, D., DeSmedt, B., Defever, E., & Reynvoet, B. (2012). Association between basic numerical abilities and mathematics achievement. *British Journal of Developmental Psychology*, *30*, 344–357.

Sasanguie, D., & Vos, H. (2018). About why there is a shift from cardinal to ordinal processing in the association with arithmetic between first and second grade. *Developmental Science*, *21*, e12653.

Schneider, M., Beeres, K., Coban, L., Merz, S., Schmidt, S.S., Stricker, J., & DeSmedt, B. (2017). Associations of non-symbolic and symbolic numerical magnitude processing with mathematical competence: A meta-analysis. *Developmental Science*, *20*, e12372.

Sella, R., Lucangeli, D., & Zorzi, M. (2019). Spatial order relates to the exact numerical magnitude of digits in young children. *Journal of Experimental Child Psychology*, *178*, 385–404.

Skwarchuk, S.L., & Anglin, J.M. (2002). Children's acquisition of the English cardinal number words: A special case of vocabulary development. *Journal of Educational Psychology, 94*, 107–125.

Steiner, A.F., Banfi, C., Finke, S., Kemény, F., Clayton, F.J., Göbel, S.M., & Landerl, K. (2021). Twenty-four or four-and-twenty: Language modulates cross-modal matching for multidigit numbers in children and adults. *Journal of Experimental Child Psychology, 202*, 104970.

Steingold, E., Spelke, E., & Kittredge, A. (2003, July). *Linguistic cues influence acquisition of number words*. Paper presented at the 25th annual conference of the Cognitive Science Society, Cambridge, MA. Retrieved on 02/13/2020, from https://pdfs.semanticscholar.org/362c/783f75 66532b360481bda6ffbd750a18f2eb.pdf

Träff, U., Levén, A., Östergren, R., & Schöld, D. (2020). Number magnitude processing and verbal working memory in children with mild intellectual disabilities. *Developmental Neuropsychology, 45*, 139–153.

Vanbinst, K., Ansari, D., Ghesquière, P., & DeSmedt, B. (2016). Symbolic numerical magnitude processing is as important to arithmetic as phonological awareness is to reading. *PLoS ONE, 11*(3), e0151045.

Vanbinst, K., Ghesquière, P., & DeSmedt, B. (2019). Is the long-term association between symbolic numerical magnitude processing and arithmetic bi-directional? *Journal of Numerical Cognition, 5*, 358–370.

VanRinsveld, A., & Schiltz, C. (2016). Sixty-twelve = seventy-two? A cross-linguistic comparison of children's number transcoding. *The British Journal of Developmental Psychology, 34*, 461–468.

Vasilyeva, M., Laski, E.V., Ermakova, A., Lai, W.-F., Jeong, Y., & Hachigian, A. (2015). Reexamining the language account of cross-national differences in base-10 number representations. *Journal of Experimental Child Psychology, 129*, 12–25.

Vinci-Booher, S., James, T.W., & James, K.H. (2016). Visual-motor functional connectivity in preschool children emerges after handwriting experience. *Trends in Neuroscience and Education, 5*, 107–120.

Vogel, S.E., Haigh, T., Sommerauer, G., Spindler, M., Brunner, C., Lyons, I.M., & Grabner, R.H. (2017). Processing the order of symbolic numbers: A reliable and unique predictor of arithmetic fluency. *Journal of Numerical Cognition, 3*, 288–308.

Vogel, S.E., Remark, A., & Ansari, D. (2015). Differential processing of symbolic numerical magnitude and order in first-grade children. *Journal of Experimental Child Psychology, 129*, 26–39.

Wellman, H.M., & Miller, K.F. (1986). Thinking about nothing: Development of concepts of zero. *The British Journal of Developmental Psychology, 4*, 31–42.

Yuan, L., Prather, R.W., Mix, K.S., & Smith, L.B. (2019). Preschoolers and multi-digit numbers: A path to mathematics through the symbols themselves. *Cognition, 189*, 89–104.

Zemlock, D., Vinci-Booher, S., & James, K.H. (2018). Visual-motor symbol production facilitates letter recognition in young children. *Reading & Writing, 31*, 1255–1271.

Ziegler, J.C., Pech-Georgel, C., Dufau, S., & Grainger, J. (2010). Rapid processing of letters, digits and symbols: What purely visual-attentional deficit in developmental dyslexia? *Developmental Science, 13*, F8–F14.

Chapter 9

The Number Line and Linear Measurement

FINALLY, perhaps one of the most interesting "technologies" for keeping track of large numerosities, and certainly one of the most powerful tools for teaching about them, is the number line.[1] This chapter will review its particular advantages as an instrument for understanding numerical relations, as well as its diagnostic value as a window into children's numerical misunderstandings. The chapter will also examine the number line's perceived direction and the role of spatial skill in understanding numerical relations, as well as ways to bring the number line into focus. Finally, just as aligning number with linear distance can provide a powerful tool for understanding and manipulating numerical relations, so it affords a model for quantifying—that is, *measuring*—continuous linear space and, by extension, any continuous linear dimension (weight, temperature, time, and so forth), often a gnarly topic for young children. Linear measurement will be taken up at the end.

THE NUMBER LINE AND NUMERICAL RELATIONS

In Chapter 8, it was noted that being able to compare the values of two numerals is the skill most closely associated with arithmetic achievement. Knowledge of the values of individual digits will let a young child know that *8* means a larger amount than *5*. But how *much* larger? How do these values relate to one another? Prior to learning formal subtraction, how can a child compare numerosities exactly? There are several options.

One could count to five and then figure out how many more number words in the sequence would get you to eight. But that would entail double counting, which is tricky.

One could count out five buttons and then see how many more would make eight or count out eight buttons and then see how many you would have to remove to make five (Figure 9.1). However, this method requires counting, which is both tedious and error-prone. Moreover, the result is difficult to remember or envision in one's head, because one heap of eight buttons is rarely configured the same way as another heap of eight buttons—a literal "heap of confusion."

DOI: 10.4324/9781003157656-12

Doing the same thing with one's fingers may be easier because fingers are all lined up (Figure 9.2), but difficult when the numerosities go above ten.

Or one could line up a set of five buttons alongside a set of eight, match them up one for one, and count the leftovers (Figure 9.3). While easier to fix in one's mind than

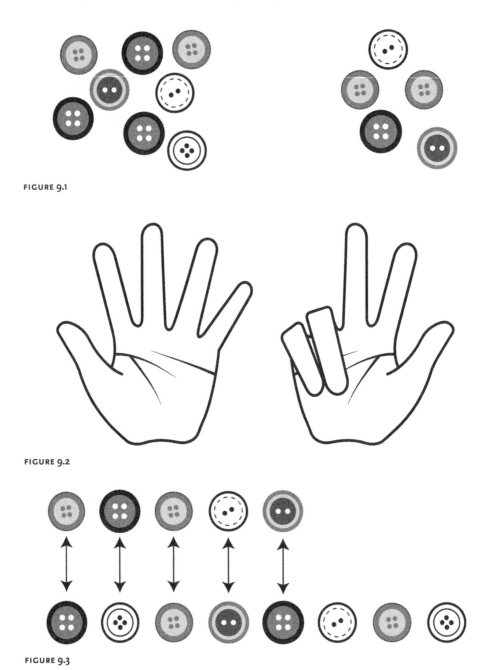

FIGURE 9.1

FIGURE 9.2

FIGURE 9.3

piles of buttons, this method is also tedious and especially error-prone with bigger numbers.

But now try this! Instead of lining up and counting individual *items*, do so instead with units of *length*. Length, then, becomes a kind of *analog* of number, where one unit of length is analogous to one countable item. A ruler is one example of units of length lined up, but a simpler version is number blocks, with each unit of length represented by a little cube and multiple units by cubes joined together in a longer block (Figure 9.4). To solve the *8 – 5* problem, one need only align the 5-block and the 8-block and count the leftover units on the 8-block. If the blocks are color-coded by length, counting and tedium are sharply reduced, significantly reducing the burden on working memory and chance of error.

Even better: Line up the blocks along a track or number line, with the units marked on it (Figure 9.5). Place a 5-block on the track, and the distance from it to *8* is easy to see, confirm with a 3-block, and remember. In this way, the burden on working memory and the chance of error are even further reduced. As noted in Chapter 1, error-free practice is essential for remembering procedural outcomes, as in basic arithmetic.

Translating discrete items into units of length is abstract, because it can be used to represent any set of countable things, just like the counting words and digits. However, representing length with physical or digital (on-screen) blocks allows children to manipulate the quantities. A more abstract version is a paper-and-pencil number line (Figure 9.6).

This single-dimension *number line* powerfully illustrates not only the cardinal (*How many*) meaning of numbers but their ordinal (*What order*) meaning as well. It also

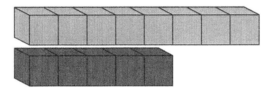

FIGURE 9.4

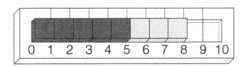

FIGURE 9.5   Number blocks on a number track.

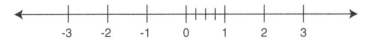

FIGURE 9.6   The number line, showing positive and negative integers, *zero*, and rational numbers.

provides a vivid, concrete illustration of the relationships between their values ("Oh! Six is here, and fifty-nine is way over there!"). An appreciation of the orderly, linear organization of number is necessary to fully understand numerical relations,[2] which in turn is crucial for arithmetic development.[3]

The number line also offers a concrete way to illustrate and compare fractional portions of unit lengths, providing a clear window into rational number. Indeed, the number line provides a clearer window into rational numbers than do the area model, fractional notation, or proportions of discrete items such as red and green marbles, as we shall see in Chapter 11.[4] By extending the number line in the opposite direction, it can also represent negative numbers, an otherwise difficult concept to understand or picture in one's mind, as discussed in Chapter 2. Importantly, because the configuration is always the same, it can serve as a stable mental template, or working model, of quantities that can be visualized, recalled, and mentally manipulated.[5] In all, it is a clear, reliable illustration (or *spatial map*) of numbers' linear order and how their quantities relate to each other.

The number line recruits and supports all the skills of budding numeracy. To use a number line, one must know the counting-word sequence, be familiar with the numerals and their names, and understand that the words and numerals represent quantities. These skills are all necessary for doing arithmetic, of course, but also for understanding a number line.[6] Individuals for whom numerical transcoding is challenging, for example, may also have difficulty with number-line placements, as studies of deaf college students and of children with transcoding difficulties due to significant working-memory deficits demonstrate.[7]

Most crucially, however, children must learn how quantities relate to each other. An understanding of numbers' linear relationships—that numbers form an ordered sequence and that each successive number is one unit bigger than the previous number—is necessary for comparing numbers[8] and learning arithmetic. This, then, is the essence of the number line as a powerful numeracy tool and the beginning of what has been called the *mental number line*. A study of five- and six-year-olds, using sequences of familiar letters or pictures of animals, found that children's ability to isolate part of a visual sequence or keep track of a visual sequence through changes predicted their arithmetic performance. Thus, it appears that understanding the positional order of quantities in sequence may help children mentally organize the numerals and their values.[9]

The child's own physical number-line drawings embody this emerging knowledge and can help make it explicit. And in so far as they reflect the child's idea of number, they can serve as a diagnostic tool, providing the teacher with a window into the child's understanding and misunderstanding of numerical relations. As a pedagogical tool, the standard physical number line can correct and clarify children's emerging ideas of numerical relations, provide a clear and memorable demonstration of numerical transformations, and expand the child's numerical horizon to include ever larger and smaller quantities.

Finally, one of the number line's most important features is that it is one-dimensional. As we saw in Chapter 8, numbers larger than *nine* are often taught with base-10 blocks organized into rods, two-dimensional flats, and three-dimensional blocks for numbers larger than *9*, *99*, and *999*, respectively. While this tool has proven an effective method for teaching place-value notation, young children have difficulty considering more than one dimension at a time. Indeed, it takes several years before they can appreciate the value represented by 10-blocks laid out over two- or three-dimensional space,[10] making the relation of values above *99* difficult to understand with such a model. These findings imply that a strictly linear embodiment of numerical relations, regardless of size, can be expected to be significantly more accessible to young children.

THE DIRECTION OF THE NUMBER LINE

The number line illustrates quantities in order from small to large, and thus by definition has a linear direction. But what direction? A casual check of the rulers and yardsticks around the house—including the ruler at the top of the computer screen as we write this—suggests that numbers grow from left to right. Logically, of course, the number line is an abstraction and its direction is arbitrary. So where did the left-to-right convention come from? International research suggests that one key source is the direction of reading. Adults and children whose language is read from left to right, such as English, also tend to think of numbers as growing in that direction, while those whose languages are read from right to left, such as Arabic, have a right-to-left idea about numbers. Illiterate adults, by contrast, do not show any directional preference.[11] However, Israeli children, whose Hebrew words are read from right to left but whose numerals are read from left to right, seem to think of numbers growing in a direction compatible with their numerical rather than word-reading direction—that is, from left to right. This suggests that word-reading direction is not the only source of numerical directional preference.[12]

In fact, there is reason to believe that there are multiple influences on the way people think about numerical direction. Time-related numbers (e.g., in two hours, five months ago) are often thought of in terms of distance or proximity to oneself and the direction one is facing, extending forward into the future or behind us into the past.[13] Some researchers attribute the left-to-right view of numerical growth to the common habit of beginning finger counting on the left hand.[14] Conversely, however, this simple association could indicate that children start counting on their left hand because that is how they think of numbers. Or perhaps some children who begin counting on their left hand do so because it frees up their dominant right hand for pointing, manipulating objects, or writing, and the association to the number line is coincidental. No one knows for sure. It is also unclear whether a child's handedness affects counting direction. One study found that young children seem to prefer to point and count along a row by beginning with the item at the end opposite from the hand used, while other researchers found no handedness effect.[15] On number-order tasks that do not involve pointing while counting, however, handedness does not seem to affect the expected direction.[16] Congenitally blind individuals, without a visual field for reference, associate low numbers to their left hand.[17] Context—reading thermometers or elevator buttons, for example—may also influence counting habits and ideas about numerical direction. Indeed, studies of children and adults that have considered all three spatial dimensions show equally strong left-to-right, bottom-to-top, and near-to-far mental views of number growth.[18]

Moreover, the left-to-right notion of number growth emerges before children learn to read. For example, when asked to count aloud a row of nine chips, pointing to each in turn, the proportion of those counting from left to right rose from 45 percent at age two and a half to 80 percent at age four and a half.[19] Preschoolers also seem to remember locations better if they are numbered from left to right.[20] How does this left-to-right image of numerical growth develop prior to reading? Studies suggest that simply paying attention to the page while being read to helps to establish a sense of conventional written—and numerical—order in young children. Additionally, the action in children's book illustrations tends to be oriented in the same direction as the text, so all of a child's directional cues are generally consistent.[21] While the sense of numerical direction is quite malleable in the early years,[22] by age nine or so, most children's left-to-right sense of numerical growth is well-established and automatic.[23]

Importantly, young children who are just learning the numbering system perform better on number-line placements, ordinal number searches, counting, symbolic numerical comparisons, and even digit naming when the direction of numerical growth remains consistently aligned to cultural norms and habits,[24] or at least consistent within a child's own activities.[25] Moreover, young primary-school children with a consistent, well-established sense of numerical direction also do better on such classroom math tasks as mental arithmetic, numerical equations, and number comparisons.[26] Like the order in which objects are counted, discussed in Chapter 6, the direction of the number line is mathematically arbitrary and irrelevant; however, while children are just starting out on their mathematical journey, it is best to stick with what makes learning about numbers easiest. For Western children, numbers grow from left to right.

CHILDREN'S MENTAL IMAGES OF NUMERICAL RELATIONS

A number line illustrates both the order of the numbers and their relative magnitudes. Thus, misunderstandings about either numerical feature can easily be recognized in children's own number line creations. When asked to draw a number line, do they space the numbers evenly, indicating that they know that all numbers differ from their immediate predecessors by the same amount? Do they line up the numbers in the correct order? If shown a number on the number line, can they name the number that comes before it? The count-word sequence in reverse is typically not learned by rote, but relies on a visual-spatial sense of ordered numerals. Having ready access to a preceding number is closely related to a child's number-comparison skill.[27]

In order to focus attention on one or another aspect of numerical thinking, researchers typically use one of three versions of the number line. Teachers can use these methods as well, to understand their students' ideas about number.

The version most similar to a child's own creation is the partially bounded number line, with *0* marked at the left end and an arrow on the right end signifying that the line

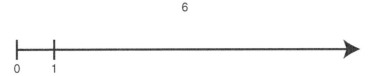

FIGURE 9.7 Partially bounded number-line estimate: If this is where *1* goes, place a hash mark on the line where you think *6* belongs.

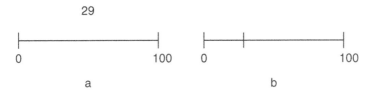

FIGURE 9.8 Bounded number-line estimate: a) Place a hash mark on the line where you think this number belongs. b) What number belongs at the hash mark?

continues (see Figure 9.7). In this task, however, a unit of length is provided. The task here is to indicate on the line where a given number belongs, using the illustrated unit as the model of one unit, an iterative process similar to measuring, except envisioned mentally.

A second and the most frequently used version is the bounded number line, with *0* marked at the left end and another number at the right end (Figure 9.8a). The children's task, then, is either to mark the line where they think a given quantity (here, *29*) belongs or to decide what number is represented by a given hash mark on the line, without counting (Figure 9.8b). Alternatively, the child is prompted with a spoken number word rather than a written numeral. Some studies also provide the child with an anchor, such as the line's midpoint. Crucially, the judgment here is proportional rather than iterative, because the distance from both endpoints needs to be considered in the placement. In that sense, the task is like judging the relative amount of water in a glass (see Figure 2.4a in Chapter 2), except in this case it requires understanding relative numerical values (e.g., Is the glass closer to empty or full? Is *7* closer to *0* or *10*?).

Importantly, in both the bounded and partially bounded number-line tasks, the child has a fresh blank number line on which to locate each number, so that previous placements do not bias subsequent choices. For the same reason, the numbers should be given in jumbled order.

A third version is the fully unbounded number line (basically just a straight line), typically used to investigate young children's ideas about the order and relative size of small numbers, as well as their direction of growth. The exercise begins with the researcher placing one number, say *6*, at the center of the line with a hash mark (Figure 9.9a). The child is then shown another number that is one more or less than the first (here *7*) and is asked to place it on the line, thereby establishing for herself both the direction of the line and the size of the unit as she envisions it (Figure 9.9b). The child

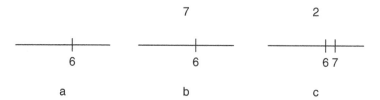

FIGURE 9.9   Unbounded number-line estimate: a) If 6 goes here, b) then where does 7 go?
c) If 6 goes here and 7 goes there, then where does 2 go?
Source: Adapted from Sella et al., 2019.

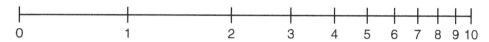

FIGURE 9.10   Skewed (logarithmic) error pattern.
Source: Adapted from Siegler & Booth, 2004.

is then shown a third number (here *2*) and asked to place it on the line (Figure 9.9c). This assesses the child's accuracy of both order and relative magnitude. With older children, any three numbers will be informative.[28]

So, what do children's number-line placements look like? Research has revealed four common, immature patterns; they are illustrated here so that teachers will understand what they mean when they see them in the classroom.

One immature pattern consists of placements that are overblown within the familiar lower number range and compressed in the unfamiliar upper range, giving it a skewed appearance. (Mathematicians would describe the pattern as a *logarithmic distribution*.) The pattern may be evident in children's own number lines or in their placements on a partially bounded number line, but is especially evident on fully bounded number lines where the upper bound further constrains upward expansion.[29] Figure 9.10 shows the hypothetical number placements of a young student who is familiar with only the smallest numbers. Interestingly, the same pattern can sometimes be seen when young children are asked to place the letters of the alphabet on a line bounded by *A* and *Z*,[30] or when they are asked to sort numbers that lie in a larger range than they are comfortable with into categories of "really small," "small," "medium," "big," and "really big."[31] The early letters and the smaller numbers feel more distinct to them because they are so much more familiar than the end of the alphabet or the big numbers.

This skewed pattern is a bit like Steinberg's iconic illustration, "The View from Ninth Avenue" (Figure 9.11), where the familiar neighborhood (in this case, the West Side of Manhattan) takes on outsized dimensions in one's mind, while the rest of the continent, the Pacific, and Asia occupy the leftover space. The view does not offer a sharp geographic picture of other cities' locations or the distances between them, although it does vaguely represent the general terrain. Similarly, in a child's mind, the large numbers are out there somewhere, but their exact locations are unclear.

FIGURE 9.11   Steinberg's "The View from Ninth Avenue" [cover ill.]. *The New Yorker Magazine.*
Source: © The Saul Steinberg Foundation/Artists Rights Society (ARS), New York.

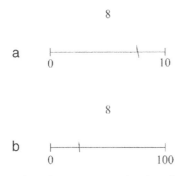

FIGURE 9.12   a) *8* correctly located on the *0-to-10* number line. b) *8* overblown on the *0-to-100*
number line.
Source: Reprinted with parental permission.

Even numbers that are accurately envisioned in a familiar number range can
become outsized in larger, unfamiliar territory,[32] as can be seen in the placements by
a seventh-grader with learning difficulties. Here, *8* is correctly placed in the familiar
range of *0* to *10* (Figure 9.12a) but is considerably overblown in the larger, less familiar
range of *0* to *100* (Figure 9.12b).

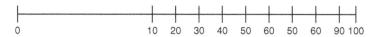

FIGURE 9.13   Bilinear error pattern, compressed in the less familiar 11-to-100 range.
Source: Adapted from Ebersbach et al., 2008; Moeller et al., 2009.

FIGURE 9.14   Placements on a 0-to-1,000 number line, where only the digits in the hundreds place were considered.
Source: Adapted from Lai et al., 2018.

Sometimes, however, the dividing line between ranges that are familiar and unfamiliar occurs at a point where the numerical notation shifts, producing a second immature pattern (see Figure 9.13). For example, the number placements might be overblown from *0* to *10* and compressed above *10*, a possible sign that the child does not understand the quantitative significance of place-value notation.[33]

Children are more likely to reveal their range of unfamiliarity in the number-line placements and categorizations that they produce themselves than on tasks that just ask them to reproduce or judge the correctness of a given number line or magnitude sorting that is presented to them.[34] Moreover, children seem to know when they are out of their "comfort zone." Researchers asked children to make number-line estimates both within their familiar number range and outside it (first grade: *0*-to-*10* and *0*-to-*100*; second grade: *0*-to-*100* and *0*-to-*1,000*; and fourth grade: *0*-to-*1,000* and *0*-to-*100,000*) and rate their confidence in doing so. The study found that children were more confident in their familiar, small-scale estimates than they were in the expanded, less familiar numerical neighborhood, as one might expect.[35]

A third immature pattern, like the second, arises from children's misunderstandings or partial understandings of place-value notation. For example, a child might locate *798* much closer to *701* than to *801* on a *0*-to-*1,000* number line (see Figure 9.14), suggesting that the child considered only the digit in the *hundreds* place.[36] In fact, some scholars suggest that children's number-line placements simply reflect their underlying knowledge (or lack thereof) of place-value.[37] However, Dutch-speaking children, whose number names are inverted (*43* is "three and forty"), do *not* have this sort of number-line placement distortion,[38] suggesting that the problem may simply lie in children's limited range of attention and working memory. In any case, it is likely that numerical notation actually interferes with number sense for some children. The same might be said of those of us for whom *4:53* on a digital clock does not convey how close we are to missing a five o'clock train with quite the same urgency as does the same time on an analog clock. Or who would happily pay $2.95 for an object we would readily pass up at $3.

A fourth immature pattern arises on a bounded number line from children's efforts to deal with the proportional nature of the task. While proportional estimates of beakers of water (or even plain straight lines) are not difficult for young children, proportions of a range of numbers are and can take a while to grasp. (Indeed, lining up the numbers on a straight line may make them easier.) In general, the pattern consists of number placements that are more accurate near key anchor points and less so in the ranges in between. For example, bounded-number-line placements of the youngest children tend to be more accurate near the *0* point than on the rest of the line, while those of first- and second-graders are typically more accurate near *0* and *100* than elsewhere. When asked about their placement strategy in one study, these young children said they had counted from the endpoints. Over the course of the school year, some of their number-line placements became more evenly distributed (i.e., accurate). Those children also performed better on a number-ordering exercise,[39] suggesting that children's number-line placements do, indeed, reflect their understanding of how numbers relate to each other across the range. By third grade or so, children begin to think about numbers proportionally. This means that they can imagine the intermediate locations of key numbers, such as *25, 50*, and *75,* on the *0*-to-*100* number line, for instance, and use them to anchor other number placements.[40] If the midpoint is not demonstrated, even young children sometimes envision one.[41] In fact, presenting the target number above the middle of the line, as in Figure 9.8a, can subtly prompt some young children to use a proportional strategy, even without a midpoint demonstration.[42] As they get acquainted with these anchor points, their other number placements may crowd around them. However, if an older child does not understand the proportional nature of the task or is befuddled by the number at the far end, like a younger child, he may simply ignore the endpoint and do what is most familiar—count up from *0*—as illustrated by this fourth-grader's effort to locate *25* on a *0*-to-*1,000* number line (Figure 9.15).[43]

Use of anchor points and a proportional strategy typically leads to more accurate number-line placements. While this raises concerns about the bounded number line's ability to reflect a "pure" picture of a child's number knowledge unclouded by strategic

FIGURE 9.15 Ignoring the upper bound and counting up from 0.
Source: Reprinted with parental permission.

considerations,[44] it is also true that imagined anchor points have a scaffolding effect in building a sense of numerical proportion, rendering the bounded number line a better pedagogical tool than open-ended lines. Indeed, studies comparing bounded and partially bounded number-line placements among children in grades two to seven found that only the bounded number-line estimates (and the proportional reasoning involved) were related to arithmetic skills.[45]

There has been much scholarly back and forth over which of these types of immature number-line patterns most accurately reflects children's ideas about number.[46] As we have seen, however, these patterns reflect differences in children's strategies, as well as number knowledge. Among four- to six-year-olds, number-line placement accuracy is more closely related to their counting skill than to proportional reasoning.[47] In fact, counting seems to be a prevalent number-line estimation strategy among young children, while older children increasingly use proportional reasoning and anchor points, reflecting their maturing number notions and growing ability to consider both endpoints.[48] Indeed, children may employ a variety of strategies to judge the accurate location of a number on a number line. Some strategies are more successful than others on any given problem, and both the mix and success of these strategies change with age and increasing number knowledge.[49]

The one thing that number-line researchers do agree on, however, is that most children's number-line placements become increasingly accurate with numerical experience, reflecting a maturing concept of the *quantitative meaning* of numerical symbols. Teachers can witness this maturation in the expansion of the child's number-line accuracy to the right for the whole numbers, to the left for negative numbers, and in the spaces for fractions and decimals.[50]

However, there are hurdles to jump along the way. Numerical notation—*22   3,698 $^7/_9$ $5^2/_3$ 3.047   -54*—is composed of many parts, including digits and other symbols that have individual meanings and their own locations or directions on the number line. Understandably, too many such parts can slow down learning and complicate the task. In fact, some scholars point to the numbers from *0* to *9* as the only true number-line "primitives"—that is, numbers that can be imagined holistically, as an uncomplicated amount.[51] Furthermore, clarity about the magnitudes symbolized by numbers and their quantitative relationships to other numbers develops from numerical experience, suggesting that it may well emerge after children demonstrate competence with place-value and algorithmic manipulation.[52] For such children, their misconceived number-line placements can come as a surprise to their teachers, who may be fooled by their students' procedural competence into thinking they understand the relative quantities that numerals represent.

Moreover, as we have seen with several other early numeracy skills, children with significant math learning difficulties are often less accurate in their number-line placements than their classmates, with a more skewed placement pattern in the same numerical range, suggesting a fragile and uncertain sense of how numbers (and the quantities they represent) relate to each other.[53] One study tracked the eye movements of a group of nine- to 11-year-old children with serious math learning problems as they placed numbers on a bounded line with only the endpoints labeled. The researchers found that these children attended to different features of the number line than did their peers and did not make effective use of endpoints or anchors.[54] The source of their confusion is not clear. As noted earlier, it may reflect a problem with place-value,[55] with reading digits, with spatial-numerical mapping, with numerical relations, or with fundamental numerical magnitude. Thus, as with any student, it would pay to ask, "How did you decide that the number belongs there?" Their strategy may reveal the source of their confusion.

One final note about negative numbers before we close this section. Children's concepts of negative numbers, as revealed in their placements on the negative side of the number line, seem to develop later than those of positive numbers.[56] However, negative values are typically not introduced until the intermediate grades. In fact, the Common Core State Standards (CCSS) recommend introducing them in sixth grade. Thus, the later development of negative numbers on the number line should not be surprising.[57] However, even introducing them as late as fourth grade can be problematic. When asked by a researcher, "Why do you think the negatives are so tricky to think about?" one fourth-grader remarked, "Because you don't learn them until like fourth grade, and then you're so used to regular numbers."[58] To our knowledge, there has been no research on the advisability of introducing children to a bidirectional number line from the very beginning in the earliest grades, although some informal classroom experiments with it have reportedly gone well.[59] Children's understanding of negative numbers is as important for learning algebra as understanding whole numbers is for learning whole-number arithmetic.[60] Indeed, one study found that Algebra I students made more negative-sign errors than errors involving fractions or arithmetic.[61] While the idea of negative numerosities is understandably baffling to young children, as discussed in Chapter 2, the extension of the number line to the left should seem quite natural and may be an easy way to introduce the topic to primary-grade students. Further research is warranted to clarify this option.

THE NUMBER LINE AND SPATIAL SKILLS

Not surprisingly, the ability to place numbers accurately on a number line—to associate number to length—is closely linked with spatial skill. In one important study, researchers found that the mental rotation skills of a group of first- and second-graders early in the school year were significantly associated with improvement in their number-line placements over the course of the year. They also found that the mental rotation and transformation skills of five-year-olds were significantly associated with their arithmetic estimation skills at age eight. The researchers concluded that spatial skills allow children to form a robust mental number line, which in turn facilitates the numerical mental manipulation necessary for arithmetic.[62]

Moreover, there is now some evidence that locating things in space—mentally or physically putting them into a spatial setting—provides a significant boost to working memory.[63] For example, number-line placement accuracy is also associated with a child's ability to remember numbers in school and daily life.[64] In this way, a reliable mental number line gives a child a place to park the numbers to be remembered and find them again.[65] Thus, learning on the number line, particularly with color-coded number blocks, should provide significant working- and long-term memory support for children with attention deficits, although to our knowledge there has been no research on this question as of the time of this writing.

In contrast, children with non-verbal learning disabilities or weak visual-spatial skills tend to make less accurate number-line estimates than those of their peers with average spatial abilities and have more trouble bisecting lines and finding the midpoint between two numbers, suggesting that understanding numerical relations is, indeed, tied to visual-spatial ability.[66]

One tell-tale sign that spatial skills influence arithmetic through a mental number line has to do with the nature of human perception. On any perceived continuum, it is more difficult to distinguish things that are close together than things that are far apart, as discussed in Chapter 2. For example, a child might have trouble remembering whether *7 + 5 = 12* or *13*, a value very close to the correct one. A study of six- to eight-year-olds found that their tendency to make such errors was *positively* related to their spatial abilities, suggesting that they rely at least in part on a mental number line, rather than just rote memory, say, in doing arithmetic.[67]

Additional evidence that number-line accuracy might be related to one's spatial abilities, unfortunately, is that elementary students' estimation skills on the *0-to-1,000* number line demonstrates a male advantage, just as do certain spatial abilities, as discussed in Chapter 5. In one study of a full range of elementary number and arithmetic abilities among children in grades one through six, *0-to-1,000* number-line placement was the only such skill to show a sex discrepancy.[68]

BRINGING THE NUMBER LINE INTO FOCUS

Abundant research attests to the strong and mutually beneficial relation, from preschool through adolescence, between children's arithmetic ability and their skill in accurately identifying where numbers belong on a number line.[69] Indeed, one meta-analysis of 41 studies found that the relation increased with age and that it was even stronger for fractions than for whole numbers.[70] (Chapter 11 takes a close look at fractions and the number line.)

Experience with the number line teaches children about numerical relationships. Young children often get this experience with board games or hopscotch. Indeed, research has demonstrated that a few sessions of guided play with a linear numerical board game can bring the number skills of low-income young children with no board game experience up to the level of their middle-class peers. (The key ingredient in the game is to have the child count up from whatever number the game piece is on—"thirty-seven . . . thirty-eight, thirty-nine, forty"—instead of counting out the number on the spinner—"one, two, three.")[71] Children with congenital blindness can learn about the linear relationship of numbers using pegs in a line on a pegboard.[72]

Number-line exercises with immediate corrective feedback can be particularly helpful in correcting misunderstanding about numerical relations. In one study, the examiner asked the child to mark on a bounded number line where a particular number belonged and then said, "After you mark where you think the number goes, I'll show you where it really goes, so you can see how close you were." In giving feedback, the examiner marked the correct location and wrote the numeral. If the placement was off by less than ten percent, the examiner said, "You can see these two marks are really quite close. How did you know to put it there?" If the placement was off by more than ten percent, the examiner said, "That's quite a bit too high/low. You can see these two marks are really quite far from each other. Why do you think that this is too high/low for [the number]?" In skewed number-line placements, the number likely to be placed farthest from its correct location is *15* on a *0-to-100* number line (or *150* on a *0-to-1,000* number line). The study found that simply pointing out that number's correct location following its inaccurate placement (Figure 9.16) had a recalibrating effect on the entire number line. When the researchers tried this strategy with a group of second- and fourth-graders, 80 percent of the children who had been corrected in that way had a remarkable turn-around, producing correct number-line placements in the whole range from then on.[73]

Readers may have the same experience when reminded that one billion is only one one-thousandth of a trillion (Figure 9.17).

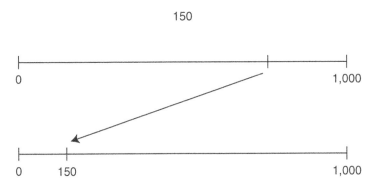

FIGURE 9.16 Corrective feedback on the placement of *150* on a *0-to-1,000* number line.
Source: Adapted from Opfer & Siegler, 2007.

FIGURE 9.17 The relationship of one billion to one trillion, as shown on a number line.

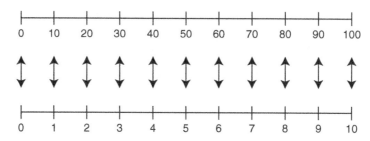

FIGURE 9.18 *0-to-10* and *0-to-100* number lines shown as scaled.
Source: Adapted from Siegler, 2016.

Understanding and correctly locating useful anchor points can also serve to align the rest of the numbers in the range, and this strategy can be taught. For example, if the goal is to help children reach an accurate view of number over a broader numerical range, guiding their location of anchor points and helping children use them correctly can have a beneficial effect, not only on their number-line placements but also on their mathematical understanding in general.[74]

Additionally, drawing attention to the relationships between smaller numbers can aid, by explicit analogy, in understanding the relationships between larger numbers,[75] such as seeing the similarity of the *0-to-1,000* number line to the *0-to-100* number line, or the *0-to-100* number line to the *0-to-10* number line (Figure 9.18).

Alert readers may be reminded here of the discussion about spatial scaling in Chapter 4. Attending to the relationships between these ranges on the number line is an exercise in scaling, or mapping, where the *0-to-10* number line is a kind of small-scale floor plan of the larger-scale *0-to-100* number line, for example. This can be a difficult concept for many children. Indeed, research reveals that young children's scaling and number-line skills are closely related.[76] Fortunately, numerical scaling is teachable: A study of children in grades two, three, and six found that progressively aligning number lines of increasing orders of magnitude (see Figure 9.18), using color-coded illustrations to draw attention to the scalar relations, led to greater accuracy and linearity at higher orders of magnitude.[77] And other researchers have begun to look at classroom mapping exercises as a way to support related math skills.[78]

LINEAR MEASUREMENT

Daily life is full of number lines in the form of rulers and tape measures. Like a number line, a ruler or tape measure consists of numbers lined up, equally spaced and in order. Aligned with objects, these instruments can quantify length, or more generally, the distance between two points. By extension, the same "technology" can be applied to measuring other uncountable dimensions such as temperature, weight, and time.

However, unlike counting out cookies, say, quantifying distance and the rest requires both ordered numbers and a *standard comparison unit*. In Chapter 2, the relative quantities obtained through subjective sizing up of continuous amounts were noted to be quite blurry and approximate. With the acquisition of a counting system and the development of standard comparison units, however, continuous amounts can be quantified—*measured*—with significantly more precision.[79]

Children's measurement skills develop significantly between preschool and second grade. Children typically begin by simply aligning two objects to see which is longer or taller, or by comparing both to a third object. Later, they compare two objects by roughly aligning other objects of various lengths end to end along each of them. Eventually, they understand that comparison objects need to be the same length and that different-length comparison objects will result in different measurements, and they can begin to use rulers. Cognitive development is rarely orderly, however, and children use a mix of mature and immature strategies throughout their early learning.[80]

In addition to the requirement for equal-sized comparison units, there are two other aspects of linear measurement that are especially gnarly for young children. The first is that standard rulers and measuring tapes (in fact, even the typical number line) are usually configured with the counting numerals aligned with hash marks to the right of each unit of length and an implied *zero* at the starting point on the left, as in Figure 9.19a. That is, the hash mark labeled *9*, say, indicates, "Nine spaces get you to here." This can be confusing for young children, who do not understand this location meaning and who are accustomed to counting *things* (e.g., hash marks) rather than the spaces between them, beginning with "one." Critically, it is the spaces *between* the hash marks that represent the comparative units of length (Figure 9.19b).

Several studies have attempted to solve this problem, producing a number of viable solutions. In one study, researchers compared four- and five-year-olds' performance on a traditional *0*-to-*10* bounded number-line task ("If this end is zero and this end is ten, where would seven be?") with their performance when asked, "If the froggy starts here, where will it land after seven hops?" (Figure 9.20). They found that the

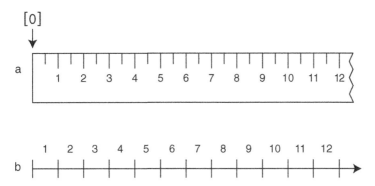

FIGURE 9.19   a) A traditional measuring tape, with numbers at the hash marks to the right of the spaces. b) A number line shown as a string of linear units labeled with numbers.

FIGURE 9.20 The frog hops toward the fly. If he lands on *1* after his first hop, where will he land on his seventh hop?

Source: Adapted from Reid et al., 2015.

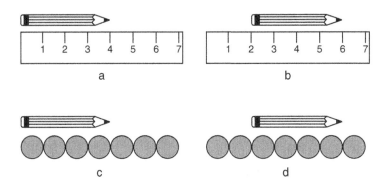

FIGURE 9.21 a) Pencil aligned with end of ruler. b) Pencil shifted away from end of ruler. c) Pencil aligned with end of a row of coins. d) Pencil shifted away from end of a row of coins.

Source: Adapted from Solomon et al., 2015.

children were more accurate on the concrete task in which they were counting hops (spans) instead of places on the line and there were no confusing marks or numerals in the way.[81] Despite the *10* at the end, the focus on this task is on the iteration of the standard unit, not on the proportional distance between the ends, much like the partially bounded number-line task.

Looking at somewhat older children, researchers trained kindergartners and second-graders how to measure the length of an object using one of four different methods: 1) the traditional method of measuring using a numbered ruler, aligning the object with its left endpoint (Figure 9.21a); 2) using a ruler with the object shifted away from the ruler's endpoint (Figure 9.21b); 3) aligning the object with the left endpoint of a row of equal-sized coins (Figure 9.21c); and 4) shifting the object away from the endpoint of the row of coins (Figure 9.21d). The children did well with all methods, except for the second one (the object shifted on the ruler), where the children performed as if they had guessed. The researchers concluded that children's ideas about rulers are so intertwined with countable hash marks and reading the number aligned with the end of the object that they miss the idea that measurement is about countable spatial intervals. They speculated that a numberless ruler might be the best measurement teaching tool.[82]

The second aspect of linear measurement that gives young children trouble is scale. Modern measurement units typically come in nested sets: Inches-feet-yards-miles. Seconds-minutes-hours-days-weeks-years-decades-centuries. Not only do children need to associate the individual scales with the objects and events they typically measure, but they also must learn the highly variable relationships between the scales. To investigate the development of time-scale knowledge, researchers asked children aged three to six years old, "Farmer Brown [jumped] for [a minute]. Captain Blue [jumped] for [an hour]. Who [jumped] more, Farmer Brown or Captain Blue?" with different actions (jumped, slept, cried, played, danced, talked) and durations (hours, seconds, minutes, days, weeks, months, years) variously paired in the story. The three-year-olds performed as if guessing, while the older children improved steadily with age. In a subsequent, related study of four- to seven-year-olds, when a number word was substituted for "a(n)" in the question (e.g., "Farmer Brown jumped for three minutes . . ."), even the six-year-olds did not know that two hours was longer than three minutes. In a third related study, children aged five to seven and adults were asked to order time words (hour, second, minute, day) and durations (two hours, six hours, nine minutes, and three minutes) on timelines. Here, researchers found that prior to formal instruction (ages four and five), children know from ambient talk that *hours* and such refer to time and that while they might know that an hour is longer than a minute, they have no idea how much longer. As with number words, young children must know the names of the days of the week or months of the year before they can link them to familiar durations.[83]

Moreover, analog clocks are not designed to clarify the relationships between the scales. The distance traveled by the hour hand in 60 minutes is not the same as the distance traveled by the minute hand in 60 seconds. Furthermore, hours, minutes, and seconds co-vary, such that the movement of one hand necessarily involves the movement of the other two. And unlike the number line, the clock is cyclical (placing the *zero* point at *12*, for example). Observations such as these have prompted some researchers to conclude that the primary grades are too early to teach time on an analog clock.[84] Alternatively, it might simply be less distracting to have three separate, one-handed clocks to compare seconds, minutes, and hours; research on this option would be valuable if analog clocks remain in use. Time knowledge does improve with age, however, particularly between the ages of six and eight, when it is strongly linked to numerical skills and number-line estimation.[85]

While learning how to measure can be confusing for all children, other factors can contribute to difficulty learning how to measure. One such factor is insufficient inhibitory control, an all-purpose executive function discussed in Chapter 1. One study found that young children's ability to gradually adopt more mature measurement strategies depended in part on their capacity to control their impulses.[86] Research with somewhat older elementary students also found that socioeconomic status can affect children's measurement skills and that boys tend to be better at visualizing and conceptualizing measurement problems, while girls tend to rely on algorithms and computation, much as discussed in Chapter 5 about math problems in general.[87]

Finally, learning how to measure with a ruler or tape measure is an effective way for children to figure out numerical relations, just as we saw with the number line. In a study of six-year-olds, those who received measurement instruction improved not only on their number-line placements but also on numerical comparisons significantly more than did their classmates who did not receive such instruction.[88]

CONCLUSION

Mapping number onto linear space is a powerful way to demonstrate both the ordinal and cardinal dimensions of number and how quantities relate to each other. It is also a solid foundation on which to build arithmetic competence, as we will demonstrate in the Activities section of Chapter 10. Children's own number lines provide a window into their understanding of numerical relations. Finally, although modern measurement systems have complicated this simple mapping, linear number-space mapping also forms the foundation of linear measurement.

ACTIVITIES

Number Line

ACTIVITY 9.1: Walk the Life-Sized Number Path

Objective: To learn the relative magnitude of numbers. Make two adjacent life-sized number paths using chalk on the playground or tape on the classroom floor or down the school hallway. In a number path, the numbers are in the rectangular spaces where the children step. Vary the length of the number paths based on the needs of the children. Use a spinner with numbers *1* to *3* for shorter number paths and a die with numbers *1* to *6* for longer number paths.

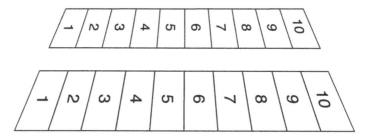

■ **First:** Put the children in groups of three, in which one child rolls the die or spins the spinner and reads the number aloud while the other two walk along the number path. (Hopping along the path is another option.) For example, the die roller rolls the number *3*. The first walker starts at *zero* (behind the first step) and walks three spaces while calling aloud, "One, two, three." The die roller rolls again and calls out, "Two." The second walker starts at *zero* and walks two spaces while calling aloud, "One, two." If the next roll of the die is *4*, the first walker continues forward, counting on from *3*, saying, "Four, five, six, seven." The children take turns walking the number path and counting on from their location. The first child to make it to the end is the winner. Alternatively, at the end, the child turns around and walks backward to *zero*, counting off "Ten, nine, eight," and so forth, and the first child to reach *zero* is the winner.

■ **Next:** Using the same two adjacent number paths, as each child walks along their respective number path, they pass a ball back and forth to one another to emphasize the distance between numbers. For example, one child walks to the number *5* and passes the ball to their partner, who is standing on the number *7* on the adjacent number path. Then their partner walks to the number *10* and tosses the ball back. It takes more effort to throw the ball from *5* to *10*, which is a greater distance, than throwing the ball from *5* to *7*.

ACTIVITY 9.2: Race to 100[89]

Objective: To learn the sequence and relationship of numbers between *zero* and *one hundred*, including base-10 concepts, using a *1*-to-*100* number chart organized in a 10 × 10 matrix (see Figure 8.2b in Chapter 8). This activity uses a number chart, which is a stacked version of a number line, because of the impracticality of using a *0-to-100* number line in the classroom. Children take turns moving their token along the numerical sequence. The player who reaches *100* first is the winner. Rapid learning with carryover in number-line estimation, numeral identification, and the ability to count on from numbers occurs when children count on from the number on the square where they began the turn (e.g., a child on *23* who rolls a *3* would say, "twenty-four, twenty-five, twenty-six.").[90] Beginning players can use one die and can later progress to using two dice.

■ **First:** The children and an adult take turns rolling one die or using a *1*-to-*6* spinner and then move their token forward on the number chart. The adult can model counting on from the number on which they start and then help the children use the counting-on method when it is their turn. If they have difficulty keeping track of the number of spaces to move forward, they can use their fingers to track the spaces while counting on aloud. Alternatively, they can count the number of spaces to move forward first by saying "one, two, three" if they roll a *3*, and then go back and say the numbers in the counting-on format: "Twenty-four, twenty-five, twenty-six . . . I landed on twenty-six!"

- **Next:** The children can play with each other without an adult using the same format as noted earlier.
- **Next:** To add increased awareness of base-10 concepts, add a rule that if they land on one of the *fives* or *tens* (*5, 10, 15, 20, 25, 30*, etc.), they get to move an additional ten spaces from that number. The children should say both final numbers, such as "twenty-five and ten more is thirty-five."
- **Next:** The children pick a "magic number" in the *ones* place, and when a player lands on that number, they move an additional ten spaces. So, if *3* is the magic number and a child lands on *23*, the child can move an additional ten spaces to *33*.

ACTIVITY 9.3: Number Path Cover-Up

Objective: To identify the location of hidden numbers on a *1*-to-*20* laminated number path on which the numbers are labeled in the center of each space (see Activity 8.3 Figure). Cover all the spaces for numbers *2* through *19* with sticky notes, leaving the spaces labeled *1* and *20* visible. You can vary the length of the number path based on the range of numbers that the children are learning. On a longer number path, also leave the midpoint number visible.

- **First:** Have the children identify the location of a number on the number path without counting. The children should eyeball the location of a number, which involves making a proportional estimation. The teacher can point to the visible *1* and *20* while asking, "Where is the number seven on the number path?" After the children guess the location of the number, lift up the sticky note and give immediate feedback about their accuracy. If their guess was incorrect, reveal the correct location. Repeat with various numbers.
- **Next:** Remind the children of the visible starting and ending numbers on the number path. Point to a sticky note and ask, "What number goes here on the number path?" As earlier, the children should eyeball their estimation without counting. After the children guess the hidden number, give immediate feedback as before.
- **Next:** In the same activity, after the children name the number hidden underneath a sticky note, then ask, "What number comes *after*?" and "What number comes *before*?" The ability to name the preceding number is an especially important math skill that helps children to compare numbers.[91] For example, after a child identifies the number *11*, ask, "What number comes after eleven?" and "What number comes before eleven?" Provide immediate corrective feedback by lifting those sticky notes.

ACTIVITY 9.4: Marking the Number Line

Objective: To develop children's mental number line. For each step listed, provide an empty laminated number line with the *0* and *100* endpoints clearly marked. Have a second completed number line marked in multiples of *five* available to provide immediate feedback to the children, who can correct their marks if needed. *Note:* In this activity and the activities that follow, the numbers will be labeled in the usual way, at the hash marks to the right of their respective spaces.

- **First:** Have the children mark where *50* should be and then immediately compare their mark with the completed number line. Talk about *50* being halfway between *0* and *100*.
- **Next:** Using a new empty number line, have the children mark where *25*, *50*, and *75* should be. Talk about *25* being halfway between *0* and *50* and *75* being halfway between *50* and *100*.
- **Next:** Using a new empty number line, have the children mark numbers that are multiples of *ten* and, once they are proficient with those numbers, mark numbers that are multiples of *five*.
- **Next:** For review, have the children fill in a complete number line, beginning with *50*, then *25* and *75*, and then the remaining multiples of *five*.

ACTIVITY 9.5: Scaling Up

Objective: To estimate the position of a number by scaling up and making an analogy based on the position of a related, single-digit number on the *0-to-10* number line. The aligned structure of the number lines stacked one above the other should help children to make these numerical estimates in increasingly larger number ranges (see Figure 9.18).[92]

- **First:** Draw two vertically aligned empty number lines. Label the top number line *0* on the left and *100* on the right. Label the bottom number line *0* on the left and *10* on the right. The lines should not be labeled with any other numbers or hash marks. Mark where the number *3* goes on the *0-to-10* number line and ask the children to indicate where *30* goes on the *0-to-100* number line. Provide immediate feedback (corrective if needed) about the accuracy of their placements. Continue with other related numbers (e.g., *2* and *20*, *5* and *50*) with continued feedback. Eventually, children can work in pairs: One child chooses a single-digit number and places it on the *0-to-10* number line and the other child places the corresponding two-digit number on the *0-to-100* number line.
- **Next:** Draw three vertically aligned empty number lines: *0-to-1,000* on the top, *0-to-100* in the middle, and *0-to-10* on the bottom, with no other visible numbers or hash marks. As earlier, mark where a single-digit number goes on the *0-to-10* number line and ask the children to indicate where the corresponding two-digit

number goes on the *0-to-100* number line and where the corresponding three-digit number goes on the *0-to-1,000* number line.

Measurement

ACTIVITY 9.6: Create a Ruler[93]

Objective: To learn the principle of measuring with equal-sized units. Children create their own numberless rulers to learn that measurement is about units of length.

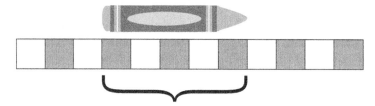

The crayon is 5 units long.

- **First:** Provide the children with strips of paper marked in equal-length units and have the children color them so that adjacent units are different colors. Collect various objects to measure with this numberless, child-made ruler. Demonstrate how to measure by aligning the object with the ruler (at the start of any unit along its length) and counting the number of spaces that span the length of the object (see Figure above). Then move the object so that it lines up with the left end of the ruler and demonstrate that the length of the object has not changed. It takes up the same distance, or number of units, on the ruler.
- **Next:** After measuring multiple objects in this manner, suggest that the children might save themselves a lot of counting by numbering the spaces consecutively, beginning on the left end of the ruler. The children discover that when the *spaces* are numbered, they can simply align the left end of the ruler with one end of an object and read out the number of the last space that aligns with the object to arrive at its length.

ACTIVITY 9.7: Comparing the Size Versus the Number of Units[94]

Objective: To improve children's understanding of the relationship between the number of units and the size of the units of measurement. As the children measure, discuss how each hash mark indicates the end of a space so that counting the number of hashmarks tells them how much space the object occupies, or the length of the object.

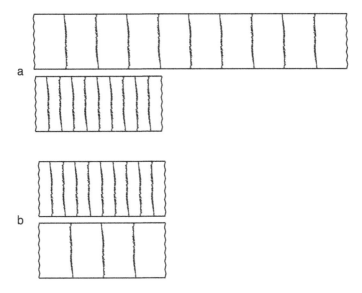

- **First:** Present the children with a strip of paper. Using a centimeter ruler, the children measure and cut the paper ten centimeters long. They should mark each of the centimeters on the paper (see Figure a). Then using an inch ruler, have the children measure and cut a second strip of paper ten inches long. They should mark each of the inches on the paper. Compare the two strips of paper and discuss how the lengths of the strips are the same number of units (ten), but a centimeter is shorter than an inch, so ten centimeters will be shorter than ten inches.
- **Next:** Start with the ten-centimeter strip of paper that the children cut in the previous step. Have the children cut a second strip of paper the same length and measure the second strip of paper in inches. Mark the inches on the paper and compare the length of the two strips of paper (see Figure b). The second strip will be just under four inches in length, so you can round up and explain that ten centimeters is the same as about four inches. Discuss how the strips are the same length but that the centimeter strip has more units because each unit is smaller.

NOTES

1 Stern & Stern, 1971/2022—sternmath.com/cda.
2 Sella et al., 2017.

3 Malone et al., 2021.

4 Begolli et al., 2020; Gunderson et al., 2019.

5 Yousif et al., 2021.

6 Friso-van den Bos et al., 2014; Xu et al., 2021.

7 Bull et al., 2011; Toll & VanLuit, 2013.

8 Sella et al., 2017.

9 Cheung & Lourenco, 2019.

10 Barrett et al., 2017.

11 Shaki et al., 2012.

12 Feldman et al., 2019.

13 Kolesari & Carlson, 2018.

14 Fischer, 2008.

15 Patro et al., 2015; J. Opfer, personal communication, October 2, 2007.

16 Opfer & Furlong, 2011.

17 Crollen et al., 2013.

18 Aleotti et al., 2020; Cooney et al., 2021.

19 Opfer et al., 2010.

20 Opfer & Furlong, 2011.

21 Göbel et al., 2018.

22 Göbel et al., 2018.

23 VanGalen & Reitsma, 2008.

24 Ebersbach, 2015; McCrink et al., 2014.

25 Rinaldi et al., 2016.

26 Georges et al., 2017.

27 Sella & Lucangeli, 2020.

28 Sella et al., 2020a, 2020b.

29 Kim & Opfer, 2017.

30 Hurst et al., 2014.

31 Laski & Siegler, 2007.

32 Siegler & Opfer, 2003.

33 Moeller et al., 2009.

34 Ebersbach, 2016.

35 Wall et al., 2016.

36 Lai et al., 2018.

37 Dietrich et al., 2016.

38 Savelkouls et al., 2020.

39 Xu, 2019.

40 Link et al., 2014a.

41 Zax et al., 2019.

42 Dackermann et al., 2018.

43 Barth et al., 2011.

44 Cohen & Quinlan, 2018.

45 Georges & Schiltz, 2021; Jung et al., 2020; Link et al., 2014b.

46 Opfer et al., 2016; Slusser & Barth, 2017.

47 Yuan et al., 2020.

48 White & Szűcs, 2012.

49 Rouder & Geary, 2014; Siegler, 1996; Sullivan & Barner, 2014.
50 Siegler & Lortie-Forgues, 2014.
51 Tzelgov et al., 2015.
52 Siegler & Opfer, 2003.
53 Sella et al., 2013.
54 Van't Noordende et al., 2016.
55 Dietrich et al., 2016.
56 Brez et al., 2016.
57 Aqazade & Bofferding, 2021.
58 Bofferding, 2014, p. 194.
59 Aze, 1989; Behrend & Mohs, 2006.
60 Young & Booth, 2020.
61 Booth et al., 2014.
62 Gunderson et al., 2012.
63 Yousif et al., 2021.
64 Thompson & Opfer, 2016.
65 Fazio et al., 2016.
66 Crollen & Noël, 2015; Crollen et al., 2015.
67 Gibson & Maurer, 2016.
68 Hutchison et al., 2019.
69 Friso-van den Bos et al., 2015.
70 Schneider et al., 2018.
71 Ramani & Siegler, 2008.
72 Szűcs & Csépe, 2005.
73 Opfer & Siegler, 2007.
74 Opfer et al., 2016.
75 Siegler, 2016.
76 Möhring et al., 2018.
77 Thompson & Opfer, 2010.
78 Jirout et al., 2018.
79 For a delightful and fascinating history of measurement, see Cooperrider & Gentner, 2019.
80 Barrett et al., 2017.
81 Reid et al., 2015.
82 Solomon et al., 2015.
83 Tillman & Barner, 2015.
84 Earnest et al., 2018.
85 Labrell et al., 2016.
86 Ren et al., 2019.
87 Casey et al., 2011; Vasilyeva et al., 2009.
88 Vasilyeva et al., 2021.
89 Adapted and derived from Laski & Siegler, 2014.
90 Siegler & Ramani, 2009.
91 Sella & Lucangeli, 2020.
92 Thompson & Opfer, 2010.
93 Adapted from Solomon et al., 2015.
94 Derived from Battista, 2006.

REFERENCES

The following references were cited in this chapter. For additional selected references relevant to this chapter, please see Chapter 9 Supplemental References in eResources.

Aleotti, S., DiGirolamo, F., Massaccesi, S., & Priftis, K. (2020). Numbers around Descartes: A preregistered study on the three-dimensional SNARC effect. *Cognition, 195,* 104111.

Aqazade, M., & Bofferding, L. (2021). Second and fifth graders' use of knowledge-pieces and knowledge-structures when solving integer addition problems. *Journal of Numerical Cognition, 7,* 82–103.

Aze, I. (1989). Negatives for little ones? *Mathematics in School, 18*(2), 16–17.

Barrett, J.E., Clements, D.H., & Sarama, J. (Eds.). (2017). *Children's measurement: A longitudinal study of children's knowledge and learning of length, area, and volume.* National Council of Teachers of Mathematics.

Barth, H., Slusser, E., Cohen, D., & Paladino, A.M. (2011). A sense of proportion: Commentary on Opfer, Siegler, and Young. *Developmental Science, 14,* 1205–1206.

Battista, M.T. (2006, Oct.). Understanding the development of students' thinking about length. *Teaching Children Mathematics, 13,* 140–146.

Begolli, K.N., Booth, J.L., Holmes, C.A., & Newcombe, N.S. (2020). How many apples make a quarter? The challenge of discrete proportional formats. *Journal of Experimental Child Psychology, 192,* 104774.

Behrend, J.L., & Mohs, L.C. (2006, Jan.). From simple questions to powerful connections: A two-year conversation about negative numbers. *Teaching Children Mathematics, 12,* 260–264.

Bofferding, L. (2014). Negative integer understanding: Characterizing first graders' mental models. *Journal for Research in Mathematics Education, 45,* 194–245.

Booth, J.L., Barbieri, C., Eyer, F., & Paré-Blagoev, E.J. (2014). Persistent and pernicious errors in algebraic problem solving. *Journal of Problem Solving, 7,* 10–23.

Brez, C.C., Miller, A.D., & Ramirez, E.M. (2016). Numerical estimation in children for both positive and negative numbers. *Journal of Cognition and Development, 17,* 341–358.

Bull, R., Marschark, M., Sapere, P., Davidson, W.A., Murphy, D., & Nordmann, E. (2011). Numerical estimation in deaf and hearing adults. *Learning and Individual Differences, 21,* 453–457.

Casey, B.M., Dearing, E., Vasilyeva, M., Ganley, C.M., & Tine, M. (2011). Spatial and numerical predictors of measurement performance: The moderating effects of community income and gender. *Journal of Educational Psychology, 103,* 296–311.

Cheung, C.-N., & Lourenco, S.F. (2019). Does 1 + 1 = 2nd? The relations between children's understanding of ordinal position and their arithmetic performance. *Journal of Experimental Child Psychology, 187,* 104651.

Cohen, D.J., & Quinlan, P.T. (2018). The log-linear response function of the bounded number-line task is unrelated to the psychological representation of quantity. *Psychonomic Bulletin & Review, 25,* 447–454.

Cooney, S.M., Holmes, C.A., & Newell, F.N. (2021). Children's spatial-numerical associations on horizontal, vertical, and sagittal axes. *Journal of Experimental Child Psychology, 209,* 105169.

Cooperrider, K., & Gentner, D. (2019). The career of measurement. *Cognition, 191,* 103942.

Crollen, V., Dormal, G., Seron, X., Lepore, F., & Collignon, O. (2013). Embodied numbers: The role of vision in the development of number-space interactions. *Cortex, 49,* 276–283.

Crollen, V., & Noël, M.-P. (2015). Spatial and numerical processing in children with high and low visuospatial abilities. *Journal of Experimental Child Psychology, 132,* 84–98.

Crollen, V., Vanderclausen, C., Allaire, F., Pollaris, A., & Noël, M.-P. (2015). Spatial and numerical processing in children with non-verbal learning disabilities. *Research in Developmental Disabilities, 47,* 61–72.

Dackermann, T., Kroemer, L., Nuerk, H.-C., Moeller, K., & Huber, S. (2018). Influences of presentation format and task instruction on children's number line estimation. *Cognitive Development, 47,* 53–62.

Dietrich, J.F., Huber, S., Dackermann, T., Moeller, K., & Fischer, U. (2016). Place-value understanding in number line estimation predicts future arithmetic performance. *British Journal of Developmental Psychology, 34,* 502–517.

Earnest, D., Gonzales, A.C., & Plant, A.M. (2018). Time as a measure: Elementary students positioning the hands of an analog clock. *Journal of Numerical Cognition, 4,* 188–214.

Ebersbach, M. (2015). Evidence for a spatial-numerical association in kindergartners using a number line task. *Journal of Cognition and Development, 16,* 118–128.

Ebersbach, M. (2016). Development of children's estimation skills: The ambiguous role of their familiarity with numerals. *Child Development Perspectives, 10,* 116–121.

Ebersbach, M., Luwel, K., Frick, A., Onghena, P., & Verschaffel, L. (2008). The relationship between the shape of the mental number line and familiarity with numbers in 5- to 9-year old children: Evidence for a segmented linear model. *Journal of Experimental Child Psychology, 99,* 1–17.

Fazio, L.K., Kennedy, C.A., & Siegler, R.S. (2016). Improving children's knowledge of fraction magnitudes. *PLoS ONE, 11*(10), 0165243.

Feldman, A., Oscar-Strom, Y., Tzelgov, J., & Berger, A. (2019). Spatial-numerical association of response code effect as a window to mental representation of magnitude in long-term memory among Hebrew-speaking children. *Journal of Experimental Psychology, 181,* 102–109.

Fischer, M.H. (2008). Finger counting habits modulate spatial-numerical associations. *Cortex, 44,* 386–392.

Friso-van den Bos, I., Kolkman, M.E., Kroesbergen, E.H., & Leseman, P.P.M. (2014). Explaining variability: Numerical representations in 4- to 8-year-old children. *Journal of Cognition and Development, 15,* 325–344.

Friso-van den Bos, I., Kroesbergen, E.H., vanLuit, J.E.H., Xenidou-Dervou, I., Jonkman, L.M., van der Schoot, M., & vanLieshout, E.C.D.M. (2015). Longitudinal development of number line estimation and mathematics performance in primary school children. *Journal of Experimental Child Psychology, 134,* 12–29.

Georges, C., Hoffmann, D., & Schiltz, C. (2017). Mathematical abilities in elementary school: Do they relate to number-space associations? *Journal of Experimental Child Psychology, 161,* 126–147.

Georges, C., & Schiltz, C. (2021). Number line tasks and their relation to arithmetics in second to fourth graders. *Journal of Numerical Cognition, 7,* 20–41.

Gibson, L.C., & Maurer, D. (2016). Development of SNARC and distance effects and their relation to mathematical and visuospatial abilities. *Journal of Experimental Child Psychology, 150,* 301–313.

Göbel, S.M., McCrink, K., Fischer, M.H., & Shaki, S. (2018). Observation of directional storybook reading influences young children's counting direction. *Journal of Experimental Child Psychology, 166,* 49–66.

Gunderson, E.A., Hamdan, N., Hildebrand, L., & Bartek, V. (2019). Number line unidimensionality is a critical feature for promoting fraction magnitude concepts. *Journal of Experimental Child Psychology, 187,* 104657.

Gunderson, E.A., Ramirez, G., Beilock, S.L., & Levine, S.C. (2012). The relation between spatial skill and early number knowledge: The role of the linear number line. *Developmental Psychology, 48,* 1229–1241.

Hurst, M., Monahan, K.L., Heller, E., & Cordes, S. (2014). 123s and ABCs: Developmental shifts in logarithmic-to-linear responding reflect fluency with sequence values. *Developmental Science*, 17, 892–904.

Hutchison, J.E., Lyons, I.M., & Ansari, D. (2019). More similar than different: Gender differences in children's basic numerical skills are the exception not the rule. *Child Development*, 90, e66–e79.

Jirout, J.J., Holmes, C.A., Ramsook, K.A., & Newcombe, N.S. (2018). Scaling up spatial development: A closer look at children's scaling ability and its relation to number knowledge. *Mind, Brain, and Education*, 12, 110–119.

Jung, S., Roesch, S., Klein, E., Dackermann, T., Heller, J., & Moeller, K. (2020). The strategy matters: Bounded and unbounded number line estimation in secondary school children. *Cognitive Development*, 53, 100839.

Kim, D., & Opfer, J.E. (2017). A unified framework for bounded and unbounded numerical estimation. *Developmental Psychology*, 53, 1088–1097.

Kolesari, J., & Carlson, L. (2018). How the physicality of space affects how we think about time. *Memory & Cognition*, 46, 438–449.

Labrell, F., Mikaeloff, Y., Perdry, H., & Dellatolas, G. (2016). Time knowledge acquisition in children aged 6 to 11 years and its relationship with numerical skills. *Journal of Experimental Child Psychology*, 143, 1–13.

Lai, M., Zax, A., & Barth, H. (2018). Digit identity influences numerical estimation in children and adults. *Developmental Science*, 21, e12657.

Laski, E.V., & Siegler, R.S. (2007). Is 27 a big number? Correlational and causal connections among numerical categorization, number line estimation, and numerical magnitude comparison. *Child Development*, 78, 1723–1743.

Laski, E.V., & Siegler, R.S. (2014). Learning from number board games: You learn what you encode. *Developmental Psychology*, 50, 853–864.

Link, T., Huber, S., Nuerk, H.-C., & Moeller, K. (2014a). Unbounding the mental number line: New evidence on children's spatial representation of numbers. *Frontiers in Psychology*, 4, 1021.

Link, T., Nuerk, H.-C., & Moeller, K. (2014b). On the relation between the mental number line and arithmetic competencies. *The Quarterly Journal of Experimental Psychology*, 67, 1597–1613.

Malone, S.A., Pritchard, V.E., & Hulme, C. (2021). Separable effects of the approximate number system, symbolic number knowledge, and number ordering ability on early arithmetic development. *Journal of Experimental Child Psychology*, 208, 105–120.

McCrink, K., Shaki, S., & Berkowitz, T. (2014). Culturally driven biases in preschoolers' spatial search strategies for ordinal and non-ordinal dimensions. *Cognitive Development*, 30, 1–14.

Moeller, K., Pixner, S., Kaufmann, L., & Nuerk, H.-C. (2009). Children's early mental number line: Logarithmic or decomposed linear? *Journal of Experimental Child Psychology*, 103, 503–515.

Möhring, W., Frick, A., & Newcombe, N.S. (2018). Spatial scaling, proportional thinking, and numerical understanding in 5- to 7-year-old children. *Cognitive Development*, 45, 57–67.

Opfer, J.E., & Furlong, E.E. (2011). How numbers bias preschoolers' spatial search. *Journal of Cross-Cultural Psychology*, 42, 682–695.

Opfer, J.E., & Siegler, R.S. (2007). Representational change and children's numerical estimation. *Cognitive Psychology*, 55, 169–195.

Opfer, J.E., Thompson, C.A., & Furlong, E.E. (2010). Early development of spatial-numeric associations: Evidence from spatial and quantitative performance of preschoolers. *Developmental Science*, 13, 761–771.

Opfer, J.E., Thompson, C.A., & Kim, D. (2016). Free versus anchored numerical estimation: A unified approach. *Cognition*, 149, 11–17.

Patro, K., Nuerk, H.-C., & Cress, U. (2015). Does your body count? Embodied influences on the preferred counting direction of preschoolers. *Journal of Cognitive Psychology*, 27, 413–425.

Ramani, G.B., & Siegler, R.S. (2008). Promoting broad and stable improvements in low-income children's numerical knowledge through playing number board games. *Child Development, 79*, 375–394.

Reid, E.E., Baroody, A.J., & Purpura, D.J. (2015). Assessing young children's number magnitude representation: A comparison between novel and conventional tasks. *Journal of Cognition and Development, 16*, 759–779.

Ren, K., Lin, Y., & Gunderson, E.A. (2019). The role of inhibitory control in strategy change: The case of linear measurement. *Developmental Psychology, 55*, 1389–1399.

Rinaldi, L., Gallucci, M., & Girelli, L. (2016). Spatial-numerical consistency impacts on preschoolers' numerical representation: Children can count on both peripersonal and personal space. *Cognitive Development, 37*, 9–17.

Rouder, J.N., & Geary, D.C. (2014). Children's cognitive representation of the mathematical number line. *Developmental Science, 17*, 525–536.

Savelkouls, S., Williams, K., & Barth, H. (2020). Linguistic inversion and numerical estimation. *Journal of Numerical Cognition, 6*, 263–274.

Schneider, M., Merz, S., Stricker, J., DeSmedt, B., Torbeyns, J., Verschaffel, L., & Luwel, K. (2018). Associations of number line estimation with mathematical competence: A meta-analysis. *Child Development, 89*, 1467–1484.

Sella, F., Berteletti, I., Lucangeli, D., & Zorzi, M. (2017). Preschool children use space, rather than counting, to infer the numerical magnitude of digits: Evidence for a *spatial mapping principle. Cognition, 158*, 56–67.

Sella, F., & Lucangeli, D. (2020). The knowledge of the preceding number reveals a mature understanding of the number sequence. *Cognition, 194*, 104104.

Sella, F., Lucangeli, D., Cohen Kadosh, R., & Zorzi, M. (2020a). Making sense of number words

and Arabic digits: Does order count more? *Child Development, 91*, 1456–1470.

Sella, F., Lucangeli, D., & Zorzi, M. (2019). Spatial order relates to the exact numerical magnitude of digits in young children. *Journal of Experimental Child Psychology, 178*, 385–404.

Sella, F., Lucangeli, D., & Zorzi, M. (2020b). The interplay between spatial ordinal knowledge, linearity of number-space mapping, and arithmetic skills. *Cognitive Development, 55*, 100915.

Sella, F., Lucangeli, D., Zorzi, M., & Berteletti, I. (2013). Number line estimation in children with developmental dyscalculia. *Learning Disabilities: A Contemporary Journal, 11*, 41–49.

Shaki, S., Fischer, M.H., & Göbel, S.M. (2012). Direction counts: A comparative study of spatially directional counting biases in cultures with different reading directions. *Journal of Experimental Child Psychology, 112*, 275–281.

Siegler, R.S. (1996). *Emerging minds: The process of change in children's thinking.* Oxford University Press.

Siegler, R.S. (2016). Magnitude knowledge: The common core of numerical development. *Developmental Science, 19*, 341–361.

Siegler, R.S., & Booth, J.L. (2004). Development of numerical estimation in young children. *Child Development, 75*, 428–444.

Siegler, R.S., & Lortie-Forgues, H. (2014). An integrative theory of numerical development. *Child Development Perspectives, 8*, 144–150.

Siegler, R.S., & Opfer, J.E. (2003). The development of numerical estimation: Evidence for multiple representations of numerical quantity. *Psychological Science, 14*, 237–243.

Siegler, R.S., & Ramani, G.B. (2009). Playing linear number board games—but not circular ones—improves low-income preschoolers' numerical understanding. *Journal of Educational Psychology, 101*, 545–560.

Slusser, E., & Barth, H. (2017). Intuitive proportion judgment in number-line estimation: Converging evidence from multiple tasks. *Journal of Experimental Child Psychology, 162,* 181–198.

Solomon, T.L., Vasilyeva, M., Huttenlocher, J., & Levine, S.C. (2015). Minding the gap: Children's difficulty conceptualizing spatial intervals as linear measurement units. *Developmental Psychology, 51,* 1564–1573.

Stern, C., & Stern, M.B. (1971/2022). *Children discover arithmetic: An introduction to structural arithmetic* (Rev.). Harper & Row.

Sullivan, J., & Barner, D. (2014). The development of structural analogy in number-line estimation. *Journal of Experimental Child Psychology, 128,* 171–189.

Szűcs, D., & Csépe, V. (2005). The parietal distance effect appears in both the congenitally blind and matched sighted controls in an acoustic number comparison task. *Neuroscience Letters, 384,* 11–16.

Thompson, C.A., & Opfer, J.E. (2010). How 15 hundred is like 15 cherries: Effect of progressive alignment on representational changes in numerical cognition. *Child Development, 81,* 1768–1786.

Thompson, C.A., & Opfer, J.E. (2016). Learning linear spatial-numeric associations improves accuracy of memory for numbers. *Frontiers in Psychology, 7,* 24.

Tillman, K.A., & Barner, D. (2015). Learning the language of time: Children's acquisition of duration words. *Cognitive Psychology, 78,* 57–77.

Toll, S.W.M., & VanLuit, J.E.H. (2013). The development of early numeracy ability in kindergartners with limited working memory skills. *Learning and Individual Differences, 25,* 45–54.

Tzelgov, J., Ganor-Stern, D., Kallai, A., & Pinhas, M. (2015). Primitives and non-primitives of numerical representations. In R. Cohen Kadosh & A. Dowker (Eds.), *The Oxford handbook of numerical cognition* (pp. 45–66). Oxford University Press.

VanGalen, M.S., & Reitsma, P. (2008). Developing access to number magnitude: A study of the SNARC effect in 7- to 9-year-olds. *Journal of Experimental Child Psychology, 101,* 99–113.

Van't Noordende, J.E., vanHoogmoed, A.H., Schot, W.D., & Kroesbergen, E.H. (2016). Number line estimation strategies in children with mathematical learning difficulties measured by eye tracking. *Psychological Research, 80,* 368–378.

Vasilyeva, M., Casey, B.M., Dearing, E., & Ganley, C. (2009). Measurement skills in low-income elementary school students: Exploring the nature of gender differences. *Cognition and Instruction, 27,* 401–428.

Vasilyeva, M., Laski, E.V., Veraksa, A., & Bukhalenkova, D. (2021). Leveraging measurement instruction to develop kindergartners' numerical magnitude knowledge. *Journal of Educational Psychology, 113,* 1354–1369.

Wall, J.L., Thompson, C.A., Dunlosky, J., & Merriman, W.E. (2016). Children can accurately monitor and control their number-line estimation performance. *Developmental Psychology, 52,* 1493–1502.

White, S.L.J., & Szűcs, D. (2012). Representational change and strategy use in children's number line estimation during the first years of primary school. *Behavioral and Brain Functions, 8,* 1.

Xu, C. (2019). Ordinal skills influence the transition in number line strategies for children in grades 1 and 2. *Journal of Experimental Child Psychology, 185,* 109–127.

Xu, C., Burr, S.D.L., Douglas, H., Susperreguy, M.I., & LeFevre, J.-A. (2021). Number line development of Chilean children from preschool to the end of kindergarten. *Journal of Experimental Child Psychology, 208,* 105144.

Young, L.K., & Booth, J.L. (2020). Don't eliminate the negative: Influences of negative number magnitude knowledge on algebra performance and learning. *Journal of Educational Psychology, 112,* 384–396.

Yousif, S.R., Rosenberg, M.D., & Keil, F.C. (2021). Using space to remember: Short-term spatial structure spontaneously improves working memory. *Cognition, 214,* 104748.

Yuan, L., Prather, R., Mix, K.S., & Smith, L.B. (2020). Number representations drive number-line estimates. *Child Development, 91,* e952–e967.

Zax, A., Slusser, E., & Barth, H. (2019). Spontaneous partitioning and proportion estimation in children's numerical judgments. *Journal of Experimental Child Psychology, 185,* 71–94.

Part IV

Arithmetic

"Many characteristics of arithmetic learning reflect the nature of the system doing the learning rather than the instruction per se."

Patrick Lemaire and Robert Siegler, 1995[1]

DOI: 10.4324/9781003157656-13

It may come as a surprise to someone preparing to teach basic arithmetic that most children—at least those who have the rudiments of the tools of numeracy, as discussed in the previous section of this book—enter school with some notion of how to solve arithmetic problems. Of course, they do not yet know the procedural intricacies of regrouping or doing long division. Nor can most of them say, off the top of their head, what the sum of *8* and *6* is.

But neither are they blank slates. Most kindergartners know, for example, that 1) when you combine two amounts, you wind up with more and 2) when you take something away, you wind up with less.[2] That is, they appreciate how sets of discrete amounts relate to each other and how they can change. The study of arithmetic, then, is the process of coming up with ways to be ever more precise and efficient in describing those relationships and changes over ever larger (whole number) and smaller (rational number) amounts, as well as understanding the similarities and differences characterizing these two sorts of numbers and how they are manipulated.[3]

Part IV begins with these "unblank" slates and traces arithmetic development as children experience it—how children use what they know to solve easy, familiar problems; how they overcome not knowing quite enough to solve ever-harder, novel ones; and how teachers can help them do that. Chapter 10 explores this evolution with whole numbers. Chapter 11 takes the reader on a walk with children through the looking glass into the world of rational numbers, where nearly everything is the opposite of what it seems. And Chapter 12 explores the challenges of doing arithmetic when it is couched in the opaque language of story problems.

A pedagogical note is in order here. One goal in writing this book was to reach all children. However, there is significant variability in the ease with which children catch on to ideas, both across children and across ideas. This section deals with arithmetic, the heart of elementary mathematics. Much of the research explores the topic through the eyes of the child and describes their "discoveries" of arithmetic principles and problem-solving strategies. For some children, these discoveries will come easily with teacher guidance and arithmetic experience. Other children, however, will need to be led to them, and some will need to be taught them explicitly.[4] In the Activities sections of these chapters, we have taken the most explicit, systematic approach to make sure that all children will benefit. The activities and materials are relatively transparent, however, and should provide fertile ground for all students.

NOTES

1 Lemaire & Siegler, 1995, p. 95, reprinted with permission.
2 Canobi & Bethune, 2008.
3 Siegler & Braithwaite, 2017.
4 Gersten et al., 2009; Kirschner et al., 2006.

REFERENCES

The following references were cited in this introduction. For additional selected references relevant to this introduction, please see Part IV Supplemental References in eResources.

Canobi, K.H., & Bethune, N.E. (2008). Number words in young children's conceptual and procedural knowledge of addition, subtraction and inversion. *Cognition, 108*, 675–686.

Gersten, R., Chard, D.J., Jayanthi, M., Baker, S.K., Morphy, P., & Flojo, J. (2009). Mathematics instruction for students with learning disabilities: A meta-analysis of instruction components. *Review of Educational Research, 79*, 1202–1242.

Kirschner, P.A., Sweller, J., & Clark, R.E. (2006). Why minimal guidance during instruction does not work: An analysis of the failure of constructivist, discovery, problem-based, experiential, and inquiry-based teaching. *Educational Psychologist, 41*, 75–86.

Lemaire, P., & Siegler, R.S. (1995). Four aspects of strategic change: Contributions to children's learning of multiplication. *Journal of Experimental Psychology: General, 124*, 83–97.

Siegler, R.S., & Braithwaite, D.W. (2017). Numerical development. *Annual Review of Psychology, 68*, 187–213.

Chapter 10

Whole-Number Arithmetic

CHILDREN wrap their minds around arithmetic beginning with what is most familiar: the counting routine with fingers or objects. However, with experience and growing confidence, most children discover or are led to shortcuts to this tedious approach that are either quicker or more frequently accurate, or both, and that work better for them, depending on the particular problem. They also discover that sometimes they simply remember a solution because they have seen the problem so often and that retrieving a solution from memory saves them a lot of time and work and lets them focus on the more difficult aspects of the problem. Finally, while they may understand the numbers and the operation in such problems as $3 + 4 =$ ___, it is often the case that no one has adequately explained to them exactly what the "=" means, leaving many to assume it means, "What's the answer?"

This chapter reviews what researchers have discovered about children's arithmetic strategies and the importance of having several of them at one's fingertips. It also examines what is known about retrieval as a strategy, how children remember solutions, and the sorts of problems for which children find retrieval most useful. Basic language skills are critical for arithmetic mastery, and the chapter discusses the common arithmetic difficulties experienced by children with various language-related learning difficulties. But first it explores the critical and surprisingly gnarly problem of the *equivalence* meaning of the equal (=) sign.

THE = SIGN

For young students intently focused on figuring out solutions to problems involving arithmetic operations, the innocuous little = sign, typically (and cryptically) expressed as "is" or "equals," is understandably often overlooked, or may implicitly signify "now give an answer," or simply serve as a mark conveniently separating the problem from their answer. Most teachers undoubtedly understand that the amount represented by the problem on the left is the same amount as the (correct) answer on the right. However, the "is-the-same-amount-as" relational meaning of "equals" often does not get explicitly taught to their students. Nor does the incorrect answer get explained as "is NOT the same amount as."

DOI: 10.4324/9781003157656-14

If math education ended at basic arithmetic, the fuzziness of understanding the = sign would not be a problem. However, math education continues on, and the complex mathematical statements of algebra require a more precise meaning for the = sign. Abundant research shows that young children who can solve the problem *5 + 2 = ___* are baffled by the problem *5 + 2 = 4 + ___* and even more so by *5 + 2 = ___ + 4*.[1] Those students who are particularly diligent about doing what they are told—a group somewhat more over-represented among girls than boys—simply do what they normally do to solve traditional (*5 + 2 = ___*) problems: They add up all the numbers.[2] For example, they might conclude that the answer to *5 + 2 = ___ + 4* is *11*. With growing confidence in their arithmetic skills, some children relax enough to think and to tolerate a more flexible way of doing things;[3] however, confusion persists through middle school, high school, and even among well-educated adults.[4] The ability to understand "=" in relational terms ("is the same amount as"), rather than operational terms ("here's my answer"), is closely associated with elementary students catching on to pre-algebraic statements and with middle-schoolers' success in early algebra.[5] Indeed, a study of children in grades six through eight who began learning algebra in grade six found that 75 percent of those who grasped the relational meaning of "=" used algebra to solve linear equations, while fewer than 20 percent of those who held to the operational definition did so.[6] Among high-school students, understanding the implication of two amounts being the same—that one can be substituted for the other—further predicted algebraic success.[7] The persistence of the confusion is understandable: A 2006 review of four middle-school textbook series revealed that textbooks rarely use "=" in a relational context and do not explicitly teach its meaning.[8]

Confusion and misunderstanding begin with the use of the = sign in earliest written arithmetic, so the problem requires an early solution. Researchers highly familiar with the problem recommend explicit instruction in relational thinking outside the arithmetic context, as well as in a variety of problem formats, as early as the primary grades. Second-grade interventions beginning with concrete examples that gradually become more abstract, along with requiring children to compare and explain different problem formats and problem-solving strategies, have been shown to improve children's understanding of mathematical equivalence and their accuracy on novel problems.[9] Similar success was found when second-graders practiced addition problems that were variously set out with the operation on the right side or the left, with the = sign replaced by "is equal to" and by organizing the workbook such that several problems in a row all had the same sum.[10] Another proposed solution that has shown some benefit is to present the problem in non-symbolic (dots) and symbolic (digits) terms simultaneously.[11]

A third method, noted in Chapter 5, is training in the unrelated skill of two-dimensional rotation—mentally combining puzzle-type pieces and imagining the resulting figure—which, remarkably, was found to improve performance on missing-term problems (*4 + ___ = 12*) among six- to eight-and-a-half-year-olds.[12]

In the activities at the end of this chapter, we translate "=" as "is the same amount as."

The potential for confusion about non-numerical mathematical symbols does not end with the = sign. Formal mathematics is replete with symbols that are open to all kinds of misunderstandings. Why say "plus" for +, when the more familiar "and"—as in, "three and five more"—or even "added to" or "combined with" would do as well? Why does one use the subtraction sign (–) to label negative numbers? Do the common "goes into" and "divided by" meanings of the division radical and ÷ sign signify the same meaning as "going into" a room or "dividing by" a wall? And wouldn't *4 × 5* be more comprehensible as simply "four fives," rather than "four times five"? Not surprisingly, research has found that adults' knowledge of math symbols and their proper use is linked to their knowledge of whole-number arithmetic, fraction and algebra procedures, and even story-problem solving.[13]

STRATEGIES

Even prior to any formal arithmetic education, children can be quite inventive in devising strategies to predict the results of numerical changes.[14] Because children know how these changes work—that adding one amount to another means the sum will not be smaller than either, for example—children's early solution efforts are often remarkably on the right track. In one study of four-year-olds on problems with numbers summing no higher than 15, for example, more than 80 percent of them predicted the answers to subtraction problems as being smaller, and those to addition problems as being larger, than the first addend. That is not to say that those solutions were necessarily accurate, just that children do have an idea of what sort of answer is required. Indeed, more than 70 percent of those four-year-olds' predictions were off by only one.[15] Moreover, research has shown that most children use several different strategies right out of the gate to solve such problems—and continue to do so through adulthood, including immature and inefficient ones when necessary.[16]

Researchers have studied how children think and strategize by watching closely how they work their way through hundreds of arithmetic problems and by asking them how they did each one. These studies are called *microgenetic* because they obtain a very close-up view of how strategies come about, ebb, flow, and change—that is, how children learn.[17] Table 10.1 summarizes some of the strategies that children most commonly use as they learn addition, subtraction, multiplication, and division. Close readers will discover in that list many strategies that they have not only observed their students use, but that they themselves have used, probably in the past week.

FIGURE 10.1

Source: For Better or for Worse © 2015 Lynn Johnston Productions. Dist. By Andrews McMeel Syndication. Reprinted with permission. All rights reserved.

TABLE 10.1 Some Strategies Used by Children (and Adults!) to Solve Addition, Subtraction, Multiplication, and Division Problems

Strategy	Example
ADDITION	$3 + 5 =$
No response	
Guess	"9?"
Count from 1 using fingers or objects ("sum")	"1, 2, 3 . . . 1, 2, 3, 4, 5 . . . 1, 2, 3, 4, 5, 6, 7, 8 . . . 8!"
Short-cut count using fingers or objects	"1, 2, 3, 4, 5, 6, 7, 8 . . . 8!"
Count silently fingers or objects	[Counts in head] . . . "8!"
Recognize finger or object total	"1, 2, 3 . . . 1, 2, 3, 4, 5 . . . 8!"
Count second addend on to first addend, with or without fingers or objects	"3 . . . 4, 5, 6, 7, 8 . . . 8!"
Count smaller addend on to larger addend ("min"), with or without fingers or objects	"5 . . . 6, 7, 8 . . . 8!"
Decomposition, with partial retrieval from memory ("decomp")	"3 + 3 = 6 . . .+2 = 8 . . . 8!" or "5 + 5 = 10 . . .-2 = 8 . . . 8!"
Retrieval from memory ("retrieval")	"8!"
SUBTRACTION	$17 - 4 =$
No response	
Guess	"12?"
Count down from minuend by the subtrahend, with or without fingers	"17 . . . 16, 15, 14, 13 . . . 13!"
Count up from subtrahend to minuend, with or without [fingers]	"4 . . . 5[1], 6[2], 7[3], 8[4], 9[5], 10[6], 11[7], 12[8], 13[9], 14[10], 15[1], 16[2], 17[3] . . . uh . . . [looks at fingers] . . . 13!"
Delete 10, then put back in	"7 . . . 6, 5, 4 . . . 3 . . . 13!"
Use reference to known addition fact	"3 + 4 = 7 . . . 13 + 4 = 17 . . . 13!" or "7 – 4 = 3 . . . 17 – 4 = 13 . . . 13!"
Retrieval	"13!"
MULTIPLICATION	$9 \times 5 =$
No response	
Write tally marks, then count sets of them	||||| ||||| ||||| ||||| ||||| ||||| ||||| ||||| ||||| "45!"
Repeated addition	"5 + 5 + 5 + 5 + 5 + 5 + 5 + 5 + 5 = 45 . . . 45!"
Well-learned skip-counting, with [fingers]	"5[1], 10[2], 15[3], 20[4], 25[5], 30[6], 35[7], 40[8], 45[9] . . . 45!"
Partial retrieval from memory, and addition or subtraction	"8 × 5 = 40 . . . 40 + 5 = 45 . . . 45!" or "10 × 5 = 50 . . . 50 – 5 = 45 . . . 45!"
9s rule finger trick	"4 fingers before 5, and 5 fingers after 5 . . . 45!"
Write the problem before responding orally	$9 \times 5 = 45$ . . . "45!"
Retrieval from memory	"45!"
DIVISION	$12 \div 4 =$
Repeated addition, with [fingers]	"4 + 4[2] = 8 . . . 8 + 4[3] = 12 . . . 3!"
Multiplication retrieval	"4 × 3 = 12 . . . 3!"
Retrieval	"3!"

Sources: Lemaire & Siegler, 1995; Mabbott & Bisanz, 2003; Robinson et al., 2006; Siegler, 1987; Siegler, 1989; Siegler & Crowley, 1994; Siegler & Shrager, 1984.

FIGURE 10.2

Although many students readily discover and continue to use multiple strategies for solving problems, the selection, configuration, flexibility, proficiency, efficiency, and frequency of use of those strategies and their execution evolve with age and experience.[18] Moreover, children may not even be aware of the strategy they are using until they try to explain it to someone else.

What follows here are researchers' observations of that developmental trajectory among children in preschool through second grade as they learn addition.[19] The examples here are particular to addition, but the same complex trajectory of strategy development from lesser to greater efficiency—what one scholar has described as "overlapping waves"[20]—applies generally to all operations and to many other math skills as well.

Typically, preschoolers begin calculating sums by counting, although many simply guess and others already know some solutions by heart. Among the youngest children, counting with fingers or objects or simply putting up fingers tend to be reasonably accurate strategies, albeit slow, while retrieval from memory is the fastest but not yet as reliable. Researchers found that a group of four- and five-year-olds working with the addends *1* to *5* used overt counting strategies on 36 percent of the problems they were given. They solved the remaining problems more quickly, but not as accurately, by guessing or retrieving the answer from memory.[21] As noted in Chapter 7, fingers provide an accessible concrete referent for the counting sequence. They can also help children keep track of where they are in the count and in the overall solution. Fingers thus support working memory and provide a springboard for early arithmetic.[22]

Importantly, experience plays a major role in the evolution of strategy choice. The intermediate stage of exposure to a math topic is particularly ripe for strategy discovery and variability. Indeed, a study of 106 children one year into multiplication instruction found that three percent used only one strategy and nearly 90 percent used three or more.[23]

Useful Discoveries

With enough practice, several discoveries or advances during these early years can make doing sums more efficient. Note that the order in which children make these discoveries and the amount of intervention required vary considerably from child to child. Also, "discoveries" here may certainly include hard-won insight facilitated by explicit, systematic instruction when necessary.

One such advance is automatically recognizing the numbers represented by various finger configurations, obviating the need to count the two addends individually or even count up the total.

Another discovery (again, given enough practice) is what has been called the *min strategy*, the gold-standard of counting strategies in that it is typically the fastest. The min strategy involves figuring out which is the larger addend, reversing the addends' order if the larger one was second, saying the larger number, and counting the smaller (minimum) addend to it—all the while simultaneously keeping track of the running total and number of counts. For example, in *3 + 6*, the child needs to recognize that *6* is the larger number, think of it as the starting number, say "six," and then count up three from there ("six . . . seven, eight, nine"). Using fingers can help the child keep track of the *3* while counting the "seven, eight, nine." Interestingly, researchers found that naming the larger number to start the counting process is often the last piece of the strategy to fall into place. A small study of kindergartners found that nearly half of them used the min strategy on at least one of the ten problems they were given. However, even when kindergartners have not yet discovered the min strategy for themselves, they recognize it as a reasonable approach when they see others use it.[24] Studies of first-graders found that nearly all of them use the min strategy by the end of that year. For those who do not, however, instructing them in the strategy's subskills—counting up from an arbitrary number, thinking of the larger addend as a word in the counting sequence, and beginning the added-on count with the next counting word—enable most of them to use the min strategy thereafter.[25] Just as counting from "one" and guessing decline in use as kindergartners and first-graders gain proficiency with more advanced strategies, so does the min counting strategy fade as children get better at retrieving sums to *20* during second grade. Notably, however, none of the strategies completely disappear from use, though all typically become faster and more accurate.[26]

Taking a microscope to the behavior of four- to six-year-olds, researchers found that children took highly variable amounts of time to discover the min strategy. More-over, in the period leading up to and including the discovery, the solution times were twice as long as those on other problems, with long pauses and "um's" and "er's" in speech before beginning, false starts in using the new approach, and slower counting. These behaviors suggested the sort of heightened cognitive activity that often leads to new discoveries. Curiously, most of the discoveries did not necessarily involve explicit insight or occur on the sorts of problems for which the min strategy might be ideal, such as those with one small addend. Nor did children use it or generalize it to other problems very frequently thereafter. However, in one study, researchers later presented the four- and five-year-olds with a more challenging problem, such as *2 + 21 = ____*.

At this point, the children who had previously discovered the min strategy used it on this problem and began to use it more frequently, while those who had not discovered it were overwhelmed by this more difficult problem. These important findings suggest that having a variety of different strategies at one's disposal allows children to adapt to new and more difficult problems, even though the children may not use them very often or find them useful on other problems.[27]

A third discovery is that with enough experience, children find that they can *retrieve* a solution to a problem from memory, although it may take a while for them to feel confident that they remember it accurately. (If they do not yet feel confident and think it is very important to be accurate, they will likely pick a back-up counting strategy instead.) On other, harder problems, especially those with bigger numbers, children may find that they recall a sum that will get them partway to the solution, a strategy called *decomposition* (see Table 10.1 for an example).

Despite the potential speed and accuracy of the retrieval approach for one-digit addition problems, it is used with surprisingly little frequency. A study completed in the late 1980s found that the percentage of problems on which retrieval was used was 53 percent among second-graders, 76 percent among third-graders, 69 percent among fourth- and sixth-graders, and 72 percent among college students.[28] By the end of second grade, children are typically quite accurate at one-digit addition, with speed of execution continuing to increase into adolescence. Remarkably, however, a large study of American adolescents found considerable differences in strategy choices; those students who continued to rely chiefly on counting strategies were also struggling with math in general. The researchers concluded that an important intervention might be simply to help those students advance to more mature strategies.[29]

A series of international studies sheds light on cross-national differences in the use of retrieval and decomposition. Among Chinese and American children in kindergarten through third grade, researchers found that Chinese children use base-10 decomposition more frequently and shift to retrieval earlier than do their American peers. The researchers attributed these differences in part to the linguistic differences noted in Chapter 6 and in part to Chinese children's more frequent early instructional exposure.[30] A study of American and Taiwanese first-graders presented with one-digit and complex two-digit addition problems found that all children's choice of strategies varied depending on the problem's difficulty. However, the skills that set apart the top students with the strongest performance on the two-digit problems (in both countries) were knowledge of the base-10 notational structure, fluent recall of one-digit sums, and the frequent use of decomposition.[31] Interestingly, among a large multinational group of first-graders, the fluent use of retrieval on simple problems and the use of decomposition on complex problems set Taiwanese girls apart from American and Russian girls, who tended to use less mature counting strategies more frequently. No sex differences in strategy choices were found in Taiwan, and no cross-national differences were found among boys.[32]

A fourth set of discoveries is that numbers can be added in any order (the *commutativity* principle) and that when addition and subtraction operations are in the same problem, they can be accomplished in any order (the *associativity* principle). Practically speaking, this means that if children can remember the solution to *6 + 2 = ___*, they also know the solution to *2 + 6 =* ___. It also means that one can make the problem *5 + 6 – 1 =* ___ a bit easier by subtracting *6 – 1* first, then adding *5 + 5*. Or simplify the work involved in *27 + 5 – 23 =* ___ by rearranging the problem to look like this: *27 – 23 + 5 =* ___. Researchers found that using these principles spontaneously in solving problems was tied to greater use of decomposition and retrieval and to flexible and efficient problem-solving among six- to eight-year-olds. Unfortunately, the associativity principle is surprisingly underutilized for shortcuts in elementary school (where it is typically used on only ten to 25 percent of the problems for which it would be appropriate), as well as in older age groups (about 30 percent in middle school and only 50 to 60 percent even in adulthood). Thus, researchers speculate whether some teachers themselves may not be entirely comfortable with it and shy away from teaching it.[33]

Finally, a fifth discovery is that *a + b – b = a* (the *inversion* principle of addition and subtraction). This is simply the application to formal arithmetic of the idea that many children grasp early on—namely, if you add one amount to another and then take it away again, you wind up with the amount you started with. As with the commutativity and associativity discoveries, the inversion discovery has also been linked to arithmetic success in first- and second-graders.[34] Compared with the associativity principle, inversion shortcuts enjoy significantly more use: 35 to 60 percent of the time in elementary school, and by age 14, up to 90 to 95 percent of the time for addition-subtraction problems. However, among second- to fourth-graders, while conceptual understanding was greater for inversion than for associativity, there was little growth in either from grade to grade. Moreover, there were large individual differences in understanding. Notably, the inverse relation between multiplication and division is more challenging and takes longer to discover. Seven- and eight-year-olds in one study were not yet able to grasp the connection between doubling an amount and then cutting the result in half, even when demonstrated with sets of objects. Even among adolescents and adults, the utilization rate is only 70 to 75 percent for multiplication-division problems.[35]

Common Errors

Not surprisingly, young children make errors when they first start out, but the errors they make are much less random than one might expect and are related to several factors. For example, small-value problems tend to be executed more accurately than large-value problems for several reasons. One is that children tend to be given more opportunities to solve small problems than large problems, and experience matters. Classroom lessons, textbooks, and picture books that offer children more contact with low-value problems, ties, or skip-counting, say, than with the higher-value, more difficult problems contribute to a disparity in expertise. A second factor is that it is more difficult to generate consistently accurate solutions to high-value problems using counting-based strategies, leading to fuzzier memories of them. And for children whose best or only recourse for a given problem is to guess the solution, there is simply a greater range of reasonable guesses for large sums than for small ones.[36]

Other types of errors include mistakenly associating the answer to another bit of familiar information. For example, a child might confuse the answer with a number-line neighbor, as we saw in Chapter 9.[37] Or slip into the counting sequence and offer as an answer the next number up from the second addend (*3 + 5 = 6*). Among older children learning several operations, it is not uncommon to confuse problems featuring the same numbers but different operations, making it difficult to keep them straight in memory—e.g., *8 + 4 = 32* and *8 × 4 = 12*—confusion known as *table interference*.[38] Beginning the study of multiplication can slow down children's responses to addition problems and make them less accurate as children struggle to disentangle the two operations in their heads. In one study, table interference accounted for four percent of second-graders' errors, 14 percent of third-graders' errors, and 48 percent of fourth-graders' errors on addition problems. Not surprisingly, such errors were more frequent when children's practice on addition and multiplication was intermixed in an exercise.[39]

Some distractible children may be unusually prone to interference errors, however, because of general difficulty in inhibiting irrelevant information that may make it difficult to keep the solutions straight in memory.[40] Conversely, children with significant general math difficulties often evidence *less* of this interference than typical math students, either because they have not learned the related solutions or because the related solutions are meaningless to them. For them, the typical table-interference difficulty may arise only much later in school.[41] Similarly, unlike most typical students, they may not be tempted by answers that are close to the correct ones—e.g., *6 × 8 = 49*—because of a poorly established mental number line[42] and, indeed, often produce results that are way off. However, they may be *more* inclined to make counting-sequence errors because the verbal sequence does not require that one actually think of the number words as quantities. Or they may not recognize the implausibility of their multiplication solutions because they have not picked up the useful regularities that result from multiplying by *5* or those involving the odd or even nature of the operands. In short, the multiplication solutions of such students reveal a lack of the number sense—that is, a sense of numbers' magnitudes and the effect that arithmetic operations have on them—that helps their peers rethink off-base answers.[43] Moreover, there is some brain-imaging evidence that children with significant math learning difficulties have less differentiated neural representations for different numerical operations than do their classmates without such difficulties.[44]

Finally, errors may arise for a host of other predictable reasons. For example, one might mistakenly choose a strategy that requires more working or long-term memory than one has available. Or be forced to choose between speed and accuracy in selecting a particular strategy for a particular problem. On written problems featuring multiple terms and operations, some children are fooled by the spacing in deciding the order in which to execute the operations (e.g., *2+3 × 4 = ___*).[45] And some children have more trouble tracking place-values when problems are presented horizontally rather than vertically.[46] Indeed, problem characteristics such as those mentioned here—as well as children's own cognitive strengths and weaknesses, their ability to focus and sustain attention, their confidence in what they know, their anxiety or perfectionism, even their eagerness to just get a problem over with—in the context of external demands all play a role in children's often minute-to-minute decisions about the strategy that they think will work best on any given problem, given the alternatives available to them. A child's progress in strategy choice can be slow and highly uneven, and generalization of known strategies also takes a long time. However, these strategy choices become increasingly adaptive with age and experience.[47]

Pedagogical Implications

Several critical research findings have important implications for the classroom.[48] One is that broad early strategy variability predicts later learning. Using several strategies both reflects and supports wider learning and helps children solve a larger assortment of problems, both currently and in the future. Strategy maturation is reflected in important brain circuitry development as well.[49] If young children are stuck on one strategy, it may mean that they have had insufficient experience with numbers, or that they lack cognitive flexibility, or that they are fearful of venturing beyond a strategy that worked well once.[50] For some children, getting stuck on one immature strategy may signal serious difficulties in understanding quantities. When a group of seventh-graders were given a choice of using their fingers, fact retrieval, or counting to do simple subtraction, 94 percent of the weakest math students were still using their fingers, compared with 42 percent of typical math students.[51] Persistent single-strategy use is a red flag that requires attention.

Second, most children will continue to use both immature and more sophisticated approaches throughout their education, although over time, their use of counting strategies will decrease as they realize they can solve the problem just as well with less work using retrieval and decomposition. As noted, this pattern reflects ideas coexisting and competing with each other in the mind. Thus, strategy choice will fluctuate for all kinds of reasons, a normal pattern for both children and adults.[52]

Third, children learn better when they can choose their own strategies and pick the one they want to use. However, a teacher can spark ideas by providing feedback on a problem and then asking the student, "How do you think I knew that?" Additionally, asking why a student thinks correct answers are correct, or why incorrect answers are incorrect, is another useful technique to challenge their thinking.[53] While it may be difficult to impose a new strategy on a student, for those who require more structure, teachers should offer guidance or explicit instruction, including modeling their own use of a strategy and thinking aloud as they solve a problem. Asking questions can also help: "How did you figure out the answer?" or "Can you think of another way to get the answer?"

Fourth, there is no rule that dictates for every student whether conceptual knowledge or procedural knowledge comes first. Although there is some disagreement about this, some children learn better one way, some the other way. Some researchers suggest that the best teaching approach is to link them with equal emphasis.[54]

Fifth, as discussed in Chapter 1, children's gestures often reveal fresh ideas, even when they cannot put words to them. Occasions when children's problem-solving gestures and words are at odds are often a prelude to new learning and insight.[55] Teachers will want to keep their eyes open for such discrepancies. Teachers can also model and encourage concept-relevant gestures.

Finally, the foregoing discussion begs the question, *What role, if any, is there for teaching the standard computational procedures (e.g., carrying and borrowing)?* One research team asked that question by observing the addition and multiplication skills of second-, third-, and fourth-graders whose teachers did teach the procedures (the "procedures" group) or did not teach the procedures (the "no procedures" group). All students were given a horizontally presented addition problem with one-, two-, and three-digit terms (e.g., *6 + 53 + 185 = ___*) and asked to solve it without paper and pencil. Students were also given other grade-appropriate addition and multiplication problems vertically presented (properly or improperly aligned) and asked to solve them and explain their reasoning using chips. The study found that the "no procedures" group produced significantly more correct answers on the initial three-term addition problems than the "procedures" group and that their errors were more reasonable. Moreover, although most students were accurate in their solution to the other problems, significantly more "no procedures" students could adequately explain their answers than could the "procedures" students (83 percent versus 23 percent in second grade, and 92 percent versus five percent in third grade).[56] These results may persuade some against explicitly teaching the computational procedures.

However, the procedures did result in correct answers for many of the problems and are legitimate strategies that, once mastered, can provide highly efficient methods for doing complex calculations. Perhaps a better way to interpret the findings of the foregoing study, then, is that some students may have mastered the procedures without understanding the underlying concepts or the nature of multi-digit numbers and place-value. Thus, the conclusion may really be that learning computational procedures *instead of* developing a thorough understanding of numbers, their notation, and how they relate to each other and can change can be worse than not learning them at all. There is every reason here to believe that teaching the procedures *along with* the underlying concepts—as additional, potentially useful strategies compatible with children's own understanding of numerical transformations—would enhance their arithmetic education.

ARITHMETIC FACTS

Retrieving the solution to a single-digit arithmetic problem from memory is the fastest strategy, and with sufficient mastery, it is also as accurate as the slower, counting-based methods. One advantage of having single-digit solutions easily accessible in memory is that it frees up cognitive resources for the more demanding aspects of complex problem-solving. As noted in the research cited earlier on complex addition, fast and accurate retrieval, along with knowledge of the base-10 notational system and use of the decomposition strategy, are strongly associated with arithmetic achievement. Thus, having single-digit solutions firmly planted in memory is essential for long-term arithmetic success.

A question for research, then, is: *How does one commit the single-digit solutions to memory?* One obstacle, of course, is that the number of pair-wise solutions in a system with ten digits (*0–9*) and four operations is enormous. Thus, a second question is: *Is it possible to focus on only a manageable and memorizable number of such solutions?*

We take these two questions up in the next two sections.

Remembering Solutions

Experience governs what people remember. Every time a child figures out a solution to a single-digit problem, that solution gets mentally associated with the problem. Unfortunately, that is the case whether or not the solution is correct. The more frequently the solution is incorrect, the more difficult it is to remember the correct one. Rather than having one clean, crisp mental picture of the correct solution, one winds up with a fuzzy cloud of possible solutions in mind. When asked to solve the same problem again, the child will have a much less reliable mental source of information, resulting in a longer search through memory, a higher probability of coming up with an incorrect answer again, or necessary recourse to even more time-consuming back-up strategies.

Conversely, the more frequently the child arrives at the correct solution, the clearer will be his mental image of it and the more likely it will come to mind the next time he tackles that problem. Moreover, the frequency of exposure to a given problem also matters. Even if a child arrives at the correct solution to a problem on all attempts, the solution will be much more reliably etched in memory after 50 such attempts than after three.[57] Thus, beginning with slow but very reliably accurate strategies through error-free practice and building gradually, through many efforts, to quicker approaches promises the best chance of remembering the correct solution to a given problem.

Which Facts?

Not all solutions to single-digit problems need to be committed to memory. Several arithmetic principles, some of which have already been discussed, can narrow the job considerably. It must be stated at the outset, however, that children need to understand these principles well in order to benefit from them. Guided experience, instruction, and lots of practice are required.

The first useful principle is the *inverse relation* of addition and subtraction and of multiplication and division. An example of this principle as it applies to addition and subtraction is: if *6 + 3 = 9*, then *9 – 3 = 6* and *9 – 6 = 3*. That is, if you start out with two amounts and add them together, then taking either amount away again will leave the other amount you started with. Thus, if you know that *6 + 3 = 9*, you also know that *9 – 3 = 6* and that *9 – 6 = 3*. If a child understands that this principle is always true, then knowing the one addition fact (*6 + 3 = 9*) automatically provides the two related subtraction facts. The two key pieces here are that the child understands the principle and that the child remembers the addition fact. Structuring problem-solving practice around well-chosen examples—e.g., solving the addition problem with corrective feedback first, then the subtraction problems with the addition problem still in view—should help children discover and use these principles.[58]

The same inversion principle applies to multiplication and division. If a child knows that *3 × 4 = 12* and understands that multiplication and division have an inverse relationship, then he also knows that *12 ÷ 3 = 4* and *12 ÷ 4 = 3*. The one small exception to this rule is that dividing by *zero* is not a meaningful operation. Thus, there is only one legitimate inverse, not two, for any problem involving multiplying by *zero*, a fact that must be taught.

As it turns out, most children rely on retrieval of addition facts when solving subtraction problems, while direct retrieval of subtraction facts tends to be confined to problems involving *one (6 – 1 = 5*, or *7 – 6 = 1)*.[59] A study of children's single-digit division strategies (to *72 ÷ 9 = ___*) revealed that fourth-graders rely heavily on repeated addition (*9 + 9 +. . .*), while fifth- through seventh-graders rely on their known multiplication facts (*9 × 8 = 72*), a quick and reliable strategy. In all four grades, children used direct retrieval of division facts less than 20 percent of the time, with its frequency of use unchanged across grades.[60] In sum, then, committing addition and multiplication facts to memory, along with understanding and practicing their application to subtraction and division problems, should suffice.[61]

A second useful principle, introduced in the discussion of strategies, is the *commutative property* of addition and of multiplication. Commutativity means that *6 + 3* is the same amount as *3 + 6* and that *6 × 3* is the same amount as *3 × 6*. That is, the order of the terms does not matter within each of these operations. (Technically, *6 × 3* means six *threes*, while *3 × 6* means three *sixes*. But for computational purposes, it is useful to discover that the outcomes are the same.) Thus, a student who knows the solution to the problem *6 + 3 = ___* also knows the solution to the problem *3 + 6 = ___*, further reducing the number of facts to be explicitly committed to memory.

A third useful principle, the *identity properties* of the four operations, can also help reduce the burden on memory. The identity property of addition and subtraction means that adding *zero* to, or subtracting *zero* from, a number will always result in that number itself (e.g., *5 + 0 = 5* and *5 – 0 = 5*). Similarly, the identity property of multiplication and division means that multiplying or dividing any number by *one* will always result in that number itself (e.g., *5 × 1 = 5* and *5 ÷ 1 = 5*). The numbers *one* and *zero* bring with them other regularities as well. For example, multiplying any number by *zero* always results in *zero* (as noted, there is no legitimate division inverse of this property). And adding *one* to any number always results in the next number up the counting sequence. Giving students lots of experience with *zero* and *one* should make it easy to bring home these regularities.

Finally, some of the remaining facts are attached to relatively easy-to-remember verbal sequences, such as skip-counting by *two* (which covers addition ties, as well as multiples of *two*) and by *five*. Again, provided that students participate in discovering them and understand the underlying concepts, these regularities should help to ease the burden on memory.

Altogether then, when these strategies for remembering some of the solutions are taken into account, only 25 addition facts (*2 + 3* to *8 + 9*) and 21 multiplication facts (*3 × 3* to *9 × 9*, without the multiples of *5*) remain to commit to memory. Limiting the store of facts in memory should be particularly helpful to students with significant attention deficits, provided they understand the principles that allow them access to the remaining combinations.

One further point is in order here. It is reasonable to be concerned that children will simply commit arithmetic facts to rote verbal memory without connecting them to the values they represent. A brain-activation study of multiplication demonstrated that most typical fifth-graders do associate the products with their quantities.[62] However, the same may not be true of children who never made a firm connection between symbolic numbers and their quantitative meaning.

LANGUAGE AND ARITHMETIC

As noted in Chapter 8, one prerequisite skill for formal arithmetic is transcoding—that is, being able to automatically connect the written digit (*3*) to the spoken word ("three"). The development of language and symbolic arithmetic is closely tied, such that by adulthood the two functions are closely aligned in the brain as well.[63] Symbolic arithmetic requires several underlying language skills. One such skill is receptive syntax—that is, understanding how the order of words in a statement contributes to the statement's meaning. First- and second-graders who have difficulty with spoken syntax were found to have trouble with simple written numerical statements (e.g., *1 + 2 = 3*).[64] A second relevant language skill is phonological awareness—that is, discerning the sounds of language, as discussed in Chapter 6. A deficit in phonological awareness or auditory processing can interfere quite specifically with efficient arithmetic fact retrieval,[65] and studies of deaf adults found notable difficulty with arithmetic as well.[66] A third important language skill is rapid automatic naming (RAN)—that is, the ability to automatically state the name of a familiar object. RAN is strongly linked to arithmetic fluency, as one might imagine.[67] Indeed, a longitudinal study from kindergarten through eighth grade of children with severe math learning difficulties found a pronounced deficit in rapid automatic naming.[68] These children may mean to say one number but end up saying another, or they may say one number and write it differently.

Deficits in these linguistic skills spell arithmetic trouble for children with specific developmental language impairments (see Textbox 10.1). Research has found pervasive difficulty with arithmetic among these children, including counting, calculations, and fact mastery. While many of them show typical arithmetic growth patterns, they often fail to catch up to their peers.[69] In fact, one ten-year follow-up of a small group of preschoolers with a specific language impairment found that three-quarters of them scored below the 25th percentile in math in adolescence.[70]

TEXTBOX 10.1

As a high school freshman taking algebra 1, George was unable to recall math facts (despite much previous effort) due to his central auditory processing disorder (CAPD). Although he understood the concepts of algebra, he was slow and inaccurate with all arithmetic, which had a negative and painful impact on him in class. During the summer before his sophomore year, George was determined to learn math facts for all arithmetic operations, and he did so using physical and written number lines and blocks as described in this chapter. His hard work paid off, and he was very successful learning with this method. When he returned to school in the fall, he had the same math teacher for geometry. The teacher was shocked at how well George did that year and said he had gone from being one of his most struggling math students to one of his best. George is now a successful honors engineering student in college. Learning with the number line can be a powerful tool at any age.

Children (and adults) with dyslexia are also typically found to have phonological and rapid naming deficits that underlie their reading difficulties and for this reason frequently run into trouble with arithmetic as well.[71] One study of third-graders with dyslexia found that they were eight and a half times more likely than their typically reading classmates to have an arithmetic fact-fluency deficit.[72] As noted earlier, addition and multiplication facts are more likely to be retrieved, while subtraction and division facts are typically derived from them. This means that addition and multiplication facts are more likely to depend on verbal memory. One brain study found evidence that children with dyslexia do not activate the language circuits as most children do when performing addition, suggesting that language-network disruption in many children with dyslexia may contribute to their arithmetic difficulties.[73] On the other hand, as noted in Chapter 8, first-graders with weak math skills can sometimes get a boost if they have strong reading skills.[74]

Conversely, many individuals who are blind from birth, and who therefore lack the benefits of written arithmetic, may nevertheless have particularly strong skills in verbal working memory and in the verbal routines required for retention of multiplication facts, for example, at which they have been found to excel.[75]

What about children who are bilingual? Large-scale studies of American children from homes where Spanish or Asian languages are spoken suggest that which non-English language the family speaks is not relevant to their child's math education. For many such children who become proficient in English in the years before formal schooling, learning math does not seem to be hampered by their bilingualism, and those who do start kindergarten behind in math (for a variety of reasons) generally catch up to their native-English-speaking peers by the end of fifth grade. Findings also suggest that the math difficulties of many bilingual students have as much to do with social factors, such as poverty, the disruption that immigration causes, or the lack of math-related early experience, as the language differences, per se.[76] A close look at children who are not yet proficient in English at the start of formal schooling, however, reveals that even those who perform comparably to their native-English-speaking classmates in basic and multi-digit addition and subtraction at the start of first grade often fall behind by the end of that year. The researchers attribute their lag to the difficult language of arithmetic, such as the multiple words for subtraction (*minus, take away, less*), making clear that arithmetic is not just numbers and symbols.[77] Other researchers found that bilingual students in grades three through five are more fluent in retrieving multiplication facts—a heavily linguistic task, as we have seen—when the problem is posed in the language in which they learned them.[78] Thus, children whose English is still fragile at the start of formal education in English-speaking classrooms may struggle with math for linguistic reasons.

CONCLUSION

Whole-number arithmetic is where children first learn to put the tools of numeracy to work as they figure out how to calculate the results of combining, subtracting, multiplying, and dividing up ever-larger quantities without laboriously counting them out. In the process, children acquire even more tools: the fundamental principles that govern these transformations, a store of basic facts, and more useful vocabulary and written symbols.

ACTIVITIES

Introduction

To learn the concepts of arithmetic and not just memorize equations, students need to develop a strong number sense and reliable mental number line. Students learn these concepts by first using a physical number line and then creating and using their own written number lines. As described in Chapter 9, the number line provides a memorable visual template to help students learn and remember the most basic numerical and arithmetic relationships. Another advantage of this method is that it provides an opportunity for error-free practice without the heavy counting burden on working memory imposed by traditional methods and provides a concrete, orderly, and predictable way of learning.

Most of these activities rely on the use of solid, color-coded number blocks in graduated sizes from one to ten, as well as a compatible *0*-to-*100* number track or number line with a barrier at *0* to prevent the blocks from slipping out of place. (For readability in what follows, we will refer to all number tracks and number lines as "number lines.") As of this writing, Stern Math number blocks and tracks[79] and Didax number tracks with Unifix cubes[80] are readily available. Though physical number tracks provide the most concrete learning, if they are not available, the Toy Theater website has a free online number line with moveable blocks.[81] After children have had practice using blocks on a number line, they should be encouraged to draw and use their own number lines. The time needed to make this transition may vary widely among children. The activities that follow are ones that are designed to introduce children to basic arithmetic, the principles that govern it, and the most efficient problem-solving strategies. The most critical factor is that the operations be taught and practiced *systematically*, introducing the numbers in the order given, with the goal of helping children develop a reliable mental number line.

Equivalence

ACTIVITY 10.1: Symbolic Equivalence

Objective: To understand that the equal sign (=) represents equivalence and should be read as "is the same amount as." This activity comes first in order to stress the importance of equivalence and the "equivalent" understanding of the equal sign for all mathematical thinking.

- **First:** Start with ten of the same type of counters, such as ten chips. Write an equal sign in the middle of a white board or piece of paper. Place three counters to the left and right of the equal sign and pointing to the equal sign say, "Three is the same amount as three. The equal sign means 'is the same amount as.'"
- **Next:** Place one counter to the left of the equal sign and four to the right. Ask children if the two sides are the same amount, and when they say no, ask them what they need to do to make the two sides the same amount. Place three more counters on the left, and then write the equation $3 + 1 = 4$, and pointing to the respective parts of the equation, say, "Three and one are the same amount as four." Complete a few more examples in this manner, varying the transformation and the side requiring the transformation (e.g., $1 = 4 - 3$).

Arithmetic

The following arithmetic activities are designed to allow children to develop a deep sense of numerical relationships that builds the foundation to mathematical thinking and problem-solving, not memorization. They incorporate the beauty and simplicity of the base-10 system of arithmetic and are designed to help children develop a strong mental number line. This knowledge can then be applied to solving curricular problems in the math classroom with greater success. Finally, these activities are based on the principle of error-free practice to reduce exposure to incorrect results.

Addition and Subtraction Activities

The steps for addition and subtraction can be completed as follows:

1. First, use number blocks and number lines without equations.
2. Then, include written equations while using the blocks and number lines.
3. Finally, complete written equations alone (with the number line available if needed).

ACTIVITY 10.2: Adding and Subtracting One on the Number Line

Objective: To learn the meaning of addition and subtraction. To understand that each number is succeeded by a unique number and that that number is the next number in the number-word sequence. To learn how to write an arithmetic statement (*equation*). Finally, to understand the inverse relation and identity principle of addition and subtraction.

■ **First:** While placing one unit-block on the number line at a time, beginning at *0*, and pointing to the numerals on the number line, say: "Zero and one more is the same amount as one. See? And one and one more is the same amount as two. Two and one more is the same amount as three. Now you try it. What's next?" The children continue placing one more block at a time and saying the equation aloud until reaching, "Nine and one more is the same amount as ten."

■ **Next:** Say, "OK! Now here we have a total of ten." Then while taking away one unit-block from the number line at a time, beginning at *10*, say: "Ten take away one is the same amount as nine. See? Nine take away one is the same amount as eight. Now you try it. What's next?" The children continue through "One take away one is the same amount as zero."

■ **Next:** Begin again and demonstrate how to write the equations for adding and subtracting one, including the symbols for *and* (+), *take away* (−), and *is the same amount as* (=). Hand the child a unit-block and say, "Let's begin again." When the children say, "Zero and one more is the same amount as one," demonstrate how that is written ($0 + 1 = 1$). Have them continue adding one unit at a time and writing each equation in turn for themselves. When they complete the task to *10*, have them take one unit away and demonstrate how that is written ($10 − 1 = 9$). Have them continue taking away one unit at a time and writing each equation in turn for themselves.

■ **Next:** The children complete the written equations without placing the blocks on the number line. If they are unsure of a solution, they should look at the number line so they practice in an error-free manner.

ACTIVITY 10.3: Two-Number Combinations That Add to 10

Objectives: To learn two-number combinations to *10*, which are the most important set of number combinations for children to master and will lead to flexible thinking for all further arithmetic, including composition and decomposition of numbers. To learn the commutativity principle of addition, the inverse relation of addition and subtraction, and equivalence. Throughout this activity, the teacher can provide a model first by saying and writing the content and then having the children do so.

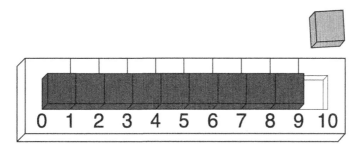

- ▥ **First:** Place a 10-block on the number line. Say, "Ten and zero is the same amount as ten, and ten take away zero is the same amount as ten." Demonstrate the written equations (*10 + 0 = 10; 10 − 0 = 10*). Following this model, the children say and do the same thing.
- ▥ **Next:** Place a 9-block on the number line and then a unit-block next to it, while the children say, "Nine and one is the same amount as ten." Demonstrate the written equation (*9 + 1 = 10*). Then they take the unit-block off the number line (see Figure), saying, "Ten take away one is the same amount as nine" and demonstrate the written equation (*10 − 1 = 9*).
- ▥ **Next:** *With the same blocks*, place the unit-block on the number line *first* and *then* place the 9-block on the number line next to it, while the children say, "One and nine is the same amount as ten" and write the equation (*1 + 9 = 10*). Comment: "Well, look at that! One and nine is the same amount as nine and one!" Write the equivalence equation *9 + 1 = 1 + 9*. Then they take the 9-block off the number line, saying, "Ten take away nine is the same amount as one" and write the equation (*10 − 9 = 1*). Ask them what they notice and whether it is easier to add from the larger number or the smaller number.
- ▥ **Next:** Continue the pattern consecutively with numbers in descending order, with *8 + 2* next. Demonstrate every combination to *10* with number blocks on a number line. Alternatively, the blocks can be aligned to demonstrate the combinations to *10*, as shown in the next Figure. For each pair that sums to *10*, the children begin with the larger block first, then switch the blocks around so that the smaller block is first, reciting the equations and writing the respective addition and subtraction equations, including the addition equivalence equation, e.g., *8 + 2 = 2 + 8*.

Continue until all combinations to *10* have been considered. Direct the children's attention to, and guide a discussion around, the observations that, for example, *7 + 3* comes to the same amount as *3 + 7* and that if *7 + 3 = 10*, then *10 – 7 = 3* and *10 – 3 = 7*.

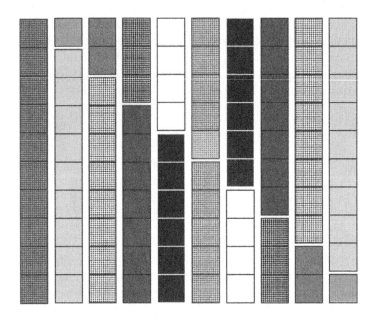

- **Next:** The children practice the combinations in jumbled order by placing pairs of blocks that add to *10* on the number line and writing the four related equations and the equivalence equation. Discuss how the addition facts can help solve the subtraction facts by adding up (*10 – 7 = __ can be rewritten as 7 + ___ = 10*).

ACTIVITY 10.4: Further Addition and Subtraction

Objective: To learn increasingly complex addition and subtraction in a way that helps develop a child's mental number line and encourages mathematical thinking while reducing the burden on word retrieval and memorization. Children complete the operations shown here as their skills develop.

Teachers can use a corresponding verbal model, as provided earlier in Activity 10.3, along with number blocks and the number line, for the following operations.

- **Doubles, doubles plus *1* and minus *1*.** Children tend to learn the doubles combinations easily (*2 + 2 = 4; 3 + 3 = 6;* etc., through *10 + 10 = 20*). Arithmetic understanding is further enhanced by adding and subtracting *1* from the doubles (*2 + 3; 2 + 1*). The children use two 2-blocks first, then one 2-block and one 3-block to improve visualization of the concept. Help the children discover that adding two of the same number always results in an even number, whereas adding two consecutive numbers always results in an odd number.

- **Composition of numbers *2* through *9*.** The children create all the two-number combinations for each of the numbers *2* through *9* (for example, for *9*: *8 + 1*; *7 + 2*; *6 + 3*; *5 + 4*). Subtraction of these combinations is introduced at the same time (*9 − 8 = 1*; *9 − 1 = 8*).
- **Adding the base-10 way.** Add on from "ten" saying, "Ten and one, the name is eleven. Ten and two, the name is twelve. Ten and three, the name is thirteen . . . two tens, the name is twenty, two tens and one, the name is twenty-one, etc."
- **Single-digit addition of all numbers *1* to *10* and corresponding subtraction.** The children use the many strategies that they have been learning. For example, if adding *5 + 8*, they can first use the commutative and min strategy to change the order to *8 + 5*. They can also use decomposition to break *5* into *2* and *3*, add *8* and *2* to get *10*, and add *3* more to reach *13*. At this stage, the children use as many strategies as they can. Once they get to *13* with this problem, they can then subtract *5* or *8* using decomposition. The children also use the strategy of doubles, doubles plus *1*, and doubles minus *1* to help them solve equations when possible. The children can share and discuss the different strategies that they use to solve these equations.
- **Adding multiples of *10* to reach *100*, subtracting from *100*.** Using the skills of adding to *10*, children add two multiples of *10* to reach *100* (*90 + 10 = 100*; *80 + 20 = 100*; *100 − 80 = 20*; etc.). This skill is a critical component of addition and subtraction using decomposition of larger numbers.
- **Adding to the next multiple of *10*, subtracting to the previous multiple of *10*.** Using the skills of adding to *10*, children add and subtract to get to the next number that has a *0* in the *ones* place. For example: *12 + 8 = 20*; *34 + 6 = 30*; *47 + 3 = 50*; *63 − 3 = 60*.
- **Using decomposition for addition and subtraction of one- and two-digit numbers.** Using blocks at first or a *1–100* number chart, children use their experience from composition of numbers through *9* to get to the next number ending in a *0* and then complete the operation. *27 + 6 = 27 + 3 + 3*; *27 + 3* is *30* and *3* more is *33*; *33 − 6* can be decomposed as *33 − 3 − 3 = 30 − 3 = 27*.

ACTIVITY 10.5 Double-Digit Addition and Subtraction

Objective: To learn to use the earlier principles and strategies with larger numbers. In addition to or in place of the number line, a *1–100* number chart can be used.

- **Decomposition strategy:** Present an addition problem with a sum of less than *100*, such as *45 + 23*. Demonstrate and explain how to decompose each addend into *tens* and *ones*: "Forty-five is four tens and five ones. Twenty-three is two tens and three ones. We can add the tens and ones separately."

(40 + 20) + (5 + 3) = 60 + 8 = 68. Have children start by placing the 10-blocks onto the number line (or point to the *10*s on the number chart) and describe their actions: "Four tens and two tens is the same amount as six tens, or sixty." Then children add the ones and explain: "Five and three is the same amount as eight. Sixty and eight more is the same amount as sixty-eight." Discuss how you reached the sum by decomposing, or separating, each addend into *tens* and *ones* and separately combining the *tens* and *ones*. It is helpful to write down the process alongside the number line so that children can see how their actions on the number line can be expressed with symbols. This process can be completed in reverse for subtraction and can immediately follow the addition.

- **Jump strategy:** Children add in increments of *tens* and *ones*, starting from one addend. Present an addition problem with a sum of less than *100*, such as *12 + 79*. Discuss that you should start adding from the larger addend, *79* in this case. Children create *79* on the number line. Explain how to decompose the other addend into *tens* and *ones*: "Twelve is one ten and two ones. Let's add the tens first." Children add the *tens* on the number line and explain: "Seventy-nine and ten is the same amount as eight-nine." Then children add the ones: "Eighty-nine and two is the same amount as ninety-one." Write children's actions alongside the number line using symbols: *12 + 79 = 79 + 12; 79 + 10 = 89; 89 + 2 = 91*. This process can be completed in reverse with subtraction and immediately follow the addition.

- **Adding-up strategy for subtraction:** Children use addition to solve subtraction problems by counting up from the number being subtracted. Many children find addition easier than subtraction, and this strategy also reinforces the direct relationship of addition and subtraction. Present a subtraction problem, such as *91 – 56*. A *1–100* number chart can easily be used here. Or children create *56* on the number line and add blocks until they reach *91*. Explain, "We start at fifty-six. Let's count up while adding by ten: sixty-six, seventy-six, eighty-six—that's three tens. We're getting close to ninety-one, so how do we finish getting there? Let's add four to get to ninety and then add one more to get to ninety-one (or just add five). Three tens and five is thirty-five. Fifty-six and thirty-five is the same amount as ninety-one, so ninety-one take away thirty-five is the same amount as fifty-six." *56 + 35 = 91*, so *91 – 35 = 56*.

Multiplication and Division Activities

A Note on Language

In the following activities, we jettison the confusing terms *times*, *divided by*, and *goes into* in favor of language that reflects the actual meaning of the operation:

- *4 × 5* is read as "four fives."
- *4 × 5 = 20* is read as "four fives is the same amount as twenty" or "there are four fives in twenty."

- *20 ÷ 5* is read as "twenty broken into fives."
- *20 ÷ 5 = 4* is read as "twenty broken into fives, there are four fives," or "there are four fives in twenty."

Using this language provides a clearer introduction to the operations. In the United States, math curricula are inconsistent with the language of multiplication and division, and *4 × 5* is usually not explicitly taught as meaning four *fives*. Commercial flash cards almost always flip the order we suggest, with *4 × 5* meaning "*five* four times," which is syntactically reversed and makes it more difficult to foster mathematical thinking.

Importantly, when children learn multiplication on the number line, using the order and language of three *fours* (*3 × 4*) followed by four *fours* (*4 × 4*) followed by five *fours* (*5 × 4*), it means that each successive equation reflects adding four more. Children can use this mathematical thinking to learn multiplication, to skip-count up or down if they cannot retrieve an answer, and to provide an overall organization to these math facts. When equations are presented non-sequentially or without this explicit instruction, children are less likely to learn this mathematical thinking, and it simply becomes a verbal memorization task. Children with dyslexia, other language impairments, and attention disorder often have a very difficult time memorizing arithmetic facts, especially when they are presented in random order without manipulatives, logic, or mathematical reasoning. In that case, all the arithmetic facts sound the same. Conventional mathematical terminology, such as "four times five," can be used once children master the meaning of the operations and mathematical thinking.

ACTIVITY 10.6 Multiplication and Division: What Does It Mean?

Objective: To learn the meaning of multiplication and division; to develop a logical, sequential, and predictable mastery of multiplication and division facts; and to develop the mental number line. The following activity will:

1. Use number blocks and a number line along with written equations.
2. Use a drawn number line and written equations.
3. Use written equations in mixed-up order to master fluency.

This method also ensures error-free practice.

- **First:** Place a 10-block at *0* on a *0*-to-*100* number line, and pointing to the *10* on the number line, say "One ten is the same amount as ten," and write the equation *1 × 10 = 10*. Place a second 10-block next to the first 10-block along the number line and pointing to the *20* on the number line say, "Two tens is the same amount as twenty—'twenty' actually means two tens," and have the children write *2 × 10 = 20*. Continue in this manner until reaching ten tens and writing *10 × 10 = 100*.

- **Next:** Immediately transition to division, keeping the 10-blocks on the number line. Say, "When one hundred is divided into 10-blocks, there will be ten 10-blocks," and have the children write *100 ÷ 10 = 10*. Take one of the 10-blocks off the number line and say, "When ninety is broken up into 10-blocks, there will be nine 10-blocks," and have the children write *90 ÷ 10 = 9*. Continue in this manner until reaching *10* on the number line.

- **Next:** Provide the students with a worksheet that has a number line at the top. The number line should be marked into ten equal segments with hash marks labeled above and with the numbers *0* to *10* to serve as multipliers (see Figure a). First, have the children fill in the multiples of *10* on the number line below each multiplier (see Figure b). The number *10* is written on the left end of the number line to indicate what number is being multiplied. The children can read the number line using the language of multiplication as follows: "One *10* is *10*, two *10*s are *20*, three *10*s are *30*, . . .," first pointing to the multiplier number above the hash mark on the number line, then the *10* on the left end, then the multiple below. Division can be completed in the reverse order as shown earlier. If students are unsure of the next multiple as they are writing in the numbers on the number line, they can use the strategies described next to find the answer, an essential part of the process. Filling in the number line is a critical step in learning multiplication and division and should be repeated until it is automatic. Have the children alternate between filling in the number line and completing the *10*s multiplication and division equations in numerical sequence in the empty space below the number line. For a printable number line template and instructions for using it as described in this chapter, please see the online Supplemental eResources that accompany this book.

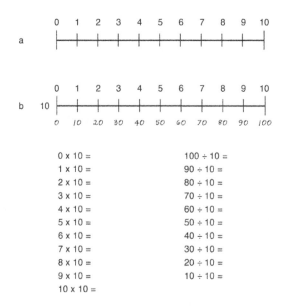

■ **Next:** Children complete the *10*s multiplication and division equations in mixed-up order and without the number line unless it is needed to avoid errors.

■ **Next:** Once multiplication and division with *10*s is familiar and at least close to mastered, proceed with the other numbers that are less than *10*. Skip-counting by *5*s is fairly easy for most children, so moving to *5*s next is often successful. After *5*s, the following sequence can be used: *1, 0, 2, 3, 4, 9, 6, 7, 8.*

■ **Next:** Practice skip-counting aloud in unison forward and backward for each number set.

■ **Next:** Include interleaved practice solving multiplication and division equations with all the numbers that children have practiced and are more confident with to help increase fluency. For children with significant attention deficits, introduce interleaved practice gradually, so that they are not overwhelmed by the change.

Strategies for Multiplication and Division

■ **Decomposition:** Children can use decomposition to help solve equations. For instance, if they are working on multiplying *6*s and they know that $6 \times 6 = 36$ but are unsure of 7×6, they can add the last *6* by decomposing *6* into *4* and *2*, then adding *36* and *4* to get *40*, and then adding *2* more to get *42*.

■ **What do I know?** If they are unsure of 9×6, they can rely on their secure knowledge of $10 \times 6 = 60$ and know that 9×6 means *6* less than *60*, so it must be *54*.

■ **Inverse relationship of multiplication and division:** Division can be more challenging for children to visualize, so they can turn it into multiplication. $24 \div 6$ can be thought of as *how many 6s are in 24?*

■ **Single-digit addition and subtraction:** If they know that $6 \times 6 = 36$ but are unsure of 7×6, another strategy is to use knowledge of doubles and single-digit addition and subtraction. They know that $6 + 6 = 12$, so $36 + 6$ results in the one's place being a *2*, so it must be *42*.

■ **Visualization of the number line or number chart:** Children can utilize their mental number line to visualize moving up and down the number line.

■ **Fingers:** Children can use their fingers to count up or down if necessary for older children if they were delayed in developing this skill.

NOTES

1 Hornburg et al., 2018.
2 Hornburg et al., 2017.
3 McNeil, 2007.
4 Chesney et al., 2013; DeCaro, 2016; Simsek et al., 2019.
5 Fyfe et al., 2018; Matthews & Fuchs, 2020.

6 Knuth et al., 2006.

7 Simsek et al., 2019.

8 McNeil et al., 2006.

9 McNeil et al., 2019.

10 McNeil et al., 2015.

11 Sherman & Bisanz, 2009.

12 Cheng & Mix, 2014.

13 Douglas et al., 2020.

14 Siegler, 2003.

15 Zur & Gelman, 2004.

16 Siegler, 2007.

17 Siegler, 2006.

18 Siegler, 2007.

19 Siegler, 1996.

20 Siegler, 1996, pp. 86–92.

21 Siegler & Robinson, 1982.

22 Siegler & Braithwaite, 2017.

23 Reed et al., 2015.

24 Siegler & Crowley, 1994.

25 Secada et al., 1983.

26 Siegler, 1987.

27 Siegler & Jenkins, 1989.

28 Ladd, 1987; cited in Siegler, 1996, p. 97.

29 Rhodes et al., 2019.

30 Geary et al., 1996.

31 Vasilyeva et al., 2015.

32 Shen et al., 2016.

33 Eaves et al., 2021.

34 Ching & Nunes, 2017.

35 Eaves et al., 2021; McCrink et al., 2017; Robinson & Dubé, 2009.

36 Siegler, 1996; Siegler & Shrager, 1984.

37 Gibson & Maurer, 2016.

38 Siegler, 1996, pp. 161–162.

39 Miller & Paredes, 1990.

40 DeVisscher & Noël, 2014.

41 Rotem & Henik, 2015.

42 Gibson & Maurer, 2016.

43 Rotem & Henik, 2020.

44 Chen et al., 2021.

45 Harrison et al., 2020.

46 Lemaire & Callies, 2009.

47 Siegler, 1996.

48 Siegler, 2003, 2007.

49 Peters & DeSmedt, 2018.

50 Reed et al., 2015.

51 Ostad, 2000.

52 Siegler, 2003.

53 Siegler, 1996, 2003.

54 Siegler, 2003.

55 Church, 1999.

56 Kamii & Dominick, 1997.

57 Siegler, 1996, pp. 155–164.

58 Paliwal & Baroody, 2020.

59 Barrouillet et al., 2008.

60 Robinson et al., 2006.

61 Walker et al., 2014.

62 Grenier et al., 2020.

63 Sokolowski et al., 2017.

64 Chow & Ekholm, 2019.

65 DeSmedt et al., 2010.

66 Andin et al., 2014.

67 Koponen et al., 2017.

68 Mazzocco & Grimm, 2013.

69 McLeod et al., 2019.

70 Aram et al., 1984.

71 DeClercq-Quaegebeur et al., 2018; Rinne et al., 2020.

72 Vukovic et al., 2010.

73 Evans et al., 2014.

74 Erbeli et al., 2021.

75 Dormal et al., 2016.

76 Han, 2012; Hartanto et al., 2018; Roberts & Bryant, 2011.

77 Martin & Fuchs, 2019.

78 Cerda et al., 2019.

79 www.sternmath.com

80 www.didax.com/unifix-1-120-number-line.html

81 https://toytheater.com/number-line/

REFERENCES

The following references were cited in this chapter. For additional selected references relevant to this chapter, please see Chapter 10 Supplemental References in eResources.

Andin, J., Rönnberg, J., & Rudner, M. (2014). Deaf signers use phonology to do arithmetic. *Learning and Individual Differences, 32,* 246–253.

Aram, D.M., Ekelman, B.L., & Nation, J.E. (1984). Preschoolers with language disorders ten years later. *Journal of Speech and Hearing Research, 27,* 232–244.

Barrouillet, P., Mignon, M., & Thevenot, C. (2008). Strategies in subtraction problem solving in children. *Journal of Experimental Child Psychology, 99,* 233–251.

Cerda, V.R., Grenier, A.E., & Wicha, N.Y.Y. (2019). Bilingual children access multiplication facts from semantic memory equivalently across languages: Evidence from the N400. *Brain and Language, 198,* 104679.

Chen, L., Iuculano, T., Mistry, P., Nicholas, J., Zhang, Y., & Menon, V. (2021). Linear and nonlinear profiles of weak behavioral and neural differentiation between numerical operations in children with math learning difficulties. *Neuropsychologia, 160,* 107977.

Cheng, Y.-L., & Mix, K.S. (2014). Spatial training improves children's mathematics ability. *Journal of Cognition and Development, 15,* 2–11.

Chesney, D.L., McNeil, N.M., Brockmole, J.R., & Kelley, K. (2013). An eye for relations: Eye-tracking indicates long-term negative effects of operational thinking on understanding of math equivalence. *Memory & Cognition, 41,* 1079–1095.

Ching, B.H.-H., & Nunes, T. (2017). The importance of additive reasoning in children's mathematical achievement: A longitudinal study. *Journal of Educational Psychology, 109,* 477–508.

Chow, J.C., & Ekholm, E. (2019). Language domains differentially predict mathematics performance in young children. *Early Childhood Research Quarterly, 46,* 179–186.

Church, R.B. (1999). Using gesture and speech to capture transitions in learning. *Cognitive Development, 14,* 313–342.

DeCaro, M.S. (2016). Inducing mental set constrains procedural flexibility and conceptual understanding in mathematics. *Memory & Cognition, 44,* 1138–1148.

DeClercq-Quaegebeur, M., Casalis, S., Vilette, B., Lemaitre, M.-P., & Vallée, L. (2018). Arithmetic abilities in children with developmental dyslexia: Performance on French ZAREKI-R Test. *Journal of Learning Disabilities, 51,* 236–249.

DeSmedt, B., Taylor, J., Archibald, L., & Ansari, D. (2010). How is phonological processing related to individual differences in children's arithmetic skills? *Developmental Science, 13,* 508–520.

DeVisscher, A., & Noël, M.-P. (2014). Arithmetic facts storage deficit: The hypersensitivity-to-interference in memory hypothesis. *Developmental Science, 17,* 434–442.

Dormal, V., Crollen, V., Baumans, C., Lepore, F., & Collignon, O. (2016). Early but not late blindness leads to enhanced arithmetic and working memory abilities. *Cortex, 83,* 212–221.

Douglas, H., Headley, M.G., Hadden, S., & LeFevre, J.-A. (2020). Knowledge of mathematical symbols goes beyond numbers. *Journal of Numerical Cognition, 6,* 322–354.

Eaves, J., Gilmore, C., & Attridge, N. (2021). Conceptual knowledge of the associativity principle: A review of the literature and an agenda for future research. *Trends in Neuroscience and Education, 23,* 100152.

Erbeli, F., Shi, Q., Campbell, A.R., Hart, S.A., & Woltering, S. (2021). Developmental dynamics between reading and math in elementary school. *Developmental Science, 24,* e13004.

Evans, T.M., Flowers, D.L., Napoliello, E.M., Olulade, O.A., & Eden, G.F. (2014). The functional anatomy of single-digit arithmetic in children with developmental dyslexia. *NeuroImage, 101,* 644–652.

Fyfe, E.R., Matthews, P.G., Amsel, E., McEldoon, K.L., & McNeil, N.M. (2018). Assessing formal knowledge of math equivalence among algebra and pre-algebra students. *Journal of Educational Psychology, 110,* 87–101.

Geary, D.C., Bow-Thomas, C.C., Liu, F., & Siegler, R.S. (1996). Development of arithmetical competencies in Chinese and American children: Influence of age, language, and schooling. *Child Development, 67,* 2022–2044.

Gibson, L.C., & Maurer, D. (2016). Development of SNARC and distance effects and their relation to mathematical and visuospatial abilities. *Journal of Experimental Child Psychology, 150,* 301–313.

Grenier, A.E., Dickson, D.S., Sparks, C.S., & Wicha, N.Y.Y. (2020). Meaning to multiply: Electrophysiological evidence that children and adults treat multiplication facts differently. *Developmental Cognitive Neuroscience, 46,* 100873.

Han, W.-J. (2012). Bilingualism and academic achievement. *Child Development, 83,* 300–321.

Harrison, A., Smith, H., Hulse, T., & Ottmar, E.R. (2020). Spacing out! Manipulating spatial features in mathematical expressions affects performance. *Journal of Numerical Cognition*, 6, 186–203.

Hartanto, A., Yang, H., & Yang, S. (2018). Bilingualism positively predicts mathematical competence: Evidence from two large-scale studies. *Learning and Individual Differences*, 61, 216–227.

Hornburg, C.B., Rieber, M.L., & McNeil, N.M. (2017). An integrative data analysis of gender differences in children's understanding of mathematical equivalence. *Journal of Experimental Child Psychology*, 163, 140–150.

Hornburg, C.B., Wang, L., & McNeil, N.M. (2018). Comparing meta-analysis and individual personal data analysis using raw data on children's understanding of equivalence. *Child Development*, 89, 1983–1995.

Kamii, C., & Dominick, A. (1997). To teach or not to teach algorithms. *Journal of Mathematical Behavior*, 16, 51–61.

Knuth, E.J., Stephens, A.C., McNeil, N.M., & Alibali, M.W. (2006). Does understanding the equal sign matter? Evidence from solving equations. *Journal for Research in Mathematics Education*, 37, 297–312.

Koponen, T., Georgiou, G., Salmi, P., Leskinen, M., & Aro, M. (2017). A meta-analysis of the relation between RAN and mathematics. *Journal of Educational Psychology*, 109, 977–992.

Ladd, S.F. (1987). *Mental addition in children and adults using chronometric and interview paradigms*. Unpublished doctoral dissertation, University of Northern Colorado, Greeley.

Lemaire, P., & Callies, S. (2009). Children's strategies in complex arithmetic. *Journal of Experimental Child Psychology*, 103, 49–65

Lemaire, P., & Siegler, R.S. (1995). Four aspects of strategic change: Contributions to children's learning of multiplication. *Journal of Experimental Psychology: General*, 124, 83–97.

Mabbott, D.J., & Bisanz, J. (2003). Developmental change and individual differences in children's multiplication. *Child Development*, 74, 1091–1107.

Martin, B.N., & Fuchs, L.S. (2019). The mathematical performance of at-risk first graders as a function of limited English proficiency status. *Learning Disability Quarterly*, 42, 244–251.

Matthews, P.G., & Fuchs, L.S. (2020). Keys to the gate? Equal sign knowledge at second grade predicts fourth-grade algebra competence. *Child Development*, 91, e14–e28.

Mazzocco, M.M.M., & Grimm, K.J. (2013). Growth in rapid automatized naming from grades K to 8 in children with math or reading disabilities. *Journal of Learning Disabilities*, 46, 517–533.

McCrink, K., Shafto, P., & Barth, H. (2017). The relationship between non-symbolic multiplication and division in childhood. *The Quarterly Journal of Experimental Psychology*, 70, 686–702.

McLeod, S., Harrison, L.J., & Wang, C. (2019). A longitudinal population study of literacy and numeracy outcomes for children identified with speech, language, and communication needs in early childhood. *Early Childhood Research Quarterly*, 47, 507–517.

McNeil, N.M. (2007). U-shaped development in math: 7-year-olds outperform 9-year-olds on equivalence problems. *Developmental Psychology*, 43, 687–695.

McNeil, N.M., Fyfe, E.R., & Dunwiddie, A.E. (2015). Arithmetic practice can be modified to promote understanding of mathematical equivalence. *Journal of Educational Psychology*, 107, 423–436.

McNeil, N.M., Grandau, L., Knuth, E.J., Alibali, M.W., Stephens, A.C., Hattikudur, S., & Krill, D.E. (2006). Middle-school students' understanding of the equal sign: The books they read can't help. *Cognition and Instruction*, 24, 367–385.

McNeil, N.M., Hornburg, C.B., Brletic-Shipley, H., & Matthews, J.M. (2019). Improving children's understanding of mathematical equivalence via an intervention that goes beyond nontraditional arithmetic practice. *Journal of Educational Psychology*, 111, 1023–1044.

Miller, K.F., & Paredes, D.R., (1990). Starting to add worse: Effects of learning to multiply on children's addition. *Cognition, 37*, 213–242.

Ostad, S.A. (2000). Cognitive subtraction in a developmental perspective: Accuracy, speed-of-processing and strategy-use differences in normal and mathematically disabled children. *Focus on Learning Problems in Mathematics, 22*, 18–31.

Paliwal, V., & Baroody, A.J. (2020). Fostering the learning of subtraction concepts and the subtraction-as-addition reasoning strategy. *Early Childhood Research Quarterly, 51*, 403–415.

Peters, L., & DeSmedt, B. (2018). Arithmetic in the developing brain: A review of brain imaging studies. *Developmental Cognitive Neuroscience, 30*, 265–279.

Reed, H.C., Stevenson, C., Broens-Paffen, M., Kirschner, P.A., & Jolles, J. (2015). Third graders' verbal reports of multiplication strategy use: How valid are they? *Learning and Individual Differences, 37*, 107–117.

Rhodes, K.T., Lukowski, S., Branum-Martin, L., Opfer, J., Geary, D.C., & Petrill, S.A. (2019). Individual differences in addition strategy choice: A psychometric evaluation. *Journal of Educational Psychology, 111*, 414–433.

Rinne, L.F., Ye, A., & Jordan, N.C. (2020). Development of arithmetic fluency: A direct effect of reading fluency? *Journal of Educational Psychology, 112*, 110–130.

Roberts, G., & Bryant, D. (2011). Early mathematics achievement trajectories: English-language learner and native English-speaker estimates, using the Early Childhood Longitudinal Survey. *Developmental Psychology, 47*, 916–930.

Robinson, K.M., Arbuthnott, K.D., Rose, D., McCarron, M.C., Globa, C.A., & Phonexay, S.D. (2006). Stability and change in children's division strategies. *Journal of Experimental Child Psychology, 93*, 224–238.

Robinson, K.M., & Dubé, A.K. (2009). Children's understanding of addition and subtraction concepts. *Journal of Experimental Child Psychology, 103*, 532–545.

Rotem, A., & Henik, A. (2015). Sensitivity to general and specific numerical features in typical achievers and children with mathematics learning disability. *The Quarterly Journal of Experimental Psychology, 68*, 2291–2303.

Rotem, A., & Henik, A. (2020). Multiplication facts and number sense in children with mathematics learning disabilities and typical achievers. *Cognitive Development, 54*, 100866.

Secada, W.G., Fuson, K.C., & Hall, J.W. (1983). The transition from counting-all to counting-on in addition. *Journal for Research in Mathematics Education, 14*, 47–57.

Shen, C., Vasilyeva, M., & Laski, E.V. (2016). Here, but not there: Cross-national variability of gender effects in arithmetic. *Journal of Experimental Child Psychology, 146*, 50–65.

Sherman, J., & Bisanz, J. (2009). Equivalence in symbolic and nonsymbolic contexts: Benefits of solving problems with manipulatives. *Journal of Educational Psychology, 101*, 88–100.

Siegler, R.S. (1987). The perils of averaging data over strategies: An example from children's addition. *Journal of Experimental Psychology: General, 116*, 250–264.

Siegler, R.S. (1989). Hazards of mental chronometry: An example from children's subtraction. *Journal of Educational Psychology, 81*, 497–506.

Siegler, R.S. (1996). *Emerging minds: The process of change in children's thinking*. Oxford University Press.

Siegler, R.S. (2003). Implications of cognitive science research for mathematics education. In J. Kilpatrick, W.B. Martin, & D.E. Schifter (Eds.), *A research companion to principles and standards for school mathematics* (pp. 219–233). National Council of Teachers of Mathematics.

Siegler, R.S. (2006). Microgenetic analyses of learning. In D. Kuhn, R.S. Siegler, W. Damon, & R.M. Lerner (Eds.), *Handbook of child psychology: Cognition, perception, and language* (pp. 464–510). John Wiley & Sons.

Siegler, R.S. (2007). Cognitive variability. *Developmental Science, 10,* 104–109.

Siegler, R.S., & Braithwaite, D.W. (2017). Numerical development. *Annual Review of Psychology, 68,* 187–213.

Siegler, R.S., & Crowley, K. (1994). Constraints on learning in nonprivileged domains. *Cognitive Psychology, 27,* 194–226.

Siegler, R.S., & Jenkins, E.A., (1989). *How children discover new strategies.* Psychology Press.

Siegler, R.S., & Robinson, M. (1982). The development of numerical understandings. *Advances in Child Development and Behavior, 16,* 241–312.

Siegler, R.S., & Shrager, J. (1984). *Strategy choices in addition and subtraction: How do children know what to do?* Origins of cognitive skills: The 18th annual Carnegie symposium on cognition (pp. 229–292). Pittsburgh, PA.

Simsek, E., Xenidou-Dervou, I., Karadeniz, I., & Jones, I. (2019). The conception of substitution of the equals sign plays a unique role in students' algebra performance. *Journal of Numerical Cognition, 5,* 24–37.

Sokolowski, H.M., Fias, W., Mousa, A., & Ansari, D. (2017). Common and distinct brain regions in both parietal and frontal cortex support symbolic and nonsymbolic number processing in humans: A functional neuroimaging meta-analysis. *NeuroImage, 146,* 376–394.

Vasilyeva, M., Laski, E.V., & Shen, C. (2015). Computational fluency and strategy choice predict individual and cross-national differences in complex arithmetic. *Developmental Psychology, 51,* 1489–1500.

Vukovic, R.K., Lesaux, N.K., & Siegel, L.S. (2010). The mathematics skills of children with reading difficulties. *Learning and Individual Differences, 20,* 639–643.

Walker, D., Bajic, D., Mickes, L., Kwak, J., & Rickard, T.C. (2014). Specificity of children's arithmetic learning. *Journal of Experimental Child Psychology, 122,* 62–74.

Zur, O., & Gelman, R. (2004). Young children can add and subtract by predicting and checking. *Early Childhood Research Quarterly, 19,* 121–137.

Chapter 11

Rational Numbers and Operations

RATIONAL numbers are the gateway to algebra and higher mathematics.[1] Two-thirds of the U.S. labor force use them in their daily work, including 82 percent of those in the highest-paid jobs.[2] Daily life is full of them: taxes, weather forecasts, discounts, health decisions, recipes, crafts, sports, politics, even this paragraph.

Yet rational numbers bring out the irrational in many students who are trying to learn them and in many adults who never did. There are good reasons for this, particularly for those who had little trouble mastering whole-number arithmetic and feel frustrated by not understanding something that looks so much like what they already know.

Indeed, feeling like rational numbers look familiar—*and yet do not always behave the way one would expect them to*—is precisely the source of the difficulty for many.[3] The experience is a bit like peering into Alice's looking-glass, where everything looks familiar but is the opposite of what one expects.[4] Rational numbers do bear several features of whole numbers but because of important differences do not behave like them under many circumstances (see Table 11.1). That is not to say that whole-number knowledge is not necessary for learning fractions. It certainly is, and children without it are almost guaranteed to have difficulty learning fractions.[5] Psychologically speaking, however, the sight of familiar digits seems to impel many children (and adults![6]) to treat rational numbers as whole numbers, an extremely stubborn habit that researchers have dubbed *whole-number bias*.[7]

As with whole numbers and whole-number arithmetic, comprehending what a rational number is, what quantity it stands for, and how it relates to other quantities is key to a firm understanding of rational-number arithmetic.[8] This chapter begins with a discussion of the nature of rational numbers. Rational-number arithmetic comprises the second part of the chapter, where the research has focused on identifying what makes it so difficult for children to learn.

WHAT IS A RATIONAL NUMBER?

We start with the definition: A *rational number* is any number that can be expressed as a ratio of two integers—easy to remember as *ratio*-nal—and written as a *fraction* % (e.g., ¾),

DOI: 10.4324/9781003157656-15

where *b* cannot equal *zero*. (Because students are introduced to rational numbers before negative numbers, we will focus our discussion on the positive rational numbers and *zero*.) A *decimal fraction* is the special case when *b* equals a power of *10* (³⁄₁₀ or *.3;* ³⁄₁₀₀ or *.03;* ³⁄₁₀₀₀ or *.003*). A *percent* is the special case when *b* equals *100* (³⁄₁₀₀ or *.03* or *3 percent*). A whole number is the special case when *b* equals *1* or *a* equals *b* (⁴⁄₁ = *4;* ⁴⁄₄ = *1*). Simply put, rational numbers look like this: ³⁄₇, and this: *2.36*, and this: *0.3̄3̄*, and this: *89%*. Rational numbers are what allow us to quantify proportional relationships exactly, as an amount that can be compared to other proportional amounts, just as whole numbers allow us to quantify and compare collections of objects exactly. In measurement, rational numbers are what allow us to quantify parts of an inch, or pound, or degree, or dollar. Yes, all whole numbers *are* rational numbers, as noted earlier. The reverse, however, is not true; that is, only the rational numbers expressible as ⁿ⁄₁ or ⁿ⁄ₙ are whole numbers. For the most part, it is the non–whole-number rational numbers that create problems for students, and those will be the focus of this chapter.

Counting Gets in the Way

The alert reader will remember that in Chapter 2 we discussed the finding that young children understand the concept of proportion and that they are actually more inclined to think in proportional than absolute terms—that is, in terms of how full the milk bottle is, rather than how much milk there is. Before counting is well-established, preschoolers

TABLE 11.1 Similarities and Differences Between Whole Numbers and Rational Numbers

Whole Numbers	*Rational Numbers*
SIMILARITIES:	
Both are taught in math class and used in daily life.	
Both identify quantities (magnitudes).	
Both can be represented as distance on a line.	
Both can be ordered by magnitude.	
Both can be written in rational number notation.	
The smallest of each is *zero*.	
Both permit addition, subtraction, multiplication, and division.	
Both are infinite in number.	
DIFFERENCES:	
Represent unique quantities of whole units.	Represent whole units and parts of whole units.
Answers *How many?*	Answers *What part of?*
Units cannot be subdivided.	Can be subdivided infinitely.
Units have unique successors.	Rational numbers do not have successors.
The smallest non-*zero* whole number is one unit.	There is no smallest non-*zero* rational number.
Successive whole numbers get larger at a steady rate.	As denominators get larger at a steady rate, unit fractions get smaller at an uneven rate.

Note: Refers to only the non-negative rational numbers.

can also make some sense of discrete proportion as well.[9] However, research with schoolchildren all the way up through sixth grade has found that children's understanding of proportion is robust, but only of continuous proportions (milk); when it comes to discrete proportions (cookies), counting gets in the way.

Figure 11.1 shows three different versions of the same problem: Judge which of the two proportions on the right is the same as the proportion on the left. As one can see, the version in the left panel contains continuous elements, the middle version contains equal-sized segments, and the third illustrates the same problem with discrete items. Third-, fourth-, and fifth-graders in this study found the continuous version easiest and the fully discrete version the hardest. The most fraction-savvy students were able to match proportions in all three versions. However, children with weak fraction knowledge succeeded only on the continuous version.[10] The results of a study of the very weakest math students were even more discouraging. That study found that fewer than half of them could rank-order such unsegmented, continuous proportional quantities even in eighth grade.[11] (See Activity 2.7 in Chapter 2 for an illustration of such a task.)

Using segmented versus unsegmented spinners to compare proportions had the same result: All the children failed when the spinners were marked in segments (Figure 11.2b), but even kindergartners showed some understanding on the unsegmented spinners (Figure 11.2a). Importantly, in judging the segmented spinners, the

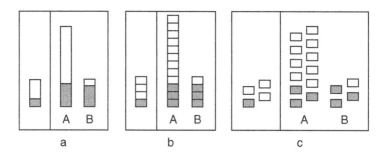

FIGURE 11.1 a) Continuous proportion. b) Segmented proportion. c) Discrete proportion.
Source: Derived from Begolli et al., 2020. © Elsevier Science & Technology Journal

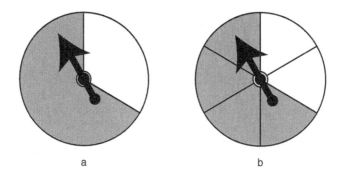

FIGURE 11.2 a) Continuous spinner. b) Segmented spinner.
Source: Adapted from Jeong et al., 2007.

children took into account only the number of segments in the "winning" color and not the relationship between them and the total number of segments.[12] Thus, it seems that when faced with discrete items, children's default strategy is to count, counting only the interesting bits and ignoring the relationship.

To be clear: Counting is important for fractions as long as both the parts of interest and the total number of parts in the whole are considered together as a proportion. In fact, studies show that adults tend to use fractions to express proportions of small numbers of countable entities, where exact enumeration is easy and necessary, and to use whichever form is easiest and expresses the desired level of precision for large-numerosity and continuous proportions.[13] Indeed, to quantify precisely, counting is required—in proportions as in measuring (see Chapter 9). The question, then, is: *Is there a way to introduce fractions, while keeping children's attention focused on proportion?* Researchers have tried several techniques. What follows is a description of some successful ones; note that they are not necessarily mutually exclusive.

One method that seems to have worked quite well with fourth-graders is for them to spend time refining their judgment of continuous proportions (as in the first panel of Figure 11.1) prior to considering discrete proportions. For example, researchers asked two groups of children in kindergarten, second grade, and fourth grade to make judgments similar to those in Figure 11.1. One group first spent time working on continuous proportions before moving on to discrete proportions, while the other group worked on discrete problems only. The researchers found that the fourth-graders, in particular, benefited from the practice with continuous amounts, with significantly better performance on subsequent discrete proportions than those without such preparation.[14]

A second method focuses on continuous versus discrete amounts by way of language. Proportional language is devilishly difficult for young children,[15] a situation compounded when numbers are thrown into the mix. Researchers taught five-, six-, and seven-year-olds the names for different proportions using illustrations like the ones in Figure 11.3. One group of children was told that the shaded portions of Figure 11.3a, b, and c were called a *blick*. A second group was told that the shaded portions of Figure 11.3a and b were called *four blicks* and that the shaded portion of Figure 11.3c was called *eight daxes*. The third group was shown an unshaded version of Figure 11.3a or b and was told, "Here are seven blicks. I'm going to color four blicks. This [pointing to the now-colored portion] is called four-out-of-seven blicks." Thus, the children's attention was drawn to the proportion with or without the use of counting and number words. On a subsequent proportion-matching task, the children in the first condition ("It's a blick") were more likely to use proportion to match similar displays than any of the other children, who were distracted by the numbers and counted segments. The researchers concluded that different fraction labels shape children's thinking about proportion differently, even when they view the same illustrations, and that introducing counting and number words prematurely will make it difficult for the children to assess proportion.[16] The goal is to maintain children's attention on the *proportional relationship*, not on the parts alone.

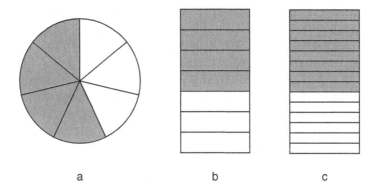

a   b   c

FIGURE 11.3 Blicks and daxes.

Source: Adapted from Hurst & Cordes, 2019.

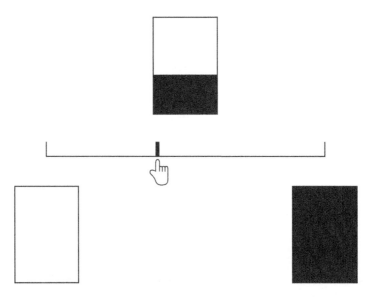

FIGURE 11.4 Indicate where the proportion would fall between empty on the left and full on the right.

Source: Adapted from Gouet et al., 2020.

A third approach introduces third- and fourth-graders to the idea of quantifying proportions by beginning with percentages, with reference to only the most familiar proportions (50 percent, 25 percent), then gradually introducing decimal fractions and *then* fractions. The focus is on continuous proportional amounts, as represented by beakers of fluid or the number line. The advantages of beginning with percentages are that 1) hundredths are familiar to children through their experience with money and coinage and 2) a denominator as large as *100* is too big to invite counting and thus ideal for judging proportions of continuous amounts. In a small study of a 20-session percentages intervention assessed against the standard curriculum, the intervention group demonstrated a richer understanding of rational numbers and was less inclined to treat them as whole numbers. When asked to explain their strategies, they also made more frequent reference to proportion, and halving strategies were common.[17] Thus, a pedagogical sequence that begins with percentages and ends with fractions would flow *with* the normal developmental current rather than against it, easing the cognitive burden on the student. It would also align better with common adult preferences and uses of rational numbers.

A fourth approach is illustrated in Figure 11.4. In this exercise, fourth-graders were asked to view a continuous proportion on a screen and click on the horizontal line segment to indicate where that proportion would fall between the two illustrated extremes. Compared to classmates who were asked to simply indicate whether or not the target proportion was more than one-half, those with the more exacting training subsequently improved not only on similar judgments using pencil and paper but on symbolic proportional judgments as well.[18]

Teaching Rational Numbers on the Number Line

The last method just mentioned essentially encourages children to think of proportion as distance along a line. Rational numbers, like whole numbers, can legitimately be represented this way, and one advantage of this approach is that children as young as second grade can easily compare ratios of line lengths.[19] Moreover, success in fraction number-line estimation is a particularly good predictor of subsequent math achievement.[20] One limitation of teaching rational numbers on the number line is that it is abstract and certainly more divorced from a child's daily life experience than math-class pizza figures; and, in fact, not all such pedigogical efforts have been successful.[21]

However, researchers point out numerous advantages that make up for this limitation. First, research has shown that students are less likely to think of lines as things to be sliced—partitioned into discrete parts—compared to pizzas. Thus, students are less likely to default to a counting strategy and more likely to consider continuous proportion.[22]

Second, it treats rational numbers as a measurement tool, in that they describe distance along a line, just as whole numbers do. In practical terms, it addresses the presumably already familiar problems of parts and leftovers—what to do when the object that one is measuring is shorter or a little bit longer than a foot or meter, for example. In this capacity, they extend the idea of a hierarchical system of fractional sub-units—inches, feet, yards, and miles, say, or ounces and pounds—and the increased precision they afford. The metric system, of course, is nested more transparently, with exponentially related sub-units.

Third, reducing the proportional representation to a single linear dimension removes the distraction of a second dimension, such as the width of a beaker or the overall area of a pizza, allowing children to focus on the proportion of interest, the linear relationship of a part to a whole. Locating rational numbers along a single dimension demonstrates and facilitates the notion that rational numbers can be ordered and their magnitudes compared.[23] Understanding and comparing the relative quantities represented by rational numbers is difficult. However, most young children understand the concept of "half," as discussed in Chapter 2, and generally find it easiest to compare proportions to one half or across the half-point divide. Among typical students, this "half advantage" is evident in fourth grade, first for proportional illustrations and then symbolic fractions, but disappears as students become more competent with other proportions. However, some students with exceptional math difficulty do not even begin to show this "half advantage" until seventh grade and continue to struggle with it through middle school.[24] In a large study of at-risk fourth-graders' ability to arrange symbolic fractions in order from smallest to largest magnitude, researchers found that 81 percent of their responses were incorrect and that 65 percent of the ordering errors were due to whole-number bias. For example, a student might ignore the denominator and use only the numerator to order the fractions ($\frac{1}{2} < \frac{2}{8} < \frac{3}{4}$), or vice versa ($\frac{1}{2} < \frac{3}{4} < \frac{2}{8}$). Furthermore, students' number-line fraction estimation skills were closely related to their fraction ordering ability, as one might predict.[25] Teaching fractions on the one-dimensional number line, where their values can be easily ordered and compared (and the halfway point is obvious) can help to free students from misleading notation and clarify how rational number magnitudes are related to each other, just as it does for whole numbers (see Chapter 9).

A fourth advantage of teaching rational numbers on a number line is that it is relatively easy to demonstrate their density on it, a difficult concept rarely addressed explicitly in standard instruction.[26] While discrete whole numbers are represented on the number line as a series of distances from *zero*, each of them one unit longer than the one before it, rational numbers are packed along the line so densely that between any two of them, there is always another. The density concept is one that children may arrive at slowly, if at all. As noted in Chapter 9, children come to grasp the magnitude of ever smaller rational numbers gradually over the course of their numerical development.[27]

Research has shown that the concept of rational-number density is stubbornly resistant to comprehension among children and adults alike.[28] When researchers asked children in grades three, four, and five whether there are other fractions between $\frac{3}{5}$ and $\frac{4}{5}$ or other decimals between *0.3* and *0.4*, few students were confident that there were.[29] Similar studies of middle- and high-school students revealed the same befuddlement. For example, researchers asked students in grades seven, nine, and 11 to indicate how many numbers there are in the interval between a given whole number and decimal (e.g., *7* and *7.001*), between two decimals (e.g., *0.1* and *0.2*), or between two fractions (e.g., $\frac{3}{5}$ and $\frac{4}{5}$). The answer choices were a) no other number; b) a finite number of decimals; c) a finite number of fractions; d) an infinite number of decimals; e) an infinite number of fractions; f) infinitely many numbers, and they can take different forms, such as decimals, fractions, and non-terminating decimals; or g) "none of the above; I believe that. . . ." Results revealed that students in all three grades viewed both fractions and decimals like whole numbers, with empty intervals between them and successors.[30]

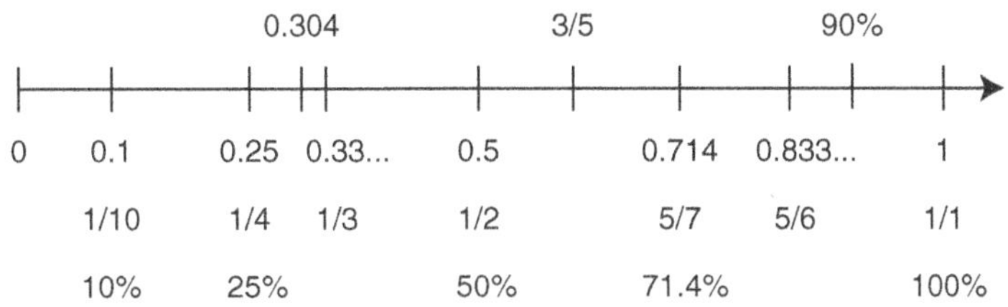

	0.304		3/5		90%	

0	0.1	0.25	0.33...	0.5	0.714	0.833...	1
	1/10	1/4	1/3	1/2	5/7	5/6	1/1
	10%	25%		50%	71.4%		100%

FIGURE 11.5 The number line accommodates rational numbers in all notations.

FIGURE 11.6 Zooming in on ever smaller subdivisions of the number line.

A fifth, related advantage of teaching rational numbers on the number line is that it can illustrate that all rational numbers can be located on the same number line, regardless of notation (Figure 11.5). In the study just cited, most students believed that only decimals could lie between decimals and only fractions could lie between fractions.[31]

Thus, a sixth advantage of the number line is that it can demonstrate that rational numbers do not have a "successor"—that is, a next number—the way that whole numbers do, because the interval between a rational number and the "next" one can always be subdivided (see Figure 11.6). By the same token, it can be used to show that there is no "smallest" (non-*0*) rational number, in contrast to the role of *1* for the natural (counting) numbers, because the interval between a rational number and *0* can also be subdivided.

A seventh advantage of the number line is that it can easily be used to demonstrate the inverse relationship between the size of the unit fraction and the numerosity of such units within the whole-number unit (see Figure 11.7), where unit fractions are those of the form ½, ⅓, ¼, ⅕. . . . Similarly, unit decimal fractions are those of the form *0.1, 0.01, 0.001.* . . .[32] In plain English: The smaller the size of the part, the more parts there are in the whole and, conversely, the more (equal-sized) parts there are crammed between two whole numbers, the smaller they are. Most children, even the youngest, understand that if they had to share their licorice stick fairly, it would be much to their advantage

FIGURE 11.7 Unit fractions on the number line.

to have to share it with only one friend than with the whole class. The number line can illustrate this relationship abstractly. Unfortunately, understanding the relationship between size and numerosity of parts is made especially difficult by the use of whole numbers in fractional notation. Research found that middle-schoolers and even well-educated adults were slower and less accurate in verifying that $1/13 > 1/30$ than that $12/13 > 1/13$,[33] suggesting that this looking-glass characteristic of denominators, where big means small and small means big, makes the relationship between unit-fraction size and numerosity especially confusing. The problems inherent in fractional notation will be discussed further in the next section.

An eighth, and related, advantage of the number line has to do with the fact that fractions' numerators and denominators affect their size very differently. Mathematically speaking, the numerators have a linear relationship with the size of the fraction, while the denominators have a power relationship with the fractional value. In plain English, this means that while the values of fractions with the same denominator increase at an even rate as the numerator increases—in equal-sized steps along the number line, just like whole numbers (Figure 11.8a)—unit fractions get small very quickly at first and then diminish more slowly as their denominators get bigger (Figure 11.8b). If this sounds vaguely familiar, it should. In Chapter 9, we noted that young children have a skewed view of whole numbers, such that the small, familiar numbers take on individual importance and are highly distinguishable, while larger numbers seem both generically big and much less distinguishable (see Figure 9.10 in Chapter 9). Ironically, that means that young children may do a better job of placing unit fractions on a *0*-to-*1* number line than older children, treating the denominators much as they do whole numbers but in the opposite direction, with the unit fractions blurring into generic tininess as they approach *0*—which they do![34] In middle school, understanding the behavior of unit fractions on the number line predicts children's readiness for algebra, suggesting that the number line is where fractions should be taught.[35]

In Chapter 9, as the reader may recall, number-line landmarks—familiar points along the number line to help orient the student—were briefly discussed, in particular regarding their potential role in guiding proportional reasoning with whole numbers. This raises the question of whether *0*-to-*1* number-line landmarks might increase children's grasp of rational numbers and, if so, which landmarks? To answer these questions, researchers asked fifth-graders to place fractions where they belong on *0*-to-*1* number lines, as well as on *0*-to-*5* number lines for improper fractions, and to explain their decisions. The children were divided up into groups, and each group was asked to place the fractions on one of the number-line configurations in Table 11.2. The children were subsequently asked to compare fractions from the same series.

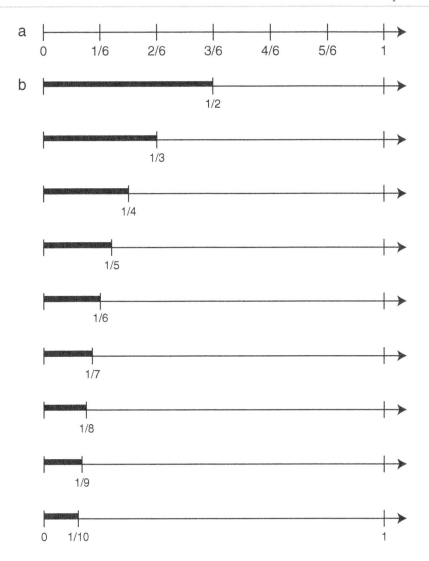

FIGURE 11.8 a) Same-denominator fractions with increasing numerators. b) Unit fractions with increasing denominators.

With the exception of ½, the researchers found that on the *0-to-1* number lines, fraction labels reduced children's accuracy and also interfered with their later fraction comparisons. The children who used number lines with only ½ labeled, or with unlabeled hashmarks, or with no landmarks at all performed better on both tasks. In contrast, the whole-number labels on the *0-to-5* number line improved the children's performance with mixed fractions, perhaps because it encouraged the children to use a mixed-number strategy to locate them.[36]

TABLE 11.2 Landmark Configurations Used by Fifth-Graders in 0-to-1 and 0-to-5 Number-Line Fraction Estimations

0 - 1		0 - 5
＊ 0 ———————————— 1	＊ 0 — $\frac{1}{4}$ — $\frac{1}{2}$ — $\frac{3}{4}$ — 1	＊ 0 ———————————— 5
＊ 0 ++++++ 1	0 — $\frac{1}{5}$ — $\frac{2}{5}$ — $\frac{3}{5}$ — $\frac{4}{5}$ — 1	0 1 2 3 4 5
＊ 0 — $\frac{1}{2}$ — 1	0 $\frac{1}{10}\frac{2}{10}\frac{3}{10}\frac{4}{10}\frac{5}{10}\frac{6}{10}\frac{7}{10}\frac{8}{10}\frac{9}{10}$ 1	

Note: ＊ = configurations leading to improved performance on fraction number-line placement and subsequent fraction comparisons.

Source: Adapted from Siegler & Thompson, 2014.

As of the time of this writing, there have been a dozen or so intervention studies, involving both typical students[37] and those at risk for math learning difficulties,[38] examining the number line as a tool for teaching fractions, where the fraction is represented by part of a line segment rather than as a section of area—more like measuring with a ruler than slicing a pizza. Some approaches employed explicit instruction[39] or number-line placement games.[40] One set of interventions began with the integers and then linked fractions to them, all on the number line.[41] Others actually found that the best route to fraction understanding was by an implicit number-line analogy to whole numbers, despite all the fraction trouble that whole numbers typically give students, as we have seen. If the analogy is set up correctly, however, it appears to work exceptionally well. For example, one study found that students who could place *3* on a *0-to-8* number line—and most of the third- through fifth-graders in the study could—were then able to figure out, without explicit instruction, where ⅜ belonged on a *0-to-1* number line if the two number lines were properly aligned (see Figure 11.9). In fact, the accuracy of children's whole-number number-line placements is linked to the accuracy of their fraction placements, such that students who do well or poorly with one tend to do well or poorly with the other.[42] Most importantly, the studies that compared the linear (number line) to the area (pizzas, rectangles) approach found that students (some as young as second grade) who learned fractions on the number line developed a significantly more accurate notion of fractions and their relation to other fractions and whole numbers than did those students who learned by the prevailing area model.[43] Moreover, the number-line approach narrowed the gap between at-risk and typical students.[44]

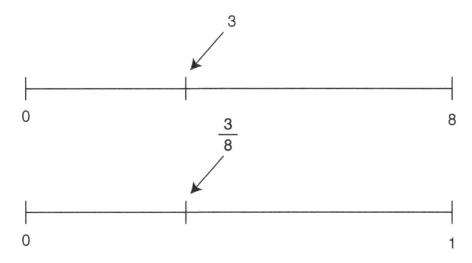

FIGURE 11.9   Scaling *3* on a *0-to-8* number line to *⅜* on a *0-to-1* number line.
Source: Adapted from Yu et al., in press.

Notation Gets in the Way

One major reason that many students have difficulty with rational numbers is that, unlike their much tidier whole-number siblings, rational numbers look complicated and messy. What they have in common is that they are expressed in ordinary, base-10 numerals. In a whole-number study cited in Chapter 8, researchers also presented children aged three to seven with some cookies and a box and asked them to put in "a half" or "a quarter" cookie and then to write a reminder of the amount on a sticky note. Only a few children represented the fraction in proper symbolic form, while nearly half wrote them as whole numbers, and the rest left the sticky note blank. Although the three-year-olds could distribute half a cookie, only the seven-year-olds could represent that amount on paper.[45]

Beyond their shared base-10 numerals, however, there are many ways that whole numbers and rational numbers are different (see Table 11.3). Indeed, whole number, fraction, and decimal fraction notation can look so different from each other that even some high-schoolers think of them as belonging to different number lines.[46] Studies have looked into the reasons for students' confusion, as well as some ways to clarify their thinking. We take up fractions first, then decimals.

The most common error that young children make when they are first shown a fraction is to interpret the numerator and denominator as representing two unrelated amounts, and even to ignore one in favor of the other. Thus, when asked to identify the segmented, shaded figure (see Figure 11.10) that best illustrates a fraction—say, ⅗—most first-graders will point to the drawing with three parts shaded and five parts unshaded, or what would be properly expressed as ⅜.[47] The misconception is stubborn: Even many middle-schoolers remain confused. In a study of sixth- and eighth-graders,

TABLE 11.3   Some Similarities and Differences in the Notation of Whole Numbers and Rational Numbers

Whole Numbers	*Rational Numbers*	
SIMILARITIES:		
Notations include numerals composed of the digits *0* to *9* and conform to the base-10 system, with a numeral's leftmost digit the largest in order of magnitude and the rightmost digit the smallest in order of magnitude.		
DIFFERENCES:		**EXAMPLES:**
Written forms have only one format.	Written forms include three formats and one combined format.	$\frac{3}{7}$, 29%, 0.0376, 85.6%
A number is written only one way.	A fractional amount can be written in infinitely many ways.	$\frac{3}{7}$, $\frac{6}{14}$, $\frac{12}{28}$, $\frac{24}{56}$, . . .
Written form is composed of digits only.	Written forms require additional symbols.	/, ., %
Written form contains only one numeral.	Written form of fractions contains two numerals.	$\frac{3}{7}$
More digits signify larger quantities.	More digits may signify either larger or smaller quantities.	0.7 < 0.715 < 0.72 < 0.723 < 0.9 $\frac{5}{37} < \frac{1}{5} < \frac{3}{5}$
The value of a number can be determined by its order in the verbal counting sequence.	There is no verbal counting sequence because rational numbers are infinitely divisible.	
Numerals may not include place-holder *0*s to the left.	Decimal fractions may include place-holder *0*s to the left.	0.0034, 0.70
Spoken forms include only cardinal and singular ordinal terms.	Spoken forms include cardinal, singular and plural ordinal, and other terms.	*One-third, three-sevenths, five percent*

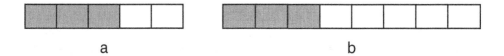

a   b

FIGURE 11.10   a) ⅗ correctly identified. b) ⅜ incorrectly identified as ⅗.

about a third of the students based their number-line placements on just the numerator or denominator.[48]

Some researchers have looked to language to help children learn the *whole* meaning of the denominator. As we saw with whole-number counting (Chapter 6), the East Asian languages are in some ways more number-friendly than English, and this applies to fractions as well. For example, the Chinese term for the cumbersome word *denominator* is "fen mu" ("fraction mother") and for *numerator*, "fen zi" ("fraction child"), vivid, concrete reminders of the tight relational nature of fractions. Language can focus attention on the part-whole relationship in other ways as well. For example, the Chinese expression for ¾ is "of four parts three," naming the denominator first. Korean makes the relationship even clearer: "of four *equal* parts three."[49] Furthermore, these terms eliminate ordinal "-ths" terminology for the denominator, a highly problematic aspect of fraction notation. Indeed, in one study, fewer than half of English-speaking fourth-graders could name ordinals higher than "thirtieth."[50] In another study, a simple rephrasing in English from "three-fifths" to "of five parts three" helped even first-graders understand the part-whole relational meaning of the fraction and to resist the universal compulsion to simply regard the numerator and denominator as two parts.[51]

The relation of the amount represented by the individual numerals to the amount represented by the fraction itself can be especially problematic for some children well into middle school. This difficulty is most evident as children attempt to compare fractions.[52] One study followed a group of children from the fall of fourth grade through the spring of sixth grade. At one timepoint in each grade, the researchers gave them pairs of fractions and asked them to indicate the larger fraction in each pair. The pairs were designed as follows: unit fractions ($\frac{1}{3}$ v. $\frac{1}{2}$); fractions with equal numerators ($\frac{2}{4}$ v. $\frac{2}{3}$) or denominators ($\frac{7}{12}$ v. $\frac{9}{12}$); reciprocals ($\frac{3}{2}$ v. $\frac{2}{3}$); fractions with components that differed in opposite directions ($\frac{3}{10}$ v. $\frac{2}{12}$); and pairs in which the large-components fraction was smaller than the small-components fraction ($\frac{50}{100}$ v. $\frac{16}{17}$). In the beginning, the children focused on the size of the individual whole-number components, revealing whole-number bias. However, some children began to point to the fraction with the smaller components, revealing the dawn of understanding that with fractions, smaller numerals can mean bigger fractions. Eventually, most of them learned to judge the fraction size according to the relation of the numerals—that is, to recognize fractions as proportional magnitudes. Interestingly, those children who could do this most successfully were those with the most accurate whole-number number-line placements.[53]

Whole-number bias can be spotted in other ways as children compare fractions. For example, if they take just as long to compare fractions with large differences ($\frac{6}{7}$ v. $\frac{2}{6}$) as they do those with small differences ($\frac{6}{7}$ v. $\frac{5}{6}$), it may indicate a piece-meal strategy. Fraction judgments obey the same Weber's law as whole-number judgments: The farther apart they are, the easier they are to distinguish (see Chapter 9). When fractions that are very different in magnitude take a long time to compare, the child is probably not automatically viewing the fractions as global magnitudes, but as separate bits.[54] Sometimes children just ignore the denominators, perhaps because the numerators behave more like familiar whole numbers; and sometimes they ignore the numerator. If a child takes longer to compare fractions with common numerators than those with common denominators, it may be because whole-number notions about the denominators are interfering.[55] Perhaps because of the special challenges posed by fractional notation, researchers have found that a student's grasp of fraction magnitudes is tied to their success with algebra.[56] And their grasp of fraction magnitudes depends on their grasp of numerator-denominator relations.[57]

The truth is, however, the two-part nature of fractional notation makes it difficult for most people to grasp an amount written as a fraction as quickly and automatically as they do an amount written as a whole number.[58] On and off the number line, fractions pose a cognitive burden on children, well-educated adults, and even math professors,[59] an experience reflected in a different strength and pattern of brain activation from that elicited by whole numbers and even decimal fractions.[60]

Although many children come to understand decimal fractions earlier than they do fractions, decimal notation can also spell trouble for some children.[61] Students' misconceptions about the quantities represented by decimal notation can be seen most clearly in the errors they make while comparing decimal fractions or attempting to locate them on the unit number line. One of the most common misunderstandings is that more digits signify a bigger quantity (*0.85 < 0.624*), again reflecting whole-number bias.[62] Indeed, one study found that some students with the very weakest math skills thought that decimal-fraction values less than *1* were greater than a whole number (*0.46 > 1*) for the same reason.[63] On the unit number line, the misconception may reveal itself when students place 0.9 close to *0* (Figure 11.11) in the belief that one-digit decimal fractions are the smallest.

In a study of middle-schoolers, researchers found that practice with fractions prior to decimal fraction practice reduced students' whole-number bias, but also increased their tendency to judge decimal fractions with fewer digits as being *larger (.23 > 0.97982)*, a new misconception overgeneralized from their just-prior experience with fraction denominators. On the unit number line, the student might misplace the decimal fractions from large to small according to their number of digits, with the single-digit decimal fractions, in this case, close to *1* (Figure 11.12). Researchers found that this misconception develops a bit later than those based on whole-number bias, after the child knows something about fractions.[64]

Another common source of decimal-notation confusion is the role of *0*, again a manifestation of whole-number bias. In whole-number notation, *0*s at the far left are not quantitatively meaningful and can be ignored, while placeholder *0*s at the far right serve to make the number larger. Confused students might assume that the same pattern holds for decimal fractions. On the unit number line, this befuddlement may manifest itself in a placement that ignores a placeholding *0* (Figure 11.13). In decimal fraction comparisons, it might cause difficulty in comparing decimal fractions with leading (*0.04* v. *0.4*) or trailing (*0.40* v. *0.4*) *0*s.[65]

FIGURE 11.11   Misunderstanding: More digits signify a larger quantity.

FIGURE 11.12   Misunderstanding: More digits signify a smaller quantity.

FIGURE 11.13   Misunderstanding: Ignore placeholding *0*.

RATIONAL-NUMBER ARITHMETIC

Understanding the nature of rational numbers is necessary for learning rational-number arithmetic. However, it is not sufficient. It is also important for students to understand the concepts and procedures of whole-number arithmetic. Indeed, one study that followed students from early elementary school through middle school found that knowledge of basic addition facts in first grade predicted their fraction-arithmetic skills in eighth grade,[66] and another found that middle-schoolers' knowledge of whole-number division was closely associated with their growth in fraction arithmetic skills.[67] Students still floundering with these basic skills will likely have a hard time with fraction arithmetic.

In addition to lacking whole-number skills, other reasons that many students have difficulty with rational-number arithmetic include the large number of often complex procedures, some of which do not make intuitive sense and may or may not bear any obvious relation with the same operations on whole numbers or even with each other.[68]

For example, fraction addition when the denominators are equal ($\frac{1}{5} + \frac{2}{5} = \frac{3}{5}$) is straightforward, intuitively accessible, and comparable to whole-number addition. In contrast, fraction addition when the denominators are unequal ($\frac{3}{5} + \frac{2}{7} = \frac{31}{35}$) is not. In a series of studies of children in grades four through eight (in a district in which equal-denominator addition is taught in fourth grade and unequal-denominator addition in fifth), researchers found that unequal-denominator addition baffled children all the way through middle school. When the researchers asked the children in grades four and five to estimate whether each of a series of such unequal-denominator sums was closer to $\frac{1}{2}$ or *1* or *1½*, nearly half of the students performed no better than if they had guessed. This was true even though many of them made reasonable estimates of the individual fraction addends on a *0*-to-*1* number line. That is, they understood the value of each fraction, but had only a dim idea of what their joint value would be if the fractions were added together. (Students who accurately estimated the sum also made accurate estimates of the individual addends.) When the researchers asked sixth- and seventh-graders to estimate both the fractions' values and the values of their sums on number lines, the results were the same. Moreover, when those estimates were compared with the same students' estimates of whole numbers and their sums, researchers found that the whole-number estimates were better than the fraction estimates, particularly the fraction sum estimates, which were very inaccurate. And when the same tasks were given to eighth-graders and advanced-math seventh-graders, where they could express their fraction-sum estimates orally in whatever terms they chose, the results were still the same. Even the hint to "think about the size of each fraction first, then add" did not help. The most remarkable finding was that some of the middle-schoolers' fraction-sum estimates were often less than their estimate of one of the addends, violating the expected *direction of effects principle* that holds for whole numbers as well as fractions—namely, if you add two amounts, you will wind up with more than either of those amounts individually.[69]

Confusing the directional effects of arithmetic operations is one of the most common difficulties in learning rational numbers. Even for older students and adults, fraction multiplication and division are especially problematic where the effects run opposite to those expected for the same operations with whole numbers—that is, with proper fractions (i.e., fractions with values less than *1*), multiplying means winding up with *less* and dividing means winding up with *more*. This confusion was demonstrated in a study of children in grades six and eight, as well as in pre-service elementary school teachers. Study participants were asked to verify (i.e., decide if true or false), without calculating, a series of statements that looked like this: $^{41}/_{66} \times {}^{19}/_{35} > {}^{41}/_{66}$? And $^{37}/_{19} \times {}^{58}/_{36} > {}^{37}/_{19}$? And $^{31}/_{56} \div {}^{17}/_{42} > {}^{31}/_{56}$? And $^{51}/_{16} \div {}^{47}/_{33} > {}^{51}/_{16}$? (Note that some problems contained two proper fractions and some two improper fractions.) Participants were also asked to place fractions on number lines and to calculate arithmetic with simple fractions containing equal and unequal denominators to gauge their sense of numerical value and their procedural skills, respectively. The results demonstrated that both middle-schoolers and pre-service teachers performed as if they were randomly guessing on multiplication and division involving proper fractions. Importantly, this was true even among participants with good estimates of the individual fractions' values and with solid mastery of basic fraction arithmetic procedures. By contrast, math and science college majors given the same tasks showed no sign of confusion about the direction of these fraction-arithmetic effects. Similar results were obtained for decimal-fraction multiplication and division using comparable methods. Altogether, these findings led researchers to conclude that many students become proficient in fraction arithmetic procedures without any understanding of what they mean or any way to judge the reasonableness of their answers.[70]

A second major reason for fraction-arithmetic difficulty is the fact that the procedures share some features but not others, leading children to muddle them and overgeneralize the procedures for one operation to the procedures for another. For example, as noted, addition of same-denominator fractions is nearly as straightforward as whole-number addition: $^{2}/_{5} + {}^{4}/_{5} = {}^{6}/_{5}$. However, the multiplication procedure is not analogous: $^{2}/_{5} \times {}^{4}/_{5} \neq {}^{8}/_{5}$. (The fact that children frequently apply addition procedures to multiplication problems is particularly curious, because the fraction multiplication procedure does not vary with denominator equality as the addition procedure does and is therefore simpler.) Decimal fraction procedures get similarly mixed up with each other. For example, to multiply two decimal fractions, it is not necessary to align the decimal points (i.e., place-values) prior to computing, while it is required for addition, lest this happen: $0.35 + 0.4 = 0.39$. Overgeneralizing addition and subtraction procedures typically accounts for a large proportion of middle-schoolers' errors on fraction multiplication and division problems.[71]

A third significant reason for fraction arithmetic difficulty is the impenetrability of what fraction multiplication and division mean. Children's working analogies for those operations with whole numbers are relatively straightforward: Multiplication is like repeated addition, and division is like sharing fairly. But what does $^{2}/_{3}$ times $^{5}/_{7}$ mean? Or $^{7}/_{9}$ divided by $^{2}/_{5}$? Matters are not made any easier by the fact that fraction division ($1^{3}/_{4} \div {}^{1}/_{2}$, say) actually has three different models—measurement (*How many ½-foot lengths are there in something that is 1¾ feet long?*), partitive (*If ½ a length is 1¾ feet, how long is the whole?*), and product and factors (*If one side of a 1¾-square foot rectangle is ½ foot, how long is the other side?*)—and multiple ways to compute the answer.[72]

A large-scale study of fraction addition and multiplication utilizing computer simulation and student data revealed that the three most frequent consistent strategies were correct strategies, strategies guided by whole-number bias, and strategies involving overgeneralization of addition approaches to multiplication. On the problems approached correctly, accuracy was above average. Furthermore, overall math achievement was higher among those using correct and overgeneralization strategies than it was among those employing whole-number methods or other variable approaches.[73]

The questions, then, are: *What accounts for such a high rate of misunderstanding?* And: *What can be done about it?*

One problem may lie with the textbooks.[74] For example, it was found that, among problems with unequal denominators, textbooks typically have twice as many multiplication practice problems as those calling for the more difficult addition or subtraction; the reverse pattern was true for problems with equal denominators.[75] Similarly, textbooks were found to offer addition and subtraction more frequently involving two decimal fractions than a whole number and a decimal fraction, while on multiplication and division practice, the opposite pattern applied.[76] One study looked at students' notions of what typical problems look like (e.g., *What operands should go here:* □ + □? or *What operation should go here:* ¾ □ ⅙? or *Guess which is the problem?*) and found that students' associations paralleled the problems in their textbooks. For example, students associated equal-denominator operands with addition and subtraction and whole number-fraction pairs with multiplication and division. These findings led the researchers to conclude that students learn spurious associations between operand features and operations and to encourage publishers (and teachers) to provide more varied and less predictable practice opportunities. The same study was done in China, with the same results. Yet Chinese students demonstrate less direction-of-effects confusion than U.S. students, suggesting that the textbooks are not the only source of difficulty. One cross-national difference is that Chinese students spend more time practicing fraction arithmetic (indicating a potential need for more practice time in the United States)[77] and are taught the rationales for fraction arithmetic procedures.[78]

Several teaching recommendations emerge from these findings. One is to provide explicit instruction on strategies for the four operations as they apply to fractions with equal and unequal denominators and to practice strategy selection alone, without doing the actual computations. Once the students have mastered the operations, having them practice on sets of mixed operations would focus their attention on strategy selection. (Blocked practice, as described in Chapter 1, tends to foster overgeneralization.[79]) Similarly, students should be challenged to reason through their strategy for aligning place-values and decimal points while practicing decimal fraction arithmetic, rather than just giving students pre-aligned problems to calculate.[80] Fraction division seems to be the gnarliest operation, with errors reflecting insufficient practice, overgeneralization from earlier learned operations, and incorrect executions of the correct algorithm.[81] Yet textbooks typically provide more practice with multiplication than division. Interestingly, the opposite case is true for Korean textbooks, which favor the more challenging division problems, perhaps a better pedagogical plan.[82]

Additionally, as we have seen in much of early arithmetic, language can help significantly in clarifying concepts. For example, as suggested in Chapter 10, one can substitute *of* for *times* in multiplication, as in *How much is ⅓ of ⅙?* for ⅓ × ⅙. Language can also help distinguish the conceptual difference between dividing a small fraction by a large one versus a large one by a small one. Thus, for ⅓ ÷ ⅚: *How much of ⅚ is ⅓?* And for ⅚ ÷ ⅓: *How many ⅓s are in ⅚?*

Some have wondered, *Should concepts be taught first, prior to procedures?* A study addressed that question in a decimal-fraction intervention and found that instruction that repeatedly went back and forth between the concept and the procedure was more successful in teaching the procedure than was a concept-first approach, while students learned the concepts equally well with both approaches.[83] Critically, most researchers note that knowledge of fraction magnitudes and fraction arithmetic bolster each other and recommend that they be taught hand-in-hand.[84]

Others have tried a learning-by-analogy approach. For example, one study found that students who practiced whole-number division prior to a lesson on fraction division learned better than those who practiced other fraction operations first.[85] One particularly effective way of teaching fraction division by analogy to whole-number division is on the number line. If the solution to *8 ÷ 2* lies in figuring out how many *2s* you would have to line up to reach *8* (Figure 11.14a), then the solution to *8 ÷ ½* would lie in figuring out how many *½s* you would have to line up to reach *8* (essentially the meaning of "goes into") (Figure 11.14b). When children tackled the whole-number problem on the number line first, they could figure out how to solve the fraction problem. (Note here that the researchers had pre-segmented the fraction number line into divisor units, in this case halves, as can be seen in Figure 11.14b.) Importantly,

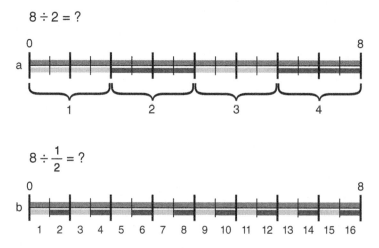

FIGURE 11.14 a) *8 ÷ 2* on the number line. b) *8 ÷ ½* on the number line.

children had a significantly easier time with this problem on the number line than by using the area model (circles and rectangles) or no visual model.[86] However, the analogy approach can be tricky. When *explicit* links between whole-number and fraction division were made during such lessons, performance was poor, suggesting that explicit linking can produce misconceptions about the newly learned material, in this case fraction division.[87]

Finally, there are several classroom exercises that can draw children's attention to the meaning of operations on fractions. One is to practice predicting the effects of the various operations on the relative size (direction) of the results—e.g., "In this problem, do you think the answer will be more or less than the first operand? Than the second operand? Why?"[88] Another is to assess the plausibility of computational results and to explain why they do or do not make sense.[89]

CONCLUSION

A child's ability to understand what rational numbers are—that they represent proportional magnitudes and can be ordered—and to manipulate them arithmetically opens the world of algebra and more abstract mathematics, not to mention the ability to cope with the everyday demands of adult life. If the villain of this tale is the child's entrenched whole-number habits, as well as rational numbers' peculiar notation, plethora of procedures, and impenetrable meaning of some rational-number operations, then the hero is the number line, along with explicit hand-in-hand instruction of concepts and procedures, lots of strategy practice, and some simple language alterations. An explicit number-line approach has proven particularly useful for children experiencing significant difficulty with fractions.[90] Making adjustments to the current curriculum and textbooks will certainly take time. Providing these sorts of opportunities to pre-service teachers to refresh or relearn rational number concepts and arithmetic might be a very fruitful first step.

ACTIVITIES

Rational Numbers

Introduction

Rational numbers can be challenging both in the underlying concepts and the language we use to talk about them. In the following activities, we do not address the procedures for rational number arithmetic, since they are a standard part of instruction. Instead, we tackle the foundational concepts and provide suggestions for using language that makes the concepts easier to grasp. Perhaps the trickiest language components are the

English-language terms for fractional numbers: half, third, thirds, fourt*h*, fourt*hs*, and so on. The terms *half* and *third (thirds)* are their own terms and do not follow the same rule as the rest of the fractional numbers, which add *th* or *ths* to the end of number names. These sounds are difficult to process, and it can be helpful to have students say these words while exaggerating the *th* or *ths* sounds: *fourTHS, fifTHS*, and so on. Discuss the meaning of these endings for rational number names.

ACTIVITY 11.1: Introduction to Rational Numbers by Visualizing Percentages First

Objective: To learn the concept of rational numbers by visualizing percentages first.[91] Using a continuous quantity such as water helps students understand rational numbers better than using discrete (countable) quantities such as buttons. Students understand the basic concept of percentages more easily than fractions,[92] so percentages can be a bridge to learning fractions. We use beakers of water here; alternatively, one could provide drawings of beakers that the students can color to the designated levels.

■ **First:** Fill three beakers to the top with water and line them up. Describe the beakers as "one hundred percent full." Note that *percent* means *per one hundred* (*cent* means *one hundred*). Next, pour out half of the water from the second beaker, point to its new level, and describe it as "half full." Discuss that half of *one hundred* is *50*, so the beaker is "fifty percent full." Label that beaker *50%*. Next, empty half of the water from the third full beaker and then, pointing to the next midpoint, pour out half of that water, describing it now as "twenty-five percent full." Discuss that *25* is half of *50*, so *25 percent* is half of *50 percent*, and label it *25%*. Next, pour the water from the half-full beaker into the beaker that is 25 percent full and discuss what the label should be (*75%*).

■ **Next:** In a similar way, demonstrate other percentages. Begin with 100 percent full, then pour a very small amount out to demonstrate *99 percent*, which means "almost full." Begin again with zero percent full, which means "empty," then add a very small amount of water to demonstrate *one percent*, or "almost empty."

■ **Next:** Mark ten equal-height segments on a beaker, such that the tenth segment corresponds to the full beaker. Fill the beaker with water in increments, beginning with ten percent, then 20 percent, and so on until reaching 100 percent. Have students name and write each percentage level and discuss their relationship.

■ **Next:** Fill one beaker to 20 percent full and a second beaker to 30 percent full, then ask the students to predict what percentage full the first beaker will be if the water in the second beaker is poured into the first beaker. Pour the water into the first beaker and discuss.

■ **Next:** Combine various amounts of water, have students make observations, and discuss the outcomes.

ACTIVITY 11.2: Translating Percentages to Decimal Fractions

Objective: To learn the meaning of decimal fractions.

■   **First:** Explain that two-place decimal fractions measure the percentage of the distance between two whole numbers, such as *0* and *1*, *1* and *2*, etc. First describe that one total beaker-full is equivalent to 100 percent and relate it to the decimal whole number *one*, expressed in decimal notation as *1.00*. Now, relate *50%* on the beaker with *.50* and write *50%* and *.50* next to each other, also saying "fifty one-hundredths." One-half of *1* is *.50*. Do the same with *25%* and *.25*, saying, "twenty-five one-hundredths," then *75%* and *.75* ("seventy-five one-hundredths"), then *99%* and *.99* ("ninety-nine one-hundredths"), then *1%* and *.01* ("one one-hundredth").

■   **Next:** Proceed to tenths. Mark a beaker in ten equal-height segments. Beginning with an empty beaker, write *0%* and *.00*. Add water to the beaker to the first tenth, then write *10%* and *.10* and say, "ten one-hundredths." Fill in the segments of the beaker for each tenth, then write and say the percentage and decimal fraction representation until reaching a full beaker, then writing *100%* and *1.00*, saying both "one" and "one-hundred one-hundredths," which mean the same thing. Emphasize that the full beaker is written as *1.00*, meaning that it is one full beaker and no more.

ACTIVITY 11.3: Connecting Percentages and Decimal Fractions to Fractions

Objective: To learn the connection between fractions, percentages, and decimal fractions.

■   **First:** Introduce fractions in terms of percentages and decimals. Repeat the first level of Activity 11.2, and this time include the fractions that correspond to the percentages and decimals. The English language of percents, decimals, and fractions is messy, and it will take students time and practice to master it. Introduce the language and notation of the written fraction ½ by pointing to the denominator *2* and saying, "of two equal parts" then pointing to the numerator, saying "one." Point to the beaker that is one-half full and say, "One of two equal parts is full of water, and the other part does not contain water. Of two equal parts, one is full." Then connect the fraction ½ with *50 percent*, which means *50* of *100*, and point out that there are two *50*s in *100*. Of two equal parts of *100*, one part is *50*. Then connect the decimal fraction *.50* with the fraction ½ and *50 percent* in a similar way. Next, introduce the fraction ¼, pointing to the denominator *4* and saying, "of four equal parts," then pointing to the numerator and saying, "One. Of four equal parts, one." Connect that there are four *25*s in *100* and that *25 percent* is the same as one of four equal parts needed to get to *100*. Or, of four equal parts, one. Continue this reasoning with the decimal fraction *.25*, then with the connection to *75 percent*, *.75*, and *¾*.

■ **Next:** Repeat the "tenths" lesson of Activity 11.2, this time including the fractions with the percentage and decimal. Discuss that there are a total of ten equal segments in the beaker, so that *10* is the denominator, representing the total number of equal segments. Begin again with an empty beaker and *0%*, *.00*, and now add the fraction *⁰⁄₁₀*. Write and say each amount. Proceed as earlier, adding one-tenth at a time, writing out and saying the fraction with each segment.

ACTIVITY 11.4: Introducing Fractions by Partitioning Length Models

Objective: To learn the concept of fractions on the number line.

■ **First:** Students start with several paper strips of the same length. First, take one paper strip and pretend that it is a candy bar that two friends want to share. Say, "What should we do?" The students will likely suggest splitting it in half. "Yes, to be fair, fold it into two equal-length pieces." Have the students fold the paper strip in half and mark along the fold. Discuss how the whole paper strip was divided into two equal-length parts. Label each fractional part with *½*, explaining that each segment represents one (*numerator*) of two (*denominator*) equal-length parts.

■ **Next:** Take another paper strip and say, "Now let's pretend that this paper strip is a candy bar again, but this time there are four friends. What should we do?" The students fold this paper strip in half and then in half again, drawing lines along the folds to indicate the segments. Discuss how the whole candy bar was divided into four equal-length parts and students label each fraction part with *¼* while saying (and pointing to the four parts), "Of four equal parts, one." In the same manner, the students fold and mark a third paper strip three times into eighths, as if sharing the candy bar equally among eight friends. The students label each fraction part with *⅛*. Talk about how the more equal parts the same sized strip (or candy bar) is divided into, the smaller each part is.

■ **Next:** The students draw a number line that is the same length as the paper strips (see Figure). Explain that we can use the number line to show fractions. Since each paper strip represents one whole, the students can label the number line *0* on the left and *1* on the right. Start with the paper strip marked into halves. Align the paper strip directly above the number line. Say, "The denominator *two* tells us that we need to make two equal-length parts. Let's split the number line into two equal-length parts, just like the paper strip." Have students draw a hash mark across the midpoint of the number line and label it *½*. Explain that when marking a number line, the hash mark is labeled to indicate the space between *0* and the hash mark. Aligned with the *1* on the end, have them write *²⁄₂* to show that *²⁄₂* represents the whole strip of paper and is the same amount as *1* and can also be written as *²⁄₂ = 1*. Two of two equal parts is one whole strip.

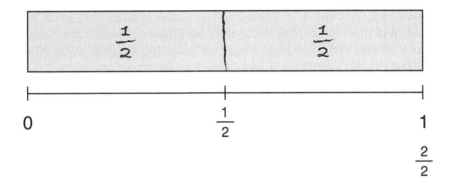

- **Next:** In the same manner, use the remaining strips to mark the number line into fourths and eighths. The number line will be numbered sequentially, unlike the individual segments of the paper strips, which were all labeled ¼ or ⅛. The number line will be labeled as ¼, ²⁄₄, ¾, ⁴⁄₄. Again, point out that ⁴⁄₄ = *1*, saying, "Four fourths is the same amount as one. Four of four equal parts means having the whole amount."

A Note About Fraction Number Lines

The following activities include the use of fraction number lines. As discussed extensively in the science section of this chapter, the fraction number line is the most advantageous way for students to develop a robust understanding of fractions. A variety of printable fraction number lines can easily be found online. Teachers and students can also create their own fraction number lines and templates. Finally, a very useful interactive fraction number line can be found online on the Math is Fun website[93] and can be used in the following activities.

ACTIVITY 11.5: Unit Fractions

Objective: To learn about unit fractions and the relation of their magnitude to the magnitude of their denominators. Students identify, label, and discuss the unit fraction. Create a number line with *0* labeled on the left and *1* labeled on the right. Fraction tiles can be used to help students draw the length of the number line with the whole unit tile and to produce accurate placements of the unit fractions by aligning them with the number line. Printable fraction number lines can also be used as a guide if fraction tiles are not available.

- **First:** Begin with marking the number line with ½. Explain that the denominator *2* means you should partition the number line into two equal-length parts. Have the students partition the number line and label where ½ belongs. Discuss how ½ is a unit fraction because its numerator is *1*. Discuss that the magnitude of the fraction ½ is halfway between *0* and *1*.

■ **Next:** Mark and label ⅓, ¼, and ⅕ on the same number line, using fraction tiles or a printed number line as a guide (see Figure). Draw the students' attention to the relationship between the denominator and the magnitude of the unit fraction. As the denominator increases, the magnitude of the unit fraction decreases, just like the more friends you share a candy bar equally with, the smaller the piece that each person gets. Point to where unit fractions with increasingly larger denominators would go on the number line, each time getting closer to *0*.

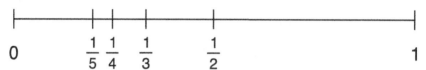

■ **Next:** Ask the students if the fraction will ever be as small as *zero* as the denominators get bigger and bigger and bigger.
■ **Next:** Write out pairs of fractions to compare their magnitude and ask which fraction of the pair is greater or lesser, such as: ½ and ⅓, ⅙ and ⅑, ¹⁄₁₀ and ¹⁄₂₀.

ACTIVITY 11.6: Comparing Fractions of Increasing Magnitude

Objective: To learn to compare the magnitude of fractions with a difference of one between the numerator and denominator. Fraction tiles are used in this activity to draw accurate placements on the number line as described in Activity 11.5.

■ **First:** Mark ½ on a number line bounded with *0* and *1*. Inform the students that together you will mark new fractions on the number line. In these new fractions, the numerator and denominator each increases by one each time, and the difference between the numerator and denominator is only one. Creating new number lines or using the number lines in the unit fractions in Activity 11.5, have the students mark ⅔, ¾, ⅘. These fraction placements require students to use multiple fraction tiles in the following manner. For ⅔, take two ⅓-tiles, align them with the drawn number line, and mark the spot equivalent to ⅔. For ¾, take three ¼-tiles, align them with the number line, and mark ¾ in the correct spot. Continue as such.
■ **Next:** Note that for each of these successive fractions, their magnitude increases and they get closer to *1* on the number line. Now, create a composite number line for all these fractions that have a difference of one between the numerator and denominator on one number line. Place ⅔, ¾, and ⅘ on it. Then have the students place the following fractions on the number line, using fraction tiles or preprinted number lines to help if needed: ⅚, 6/7, and ⅞. Discuss that the more total equal parts upon which a fraction is based (the larger the denominator), the closer it gets to *1*, reflecting greater magnitude. Contrast this concept with unit fractions

in Activity 11.5, in which the more total parts upon which the fraction is based (the larger the denominator), the closer the unit fraction gets to *zero*.

■ **Next:** Create a number line with both unit fractions and fractions with a numerator that is one less than the denominator. Discuss the students' observations.

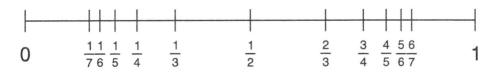

■ **Next:** Write out pairs of fractions to compare their magnitude and ask which fraction of the pair is greater or lesser such as: $\frac{1}{2}$ and $\frac{2}{3}$, $\frac{5}{6}$ and $\frac{8}{9}$, $\frac{3}{4}$ and $\frac{11}{12}$. Students should learn to recognize the fraction with the greater (or lesser) magnitude without calculation.

ACTIVITY 11.7: Half and Close to Half

Objective: To learn about fractions that are equivalent to *one-half* and fractions that are just under and over *one-half*. Students who understand the placement of *one-half* or close to *one-half* on the number line have more accurate judgment of fraction magnitude overall, known as the *half advantage*.[94]

■ **First:** The students mark $\frac{1}{2}$ on a bounded number line with *0* and *1* on the two ends.
■ **Next:** Have students mark another bounded number line into fourths. Ask the students if $\frac{1}{2}$ and $\frac{2}{4}$ are equivalent fractions and discuss. Then ask them about the relationship of *two* and *four* in the $\frac{2}{4}$ fraction, saying, "Yes, two is half of four, and two-fourths is the same magnitude and proportion as one-half."
■ **Next:** Ask students what half of *six* is, and when they say "three," ask them to mark $\frac{3}{6}$ on the first number line marked with $\frac{1}{2}$. They can write $\frac{3}{6}$ underneath the $\frac{1}{2}$ mark, showing they are in the same spot on the number line. Continue with even denominators (e.g., *8* and *10*), asking what half of the denominator is and marking it on the number line ($\frac{4}{8}$ and $\frac{5}{10}$). Discuss that for fractions equivalent to $\frac{1}{2}$, the numerator will always be half of the denominator.
■ **Next:** Discuss denominators that are odd numbers and cannot be evenly divided in half, so they cannot be the equivalent of $\frac{1}{2}$. Present fractions with odd-number denominators that are just under $\frac{1}{2}$ and just over $\frac{1}{2}$: $\frac{1}{3}$ and $\frac{2}{3}$, $\frac{2}{5}$ and $\frac{3}{5}$, $\frac{3}{7}$ and

¹/₇, ⁴/₉ and ⁵/₉. The students make number lines with each pair of odd-denominator fractions. Fraction tiles may be used as a guide for placement if needed. Discuss that the first fraction in each pair is less than ¹/₂ (or closer to *0*) and the second fraction in each pair is greater than ¹/₂ (or closer to *1*).

■ **Next:** Experiment with placing more pairs of odd-denominator fractions just below and above ¹/₂ on the number line. Discuss what happens to the placements of the odd-denominator fractions as the denominators increase. The greater the denominator, the more segments on the number line and the closer the odd-denominator fraction pairs get to ¹/₂ (but can never equal ¹/₂).

ACTIVITY 11.8: Decimal and Fraction Number-Line Zoom-In to Hundredths and Thousandths

Objective: To learn decimal place-value and density using the number line.[95] To help students learn the meaning of rational numbers and their relationships.

■ **First:** Mark ten equal segments on a *0*-to-*1* number line. Have students label the hash marks from *.00* to *1.00* with *.1*, *.2*, *.3*, . . ., while saying, "one-tenth," "two-tenths," "three-tenths," etc. Emphasize that since there are ten equal segments between *0* and *1*, the decimal fractions are in *tenths*.

```
.00  .1  .2  .3  .4  .5  .6  .7  .8  .9  1.00
```

■ **Next:** Zoom in on the segment from *.0* to *.1* first, then draw an arrow to a new full-length number line and label its endpoints *.00* and *.1*. Mark ten new equal segments on that line (see Figure below). Discuss that if each segment of the tenths number line had ten segments, there would be 100 segments altogether from *0* to *1*. Therefore, decimals will now be in *hundredths*. Have students label the hash marks and name the decimal fractions from *.00* to *.1* and then from *.1* to *.2* on a new zoom-in number line. Help the students name the decimal fractions, saying, "one-hundredth," "two-hundredths," etc., up to "ten-hundredths."

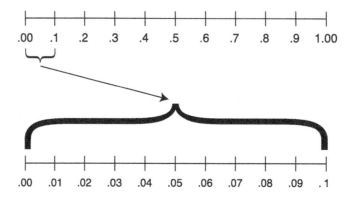

- **Next:** Zoom in on the segment from *.00* to *.01*. Mark ten equal segments on that line and discuss that if each segment of the hundredths number line had ten equal segments, there would be 1,000 equal segments altogether from *0* to *1*! Therefore, decimals in that range will be in the thousandths. Talk about how 1,000 equal segments are a lot of segments! Have students label the hash marks and name the decimal fractions.

- **Next:** Repeat this activity but with proper fractions, zooming in first to *tenths*, then *hundredths*, then *thousandths*.

Rational-Number Arithmetic

ACTIVITY 11.9: Basic Concepts and Procedures of Fraction Addition and Subtraction

Objective: To learn the initial concepts and procedures of adding and subtracting fractions. To predict the direction of the outcome for fraction addition and subtraction. This activity can be completed with common fraction tiles aligned with a bounded number line from *0* to *1*. If these are not available, it can be completed using paper strips as described in Activity 11.4.

- **First:** Draw a *0*-to-*1* bounded number line that matches the length of the whole one fraction tile and segment it into fourths. Students line up two of the $\frac{1}{4}$-tiles on the number line beginning at *0*. Ask how many fourths they have now. Model writing and saying the equation $\frac{1}{4} + \frac{1}{4} = \frac{2}{4}$ ("One-fourth plus one-fourth is the same amount as two-fourths"). Then say, "Yes, of four equal parts (while pointing to the *4* in $\frac{2}{4}$), we now have two (pointing to the *2* in $\frac{2}{4}$). Or we could say we have two of four equal parts." The students then take another $\frac{1}{4}$-tile and line it up with the first two along the number line and say and write $\frac{2}{4} + \frac{1}{4} = \frac{3}{4}$. Discuss that the number of four total parts did not change, so the denominator did not change, but the number of fourths did change, so only the numerator changed in the equation. "Of four parts, we now have three." Have the students line up the fourth $\frac{1}{4}$-tile with the others along the number line. Write the equation $\frac{3}{4} + \frac{1}{4} = \frac{4}{4}$, saying, "Now we have all four parts, so we have the whole four-fourths, which we can also write as one. Four-fourths is the same amount as one."

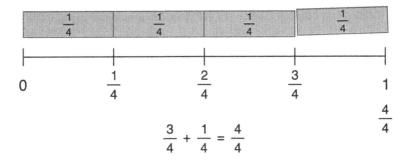

- **Next:** Complete the previous sequence in reverse to demonstrate fraction subtraction. Begin with ¾ and subtract (take away) ¼, write and say the equation, and talk about the answer as, "Three-fourths; of four equal parts, we now have three, or three of four equal parts." Continue the progression down to ¾.

- **Next:** Repeat this with the ⅛-tiles (or any different set of fraction tiles). Complete a variety of addition and subtraction problems, saying and writing the equations, and using the language of parts ("Of eight equal parts, three," or "Three of eight equal parts").

- **Next:** Write out several of the fraction addition problems from the earlier exercise. Ask the students if adding fractions together always results in more. They should have enough experience to observe that adding fractions together always results in a greater magnitude, just as with whole numbers. If they are not sure, continue to write out equations and plot them on the number line until they fully understand the concept.

- **Next:** Write out several of the fraction subtraction problems from the previous activity. Ask the students if subtracting fractions always results in less than the first fraction, and they should conclude that subtracting fractions always results in less, just as with subtracting whole numbers. If they are not sure, continue to write out equations, and align the number tiles with the number line until they fully understand the concept.

ACTIVITY 11.10: Making Sense of Fraction Addition and Subtraction With Unlike Denominators

Objective: To learn why like denominators are needed for fraction addition and subtraction. To predict the direction of the outcome for fraction addition and subtraction. The procedures for finding like denominators is not presented, since it is a common part of every curriculum, but the reasoning for like denominators is discussed.

- **First:** Students pick a variety of fraction tiles (¼, ⅙, ⅛, etc.), then line up any two of the tiles on a bounded fraction number line beginning at *0*. Ask students if adding the fractions results in more or less without naming the total amount. Discuss that adding and subtracting fractions with unlike denominators is difficult, since there is not a concise name without like denominators. Align a variety of tiles with unlike denominators on the number line, adding some and subtracting some without any calculation. Simply ask if there is more or less as the result of the addition or subtraction. Students should observe that adding any two fractions with different denominators will always result in more, even if the result cannot be named concisely for the new fraction total.[96]

- **Next:** Remind students of the following:

  - When adding or subtracting fractions with the same denominator, the total number of equal parts that makes the whole does not change, only the number of those parts that you have changes.

- When adding or subtracting fractions with different denominators, you wind up with a combination of different sized parts, thus making it difficult to name the result concisely.
- When adding fractions (and whole numbers), the total is always more.
- When subtracting fractions (and whole numbers), the result is always less than the first fraction (or whole number) in the equation.
- **Next:** Now experiment: What would happen if we added the denominators in the following equation: $\frac{3}{6} + \frac{1}{4} = \frac{4}{10}$. Does that make sense? *Four-tenths* is less than *one-half* on the number line, yet the equation started with an equivalent to *one-half* and even more was added. The result cannot be less than half! Place the related fraction tiles on a number line to show that the result would have to be more even if we do not have a concise answer. Adding the numerators together and then the denominators together will always result in less and always be incorrect. Experiment with other fraction addition problems with unlike denominators and demonstrate that if the denominators are added together, the result will always result in less instead of more and will not make sense.
- **Next:** Experiment with fraction subtraction with unlike denominators and subtract the numerators and denominators. $\frac{3}{6} - \frac{1}{4} = \frac{2}{2}$. Does that make sense? No! The result in the equation is greater than the first fraction in the equation, which cannot be correct for subtraction of fractions or whole numbers. Experiment with other fraction subtraction problems, demonstrating that subtracting the denominators will always result in more instead of less and does not make sense.
- **Next:** Write the equation $\frac{1}{2} + \frac{1}{4}$. Discuss that to name the result of this equation, the denominators need to be alike. Using fraction tiles, align a $\frac{1}{2}$-tile and two $\frac{1}{4}$-tiles. Place them on the bounded *0-to-1* number line and discuss $\frac{2}{4}$ and $\frac{1}{2}$ are equivalent fractions because they are at the same spot on the number line. Further discuss that converting unlike denominators to like denominators is always accomplished by dividing one or both the denominators into more parts until the denominators are the same. Since $\frac{1}{2}$ is the same amount as $\frac{2}{4}$, we can substitute $\frac{2}{4}$ for $\frac{1}{2}$ in the equation: $\frac{2}{4} + \frac{1}{4} = \frac{3}{4}$.

ACTIVITY 11.11: Fraction Multiplication: What It Means and Direction of Outcome

Objective: To learn to predict the direction of the outcome of fraction multiplication based on whether multiplying by more than *one* or less than *one*.[97] This lesson can be taught on the number line or using beakers of water.

- **First:** Review whole-number multiplication to show that it always results in more than either number in the equation ($6 \times 9 = 54$).
- **Next:** Tell students that you have BIG NEWS! When multiplying by a fraction that is less than *one* (a proper fraction), the result will ALWAYS BE LESS than the number being multiplied!

- **Next:** It is easier to understand multiplying by a proper fraction when using the word *of* instead of *times*: "one-half *of* four," instead of "one-half *times* four," which does not have a clear meaning. Provide a list of proper fraction multiplication problems and have students practice reading them aloud using this language: *¾ × 3* read as, "Three-fourths of three."

- **Next:** Ask students to imagine one-half or one-fourth of a variety of things such as an elephant, a bus, a football field, a school, or anything else that is fun and silly. Ask students if their images are more or less than the original thing. Taking one-half of something means that you are taking a part of it, or a *fraction* of it. Students can share their imagined ideas.

- **Next:** Transition to fraction tiles. Take two whole tiles and write the equation: *½ × 2 = ___* (expressed as "one-half of two"). Take one of the whole tiles away, leaving one whole tile. Ask the students to describe what happened when multiplying by *½*.

- **Next:** Align a *½*-tile with a bounded number line, with one end at *0*. Write the equation *¼ × ½* (expressed as "one-fourth of one-half"). Take eight *⅛*-tiles and align them with the bounded number line and the *½*-tile. Four of the *⅛*-tiles will fit between *0* and *½* on the number line, and the other four *⅛*-tiles will fit from *½* to *1* on the number line. Finish writing the equation as *¼ × ½ = ⅛*. Discuss that the result of multiplying two proper fractions is less than either of the original fractions.

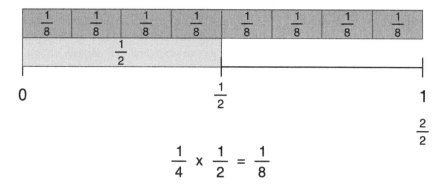

- **Next:** Rewrite the equation as *½ × ¼*. Knowing the commutative principle will let students know that the answer is the same as *¼ × ½* (expressed as "one-fourth of one-half"), but what does it mean? Align the *¼*-tile with the number line, then put two *⅛*-tiles underneath the *¼*-tile. A half of one-fourth is one-eighth: *½ × ¼ = ⅛*.

- **Next:** Present another multiplication problem with two proper fractions such as *⅓ × ¾* and have students predict the result. Complete the calculation using fraction multiplication procedures (numerator times numerator, denominator times denominator) and fraction tiles. Note that when multiplying *any* number by a proper fraction, the resulting number will always be less than that number. Then reverse the order of the fractions ($\frac{3}{4} \times \frac{1}{3}$) to show that the result will always be less than both fractions.

- **Next:** Compare $\frac{9}{10} \times 2$ with $\frac{1}{10} \times 2$. Have the students predict and then discuss the difference in the outcomes. In simple terms, $\frac{9}{10}$ is close to *one*, so you could say, "Nine-tenths of two is like *most of* two," whereas $\frac{1}{10}$ is close to *zero*, so you could say, "One-tenth of two is *just a little bit of* two." The closer the proper fraction is to *zero*, the less the outcome will be, since it means taking a small part. The greater the magnitude of the proper fraction (i.e., the closer to *1*), the greater the magnitude of the outcome, and the closer the result will be to the multiplicand (in this case, the multiplicand is *2*).

- **Next:** Complete the same steps as previously, using decimal fractions that are less than *one*. The same concepts will apply. Multiplying by a decimal fraction less than *one* will result in a smaller amount.

- **Next:** Point to or write out some improper and mixed fractions on a number line and ask students if their values are more or less than *one*. Once they are confident that they are all more than *one*, ask them to predict if the result of multiplying with a fraction or decimal fraction greater than *one* will result in more or less, such as $2\frac{1}{2} \times 3$, or 2.5×3. If they are unsure, remind them that they are multiplying with a *whole number and a little more*, so the result will always be more, just as with multiplying with any whole numbers.

- **Next:** Using the nine problem triads provided here, practice predicting—without calculating—whether the result will be more than, less than, or the same amount as each of the two factors and explain why. When students master these lists, scramble up the order of problems and then the sets, to make it more challenging.

- $\frac{8}{10} \times 2 =$ $\frac{10}{10} \times 2 =$ $\frac{12}{10} \times 2 =$
- $.9 \times 2 =$ $1.0 \times 2 =$ $1.1 \times 2 =$
- $\frac{1}{5} \times \frac{3}{4} =$ $\frac{5}{5} \times \frac{3}{4} =$ $\frac{7}{5} \times \frac{3}{4} =$
- $.80 \times .75 =$ $1.0 \times .75 =$ $1.2 \times .75 =$
- $\frac{2}{9} \times \frac{5}{9} =$ $\frac{9}{9} \times \frac{5}{9} =$ $\frac{10}{9} \times \frac{5}{9} =$
- $\frac{3}{4} \times 2\frac{3}{4} =$ $1 \times 2\frac{3}{4} =$ $2\frac{3}{4} \times 2\frac{3}{4} =$
- $\frac{4}{5} \times \frac{4}{3} =$ $\frac{4}{4} \times \frac{4}{3} =$ $\frac{4}{2} \times \frac{4}{3} =$
- $.12 \times .95 =$ $1.0 \times .95 =$ $9.5 \times .95 =$
- $.34 \times 1.2 =$ $1.0 \times 1.2 =$ $1.1 \times 1.2 =$

ACTIVITY 11.12: Fraction Division: Direction of the Outcome

Objective: To learn the meaning of fraction division and to predict the direction of the outcome of fraction division based on whether dividing by more than *one* or less than *one*. Fraction division is difficult to understand, and the goal of this activity is to provide understanding of what happens during fraction division. We do not address the procedure for fraction division, since that is a part of every curriculum. For each of the equations shown, students can perform the procedure for fraction division to see that the procedure results in the same amount as the number line and fraction tile result.

- **First:** Provide the students with some simple whole-number division problems such as *12 ÷ 4 = 3*. Ask the students if division always results in less than the dividend (the first number) and have them explain their reasoning. If needed, discuss that the dividend is being divided, or broken into, whole segments. In the earlier problem, there are three segments of four in *12*. Or, if *12* is broken into segments of *four*, there will be three of those segments.
- **Next:** Tell the students that you have MORE BIG NEWS! When dividing by a fraction that is less than *one* (a proper fraction), the result will ALWAYS BE MORE than the number being divided!
- **Next:** Discuss that when dividing by a proper fraction, it is often easier to conceptualize by using the following language: *2 ÷ ½ = 4* expressed as, "Two divided into segments of one-half, there will be four one-half segments. Or there are four one-half segments in two."
- **Next:** Using fraction tiles, align two whole segments along a number line bounded by *0* on the left and *2* on the right. Take four *½*-tiles and align them below the two whole segments and number line. Write the equation *2 ÷ ½ = 4* and have the students discuss the meaning of the equation in relation to the fraction tiles and number line. When dividing any number by a proper fraction (less than *one*), more of those small segments are needed to complete the whole dividend. Dividing by a proper fraction results in more than the dividend (first number).

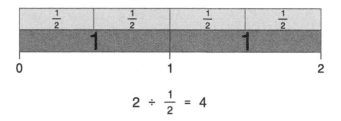

$$2 \div \frac{1}{2} = 4$$

- **Next:** Using fraction tiles and the same bounded number line, first write the equation *2 ÷ ¼ = 8*, then align the respective tiles and the number line. Ask the students to discuss what happened when the dividend *2* was divided into even smaller segments of *¼*. Ask if it is true or false that dividing by a proper fraction results in MORE and have students explain their reasoning.
- **Next:** Write out the equation *2½ ÷ ¼ = 10* and read it aloud: "Two and one-half divided into segments of one-fourth is the same amount as ten one-fourth segments, or there are ten one-fourth segments in two and one-half." Here we have a mixed fraction divided by a proper fraction. Using fraction tiles, align two whole tiles and a *½*-tile. Below these tiles, align ten *¼*-tiles. Discuss what division of fractions means with mixed fractions.

- **Next:** Write out the equation $\frac{1}{2} \div \frac{1}{8} = 4$ and read it aloud: "One-half divided into segments of one-eighth is the same amount as four one-eighth segments." There are four one-eighth segments in one-half. Here we have a proper fraction divided by a proper fraction that results in a number larger than either fraction. Align a $\frac{1}{2}$-tile below a bounded *0*-to-*1* number line and then place four $\frac{1}{8}$-tiles below the $\frac{1}{2}$-tile.
- **Next:** Write out the equation $3 \div 1\frac{1}{2} = 2$. Invite students to notice what is different about this equation than the previous equations in this activity. Discuss that this equation involves dividing by an improper fraction which has a value of more than *one*. When dividing by an improper fraction, the direction of the outcome will follow the rules of whole-number division since it means dividing by a "whole number and a little more." Use fraction tiles or draw a number line to demonstrate this equation.
- **Next:** Working in small groups, have students create their own fraction division problems and solve them using the fraction tiles and/or number line, then share their work with the whole class.

ACTIVITY 11.13: Fraction Arithmetic: Same Numbers, Different Operations[98]

Objective: To learn the relationship of fraction arithmetic operations through explicit practice using the same numbers for all operations.

- **First:** Present students with the fractions shown here, and have them predict whether the result of each of the arithmetic operations will result in more or less than the first number in the equation.
- **Next:** The students complete all four operations of addition, subtraction, multiplication, and division on the same fractions. Discuss the outcomes.

  - $\frac{3}{6} + \frac{2}{6}$ $\frac{3}{6} - \frac{2}{6}$ $\frac{3}{6} \times \frac{2}{6}$ $\frac{3}{6} \div \frac{2}{6}$
  - $2\frac{1}{3} + 1\frac{1}{3}$ $2\frac{1}{3} - 1\frac{1}{3}$ $2\frac{1}{3} \times 1\frac{1}{3}$ $2\frac{1}{3} \div 1\frac{1}{3}$
  - $4 + \frac{1}{3}$ $4 - \frac{1}{3}$ $4 \times \frac{1}{3}$ $4 \div \frac{1}{3}$
  - $\frac{2}{3} + \frac{1}{6}$ $\frac{2}{3} - \frac{1}{6}$ $\frac{2}{3} \times \frac{1}{6}$ $\frac{2}{3} \div \frac{1}{6}$
  - Pick any additional fraction pairs and continue the practice.

ACTIVITY 11.14: What's the Operation?

Objective: To learn to recognize the result of different operations with fractions and decimals.

- **First:** Without calculating, and knowing only the principles governing the direction of the outcome of fraction arithmetic, students figure out what the operation □ (+, −, ×, ÷) is. Have students explain their reasoning.

Write the correct operation in each □:

- $\frac{1}{3}$ □ $\frac{2}{3}$ = $\frac{2}{9}$
- $\frac{4}{5}$ □ $\frac{7}{5}$ = $\frac{11}{5}$
- $\frac{3}{4}$ □ $\frac{1}{4}$ = $\frac{2}{4}$
- $\frac{3}{4}$ □ $\frac{1}{4}$ = 3
- 4.0 □ $.5$ = 8
- $.25$ □ 1.50 = 1.75
- $.87$ □ $.62$ = $.25$
- $.60$ □ $.25$ = $.15$

ACTIVITY 11.15: Connecting the Area Model to the Number Line

Objective: To learn what the area model means in terms of the number line. Area models are frequently used to represent fractions in math curricula and classroom activities. However, research suggests that using a linear model results in a richer understanding of fractions than using area models.[99] In this activity, students connect an area model represented by fractions of a circle to the number line to gain a better understanding of the area models they will experience in most classrooms.

- **First:** Give the students a blank number line and have them label the number line with *0* on one end and *1* on the other end. Then ask them to mark the number line with $\frac{0}{2}$, $\frac{1}{2}$, and $\frac{2}{2}$. Next, have the students draw circles under each of those fractions on the number line, then divide the circles into two equal parts. For the circle beneath $\frac{1}{2}$, have them shade in one-half of the circle, and for the circle beneath $\frac{2}{2}$, have them shade in both halves of the circle. Engage the students in a discussion of the relationship of the circles and the fractions on the number line.
- **Next:** On separate number lines, continue with *thirds, fourths, fifths, sixths,* and so on, following the same procedure as earlier to create a number line with the respective fractions and corresponding circles. (See Figure for a number line divided into *fifths*, with the corresponding circles.)

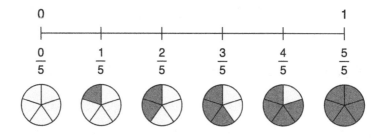

- **Next:** Provide more blank number lines and a mixed-up variety of fractions and have the students mark the blank number lines and draw the corresponding circles that match.

NOTES

1 Siegler et al., 2012.
2 Handel, 2016.
3 Lortie-Forgues et al., 2015.
4 Carroll & Gardner, 1865/1970.
5 Namkung et al., 2018.
6 Coulanges et al., 2021; Stricker et al., 2021.
7 Alibali & Sidney, 2015.
8 Siegler & Pyke, 2013; vanHoof et al., 2018.
9 Mix et al., 1999.
10 Begolli et al., 2020; Park et al., 2021.
11 Mazzocco & Devlin, 2008.
12 Jeong et al., 2007.
13 Tian et al., 2020.
14 Boyer & Levine, 2012.
15 Vanluydt et al., 2021.
16 Adapted from the protocol of Hurst & Cordes, 2019.
17 Moss & Case, 1999.
18 Gouet et al., 2020.
19 Kalra et al., 2020.
20 Vamvakoussi et al., 2018.
21 Tian et al., 2021a.
22 Hurst et al., 2020.
23 Gunderson et al., 2019; Moss & Case, 1999.
24 Mazzocco et al., 2013.
25 Malone & Fuchs, 2017.
26 McMullen & vanHoof, 2020.
27 Siegler & Lortie-Forgues, 2014.
28 Shtulman & Valcarcel, 2012.
29 McMullen et al., 2015.
30 Vamvakoussi & Vosniadou, 2010.
31 Vamvakoussi & Vosniadou, 2010.
32 Booth & Newton, 2012.
33 Meert et al., 2010; Shtulman & Valcarcel, 2012.
34 Opfer & DeVries, 2008.
35 Booth & Newton, 2012.
36 Siegler & Thompson, 2014.
37 Hamdan & Gunderson, 2017; Moss & Case, 1999; Saxe et al., 2013.
38 Dyson et al., 2020.
39 Fuchs et al., 2013.
40 Dyson et al., 2020; Fazio et al., 2016.
41 Saxe et al., 2013.
42 Fazio et al., 2016; Yu et al., in press.
43 Dyson et al., 2020; Fuchs et al., 2013; Gunderson et al., 2019; Saxe et al., 2013; Sidney et al., 2019.
44 Fuchs et al., 2013.

45 Bialystok & Codd, 2000.

46 Vamvakoussi & Vosniadou, 2010.

47 Miura et al., 1999.

48 Siegler & Pyke, 2013.

49 Lim, 2001; Miller et al., 2005.

50 Miller et al., 2000.

51 Paik & Mix, 2003.

52 Braithwaite & Siegler, 2018b.

53 Rinne et al., 2017.

54 Gabriel et al., 2013.

55 Meert et al., 2010.

56 Hurst & Cordes, 2018.

57 Mou et al., 2016.

58 Zhang et al., 2014.

59 DeWolf et al., 2014; Obersteiner et al., 2013.

60 DeWolf et al., 2016.

61 VanHoof et al., 2018.

62 Rittle-Johnson et al., 2001.

63 Mazzocco & Devlin, 2008.

64 Durkin & Rittle-Johnson, 2015; Ren & Gunderson, 2019.

65 Durkin & Rittle-Johnson, 2015; Resnick et al., 2019.

66 Bailey et al., 2014.

67 Siegler & Pyke, 2013.

68 Alibali & Sidney, 2015; Christou, 2015; Siegler & Lortie-Forgues, 2017.

69 Braithwaite et al., 2018.

70 Lortie-Forgues & Siegler, 2017; Obersteiner et al., 2016; Siegler & Lortie-Forgues, 2015.

71 Hiebert & Wearne, 1985; Siegler & Pyke, 2013.

72 Ma, 1999.

73 Braithwaite et al., 2019.

74 Siegler et al., 2020.

75 Braithwaite et al., 2017.

76 Tian et al., 2021b.

77 Braithwaite & Siegler, 2018a.

78 Ma, 1999.

79 Braithwaite et al., 2017.

80 Hiebert & Wearne, 1985.

81 Siegler et al., 2020.

82 Braithwaite et al., 2017.

83 Rittle-Johnson & Koedinger, 2009.

84 Bailey et al., 2017.

85 Sidney & Alibali, 2015.

86 Sidney et al., 2019.

87 Sidney, 2020; Sidney & Alibali, 2015.

88 Siegler & Lortie-Forgues, 2015.

89 Braithwaite et al., 2017.

90 Barbieri et al., 2020.

91 Moss & Case, 1999.
92 Moss & Case, 1999.
93 www.mathsisfun.com/numbers/fraction-number-line.htm
94 Mazzocco et al., 2013.
95 McMullen & vanHoof, 2020.
96 Braithwaite & Siegler, 2021.
97 Siegler & Lortie-Forgues, 2015.
98 Siegler et al., 2020.
99 Sidney et al., 2019.

REFERENCES

The following references were cited in this chapter. For additional selected references relevant to this chapter, please see Chapter 11 Supplemental References in eResources.

Alibali, M.W., & Sidney, P.G. (2015). Variability in the natural number bias: Who, when, how, and why. *Learning and Instruction, 37*, 56–61.

Bailey, D.H., Hansen, N., & Jordan, N.C. (2017). The codevelopment of children's fraction arithmetic skill and fraction magnitude understanding. *Journal of Educational Psychology, 109*, 509–519.

Bailey, D.H., Siegler, R.S., & Geary, D.C. (2014). Early predictors of middle school fraction knowledge. *Developmental Science, 17*, 775–785.

Barbieri, C.A., Rodrigues, J., Dyson, N., & Jordan, N.C. (2020). Improving fraction understanding in sixth graders with mathematics difficulties: Effects of a number line approach combined with cognitive learning strategies. *Journal of Educational Psychology, 112*, 628–648.

Begolli, K.N., Booth, J.L., Holmes, C.A., & Newcombe, N.S. (2020). How many apples make a quarter? The challenge of discrete proportional formats. *Journal of Experimental Child Psychology, 192*, 104774.

Bialystok, E., & Codd, J. (2000). Representing quantity beyond whole numbers: Some, none, part. *Canadian Journal of Experimental Psychology, 54*, 117–128.

Booth, J.L., & Newton, K.J. (2012). Fractions: Could they really be the gatekeeper's doorman? *Contemporary Educational Psychology, 37*, 247–253.

Boyer, T.W., & Levine, S.C. (2012). Child proportional scaling: Is 1/3 = 2/6 = 3/9 = 4/12? *Journal of Experimental Child Psychology, 111*, 516–533.

Braithwaite, D.W., Leib, E.R., Siegler, R.S., & McMullen, J. (2019). Individual differences in fraction arithmetic learning. *Cognitive Psychology, 112*, 81–98.

Braithwaite, D.W., Pyke, A.A., & Siegler, R.S. (2017). A computational model of fraction arithmetic. *Psychological Review, 124*, 603–625.

Braithwaite, D.W., & Siegler, R.S. (2018a). Children learn spurious associations in their math textbooks: Examples from fraction arithmetic. *Journal of Experimental Psychology: Learning, Memory, and Cognition, 44*, 1765–1777.

Braithwaite, D.W., & Siegler, R.S. (2018b). Developmental changes in the whole number bias. *Developmental Science, 21*, e12541.

Braithwaite, D.W., & Siegler, R.S. (2021). Putting fractions together. *Journal of Educational Psychology, 113*, 556–571.

Braithwaite, D.W., Tian, J., & Siegler, R.S. (2018). Do children understand fraction addition? *Developmental Science, 21*, e12601.

Carroll, L., & Gardner, M. (1865/1970). *The Annotated Alice* (pp. 167–345). Forum Books.

Christou, K.P. (2015). Natural number bias in operations with missing numbers. *ZDM Mathematics Education, 47*, 747–758.

Coulanges, L., Abreu-Mendoza, R.A., Varma, S., Uncapher, M.R., Gazzaley, A., Anguera, J., & Rosenberg-Lee, M. (2021). Linking inhibitory control to math achievement via comparison of conflicting decimal numbers. *Cognition, 214*, 104767.

DeWolf, M., Chiang, J.N., Bassok, M., Holyoak, K.J., & Monti, M.M. (2016). Neural representations of magnitude for natural and rational numbers. *NeuroImage, 141*, 304–312.

DeWolf, M., Grounds, M.A., Bassok, M., & Holyoak, K.J. (2014). Magnitude comparison with different types of rational numbers. *Journal of Experimental Psychology: Human Perception and Performance, 40*, 71–82.

Durkin, K., & Rittle-Johnson, B. (2015). Diagnosing misconceptions: Revealing changing decimal fraction knowledge. *Learning and Instruction, 37*, 21–29.

Dyson, N.I., Jordan, N.C., Rodrigues, J., Barbieri, C., & Rinne, L. (2020). A fraction sense intervention for sixth graders with or at risk for mathematics difficulties. *Remedial and Special Education, 41*, 244–254.

Fazio, L.K., Kennedy, C.A., & Siegler, R.S. (2016). Improving children's knowledge of fraction magnitudes. *PLoS ONE, 11*(10), e0165243.

Fuchs, L.S., Schumacher, R.F., Long, J., Namkung, J., Hamlett, C.L., Cirino, P.T., Jordan, N.C., Siegler, R.S., Gersten, R., & Changas, P. (2013). Improving at-risk learners' understanding of fractions. *Journal of Educational Psychology, 105*, 683–700.

Gabriel, F.C., Szűcs, D., & Content, A. (2013). The development of the mental representations of the magnitude of fractions. *PLoS One, 8*(11), e80016.

Gouet, C., Carvajal, S., Halberda, J., & Peña, M. (2020). Training nonsymbolic proportional reasoning in children and its effects on their symbolic math abilities. *Cognition, 197*, 104154.

Gunderson, E.A., Hamdan, N., Hildebrand, L., & Bartek, V. (2019). Number line unidimensionality is a critical feature for promoting fraction magnitude concepts. *Journal of Experimental Child Psychology, 187*, 104657.

Hamdan, N., & Gunderson, E.A. (2017). The number line is a critical spatial-numerical representation: Evidence from a fraction intervention. *Developmental Psychology, 53*, 587–596.

Handel, M.J. (2016). What do people do at work? A profile of U.S. jobs from the survey of workplace Skills, Technology, and Management Practice (STAMP). *Journal of Labor Market Research, 49*, 177–197.

Hiebert, J., & Wearne, D. (1985). A model of students' decimal computation procedures. *Cognition and Instruction, 2*, 175–205.

Hurst, M.A., & Cordes, S. (2018). Children's understanding of fraction and decimal symbols and the notation-specific relation to pre-algebra ability. *Journal of Experimental Child Psychology, 168*, 32–48.

Hurst, M.A., & Cordes, S. (2019). Talking about proportion: Fraction labels impact numerical interference in non-symbolic proportional reasoning. *Developmental Science, 22*, e12790.

Hurst, M.A., Massaro, M., & Cordes, S. (2020). Fraction magnitude: Mapping between symbolic and spatial representations of proportion. *Journal of Numerical Cognition, 6*, 204–230.

Jeong, Y., Levine, S.C., & Huttenlocher, J. (2007). The development of proportional reasoning: Effect of continuous v. discrete quantities. *Journal of Cognition and Development, 8*, 237–256.

Kalra, P.B., Binzak, J.V., Matthews, P.G., & Hubbard, E.M. (2020). Symbolic fractions elicit an analog magnitude representation in school-age children. *Journal of Experimental Child Psychology, 195*, 104844.

Lim, B.S. (2001). Relationships between linguistics and understanding fractions by monolingual English speaking students and bilingual Korean American students. *Focus on Learning Problems in Mathematics, 23,* 85–101.

Lortie-Forgues, H., & Siegler, R.S. (2017). Conceptual knowledge of decimal arithmetic. *Journal of Educational Psychology, 109,* 374–386.

Lortie-Forgues, H., Tian, J., & Siegler, R.S. (2015). Why is learning fraction and decimal arithmetic so difficult? *Developmental Review, 38,* 201–221.

Ma, L.-P. (1999). *Knowing and teaching elementary mathematics.* Lawrence Erlbaum Associates.

Malone, A.S., & Fuchs, L.S. (2017). Error patterns in ordering fractions among at-risk fourth-grade students. *Journal of Learning Disabilities, 50,* 337–352.

Mazzocco, M.M.M., & Devlin, K.T. (2008). Parts and "holes": Gaps in rational number sense among children with vs. without mathematical learning disabilities. *Developmental Science, 11,* 681–691.

Mazzocco, M.M.M., Myers, G.F., Lewis, K.E., Hanich, L.B., & Murphy, M.M. (2013). Limited knowledge of fraction representations differentiates middle school students with mathematics learning disability (dyscalculia) versus low mathematics achievement. *Journal of Experimental Psychology, 115,* 371–387.

McMullen, J., Laakkonen, E., Hannula-Sormunen, M., & Lehtinen, E. (2015). Modeling the developmental trajectories of rational number concept(s). *Learning and Instruction, 37,* 14–20.

McMullen, J., & vanHoof, J. (2020). The role of rational number density knowledge in mathematical development. *Learning and Instruction, 65,* 101228.

Meert, G., Grégoire, J., & Noël, M.-P. (2010). Comparing the magnitude of two fractions with common components: Which representations are used by 10- and 12-year-olds? *Journal of Experimental Child Psychology, 107,* 244–259.

Miller, K.F., Kelly, M., & Zhou, X. (2005). Learning mathematics in China and the United States:

Cross-cultural insights into the nature and course of preschool mathematical development. In J.I.D. Campbell (Ed.), *Handbook of mathematical cognition* (pp. 163–178). Psychology Press.

Miller, K.F., Major, S.M., Shu, H., & Zhang, H. (2000). Ordinal knowledge: Number names and number concepts in Chinese and English. *Canadian Journal of Experimental Psychology, 54,* 129–139.

Miura, I.T., Okamoto, Y., Vlahovic-Stetic, V., Kim, C.C., & Han, J.H. (1999). Language supports for children's understanding of numerical fractions: Cross-national comparisons. *Journal of Experimental Child Psychology, 74,* 356–365.

Mix, K.S., Levine, S.C., & Huttenlocher, J. (1999). Early fraction calculation ability. *Developmental Psychology, 35,* 164–174.

Moss, J., & Case, R. (1999). Developing children's understanding of the relational numbers: A new model and an experimental curriculum. *Journal for Research in Mathematics Education, 30,* 122–147.

Mou, Y., Li, Y., Hoard, M.K., Nugent, L.D., Chu, F.W., Rouder, J.N., & Geary, D.C. (2016). Developmental foundations of children's fraction magnitude knowledge. *Cognitive Development, 39,* 141–153.

Namkung, J.M., Fuchs, L.S., & Koziol, N. (2018). Does initial learning about the meaning of fractions present similar challenges for students with and without adequate whole number skill? *Learning and Individual Differences, 61,* 151–157.

Obersteiner, A., vanDooren, W., vanHoof, J., & Verschaffel, L. (2013). The natural number bias and magnitude representation in fraction comparison by expert mathematicians. *Learning and Instruction, 28,* 64–72.

Obersteiner, A., vanHoof, J., Verschaffel, L., & vanDooren, W. (2016). Who can escape the natural number bias in rational number tasks? A study involving students and experts. *British Journal of Psychology, 107,* 537–555.

Opfer, J.E., & DeVries, J.M., (2008). Representational change and magnitude estimation: Why young children can make more accurate salary comparisons than adults. *Cognition, 108*, 843–849.

Paik, J.H., & Mix, K.S. (2003). U.S. and Korean children's comprehension of fraction names: A reexamination of cross-national differences. *Child Development, 74*, 144–154.

Park, Y., Viegut, A.A., & Matthews, P.G. (2021). More than the sum of its parts: Exploring the development of ratio magnitude versus simple magnitude perception. *Developmental Science, 24*, e13043.

Ren, K., & Gunderson, E.A. (2019). Malleability of whole-number and fraction biases in decimal comparison. *Developmental Psychology, 55*, 2263–2274.

Resnick, I., Rinne, L., Barbieri, C., & Jordan, N.C. (2019). Children's reasoning about decimals and its relation to fraction learning and mathematics achievement. *Journal of Educational Psychology, 111*, 604–618.

Rinne, L.F., Ye, A., & Jordan, N.C. (2017). Development of fraction comparison strategies: A latent transition analysis. *Developmental Psychology, 53*, 713–730.

Rittle-Johnson, B., & Koedinger, K. (2009). Iterating between lessons on concepts and procedures can improve mathematics knowledge. *British Journal of Educational Psychology, 79*, 483–500.

Rittle-Johnson, B., Siegler, R.S., & Alibali, M.W. (2001). Developing conceptual understanding and procedural skill in mathematics: An iterative process. *Journal of Educational Psychology, 93*, 346–362.

Saxe, G.B., Diakow, R., & Gearhart, M. (2013). Towards curricular coherence in integers and fractions: A study of the efficacy of a lesson sequence that uses the number line as the principal representation context. *ZDM Mathematics Education, 45*, 343–364.

Shtulman, A., & Valcarcel, J. (2012). Scientific knowledge suppresses but does not supplant earlier intuitions. *Cognition, 124*, 209–215.

Sidney, P.G. (2020). Children's learning from implicit analogies during instruction: Evidence from fraction division. *Cognitive Development, 56*, 100956.

Sidney, P.G., & Alibali, M.W. (2015). Making connections in math: Activating a prior knowledge analogue matters for learning. *Journal of Cognition and Development, 16*, 160–185.

Sidney, P.G., Thompson, C.A., & Rivera, F.D. (2019). Number lines, but not area models, support children's accuracy and conceptual models of fraction division. *Contemporary Educational Psychology, 58*, 288–298.

Siegler, R.S., Duncan, G.J., Davis,-Kean, P.E., Duckworth, K., Claessens, A., Engel, M., Susperreguy, M.I., & Chen, M. (2012). Early predictors of high school mathematics achievement. *Psychological Science, 23*, 691–697.

Siegler, R.S., Im, S.-H., Schiller, L., Tian, J., & Braithwaite, D. (2020). The sleep of reason produces monsters: How and when biased input shapes mathematics learning. *Annual Review of Developmental Psychology, 2*, 413–435.

Siegler, R.S., & Lortie-Forgues, H. (2014). An integrative theory of numerical development. *Child Development Perspectives, 8*, 144–150.

Siegler, R.S., & Lortie-Forgues, H. (2015). Conceptual knowledge of fraction arithmetic. *Journal of Educational Psychology, 107*, 909–918.

Siegler, R.S., & Lortie-Forgues, H. (2017). Hard lessons: Why rational number arithmetic is so difficult for so many people. *Current Directions in Psychological Science, 26*, 346–351.

Siegler, R.S., & Pyke, A.A. (2013). Developmental and individual differences in understanding of fractions. *Developmental Psychology, 49*, 1994–2004.

Siegler, R.S., & Thompson, C.A. (2014). Numerical landmarks are useful—except when they're not. *Journal of Experimental Child Psychology, 120*, 39–58.

Stricker, J., Vogel, S.E., Schöneburg-Lehnert, S., Krohn, T., Dögnitz, S., Jud, N., Spirk, M., Windhaber, M.-C., Schneider, M., & Grabner, R.H. (2021). Interference between naïve and scientific theories occurs in mathematics and is related to mathematical achievement. *Cognition, 214*, 104789.

Tian, J., Bartek, V., Rahman, M.Z., & Gunderson, E.A. (2021a). Learning improper fractions with the number line and the area model. *Journal of Cognition and Development, 22*, 305–327.

Tian, J., Braithwaite, D.W., & Siegler, R.S. (2020). How do people choose among rational number notations? *Cognitive Psychology, 123*, 101333.

Tian, J., Braithwaite, D.W., & Siegler, R.S. (2021b). Distributions of textbook problems predict student learning: Data from decimal arithmetic. *Journal of Educational Psychology, 113*, 516–529.

Vamvakoussi, X., Christou, K.P., & Vosniadou, S. (2018). Bridging psychological and educational research on rational number knowledge. *Journal of Numerical Cognition, 4*, 84–106.

Vamvakoussi, X., & Vosniadou, S. (2010). How many decimals are there between two fractions? Aspects of secondary school students' understanding of rational numbers and their notation. *Cognition and Instruction, 28*, 181–209.

VanHoof, J., Degrande, T., Ceulemans, E., Verschaffel, L., & vanDooren, W. (2018). Towards a mathematically more correct understanding of rational numbers: A longitudinal study with upper elementary school learners. *Learning and Individual Differences, 61*, 99–108.

Vanluydt, E., Supply, A.-S., Verschaffel, L., & vanDooren, W. (2021). The importance of specific mathematical language for early proportional reasoning. *Early Childhood Research Quarterly, 55*, 193–200.

Yu, S., Kim, D., Fitzsimmons, D.J., Mielicki, M.K., Thompson, C.A., & Opfer, J.E. (in press). From integers to fractions: Developing a coherent understanding of proportional magnitude. *Developmental Psychology, 59*.

Zhang, L., Fang, Q., Gabriel, F.C., & Szűcs, D. (2014). The componential processing of fractions in adults and children: Effects of stimuli variability and contextual interference. *Frontiers in Psychology, 5*, 981.

Chapter 12

Written Story Problems

Mr. Martinez's swimming pool is 36 feet long and 24 feet wide. Mr. Martinez wants to build a wooden fence around it, leaving a 6-foot-wide strip of lawn all around the pool. How much will the fence cost if 3 feet of fencing costs $10 (cost inclusive of all materials and labor)?[1]

To the adult eye, written story problems like this one look simple and straightforward. The information is all there, so all one must do is add here, multiply there, and you have your answer. To a child's eye, however, they are the most complex tasks in elementary arithmetic. That is because story problems call upon every academic and cognitive skill the child has acquired so far—basic arithmetic facts, numerical relations, strategies, and procedures; vocabulary, verbal comprehension, reasoning, and reading—not to mention attention, inhibition, cognitive flexibility, and working memory. Remarkably, as we will see, even these skills are sometimes not enough, and therein lies the problem. This chapter will review the sorts of academic and cognitive demands that written story problems make on young students, as well as the many ways these problems can trip children up.[2]

Before getting into those details, however, it is important to point out what a story problem is—and is not—beginning with what it is not. Contrary to appearances, a story problem (often called a "word problem") is not an exercise in real-life problem-solving. Take, for example, the typical story problem shown here. In real life, Mr. Martinez's problem is that he wants to build a fence around his pool and would like to know how much it will cost. Between this real-life version of the problem and the school version of the problem lie myriad decisions, measurements, and considerations: what materials to use and their relative costs, the additional cost of design options and maintenance, overtime charges for weekend labor, and so forth. The school version represents the tail end of a complex series of qualitative and quantitative decisions.[3]

The difficulty in the classroom is that children can sense the contrived nature of many story problems and often learn to deal with them in one of two ways. Either they side with common sense and what they know or they learn to deal with them in school mode, in which common sense and actual experience play little part. For example, in response to this question:

What will be the temperature of water in a container if you pour into it one jug of water at 80°F and one jug of water at 40°F?

DOI: 10.4324/9781003157656-16

many fifth-graders in one study replied *120°*—even though they had no trouble correctly answering:

What will the water be like if you pour hot water and cold water into one container?[4]

Real-life problems often contain irrelevant information, or have no solution, or have multiple solutions, or have a solution that does not require any arithmetic. In contrast, much of students' school experience implicitly teaches them to assume that story problems will have only relevant information and one solution, reached by the arithmetic they have been taught. When researchers asked students in grades one through six to solve story problems that were each designed to violate one of those assumptions, only 38 percent of the children responded correctly, ranging from 16 percent of first-graders to 56 percent of sixth-graders. The most difficult assumption to overcome was that a problem must have a solution (18 percent correct). The easiest of the assumptions to get past was that all information must be relevant (still only 57 percent correct),[5] perhaps because many story problems in textbooks and on standardized exams now include irrelevant details, an issue taken up later in this chapter. Unfortunately, the study failed to compare children's performance on these non-standard problems to that on the standard problems they also solved, so it is difficult to interpret these findings other than to say that such assumptions are ubiquitous and reflect a significant divide between real-world and school problem-solving experience.

So, story problems are not real-life problems. But that is not to say that real-life experience does not occasionally help with school story problems. If a student's answer to a recipe problem, for example, is three-quarters of an egg, experience might see that as a red flag indicating that the problem's goal, strategy, or results deserve review.[6] In fact, children with good real-life problem-solving skills also tend to have good school story-problem solving skills.[7] In general, however, school story problems are not lessons about real life.

Rather, story problems are contrived to teach mathematical language—that is, the meaning and syntax of verbal expressions that convey quantitative relationships and questions about them. Three steps are involved in solving a typical story problem: reading the problem, making sense of what it is asking, and solving it arithmetically. Some of those skills have been introduced in previous chapters; we will reintroduce them here as they pertain to story problems, beginning with reading the problem and then skipping to the arithmetic solution. The bulk of the chapter will then address the most difficult step for many students: understanding what the problem is asking.

VERBAL COMPREHENSION AND READING

For most students, reading well-written story problems is not unduly challenging. A well-written story problem features words, objects, and settings familiar to children at their grade level. Unfortunately for some children, even reading the words of the problem is so difficult that they never get to the math part at all. Who are these children?

Some of these children have difficulty reading because of neurodevelopmental conditions. One such condition, previously discussed in Chapter 6, is a developmental language disorder that can make it difficult for children to discriminate between words that sound similar, follow spoken syntax, understand language meaning, learn verbal sequences, and remember the words they hear. It affects both their comprehension of oral language and their ability to express themselves verbally. Reading acquisition can be challenging. Any aspect of math that depends on verbal learning (e.g., counting or remembering arithmetic facts) can be especially difficult, even though these children may be able to manage concepts that can be grasped non-verbally. Research suggests that about half of the children with a developmental language disorder or significant delay also have severe math difficulties.[8] A study of third-graders with a developmental language disorder revealed that their elementary story-problem solving skills, as demonstrated on a task in which the stories were read aloud to them, fell significantly behind those of their typical classmates.[9] Children with dyslexia, most of whom share some of the phonological speech-sounds difficulties as those with a more global developmental language disorder, have particular difficulty learning to read and may lack sufficient vocabulary knowledge or syntactic awareness to understand the problem's words and sentences.[10] Other children have little trouble reading individual words but struggle to comprehend connected text.[11] We mention them here, rather than in the section that follows on understanding what the problem is asking, because their reading comprehension difficulties are broader than simply making their way through the mathematical language. Children who are deaf or hard of hearing also typically have trouble learning to read but can benefit from being read to in American Sign Language to decipher the problem's text.[12]

A much larger group of students may have trouble understanding the basic words and sentences in these problems because they are growing up in low-income homes with few books and little opportunity to develop the necessary syntax and vocabulary.[13] Research has shown that children who are read to by parents or caregivers have been exposed to more than a million more words by the time they turn six than children who are not read to.[14] Indeed, children from low-income homes demonstrate significant disparities in language processing and vocabulary by the time they turn two, and these disparities have a negative cascading effect as the children grow.[15] Others bring to school with them ethnic and regional vernaculars, with their subtle differences in the use of common words—prepositions, conjunctions, relative pronouns—that make the often formulaic language of story problems sound foreign to their ears.[16] And many may find that story problem situations do not resemble their own life experience.

Finally, children new to English can find reading story problems particularly vexing. A long list of troubling linguistic features disadvantage these children. Problematic grammatical structures include adverbial and relative clauses, long noun and prepositional phrases, article usage, and the passive voice. Line breaks that disrupt syntax can also pose a problem. Unfamiliar vocabulary and idioms, polysemous (i.e., multi-definition) words, words without cognates in the native language, logical connectors, and terms belonging to unfamiliar, mainstream American culture (*coupon*, *baseball card*) can all prove confounding. Researchers recommend simplifying the story-problem language and providing dictionaries or glossaries for children on large-scale assessments.[17] Indeed, one study revealed that on stories with uncomplicated language, fourth-grade English-language learners performed comparably to native speakers.[18] (Of course, a certain amount of linguistic simplification across the board in textbook problems, as well as on exams, would perhaps simply reflect better writing generally.) As will be discussed later, some words and phrases frequently found in story problems are exceptionally difficult even for typical native speakers. Some of these terms are also difficult to alter because they go to the heart of the mathematical question itself.

Thus, a story problem is first and foremost a reading and language exercise.[19] All students will need to be able to read the words and sentences of the problem, or understand and remember them if the problem is read to them, before they can approach the mathematics in it.

Importantly, however, while adequate basic language and reading skills are necessary for solving story problems, they are not sufficient. As we will see, many other skills are required.

STORY-PROBLEM ARITHMETIC

As with basic reading skill, so also with basic arithmetic computation: It is necessary but not sufficient for solving story problems. Many children who can read a problem and independently do the required calculations with ease are unable to understand what the problem is asking.[20] To this point, researchers asked children at the end of first grade to answer some story problems (read aloud to them) and then to perform the same calculations independently of the stories. The children's straightforward calculations were accurate more than three times more often than were their story-problem solutions,[21] suggesting that, indeed, the trouble was in understanding the problem, not the arithmetic solution.

Nevertheless, basic arithmetic skill is necessary. While much of the arithmetic embedded in textbook story problems is relatively straightforward, there are children who struggle with it for all the many reasons discussed in the chapters leading up to this one. Children with serious difficulties in understanding numbers and how they relate to each other can be expected to have particular trouble understanding questions about numerical relationships when presented in writing. As one scholar pointed out, "It is impossible to put two numbers into a relationship unless the numbers themselves are solidly present in the child's mind."[22]

Another group of children who may have trouble with the arithmetic are students who learned some arithmetic in one language (e.g., Spanish) and then switched to a second language (e.g., English). As discussed in Chapter 10, people tend to be more fluent in verbally learned arithmetic facts (e.g., multiplication) in the language in which it is first learned.[23] Emerging bilingualism may slow such students down as they wrestle with the multiple linguistic and arithmetic demands of story problems.

Not all children use formal arithmetic strategies for solving story problems, however. As a result, the context in which an arithmetic problem is presented in the story can make a difference in the child's ability to compute the result. For example, researchers gave the following two problems to a group of third-graders:

> *Marshall wants to buy chocolates. Each chocolate costs 50 cents. He wants to buy 3 chocolates. How much money does he need?*
> *Marshall wants to buy chocolates. Each chocolate costs 3 cents. He wants to buy 50 chocolates. How much money does he need?*

The first version was easy to solve by mentally adding up "fifty plus fifty is one hundred. That's one dollar. Plus fifty cents is a dollar fifty." Without automatic knowledge of the commutativity principle of multiplication, however, the second version (of the same arithmetic problem) seemed unfeasible using the same repeated addition method, and many children gave up. When asked to write an equation, they could do so for the first version but not the second. The researchers concluded that children learn to solve problems with small multipliers, like the first one, before they learn to solve those like the second.[24]

Finally, some of the arithmetic can be expected to involve more thought, time, effort, and working memory. Multi-digit computations, particularly those requiring trading, require more cognitive resources than single-digit computations, as do counting and decomposition strategies and problems involving more than one step for solution. Other problems raise conflicts between firmly entrenched mental models (e.g., multiplication as repeated addition) and the given numbers (e.g., a decimal fraction as multiplier). Faced with this cognitive workload, students sometimes try to find easier strategies, with more or less success.[25]

WHAT IS THE PROBLEM ASKING?

At their most basic, written story problems are about quantities and their relationships. Typically, a one-step problem offers two propositions containing quantitative and relational information and asks a question that requires arithmetic to answer. The people, objects, and settings are essentially merely cover stories. For example: *Hannah went to the store to buy 6 apples. The apples cost 30 cents each. How much did Hannah's 6 apples cost?* In this story, neither Hannah nor the store nor the identity of her purchases is mathematically relevant. Strictly speaking, the problem is about six items each costing 30 cents, and the question is, *What is the total cost?* For many students, the most difficult part of solving story problems is getting past the window dressing to the stripped-down numerical relations and what the problem is asking.[26] Research has explored what makes this task so difficult; what follows are some of its findings.

Complex Grammar

Mathematical language is dense, with lots of information bits packed in tightly and little redundancy to give them air to breathe—much like income tax forms or poetry, as some have noted.[27] Adding even a single word can change the entire meaning of a math phrase. For example, *five more than three* means *3 + 5*, while *five is more than three* means *5 > 3*.[28] In this sense, mathematical language is merciless.

When such terse language is clearly and straightforwardly written, the information it conveys is usually accessible. However, not all story problems are optimally written. On the one hand, long sentences with grammatical twists and turns, such as participial phrases (. . . *leaving a 6-foot-wide strip of lawn all around the pool*), object clauses (*Ollie knew that Olga had 8 pencils*), conditional clauses (*If Maya wanted to buy 5 notebooks, . . .*), and other adverbial clauses (*After 5 kittens ran away, . . .*) can be particularly difficult to decipher, particularly if the clause comes at the beginning of a sentence.[29] These sorts of clauses can be especially draining for students with limited verbal working memory, since the information in the leading clause must be kept in mind while one is reading the rest of the sentence. Grammatical embellishments such as these are perfectly legitimate and often work well in less dense literary narrative but can drain mental resources in condensed mathematical prose. By contrast, simple and compound sentences are typically much easier to access and remember.

On the other hand, some story-problem sentences are written too telegraphically. Researchers suggest that such painfully compact sentences can be made more readable by adding just a few words here and there to loosen them up and clarify their meaning—*Robert had some marbles. He won 3 more marbles. Now he has 5 marbles. How many marbles did Robert have at the beginning?* Or, *Everett and Calvin have 9 crayons altogether. Three of these crayons belong to Everett. The rest belong to Calvin. How many crayons does Calvin have?*[30] Although this makes the problems a bit longer, their improved clarity actually reduces the cognitive demands.

Indeed, children read and write best when they can do so the way they speak, and few children speak in grammatically convoluted sentences. Neither do they typically use the passive voice, the conditional tense, or unfamiliar words. Children tend to speak in short words, although a long, familiar word such as *television* should not be a problem for most. Some experts also advise using the present tense, but a problem involving a quantitative change over time—*Zara had 3 pansies. Then Noor gave her 5 more pansies. How many pansies does Zara have now?*—would be indecipherable in a single tense. When the grammatical structure of a question is beyond their understanding, children tend to hear and respond to a less complex, more familiar question.[31] Indeed, if a child seems puzzled or produces an incorrect answer, one can often diagnose the misunderstanding by asking the child to repeat or paraphrase the question. In such cases, they are more likely to remember the question they thought they were answering than the grammatically baffling question they were asked. Such queries can be especially productive above second grade.[32]

This is not necessarily an argument for eliminating difficult elements from story problems. It is, however, a caution that any of these elements could be an obstacle to understanding what the problem is asking, particularly for children with language or reading impairments, those with reduced language exposure, and those who are new to English.[33] (Indeed, when researchers tracked children's eye movements as they read story problems, they found that low-ability students focused on different parts of the problem than high-ability students did.[34]) It is also an invitation to regard such occurrences as opportunities to teach math vocabulary and syntax.[35]

Order of the Numerical Information and Position of the Unknown

Reading is by its very nature sequential. When one reads a story problem from its beginning to its end, one takes in the information—the two bits of quantitative information, their relationship, and the question—in the order in which it appears. For example, *Billy had 3 baseball cards. Then Jillian gave him 5 more. How many baseball cards does Billy have now?* In this example, the unknown, to-be-calculated bit of information is mentioned last. This order coincides with the order most commonly encountered in standard symbolic arithmetic statements ($3 + 5 =$ ___), making the problem feel familiar. The youngest children may find problems with the larger number mentioned first ($5 + 3 =$ ___) easier, because they can use the counting-on strategy directly for adding.[36] However, sometimes story problems mention the unknown in the second, or even first, position: *Billy had some baseball cards. Then Jillian gave him 5 more. Now Billy has 8 baseball cards. How many baseball cards did Billy have in the beginning?* The symbolic arithmetic statement then reads: ___ $+ 5 = 8$, which can be confusing to children who have no experience with non-standard statements. In fact, research has found that problems with the unknown in the first position are the most difficult for young students; indeed, even college students struggle when the information in story problems is given out of the expected order.[37] Such problems are particularly vexing for children with severe math learning difficulties[38] or verbal working memory trouble.

However, when researchers instead worded the initial statement as a question—*How many baseball cards does Billy have now? Billy had 3 baseball cards. Then Jillian gave him 5 more*—children of both high and low math ability performed better than when the question appeared at the end. In fact, the improvement was more striking in children of low math ability, as well as for more difficult problems. The researchers concluded that posing the question first provides a context for the subsequent information, a kind of heads-up, making it easier to mentally organize it for solution.[39]

Finally, problems requiring the non-commutative operations of subtraction and division can present an obstacle when the order of the numbers in the problem is inconsistent with the order required for algorithmic solution. For example: *Billy and Jillian have 8 baseball cards altogether. Billy has 3 baseball cards. How many baseball cards does Jillian have?* The solution calls for subtraction, and here the numbers appear in the problem in the same order in which they should appear in the equation: $8 - 3 =$ ___. By contrast: *Billy had 3 baseball cards. Then Jillian gave him some more baseball cards. Now Billy has 8 baseball cards. How many baseball cards did Jillian give him?* In this case, the arithmetic statement still reads $8 - 3 =$ ___, but the numbers appear in the opposite order in the problem text. Such inconsistency requires more attention, working memory, mental energy, and understanding.[40] (Technically, the arithmetic statement reads $3 +$ ___ $= 8$, an equally confusing non-standard format.) Similarly, simple division problems in which the divisor appears first in the text, followed by the dividend, can demand extra attention.[41] Two-step problems create an even greater challenge. Thus, the order in which information appears in the problem can affect problem difficulty.

All that having been said, however, life often presents arithmetic problems in non-standard order, one of many good reasons for children to master non-standard equations and thoroughly understand the equivalence meaning of the = sign, as discussed in Chapter 10.

Inadequate and Irrelevant Information

As noted at the beginning of this section, the second and most crucial step in addressing a story problem is understanding the underlying mathematical relationships and question. Once those fundamentals are laid bare, the next question is: *Do I have enough information to solve this problem?* In real life, the answer is frequently *No.* The possibility that one might not have enough information, or even what sort of information one would require to solve a particular problem, is often not addressed in the classroom. Certainly, a student's overwhelming experience is that story problems do have sufficient pertinent information. It is thus understandable that they would expect this always to be the case, leaving students unprepared for real-life situations in which it is not.

Often, however, school math problems do contain irrelevant information. For example: *Hannah went to the store to buy 6 apples, a loaf of bread, and a quart of milk. The apples cost 30 cents each. How much did Hannah's 6 apples cost?* Part of the student's job here is to determine which bits of information are relevant to answering the question. In this case, the bread and milk can be ignored. The inclusion of irrelevant numbers, however, may be problematic for children with poor working memory and for children with serious math difficulties, who have specific trouble remembering numbers.[42] For example: *Hannah went to the store to buy apples, bread, and milk. If apples cost 30 cents each, a loaf of bread costs 3 dollars, and a quart of milk costs 4 dollars, how much do 6 apples cost?* As one reads the problem, working memory must hold on to *30 cents*, *3 dollars*, and *4 dollars* until the end, at which point it becomes clear that only one of those numbers is needed and the other two can be forgotten. By that time, the relevant number, *30 cents*, may well have been forgotten, too. Children know that story problems are all about the numbers, so that is where they focus their attention. If a problem contains extraneous numbers, children will find them more difficult to ignore than non-quantitative text.[43]

Thus, one significant downside to including irrelevant details is that it takes longer to read the problem, putting extra strain on attention and working memory, a particular problem for children with attention and reading difficulties. Under those circumstances, irrelevant numbers can distract and mislead the student, steering some children to the default option of just adding up all the numbers. Research has found that including irrelevant information in story problems causes a significant drop in performance, particularly among children with general learning difficulties, who may do poorly on them for reasons unrelated to their understanding of the math.[44] Researchers who tried enriching story problems in the hope of making them more interesting or giving the problem more context found that the effort produced no benefit in solution accuracy for any student.[45] Indeed, children do best with just enough information than with either too much or not enough.[46]

A second and broader downside to including irrelevant information in story problems is that irrelevant information generally does not present itself in story problems the way it does in real life. Take this problem, for example: *Hannah wants to bake three apple pies. Each pie calls for 6 apples. She goes to the grocery store, where she sees that bananas cost 29 cents each, pears cost 69 cents each, and apples, which are now on sale, cost 39 cents each. How much will Hannah have to pay for enough apples to make her pies?* In real life, Hannah would look at her recipe, figure out how many apples she will need altogether ("Let's see, three sixes is eighteen"). She would go to the store to buy 18 apples, will be glad to see they are on sale, may estimate that they will cost her less than ten dollars, pay for them, and leave. If she is particularly fond of bananas, say, she may check out their price, and may even add them to her cart. But the prices of bananas and pears, although in full view, would not have the same salience to her at that moment as the price of apples and will visually and mentally fade into the background and probably be forgotten. Written out as a story problem, however, this irrelevant information has as much visual presence as the price of apples. Indeed, the irrelevant information accounts for 17 percent of the problem's words—and 63 percent of the words conveying price information. Moreover, the information is not part of the background chaos of the grocery store—it is on the paper in front of the student, right next to the price of apples.

Most crucially, however, Hannah knows from the minute she sets out for the store that her goal is to buy 18 apples for apple pie and that, even though she may not yet know the exact cost, she will need to bring along enough money to pay for them. In most story problems, by contrast, the overriding question is often saved for last, as noted in the previous section. Irrelevant information is not irrelevant until it is considered in the context of the question.

In fact, an eye-tracking study that charted students' visual focus on different parts of the problem found that, for students at all math achievement levels solving problems with and without irrelevant information, students who kept looking back to the problem's question succeeded in solving the problem.[47] Thus, even for students without reading or attention difficulties, these story problems may pose significantly more difficulty than comparable real-life problems.

"Key Words"

> *Lila and Jeff have 5 teddy bears <u>altogether</u>. Lila has 2 teddy bears. How many teddy bears does Jeff have?*
> *Lila has read 15 books. She has read three <u>times as many</u> books as Jeff. How many books has Jeff read?*

Anyone who has spent time solving (or teaching) written story problems knows that certain words appear in them over and over again. And if one is paying close attention, one will realize that particular words and phrases seem to coincide with the operation necessary to compute the solution. Since reasoning one's way through a problem can be so difficult, particularly for children who struggle with math and reading, well-meaning educators have compiled lists of these verbal cues to assist in choosing a solution strategy.

As the two problems at the beginning of this section demonstrate, however, using "key words" as a guide to the correct operation is simply not reliable.[48] Sometimes a different operation is required.

Problems for which the required operation is inconsistent with the terms and objects embedded in them are notoriously difficult for students, requiring extraordinary mental control to disregard the operation signaled by the "key words."[49] Inconsistent problems with subtraction-cueing terms—*less, take away*, etc.—are particularly difficult for weaker students: Apparently these negative-sounding words are psychologically more compelling than words with positive connotations, such as *more* and *add*.[50] Students with significant difficulties in reading comprehension or math have the hardest time with such problems. However, any student lacking exposure to inconsistent problems or explicit instruction in solving them will find them difficult. When students are seduced by "key words," their errors are almost always the correct answer for the cued but incorrect operation. And when students are asked to recall the problem after making such an error, they are likely to mis-recall it as consistent with the cued but incorrect operation.[51]

Another confounding challenge is students' own understanding of the operation-associated terms. A researcher gave a set of cards, each with a "key" term, to a group of nine- and ten-year-olds and asked the children to sort the cards into piles according to terms that shared something in common. The terms on the cards were *add, more, sum, subtract, less, total, many, take away, compare, altogether, difference, take, equal, many left, gives away*, and *many more*. The researcher then asked the children to explain their choices. Many of them understood the terms quite literally, and the common errors were revealing. *Difference* was understood as *different* and was not sorted. *Many more* and *many* (like *take* and *take away*) were sorted into the same pile because they contained the same word. Some children sorted *many more* and *take away* together, arguing that "many more is a take-away, because when you have 54 and take away 29, you can always go and get many more," as one does in algorithmic borrowing. *Compare* and *add* were sorted together, because "when you compare groups, you put them in pairs, you join them." *Many more* was sorted with *add*, because "when you add, you get a lot more, many more." *Less* and *subtract* were grouped together, because "less refers to the smaller number under the bigger one in subtraction." *Many, left, equal, total*, and *altogether* were sorted together because of their shared position at the end of story problems. And *equal* simply meant "do the problem."[52] Other researchers found that children in grades one through three often regard *some* as an adjective, rather than a quantifier, when it appears with digits in a story problem and thus do not know what to do with it. The researchers also found that young children tend to interpret *altogether* as *each* or a command to add up all the numbers in the problem.[53]

One regularity in textbook story problems is the association of symmetric objects (i.e., objects in the same category, such as horses and cows) with the commutative operation of addition and that of asymmetric objects (i.e., functionally related objects, such as horses and horseshoes) with the non-commutative operation of division. In a 1998 review of a grades-one-to-eight textbook series, one researcher found that all of the addition story problems featured symmetric objects and 95 percent of the division problems featured asymmetric objects. What, then, is a student to make of the following problems? *One tutor sees three students on Tuesday and two on Friday. How many students does the tutor see altogether?* Or, *To make six pies, the recipe calls for 24 peaches and 30 plums. How many of each type of fruit are in each pie?* The first problem, involving the asymmetric tutor and students, requires addition, while the second problem, involving symmetric peaches and plums, requires division. Thus, solving the problem using operations suggested by the objects in the problem is no more reliable than using "key terms."[54]

In short, by-passing reasoning by relying on superficial problem regularities for a solution strategy may at best occasionally facilitate the correct answer but will preclude understanding.[55] *There are no shortcuts to understanding.*

Comparison Terms

Ms. Gonzalez has 5 students in her class. Mr. Patel has 8 students in his class. How many more students does Mr. Patel have than Ms. Gonzalez?
There are 5 birds and 3 worms. How many more birds are there than worms?[56]

In Chapter 2, we discussed how toddlers can distinguish more from less or fewer when it comes to ice cream or cookies. Subsequent chapters demonstrate that young children learn to order numbers and compare their values. They know the meanings of *more* and *less* and can answer the questions *How much?* and *How many?*

It is thus both surprising and remarkable that the common verbal expression *How many more . . . than* is one of the most difficult grammatical constructions found in story problems. The same is true for other comparatives, such as *How much more . . . than, have more than, fewer than, as old as, greater than, less than, X times as many as, X times as much as, how much taller/longer/younger*, etc.[57] They are difficult for adults,[58] elementary students,[59] and young children.[60] In one study, sixth-graders' skill on comparison problems was closely associated with their general reading comprehension, highlighting the problems' lack of verbal clarity.[61] For some children, particularly those with both math and reading impairments, experts deem these comparatives too linguistically advanced.[62] Looking closely at the expression *have more than*, researchers found that end-of-the-year first-graders seemed to interpret the expression simply as *have*—that is, not as a numerical difference but as ownership—or ignore it completely. In the former case, the student would offer one of the given numbers for an answer (in the first problem at the start of this section, the answer would be *Mr. Patel has 8 students*); in the latter case, they would employ the wrong operation (*5 + 8 = 13*).[63]

When the birds-and-worms problem at the beginning of this section was read aloud to groups of young children, 17 percent of the preschoolers and 64 percent of the first-graders got it right. However, when the question was reworded: *Suppose all the birds race over and each one tries to get a worm! How many birds won't get a worm?,* a full 83 percent of the preschoolers and all of the first-graders got it right.[64] The trouble was not the concept, it was the wording.

CLASSROOM IMPLICATIONS

With so many reasons to leave one staring blankly at a story problem, researchers have attempted to find a way to help children gain access to its meaning. These ideas sort themselves into verbal approaches and non-verbal approaches.

Words

Story problems are reading exercises involving mathematical language. Thus, some experts have suggested teaching the mathematical language directly, with lists of words and common synonyms, as one might teach a foreign language.[65] One problem with English mathematical vocabulary in particular is that many words have a mathematical meaning that is different from their non-mathematical meaning (*table, foot, yard, product, odd, sign, root*), while others sound the same as a more familiar word but have a different spelling and meaning (*sum/some, whole/hole, add/ad, four/for, two/to/too, cent/scent/sent*). These differences need to be taught explicitly.

Comparisons are central to much of math. Thus, some researchers suggest teaching the difficult comparative language right along with early addition and subtraction—e.g., *7 = 4 + 3* means "Seven is the same amount as four and three more," or "Seven is the same amount as three more than four."[66] As we have seen, a child's attempt to paraphrase a problem can often reveal the source of a misunderstanding, which can then be investigated and corrected. Indeed, the very effort to paraphrase can sometimes clarify for the student the question being asked. Several researchers have used this method successfully with children at risk for serious math learning difficulties[67] and with children new to English.[68] A related method is to present the propositions and then ask the child to come up with an appropriate question related to those propositions and answer it. Starting out with *Diego has 3 marbles and David has 8 marbles*, a child has several reasonable questions to choose from.[69] Other options for older children who have trouble sorting through the propositions in a problem is to teach them how to identify and remove extraneous information, to rearrange the order of the numerical statements, and to disentangle the question from the rest of the text.[70]

Looking at the problem as a whole, there are several ways to help children gain clarity about the question being asked. One such method is to demonstrate how two problems with different window dressing are asking the same sort of question. Here, for example, are two problems with very different characters and storylines but the same mathematical question:

> John, Shuyuan, and Jike want to start a coin collection. John has three coins, Shuyuan has seven, and Jike has six. How many coins do John, Shuyuan, and Jike have altogether?
>
> Orlee and Tamar enjoy going to baseball games together. They went to four baseball games in June, five in July, and two in August. How many baseball games did they attend altogether?

One researcher calls this approach "abstraction by intersection"—that is, by pointing out what these problems have in common, which is their mathematical structure and the kind of question they are asking.[71]

A related way to organize story problems is by the type (some researchers call it *schema*) of mathematical transformation involved. For example, among problems requiring addition or subtraction for solution, there are *change* problems (in which a quantity changes through some action), *combine* problems (in which amounts are combined into one new amount), and *compare* problems (in which amounts are compared). Explicit instruction in these distinctions, combined in some studies with practice sorting problems by type, has met with success in improving story-problem understanding and performance among young students, including those who were struggling.[72]

Schematic Diagrams

In Chapter 5, we discussed the intimate relationship between visual-spatial thinking and mathematics. One of the ways that visual-spatial thinking can be of great service to mathematical understanding is in permitting one to envision and sketch out the essential elements of a problem. Research with a large, international sample of sixth-graders reveals that visual images lead to more success than an analytic approach using just the problem's numbers.[73] In fact, children seem to implicitly understand their usefulness because they tend to create visual images spontaneously when the problems are complex or otherwise difficult.[74]

The ability to imagine and draw what the relationships between quantities in a story might look like presents the same challenge as describing those relationships in words: namely, determining what is essential and what is extraneous. Imagining a scene and seeing a scene both depend on the visual system. In human vision, the eyes send visual information to the brain, where it gets channeled into two separate neural pathways. One pathway, dubbed the "what" circuit, takes in the visual scene in all its realistic detail, much like a painting or photograph. The other pathway, dubbed the "where" circuit, takes in only the scene's elements that are relevant to immediate action, like a road map or the diagram that comes with assembly instructions. These two brain circuits influence not only the way we actually see things but the way we envision them in our imagination. The painting-like imagery generated in the "what" circuit is described as *iconic*, while the selective imagery generated in the "where" circuit is described as *schematic*. Both circuits are always available and usually work

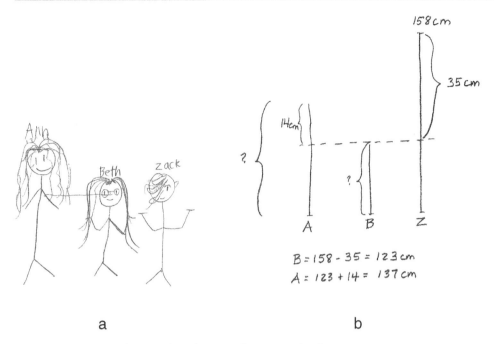

FIGURE 12.1 a) Iconic drawing. b) Schematic diagram and solution.
Source: Reprinted with parental permission.

together, but the salient elements of the scene or problem may help determine how we pay attention to it or imagine it.[75]

> *Anne is 14 centimeters taller than Beth. Beth is 35 centimeters shorter than Zack. Zack is 158 cm tall. How tall are Anne and Beth?*

Figure 12.1a shows a fifth grader's efforts to "draw something" to help her solve the problem. Other than the relative heights of Anne and Beth, there is no mathematical information in this purely iconic illustration. Figure 12.1b is a schematic diagram with all the mathematical information necessary and no extraneous information, allowing for an easy solution.

> *A man wants to visit his mother in another town. To get to his mother's house, he leaves his house and drives straight down the highway for 10 miles. Then he turns right and drives another 4 miles until he gets to a stop sign, where he turns left. His mother's house is 2½ miles down the road from the stop sign. Draw a map of his trip from his house to his mother's house.*

Figure 12.2a is a fourth-grader's attempt to draw the problem's map. While he includes some numerical information, he takes "down the highway" literally and then

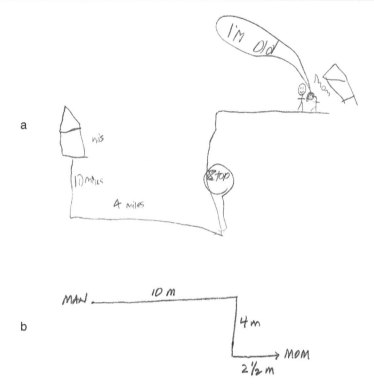

FIGURE 12.2 a) Iconic drawing with an attempted diagram. b) Schematic diagram.
Source: Reprinted with parental permission.

uses himself as a reference for the right turn. He soon loses sight of the map as he gets involved in iconically portraying the irrelevant, albeit charmingly human, aspects of the problem. A driver using this map would quickly get lost. Figure 12.2b is a schematic map, without irrelevant detail.

Neither of the two students who drew Figures 12.1a and 12.2a had been taught to diagram problems.

Research has shown that iconic-style drawings, while appealing, are generally useless as problem-solving aids. By contrast, schematic diagrams, like the ones on the right, are lean and easy to mentally take apart, rearrange, analyze piecemeal, and even set in motion. As such, they are highly useful for problem-solving.[76] In particular, they serve as a way to organize the essential elements of a problem in an easily accessible form. Moreover, while reading necessarily provides information sequentially, as previously discussed, the information in a schematic diagram—the problem's numbers and their relationships—is accessible at a glance, significantly reducing the reading and working memory required and thereby making more mental resources available to solve the problem. In fact, diagrams have been found to be especially useful to children

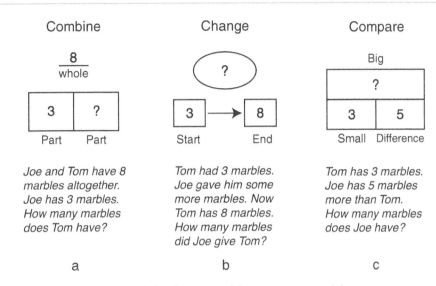

Combine	Change	Compare

8
whole

3	?
Part   Part

? (in oval)

| 3 | → | 8 |
Start   End

Big

?
3	5
Small   Difference

Joe and Tom have 8 marbles altogether. Joe has 3 marbles. How many marbles does Tom have?

Tom had 3 marbles. Joe gave him some more marbles. Now Tom has 8 marbles. How many marbles did Joe give Tom?

Tom has 3 marbles. Joe has 5 marbles more than Tom. How many marbles does Joe have?

a   b   c

FIGURE 12.3   a) Combine model. b) Change model. c) Compare model.

with reading difficulties for that reason[77] and because they are additionally devoid of extraneous detail, should be particularly useful to children with attention deficits.

The two problems presented earlier pertain to distances and so lend themselves well to schematic diagrams. But what about stories whose numbers pertain to discrete objects or other units of measurement, such as weight or time? Several researchers have devised different visual-spatial formats useful for illustrating the numerical relationships described in those stories. One such format is based on the part-part-whole relationships of numbers in many story problems, wherein two quantities are given and the third is to be computed. Figure 12.3 illustrates the forms such diagrams would take for combine, change, and compare problems, respectively.[78] These models all assume that a student will understand the numerical relationship between the given symbolic numbers. While they set up the relevant numbers for the student, they do not illustrate spatially the relative values represented by the symbols.

By contrast, another format (see Figure 12.4), which like the number line is based on the analog of linear distance, involves rectangles whose lengths are in the same relationship to each other as the numbers in the problem.[79] For children who may be uncertain about the symbolic numerical relationships, this format provides the information spatially as well, just as the number line does. In fact, a study of second-graders found that their number-line estimation skill accounted for the link between their spatial skills and story-problem performance.[80]

Other researchers, using blocks and balance scales as a kind of three-dimensional bare-bones diagram (see Figure 12.5), point out that solving story problems in which the missing information winds up on one or the other side of the balance scale is an effective way to deal with a non-standard position of the unknown in a problem and provides an introduction to algebra.[81]

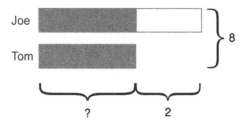

Tom and Joe each have some marbles, and together they have a total of 8 marbles. Joe has 2 more marbles than Tom. How many marbles do they each have?

FIGURE 12.4   Bar model.

FIGURE 12.5   Balance scale model.

Another familiar form of schematic diagram used in solving math problems is a graph, a two-dimensional grid with two perpendicular axes representing the variable values of two different features of the problem (e.g., age and height, distance and time, date and temperature, and so forth). The graph itself, then, represents an abstract, spatial depiction of the *relationship* of those values. Just as with maps and verbal descriptions, however, graphs can be interpreted iconically or schematically. The graph in Figure 12.6, for example, shows how the location of an object changes over time. This problem is likely more advanced than the math encountered by the students for whom this book is written, but it offers an excellent illustration of the difference between a useful schematic approach and a useless iconic approach. In

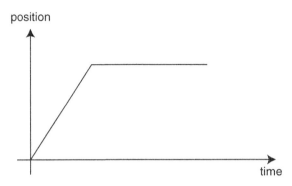

position

time

FIGURE 12.6 GRAPH MODEL.

one study, some students offered correct, schematic interpretations of this graph—for example:

> *In the first time interval, it has a constant velocity. It is moving constantly at a constant speed. In the second interval, the position is the same: it does not move.*

By contrast, other students (mis)interpreted the graph literally, as if it were a photograph:

> *Could it be just elevation or height? The car goes uphill. . . . This is a hill. It goes uphill. Then it's flat. It does not change its direction.*

Only the schematic, abstract interpretation is mathematically correct and useful for solving a problem. Those who offered such an interpretation tended to have strong visual-spatial skills, while those who offered the literal, iconic (mis)interpretation had relatively weak spatial skills. Literal graph (mis)interpretations are not limited to young children: The students in this study were all in college.[82] Spatial skills aside, however, graphs' verbal components—keys, labels, legends—may pose additional challenges and must be explicitly taught.[83]

Unfortunately, many students do not understand what a schematic diagram or graph is or how to use one to solve problems. In a study of children in grades four to seven, encompassing the full range of math ability, researchers asked students to solve some story problems, instructing them: "You may solve these problems on the paper that I have given you." If the student did not attempt to draw anything for a problem, the researcher would prompt them to try doing so. The researchers found that all students, regardless of their math ability, used diagrams poorly. Students were more likely to solve the problem correctly if they drew a schematic diagram than if they drew an iconic picture, and solution accuracy increased with prompting. The weakest math students in the study drew more iconic pictures and fewer schematic diagrams than their more able classmates.[84] Moreover, research with fourth- and sixth-graders found that girls with weak visual-spatial skills may have particular difficulty with schematic diagrams. Across skill levels, when recording their solution girls wrote calculations and boys drew diagrams.[85] These findings raise the question of whether the children's drawings were poor because they did not understand the words or the math, or their math suffered because they could not draw a diagram to guide them through the problem.

Most researchers now agree that schematic diagrams are a powerful aid to understanding and solving story problems. Indeed, one study of a group of sixth-graders with a wide range of story-problem skill found that drawing an accurate schematic diagram increased the likelihood of obtaining a correct solution to the story problem nearly six times over the chances of obtaining a correct solution using no visual representation.[86] Researchers also agree that explicit instruction on the nature of schematic diagrams and on how to construct and use them to organize the given information and set up the solution is critical for all students, not just for those who struggle. Simply directing children to "show your work," "draw a picture," "visualize the problem," or even to write "what I know and what I look for"[87] is not explicit enough for most students. Studies of third-graders with and without serious story-problem difficulties found that explicitly teaching diagramming improved children's story-problem skills more than a verbal approach or even than an approach combining visual and verbal strategies.[88] More research on explicit instruction in story-problem diagramming at different grade levels is warranted.

Another approach is to integrate explicit, teacher-led instruction with peer teaching. In a study of eighth-graders, a teacher guided students through two story problems during each of three sessions. The students, grouped in pairs, were instructed to explain the problem to each other using a schematic diagram; they later explained their solution to the whole class as well, using a schematic diagram. The researchers found that the experience led to greater spontaneous use of schematic diagrams to solve problems and concluded that using diagrams as communication tools led to the students' internalizing them for problem-solving.[89] Research on adapting peer teaching using schematic diagrams in modified form with elementary students is warranted.

Finally, two studies of fifth- and sixth-graders found that a series of interventions focused on a variety of visual-spatial activities improved not only students' spatial visualization and orientation skills but their performance on story problems as well.[90] This is another approach meriting more research.

Two cautionary notes are in order. The first concerns the effect of providing an accompanying graphic *for* students. Researchers presented weak and strong fifth-grade math students with 24 story problems that were accompanied by one of the following: a relevant equation ("bare"), an iconic picture without relevant information ("useless"), a graphic with information that could be used to solve the problem ("helpful"), and a graphic with information necessary to solve the problem ("essential"). The study found that ignoring irrelevant or redundant information in the "useless" or "helpful" graphics increased problem-solving time and that switching between, and integrating, verbal and graphic information ("essential") split children's attention and increased working memory demands, leading to diminished accuracy and increased time on the problem—for weak and strong students alike.[91] (And, of course, the "bare" equation obviated any need to reason through the problem, so was of little pedagogical use.) In other words, none of these teacher-provided aids was helpful. These findings suggest that the value of diagramming problems lies in the students' efforts to understand and solve the problem by creating a meaningful diagram *for themselves*. The teacher can help students learn how to do that by modeling the process for them.

Second, for some children and some problems, the story format is exceptionally difficult; the question then is: *Are story problems worth it?* Couching mathematical problems in text or stories may make them more appealing and teach important language, but for difficult mathematical concepts and for children with significant learning difficulties, dressing up problems in this way can make them even more inaccessible by piling on reading, vocabulary, syntactic, and working memory burdens. One study of fifth-graders learning fraction magnitude comparisons found that children with persistent math learning issues (those consistently scoring below the tenth percentile on standard math tests) performed much better with explicit instruction and demonstrations than when the problems were embedded in stories.[92] Moreover, when story problems are used heavily for assessment, some children's failure may be unrelated to their understanding of mathematics and may, instead, reflect language and reading difficulties. Thus, story-problem exams, both classroom and standard, may serve as a barrier for otherwise math-capable students who wish to access STEM opportunities, where real-life math problems are rarely embedded in written stories, but rather in spreadsheets, diagrams, and discussions.

CONCLUSION

We located this chapter near the end of the book because reading, understanding, and solving story problems draw on every academic and cognitive skill acquired in the early years of education. This means that children with neurodevelopmental or experience-based deficits in any area—vocabulary, syntax, verbal comprehension and expression, or reading; a basic sense of quantitative values or relationships; arithmetic strategies, fact knowledge, or procedures; common sense or logical reasoning; attention, cognitive control, verbal or spatial working memory, or mental flexibility—may find themselves struggling to master them. Contrary to popular impression, story problems are not about real-life problems, but about mathematical language, which can appear deceptively similar to daily, non-quantitative language and thus be particularly tricky to master. While some adjustments to the wording of the problems can help, schematic diagrams can be an especially powerful aid in reasoning through a problem and communicating that thought process to others. Meanwhile, talking out real-life problems can introduce children to both the mathematics and the reasoning necessary to solve them.

ACTIVITIES

Introduction

Story problems can be difficult for many reasons, as outlined earlier in this chapter. Students often take all the numbers in a problem and apply an operation without understanding the intent of the problem, or they might look for "key words" to help them choose an operation, but those can often be misleading. Children benefit from encouragement to read the problem slowly, explain it in their own words, and draw a schematic diagram to help process its meaning. Children may also need explicit instruction on the vocabulary, grammar, and syntax (word order) of story problems, which are often confusing, particularly if story problems are poorly written. Children can then learn to translate the problem's wording into an equation to solve.[93] Finally, students should always ask themselves, *Does this solution make sense?* and be able to explain their reasoning. This may be a particularly useful step for children prone to careless errors because of attention deficits.

ACTIVITY 12.1: What Is the Question Asking?

Objective: To learn to first identify the question and write a solution statement in a story problem. Story-problem solutions should always include a solution statement to indicate what the number in the solution represents. How many *what?* When children do not focus on what the problem is asking, they can get lost in the numbers and language of the problem. Attending to the question first helps them to identify relevant numbers, as well as irrelevant numbers, which can be particularly confusing. In order to get enough practice identifying the questions and writing solution statements, children can complete this activity without actually solving the problems.

- Given a variety of story problems, children underline the question that the problem is asking. They then write a solution statement without needing to solve the problem. *Fran has 15 blocks and 3 balls, then gives 8 blocks to Raj. How many blocks does Fran have left?* Answer: *Fran has _____ blocks left.*
- Children rewrite or retell the story problem so that the question is at the beginning of the problem instead of at the end, providing a context in which to organize the subsequent information and eliminate irrelevant information.[94] The problem here can be rewritten as: *How many blocks does Fran have left? Fran has 15 blocks and 3 balls, then gives 8 blocks to Raj. Fran has _____ blocks left.*

ACTIVITY 12.2: Schematic Diagrams

Objective: To learn how to create schematic diagrams of story problems. Using such representations increases the chance of solving a story problem correctly almost six-fold.[95] Meaningful schematic diagrams help students process the problem and language more accurately, whereas drawing the scene (iconic image) of the problem often reduces the accuracy. Many children will naturally draw the iconic scene of the problem, so they need explicit instruction in how to create schematic diagrams. Number lines, bar models, strip or tape diagrams, maps, lists, and sequences are a few examples of schematic representations.

▪ **First:** Teachers demonstrate drawing schematic diagrams to solve story problems. For example:

▪ *In a running race, Vaz is 5 yards ahead of Pat and Kris is 3 yards ahead of Vaz. How far is Kris ahead of Pat?*

Pat ——————— Vaz ——————— Kris
5 yards   3 yards

Kris is 8 yards ahead of Pat.

▪ *Ram participated in a 3-mile run. He runs each mile in 10 minutes. Because of an ankle injury, Ram had to take a 5-minute break after every mile. How much time did it take him to complete the 3-mile run?*

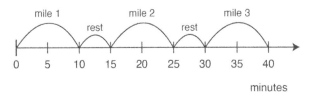

▪ *The ratio of Asha's monthly allowance to her older sister's monthly allowance is 5:3, and their total monthly allowance is $40. How much is Asha's monthly allowance?*

Asha

sister

8 parts total $40
1 part is the same amount as 40 ÷ 8 = 5
5 parts represent $25
Asha's monthly allowance is $25

■ *Paul and Jen go to the farmers market with $75. They spend $25 on vegetables, $10 on baked goods, and $30 on fruit. How much money do they have left when they go home?*

$$\underline{\text{start}} \longrightarrow \underline{\text{spend}} \longrightarrow \underline{\text{left}}$$

$$\$25$$

$$\$10$$

$$+ \ \underline{\$30}$$

$$\$75 \quad - \quad \$65 \quad = \quad \$10$$

■ **Next:** Teachers and students collaborate as a class to create different schematic diagrams of a variety of story problems. Since there is often more than one way to make a meaningful schematic diagram, sharing ideas can help students learn how to create their own diagrams for future problems.

■ **Next:** Have students work in small groups and/or independently to solve word problems by drawing schematic diagrams, and then they take turns explaining their diagrams to their peers. Peers provide feedback as well.

Language Comprehension in the Context of Story Problems

Many children misunderstand the meaning of commonly used math vocabulary, grammar, and syntax in story problems; thus, explicit instruction is often warranted.[96] It is easy to assume that children understand the meaning of common math language, so how can a teacher know if a child comprehends the problem? One way is to ask children to explain what they think a word, phrase, or sentence means within the context of the problem. Likewise, having children paraphrase the problem can be a way to assess their understanding of the question and is a successful teaching strategy overall. Children's gestures are another clue to how they understand the problem. Importantly, gestures can also help children learn the meaning of math language in isolation and in context. Children learn by observing others use gestures and by using gestures themselves. Following are examples of potentially confusing math terms, syntax, and grammar that should be clarified or taught while solving story problems with children.

■ **Key words are unreliable** when used as a strategy for solving story problems. Even though looking for key words is a commonly taught strategy, they can be misleading and result in errors. Searching for key words negates the goal of understanding the problem. Instead, children need to read the entire problem in context to determine the meaning. An example of key words being misleading is as follows: *Keisha had some stamps. Then she got 15 more stamps. At that point, she had 37 stamps altogether. How many stamps did Keisha have at first?* Despite the presence of *more* and *altogether*, the solution requires subtraction, not addition.

- **Arithmetic terms:** *together, altogether, all, in all, sum, total, more, more than, and, both, increased by, additional, extra, combined, between them, in addition to, total, raise, difference* (often confused with *different*), *minus, fewer, subtract, takes, take away, gave, less, less than, more than, remain, left, left over, lost, decreased by, reduce, how much more, how much less, how many more, how many less.*
  - Children need to understand the meaning of these terms; however, these terms should not be sought after as "key words" to determine the operation to use within a problem, since only the context will determine the operation.
- **Multiple-meaning words** can create confusion when they have different meanings in math and regular language. Examples include *odd, even, face, area, times, right, base, foot, yard, four/for, eight/ate, volume, table, two/to/too, sign.*
- **Syntax misalignment** is a common problem with subtraction language. For example, *seven less than 12* means $12 - 7$, whereas many students will write it literally as $7 - 12$. A number line in this situation can help to clarify the meaning.
- **Comparative language** using the *<-er>* ending is frequently found in story problems and often used with "difference" language. Examples include *taller, bigger, how much taller, smaller, fewer, older, younger, greater than, lesser, farther, faster, longer* (time and length). Children may ignore this ending in words, resulting in misunderstanding.
- **Superordinate categories** can be a source of confusion for children, requiring explicit instruction. For example, *Eric has 8 apples and Steve has 3 bananas. How many fruits do they have together?* Or *David has 3 dogs, Jenni has 2 geckos, and Paul has 2 dogs. How many pets do they have between them?* What may be obvious to adults may be less so for children.
- **"Is the same amount as" instead of "equals."** The word *equals* is introduced to children early on in equations and can lead them to think that the answer always follows the = sign: $2 + 3 =$ (equals) 5. When setting up equations for story problems (indeed, in all equations), it is very important for children to say and understand that the = sign should be read as *is the same amount as*. In story problems, the missing information may be in any position of an equation, including the first position, so it is essential that children understand that they are making both sides of the = sign the same amount.
- **Quantifiers** that can be surprisingly misunderstood include *some, all, only, many, also, a few,* and *a couple of.*
- **Imprecise grammar** (including confusing syntax and use of tense) is common in story problems, making them difficult to interpret. Rewording the problem is sometimes the only way to make sense of it. Teachers can model paraphrasing the question, and students can gradually increase their independence with paraphrasing the question themselves.

■ *There are 2 cows in a barn. More cows go in the barn. Then there are 6 cows in the barn. How many cows go in the barn?* (Modified from a common first-grade math book.) This problem is written in a disconnected, telegraphic style, with a constricted use of tense, making the problem difficult to decipher. The question could be reworded in the following way: *There were 2 cows in a barn. Then more cows walked in, so there was now a total of 6 cows in the barn. How many cows walked into the barn?*

ACTIVITY 12.3: Number-Free Story Problems

Objective: To learn the structure of story problems and to identify the operations within them. Any story problem can be changed into a number-free story problem using one of two different methods. The first method is to present a hypothetical situation that focuses on discovering the operation that could be used to solve it. The second method is to cover the numbers in the problem, discuss what the problem means, determine the operations needed to solve it, and then reveal the numbers to finish solving it. Using number-free story problems eliminates the chance that children will look for the numbers in the problem, perform an operation without understanding the problem, or just give an answer as quickly as possible.

■ **Hypothetical situation method:** Introduce number-free story problems. Children explain their reasoning as they describe the operations needed. Examples are as follows:

■ *If you know the length of a rectangular rug and the area, how can you find the width of the rug?*

■ *Two children collect rocks and count the total between them. If you know how many the first child collected, how can you determine how many the second child collected?*

■ *If you know the total number of pencils to be divided evenly in a class and how many children are in the class, how can you determine how many pencils each child gets?*

■ **Cover the numbers:** Present story problems in which the numbers are covered, which helps children to focus on the meaning of the problem without getting distracted by the numbers. First, have the children discuss what the problem means and make a plan for how to solve it. Then reveal the numbers and have the children carry out their solution plan. Examples are as follows:

■ *Last Monday, the sweet pea plant was __ centimeters tall. This Monday, the plant was __ centimeters tall. How much did the sweet pea plant grow in a week?*

■ *The aquarium has __ starfish. Each starfish has __ arms. How many arms do all the starfish in the aquarium have in total?*

ACTIVITY 12.4: Worked Solutions and Paraphrasing

Objective: To learn how to understand and solve a story problem without any pressure to produce a solution. Students with the most persistent difficulty with story problems may benefit the most from this strategy. Students read a story problem with the solution already provided so that they can focus on the meaning of the problem and how to solve it.[97] With increasing complexity of language, students learn to paraphrase the story problem to improve their problem-solving ability.[98]

- **First:** Provide students with simple, single-step story problems that *include the answer*. Surprise! Read the problem together, then determine the meaning of the problem, the relationship of the numbers, and the operation that is needed to arrive at the solution already provided. By providing the solution with the problem, students' anxiety and their impulse to guess is eliminated. Create schematic diagrams and number lines to depict the problem. The goal at this stage is for the student to determine the process for solving the problem without the pressure to "get the answer." Use a variety of problems that require different operations.

- **Next:** Provide single-step story problems that *include the answer* but that contain potentially confusing vocabulary, grammar, and syntax; misleading "key words"; and irrelevant information. Rewrite the problem for the students in a manner that is easier to understand and compare both versions of the problem. The children determine the meaning, decide what operation is needed, and explain their reasoning.

  - Example: *Jerome has 27 balls altogether in a basket after his friend gave him 12 balls and 1 frisbee for his birthday. How many balls did Jerome have to start?* Teacher rewrites the problem as: *Jerome first had a basket of balls, then his friend gave him 12 more balls to put in the basket, which made a total of 27 balls. How many balls did Jerome have in the basket at first? Jerome had 15 balls in the basket at first. ___ + 12 = 27 balls.*

- **Next:** Provide story problems with two or more steps that *include the answer*. Tell students how many steps are needed. Paraphrase the problem together in simplified language, take out irrelevant information, and use schematic diagrams and number lines as indicated. Students determine and complete the steps required.

- **Next:** Increase student independence gradually by including the following steps: Students first paraphrase the question themselves. Then teachers ask guiding questions, provide similar problems but without simplifying the language, provide partial steps, and provide similar types of problems already completed but without providing the answer.

ACTIVITY 12.5: Schema-Based Story-Problem Intervention

Objective: To learn about story-problem types (*schemas*) and use the corresponding strategies to solve the problem. Schemas are used to recognize new problems as similar to previously seen problems. Researchers have studied and refined schema-based instruction for many years to include language comprehension and ensure transfer to novel problems. This activity will outline the basics of the schema approach; however, a complete description is beyond the scope of this chapter. Fortunately, Pirate Math Equation Quest[99] is a free online resource that provides complete and detailed teacher instruction, scripts, and student materials for schema instruction. Research has found a positive impact of the Pirate Math program on children's ability to solve story problems.[100] Children follow the acronym RUN: Read the problem, Underline the question and label, cross out irrelevant information, and Name the problem type (i.e., choose the correct schema). Then they can set up the equation, using x to represent the missing information, and solve the problem.[101] Emphasis is also placed on solving for x by balancing the two sides of the equation, with the = sign read as *is the same amount as*.

- Solve **Combine** or **Total** problems, which consist of adding parts to make a total or whole: Part + Part = Total. *Ruth had 6 shells, Lou had 10 shells, and Gracie had 3 shells. The shells were of different colors and shapes. They put all their shells in a glass jar. How many shells were in the jar? Equation: 6 + 10 + 3 = x shells.*
- Solve **Difference** or **Compare** problems, in which greater and lesser amounts are compared to determine the difference between them: Greater – Lesser = Difference. *Paul has 12 marbles in a jar and Akeem has 7 marbles in a box. How many more marbles does Paul have than Akeem? Equation: 12 – 7 = x marbles.* In these problems, there is no time element and different categories can be compared; for example: *There are 15 dogs and 7 cats at the pet store. There are also 5 ferrets. How many more dogs are there than cats?*
- Solve **Change** problem types that include a time element. There is a starting amount followed by an action that causes a change and then an ending amount: Start Amount +/– a Change Amount = End Amount. *Juwan had $15 in his piggy bank, then he mowed 2 lawns on his street. After mowing the lawns, Juwan had $45 in his piggy bank. How much money did he earn for mowing the 2 lawns? Equation: 15 + x = 45 dollars.*

ACTIVITY 12.6: Multistep Story Problems

Objective: To learn strategies for solving multistep story problems in a collaborative context. Students benefit from explaining their reasoning and listening to the reasoning of other students and their teacher to solve multistep story problems.

- **First:** Students carefully read the story problem and write a solution statement as outlined in Activity 12.1.
- **Next:** Students collaborate to draw a schematic diagram of the problem. To do so, they can ask the following questions: *What do I need to know to solve this problem? What do I already know? What do I need to find out first, and how do I translate that into an equation? What do I need to find out next and translate that into an equation?*
- **Next:** Students collaborate to write the equations and solve the problem. Then they ask, *Does this solution make sense?* and explain their reasoning.

ACTIVITY 12.7: Students Write Their Own Story Problems

Objective: To learn the structure of story problems by students creating their own.

- **First:** Students work in groups to create their own story problems. At first, teachers can provide equations from which the students can create story problems, and eventually the students can create their own. The students then share their story problems with other groups in the class.
- **Next:** Students create story problems independently and then share them with peers, who provide feedback.

ACTIVITY 12.8: Math in My Life

Objective: To learn about the need for math in familiar people's personal and working daily lives and how math stays relevant throughout a person's life.

- Teachers can invite students, parents, grandparents, other teachers, school personnel (nurse, food services, custodian), administrative staff (including the principal), and members of the community (e.g., business leaders) to present situations in their own lives that require them to use math in some way related to what students are learning in class. For example, an animal shelter employee could present the problem of calculating how much food they need to buy for the number of cats or dogs that are in the shelter. The physical education teacher could present the problem of how many teams for a given activity need to be formed given the number of students in the grade and the size of the teams. Individuals can present the problem that needs to be solved and invite children to ask questions and collaborate to solve it. Invite people to think of the many situations in their lives in which they use math and present them to students.

Summary

The following steps provide a summary of the main ideas in the activities listed.

- Children first read the story problem, identify the question, and label the final answer.
- Visualize the problem and draw a diagram.
- Check the diagram to make sure it represents all the relevant parts of the problem (and none of the irrelevant parts).
- Determine the number of steps (or equations) that are needed to solve the problem.
- Set up and solve the equation.
- Check to make sure the final answer makes sense.[102]

NOTES

1   Nesher, 1980.
2   Daroczy et al., 2015.
3   Nesher, 1980.
4   Nesher, 1980.
5   Jiménez & Verschaffel, 2014.
6   Bassok, 2001.
7   Fitzpatrick et al., 2020.
8   Shalev et al., 2000.
9   Cowan et al., 2005.
10 Peake et al., 2015.
11 Pimperton & Nation, 2010.
12 Pagliaro & Ansell, 2012.
13 Fuchs et al., 2018.
14 Logan et al., 2019.
15 Fernald et al., 2013.
16 Orr, 1987.
17 Kieffer et al., 2012.
18 Martinello, 2008.
19 Fuchs et al., 2018.
20 Daroczy et al., 2015.
21 Cummins et al., 1988.
22 Kamii, 1980; cited in Riley et al., 1983, p. 191.
23 Spelke & Tsivkin, 2001.
24 Brissiaud & Sander, 2010.
25 DeCorte et al., 1988.
26 Nesher & Teubal, 1975.
27 Munro, 1979; Perera, 1980.
28 Nesher & Teubal, 1975.
29 Perera, 1980.

30 DeCorte et al., 1985.
31 Lean et al., 1990; Noonan, 1990; Perera, 1980; Riley et al., 1983.
32 Cummins et al., 1988.
33 Larsen et al., 1978.
34 DeCorte et al., 1990.
35 Rothman & Cohen, 1989.
36 Riley et al., 1983.
37 Lewis & Mayer, 1987.
38 García et al., 2006.
39 Thevenot et al., 2007.
40 Munro, 1979.
41 Riley et al., 1983.
42 Peng & Fuchs, 2016.
43 Ng et al., 2017.
44 Parmar et al., 1996.
45 Cummins et al., 1988; Vicente et al., 2007.
46 Leong & Jerred, 2001.
47 Cook & Rieser, 2005.
48 Nesher & Teubal, 1975; Swanson et al., 2013.
49 Lubin et al., 2013.
50 Deschamps et al., 2015.
51 Pape, 2003.
52 Warren, 2003.
53 Cummins et al., 1988.
54 Bassok et al., 1998.
55 Bassok, 2001.
56 Hudson, 1983.
57 Lean et al., 1990.
58 Deschamps et al., 2015.
59 Lean et al., 1990.
60 Hudson, 1983.
61 Boonen et al., 2013.
62 Lean et al., 1990; Powell et al., 2009.
63 Cummins et al., 1988.
64 Hudson, 1983.
65 Rothman & Cohen, 1989.
66 Lean et al., 1990.
67 Moran et al., 2014.
68 Kong & Swanson, 2019.
69 Cummins et al., 1988.
70 Cohen & Stover, 1981; Swanson et al., 2013.
71 Bassok, 2003.
72 Fuchs et al., 2021.
73 Lowrie, 2020.
74 Lowrie & Kay, 2001.
75 Milner & Goodale, 2008.

76 Boonen et al., 2014.
77 Lee et al., 2009; Moyer et al., 1984.
78 Fuson & Willis, 1989; Swanson et al., 2013.
79 Cai et al., 2011.
80 Tam et al., 2019.
81 Kilpatrick, 2011; Powell et al., 2020.
82 Kozhevnikov et al., 2007.
83 Lowrie et al., 2019.
84 Hembree, 1992; VanGarderen et al., 2012.
85 Tartre, 1990; Vasilyeva et al., 2009.
86 Boonen et al., 2014.
87 Goulet-Lyle et al., 2020.
88 Csikos et al., 2012; Swanson et al., 2013.
89 Uesaka & Manalo, 2007.
90 Lowrie et al., 2017, 2019.
91 Berends & vanLieshout, 2009.
92 Herold et al., 2020.
93 Fuchs et al., 2021.
94 Thevenot et al., 2007.
95 Boonen et al., 2014.
96 Fuchs et al., 2021.
97 Kirschner et al., 2006.
98 Moran et al., 2014.
99 www.piratemathequationquest.com
100 Fuchs et al., 2021.
101 Powell et al., 2020.
102 Adapted from vanGarderen, 2007.

REFERENCES

The following references were cited in this chapter. For additional selected references relevant to this chapter, please see Chapter 12 Supplemental References in eResources.

Bassok, M. (2001). Semantic alignments in mathematical word problems. In D. Gentner, K.J. Holyoak, & B.N. Kokinov (Eds.), *The analogical mind: Perspectives from cognitive science* (pp. 401–433). MIT Press.

Bassok, M. (2003). Analogical transfer in problem solving. In J.E., Davidson & R.J. Sternberg (Eds.), *The psychology of problem solving* (pp. 343–369). Cambridge University Press.

Bassok, M., Chase, V.M., & Martin, S.A. (1998). Adding apples and oranges: Alignment of semantic and formal knowledge. *Cognitive Psychology, 35,* 99–134.

Berends, I.E., & vanLieshout, E.C.D.M. (2009). The effect of illustrations in arithmetic problem-solving: Effects of increased cognitive load. *Learning and Instruction, 19,* 345–353.

Boonen, A.J.H., van der Schoot, M., vanWesel, F., deVries, M.H., & Jolles, J. (2013). What underlies successful word problem solving? A path analysis in sixth grade students. *Contemporary Educational Psychology, 38,* 271–279.

Boonen, A.J.H., vanWesel, F., Jolles, J., & van der Schoot, M. (2014). The role of visual representation type, spatial ability, and reading comprehension in word problem solving: An item-level analysis in elementary school children. *International Journal of Educational Research, 68,* 15–26.

Brissiaud, R., & Sander, E. (2010). Arithmetic word problem solving: A Situation Strategy First framework. *Developmental Science, 13,* 92–107.

Cai, J., Ng, S.F., & Moyer, J.C. (2011). Developing students' algebraic thinking in earlier grades: Lessons from China and Singapore. In J.C. Cai & E. Knuth (Eds), *Early algebraization: A global dialogue from multiple perspectives* (pp. 25–41). Springer.

Cohen, S.A., & Stover, G. (1981). Effects of teaching sixth-grade students to modify format variables of math word problems. *Reading Research Quarterly, 16,* 175–200.

Cook, J.L., & Rieser, J.J. (2005). Finding the critical facts: Children's visual scan patterns when solving story problems that contain irrelevant information. *Journal of Educational Psychology, 97,* 224–234.

Cowan, R., Donlan, C., Newton, E.J., & Lloyd, D. (2005). Number skills and knowledge in children with specific language impairment. *Journal of Educational Psychology, 97,* 732–744.

Csíkos, C., Szitányi, J., & Kelemen, R. (2012). The effects of using drawings in developing young children's mathematical word problem solving: A design experiment with third-grade Hungarian students. *Educational Studies in Mathematics, 81,* 47–65.

Cummins, D.D., Kintsch, W., Reusser, K., & Weimer, R. (1988). The role of understanding in solving word problems. *Cognitive Psychology, 20,* 405–438.

Daroczy, G., Wolska, M., Meurers, W.D., & Nuerk, H.-C. (2015). Word problems: A review of linguistic and numerical factors contributing to their difficulty. *Frontiers in Psychology, 6,* 348.

DeCorte, E., Verschaffel, L., & DeWin, L. (1985). Influence of rewording verbal problems on children's problem representations and solutions. *Journal of Educational Psychology, 77,* 460–470.

DeCorte, E., Verschaffel, L., & Pauwels, A. (1990). Influence of the semantic structure of word problems on second graders' eye movements. *Journal of Educational Psychology, 82,* 359–365.

DeCorte, E., Verschaffel, L., & vanCoillie, V. (1988, Apr. 5–9). *Influence of number size, problem structure and response mode on children's solutions of multiplication word problems.* Paper presented at the Annual Meeting of the American Educational Research Association, New Orleans, LA.

Deschamps, I., Agmon, G., Loewenstein, Y., & Grodzinsky, Y. (2015). The processing of polar quantifiers, and numerosity perception. *Cognition, 143,* 115–128.

Fernald, A., Marchman, V.A., & Weisleder, A. (2013). SES differences in language processing skill and vocabulary are evident at 18 months. *Developmental Science, 16,* 234–248.

Fitzpatrick, C.L., Hallett, D., Morrissey, K.R., Yıldız, N.R., Wynes, R., & Ayesu, F. (2020). The relation between academic abilities and performance in realistic word problems. *Learning and Individual Differences, 83–84,* 101942.

Fuchs, L.S., Gilbert, J.K., Fuchs, D., Seethaler, P.M., & Martin, B.L.N. (2018). Text comprehension and oral language as predictors of word-problem solving: Insights into word-problem solving as a form of text comprehension. *Scientific Studies of Reading, 22,* 152–166.

Fuchs, L.S., Seethaler, P.M., Sterba, S.K., Craddock, C., Fuchs, D., Compton, D.L., Geary, D.C., & Changas, P. (2021). Closing the word-problem achievement gap in first grade: Schema-based word-problem intervention with embedded language comprehension instruction. *Journal of Educational Psychology, 113,* 86–103.

Fuson, K.C., & Willis, G.B. (1989). Second graders' use of schematic drawings in solving addition and subtraction word problems. *Journal of Educational Psychology, 81*, 514–520.

García, A.I., Jiménez, J.E., & Hess, S. (2006). Solving arithmetic word problems: An analysis of classification as a function of difficulty in children with and without arithmetic LD. *Journal of Learning Disabilities, 39*, 270–281.

Goulet-Lyle, M.-P., Voyer, D., & Verschaffel, L. (2020). How does imposing a step-by-step solution method impact students' approach to mathematical word problem solving? *ZDM Mathematics Education, 52*, 139–149.

Hembree, R. (1992). Experiments and relational studies in problem solving: A meta-analysis. *Journal for Research in Mathematics Education, 23*, 242–273.

Herold, K.H., Bock, A.M., Murphy, M.M., & Mazzocco, M.M.M. (2020). Expanding task instructions may increase fractions problem difficulty for students with mathematics learning disability. *Learning Disability Quarterly, 43*, 201–213.

Hudson, T. (1983). Correspondences and numerical differences between disjoint sets. *Child Development, 54*, 84–90.

Jiménez, L., & Verschaffel, L. (2014). Development of children's solutions of non-standard arithmetic word problem solving. *Journal of Psychodidactics, 19*, 93–123.

Kamii, C. (1980, Apr.). *Equations in first-grade arithmetic: A problem for the "disadvantaged" or for first graders in general?* Paper presented at the annual meeting of the American Educational Research Association, Boston, MA.

Kieffer, M.J., Rivera, M., & Francis, D.J. (2012). *Practical guidelines for the education of English language learners: Research-based recommendations for the use of accommodations in large-scale assessments. 2012 update.* RMC Research Corporation, Center on Instruction.

Kilpatrick, J. (2011). Commentary on part I. In J.C. Cai & E. Knuth (Eds.), *Early algebraization: A global dialogue from multiple perspectives* (pp. 125–130). Springer.

Kirschner, P.A., Sweller, J., & Clark, R.E. (2006). Why minimal guidance during instruction does not work: An analysis of the failure of constructivist, discovery, problem-based, experiential, and inquiry-based teaching. *Educational Psychologist, 41*, 75–86.

Kong, J.E., & Swanson, H.L. (2019). The effects of a paraphrasing intervention on word problem-solving accuracy of English learners at risk of mathematics disabilities. *Learning Disability Quarterly, 42*, 92–104.

Kozhevnikov, M., Motes, M.A., & Hegarty, M. (2007). Spatial visualization in physics problem solving. *Cognitive Science, 31*, 549–579.

Larsen, S.C., Parker, R.M., & Trenholme, B. (1978). The effects of syntactic complexity upon arithmetic performance. *Learning Disability Quarterly, 1*(4), 80–85.

Lean, G.A., Clements, M.A., & DelCampo, G. (1990). Linguistic and pedagogical factors affecting children's understanding of arithmetic word problems: A comparative study. *Educational Studies in Mathematics, 21*, 165–191.

Lee, K., Ng, E.L., & Ng, S.F. (2009). The contributions of working memory and executive functioning to problem representation and solution generation in algebraic word problems. *Journal Educational Psychology, 101*, 373–387.

Leong, C.K., & Jerred, W.D. (2001). Effects of consistency and adequacy of language information on understanding elementary mathematics word problems. *Annals of Dyslexia, 51*, 275–298.

Lewis, A.B., & Mayer, R.E. (1987). Students' miscomprehension of relational statements in arithmetic word problems. *Journal of Educational Psychology, 79*, 363–371.

Logan, J.A.R., Justice, L.M., Yumuş, M., & Chaparro-Moreno, L.J. (2019). When children are not read to at home: The million word gap. *Journal of Developmental and Behavioral Pediatrics, 40*, 383–386.

Lowrie, T. (2020). The utility of diagrams in elementary problem solving. *Cognitive Development*, *55*, 100921.

Lowrie, T., & Kay, R. (2001). Relationship between visual and nonvisual solution method and difficulty in elementary mathematics. *Journal of Educational Research*, *94*, 248–255.

Lowrie, T., Logan, T., & Hegarty, M. (2019). The influence of spatial visualization training on students' spatial reasoning and mathematics performance. *Journal of Cognition and Development*, *20*, 729–751.

Lowrie, T., Logan, T., & Ramful, A. (2017). Visuospatial training improves elementary students' mathematics performance. *British Journal of Educational Psychology*, *87*, 170–186.

Lubin, A., Vidal, J., Lanoë, C., Houdé, O., & Borst, G. (2013). Inhibitory control is needed for the resolution of arithmetic word problems: A developmental negative priming study. *Journal of Educational Psychology*, *105*, 701–708.

Martinello, M. (2008). Language and the performance of English-language learners in math word problems. *Harvard Educational Review*, *78*, 333–368.

Milner, A.D., & Goodale, M.A. (2008). Two visual systems re-viewed. *Neuropsychologia*, *46*, 774–785.

Moran, A.S., Swanson, H.L., Gerber, M.M., & Fung, W. (2014). The effects of paraphrasing interventions on problem-solving accuracy for children at risk for math disabilities. *Learning Disabilities Research & Practice*, *29*, 97–105.

Moyer, J.C., Sowder, L., Threadgill-Sowder, J., & Moyer, M.B. (1984). Story problem formats: Drawn versus verbal versus telegraphic. *Journal for Research in Mathematics Education*, *15*, 342–351.

Munro, J. (1979). Language abilities and maths performance. *The Reading Teacher*, *32*, 900–915.

Nesher, P. (1980). The stereotyped nature of school word problems. *For the Learning of Mathematics*, *1*, 41–48.

Nesher, P., & Teubal, E. (1975). Verbal cues as an interfering factor in verbal problem solving. *Educational Studies in Mathematics*, *6*, 41–51.

Ng, J., Lee, K., & Khng, K.H. (2017). Irrelevant information in math problems need not be inhibited: Students might just need to spot them. *Learning and Individual Differences*, *60*, 46–55.

Noonan, J. (1990). Readability problems presented by mathematics text. *Early Child Development and Care*, *54*, 57–81.

Orr, E.W. (1987). *Twice as less: Black English and the performance of Black students in mathematics and science*. W.W. Norton.

Pagliaro, C.M., & Ansell, E. (2012). Deaf and hard of hearing students' problem-solving strategies with signed arithmetic story problems. *American Annals of the Deaf*, *156*, 438–458.

Pape, S.J. (2003). Compare word problems: Consistency hypothesis revisited. *Contemporary Educational Psychology*, *28*, 396–421.

Parmar, R.S., Cawley, J.F., & Frazita, R.R. (1996). Word problem-solving by students with and without mild disabilities. *Exceptional Children*, *62*, 415–429.

Peake, C., Jiménez, J.E., Rodríguez, C., Bisschop, E., & Villarroel, R. (2015). Syntactic awareness and arithmetic word problem solving in children with and without learning disabilities. *Journal of Learning Disabilities*, *48*, 593–601.

Peng, P., & Fuchs, D. (2016). A meta-analysis of working memory deficits in children with learning difficulties: Is there a difference between verbal domain and numerical domain? *Journal of Learning Disabilities*, *49*, 3–20.

Perera, K. (1980). The assessment of linguistic difficulty in reading material. *Educational Review*, *32*, 151–161.

Pimperton, H., & Nation, K. (2010). Understanding words, understanding numbers: An exploration of the mathematical profiles of poor comprehenders. *British Journal of Educational Psychology*, *80*, 255–268.

Powell, S.R., Berry, K.A., & Barnes, M.A. (2020). The role of pre-algebraic reasoning within a word-problem intervention for third-grade students with mathematics difficulty. *ZDM Mathematics Education, 52,* 151–163.

Powell, S.R., Fuchs, L.S., Fuchs, D., Cirino, P.T., & Fletcher, J.M. (2009). Do word-problem features differentially affect problem difficulty as a function of students' mathematics difficulty with and without reading difficulty? *Journal of Learning Disabilities, 42,* 99–110.

Riley, M.S., Greeno, J.G., & Heller, J.I. (1983). Development of children's problem-solving ability in arithmetic. In H.P. Ginsburg (Ed.), *The development of mathematical thinking* (pp. 153–196). Academic Press.

Rothman, R.W., & Cohen, J. (1989). The language of math needs to be taught. *Academic Therapy, 25,* 133–142.

Shalev, R.S., Auerbach, J., Manor, O., & Gross-Tsur, V. (2000). Developmental dyscalculia: Prevalence and prognosis. *European Child & Adolescent Psychiatry, 9,* II/58-II/64.

Spelke, E.S., & Tsivkin, S. (2001). Language and number: A bilingual training study. *Cognition, 78,* 45–88.

Swanson, H.L., Lussier, C., & Orosco, M. (2013). Effects of cognitive strategy interventions and cognitive moderators on word problem solving in children at risk for problem solving difficulties. *Learning Disabilities Research & Practice, 28,* 170–183.

Tam, Y.P., Wong, T.T.-Y., & Chan, W.W.L. (2019). The relation between spatial skills and mathematical abilities: The mediating role of mental number line representation. *Contemporary Educational Psychology, 56,* 14–24.

Tartre, L.A. (1990). Spatial skills, gender, and mathematics. In E. Fennema & G. Leder (Eds.), *Mathematics and gender* (pp. 27–59). Teachers College Press.

Thevenot, C., Devidal, M., Barrouillet, P., & Fayol, M. (2007). Why does placing the question before an arithmetic word problem improve performance? A situation model account. *The Quarterly Journal of Experimental Psychology, 60,* 43–56.

Uesaka, Y., & Manalo, E. (2007). *Peer instruction as a way of promoting spontaneous use of diagrams when solving math word problems.* Proceedings of the 29th annual meeting of the Cognitive Science Society, University of California, Merced, CA.

VanGarderen, D. (2007). Teaching students with LD to use diagrams to solve mathematical word problems. *Journal of Learning Disabilities, 40,* 540–553.

VanGarderen, D., Scheuermann, A., & Jackson, C. (2012). Examining how students with diverse abilities use diagrams to solve mathematics word problems. *Learning Disability Quarterly, 36,* 145–160.

Vasilyeva, M., Casey, B.M., Dearing, E., & Ganley, C.M. (2009). Measurement skills in low-income elementary school students: Exploring the nature of gender differences. *Cognition and Instruction, 27,* 401–428.

Vicente, S., Orrantia, J., & Verschaffel, L. (2007). Influence of situational and conceptual rewording on word problem solving. *British Journal of Educational Psychology, 77,* 829–848.

Warren, E. (2003). Language arithmetic and young children's interpretations. *Focus on Learning Problems in Mathematics, 25,* 22–35.

Chapter 13

Early Math Screening
Spotting the Red Flags and Skill Gaps

> *One does not advance the swimming ability of ducks by throwing the eggs in the water.*
> Multatuli (Edward Douwes Dekker), novelist, 1820–1887

B Y this point in the tale, the attentive reader will have correctly concluded that, from the vantage point of a child's mind, learning mathematics is devilishly complex. At the very least, learning math requires paying attention, which means blocking out the myriad other thoughts clamoring for it. Learning math also requires adequate perception: the ability to see the materials, one's paper, and what the teacher is writing clearly and the ability to hear and interpret the sounds of speech accurately. Learning math requires facility with language, including the ability to speak it, to understand it, and to grow it—to absorb new words, what they mean, and the world of ideas they open up. Learning math also requires a sense of how the physical world is cobbled together—knowing where one is in the environment and how objects relate to each other and move in space—and of quantity, the more and less of things, and how that is expressed in words and written symbols. Finally, learning math requires abundant experience with quantity and numbers—ideally with adult-guided experience—because the mind cannot grow or learn without it.

By the time a child enters kindergarten, she should have at least a nodding acquaintance with some of the tools of numeracy. She should be able to recite the beginning of the sequence of counting words in the correct order. She should know how to tag objects with them, understand that the last tag used tells how many objects there are (at least for the smallest numbers), and know that the words in the counting sequence stand for progressively larger quantities of objects. She should know that her fingers are useful for keeping track of the objects counted, for showing someone how many things there are (or how old she is), and for calculating small sums. She should know a few of the numerical symbols. And, importantly, she should know that the counting words and their symbols stand for different (unique) quantities and that any given quantity is more or less than other quantities.

That is a tall order! Remarkably, many children enter kindergarten well enough equipped with these prerequisite skills to learn from the math instruction offered in

DOI: 10.4324/9781003157656-17

school. That is not to say that all children are equally equipped with any of them—it is reasonable to expect that there will be differences within any kindergarten classroom on any of these abilities. It is also the case that children will learn *more* about each of these tools every year in school. Overall, however, many children will come to kindergarten ready to benefit from the curriculum.

Many children, however, will not, and that is worrisome. One study that followed the math progress of a wide sampling of kindergartners through the school year found that their math skill developed along one of four paths: 1) began kindergarten with good skills and remained at a high level; 2) began kindergarten with weak skills but showed good growth through the year; 3) began kindergarten with good skills but had trouble by spring; and 4) began kindergarten with weak skills and showed little growth through the year. When the researchers then followed their math progress through fifth grade, they found that growth was the strongest in the first group and diminished in each group in turn, with the lowest growth in the last group. Specifically, the researchers found that those whose math performance measured below the tenth percentile at the beginning and end of kindergarten had a 70 percent chance of remaining below the tenth percentile five years later.[1] Another longitudinal study found that students performing in the 25th percentile in *seventh grade* had started first grade behind their classmates in math. Although by third grade the growth *rate* of their math skills had normalized, they nevertheless remained at the bottom of the class through seventh grade.[2] Indeed, one very large longitudinal study found that numerical knowledge at age four and a half predicts math achievement through age 15, even after accounting for early differences in reading, general cognitive skills, and other family and child characteristics. Moreover, *growth* in math between age four and a half and first grade was an even stronger predictor of adolescent math achievement.[3]

For children who are struggling at the end of kindergarten and for their teacher and subsequent teachers, this is discouraging news. Without a rock-solid foundation, children cannot hope to master more advanced concepts and procedures, and certainly not at the pace set by teachers anxious to meet target grade standards. This includes many children who might otherwise be perfectly able to learn math, given the proper and necessary fundamentals. The pressure in recent years to bring the first-grade math curriculum down to kindergarten[4] can only make matters worse. Persistent significant math difficulty bodes poorly for success in high-school math, the search for lucrative job opportunities, and even the basic math tasks of daily adult life. Textbox 13.1 tells the story of Daisy, an otherwise highly successful college student whose life ambitions nearly got derailed because some of her math skills remained at the second-grade level.

As discussed throughout this book, children can have trouble learning math for many reasons. We wrote the book because we felt that understanding the recent discoveries of cognitive science, hitherto unavailable to most educators, could help teachers reach many of the children who, like Daisy, get left behind in the earliest grades. Mathematics is a discipline that builds upon itself. Thus, much of the book's focus has been

TEXTBOX 13.1

Daisy, a 19-year-old sophomore at a nationally competitive university, was referred for evaluation because she was having difficulty with her math-related courses. She had a passion for science and hoped to become a doctor, so her difficulty with math-based science classes was particularly frustrating.

She reported that, "I love science because it's all concepts. And I really understand the concepts in math, it's just that I don't *do* it correctly." Following a chemistry test, her professor noted that she had set up every problem properly, yet every answer was incorrect. Her mistakes included scrambling the order of digits in numbers ("*29* and *92* look the same to me") and entering numbers incorrectly on her calculator. On the next exam, which was low on calculation demands, she earned a perfect grade and finished before the rest of the class. In general, she found all calculations difficult but subtraction more so than addition ("Six hundred minus one hundred makes sense, but *629 – 192* doesn't—what's *29 – 92*?"). She often constructed number lines to help her calculate but felt that she did not always make them correctly. Moreover, in reading, she had to work harder to remember quantitative facts, such as dates, than non-quantitative facts. She had to count on her fingers to know the month in a date like 4/16/17, because she did not associate months to numbers, and had difficulty visualizing such dimensions as length, size, weight, and distance when expressed in numbers.

Daisy had always had difficulty with numbers. In elementary school, she had trouble naming numbers and calculating, and she never learned the basic arithmetic facts. As a college student, she still carried her flash cards around in her car and Googled arithmetic algorithms as needed. As a child, she also had difficulty learning to tell time. Even in musical notation, despite years of music lessons, "I could write a half-note, but I couldn't connect it to duration." Learning to count money was also difficult, and to this day she finds the calculations around credit cards and interest rates "mysterious." Her math learning disability was not diagnosed until middle school, and throughout middle and high school she worked "three to four times harder than anyone else in math," with strong support from her family, who excelled in math. "My proudest accomplishment was my C in calculus."

By contrast, she found trigonometry and geometry "pretty easy" because they are "more visual." As a child, she loved puzzles and building with blocks. She was excited about her organic chemistry course because it required mostly three-dimensional visualization of molecules, the sort of puzzle she enjoyed the most. Her "dream job" would be as a heart or brain surgeon.

An extensive psychometric evaluation revealed that Daisy was an exceptionally bright young woman, with verbal, visual-spatial, memory, and overall reasoning skills solidly above average for her level of education. Her reading was excellent, with no evidence of dyslexia. Findings left open the possibility of attention deficit-hyperactivity disorder (ADHD) but were inconclusive, although subsequent evaluation supported an ADHD diagnosis.

Analysis of Daisy's math skills revealed significant difficulty with written numbers. When asked to find the two matching numerals from among *73 37 53 75 35 37*, she was accurate but very slow. On this task she performed at the ninth percentile and complained that all the numerals looked the same to her. Even when not under time pressure, she occasionally misread numbers (e.g., mistook $^{12}/_{13}$ for $^{13}/_{12}$). By contrast, she had no difficulty reading words and could rapidly match and discriminate small, abstract shapes, suggesting that her visual difficulty was specific to math symbols (and the quantitative aspect of music symbols).

She also reported trouble remembering numbers, including her family's birthdays and ages, and she mentally scrambled the last four digits of an often-called family phone number ("0411—no, 4141—no, 4411, that's it!"). Thus, symbolic numbers gave her particular difficulty, even if she was not required to manipulate them mathematically. By contrast, her ability to determine the larger of two sets of dots measured above the 90th percentile.

Her knowledge of basic arithmetic facts was weak and spotty, with performance on a timed fact test measuring at the second percentile. Her responses were all correct, but because she calculated most of the problems on her fingers, she was exceptionally slow.[5]

She had an equally poor grasp of calculation algorithms and compensated instead by decomposing the operands. For example, to add *326 + 291*, given a pencil and plenty of paper, she first added *300 + 200* to get *500*. Then she figured that *26 + 91* "would equal at least another hundred." She understood that her remaining task was to subtract *9* from *26*, which she did on her fingers. On other problems, she transformed all subtraction, multiplication, and division problems into equivalent addition problems to make computation easier. When asked to first mentally *estimate* the results of the same problems, her estimates were reasonable.

The same pattern was evident in her understanding of rational numbers, where she knew what the problem was asking and could set it up correctly but was unable to solve it. She could easily determine the larger of two fractions (e.g., $^4/_7 > ^5/_{11}$, $^2/_8 > ^2/_9$), reduce fractions, and round up decimals. Thus, for the most part, the symbolic calculations, not the quantities themselves, were the problem, although she had difficulty locating very large numbers on a number line.

Feedback from the evaluation led her to a better understanding of her difficulties and a willingness to press her professors for math explanations in terms she could understand. She also found multiple ways to manage her distractibility and unreliable calculator skills. With the benefit of extra time allotted for exams requiring calculations, her good grasp of concepts, and a growing number sense, she graduated with honors, with a major in studio art and a minor in chemistry. Since graduation, she has worked in medical research and very successfully completed her remaining pre-med requirements.

on the early years because without a rock-solid foundation, there can be no enduring structure. The pedagogical approach and activities offered herein are designed to reach most struggling students and provide a firm foundation for all students. Moreover, as the alert reader may have noticed, many of the suggested activities are quite different from those in most standard curricula. For children whom the standard curriculum has failed to reach, we trust that this will be a welcome relief. Importantly, we have resisted attaching grade levels to any of the activities, simply because the activities are useful for a child at any age who still lacks that skill. Math is not about age or grade level—it is about skills and understanding.

As with all foundation building, the process must begin early. As of this writing, many states are considering mandating kindergarten screening for signs of possible reading difficulty. It is equally urgent that kindergarten teachers know early in the school year which students have significant gaps in their numeracy skills as well. As noted, formal arithmetic instruction typically now begins in kindergarten. This means that students who do not yet understand what numbers are and how they relate to each other will be at a tremendous disadvantage straight out of the starting gate. Screening at the start of kindergarten is absolutely critical. This chapter will look at some of the screening approaches available to teachers to spot the red flags in the perceptual, cognitive, and experiential supports for math learning detailed throughout the book and at the start of this chapter. We will then look at ways to screen for gaps in an incoming kindergartner's numeracy skills and remind readers where to look in this book for ways to close those gaps.

ASSESSING THE SUPPORT SYSTEM

At the start of this chapter, we listed perceptual, cognitive, and experiential prerequisites to math learning. Deficits in any of these put children at risk for math learning difficulties. Large-scale, nationally representative, longitudinal studies found that the two most frequent risk factors for persistent math learning trouble are poverty and significant math difficulties upon kindergarten entry.[6] Additional significant risk factors include inattention and weak spatial skills, as well as reading and other language disabilities. We will address poverty first.

Poverty

Not all children from poor families enter kindergarten inadequately prepared for school math,[7] and many who are unprepared are not poor. However, the exigencies of poverty—limited resources, not just of money but especially of parental time and, frequently, parental education—can make it difficult for parents to provide the kind of early supports described in the first three parts of this book.[8] In one study, for example, preschool children from middle-class homes reported twice as much experience playing numerical board games, such as Chutes and Ladders, at home and with relatives and friends as their poorer classmates did. Among low-income children, the amount of board-game experience they reported was closely linked to their ability to locate numbers on a number line, compare quantities, identify digits, count, and learn numerical transformations. Playing card games was linked with numerical comparison ability.[9] Parental influence on the growth of children's language in general, and math language in particular, which is often diminished in less educated families, also privileges middle-class children.[10] Moreover, children of poverty frequently lack the regular medical care that children from middle-class families take for granted, leaving them with undiagnosed and untreated conditions related to vision and attention deficits, lead exposure, and persistent hunger, among others, that can significantly interfere with learning.[11]

How do these children's math difficulties manifest themselves in the kindergarten classroom? One study found that, overall, low-income *kindergartners* performed like middle-class *preschoolers* on such tasks as numerical comparison. Many were unable to judge which is more, *5* or *4*? Or which number means almost the same amount as *5*: *6* or *2*? Kindergartners from wealthier families answered the *5* v. *4* comparison correctly 96 percent of the time, while those from low-income families were correct only 18 percent of the time.[12] Low-income children's early disadvantage is seen most often on verbal tasks, particularly those demanding knowledge of the amount a number word stands for. Indeed, the age at which a child can create a set of five or six items upon request strongly predicts math readiness at the start of first grade.[13] Thus, these children often have trouble with counting (up from one and up or down from other numbers), naming written numerals, comparing numerical magnitudes, and simple numerical transformations. They have particular difficulty with story problems, on which they are four times more likely than their wealthier classmates to start out weak and show little growth over the kindergarten year. They also tend not to begin using their fingers to represent number words until first grade. This delay means that by second grade, when many middle-class children are developing sophisticated methods of solving more complex arithmetic problems and can already retrieve the results of many simple ones from memory, low-income classmates are still using immature finger-counting strategies.[14] Understandably, districts in low-income communities are concerned about their students' failure to meet curriculum standards. However, ratcheting up the kindergarten curriculum and pedagogical methods to first-grade level, a practice common in these districts[15] and most others around the country, is bound to be counter-productive. Without a foundation, the house cannot stand.

Do these low-income children with such significant delays at the start of school ever catch up? Some do. Many do not, including the majority of such children who have no inherent reason for math failure other than their lack of necessary early experience. As described earlier, children begin kindergarten with either adequate or weak numeracy skills; among those with weak skills, some grow and others fail to grow during that school year. Children from low-income families are over-represented in this last group and under-represented in the others.[16] And while they may show growth after that, they do not, on average, ever catch up, particularly if they have additional learning or behavioral problems.[17] One study found that those children with stronger language and executive skills fared better.[18] Several research teams have devised interventions for these children at the preschool, kindergarten, or first-grade level. However, those who have followed children into the later grades have concluded that unless there is significant concurrent growth in executive functions, ongoing intensive intervention up through the elementary grades is necessary to meet the complex challenges these children present.[19]

Clearly, poverty is a red flag. It does not mean that children from low-income families will necessarily be unprepared for kindergarten math, but it does mean that they should be considered at risk. It also means that the teacher needs to get to know his students and their family resources at the very start of the school year so that he knows whom he must keep an eye on. If math screening is not universal, then these children should be selected for screening. The Common Core prescribes that certain math topics be covered in kindergarten, but it does not prescribe where to begin. Universal screening at the beginning of the year in low-income community kindergartens—in all kindergartens, for that matter—would give the teacher an idea of where to start, to make sure of reaching all students. If the school or district does not have the resources for such screening, then teachers should assume that it is a safe bet to start with earlier math skills and secure them before introducing the kindergarten curriculum, to give all children a chance to learn.

Inattention

As we discussed at the outset of this book, attention and the executive functions, particularly working memory, are essential for math learning from the very beginning.[20] Mental disengagement even in kindergarten can have long-lasting effects on math achievement. Of course, children's ability to attend and control themselves develops with age and adult guidance, and typical kindergartners do not have the attention and self-control of fifth-graders or adults. In the discussion that follows, we refer to attention that is weaker than expected for young kindergartners. It is also assumed that the kindergarten school day is structured to accommodate the attention span of a typical kindergartner.

What do age-inappropriate inattention and diminished executive control look like in a kindergartner? Inattentive children are typically notably distractible. Sometimes those distractions reside in the classroom or out the window, but for other children the distractions are internal in the form of preoccupations, daydreams, meandering thoughts, or worries. Inattention might have a hyperactivity component, manifesting as fidgety or impulsive behavior, such as responding to a question without taking time to think about it. But it might not. Thus, children who stare out the window, or even those who look like they are paying attention in class but simply do not register anything that was said or done, should be of equal concern. In one large-scale longitudinal study of math learning from kindergarten through third grade, student disengagement had more of an impact on math growth than did time spent on instruction. Moreover, this effect was the strongest among the lowest-performing students and a major reason for their failure to grow in math over the primary school years.[21] As we saw, attention and the executive functions are fragile and easily disrupted by lack of sleep, momentary upset, psychological trauma, depression, hunger, pressing social or emotional concerns, or illness. Often this disruption is short-lived, and the child is soon herself again.

However, sometimes it is not, and attention remains unstable. Persistent inattention might signal ADHD, which, like specific learning disorders, is itself a neurodevelopmental disorder. It has been estimated that between 11 percent and 31 percent of students with ADHD have serious math difficulties (depending on how "serious" is defined).[22] Conversely, among students with serious math difficulties, about one in four has ADHD.[23] In both cases, the incidence is much higher than in students without one or the other of the conditions. Among very bright students, whose frequent errors are often rationalized as just careless, an ADHD diagnosis can easily be missed, as we saw in the college student vignette in Chapter 1.

Whatever the cause for inattention or disengagement, the behavior is a red flag for serious math trouble—indeed, for learning in general. Unfortunately, little learning will happen until the cause of the problem is understood and properly addressed, usually with the assistance of other professionals, who may also be able to advise the teacher on how to accommodate the child's needs in the classroom. Importantly, the classroom teacher is in a unique position to observe the behavior because few settings demand as much focused and sustained attention as long hours in the classroom. In a national sample, 13 percent of kindergartners were rated as having attention problems by their parents versus 34 percent as rated by their teachers.[24] In fact, the teacher's behavioral ratings of the child on standardized rating scales are always a crucial piece of the assessment puzzle. They are also a crucial piece of the educational puzzle, since the classroom is where most of a child's formal learning will take place.

Language Deficits

Throughout this book, we have stressed the importance of language for math learning. This means that children with developmental deficits in language are at risk for math learning difficulties. Indeed, of the children in one study who had been diagnosed with a developmental language disorder in kindergarten, 55 percent of them were found to have serious math difficulties by fifth grade—more than ten times the rate in the general population (again, depending on how "serious" is defined).[25] As noted earlier in the book, deficits in two key linguistic skills can cause significant math learning difficulty. One is phonological awareness—the brain's ability to process the sounds of language. The other is the ability to retrieve verbal information, including the names of digits, rapidly and automatically from memory, or *rapid automatic naming* (*RAN*). The first deficit makes it difficult to understand instruction, learn the count-word sequence, calculate orally using objects, keep track of verbal information in working memory, and understand place-value. It may also delay the ability to connect numerical symbols with the quantities they stand for. And both deficits make it difficult to retrieve arithmetic facts from memory; this is particularly true of multiplication facts, for which it is difficult to recruit compensatory procedural or visual strategies. Although many students with these language deficits understand the arithmetic principles, they are often severely hampered in solving arithmetic problems.[26]

Developmental deficits in these language skills—phonological awareness and rapid automatic naming—are the two principal underlying deficits that can characterize many children with severe difficulty learning to read, a condition known as *dyslexia*.[27] And, indeed, many elementary school students with dyslexia have the same difficulty with the verbal aspects of math, noted earlier.[28] For example, in one study, third-graders with dyslexia were eight and a half times more likely than classmates without dyslexia to have a deficit in arithmetic fact-retrieval fluency.[29] There are other, less common, reasons for reading difficulty, such as the tendency to confuse the position of letters in words; however, one small study of children and adolescents with that visually based problem revealed that only a few of them confused the position of digits in multi-digit numerals.[30] In a review of 36 relevant studies, researchers concluded that people with significant math difficulty are about twice as likely to have associated reading difficulty as are those with typical math abilities.[31] Moreover, the risk of having serious trouble with reading *and* math is significantly higher in children from families with a history of language and reading disorders.[32] Children with significant trouble in both math and reading (and normal-range intelligence) often have serious difficulties learning, and there is some evidence that their brain circuitry is somewhat different from that of children with one or the other of the difficulties in isolation.[33]

Clearly, then, developmental language deficits represent a red flag for math learning. Fortunately, they can be detected in kindergarten prereaders by screening. As noted earlier, as of this writing many states have approved or are considering mandatory universal kindergarten reading screening. Although it is not yet clear how that screening will be structured, proper reading screening looks specifically for deficits in phonological awareness and RAN. In one study of five-year-old kindergartners, measures of phonological awareness and numeral naming predicted not only early reading but also early arithmetic difficulties.[34] These screening results will be another crucial resource in the effort to determine who may be at risk for math learning difficulties.[35] Moreover, many of those states considering mandating universal reading screening are also considering mandating that schools provide appropriate structured literacy programs, which may also improve those children's verbally based math skills.

Spatial Skill Deficits

Most assessments of early numeracy do not include investigation of spatial skills. As discussed in Chapter 5, spatial skills are deeply connected to mathematics at all levels; in fact, this link is already evident in preschool and kindergarten and is associated with the development of a functional mental number line.[36] Moreover, deficits in these skills can be devastating, particularly for children from low-income families, as we saw in Chapter 5, as well as for girls—large-scale studies estimate that roughly two out of every three children with an isolated math disability and three out of every four children with combined math and reading disabilities are girls.[37] For that reason, spatial skills belong on the list of potential screening items—in particular, mental transformation and rotation. There are two additional reasons for screening spatial skills. One is that they are remediable, as discussed in Chapter 5; because of their impact on math learning, the earlier they are tackled, the better. The second reason is that they are silent. Except perhaps for art or gym classes, where deficits in visual-spatial skills may become obvious, the connection between spatial skill and most school subjects is not well known or easily recognized. Thus, it is highly unlikely that a spatial deficit will be discovered, leaving any consequent math difficulties shrouded in mystery. A few minutes of testing in kindergarten, along with the necessary remedial work,[38] could help get in front of the problem.

Evaluating spatial abilities in five-year-olds requires well-designed, though not necessarily costly, procedures. As discussed in Chapter 4, in the kindergarten age range, mental rotation is most effectively assessed with two-dimensional puzzle tasks. One method requires mentally rotating and moving geometric puzzle pieces so they fit together and then envisioning the whole, much like doing a jigsaw puzzle in your head (see Figure 4.6 in Chapter 4).[39] Another method requires mentally rotating an asymmetric puzzle piece and its mirror image to determine which fits into a matching slot or hole.[40] We include the first of these methods, which has also worked well in a digitized version, in Table 13.2.[41] However, both methods have been associated with kindergartners' math performance and should work well as a spatial skill screener.[42]

Another math-relevant visual-spatial skill that can be screened easily at kindergarten entry is visual-graphomotor integration—the brain's ability to coordinate what the eye sees with hand motion in drawing and writing, for example—for which there is an adequate measure[43] and treatment.[44] Figure 13.1 illustrates the attempt of a fourth-grader with visual-graphomotor integration difficulties to copy the shape on the left, a task that children without such difficulties can typically do correctly by the time they are eight. Such difficulties can interfere with a child's efforts to organize numbers on the page, set up problems adequately for solution, and diagram story problems.

The potential consequences for math learning due to deficits in both language and spatial skills are illustrated in Textbox 13.2, which describes the travails of a child who, like Daisy, did not have the benefit of early screening.

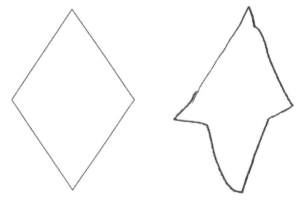

FIGURE 13.1 The attempt of a fourth-grader with visual-graphomotor integration difficulty to copy a diamond.

Source: Reprinted with parental permission.

TEXTBOX 13.2

In preschool, Sophia was delayed in her speech and language development and began speech therapy. Although she could not read even simple words such as *cat* and *dog* in kindergarten, her school did not screen her for dyslexia or phonological processing. During kindergarten, she was unable to keep up with her peers in math because the school math curriculum was heavily language- and reading-based with story problems used for instruction, making math inaccessible for her. Sophia was pulled out of class and away from her peers for most of the day, despite having tested in the average range for cognitive ability. By the start of third grade, Sophia still could not read even three-letter words, and she was unable to complete single-digit addition or subtraction. Sophia felt bad about herself and longed to be with her peers in the classroom. She was diagnosed with dyslexia and phonological processing disorder by an outside professional at the beginning of third grade, and her parents negotiated with the school to switch her reading instruction to a structured literacy program designed for children with dyslexia. Sophia worked very hard to learn to read in school and with her dedicated parents at home using the structured approach. By the third trimester of fourth grade, Sophia was reading at grade level, and her parents successfully fought to have her join her peers in the mainstream classroom again for the full day, much to Sophia's overwhelming delight!

However, in fourth grade, Sophia still could not add two numbers to *ten*, complete single-digit addition or subtraction, or place numbers accurately on a *0*-to-*100* number line. Her visual-spatial skills were also very weak, and she could not put together and rotate puzzle pieces accurately, copy simple geometric shapes, or recognize shapes in their mirror image, and she had difficulty writing letters and numbers in their proper orientation. Toward the end of fourth grade, Sophia began an intensive intervention to learn the foundations of math as outlined in this book, and even though she was in fourth grade, she was taught how to use her fingers, count the base-10 way, and use number blocks and a number line to learn arithmetic. She also worked on her visual-spatial skills through playing spatial games and drawing figures and geometric shapes in different orientations, with a focus on learning to draw the mirror image. By the beginning of fifth grade, she had developed a much stronger foundation in math.

Now, Sophia is a delightful and creative fifth-grader. Her challenge is to use her blossoming math skills in the mainstream class with the complex language-based math curriculum. Her math facts are not yet automatic, so she is allowed to use a multiplication table and a calculator at appropriate times. She is doing well on all her math tests and now enjoys math as her favorite class. She must work hard to make up for all that she missed, even learning how to take a math test, and early screening and appropriate intervention could have saved Sophia some of the suffering she endured. However, she is living proof that building the conceptual foundations of math can lead to success for even older and the most struggling students. Her teachers enjoy having her in their classroom and are impressed with all that she contributes.

ASSESSING EARLY NUMERACY

Kindergarten is the year when children make the transition from the informal mathematics of home and preschool to the formal mathematics of elementary school, and many will be taught to solve quantitative problems using the tools of numeracy described in Chapters 6 through 9. Although the Common Core State Standards for kindergarten outline the skills a child will need to master before moving on to first grade,[45] they cannot tell a teacher where to start, because they have no way of knowing what the child already knows. The chief question a kindergarten teacher will need to answer is, *What is in a child's numeracy toolbox when she walks into school on the first day?*

As we have seen throughout this book, the stakes are high, and this is where a numeracy screener can be valuable. In the years leading up to the writing of this book, scholars have made a concerted effort to figure out what sorts of questions can most reliably and efficiently detect the gaps in a young child's early numeracy skills.[46] Indeed, several such instruments are available, although not all of them are designed for kindergarten screening; no doubt more will be available by the time the reader has this book in hand.[47] It is well beyond the scope of this book to review them here. Instead, we will look at the important considerations a teacher or school district will want to keep in mind in thinking about how to screen their entering kindergartners.

Of course, in an ideal world, each kindergartner would walk into school on the first day with the report of a comprehensive numeracy evaluation. The teacher could then figure out which children lacked which skills and plan instruction accordingly.

But this is not an ideal world. Nor is it realistic to think about providing such a comprehensive evaluation for the whole class once school begins. Such evaluations are expensive in terms of teacher and student time, as well as in labor and materials. Thus, the object is to develop or find a screener that will identify as efficiently as possible which students have gaps in their skills and what those gaps are.

As of this writing, there is no such perfect screener. As noted earlier and throughout this book, even basic numeracy is a complex set of skills, and incoming kindergartners could have gaps in any of them.

This does not mean that screeners are useless, however. Far from it. Research has revealed several early numeracy tasks that signal quite effectively a critical gap in a child's understanding of number. District administrators should understand how to evaluate a screener's usefulness. An ideal screener will be normed, which means it will be able to compare one child's performance against the performance of other children in the general population who are entering kindergarten. In addition to their obvious relevance to a district's resource allocation decisions, normative scores can give a teacher a sense of where her students fit into the big picture. Unfortunately, testing a large, demographically representative sample of children to establish norms can be expensive, affecting the cost of the screener. Importantly, an ideal screener will also give a teacher information about a child's performance in relation to standards set by the school's kindergarten curriculum.

Several academic studies have undertaken to investigate what young children know, using demographically representative samples of children. The findings from one such study are shown in Table 13.1. As one can see, the number of children in this study was substantial, although certainly not large enough for norming purposes. The children came

TABLE 13.1   Early Numeracy Skills of Kindergarten Entry–Age Children

Skill	*Limit*	*% Who Succeeded*	
		Age 5	*Age 5 1/2*
Number of children in the study		183	90
Verbally count up to:	5	96	100
	10	90	99
	15	60	87
	20	51	77
	25	46	70
	40	19	41
	100	7	19
Point to and count dots in a row up to:	3	96	100
	6	85	93
	11	72	87
	14	61	87
	16	54	80
Cardinality: How many dots are there?	3	96	100
	6	86	92
	16	65	87
Cardinality: Give me __ (objects)	3	87	94
	4	83	92
	8	66	87
	16	33	53
Name numerals up to numeral:	1	96	100
	8	75	91
	10	65	91
	12	38	62
	14	54	74
	15	41	63

(*Continued*)

TABLE 13.1   (Continued)

Skill	Limit	% Who Succeeded	
		Age 5	Age 5 1/2
Verbal story problems: Addition	0 + 2	65	80
	1 + 1	59	74
	2 + 2	34	60
Verbal story problems: Subtraction	1 − 1	54	67
	2 − 1	57	73
	3 − 2	54	71
	4 − 1	35	58
Symbolic addition:	0 + 2	29	42
	1 + 1	45	47
	1 + 2	41	44
	2 + 2	36	43
	1 + 3	29	37

Adapted from Litkowski et al., 2020.

from a wide range of backgrounds, with 17 percent of the five-year-olds and 11 percent of the five-and-a-half-year-olds enrolled in Head Start, and so should represent a reasonable general profile of the skills that American children typically bring with them on their first day of kindergarten.[48]

In normative terms, for any given skill at any given age, the higher the proportion of children who succeed, the more critical is the assessment of those who do not. For example, about 89 percent of five-year-olds in the study just cited could count to ten. That means it would be of considerable urgency that the 11 percent who could not count to ten be identified and taught to do so. In terms of the standards set by the curriculum, it would also be important that each child meet the benchmarks indicating readiness for instruction and that curricular instruction be withheld from a child until those benchmarks were confidently met.

Table 13.2 lists some potential screening questions emerging from research, for the most part in the order of topics presented in this book. Several can be posed in different ways depending in part on whether the testing is accomplished in person or on screen. One-on-one, in-person screening has the advantage of a teacher's being able to engage an anxious child or notice behavioral clues, such as uncertainty, and factor those into the risk assessment. The teacher can also pose probing follow-up questions if necessary. A well-designed on-screen assessment has the potential advantages of uniform administration, ease of performance timing, reduced need for personnel and materials, and automated scoring. Individual children may feel more comfortable with one mode of administration or the other. Of course, the choice also involves financial and time considerations. Importantly, these questions are not restricted to kindergartners. As noted earlier in this chapter, math is not about age or grade level, but about skills and

TABLE 13.2   Suggested Kindergarten Math Screening Items, With Reference to the Relevant Chapters in This Book

SKILL	SAMPLE QUESTIONS	NOTES	CHAPTER
SIZING UP	(Show 2 sets of dots.) Here are 2 groups of dots. Which group has more dots?	Timed or time-limited exposure.[49] Use sets too large to count quickly.	2
LANGUAGE[50]	(Show 3 pictures.) Point to the picture that shows *more*.	Only 1 of the 3 pictures illustrates the word. Use quantity words (*more, less*).	2
	(Show 3 pictures.) Point to the picture that shows *above*.	Only 1 of the 3 pictures illustrates the word. Use spatial words (*below, next to*).	4
COUNTING/ ESTIMATING	Recite the count sequence as high as you can.[51]	To 20. Assess accuracy and fluency.	3, 6
	(Set out 7 objects.) Can you count these?	Does the child point to each? 1–10, can extend to 20.	6
	(Rearrange the objects in the previous item.) Now how many are there?	Does the child have to recount?	6
	(Set out 30 objects.) Can you give me 7?[52] (Or: Can you draw 7 circles?) Now count them again.[53]	Allow for self-correction. Test 1–10 or 1–20, in random order (e.g., 3, 1, 6, 2, 4,. . . .).	6
	(Set out cards with 4 different sets of dots.) Point to the picture with ____ dots.	Ask for the numerosities in random numerical order.	6
	(Show 5 dots.) Here are some dots. (Hide them after 1 second) About how many did you see—4 or 19?[54]	1–10 or 1–20. Dots hidden to prevent counting. Choices: target ± 1 and target ± 5 or more.	2, 6
FINGERS	Can you show me with your fingers how old you are?		7
	Can you show me with your fingers how many ears I have?		7
	If you have 3 M&Ms and I have 4 M&Ms, how many M&Ms do we have altogether?	Observe for finger use.[55] Up to sum of 10.	7, 10
NUMERALS	Here are 2 pages of numbers. I'd like you to go across each row and name the numbers as quickly as possible.	Present two pages of 56 randomly ordered numerals (1–10) per page. 1-minute time limit. If child hesitates 3 seconds, say, "Skip this one and go on."[56]	8
	I'm going to say some numbers. I'd like you to write each number after I say it.	Dictate 1–10 in random order.[57] Can extend to 20.	8
	(Array numerals 1–10 randomly in a row.) Here are some numbers. Point to the number I say.	Can extend to 20.	8
	(Show 1 set of dots and 4 numerals.) Point to the numeral that shows how many dots there are.	1–10.	8
	(Show 1 numeral and 4 sets of dots.) Point to the card that shows the same number of dots as this number says.	1–10.	8

(*Continued*)

TABLE 13.2 (Continued)

SKILL	SAMPLE QUESTIONS	NOTES	CHAPTER
ORDINALITY/ NUMBER LINE[58]	(Place a hash mark with a digit on a straight line.) If this number goes on the line here (now show a second digit), where would this one go? (After that digit is placed, show a third digit.) And now where would this one go? (See Figure 9.9 for this item.)	Three digits < 10. Begin testing with second digit = first digit ±1. If child does well, use any 3 digits < 10.[59]	9
	If 0 goes at this end (point) and 10 goes at this end (point), where would 3 go? (Can extend to 20 or 100.)	3 0_____10	9
	If 0 goes at this end (point) and 10 goes at this end (point), what number would go here (point)? (Can extend to 20 or 100.)	0_____|__10	9
	(Show 2 digits and a blank space.) What number goes here?	Sets of 3 consecutive digits to 10, with first, second, or third digit missing. Oral response. 1-minute limit for as many sets as possible.[60] Can extend to 20.	6, 9
	Begin counting from 4.		6
	Count backward from 10.		6, 9
SYMBOLIC COMPARISON	I'm going to say 2 numbers. After I say them, you tell me which number means more things.[61]	Pairs of numerals 1–20. State larger number first or second randomly.	6, 9
	I'm going to say 2 numbers. After I say them, you tell me which number means fewer things.	To 20. State the smaller number first or second randomly.	6, 9
	(Show pairs of numerals.) Here are pairs of numbers. For each pair, decide which number means more and cross it out.	2-minute limit for as many as possible, 1–10,[62] or 1–20.[63] Place the larger numeral on right or left randomly.	8, 9
	(Display the digits 5, 6, and 2.) Which is almost the same amount as 5: 6 or 2?[64]	Use various targets, show in random order. Choices: target ±1 or 2 and target ±3 or more.	8, 9
	(Display three digits in a row in random order.) Which number means the most things?	Digits up to 9.[65]	8, 9
SPATIAL VISUALIZATION	(Children's Mental Transformation Task: CMTT)[66]	Best to do on screen.[67]	4
VISUAL-MOTOR INTEGRATION	(Visual-Motor Integration: VMI)[68]	If score is low, refer to occupational therapy.	

understanding. If an older child seems lost, it is perfectly reasonable to go back to these basics to understand the root of the problem.

Two crucial points are in order here. First, many large, comprehensive academic diagnostic batteries, such as the Woodcock-Johnson,[69] have relevant math subtests. These should *not* be used for screening purposes for the simple reason that it will render the battery useless for overall diagnostic assessment of that child, should the need arise. The second important point is that those adults doing the screening be trained how to do it. Screening can be time-consuming. Sometimes schools will ask their paraprofessionals to do it, or parents and grandparents will volunteer their time. Understandably, sympathetic adults are eager to see children do well and may inadvertently give the child a boost. Volunteers should be instructed on the importance of remaining objective in test administration so they do not cue children to get the correct answer and thus potentially miss being identified as needing remediation.

The list in Table 13.2 in its entirety is too comprehensive and time-consuming to be an efficient screener; moreover, it has neither been normed nor evaluated against grade standards. However, small sets of items may be useful. Research findings vary widely on which of these questions would most likely reveal the most serious gaps. No single question does so perfectly. As discussed in earlier chapters, the two most important aspects of early numeracy are a child's understanding of numbers' quantitative values and how those values relate to each other. Thus, some researchers have found that the most efficient way to uncover serious gaps in understanding is via symbolic numerical comparisons, as well as number-line placements and missing-number questions.[70] Thus, for example, if a child cannot determine which means more, *7* or *3*, it might indicate that the child does not know what *more* means, does not recognize the symbols, does not know that they stand for quantities, does not know what quantities they stand for, and/ or does not know how they relate to each other. Comprehensive follow-up questions could then determine the particular gap or gaps. On the other hand, if a child answers a series of comparison questions correctly, then the chances are good that he understands all the underlying concepts as well. Therefore, beginning screening by assessing the more complex skills may be one efficient way to determine which children may have earlier gaps in their knowledge. Those children would then necessarily require further probing in order to fully inform the teacher about where and how to target instruction.

Predictable response patterns can also help identify gaps. One study looked at the object-counting and number-line placement skills of children between the ages of three and six years and found that some children could neither count objects nor place numbers in order on a line, some could count objects but not yet place numbers in order on a line, and some could do both. When the researchers then looked at their ability to compare the quantities represented by digits, they found that only the children who could consistently place numbers correctly in relation to each other along a line were able to successfully compare digits. This finding led the researchers to conclude that children seem to rely on a mental linear spatial organization of number to understand the quantitative relationships between numbers.[71] Moreover, while most young children could name the number immediately following a given number ("What comes after six?" "Seven.")—knowledge accessible from the rote number-word sequence—being able to state the number immediately *before* a given number, like being able to compare two numbers, depends on a mental number line that one can travel forward and backward on, as on a train track.[72] Arithmetic also depends on such a mental number line,[73] although findings are mixed on whether kindergartners' physical number-line placements reliably predict their later arithmetic performance.[74] As elementary school progresses, the knowledge of numbers' relative values—their ordinality, or order on the mental number line—becomes even more important for arithmetic.[75]

A vital part of screening is monitoring progress in order to ensure that instruction is properly targeted and working. Thus, the ideal screener would include alternative test forms with different versions of each item, permitting their use for periodic re-evaluation. Alternatively, many test items, such as some of those listed in Table 13.2, could be expanded into higher number ranges. Monitoring both progress in filling in earlier gaps and, for all students, progress through the kindergarten curriculum is essential because, as discussed earlier in this chapter, some students start kindergarten with adequate skills but then do not progress, placing them at nearly equal risk for long-term persistent difficulties as those who began the year with early gaps. It is also the case that students can fluctuate significantly in their skills and growth from test point to test point; a one-time assessment may not accurately reflect their abilities. It is vital for end-of-the-year overall success that the teacher knows who those students are and can stay ahead of any potential long-term trouble. If growth is flat over the course of a few weeks, the teacher can reassess the situation and adjust intervention accordingly. Progress monitoring in the second half of the year can additionally assess growth in kindergarten skills in preparation for first grade.

Finally, as to instruction, it must begin with the basics. What tools are missing from a child's numeracy toolkit at the start of kindergarten? Different children will present with gaps in different skills.[76] The most important job is to address the fundamental concepts not yet grasped by that particular child, regardless of how basic, because without them, there is no chance for success. In the last column of Table 13.2 are the numbers of this book's chapters where the reader can find information about each skill and suggested instructional activities designed to address it. For the most part, kindergarten teachers can use them in stations around the classroom or in small-group instructional settings in or outside the classroom; some can be used as whole-class activities if the whole class can benefit from them. Some children may respond relatively quickly, as discussed in relation to the response of children from low-income environments to simple numerical board games (see Chapter 9).[77] Others may need extra support well past kindergarten. Some children may have so much difficulty that intensive intervention may be necessary from the very beginning.[78] However, identifying the gaps and stepping in to fill them quickly may significantly reduce the need to provide extra support in later grades, when the effects of a weak foundation make mastering more advanced skills exceptionally difficult. The vignette in Textbox 13.3 illustrates this advantage. For teachers of older children who did not establish a firm foundation in the earlier grades, now is the right time to locate the early gaps that are making it difficult for them to understand the more advanced material. The activities herein are appropriate for any age when they might be necessary.

TEXTBOX 13.3

Emily was delayed in her speech and language development, and she had difficulty expressing herself in a manner that others could understand, both in her articulation and in her meaning. At the age of four, she was diagnosed with a phonological processing disorder, which meant that she had difficulty discriminating and sequencing the individual sounds in words, essential components of speech, and learning new words (including those related to numbers and spatial relations such as *behind* and *below*). She participated in speech therapy, and fortunately, a reading screening in kindergarten identified her as at risk for serious reading and spelling difficulties. Her school provided a targeted structured literacy intervention to address her phonological impairment and reading needs.

  Emily also had difficulty with early math skills such as counting easily and without hesitations, counting on from her spot in number games, and adding small numbers. She also had difficulty with spatial tasks such as putting together different types of puzzle pieces, writing her letters and numbers clearly, and drawing simple shapes. She participated in a math intervention that targeted her weaknesses with activities outlined in this book, such as counting the base-10 way and using number blocks with a physical number line. She also learned to draw various geometric shapes in different orientations, letters and numerals in the proper orientation, and even pictures such as Jack and Jill, with Jill right side up and then upside down as she tumbled down the hill. Her parents followed through with home math activities and counting games, and they played visual-spatial games with Emily, such as tangrams, puzzles, Q-bitz Jr., and building with blocks.

  Emily is now a thriving second-grader who loves math and reading and who is performing at or above grade level in all areas. She is a curious, bright, and enthusiastic learner and a wonderful example of the benefit of understanding risk factors, early screening, and early intervention.

CONCLUSION

As noted in this book's preface, American children are struggling in math and failing to keep up internationally.[79] That is a serious problem for the nation. It is an especially serious problem for our children, many of whom grow to adulthood lacking the skill and confidence to manage the basic mathematical aspects of daily adult life: rent and mortgages, credit cards, health-care decisions, budgeting, taxes, following recipes, and myriad pastimes. In an increasingly technological world, weak mathematical understanding also closes them out of up-to-date and often lucrative employment opportunities—a particular disappointment for families hoping that education will help their children and future generations rise out of poverty.[80]

It is our view that the best way to solve a problem is to first understand it. Over the past two decades, there has been an explosion of research on how children learn math. This book has reviewed that effort and spelled out ways to put that knowledge to use in the classroom. As we have seen in the early chapters of this book, there are ways to make up for a paucity of experience prior to formal schooling. There is even preliminary evidence that some targeted interventions during the elementary-school years can not only improve math achievement but improve the math circuits in the brain.[81] For children who have trouble learning math, there is now abundant reason to believe they can be helped to succeed, particularly if those children and the sources of their befuddlement can be identified early. We wrote this book in the belief that the insights reported herein will allow all children to succeed.

There is much at stake.

NOTES

1 Morgan et al., 2009.
2 Geary et al., 2013.
3 Watts et al., 2014.
4 Bassok et al., 2016.
5 For a student with some similar features, see Kaufmann et al., 2011.
6 Morgan et al., 2016.
7 Scalise et al., 2021.
8 Lombardi & Dearing, 2021.
9 Siegler, 2009.
10 Jordan & Levine, 2009; Logan et al., 2019.
11 Gracy et al., 2018.
12 Griffin et al., 1994.
13 Geary et al., 2018.
14 Jordan & Levine, 2009.
15 Bassok et al., 2016.
16 Jordan & Levine, 2009.
17 Darney et al., 2013.
18 Burchinal et al., 2020.
19 Bailey et al., 2020; Clarke et al., 2020; Clements et al., 2020; Doabler et al., 2021a, 2021b; Jordan et al., 2012; Shanley et al., 2017.
20 Ribner et al., 2018; Traverso et al., 2021.
21 Bodovski & Farkas, 2007.
22 Monuteaux et al., 2005; Zentall, 2007.
23 Gross-Tsur et al., 1996.
24 West et al., 2000.
25 Shalev et al., 2000.
26 Donlan et al., 2007; Hecht et al., 2001; Koponen et al., 2017.
27 Catts et al., 2015.
28 Boets & DeSmedt, 2010; Träff & Passolunghi, 2015.

29 Vukovic et al., 2010.

30 Friedmann et al., 2010.

31 Joyner & Wagner, 2020.

32 Snowling et al., 2021.

33 Skeide et al., 2018.

34 Vanbinst et al., 2020.

35 Purpura et al., 2011.

36 Gunderson et al., 2012; Hawes et al., 2019a; Mix et al., 2016.

37 Landerl & Moll, 2010.

38 Fernández-Méndez et al., 2020; Hawes et al., 2017.

39 Levine et al., 1999; Wang et al., 2021.

40 Fernández-Méndez et al., 2020; Frick et al., 2013a, 2013b.

41 McDonald et al., 2021.

42 Fernández-Méndez et al., 2020; Gunderson & Hildebrand, 2021; Gunderson et al., 2012; McDonald et al., 2021; Wang et al., 2021.

43 Beery & Beery, 2010.

44 Dankert et al., 2003.

45 Common Core State Standards Initiative. (2021). *Preparing America's students for success:* www.corestandards.org/Math/Content/K/introduction.

46 Nelson & Powell, 2018.

47 Bugden et al., 2021; Clarke et al., 2014; Mazzocco & Vukovic, 2018.

48 Litkowski et al., 2020.

49 On screen (e.g., https://panamath.org/; Halberda & Feigenson, 2008) or paper (e.g., www.numeracyscreener.org/; Hawes et al., 2019b). Gimbert et al., 2019; Malone et al., 2020; Purpura & Logan, 2015. But see Sasanguie et al., 2014.

50 Georges et al., 2021; Toll & vanLuit, 2014.

51 Clarke et al., 2008.

52 Producing a set of a given numerosity may be more difficult than just counting a set of the same numerosity; Mou et al., 2021.

53 Krajcsi, 2021.

54 Estimation task, Seethaler & Fuchs, 2010; Pamela Seethaler, personal communication, December 16, 2020.

55 Finger use is a good sign in kindergarten; Jordan & Levine, 2009.

56 Clarke et al., 2008.

57 Malone et al., 2020.

58 Bull et al., 2021; Schneider et al., 2018. But see Ellis et al., 2021; Sutherland et al., 2021, who did not find number-line estimation strongly predictive of future math achievement.

59 Sella et al., 2019.

60 Clarke et al., 2008.

61 Griffin et al., 1994.

62 www.numeracyscreener.org/; Hawes et al., 2019b.

63 Clarke et al., 2008.

64 Griffin et al., 1994; Jordan et al., 2008.

65 Sella et al., 2019.

66 Gunderson et al., 2012; McDonald et al., 2021; Spatial Intelligence and Learning Center: www.silc.northwestern.edu/childrens-mental-transformation-task-cmtt/

67 McDonald et al., 2021.

68 Beery & Beery, 2010.

69 Woodcock et al., 2014.

70 Hawes et al., 2019b; Sella et al., 2019.

71 Sella et al., 2017.

72 Sella & Lucangeli, 2020.

73 Sella et al., 2020.

74 Bull et al., 2021; Schneider et al., 2018. But see Ellis et al., 2021; Sutherland et al., 2021.

75 Lyons et al., 2014.

76 Mazzocco & Vukovic, 2018.

77 Ramani & Siegler, 2008.

78 Zhang et al., 2020.

79 Mullis et al., 2020; Programme for International Student Assessment. Retrieved from: www.oecd.org/pisa/publications/PISA2018-CN-USA.pdf

80 Ritchie & Bates, 2013.

81 Iuculano et al., 2015; Kucian et al., 2011; Michels et al., 2018.

REFERENCES

The following references were cited in this chapter. For additional selected references relevant to this chapter, please see Chapter 13 Supplemental References in eResources.

Bailey, D.H., Fuchs, L.S., Gilbert, J.K., Geary, D.C., & Fuchs, D. (2020). Prevention: Necessary but insufficient? A 2-year follow-up of an effective first-grade mathematics intervention. *Child Development, 91*, 382–400.

Bassok, D., Latham, S., & Rorem, A. (2016). Is kindergarten the new first grade? *AERA Open, 2*(1), 1–31.

Beery, K.E., & Beery, N.A. (2010). *Beery-Buktenica developmental test of visual-motor integration* (6th ed.). N.C.S. Pearson, Inc.

Bodovski, K., & Farkas, G. (2007). Mathematics growth in early elementary school: The roles of beginning knowledge, student engagement, and instruction. *The Elementary School Journal, 108*, 115–130.

Boets, B., & DeSmedt, B. (2010). Single-digit arithmetic in children with dyslexia. *Dyslexia, 16*, 183–191.

Bugden, S., Peters, L., Nosworthy, N., Archibald, L., & Ansari, D. (2021). Identifying children with persistent developmental dyscalculia from a 2-min test of symbolic and nonsymbolic magnitude processing. *Mind, Brain, and Education, 15*, 88–102.

Bull, R., Lee, K., & Muñez, D. (2021). Numerical magnitude understanding in kindergartners: A specific and sensitive predictor of later mathematical difficulties. *Journal of Educational Psychology, 113*, 911–928.

Burchinal, M., Foster, T.J., Bezdek, K.G., Bratsch-Hines, M., Blair, C., Vernon-Feagans, L., & the Family Life Project Investigators. (2020). School-entry skills predicting school-age academic and social-emotional trajectories. *Early Childhood Research Quarterly, 51*, 67–80.

Catts, H.W., Nielsen, D.C., Bridges, M.S., Liu, Y.S., & Bontempo, D.E. (2015). Early identification of reading disabilities within in RTI framework. *Journal of Learning Disabilities, 48*, 281–297.

Clarke, B., Baker, S., Smolkowski, K., & Chard, D.J. (2008). An analysis of early numeracy curriculum-based measurement. *Remedial and Special Education, 29*, 46–57.

Clarke, B., Cil, G., Smolkowski, K., Sutherland, M., Turtura, J., Doabler, C.T., Fien, H., & Baker, S.K. (2020). Conducting a cost-effectiveness analysis of an early numeracy intervention. *School Psychology Review, 49*, 359–373.

Clarke, B., Haymond, K., & Gersten, R. (2014). Mathematics screening measures for the primary grades. In R.J. Kettler, T.A. Glover, C.A. Albers, & K.A. Feeney-Kettler (Eds.), *Universal screening in educational settings: Evidence-based decision making for schools* (pp. 199–221). American Psychological Association.

Clements, D.H., Sarama, J., Layzer, C., Unlu, F., & Fesler, L. (2020). Effects on mathematics and executive function of a mathematics and play intervention versus mathematics alone. *Journal for Research in Mathematics Education, 51,* 301–333.

Common Core State Standards Initiative. (2021). *Preparing America's students for success.* Retrieved from www.corestandards.org/Math/Content/K/.

Dankert, H.L., Davies, P.L., & Gavin, W.J. (2003). Occupational therapy effects on visual-motor skills in preschool children. *American Journal of Occupational Therapy, 57,* 542–549.

Darney, D., Reinke, W.M., Herman, K.C., Stormont, M., & Ialongo, N.S. (2013). Children with co-occurring academic and behavior problems in first grade: Distal outcomes in twelfth grade. *Journal of School Psychology, 51,* 117–128.

Doabler, C.T., Clarke, B., Kosty, D., Fien, H., Smolkowski, K., Liu, M., & Baker, S.K. (2021a). Measuring the quantity and quality of explicit instructional interactions in an empirically validated Tier 2 kindergarten mathematics intervention. *Learning Disability Quarterly, 44,* 50–62.

Doabler, C.T., Clarke, B., Kosty, D., Maddox, S.A., Smolkowski, K., Fien, H., Baker, S.K., & Kimmel, G.L. (2021b). Kindergartners at risk for severe mathematics difficulties: Investigating tipping points of core mathematics instruction. *Journal of Learning Disabilities, 54,* 97–110.

Donlan, C., Cowan, R., Newton, E.J., & Lloyd, D. (2007). The role of language in mathematical development: Evidence from children with specific language impairments. *Cognition, 103,* 23–33.

Ellis, A., Susperreguy, M.I., Purpura, D.J., & Davis-Keen, P.E. (2021). Conceptual replication and extension of the relation between the number line estimation task and mathematical competence across seven studies. *Journal of Numerical Cognition, 7,* 435–452.

Fernández-Méndez, L.M., Contreras, M.J., & Elosúa, M.R. (2020). Developmental differences between 1st and 3rd year of Early Childhood Education (preschool) in mental rotation and its training. *Psychological Research, 84,* 1056–1064.

Frick, A., Ferrara, K., & Newcombe, N.S. (2013a). Using a touch screen paradigm to assess the development of mental rotation between 3 1/2 and 5 1/2 years of age. *Cognitive Processing, 14,* 117–127.

Frick, A., Hansen, M.A., & Newcombe, N.S. (2013b). Development of mental rotation in 3- to 5-year-old children. *Cognitive Development, 28,* 386–399.

Friedmann, N., Dotan, D., & Rahamim, E. (2010). Is the visual analyzer orthographic-specific? Reading words and numbers in letter position dyslexia. *Cortex, 46,* 982–1004.

Geary, D.C., Hoard, M.K., Nugent, L., & Bailey, D.H. (2013). Adolescents' functional numeracy is predicted by their school entry number system knowledge. *PLoS ONE, 8*(1), e54651.

Geary, D.C., vanMarle, K., Chu, F.W., Rouder, J., Hoard, M.K., & Nugent, L. (2018). Early conceptual understanding of cardinality predicts superior school-entry number-system knowledge. *Psychological Science, 29,* 191–205.

Georges, C., Cornu, V., & Schiltz, C. (2021). The importance of visuospatial abilities for verbal number skills in preschool: Adding spatial language to the equation. *Journal of Experimental Psychology, 201,* 104971.

Gimbert, F., Camos, V., Gentaz, E., & Mazens, K. (2019). What predicts mathematics achievement? Developmental change in 5- and 7-year-old children. *Journal of Experimental Child Psychology, 178,* 104–120.

Gracy, D., Fabian, A., Basch, C.H., Scigliano, M., MacLean, S.A., MacKenzie, R.K., & Redlener,

I.E. (2018). Missed opportunities: Do states require screening of children for health conditions that interfere with learning? *PLoS ONE, 13*(1), e0190254.

Griffin, S.A., Case, R., & Siegler, R.S. (1994). Rightstart: Providing the central conceptual prerequisites for first formal learning of arithmetic to students at risk for school failure. In K. McGilly (Ed.), *Classroom lessons: Integrating cognitive theory and classroom practice* (pp. 25–49). MIT Press.

Gross-Tsur, V., Manor, O., & Shalev, R.S. (1996). Developmental dyscalculia: Prevalence and demographic features. *Developmental Medicine and Child Neurology, 38*, 25–33.

Gunderson, E.A., & Hildebrand, L. (2021). Relations among spatial skills, number line estimation, and exact and approximate calculation in young children. *Journal of Experimental Child Psychology, 212*, 105251.

Gunderson, E.A., Ramirez, G., Beilock, S.L., & Levine, S.C. (2012). The relation between spatial skill and early number knowledge: The role of the linear number line. *Developmental Psychology, 48*, 1229–1241.

Halberda, J., & Feigenson, L. (2008). Developmental change in the acuity of the "number sense": The approximate number system in 3-, 4-, 5-, and 6-year-olds and adults. *Developmental Psychology, 44*, 1457–1465.

Hawes, Z., Moss, J., Caswell, B., Naqvi, S., & MacKinnon, S. (2017). Enhancing children's spatial and numerical skills through a dynamic spatial approach to early geometry instruction: Effects of a 32-week intervention. *Cognition and Instruction, 35*, 236–264.

Hawes, Z., Moss, J., Caswell, B., Seo, J., & Ansari, D. (2019a). Relations between numerical, spatial, and executive function skills and mathematics achievement: A latent-variable approach. *Cognitive Psychology, 109*, 68–90.

Hawes, Z., Nosworthy, N., Archibald, L., & Ansari, D. (2019b). Kindergarten children's symbolic number comparison skills relates to 1st grade mathematics achievement: Evidence from a two-minute paper-and-pencil test. *Learning and Instruction, 59*, 21–33.

Hecht, S.A., Torgesen, J.K., Wagner, R.K., Rashotte, C.A. (2001). The relations between phonological processing abilities and emerging individual differences in mathematical computational skills: A longitudinal study from second to fifth grades. *Journal of Experimental Child Psychology, 79*, 192–227.

Iuculano, T., Rosenberg-Lee, M., Richardson, J., Tenison, C., Fuchs, L., Supekar, K., & Menon, V. (2015). Cognitive tutoring induces widespread neuroplasticity and remediates brain function in children with mathematical learning disabilities. *Nature Communications, 6*, 8453.

Jordan, N.C., Glutting, J., Dyson, N., Hassinger-Das, B., & Irwin, C. (2012). Building kindergartners' number sense: A randomized controlled study. *Journal of Educational Psychology, 104*, 647–660.

Jordan, N.C., Glutting, J., & Ramineni, C. (2008). A number sense assessment tool for identifying children at risk for mathematical difficulties. In A. Dowker (Ed.), *Mathematical difficulties: Psychology and intervention* (pp. 45–58). Academic Press.

Jordan, N.C., & Levine, S.C. (2009). Socioeconomic variation, number competence, and mathematics learning difficulties in young children. *Developmental Disabilities Research Reviews, 15*, 60–68.

Joyner, R.E., & Wagner, R.K. (2020). Co-occurrence of reading disabilities and math disabilities: A meta-analysis. *Scientific Studies of Reading, 24*, 14–22.

Kaufmann, L., Pixner, S., & Göbel, S.M. (2011). Finger usage and arithmetic in adults with math difficulties: Evidence from a case report. *Frontiers in Psychology, 2*, 254.

Koponen, T., Georgiou, G., Salmi, P., Leskinen, M., & Aro, M. (2017). A meta-analysis of the relation between RAN and mathematics. *Journal of Educational Psychology, 109*, 977–992.

Krajcsi, A. (2021). Follow-up questions influence the measured number knowledge in the Give-a-number task. *Cognitive Development, 57*, 100968.

Kucian, K., Grond, U., Rotzer, S., Henzi, B., Schön-mann, C., Plangger, F., Gälli, M., Martin, E., vonAster, M. (2011). Mental number line training in children with developmental dyscalculia. *NeuroImage*, *57*, 782–795.

Landerl, K., & Moll, K. (2010). Comorbidity of learning disorders: Prevalence and familial transmission. *The Journal of Child Psychology and Psychiatry*, *51*, 287–294.

Levine, S., Huttenlocher, J., Taylor, A., & Langrock, A. (1999). Early sex differences in spatial skill. *Developmental Psychology*, *35*, 940–949.

Litkowski, E.C., Duncan, R.J., Logan, J.A.R., & Purpura, D.J. (2020). When do preschoolers learn specific mathematics skills? Mapping the development of early numeracy knowledge. *Journal of Experimental Child Psychology*, *195*, 104846.

Logan, J.A.R., Justice, L.M., Yumuş, M., & Chaparro-Moreno, L.J. (2019). When children are not read to at home: The million word gap. *Journal of Developmental and Behavioral Pediatrics*, *40*, 383–386.

Lombardi, C.M., & Dearing, E. (2021). Maternal support of children's math learning in associations between family income and math school readiness. *Child Development*, *92*, e39-e55.

Lyons, I.M., Price, G.R., Vaessen, A., Blomert, L., & Ansari, D. (2014). Numerical predictors of arithmetic success in grades 1–6. *Developmental Science*, *17*, 714–726.

Malone, S.A., Burgoyne, K., & Hulme, C. (2020). Number knowledge and the approximate number system are two critical foundations for early arithmetic development. *Journal of Educational Psychology*, *112*, 1167–1182.

Mazzocco, M.M.M., & Vukovic, R. (2018). How SLD manifests in mathematics. In V.C. Alfonso & D.P. Flanagan (Eds.), *Essentials of specific learning disability identification* (2nd ed., pp. 59–102). John Wiley & Sons, Inc.

McDonald, J.A., Merkley, R., Mickle, J., Collimore, L.-M., Hawes, Z., & Ansari, D. (2021). Exploring the implementation of early math assessments in kindergarten classrooms: A research-practice collaboration. *Mind, Brain, and Education*, *15*, 311–321.

Michels, L., O'Gorman, R., & Kucian, K. (2018). Functional hyperconnectivity vanishes in children with developmental dyscalculia after numerical intervention. *Developmental Cognitive Neuroscience*, *30*, 291–303.

Mix, K.S., Levine, S.C., Cheng, Y.-L., Young, C., Hambrick, D.Z., Ping, R., & Konstantopoulos, S. (2016). Separate but correlated: The latent structure of space and mathematics across development. *Journal of Experimental Psychology; General*, *145*, 1206–1227.

Monuteaux, M.C., Faraone, S.V., Herzig, K., Navsaria, N., & Biederman, J. (2005). ADHD and dyscalculia: Evidence for independent familial transmission. *Journal of Learning Disabilities*, *38*, 86–93.

Morgan, P.L., Farkas, G., Hillemeier, M.M., & Maczuga, S. (2016). Who is at risk for persistent mathematics difficulties in the United States? *Journal of Learning Disabilities*, *49*, 305–319.

Morgan, P.L., Farkas, G., & Wu, Q. (2009). Five-year growth trajectories of kindergarten children with learning difficulties in mathematics. *Journal of Learning Disabilities*, *42*, 306–321.

Mou, Y., Zhang, B., Piazza, M., & Hyde, D.C. (2021). Comparing set-to-number and number-to-set measures of cardinal number knowledge in preschool children using latent variable modeling. *Early Childhood Research Quarterly*, *54*, 125–135.

Mullis, I.V.S., Martin, M.O., Foy, P., Kelly, D.L., & Fishbein, B. (2020). *TIMSS 2019 international results in mathematics and science*. Retrieved from https://timssandpirls.bc.edu/timss2019/international-results/

Nelson, G., & Powell, S.R. (2018). A systematic review of longitudinal studies of mathematics difficulty. *Journal of Learning Disabilities*, *51*, 523–539.

Programme for International Student Assessment. Retrieved from www.oecd.org/pisa/publications/PISA2018-CN-USA.pdf

Purpura, D.J., Hume, L.E., Sims, D.M., & Lonigan, C.J. (2011). Early literacy and early numeracy:

The value of including early literacy skills in the prediction of numeracy development. *Journal of Experimental Child Psychology, 110,* 647–658.

Purpura, D.J., & Logan, J.A.R. (2015). The nonlinear relations of the approximate number system and mathematical language to early mathematics development. *Developmental Psychology, 51,* 1717–1724.

Ramani, G.B., & Siegler, R.S. (2008). Promoting broad and stable improvements in low-income children's numerical knowledge through playing number board games. *Child Development, 79,* 375–394.

Ribner, A., Moeller, K., Willoughby, M., Blair, C., & the Family Life Project Key Investigators. (2018). Cognitive abilities and mathematical competencies at school entry. *Mind, Brain, and Education, 12,* 175–185.

Ritchie, S.J., & Bates, T. (2013). Enduring links from childhood mathematics and reading achievement to adult socioeconomic status. *Psychological Science, 24,* 1301–1308.

Sasanguie, D., Defever, E., Maertens, B., & Reynvoet, B. (2014). The approximate number system is not predictive for symbolic number processing in kindergarteners. *The Quarterly Journal of Experimental Psychology, 67,* 271–280.

Scalise, N.R., Daubert, E.N., & Ramani, G.B. (2021). When one size does not fit all: A latent profile analysis of low-income preschoolers' math skills. *Journal of Experimental Child Psychology, 209,* 105156.

Schneider, M., Merz, S., Stricker, J., DeSmedt, B., Torbeyns, J., Verschaffel, L., & Luwel, K. (2018). Associations of number line estimation with mathematical competence: A meta-analysis. *Child Development, 89,* 1467–1484.

Seethaler, P.M., & Fuchs, L.S. (2010). The predictive utility of kindergarten screening for math difficulty. *Exceptional Children, 77,* 37–59.

Sella, F., Berteletti, I., Lucangeli, D., & Zorzi, M. (2017). Preschool children use space, rather than counting, to infer the numerical magnitude of digits: Evidence for a *spatial mapping principle. Cognition, 158,* 56–67.

Sella, F., & Lucangeli, D. (2020). The knowledge of the preceding number reveals a mature understanding of the number sequence. *Cognition, 194,* 104104.

Sella, F., Lucangeli, D., & Zorzi, M. (2019). Spatial order relates to the exact numerical magnitude of digits in young children. *Journal of Experimental Child Psychology, 178,* 385–404.

Sella, F., Lucangeli, D., Zorzi, M. (2020). The interplay between spatial ordinal knowledge, linearity of number-space mapping, and arithmetic skills. *Cognitive Development, 55,* 100915.

Shalev, R.S., Auerbach, J., Manor, O., & Gross-Tsur, V. (2000). Developmental dyscalculia: Prevalence and prognosis. *European Child and Adolescent Psychiatry, 9,* II/58–II/64.

Shanley, L., Clarke, B., Doabler, C.T., Kurtz-Nelson, E., & Fien, H. (2017). Early number skills gains and mathematics achievement: Intervening to establish successful early mathematics trajectories. *The Journal of Special Education, 51,* 177–188.

Siegler, R.S. (2009). Improving the numerical understanding of children from low-income families. *Child Development Perspectives, 3,* 118–124.

Skeide, M.A., Evans, T.M., Mei, E.Z., Abrams, D.A., & Menon, V. (2018). Neural signatures of co-occurring reading and mathematical difficulties. *Developmental Science, 21,* e12680.

Snowling, M.J., Moll, K., & Hulme, C. (2021). Language difficulties are a shared risk factor for both reading disorder and mathematics disorder. *Journal of Experimental Child Psychology, 202,* 105009.

Sutherland, M., Clarke, B., Nese, J.F.T., Cary, M.S., Shanley, L., Furjanic, D., & Durán, L. (2021). Investigating the utility of a kindergarten number line assessment compared to an early numeracy screening battery. *Early Childhood Research Quarterly, 55,* 119–128.

Toll, S.W.M., & vanLuit, J.E.H. (2014). The developmental relationship between language and low early numeracy skills throughout kindergarten. *Exceptional Children, 81,* 64–78.

Träff, U., & Passolunghi, M.C. (2015). Mathematical skills in children with dyslexia. *Learning and Individual Differences, 40,* 108–114.

Traverso, L., Tonizzi, I., Usai, M.C., & Viterbori, P. (2021). The relationship of working memory and inhibition with different number knowledge skills in preschool. *Journal of Experimental Child Psychology, 203,* 105014.

Vanbinst, K., vanBergen, E., Ghesquière, P., & DeSmedt, B. (2020). Cross-domain associations of key cognitive correlates of early reading and early arithmetic in 5-year-olds. *Early Childhood Research Quarterly, 51,* 144–152.

Vukovic, R.K., Lesaux, N.K., & Siegel, L.S. (2010). The mathematics skills of children with reading difficulties. *Learning and Individual Differences, 20,* 639–643.

Wang, S., Hu, B.Y., & Zhang, X. (2021). Kindergarteners' spatial skills and their reading and math achievement in second grade. *Early Childhood Research Quarterly, 57,* 156–166.

Watts, T.W., Duncan, G.J., Siegler, R.S., & Davis-Kean, P.E. (2014). What's past is prologue: Relations between early mathematics knowledge and high school achievement. *Educational Researcher, 43,* 352–360.

West, J., Denton, K., & Germino-Hausken, E. (2000, Feb.). *America's kindergartners.* U.S. Department of Education.

Woocock, R.W., Schrank, F., Mather, N., & McGrew, K.S. (2014). *Woodcock-Johnson IV.* Riverside Publishing.

Zentall, S.S. (2007). Math performance of students with ADHD: Cognitive and behavioral contributors and interventions. In D.B. Berch & M.M.M. Mazzocco (Eds.), *Why is math so hard for some children? The nature and origins of mathematical learning difficulties and disabilities* (pp. 219–243). Paul H. Brookes Publishing.

Zhang, X., Räsänen, P., Koponen, T., Aunola, K., Lerkkanen, M.-K., & Nurmi, J.-E. (2020). Early cognitive precursors of children's mathematics learning disability and persistent low achievement: A 5-year longitudinal study. *Child Development, 91,* 7–27.1/3-tiles

Index

Note: Page numbers in *italics* indicate figures; page numbers in **bold** indicate tables

396 *Index*

202, **203**; proportional 291–292; quantitative 61–65; spatial 100–101, 131–132; story problems 331–333, 334–336, 338–341, 341–342, 352–354; transcoding 199–201; understanding 12–13; *see also* American sign language; auditory processing; bilingual; blind; central auditory processing disorder (CAPD); deaf; developmental language disorder; dyslexia; phonological awareness; rapid automatic naming

later-greater principle 164; *see also* digits, quantitative meaning

Lemaire, Patrick 254

length, and whole-number sequence 39, *39*

Locke, John 150

logarithmic (skewed) number line distribution *see* number line, error patterns

long-term memory *see* memory, long-term

Mandarin *see* Chinese, language

mapping, scaling, floor plans *see* spatial skills, people in motion

matching numerosities 69–72

measurement: by comparison 38; linear 234–238; and misleading hash mark numbering 235–236, *235, 236*; scaling difficulties in 237; and standard comparison unit 234–235

measurement activities 242–243

mechanical reasoning *see* spatial skills, objects in motion

memory 6–11

memory, long-term 6–8; and arithmetic facts 7, 263, 267–270; and distributed *vs.* massed practice 8, 15; explicit 6; implicit 7; and language impairment 156, 372; and metacognition 8; motor 197–198; and the number line 272; and small numerosities 72; statistical learning 7; strategies 7–8

memory, short term and working 8–11; and arithmetic 272, 334; auditory 10; central executive 9; and copying small sets 65; and finger arithmetic 185, 261; and fingers and object tagging 183; and inattention 371; and the number line 221–222, 231; and numeral-naming fluency 200; and numerical order 202; and numerical syntax 228; and patterns 16; and phonological awareness 372; and processing speed 10; and schematic diagrams 344, 348–349; and sequential subitizing 59; spatial 10–11; strategies 9–10; updating 9; visual 10–11; visual-spatial, and sex differences 125–126, 129; verbal, and blind 271; verbal, and story problems 335–337; visual-spatial, training and math 121; and worked problems 14

mental control and attention *see* attention and mental control

mental number line: and arithmetic 265, 272–273, 276–277, 279–281; development of spatial-numerical association 39, 119, 241; and the number line 222; and sense of numerical order 381–382; sex differences in 125, 128–129; and spatial skill 231, 373; and working memory 232

mental paper-folding 96, *96*

mental rotation *see* spatial skills, objects in motion

Mental Rotation Test 94–96, *95*; and math 119

metacognition *see* memory, long-term

microgenetic studies 259

mind-wandering 2–3

min strategy *see* arithmetic, whole-number, strategies

mirror confusion 13, 86–87, 90, 94, *94*, 196–198, *197*; activities 102–103, 109–110; remediation 206; and sex differences 122–123; Sophia, student example 375–376; *see also* digits, recognition and writing

missing-term problems: and mental rotation 258

Mix, Kelly: toddler example (Spencer) 63–64

Morse code 59

Multatuli *see* Dekker, Edward Douwes

multidigit numerals *see* place value

multiplication, rational-number: activities 317–319, 321–322; direction of results 303–304; misunderstanding 304–307; procedural confusion 304

multiplication, whole-number: activities 278–281; bilingual 271, 333; common errors in 265; commutativity principle 269; Daisy, student example 367–368; facts 269–270; identity principle 269; inverse relation with division 269; language deficits and 372; and memory 7; procedures 267; Sophia, student example 375–376; and story problems 334; strategies **260**, 261, 264; and verbal memory 271

music instruction: instrumental training and finger gnosis 186; and spatial skill 130

National Assessment of Educational Progress (NAEP) x, 125

navigation *see* spatial skills, people in motion

negative quantities 31, 41–42, *42*; in CCSS 231; digging holes activity 51; on the number line *221*, 231

non-verbal learning difficulties: and the number line 232; and spatial working memory 11

noticing numerosity 67–68; activity 74–75